lonely planet

Hungary

Neal Bedford

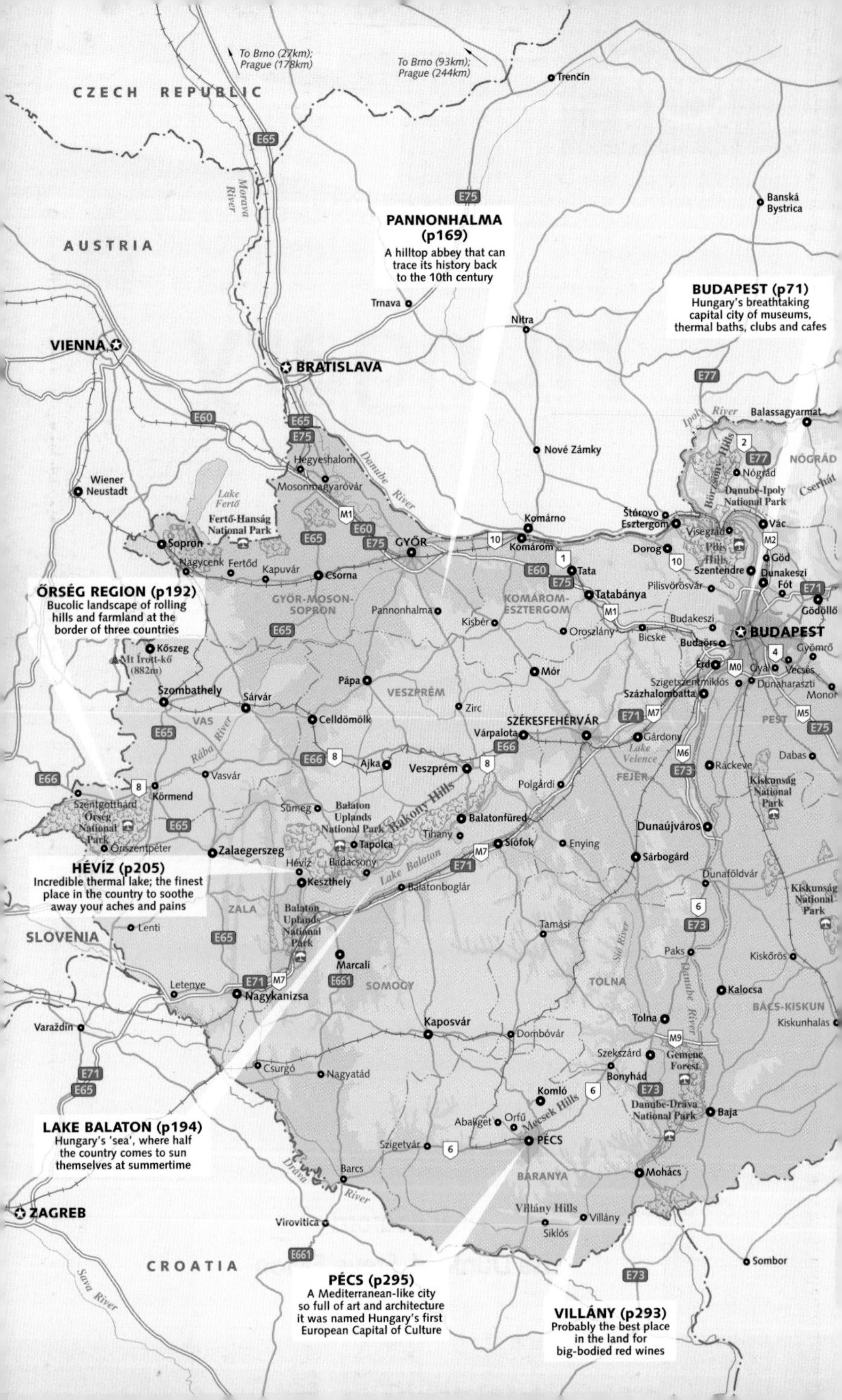

CZECH REPUBLIC
AUSTRIA
SLOVENIA
CROATIA
To Brno (27km); Prague (178km)
To Brno (93km); Prague (244km)
PANNONHALMA (p169)
A hilltop abbey that can trace its history back to the 10th century
BUDAPEST (p71)
Hungary's breathtaking capital city of museums, thermal baths, clubs and cafes
ŐRSÉG REGION (p192)
Bucolic landscape of rolling hills and farmland at the border of three countries
HÉVÍZ (p205)
Incredible thermal lake; the finest place in the country to soothe away your aches and pains
LAKE BALATON (p194)
Hungary's 'sea', where half the country comes to sun themselves at summertime
PÉCS (p295)
A Mediterranean-like city so full of art and architecture it was named Hungary's first European Capital of Culture
VILLÁNY (p293)
Probably the best place in the land for big-bodied red wines
VIENNA
BRATISLAVA
BUDAPEST
ZAGREB
Trenčín
Banská Bystrica
Trnava
Nitra
Nové Zámky
Wiener Neustadt
Hegyeshalom
Mosonmagyaróvár
Lake Fertő
Fertő-Hanság National Park
Sopron
Nagycenk
Fertőd
Kapuvár
Csorna
GYŐR
Komárno
Komárom
Tata
Tatabánya
Štúrovo
Esztergom
Visegrád
Pilis Hills
Dorog
Szentendre
Pilisvörösvár
Vác
Göd
Dunakeszi
Fót
Gödöllő
Balassagyarmat
Nógrád
NÓGRÁD
Cserhát
Börzsöny Hills
Danube-Ipoly National Park
Ipoly River
Danube River
Morava River
GYŐR-MOSON-SOPRON
Pannonhalma
Kisbér
KOMÁROM-ESZTERGOM
Oroszlány
Bicske
Budakeszi
Budaörs
Érd
Gyál
Vecsés
Gyömrő
Szigetszentmiklós
Dunaharaszti
Százhalombatta
Monor
PEST
Kőszeg
Mt Írott-kő (882m)
Szombathely
Sárvár
Pápa
VESZPRÉM
Mór
Zirc
Celldömölk
VAS
Rába River
SZÉKESFEHÉRVÁR
Várpalota
Gárdony
Lake Velence
Dabas
Ajka
Veszprém
Vasvár
Körmend
Szentgotthárd
Őrség National Park
Őriszentpéter
Sümeg
Balaton Uplands National Park
Bakony Hills
Polgárdi
FEJÉR
Ráckeve
Kiskunság National Park
Balatonfüred
Tihany
Siófok
Enying
Dunaújváros
Sárbogárd
Zalaegerszeg
Hévíz
Tapolca
Badacsony
Keszthely
Lake Balaton
Balatonboglár
Dunaföldvár
ZALA
Lenti
Tamási
Sió River
Paks
Kiskőrös
Marcali
SOMOGY
TOLNA
Letenye
Nagykanizsa
Kalocsa
BÁCS-KISKUN
Kiskunhalas
Varaždin
Kaposvár
Dombóvár
Tolna
Szekszárd
Gemenc Forest
Bonyhád
Csurgó
Nagyatád
Komló
Mecsek Hills
Danube-Dráva National Park
Baja
Abaliget
Orfű
PÉCS
Szigetvár
BARANYA
Mohács
Barcs
Dráva River
Villány Hills
Villány
Siklós
Virovitica
Sombor
Sava River
E65
E75
E77
E60
E71
E66
E73
E661
M0
M1
M2
M5
M6
M7
M9

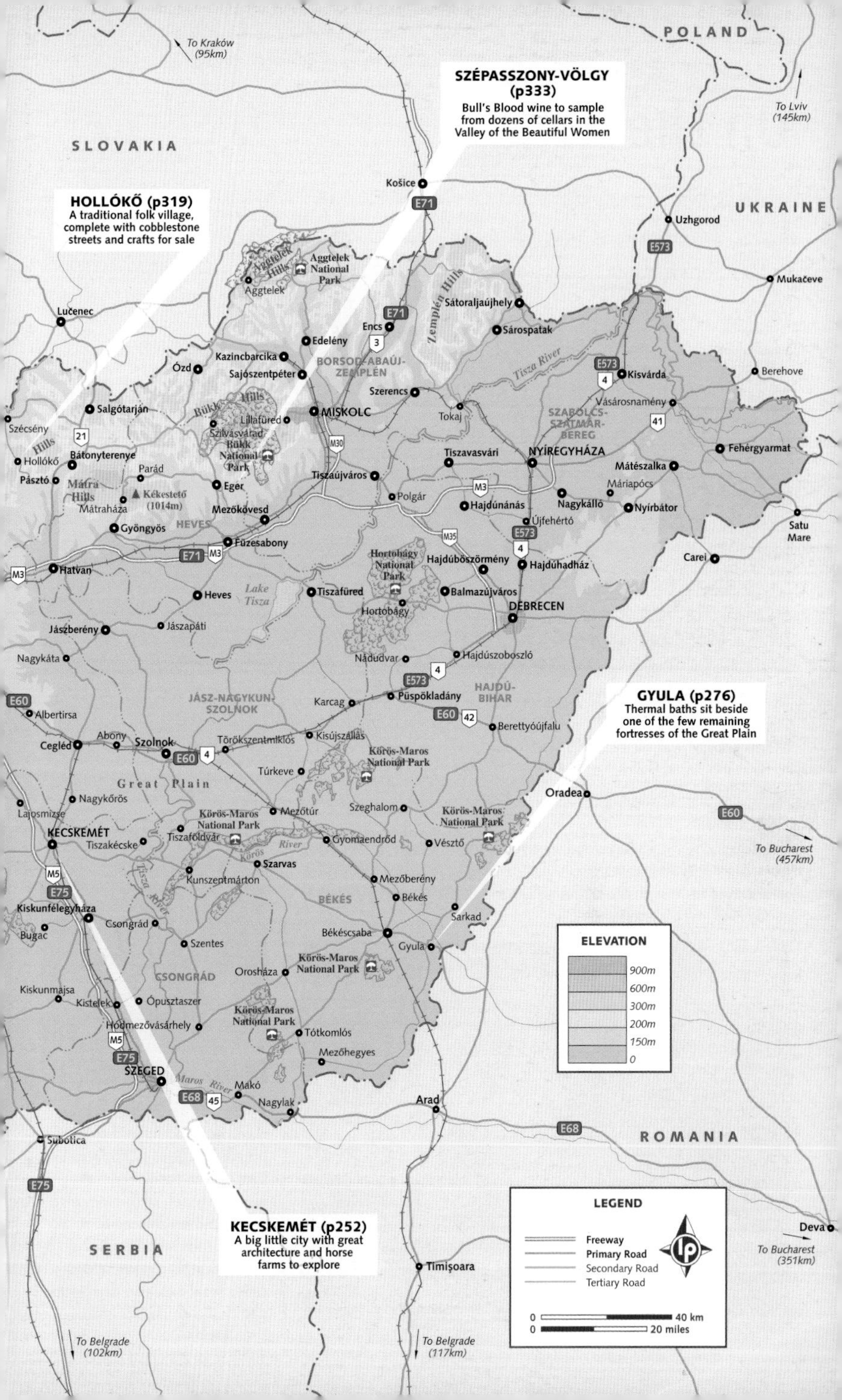

POLAND
To Kraków (95km)
SZÉPASSZONY-VÖLGY (p333)
Bull's Blood wine to sample from dozens of cellars in the Valley of the Beautiful Women
To Lviv (145km)
SLOVAKIA
UKRAINE
HOLLÓKŐ (p319)
A traditional folk village, complete with cobblestone streets and crafts for sale
Košice
E71
Uzhgorod
E573
Mukačeve
Aggtelek Hills
Aggtelek National Park
Aggtelek
Zemplén Hills
Sátoraljaújhely
Sárospatak
Lučenec
Encs
Edelény
Kazincbarcika
Ózd
Sajószentpéter
BORSOD-ABAÚJ-ZEMPLÉN
Tisza River
Kisvárda
Berehove
Szerencs
Vásárosnamény
Salgótarján
Bükk Hills
Lillafüred
MISKOLC
Tokaj
SZABOLCS-SZATMÁR-BEREG
Szécsény
Szilvásvárad
Bükk National Park
M30
Tiszavasvári
NYÍREGYHÁZA
Fehérgyarmat
Hollókő
Bátonyterenye
Parád
Mátészalka
Pásztó
Mátra Hills
Kékestető (1014m)
Eger
Tiszaújváros
M3
Máriapócs
Mátraháza
Polgár
Nagykálló
Nyírbátor
Mezőkövesd
Hajdúnánás
Gyöngyös
HEVES
Újfehértó
Satu Mare
Füzesabony
M35
Hortobágy National Park
Hajdúböszörmény
Carei
Hatvan
Hajdúhadház
Heves
Lake Tisza
Tiszafüred
Balmazújváros
DEBRECEN
Hortobágy
Jászberény
Jászapáti
Nagykáta
Nádudvar
Hajdúszoboszló
JÁSZ-NAGYKUN-SZOLNOK
HAJDÚ-BIHAR
Püspökladány
Karcag
GYULA (p276)
Thermal baths sit beside one of the few remaining fortresses of the Great Plain
E60
Albertirsa
Berettyóújfalu
Abony
Cegléd
Szolnok
Törökszentmiklós
Kisújszállás
Körös-Maros National Park
Túrkeve
Great Plain
Oradea
Nagykőrös
Lajosmizse
Mezőtúr
Szeghalom
Körös-Maros National Park
KECSKEMÉT
Tiszakécske
Tiszaföldvár
Körös River
Gyomaendrőd
Vésztő
To Bucharest (457km)
Szarvas
M5
Kunszentmárton
Mezőberény
E75
BÉKÉS
Békés
Kiskunfélegyháza
Tisza River
Sarkad
Csongrád
Bugac
Békéscsaba
Gyula
ELEVATION
900m
600m
300m
200m
150m
0
Szentes
Orosháza
Körös-Maros National Park
CSONGRÁD
Kiskunmajsa
Ópusztaszer
Kistelek
Hódmezővásárhely
Tótkomlós
Mezőhegyes
SZEGED
Maros River
Makó
E68
Nagylak
Arad
Subotica
ROMANIA
KECSKEMÉT (p252)
A big little city with great architecture and horse farms to explore
LEGEND
Freeway
Primary Road
Secondary Road
Tertiary Road
Deva
To Bucharest (351km)
SERBIA
Timişoara
0 40 km
0 20 miles
To Belgrade (102km)
To Belgrade (117km)

On the Road

NEAL BEDFORD Coordinating Author
The Seas of Stones in the Kál Basin are bizarre, filled with sandstone boulders and rocky outcrops, such as this one, known locally as the swinging rock. It doesn't so much swing as 'rock', but it's still unnerving to be standing atop a massive moving slab 3m above the ground.

LISA DUNFORD There's nothing like a big 'kettle' of *gulyás* (beef goulash soup) and a cold beverage, enjoyed under the trees after a hard horseback ride. I've been living Western-style in Texas for years now; you should have seen me bumping around in the English saddle in sandy Kiskunság National Park.

STEVE FALLON OK, this is how it works. Budding author bent on success goes to Budapest's City Park to stroke the now very shiny pen of Anonymous, the unknown chronicler at the court of King Béla III, for inspiration. The result: a bestseller. Now only you can decide whether it worked this time.

For full author biographies see p408.

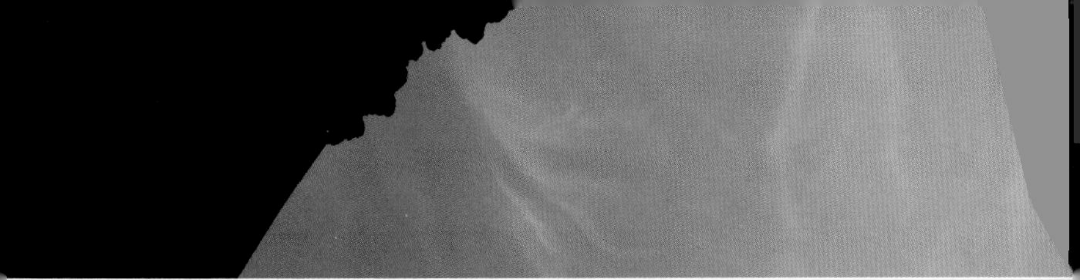

HUNGARY HITS

Hungary offers a wealth of experiences, if you know where to look. You could be riding across the plains in the afternoon, and in the evening be taking a dip in rejuvenating thermal waters. Or find yourself gazing at glorious Art Nouveau architecture before sitting down to *gulyás* (or is that *pörkölt*?) and stomach-settling *pálinka*. The following highlights are just a sample of what this unique country has in store.

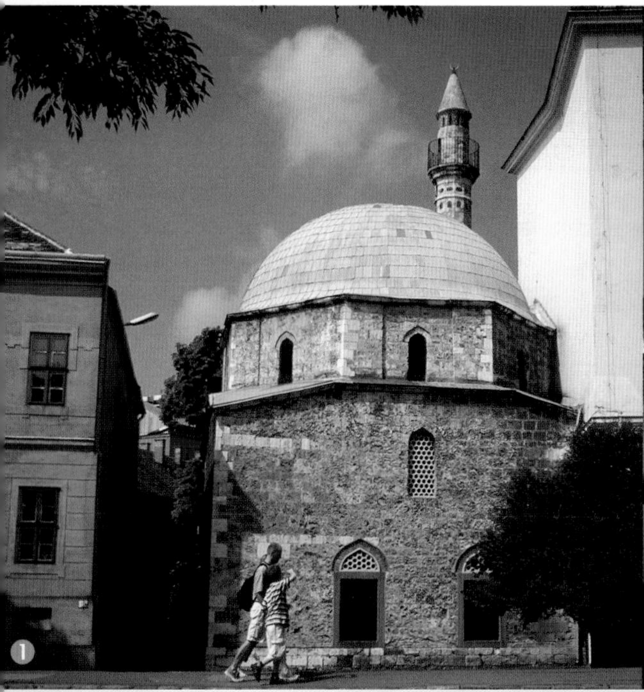

Architectural Appeal

Hungary is a treasure-trove of architectural delights. Whether it's Romanesque, Gothic, Renaissance, baroque or neoclassical you're into, the country's towns and cities have it covered. While some places may only have one or two noteworthy buildings, there are a few jammed to the hilt with impressive structures.

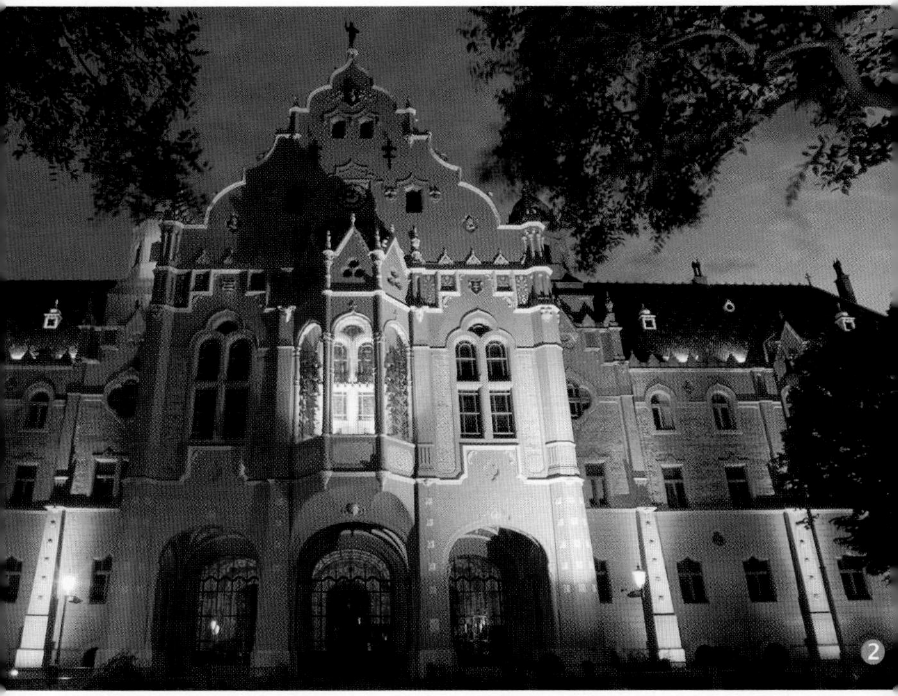

1 Pécs
This gem of a city (p295) is blessed with rarities – Turkish architecture and early Christian and Roman tombs. Its Mosque Church is the largest Ottoman structure still standing in the country, while the Pasha Hassan Jakovali Mosque has survived the centuries in exceptional condition.

2 Kecskemét
This Southern Plain city (p252) holds some surprises. Hidden behind its ring of vineyards and orchards are fine examples of Art Nouveau, such as the Ornamental Palace, Otthon Cinema and Town Hall, and if you look hard enough you'll even find a yellow brick road.

3 Hollókő
It may only consist of two streets, but Hollókő (p319) is the most beautiful of Hungary's villages. Its 60 whitewashed houses, little changed since their construction in the 17th and 18th centuries, are pure examples of traditional folk architecture.

4 Budapest
Budapest's (p71) architectural waltz through the ages begins with the Romans at Aquincum, moves on to Castle Hill's medieval streets, and hits its stride during the Art Nouveau era. The Royal Postal Savings Bank, Gresham Palace, Museum of Applied Arts and Gellért Baths are just some of its Secessionist stunners.

5 Sopron
Sopron (p171) sports the most intact medieval centre in Hungary. Its cobbled streets are lined with one Gothic or early-baroque facade after the next; a wander here is like stepping back in time. The icing on the cake is the town's Roman ruins.

Dishes & Drinks

Hungary's larder offers a cornucopia of fresh surprises, and why ignore the drinks cupboard? The country's wine – from the big-bodied reds of Villány and Somló's flinty whites to honey-gold Tokaj – is world-renowned, the fruit-flavoured *pálinka* kicks like a mule and the chocolate-brown aperitif Unicum is as bitter as a loser's tears.

2

3

❶ Gulyás vs Pörkölt

A bone of contention among Hungarians is what foreigners erroneously refer to as goulash, which here is a rich 'stew' usually made with beef or veal called *pörkölt*. *Gulyás* is actually a meat soup (p52).

❷ Wine & Pálinka

Tokaj is the 'wine of kings and the king of wines'. Still, travel around and meet (and taste) a few other 'noble' wines available here (p53). Punching much higher in the alcohol stakes is *pálinka* (p53), a strong brandy flavoured with fruit.

❸ Paprika

Many Hungarian dishes wouldn't be, well, Hungarian (or dishes for that matter) without the addition of paprika (p52), the 'red gold' spice grown around Szeged (p263) and Kalocsa (p259) that comes in varying degrees of piquancy.

❹ Sausage & Salami

Sausages and salamis are almost icons in Hungary and, like most things religious, often lead to serious rivalry. Some people swear by the 'Hungaricum' (any famous Hungarian product) known as Pick while others can't last a day without a slice of smoked sausage from Debrecen (p246) or fatty *csabai* (p274).

❺ Goose

A skein of geese (that's a gaggle in flight, doncha know) is a wondrous sight but we prefer our goose on a plate, either as goose leg with mashed potatoes and red cabbage or as the more refined goose liver sautéed with apples (p53).

Outdoor Escapades

OK, so the country has more than its fair share of high art and architecture. Still, some of the most characteristically Hungarian experiences are to be had outdoors: watch as thousands of cranes fly in, ride a Nonius horse across the *puszta,* and don't forget to soak in the thermal waters…

❶ Bird-Watching
With more than 200 resident species, several endangered, you don't have to go out of your way to bird-watch. Head to the Eastern Plain (p242) to watch autumn migrations, or to one of the many small lakes, like Kis-Balaton (p204), to see aquatic birdlife.

❷ Thermal Baths
With more than 300 thermal hot springs in public use across the country, it's not hard to find a place to take a bath. Dip in at a classic spa in Budapest (p103) or float on a thermal lake in Hévíz (p205).

❸ The Puszta
The unending plains of myth and memory are waiting to be explored in Kiskunság National Park (p257) and Hortobágy (p248). Ride yourself, or watch as Hungarian cowboys ride with five horses in hand at a staged show.

❹ Sunning & Swimming
Lake Balaton (p194) is Hungary's summer playground for sunning, swimming and sailing in resort towns that have attracted international attention in recent years. For quieter recreation, there's the nation's second-largest body of water, Lake Tisza, at Tiszafüred (p239).

Folk Forte

Preserved through generations, Hungary's folk art traditions bring everyday objects to life. Differences in colours and styles easily identify the art's originating region. You'll find exquisite detailed embroidery, pottery, hand-painted or -carved wood, dyed Easter eggs and graphic woven cloth all across the country. Some pretty garish knock-offs are out there, too.

❶ Kalocsa

Fuchsia tulips, sunburst daisies and vibrant blue hyacinths. No, this isn't a technicolour garden, it's the over-the-top wall-painting, embroidery and painted pottery that Kalocsa (p257) is known for countrywide.

❷ Bereg

The culture of the tiny villages in the far, far northeast of Hungary has much to do with their neighbours to the east. Each graphic cross-stitch pattern in the Bereg Region (p364) has a name. And the Easter eggs are brightly dyed.

❸ Mezőkövesd

You can't mistake the pom-pom-festooned headwear in the folk costume of the Matyó women. But it's the intricate embroidered roses and hand-painted flowers on dark wood furniture that are worth seeking out in Mezőkövesd (p336).

❹ Sárköz

The distinctive red-and-black striped woven fabric couldn't come from anywhere but the Sárköz region (p285) near Szekszárd. Area shepherds are also famous for the household objects they carve from horn and wood.

❺ Great Plain

The sombre black-on-black pottery of Nádudvar (p252) proves so striking the first time you see it. Or do you prefer blue-and-white designs of fish and fowl, one of three types originating in Hódmezővásárhely (p269)? To each small town, its style.

Contents

Regional Map Contents

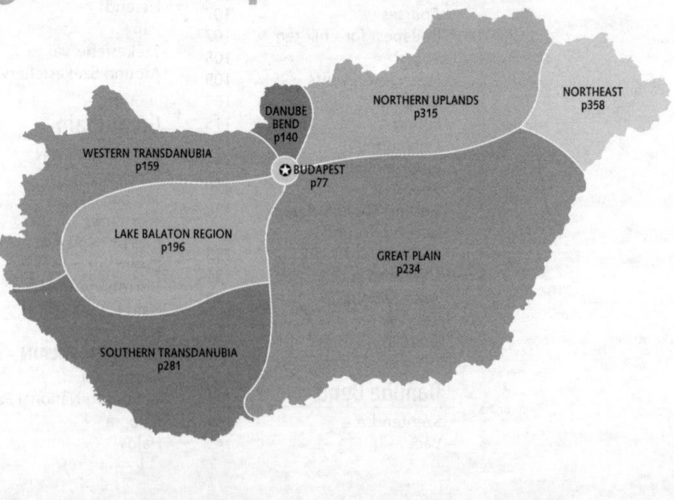

Destination Hungary

Hungary (Magyarország) has always been a little different. Ever since the Magyars secured this kidney-shaped island in a sea of Slavs over a thousand years ago, they have been going about their business as they deemed fit. Even the Soviets couldn't push their full plans through here, with the stalwart Magyars managing to engineer their own form of socialism – the watered-down, not-so-spicy 'goulash communism'.

After the fall of the Iron Curtain, Hungary, forever a country with an eye to the West (and a foot firmly planted in the East), quickly embraced capitalism and all its trappings. The economy boomed, open-plan malls magically appeared like mushrooms after a rain on the fringes of every sizeable town, and mobile-phone ownership went through the roof. Magyars began borrowing for homes and new cars (the old Trabant no longer cut it), and, unlike their Slavic neighbours, did so via cheap foreign-currency loans.

The health of Hungary's economy largely depended on foreign markets, and the government let spending spiral out of control. Then came the credit crunch. Average Hungarians were hit hard, finding themselves exposed to rising debt payments as the forint devalued against the euro and Swiss franc. In late 2008 global institutions – led by the International Monetary Fund – lent Hungary US$25 billion to help it out of the tight spot, but it remains to be seen whether the bailout will bring the failing economy back from the brink.

In recent years, the growing frustration normally kept at bay behind closed doors began to spill out onto Hungary's streets. Peaceful demonstrations turned into full-blown riots, most notably on the 50th anniversary of the 1956 Uprising, when Budapest became a battlefield between protestors and police. Hungary's nationalist movement gained new momentum in mid-2007 with the formation of the Magyar Gárda (Hungarian Guard), the strong arm of the far-right Jobbik Magyarországért Mozgalom (Movement for a Better Hungary) party. Dressed in black and proudly displaying nationalist emblems, the militant group is a disturbing sight on Hungary's streets for many Hungarians. Even though membership is small (below 500), support for the Gárda from the likes of a former defence minister and several churchmen has raised concerns.

Through it all most Hungarians have gone about their business as only Hungarians can – with a large dose of reality mixed with fierce pride for their homeland. Slowly the focus is turning from quantity to quality: boutique hotels are popping up in Budapest and Balaton; world-class restaurants are spreading out from the capital to smaller enclaves; and superior thermal retreats are replacing dated communist-era eyesores. Despite the rising tide of commercialism, Hungary's roots remain firmly entwined with its folk traditions, as a trip to any part of the country will testify to. Thankfully Hungary has held on to the one factor that makes it special – being Hungarian. What that means is different for every person, but the good thing is Magyarország likes to be different. It's been so for generations, and we hope it doesn't change.

FAST FACTS

Population: 10.045 million

GDP per head: US$13,900 (at purchasing power parity US$19,240)

Inflation: 6.7%

Unemployment: 7.4%

Size: 93,030 sq km

Internet domain: .hu

Number of mobile phones per 1000 inhabitants: 1100 (302 in 2000)

Suicide rate: 42.3 men and 11.2 women per 100,000 people, surpassed only by Belarus, Russia and Lithuania

National anthem: 'Himnusz', with the music composed by Ferenc Erkel and the lyrics written by poet Ferenc Kölcsey

Number of cinemas in 2007: 400 (down from 1960 in 1990)

Getting Started

A trip to Hungary actually requires very little advance planning. Free tourist literature abounds, maps are excellent and readily available, and staff at tourist offices, travel agencies, hotels, train stations and so on are generally helpful and knowledgeable. In fact, almost anything can be arranged after you've arrived. However, a little planning never goes amiss and it can be of great value if you have special interests or are keen on a particular activity.

WHEN TO GO

See Climate Charts (p371) for more information.

Hungary has a temperate climate with three climatic zones, so there is a certain amount of variation across the country: Mediterranean in the south, Continental in the east and Atlantic in the west.

Although it can be pretty wet in April and May, spring is just glorious throughout Hungary. The weather is usually mild and tourist crowds are small. The Hungarian summer is warm, sunny and unusually long, and the resorts can get very crowded in late July and August. If you avoid Lake Balaton and the ever-popular Mátra Hills, you should be OK. Cities come to a grinding halt in August, which Hungarians traditionally call 'the cucumber-growing season' (because that's about the only thing happening here).

Autumn is beautiful, particularly in the hills around Budapest, in the Northern Uplands and around Lake Balaton. In Transdanubia and on the Great Plain it's harvest and vintage time. November is one of the rainiest months of the year in certain parts of the country, however. Winter is the least attractive season: aside from being cold and often bleak, museums and other tourist sights close or cut their hours sharply.

COSTS & MONEY

Hungary is no longer the bargain-basement destination for foreign travellers that it once was, but it is still cheaper than most Western European countries. If you bunk down in private rooms, eat at medium-priced restaurants and travel on public transport, you should get by on €35 a day in the provinces without too much scrimping, though Budapest will cost you closer to €50 a day.

Travelling in more style and comfort – restaurant splurges with bottles of wine, a fairly active nightlife, staying in small hotels/guest houses with 'character' – will cost about twice as much (€70 in the provinces and €100 in the capital). Those putting up at hostels or college dormitories, and eating street-stall food like *burek* (pastry with filling) for lunch and at self-service restaurants for dinner, could squeak by for around €20 a day (€35 in Budapest).

For information about discounts, see p373.

DON'T LEAVE HOME WITHOUT…

- checking the visa situation and your passport expiry date (p380)
- organising a good health-insurance policy (p375)
- a few words of Hungarian, and a phrase book – a little goes a long way (p397)
- swimsuit, plastic sandals and towel – for that mandatory thermal-spa visit
- a stomach for heavy food and great wine (p51)
- ear plugs, or a penchant for tacky music – there's no escaping it in bars, restaurants and cafes

TRAVELLING RESPONSIBLY

In general, many Hungarians are largely unaware of their impact on the surrounding environment, but this is slowly changing. For example, in recent years recycling banks have been employed by local governments in the country's bigger towns and cities. As a traveller, it is impossible not to have some effect on the Hungarian environment as well, but there are a number of ways to minimise the impact.

Getting There & Around

Getting to Hungary by train or bus from most parts of Europe is a relatively easy exercise. Naturally it's more time-consuming than plane travel, but your carbon footprint is a fraction in comparison. If you do fly, consider offsetting your carbon emissions (for example on www.climatecare.org).

Within Hungary, the public transport network connects even the smallest towns and villages. Trains travel the length and breadth of the country, and where they don't go, buses do. Almost all sizeable towns and cities employ local transport options. The flat topography of Hungary makes getting around by bicycle a highly viable option; bicycles can also be transported on some trains. Unfortunately, finding establishments that rent bicycles can prove problematic, so it's best to bring your bike with you. Lake Balaton is one exception – over the summer months, bicycle-rental spots pop up like mushrooms after rain.

HOW MUCH?

Cheap/good bottle (75cL) of wine in supermarket 750/2500Ft

Bed in private room in provinces/Budapest from 3000/6000Ft

Cup of coffee in a cafe 250-500Ft

Local English-language newspaper 400-600Ft

Dinner for two at a good restaurant in the provinces/Budapest 9000/15,000Ft

Sleeping & Eating

It's easy to avoid the large, generic hotel chains in Hungary and opt for smaller, family-run establishments, therefore ensuring your forints go directly to the local community. Additionally, agrotourist accommodation, private rooms and *pensions* (see p368) are further alternatives.

Fruits, vegetables and flowers are readily available at town markets throughout Hungary; much of it is locally grown and free of chemical sprays.

TRAVEL LITERATURE

Travellers writing diary accounts usually treat Hungary rather cursorily as they make tracks for 'more exotic' Romania or places beyond. A few classic – and very personal – accounts are still available in bookshops, in libraries or on amazon.com.

- *Between the Woods and the Water* (Patrick Leigh Fermor) Describing his 1933 walk through Western and Central Europe to Constantinople as a young man, Fermor wrote the classic account of Hungary.
- *Under the Frog* (Tibor Fischer) An amusing account of the antics of two members of Hungary's elite national basketball team from the end of WWII through the 1956 Uprising.
- *Danube* (Claudio Magris) A colourful account of the author's journey through Central Europe, following the path of the Danube; written a handful of years before the fall of the Berlin Wall.
- *The Hungarian Girl Trap* (Ray Dexter) Insightful personal account of life in modern-day Budapest for an expat who, like so many others, fell in love with a beautiful Hungarian girl.
- *Hungary & the Hungarians: The Keywords* (István Bart) Subtitled 'A Concise Dictionary of Facts, Beliefs, Customs, Usage & Myths', this book will prepare you for (and guide you through) just about everything Magyar – from ABC (a kind of greengrocer under the old regime) to Zsolnay.
- *Stealing from a Deep Place* (Brian Hall) Sensitive but never cloying, the author describes his tempered love affair with the still-communist Budapest of the 1980s while completing a two-year cycle tour of Hungary, Romania and Bulgaria.

TOP PICKS

HUNGARIANS YOU SHOULD KNOW

- Béla Bartók (p47)
- Matthias Corvinus (p27)
- St Stephen (p25)
- Lajos Kossuth (p29)
- Franz Liszt (p47)
- St Margaret (p95)
- Cardinal József Mindszenty (p155)
- Sándor Petőfi (p48)
- Ferenc Rákóczi II (p29)
- József Rippl-Rónai (p45)
- István Széchenyi (p179)

HISTORICAL STRUCTURES

- Széchenyi Chain Bridge in Budapest (p92)
- Museum of Applied Arts in Budapest (p100)
- Minorite church in Eger (p333)
- Esterházy Palace at Fertőd (p177)
- Gödöllő Royal Palace (p138)
- Hortobágyi Csárda (p248)
- Benedictine Abbey Church at Ják (p185)
- Pannonhalma Abbey (p169)
- Sümeg Castle (p212)
- Art Nouveau New Synagogue in Szeged (p265)

FREE-TIME PURSUITS

- Bird-watching in the Fertő-Hanság National Park (p177)
- Canoeing or kayaking on the Tisza River (p239)
- Caving in Aggtelek (p346)
- Cycling around Lake Balaton (p195)
- Fishing in Lake Tisza (p239)
- Hiking in the Zemplén Hills (p347)
- Horse riding at Hortobágy (p248)
- Sailing on Lake Balaton (p197)
- Swimming in the thermal lake at Hévíz (p205)
- Wine tasting in the Villány region (p293)

- *The City of the Magyar or Hungary and Her Institutions in 1839–40* (Julia Pardoe) This three-volume part-travelogue, part-history by a British spinster is priceless for its vivid descriptions of events such as the devastating Danube floods of 1838.

INTERNET RESOURCES

Hungarian Home Page (www.fsz.bme.hu/hungary) Despite some links being out of date, this web portal is still a useful address listing a plethora of Hungarian home pages.

Hungarian National Tourism Organisation (www.hungary.com) Without a doubt the single best website on Hungary; it should be your first portal of call.

Hungary.hu (www.hungary.hu) Government portal with key data, but not always as up to date as it should be.

Inside Hungary (www.insidehungary.com) National news and a myriad of excellent links on everything from business to culture.

Lonely Planet (www.lonelyplanet.com) Includes summaries on Hungary, links to Hungary-related sites and travellers trading information on the Thorn Tree.

Museums in Hungary (www.museum.hu) A complete list of every museum in the land that's currently open to the public.

Itineraries

CLASSIC ROUTES

GO WEST

One to Two Weeks

Combining many of the highlights of the west of the country will give you a taste of Hungary's historical wealth and natural beauty. From **Budapest** (p71) head north through the Danube Bend region to the former artists colony of **Szentendre** (p141) and historical **Visegrád** (p149), before arriving at **Esztergom** (p153), Hungary's holiest city. The road continues west along the Danube to **Győr** (p163), an industrial city surprisingly rich in historical buildings and monuments. From here, head south to **Pannonhalma** (p169), whose awesome abbey is on Unesco's World Heritage List, and onto **Veszprém** (p223), the 'city of queens'. The scenic northern coast road of Lake Balaton, and its settlements of **Balatonfüred** (p219), **Tihany** (p215) and **Badacsony** (p207), is your next port of call. Make a quick detour to **Sümeg** (p212) and its dramatic castle before turning south again to **Pécs** (p295), the jewel of the south. Return to the capital, but take time to sample the sublime red wines of **Szekszárd** (p281) and Hungary's 'city of kings', **Székesfehérvár** (p229), along the way.

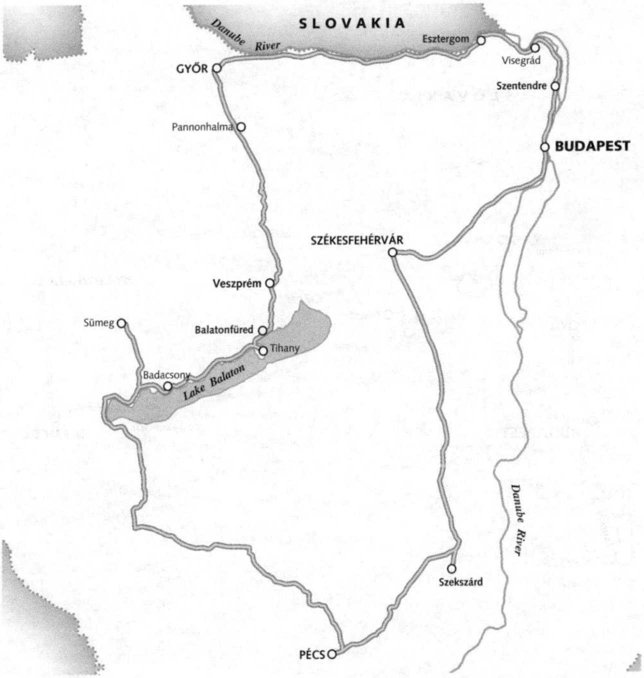

This 690km trip has something for everyone: castles, churches, palaces, thermal spas, rolling hills and Hungary's biggest lake. It's mostly an easy drive, and you could do it in a week. But with so much to see and time to recharge on the Balaton, we recommend two.

OVER HILL & BEYOND DALE

One to Two Weeks

Hungary's uplands to the north are hardly what you would call dramatic. But they have a gentle beauty all of their own, and nestled within the hills are important historical towns and traditional villages. From **Budapest** (p71) head north to **Vác** (p145), arguably the most attractive town on the Danube Bend, and then on to **Balassagyarmat** (p316), the capital of the traditional Palóc region. Continue due east to **Szécsény** (p317), site of a pivotal battle and a delightful manor house. Dip down through the rolling Cserhát Hills to **Hollókő** (p319), a 'museum town' of Hungarian traditions. From here the road winds through the eastern Cserhát and foothills of the Mátra Hills to **Gyöngyös** (p324), where you'll start a challenging drive through the hills past **Kékestető** (p328), Hungary's highest point, and scary **Recsk** (p329), site of what was once Hungary's most brutal forced-labour camp. Lovely baroque **Eger** (p330) awaits you at the end of the high road. It's then onto sprawling **Miskolc** (p340) and the traditionally sweet wines of **Tokaj** (p348) before a quick stop at **Nyíregyháza** (p358) en route to **Debrecen** (p242), nicknamed 'Calvinist Rome', the country's second-largest city. For a taste of Hungary's Great Plain head west through **Hortobágy National Park** (p248) to **Tiszafüred** (p239) and eventually back to Budapest.

You'll get both the 'ups' and 'downs' of northern and eastern Hungary – the so-called Northern Uplands and the Great Plain – on this 650km trip. There's plenty to do – from exploring historical cities like Eger and Debrecen to wine tasting in Tokaj and bird-watching in the Hortobágy region.

ROADS LESS TRAVELLED

SOUTHERN TRAILS One to Two Weeks

The southern reaches of Hungary contain relatively few major attractions and plenty of minor ones, but no matter their size, most are overlooked by travellers. Be the odd one out and make a beeline from **Budapest** (p71) to **Jászberény** (p237), home of the legendary Lehel Horn, and then turn south to **Szolnok** (p235), a working-class city and capital of the Central Plain. Continue south through **Körös-Maros National Park** (p276) to sleepy **Szarvas** (p273), whose arboretum is among the best in Hungary. **Békéscsaba** (p274), with its leafy avenues and church spires, beckons to the southeast, from where a detour to the medieval castle and thermal baths of **Gyula** (p276) is mandatory. Cross the plain to **Szeged** (p263), arguably the finest city in the region, but pause long enough to appreciate the folk art – particularly pottery – of **Hódmezővásárhely** (p269). After wandering the architecturally rich streets of Szeged and dining on spicy fish soup, head north to **Ópusztaszer** (p269), the famed spot where Árpád held the first assembly of the Magyar chieftains, and onto **Csongrád** (p271) and its traditional fishers' cottages. **Kecskemét's** (p252) splendid Art Nouveau buildings are only a short drive away, as is the legendary horse show at **Bugac** (p257) in Kiskunság National Park. From Kecskemét, head southwest to **Kalocsa** (p257) and **Baja** (p260), two towns close to the Danube, then cross the mighty river to **Mohács** (p286), site of Hungary's famous defeat at the hands of the Ottomans in 1526. Finish with wine in hand in **Szekszárd** (p281).

Take the time to discover Hungary's southern expanse on this 685km trip through the Southern Plain. Quiet rural towns, Art Nouveau architecture, regional folk art, legendary battle sites and remote national parks await you in this unspoiled corner of the *puszta*.

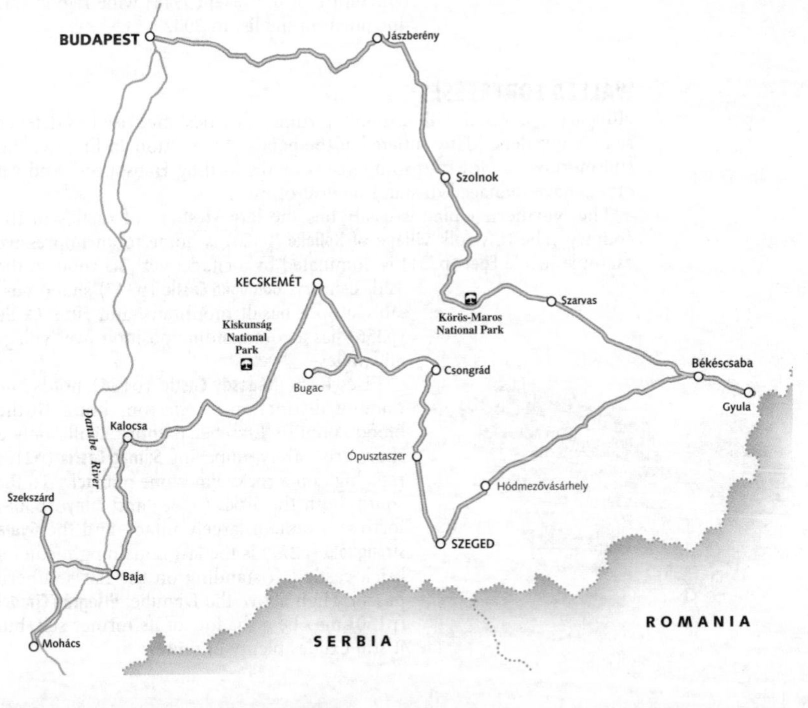

TAILORED TRIPS

UNESCO WORLD HERITAGE SITES

Hungary counts a total of one natural and seven cultural sites on the Unesco World Heritage List.

The first two to be inaugurated – in 1987 – captured the country's considerable contrasts between its rural heritage and urban achievements. The settlement of **Hollókő** (p319) was the first village in the world to make the list for its traditional architecture and folk customs, while **Budapest** (p71) – in particular Buda Castle, the banks of the Danube and Andrássy út – was deemed worthy due to its impressive city landscape.

The variety of formations and combination of tropical and climatic effects in the caves at **Aggtelek** (p346) won Hungary its only natural site in 1995; it was extended in both 2000 and 2008.

Not to be outdone, the 1000-year-old Benedictine abbey at **Pannonhalma** (p169) was added a year later in 1996, closely followed by **Hortobágy National Park** (p248) in 1999.

This century, the wonderfully decorative early Christian tombs in the heart of **Pécs** (p295) made the list in 2000; the varied landscape and rural architecture surrounding **Lake Fertő** (p177) near Sopron was added in 2001; and the age-old viticulture of the **Tokaj** (p348) wine region was included on the list in 2002.

WALLED FORTRESSES

Hungary is covered with crumbling ruins of castles once used as defence against invaders. Many suffered at the hands of the Ottoman Empire, and still more were blown to smithereens by the lording Habsburgs. And yet others have managed to stand the test of time.

The Northern Uplands easily has the largest share of castles in the country. The tiny folk village of **Hollókő** (p320) is home to an impressive example, while **Eger** (p331) is dominated by a citadel with its roots in the 12th century. **Boldogkő Castle** (p347) sits impossibly atop a basalt mountain, and **Füzér Castle** (p356) has a commanding position over village and valley.

Elsewhere, **Nádasdy Castle** (p186) holds the dubious distinction of one-time home to the blood countess Erzsébet Báthory, while only a short drive away, imposing **Sümeg Castle** (p212) rests high on a rocky limestone pinnacle. To the south, both the **Siklós** (p288) and **Zrínyi** (p308) fortresses remain largely intact, and the **Gyula stronghold** (p277) is the last remaining medieval brick castle left standing on the flat southern *puszta*. High above the Danube, **Visegrád Citadel** (p150) may be a shadow of its former self, but it still exudes plenty of power.

History

HUNGARY'S EARLY INHABITANTS

The Carpathian Basin, in which Hungary lies, has been populated for at least half a million years. Bone fragments found at Vértesszőlős, about 5km southeast of Tata (p159), in the 1960s are believed to be that old. The findings suggest that Palaeolithic and, several hundred millennia later, Neanderthal humans were attracted by the area's hot springs and the abundance of reindeer, bears and mammoths. Stone Age pottery shards and bone-tipped arrowheads have been found at Istállóskő Cave near Szilvásvárad (p338).

During the Neolithic period (5000–2500 BC), climate change forced much of the indigenous wildlife to migrate northward. As a result the domestication of animals and the early forms of agriculture appeared, simultaneously with the rest of Europe. Remnants of the Körös culture in the Szeged area of southeast Hungary (p263) suggest that these goddess-worshipping people herded sheep, fished and planted crops.

Indo-European tribes from the Balkans stormed the Carpathian Basin in horse-drawn carts in about 2000 BC, bringing with them copper tools and weapons. After the introduction of the more durable metal bronze, horses were domesticated, forts built and a military elite developed.

Over the next millennium, invaders from the west (Illyrians, Thracians) and east (Scythians) brought iron, but it was not in common use until the Celts arrived at the start of the 4th century BC. They introduced glass and crafted some of the fine gold jewellery that can still be seen in museums throughout Hungary (eg the Mór Wosinszky County Museum in Szekszárd, p281).

In about 35 BC the Romans conquered the area west and south of the Danube River, and two dozen years later occupied the Danube Bend. By AD 10 they had established the province of Pannonia, which would later be divided into Upper (Superior) and Lower (Inferior) Pannonia. Subsequent victories over the Celts extended Roman domination across the Tisza River as far as Dacia (today's Romania). The Romans introduced writing, viticulture and stone architecture, and established garrison towns and other settlements, the remains of which can still be seen in Óbuda (Aquincum in Roman times; p94), Szombathely (Savaria; p182), Pécs (Sophianae; p298) and Sopron (Scarbantia; p173).

The Corvinus Library of Hungarian History (www.hungarianhistory.com) is a font of all knowledge and an excellent first step on the subject; the links to related topics – from language to painting – are endless.

THE MIGRATION PERIOD

The first of the so-called Great Migrations of nomadic peoples from Asia reached the eastern outposts of the Roman Empire early in the 3rd century AD, and in 270 the Romans fled Dacia altogether. Within less than two

TIMELINE

AD 106	Late 430s	895–96
Roman Aquincum (in today's Óbuda) is named the administrative seat of the province of Pannonia Inferior.	Huns raze Aquincum, forcing Romans and other settlers to flee.	Nomadic Magyar tribes enter and settle in the Carpathian Basin.

centuries they were also forced to pull out of Pannonia by the Huns, whose short-lived empire had been established by Attila. (Attila had previously conquered the Magyars near the lower Volga River and for centuries these two groups were thought – erroneously – to share a common ancestry.)

Although Hungarians are in no way related to the Huns, Attila remains a very common given name for males in Hungary today.

Germanic tribes such as the Goths, Gepids and Longobards occupied the region for the next century and a half until the Avars, a powerful Turkic people, gained control of the Carpathian Basin in about 580. They in turn were subdued by the Frankish king Charlemagne in 796 and converted to Christianity. By that time the Carpathian Basin was virtually unpopulated, except for groups of Turkic and Germanic tribes on the plains and Slavs in the northern hills.

THE ORIGIN OF THE MAGYARS

The origin of the Magyars is a complex issue, not helped by the similarity (in English) of the words 'Hun' and 'Hungary', which are *not* related. One thing is certain: Magyars are part of the Finno-Ugric group of peoples who inhabited the forests somewhere between the middle Volga River and the Ural Mountains in western Siberia and began migrating as early as 4000 BC.

By about 2000 BC population growth had forced the Finnish-Estonian branch of the group to move westward, ultimately reaching the Baltic Sea. The Ugrians migrated from the southeastern slopes of the Urals into the valleys, and switched from fishing, hunting and gathering to primitive farming and raising livestock, especially horses. The Magyars' equestrian skills proved useful half a millennium later when climatic changes brought drought, forcing them to move north to the steppes.

If you'd like to learn more about the nomadic Magyars, their history, civilisation and/or art, go to http://ancientmagyarworld.tripod.com, which also offers a number of useful and interesting links.

On the plains, the Ugrians turned to nomadic herding. After 500 BC, by which time the use of iron had become widespread among the tribes, some of the groups moved westward to the area of Bashkiria in central Asia. Here they lived among Persians and Bulgars and began referring to themselves as Magyars (from the Finno-Ugric words *mon*, 'to speak', and *er*, 'man').

After several centuries another group split away and moved south to the Don River under the control of the Turkic Khazars. Here they lived among different groups under a tribal alliance called *onogur* (or '10 peoples'). This is the derivation of the word 'Hungary' in English and 'Ungarn' in German. Their last migration before the conquest of the Carpathian Basin brought them to what modern Hungarians call the Etelköz, the region between the Dnieper and lower Danube Rivers above the Black Sea.

THE CONQUEST OF THE CARPATHIAN BASIN

Nomadic groups of Magyars probably reached the Carpathian Basin as early as the mid-9th century AD, acting as mercenaries for various armies. In about 889 the Pechenegs, a fierce people from the Asiatic steppe, allied themselves with the Bulgars and attacked the Etelköz settlements. When they were

955

Hungarian raids outside the Carpathian Basin are stopped for good by German King Otto I at the battle of Augsburg.

1000

Stephen (István) is crowned 'Christian King' of Hungary at Esztergom on Christmas Day.

1083

King Stephen is canonised as St Stephen by Pope Victor III in Rome, and 20 August is declared his feast day.

attacked again in about 895, seven tribes under the leadership of Árpád – the *gyula*, or chief military commander – struck out for the Carpathian Basin. They crossed the Verecke Pass in today's Ukraine three years later.

The Magyars met almost no resistance and the tribes dispersed in three directions. The Bulgars were quickly dispatched eastward; the Germans had already taken care of the Slavs in the west; and Transylvania was wide open. Known for their ability to ride and shoot – a common Christian prayer during the so-called Dark Ages was 'Save us, O Lord, from the arrows of the Hungarians' – and no longer content with being hired guns, the Magyars began plundering and pillaging on their own, taking slaves and amassing booty. Their raids took them as far as Spain, northern Germany and southern Italy, but in the early 10th century the Magyars began to suffer a string of defeats. In 955 they were stopped in their tracks for good by the German King Otto I at the battle of Augsburg.

Strong believers in magic and celestial intervention, the ancient Magyars believed that the *turul*, a mythical hawklike bird and symbol of the nation, begat the ancestors of Árpád, the nation's first military leader.

This and subsequent defeats – their raids on Byzantium ended in 970 – left the Magyar tribes in disarray and, like the Bohemian, Polish and Russian princes of the time, they had to choose between their more powerful neighbours – Byzantium to the south and east or the Holy Roman Empire to the west – to form an alliance. In 973 Prince Géza, the great-grandson of Árpád, asked the Holy Roman Emperor Otto II to send Catholic missionaries to Hungary. Géza was baptised, as was his son Vajk, who took the Christian name Stephen (István). When Géza died in 997, Stephen ruled as prince. But on Christmas Day in the year 1000 he was crowned 'Christian King' Stephen I. Hungary the kingdom – and the nation – was born.

KING STEPHEN I & THE ÁRPÁD DYNASTY

Stephen ruthlessly set about consolidating royal authority by expropriating the land of the independent-minded clan chieftains and establishing a system of *megye* (counties) protected by fortified *vár* (castles). The crown began minting coins and, shrewdly, Stephen transferred much land to loyal (mostly German) knights. The king sought the support of the church throughout and established 10 episcopates, two of which – Kalocsa and Esztergom – were made archbishoprics. Monasteries were set up around the country and staffed by Irish, German and Italian scholars. By the time Stephen died in 1038, Hungary was a nascent Christian nation, increasingly westward-looking and multiethnic.

Despite this apparent consolidation, the next two and a half centuries until 1301 – the reign of the House of Árpád – would test the kingdom to the limit. The period was marked by dynastic intrigues and relentless struggles between rival pretenders to the throne, which weakened the young nation's defences against its powerful neighbours. There was a brief hiatus under King Ladislas I (László; r 1077–95), who ruled with an iron fist and fended off attacks from Byzantium, and under his successor Koloman the

1220
The Gothic style of architecture extends into Hungary from northern France, superseding the heavier Romanesque style.

1222
King Andrew II signs the Golden Bull, according the nobility more rights and powers.

1241–42
The Mongols sweep across Hungary, reducing the population by up to one-half.

Booklover (Könyves Kálmán), a temperate ruler who encouraged literature and art until his death in 1116.

Tensions flared up again when the Byzantine emperor made a grab for Hungary's provinces in Dalmatia and Croatia, which it had acquired early in the 12th century and, together with Slovakia and Transylvania, were referred to as the 'crown lands of St Stephen'. Béla III (r 1172–96) successfully resisted the invasion and had a permanent residence built at Esztergom (p155). Béla's son, Andrew II (András; r 1205–35), however, weakened the crown when, to help fund his crusades, he gave in to local barons' demands for more land. This led to the Golden Bull, a kind of Magna Carta signed at Székesfehérvár in 1222, which limited some of the king's powers in favour of the nobility.

When Béla IV (r 1235–70) tried to regain the estates, the barons were able to oppose him on equal terms. Fearing Mongol expansion and realising he could not count on local assistance, Béla looked to the west and brought in German settlers. He also gave asylum to Turkic Cuman (Hungarian: Kun) tribes displaced by the Mongols in the east. In 1241–42 the Mongols swept through Hungary, burning it virtually to the ground and killing an estimated one-third to one-half of its two million people.

To rebuild the country as quickly as possible, Béla, known as the 'second founding father', again encouraged immigration, inviting Germans to settle in Transdanubia, Saxons in Transylvania and Cumans on the Great Plain. He also built a string of defensive hilltop castles, including the ones at Buda (p76), Visegrád (p150) and Diósgyőr near Miskolc (p340). But in a bid to appease the lesser nobility, he handed them large tracts of land. This

THE CROWN OF ST STEPHEN

Legend tells us that it was Asztrik, the first abbot of the Benedictine monastery at Pannonhalma (p169), who presented a crown to Stephen as a gift from Pope Sylvester II around AD 1000, thus legitimising the new king's rule and assuring his loyalty to Rome over Constantinople. It's a nice story, but it has nothing to do with the object on display in the Parliament building in Budapest. That two-part crown, with its characteristic bent cross, pendants hanging on either side and enamelled plaques of the Apostles, dates from the 12th century. Regardless of its provenance, the Crown of St Stephen has become the very symbol of the Hungarian nation.

The crown has disappeared several times over the centuries, only to appear again later. During the Mongol invasions of the 13th century the crown was dropped while being transported to a safe house, giving it that slightly jaunty, skewed look. More recently, in 1945, Hungarian fascists fleeing the Soviet army took it to Austria. Eventually the crown fell into the hands of the US Army, which transferred it to Fort Knox in Kentucky. In January 1978 the crown was returned to Hungary with great ceremony – and relief. Because legal judgments in Hungary had always been handed down 'in the name of St Stephen's Crown', it was considered a living symbol and had thus been 'kidnapped'.

1301

The line of the House of Árpád ends with the death of Andrew III, who leaves no male heir, followed by a period of great turmoil.

1458–90

Medieval Hungary enjoys a golden age under the enlightened reign of King Matthias Corvinus.

1514

A peasant uprising is crushed, with 70,000 people – including its leader György Dózsa – executed.

strengthened their position and demands for more independence even further; by the time of Béla's death, anarchy gripped Hungary, and the rule of his reprobate son and heir Ladislas the Cuman (Kun László; r 1272–90), so-called because his mother was a Cuman princess, was equally unsettled. The Árpád line died out in 1301 with the death of Andrew III, who left no heir, leading to a period of great upheaval.

MEDIEVAL HUNGARY

The struggle for the Hungarian throne after the fall of the House of Árpád involved several European dynasties, but it was Charles Robert (Károly Róbert) of the French House of Anjou who, with the pope's blessing, was crowned in 1309 and ruled for more than three decades. Charles Robert was an able administrator who managed to break the power of the provincial barons, sought diplomatic links with his neighbours and introduced a stable gold currency called the florin. In 1335 Charles Robert met the Polish and Bohemian kings at the new royal palace in Visegrád to discuss territorial disputes and to forge an alliance that would smash Vienna's control of trade.

'The Árpád line died out in 1301 with the death of Andrew III, who left no heir, leading to a period of great upheaval'

Under Charles Robert's son, Louis I the Great (Nagy Lajos; r 1342–82), Hungary began to move away from being a poor state with little more than subsistence agriculture as its economic base, to become a leading power. Louis acquired territory in the Balkans as far as Dalmatia and Romania, and as far north as Poland, where he was crowned king in 1370. But his successes were short-lived and the menace of the Ottoman Turks had appeared.

As Louis had no sons, one of his daughters, Mary (r 1382–87), succeeded him. The barons rose up against this 'petticoat throne' and within a short time Mary's husband, Sigismund (Zsigmond; r 1387–1437) of Luxembourg, was crowned king. Sigismund's 50-year reign brought peace at home, and there was a great flowering of Gothic art and architecture in Hungary (see p45). But while he managed to procure the coveted crown of Bohemia and was made Holy Roman Emperor in 1433, he was unable to stop the Ottoman march up through the Balkans.

An alliance between Poland and Hungary in 1440 gave the former the Hungarian crown. When Vladislav I (Úlászló), son of the Polish Jagiellonian king, was killed fighting the Turks at Varna in 1444, János Hunyadi was made regent. A Transylvanian general born of a Wallachian (Romanian) father, János Hunyadi began his career at the court of Sigismund. His decisive victory over the Turks at Belgrade (Hungarian: Nándorfehérvár) in 1456 checked the Ottoman advance into Hungary for 70 years and assured the coronation of his son Matthias (Mátyás), the greatest ruler of medieval Hungary.

Matthias (r 1458–90), nicknamed 'the Raven' (Corvinus) from his coat of arms, very wisely maintained a mercenary force of up to 10,000 men by taxing the nobility, and it was this 'Black Army' that conquered Moravia, Bohemia and even parts of lower Austria. Not only did Matthias Corvinus

1526

Hungary is defeated at the Battle of Mohács; the ensuing Turkish occupation lasts more than a century and a half.

1541

Buda Castle falls to the Ottomans; Hungary is partitioned and shared between the Turks, the Habsburgs and the Transylvanian princes.

1566

Miklós Zrínyi and his 2500 soldiers make their heroic sally at Szigetvár Castle; Sultan Suleiman I dies in battle.

make Hungary one of Central Europe's leading powers, but under his rule the nation enjoyed its first golden age. His second wife, the Neapolitan princess Beatrix, brought artisans up from Italy who completely rebuilt and extended the Gothic palace at Visegrád (p150); the beauty and sheer size of the Renaissance residence was beyond compare in the Europe of the time.

But while Matthias busied himself with centralising power for the crown and being a good king, he ignored the growing Turkish threat. His successor Vladislav II (Úlászló; r 1490–1516) was unable to maintain even royal authority, as the members of the diet (assembly), which met to approve royal decrees, squandered royal funds and expropriated land. In May 1514 what had begun as a crusade organised by the power-hungry archbishop of Esztergom, Tamás Bakócz, turned into a peasant uprising against landlords under the leadership of soldier of fortune György Dózsa.

Though somewhat dated (it was published in 2001), *A Concise History of Hungary* by Miklós Molnár remains the most reliable 'accessible' history of the country. It covers all the major episodes and trends from earliest times till the 1990s and is never dull.

The revolt was brutally repressed by noble leader John Szapolyai (Zápolyai János). Some 70,000 peasants were tortured and executed; Dózsa himself was fried alive on a red-hot iron throne, wearing a scalding crown. The retrograde Tripartitum Law that followed the crackdown codified the rights and privileges of the barons and nobles and reduced the peasants to perpetual serfdom. By the time nine-year-old Louis II (Lajos) took the throne in 1516, he couldn't rely on either side.

THE BATTLE OF MOHÁCS & TURKISH OCCUPATION

The defeat of Louis' ragtag army by the Ottoman Turks at Mohács (p286) in 1526 is a watershed in Hungarian history. On the battlefield south of this small town in Southern Transdanubia, a relatively prosperous and independent medieval Hungary died, sending the nation into a tailspin of partition, foreign domination and despair that would be felt for centuries.

It would be unfair to put all the blame on the weak and indecisive teenaged King Louis or on his commander-in-chief, Pál Tomori, the archbishop of Kalocsa. Bickering among the nobility and the brutal response to the peasant uprising a dozen years before had severely diminished Hungary's military might, and there was virtually nothing left in the royal coffers. By 1526 Ottoman Sultan Suleiman the Magnificent had occupied much of the Balkans, including Belgrade, and was poised to march on Buda and then Vienna with a force of up to 90,000 men.

Unable – or, more likely, unwilling – to wait for reinforcements from Transylvania under the command of his rival John Szapolyai, Louis rushed south with a motley army of just over 25,000 men to battle the Turks and was defeated in less than two hours. Along with bishops, nobles and an estimated 18,000 soldiers, the king was killed – crushed by his horse and drowned while trying to retreat across a stream. John Szapolyai, who had sat out the battle in Tokaj with forces of up to 13,000, was crowned king six weeks later. Despite

1686

Austrian and Hungarian forces liberate Buda from the Turks with the help of the Polish army.

1699

Peace signed with the Ottomans at Karlowitz (now in Serbia).

1703–11

Ferenc Rákóczi II fights and loses a war of independence against the Habsburgs.

grovelling before the Turks and kissing the sultan's hand, Szapolyai was never able to exploit the power he had sought so single-mindedly.

After Buda Castle fell to the Turks in 1541, Hungary was divided into three parts. The central section, including Buda, went to the Turks, while parts of Transdanubia and what is now Slovakia were governed by the Austrian House of Habsburg and assisted by the Hungarian nobility based at Bratislava. The principality of Transylvania prospered as a vassal state of the Ottoman Empire, initially under Szapolyai's son John Sigismund (Zsigmond János; r 1559–71). Though heroic resistance continued against the Turks throughout the 16th century, most notably at Kőszeg (see the boxed text, p191), Eger (see the boxed text, p331) and Szigetvár (see the boxed text, p310), this division would remain in place for more than a century and a half.

The Turkish occupation was marked by constant fighting among the three divisions; Catholic 'Royal Hungary' was pitted against both the Turks and the Protestant Transylvanian princes. Gábor Bethlen, who ruled Transylvania from 1613 to 1629, tried to end the warfare by conquering 'Royal Hungary' with a mercenary army of Heyduck peasants and some Turkish assistance in 1620. But both the Habsburgs and the Hungarians themselves viewed the 'infidel' Ottomans as the greatest threat to Europe since the Mongols and blocked the advance.

Ottoman power began to wane in the 17th century. At the same time Hungarian resistance to the Habsburgs, who had used 'Royal Hungary' as a buffer zone between Vienna and the Turks, increased. A plot inspired by the palatine Ferenc Wesselényi was foiled in 1670 and a revolt by Imre Thököly and his army of *kuruc* (anti-Habsburg mercenaries) was quelled in 1682. But with the help of the Polish army, Austrian and Hungarian forces liberated Buda from the Turks in 1686 after a 77-day siege, leaving much of the castle in ruins. An imperial army under Eugene of Savoya wiped out the last Turkish army in Hungary at the Battle of Zenta (now Senta in Serbia) 11 years later.

Eclipse of the Crescent Moon (Géza Gárdonyi, 1901) is a *Boy's Own*–style page-turner that tells the story of the siege of Eger by the Turks in 1552 and an orphaned peasant boy who grows up to become one of the greatest (fictional) heroes in Hungarian history.

THE START OF HABSBURG RULE

The expulsion of the Turks did not result in independence, and the policies of the Catholic Habsburgs' Counter-Reformation and heavy taxation further alienated the nobility. In 1703 the Transylvanian prince Ferenc Rákóczi II assembled an army of *kuruc* forces against the Austrians at Tiszahát in northeastern Hungary. The rebels 'dethroned' the Habsburgs as the rulers of Hungary in 1706 and the war dragged on for another five years. Superior imperial forces and lack of funds, however, forced the *kuruc* to negotiate a separate peace with Vienna behind Rákóczi's back. The 1703–11 war of independence had failed, but Rákóczi was the first leader to unite Hungarians against Habsburgs. Forced into exile, Rákóczi was given asylum by the Turkish Sultan Ahmet III and lived at Tekirdağ in Thrace until his death in 1735.

1795

Seven pro-republican Jacobites are beheaded at Vérmező in Buda for plotting against the Habsburg throne.

1838

Devastating Danube flood takes a heavy toll, with three-quarters of the homes in Pest washed away and some 150 people drowned.

1848–49

War of Independence; Sándor Petőfi dies fighting, and Lajos Batthyány and 13 of his generals are executed for their roles.

Habsburg Emperor Joseph II was called the 'hatted king' because he was never actually crowned within the borders of Hungary.

Though the armistice had brought the fighting to an end, Hungary was now a mere province of the Habsburg Empire. Five years after Maria Theresa ascended the throne in 1740, the Hungarian nobility pledged their 'lives and blood' to her at the diet in Bratislava in exchange for tax exemptions on their land. Thus began the period of 'enlightened absolutism' that would continue under the rule of Maria Theresa's son, Joseph II (r 1780–90).

Under both rulers, Hungary took great steps forward economically and culturally. The depopulated areas in the east and south were settled by Romanians and Serbs, while German Swabians were sent to Transdanubia. Joseph's attempts to modernise society by dissolving the all-powerful (and corrupt) religious orders, abolishing serfdom and replacing 'neutral' Latin with German as the official language of state administration were opposed by the Hungarian nobility, and he rescinded most of these orders on his deathbed.

Dissenting voices could still be heard, and in 1795 Ignác Martonovics, a former Franciscan priest, and six other republican Jacobites were beheaded at Vérmező (Blood Meadow) in Buda for plotting against the crown.

Liberalism and social reform found their greatest supporters among certain members of the aristocracy. Count György Festetics (1755–1819), for example, founded Europe's first agricultural college at Keszthely. Count István Széchenyi (1791–1860), a true Renaissance man (see the boxed text, p179), advocated the abolition of serfdom and returned much of his own land to the peasantry, and oversaw the regulation of the Tisza and Danube Rivers for commerce and irrigation.

But the proponents of gradual reform were quickly superseded by a more radical faction who demanded more immediate action. The group included Miklós Wesselényi, Ferenc Deák and Ferenc Kölcsey, but the predominant figure was Lajos Kossuth (1802–94). It was this dynamic lawyer and journalist who would lead Hungary to its greatest-ever confrontation with the Habsburgs.

THE 1848–49 WAR OF INDEPENDENCE

In what must be one of the oddest footnotes in Hungarian history, Napoleon Bonaparte entered Hungarian territory and spent the night of 31 August 1809 in Győr, which was near a battle site.

The Habsburg Empire began to weaken as Hungarian nationalism strengthened early in the 19th century. The Hungarians, suspicious of Napoleon's policies, ignored French appeals to revolt against Vienna, and certain reforms were introduced in the 1830s: the replacement of Latin, the official language of administration, with Hungarian; a law allowing serfs alternative means of discharging their feudal obligations of service; and increased Hungarian representation in the Council of State.

The reforms carried out were too limited and far too late, however, and the wave of revolution sweeping Europe was spurring on the more radical faction. On 15 March 1848 a group calling itself the Youth of March, led by the poet Sándor Petőfi, took to the streets to press for even more radical reforms. Just

1867

Act of Compromise creates the Dual Monarchy – Austria (the empire) and Hungary (the kingdom).

1896

Millennium of the Magyar conquest of the Carpathian Basin is marked by six-month exhibition in Budapest's City Park.

1918

Austria-Hungary loses WWI in November and the political system collapses; Hungary declares itself a republic.

two days later the liberal count Lajos Batthyány was made prime minister of the new Hungarian ministry, which counted Deák, Kossuth and Széchenyi as members, and the Habsburgs even agreed (reluctantly) to abolish serfdom and proclaim equality under the law. But with the diet becoming even more defiant in its dealings with the crown, Habsburg patience wore thin.

In September 1848 Habsburg forces launched an attack at Pákozd, on the northern shore of Lake Velence some 55km southwest of Budapest, and Batthyány's government was dissolved. The Hungarians hastily formed a national defence commission and moved the government seat to Debrecen, where Kossuth was elected governor-president. In April 1849 the parliament declared Hungary's full independence and the Habsburgs were 'dethroned' for the second time.

The new Habsburg emperor, Franz Joseph (r 1848–1916), was not at all like his feeble-minded predecessor Ferdinand V (r 1835–48) and acted quickly. He sought the assistance of Tsar Nicholas I, who obliged with 200,000 troops, and appointed a series of heads of government who were inflexible on the national question. Support for the revolution was waning rapidly, particularly in areas of mixed population where the Magyars were seen as oppressors. Weak and vastly outnumbered, the rebel troops were defeated by August 1849 and Kossuth had resigned.

A series of brutal reprisals ensued. Batthyány and 13 of his generals – the so-called 'Martyrs of Arad' – were executed. (Petőfi had died in battle in July of that year and Kossuth was now in exile.) Habsburg troops then went around the country systematically blowing up castles and fortifications lest they be used by resurgent rebels.

THE DUAL MONARCHY

Hungary was again merged into the Habsburg Empire as a conquered province and 'neo-absolutism' was the order of the day. Passive local resistance and disastrous military defeats for the Habsburgs by the French and then the Prussians in 1859 and 1866, however, pushed Franz Joseph to the negotiating table with liberal Hungarians under Deák's leadership.

The result was the Act of Compromise of 1867, which fundamentally restructured the Habsburg monarchy and created the Dual Monarchy of Austria (the empire) and Hungary (the kingdom) – a federated state with two parliaments and two capitals: Vienna and Pest (Budapest when Buda, Pest and Óbuda were merged in 1873). Only defence, foreign relations and customs were directed by the old imperial administration in Vienna.

This 'Age of Dualism', which would carry on until 1918, ushered in economic, cultural and intellectual renaissance in Hungary. The middle class, dominated by Germans and Jews in Pest, burgeoned and the capital entered into a frenzy of building. Much of what you see in Budapest

John Lukacs' classic *Budapest 1900: A Historical Portrait of a City and Its Culture* (1994) is an illustrated social history presenting the Hungarian capital at the height of its *fin-de-siècle* glory.

1919

Béla Kun's Republic of Councils, the world's second communist government after the Soviet Union's, lasts for five months.

1920

Treaty of Trianon carves up much of central Europe, reducing historical Hungary by almost two-thirds.

1931

Strongman Miklós Horthy declares martial law in the face of economic unrest.

today – from the grand boulevards with their Eclectic-style apartment blocks to the Parliament building – was built at this time, thus giving the cityscape a pleasantly homogenous feel. The apex of this golden age was the six-month exhibition in 1896 celebrating the millennium of the Magyar conquest *(honfoglalás)* of the Carpathian Basin.

Paul Lendvai's lively *The Hungarians: A Thousand Years of Victory in Defeat* takes a holistic look at Hungary's past – not just political events and the people who shaped them, but why Hungarians have contributed so disproportionately, relative to their numbers, to modern sciences and arts.

But all was not well in the kingdom. The working class, based almost entirely in Budapest, had virtually no rights and the situation in the countryside remained as dismal as it had been in the Middle Ages. Despite a new law enacted in 1868 to protect their rights, minorities under Hungarian control – Czechs, Slovaks, Croatians and Romanians – were under increased pressure to 'Magyarise', and many viewed their new rulers as oppressors.

WWI & THE REPUBLIC OF COUNCILS

On 28 July 1914, a month to the day after the assassination of Archduke Franz Ferdinand, heir to the Habsburg throne, by a Bosnian Serb in Sarajevo, Austria-Hungary declared war on Serbia and entered WWI allied with the German Empire. The result was disastrous, with widespread destruction and hundreds of thousands killed on the Russian and Italian fronts. After the armistice in 1918 the fate of the Dual Monarchy – and Hungary as a multinational kingdom – was sealed with the Treaty of Trianon (see the boxed text, below).

A republic under the leadership of Count Mihály Károlyi was established just five days after the armistice was signed, but the fledgling republic would not last long. Rampant inflation, mass unemployment, the occupation of

NEVER! SAY NEVER!

In June 1920, scarcely a year and a half after the treaty ending WWI was signed, the victorious Allies drew up a postwar settlement under the Treaty of Trianon at Versailles, near Paris, that enlarged some countries, truncated others and created several 'successor states'. As one of the defeated enemy nations and with large numbers of minorities clamouring for independence within its borders, Hungary stood to lose more than most. It was reduced to 40% of its historical size and, while it was now a largely uniform, homogeneous state, millions of ethnic Hungarians in Romania, Yugoslavia and Czechoslovakia were now the minority. Hungary lost 43% of its arable land, 58% of its railroads, 60% of its forests and 83% of its iron ore resources.

'Trianon' became the singularly most hated word in Hungary and *'Nem, Nem, Soha!'* (No, No, Never!) the rallying cry during the interwar years. Many of the problems the *diktátum* – 'dictate', as the Hungarians disparagingly call the treaty – created remained in place for decades, and it has coloured Hungary's relations with its neighbours for almost a century. Hungary has now signed basic treaties with fellow EU members Romania and Slovakia renouncing all outstanding territorial claims, but the issue of ethnic Hungarian minority rights in those countries causes bilateral tensions to flare up from time to time.

1939

Nazi Germany invades Poland; Britain and France declare war on Germany two days later.

1941

Hungary joins the Axis led by Germany and Italy against the Allies in WWII.

1944

Germany invades and occupies Hungary; most Hungarian Jews are deported to Nazi concentration camps.

HUNGARY BEFORE THE 1920 TRIANON TREATY

Hungary by the Allies and dismemberment of 'Greater Hungary', and the success of the Bolshevik Revolution in Russia all combined to radicalise much of the Budapest working class. In March 1919 a group of Hungarian communists under a former Transylvanian journalist called Béla Kun took power. The so-called Republic of Councils (Tanácsköztársaság) set out to nationalise industry and private property, but Kun's failure to regain the 'lost territories' (despite getting some land back from Romania and briefly occupying Slovakia) brought mass opposition to the regime and the government unleashed a reign of 'red terror' around the country. Kun and his comrades, including Minister of Culture Béla Lugosi of *Dracula* fame, were overthrown in just five months by Romanian troops, who occupied the capital.

Miklós Jancsó's film *Csend és Kiáltás* (Silence and Cry; 1967) is a political thriller about a 'red' who takes refuge among politically suspicious peasants after the overthrow of Béla Kun's Republic of Councils in 1919.

THE HORTHY YEARS & WWII

In March 1920, in Hungary's first-ever election by secret ballot, parliament chose a kingdom as the form of state and – lacking a king – elected as its 'regent' Admiral Miklós Horthy. He embarked on a 'white terror' – every bit as brutal as the red one of Béla Kun – that attacked communists and Jews (Béla Kun and many of his aides were Jewish) for their roles in supporting the Republic of Councils. As the regime was consolidated, it showed itself to be extremely right-wing and conservative, advocating the status quo and 'traditional values' – family, state, religion. Though the country had the remnants of a parliamentary system, Horthy was all-powerful, and very few reforms were enacted.

1945

Budapest is liberated by the Soviet army in April, a month before full victory in Europe.

1946

Hungary experiences the world's worst hyperinflation, with notes worth up to 10,000 trillion pengő issued.

1949

The communists, now in complete control, announce the formation of the 'People's Republic of Hungary'.

One thing on which everyone agreed was that the return of the 'lost' territories was essential for Hungary's development. Early on Prime Minister István Bethlen was able to secure the return of Pécs, illegally occupied by Yugoslavia, and the citizens of Sopron voted in a plebiscite to return to Hungary from Austria, but that was hardly enough. Hungary obviously could not count on the victorious Allies to help recoup its land; instead, it sought help from the fascist governments of Germany and Italy.

A perplexed US president Franklin D Roosevelt asked an aide in the early days of WWII: 'Hungary is a kingdom without a king, run by a regent who's an admiral without a navy?'

Hungary's move to the right intensified throughout the 1930s, though it remained silent when WWII broke out in September 1939. Horthy hoped an alliance would not mean actually having to enter the war, but after recovering northern Transylvania and part of Croatia with Germany's help, the regent joined the German- and Italian-led Axis, declaring war on the Soviet Union in June 1941. The war was as disastrous for Hungary as WWI had been, and hundreds of thousands of Hungarian troops died while retreating from Stalingrad, where they'd been used as cannon fodder. Realising too late that his country was on the losing side again, Horthy and his prime minister began secret discussions with the Allies.

When Hitler caught wind of this in March 1944 he dispatched the German army. Under pressure, Horthy installed Ferenc Szálasi, the deranged leader of the pro-Nazi Arrow Cross Party, as prime minister in October before being deported to Germany. (Horthy would later go into exile in Portugal, where he died in 1957. Despite some public outcry, his body was taken to Hungary in September 1993 and buried in the family plot at Kenderes, east of Szolnok.)

The Arrow Cross Party moved quickly to quash any opposition, and thousands of liberal politicians and labour leaders were arrested. At the same time, the puppet government introduced anti-Jewish legislation similar to that in Germany and Jews, living in fear but still alive under Horthy, were rounded up into ghettos by the Hungarian Nazis. From May to July of 1944, less than a year before the war ended, some 450,000 men, women and children – 70% of Hungarian Jewry – were deported to Auschwitz and other labour camps, where they starved to death, succumbed to disease, or were brutally murdered by the German fascists and their henchmen.

German director Rolf Schübel's romantic drama *Ein Lied von Liebe und Tod* (Gloomy Sunday; 1999) is set in a Budapest restaurant just before the Nazi invasion and revolves around the song 'Gloomy Sunday', which was so morose it had people committing suicide in Budapest.

Hungary now became an international battleground for the first time since the Turkish occupation, and bombs began falling on Budapest. What little opposition there was internally came mainly from the communists. Fierce fighting continued in the countryside, especially near Debrecen and Székesfehérvár, but by Christmas Day 1944 the Soviet army had encircled Budapest. When the Germans and Hungarian Nazis rejected a settlement, the Provisional National Assembly at Debrecen declared war on Germany and the siege of Budapest began. By the time the German war machine had surrendered in April 1945, many of Budapest's homes, historical buildings and churches had been destroyed. The vindictive retreating Germans blew up Buda Castle and knocked out every bridge spanning the Danube.

1956

Hungary is in revolution in October; János Kádár is installed as leader.

1958

Imre Nagy and others are executed by the communist regime for their role in the Uprising.

1963

The communist government extends amnesty to those involved in the 1956 Uprising, after a UN resolution condemning the suppression of the rebellion is struck from the agenda.

THE PEOPLE'S REPUBLIC OF HUNGARY

When free parliamentary elections were held in November 1945, the Independent Smallholders' Party (FKgP) received 57% (245 seats) of the vote. In response, Soviet political officers, backed by the occupying Soviet army, forced three other parties – the Communists, Social Democrats and National Peasants – into a coalition. Limited democracy prevailed, and land-reform laws, sponsored by the communist Minister of Agriculture Imre Nagy, were enacted. In March 1946 Arrow Cross Party leader Ferenc Szálasi was found guilty of high treason and war crimes and was executed by hanging.

Within a couple of years the communists were ready to take complete control. After a disputed election was held under a complicated new electoral law in 1947, they declared their candidate, Mátyás Rákosi, victorious. The following year the Social Democrats merged with the communists to form the Hungarian Workers' Party.

Rákosi, a big fan of Stalin, began a process of nationalisation and unfeasibly rapid industrialisation at the expense of agriculture. Peasants were forced into collective farms and all produce had to be delivered to state warehouses. A network of spies and informers exposed 'class enemies' (such as Cardinal József Mindszenty; see the boxed text, p155) to the secret police, the ÁVO (ÁVH after 1949). The accused were then jailed for spying, sent into internal exile or condemned to labour camps, such as the notorious one at Recsk in the Mátra Hills (p329). It is estimated that during this period a quarter of the adult population faced police or judicial proceedings.

Bitter feuding within the party began, and purges and Stalinist show trials became the norm. László Rajk, the communist minister of the interior (which also controlled the secret police), was arrested and later executed for 'Titoism'; his successor János Kádár was tortured and jailed. In August 1949 the nation was proclaimed the 'People's Republic of Hungary'.

After the death of Stalin in March 1953 and Krushchev's denunciation of him three years later, Rákosi's tenure was up and the terror began to abate. Under pressure from within the party, Rákosi's successor, Ernő Gerő, rehabilitated Rajk posthumously and readmitted Nagy, who had been expelled from the party a year earlier for suggesting reforms. But Gerő was ultimately as much a hardliner as Rákosi and by October 1956, during Rajk's reburial, murmured calls for a real reform of the system – 'socialism with a human face' – were already being heard.

THE 1956 UPRISING

The nation's greatest tragedy – an event that rocked communism, shook the world and pitted Hungarian against Hungarian – began on 23 October, when some 50,000 university students assembled at Bem tér in Buda, shouting anti-Soviet slogans and demanding that Nagy be named prime minister. That night a crowd pulled down the colossal statue of Stalin near Heroes' Sq,

The website of the Institute for the History of the 1956 Hungarian Revolution (www.rev.hu) will walk you through the build-up, outbreak and aftermath of Hungary's greatest modern tragedy through photographs, essays and timelines.

1968

Plans for a liberalised economy are introduced, but rejected as too liberal by conservatives.

1978

The Crown of St Stephen is returned to Hungary from the USA, where it had been held since the end of WWII.

1988

János Kádár is forced to retire in May after more than three decades in power.

leaving nothing but his boots on the plinth, and shots were fired by ÁVH agents on another group gathering outside the headquarters of Hungarian Radio in Pest. Hungary was in revolution.

The next day Nagy, the reform-minded minister of agriculture, formed a government, while János Kádár was named president of the Central Committee of the Hungarian Workers' Party. At first it appeared that Nagy might be successful in transforming Hungary into a neutral, multiparty state. On 28 October the government offered amnesty to all those involved in the violence and promised to abolish the ÁVH. On 31 October hundreds of political prisoners were released and widespread (and quite violent) reprisals against ÁVH agents began. The next day Nagy announced that Hungary would leave the Warsaw Pact and declare itself neutral.

Szabadság, Szerelem (Children of Glory; 2006) by Krisztina Goda is the simplified (but effective) history of the 1956 Uprising, as seen through the eyes of a player on the Olympic water polo team and his girlfriend, who is one of the student leaders.

At this, Soviet tanks and troops crossed into Hungary and within 72 hours began attacking Budapest and other urban centres. Kádár, who had slipped away from Budapest to join the Russian invaders, was installed as leader.

Fierce street fighting continued for several days – encouraged by Radio Free Europe broadcasts and disingenuous promises of support from the West, which was embroiled in the Suez Canal crisis at the time. When the fighting was over, 25,000 people were dead. Then the reprisals began. About 20,000 people were arrested and 2000 – including Nagy and his associates – were executed. Another 250,000 refugees fled to Austria. The government lost what little credibility it had ever had and the nation some of its most talented people. As for the physical scars, look around you at so many buildings in Pest: the bullet holes and shrapnel scorings on the exterior walls still cry out in silent fury.

HUNGARY UNDER KÁDÁR

After the revolt, the ruling party was reorganised as the Hungarian Socialist Workers' Party, and Kádár began a program to liberalise the social and economic structure, basing his reforms on compromise. (His most quoted line was 'Whoever is not against us is for us' – a reversal of the Stalinist adage that 'Those not for us are against us'.) In 1968 he and the economist Rezső Nyers unveiled the New Economic Mechanism (NEM) to introduce market elements to the planned economy. But even this proved too daring for many party conservatives. Nyers was ousted and the NEM all but abandoned.

A Good Comrade: János Kádár, Communism & Hungary by Roger Gough, arguably the definitive biography of a communist official, does much to explain the tour de force that transformed Kádár from traitor and most hated man in the land to respected reformer.

Kádár managed to survive that power struggle and went on to introduce greater consumerism and market socialism. By the mid-1970s Hungary was light years ahead of any other Soviet bloc country in its standard of living, freedom of movement and opportunities to criticise the government. The 'Hungarian model' attracted much Western attention and, importantly, investment.

But things began to go pear-shaped in the 1980s. The Kádár system of 'goulash socialism', which seemed so 'timeless and everlasting' (as

1989

The electrified fence separating Hungary and Austria is removed in July; the Republic of Hungary is declared in October.

1990

The centrist MDF wins the first free elections in 43 years in April; Árpád Göncz is elected the republic's first president in August.

1991

The last Soviet troops leave Hungarian soil in June, two weeks before they were scheduled to leave.

one Hungarian writer has put it), was incapable of dealing with such 'unsocialist' problems as unemployment, soaring inflation and the largest per-capita foreign debt in the region. Kádár and the 'old guard' refused to hear talk about party reforms. In June 1987 Károly Grósz took over as premier, and less than a year later Kádár was booted out of the socialist party and retired.

RENEWAL & CHANGE

A group of reformers – among them Nyers, Imre Pozsgay, Miklós Németh and Gyula Horn – took charge. Party conservatives at first put a lid on real change by demanding a retreat from political liberalisation in exchange for their support of the new regime's economic policies. But the tide had already turned.

Throughout the summer and autumn of 1988, new political parties were formed and old ones resurrected. In January 1989 Pozsgay, seeing the handwriting on the wall as Mikhail Gorbachev launched his reforms in the Soviet Union, announced that the events of 1956 had been a 'popular insurrection' and not the 'counter-revolution' that the regime had always called it. In June some 250,000 people attended the reburial of Imre Nagy and other victims of 1956 in Budapest.

The next month, again at Pozsgay's instigation, Hungary began to demolish the electrified wire fence separating it from Austria. The move released a wave of East Germans holidaying in Hungary into the West and the opening attracted thousands more. The collapse of the communist regimes around the region had become unstoppable.

THE REPUBLIC OF HUNGARY REBORN

At their party congress in February 1989 the communists had agreed to give up their monopoly on power, paving the way for free elections in March 1990. On 23 October 1989, the 33rd anniversary of the 1956 Uprising, the nation once again became the Republic of Hungary. The party's name was changed from the Hungarian Socialist Workers' Party to the Hungarian Socialist Party (MSZP).

The last Soviet troops left Hungary in June 1991 to great fanfare, and an annual festival still marks the date, but what few people know is that the Russians actually left two weeks ahead of schedule.

The MSZP's new program advocated social democracy and a free-market economy, but this was not enough to shake off the stigma of its four decades of autocratic rule. The 1990 vote was won by the centrist Hungarian Democratic Forum (MDF), which advocated a gradual transition to full capitalism. The social-democratic Alliance of Free Democrats (SZDSZ), which had called for much faster change, came second and the socialists trailed far behind. As Gorbachev looked on from Moscow, Hungary changed political systems with scarcely a murmur, and what Hungarians now call *az átkos 40 év* (the accursed 40 years) came to a withering, almost feeble, end.

1994

The Socialists win general election and form government for the first time since the changes of 1989.

1995

Árpád Göncz of the SZDSZ, arguably the most popular politician in Hungary, is elected for a second (and, by law, final) five-year term as president of the republic.

1999

Hungary joins NATO as a fully fledged member.

In coalition with two smaller parties – the Independent Smallholders and the Christian Democrats (KDNP) – the MDF provided Hungary with sound government during its painful transition to a full-market economy. Those years saw Hungary's northern (Czechoslovakia) and southern (Yugoslavia) neighbours split along ethnic lines, and Prime Minister József Antall did little to improve Hungary's relations with Slovakia, Romania and Yugoslavia by claiming to be the 'emotional and spiritual' prime minister of the large Magyar minorities in those countries. He died in December 1993 after a long fight with cancer and was replaced by interior minister Péter Boross.

Alan Parker's 1996 film *Evita* was filmed in Budapest. The Buenos Aires cathedral on screen is St Stephen's Basilica, the grand, tree-lined boulevard is Andrássy út and the swarthy horse guards belong to the Hungarian mounted cavalry.

Despite initial successes in curbing inflation and lowering interest rates, a host of economic problems slowed the pace of development, and the government's laissez-faire policies did not help. Like most people in the region, Hungarians had, perhaps unrealistically, expected a much faster improvement in their living standards. Most of them – 76% according to a poll in mid-1993 – were 'very disappointed' with the results.

In the national elections of May 1994 the Socialist Party, led by Gyula Horn, won an absolute majority in parliament. This in no way implied a return to the past, and Horn was quick to point out that it was in fact his party that had initiated the whole reform process in the first place. (Indeed, as foreign minister in 1989 he had played a key role in opening the border with Austria.) Árpád Göncz of the SZDSZ was elected for a second five-year term as president in 1995.

THE ROAD TO EUROPE

After its dire showing in the 1994 elections, the Federation of Young Democrats (Fidesz), which until 1993 had limited membership to those aged under 35 in order to emphasise a past untainted by communism and privilege, moved to the right and added the extension 'MPP' (Hungarian Civic Party) to its name to attract the support of the burgeoning middle class. In the 1998 elections, during which it campaigned for integration with Europe, Fidesz-MPP won by forming a coalition with the MDF and the conservative Independent Smallholders. The party's youthful leader, Viktor Orbán, was named prime minister.

But despite the astonishing economic growth and other gains made by the coalition government, the electorate grew increasingly hostile to Fidesz-MPP's strongly nationalistic rhetoric and perceived arrogance. In April 2002 the largest turnout of voters in Hungarian history unseated the government in the country's most closely fought election ever and returned the MSZP, allied with the SZDSZ, to power under Prime Minister Péter Medgyessy, a free-market advocate who had served as finance minister in the Horn government. In August 2004, amid revelations that he had served as a counterintelligence officer in the late 1970s and early 1980s while working in the finance ministry, and with the government's popularity at a three-year low, Medgyessy tendered his resignation – the first collapse of a government in Hungary's postcommunist history. Sports Minister Ferenc Gyurcsány of the MSZP was named premier.

2000

Ferenc Mádl, the nominee of the Fidesz-MPP and FKgP coalition government, is elected the second president of the republic to succeed Árpád Göncz.

2004

Hungary is admitted to the EU along with nine other new member-nations.

2005

László Sólyom, law professor and founding member of the MDF, is elected third president of the republic, succeeding Ferenc Mádl.

HOME AT LAST

Hungary became a fully fledged member of NATO in 1999 and, with nine so-called accession countries, was admitted into the EU in May 2004. In June 2005 parliament elected László Sólyom, a law professor and founding member of the MDF, as the third president of the republic to succeed the outgoing Ferenc Mádl.

Gyurcsány was reappointed prime minister in April 2006 after the electorate gave his coalition 210 of the available 386 parliamentary seats. He immediately began a series of austerity measures to tackle Hungary's budget deficit, which had reached a staggering 10% of the GDP. But in September, in an incident that could have been scripted by the courtiers of Louis XIV's Versailles, just as these unpopular steps were put into place an audiotape recorded shortly after the election at a closed-door meeting of the prime minister's cabinet had Gyurcsány confessing that the party had 'lied morning, evening and night' about the state of the economy since coming to power and now had to make amends. Gyurcsány refused to resign, and public outrage led to a series of demonstrations near the Parliament building in Budapest, culminating in widespread rioting that marred the 50th anniversary of the 1956 Uprising.

Since then sometimes violent demonstrations have become a regular feature on the streets of Budapest and other large cities, especially during national holidays. The radical right-wing nationalist party Jobbik Magyarországért Mozgalom (Movement for a Better Hungary), and its uniformed militia arm, the Magyar Gárda (Hungarian Guard), have been at the centre of many of these demonstrations and riots. Many Hungarian people are deeply concerned with the rise in the activities (and some say popularity) of the extreme right.

Gyurcsány, who has been able to survive near-death blows in his political career, had his head on the block again in March 2008 when the opposition forced through a referendum on the government's health-care reform program. The referendum was soundly defeated, and the SZDSZ quit the coalition, leaving Gyurcsány to head a feeble minority government until general elections scheduled for 2010.

At the time of writing Hungary, once the success story of Eastern Europe, was still reeling from the fallout of worldwide economic collapse. Overborrowed and overspent, the country had been especially hard hit and, with such unlikely fellow travellers as Iceland, Belarus and Pakistan, had just a week before Republic Day approached the International Monetary Fund for economic assistance. It felt like a century – not less than two decades – had passed since the heady moments of 23 October 1989 when the republic of Hungary had re-emerged phoenix-like from the ashes of communism. 'Many people think that Hungary was,' wrote István Széchenyi, in his seminal work *Hitel* (Credit) in 1830. 'I like to believe that she will be!' Truer words, dear count…

2006

Socialist Prime Minister Ferenc Gyurcsány is re-elected; Budapest is rocked by rioting during the 50th anniversary celebrations of the 1956 Uprising.

2008

Government loses key referendum on health-care reform in March; SZDSZ quits coalition, leaving the socialists to form a minority government.

2008

In November, with Hungary's economy in danger of meltdown, the International Monetary Fund throws the country a US$25 billion lifeline.

The Culture

THE NATIONAL PSYCHE

When the Italian-American Nobel Prize–winning physicist Enrico Fermi (1901–54) was asked whether extraterrestrial beings existed, he replied: 'Of course they do…[and] they are already here among us. They are called Hungarians.' Dr Fermi, who had worked with two Nobel Prize–winning Hungarian scientists on the so-called Manhattan Project, which led to the development of the atomic bomb, was referring to the Magyars, an Asiatic people of obscure origins who do not speak an Indo-European language and make up the vast majority of Hungary's 10 million or so people.

Hungarians are generally not uninhibited souls like the gregarious Romanians or the sentimental Slavs. Forget about the impassioned, devil-may-care, Gypsy-fiddling stereotype – it doesn't exist here. Hungarians are a reserved and somewhat formal people. They are almost always extremely polite in social interaction, and the language can be very courtly – even when doing business with the butcher or having a haircut. A standard greeting for a man to a woman (or youngsters to their elders, regardless of sex) is *'Csókolom'* ('I kiss it' – 'it' being the hand). People of all ages – even close friends – shake hands when meeting up. But while all this civility certainly oils the wheels that turn a sometimes difficult society, it can be used to keep 'outsiders' (both foreigners and other Hungarians) at a distance.

The national anthem describes Hungary as 'long torn by ill fate' and the overall mood here is one of *honfibú*, literally 'patriotic sorrow' but really a penchant for the blues with a sufficient amount of hope to keep most people going. This mood certainly predates communism. To illustrate what she saw as the 'dark streak in the Hungarian temperament', the late US foreign correspondent Flora Lewis recounted a story in *Europe: A Tapestry of Nations* that was the talk of Europe in the early 1930s. 'It was said', she wrote, 'that a song called 'Gloomy Sunday' so deeply moved otherwise normal people [in Budapest] that whenever it was played, they would rush to commit suicide by jumping off a Danube bridge.' The song has been covered in English by many artists, including Billie Holiday, Sinéad O'Connor, Marianne Faithfull and Björk.

'Hungary's contributions to education and the sciences have been far greater than its size and population would dictate'

Hungary is a highly cultured and educated society, with a literacy rate of over 99% among those 15 years and over. School is compulsory until the age of 16. A very high 86% of the population have completed secondary school and 14% are university graduates. Hungary currently counts 19 universities.

Hungary's contributions to specialised education and the sciences have been far greater than its present size and population would dictate. A unique method of music education devised by the composer Zoltán Kodály (1882–1967) is widespread, and Budapest's Pető Institute, founded by András Pető (1893–1967) in 1945, has a very high success rate in teaching children with cerebral palsy to walk. Albert Szent-Györgyi (1893–1986) won the Nobel Prize for Physiology or Medicine in 1937 for his discovery of vitamin C; Georg von Békésy (1899–1972) won the same prize in 1961 for his research on the inner ear; and Eugene Paul Wigner (1902–95) received a Nobel Prize in 1963 for his research in nuclear physics.

LIFESTYLE

About two-thirds of all Hungarians live in towns (see p43), though many retain some connection with the countryside – be it a *nyaralóház* (summer cottage) by the lake or a hut in one of the wine-growing regions.

That's not to say traditional culture is exactly thriving in Hungary. Apart from the Busójárás festival in Mohács (p286), Farsang and other pre-Lenten carnivals are now celebrated at balls and private parties. The sprinkling of water or perfume on young girls on Easter Monday is now rare except in the village of Hollókő (p319), though the Christmas tradition of Betlehemzés, where young men and boys carry model churches containing a manger from door to door, can still be seen in some parts of the countryside. A popular event for city folk, with tenuous ties to the countryside, is the *disznótor,* which involves the slaughtering of a pig followed by a party.

Like Spaniards, Poles and many others with a Catholic background, Hungarians celebrate *névnap* (name days) along with birthdays. Name days are usually the Catholic feast day of their patron saint, but less holy names have a date, too. Most calendars in Hungary list them and it's traditional for men to give women at least a single blossom.

By and large, Hungarians tend to meet their friends and entertain outside the home at cafes and restaurants. If you are invited to a Hungarian home, bring a bunch of flowers or a bottle of good local wine (see p53).

The 'typical' Hungarian family is two children plus their married parents, but this is a model only; fewer couples are getting married before they have their first (and only) child. Of those couples who do go for marriage, more than half end up divorcing. About 16% of all Hungarian children live in single-parent (usually fatherless) households.

You can talk about anything under the sun with Hungarians – from religion and politics to whether their language really is more difficult than Japanese and Arabic – but money is a touchy subject. Traditionally, the discussion of wealth – or even wearing flashy bling and clothing – was considered gauche (though it's not so much the case nowadays). Though it's almost impossible to calculate (with the 'black economy' being so widespread and important), the average monthly salary at the time of writing was about 164,000Ft gross. The minimum wage at the start of 2008 was 69,000Ft a month, which could be increased by 20% to 60% depending on the recipient's educational qualifications.

Drinking is an important part of social life in a country that has produced wine and fruit brandies for thousands of years. Consumption is high at an annual average of 13.6 litres of alcohol per person; only citizens of Luxembourg and Ireland drink more alcohol per capita in Europe. Alcoholism in Hungary is not as visible to the outsider as it is in, say, Russia, but it's there nonetheless; official figures suggest that 10% of the population are fully fledged alcoholics. And it must be said that even social drinking is not always a happy affair and can often end (willingly) in tears. Indeed, Hungarians have an expression for this bizarre arrangement: *sírva vigadni,* or 'to take one's pleasure sadly'.

The revised edition of *Culture Shock! Hungary: A Guide to Customs & Etiquette* by Zsuzsanna Ardó goes beyond the usual anecdotal information and observations offered in this kind of book and is virtually an anthropological and sociological study of the Magyar race.

WHERE THE FIRST COME LAST

Following a practice unknown outside Asia, Hungarians reverse their names in all uses, and their 'last' name (or surname) always comes first. For example, John Smith is never János Kovács but Kovács János, while Elizabeth Taylor is Szabó Erzsébet and Francis Flour is Liszt Ferenc.

Most titles also follow the structure: Mr John Smith is Kovács János úr. Many women follow the practice of taking their husband's full name. If Elizabeth was married to John, she might be Kovács Jánosné (Mrs John Smith) or, increasingly popular among professional women, Kovácsné Szabó Erzsébet.

To avoid confusion, all Hungarian names that are translated into English in this guide are written in the usual Western manner – Christian name first – including the names of museums, theatres etc. So, Budapest's Arany János színház is the János Arany Theatre in English. Addresses are always written in Hungarian as they appear on street signs: eg Kossuth Lajos utca, Dísz tér.

A DUBIOUS DISTINCTION

Hungary has one of the world's highest suicide rates – 42.3 men and 11.2 women per 100,000 people, surpassed only by Belarus, Russia and Lithuania. Psychologists are still out to lunch as to why this phenomenon has persisted for more than a century and a half. Some say that Hungarians' inclination to gloom leads to the ultimate act of despair. Others link it to a phenomenon not uncommon here in the late 19th century. As the Hungarian aristocracy withered away, the *kisnemesség* (minor nobility), some of whom were no better off than the local peasants, would do themselves in to 'save their name and honour'. As a result, suicide was – and is – not looked upon dishonourably as such. Victims may be buried in hallowed ground and the euphemistic sentence used in newspaper obituaries is 'János Kovács/Erzsébet Szabó died suddenly and tragically.' Some 63% of suicides are by hanging.

While some Hungarian men can be sexist in their thinking, women generally do not suffer any particular form of harassment (though domestic violence and rape get relatively little media coverage here). Most men are effusively polite to women. Women may not be made to feel especially welcome when eating or drinking alone, but it's really no different to most other countries in Europe.

Life expectancy in Hungary is very low by European standards: just over 69 years for men and almost 78 for women. The nation also has one of Europe's lowest birth rates – 9.6 per 1000 people, with a population growth of -0.25%. Sadly, it also claims one of the highest rates of suicide (see the boxed text, above) in the world.

There's not much gay or lesbian life in the countryside unless you take it with you; both communities keep a very low profile outside the capital. But one recent change that may see an end to that is a new law, which goes into effect in 2009, allowing same-sex couples to register a civil partnership. This arrangement will carry many of the rights and obligations of marriage, including inheritance, taxation and other financial matters, but not adoption.

Hungarians let their hair – and most of their clothes – down in summer at lake and riverside resorts; going topless is almost the norm for women here. In warm weather everywhere you'll see more public displays of affection on the streets than perhaps any place else in the world. It's all very romantic, but beware: in the more remote corners of city parks you may even stumble upon more passionate displays.

ECONOMY

With the world's financial markets in freefall at the time of writing, Hungary's economy, already on its knees, was in danger of meltdown. After intense negotiations, in November 2008 the International Monetary Fund threw Hungary a US$25 billion lifeline, but one with strings attached requiring severe austerity.

Once the region's success story, Hungary has been living off borrowed money for years. In his first term, Prime Minister Ferenc Gyurcsány bolstered his popularity by cutting taxes, increasing child support subsidies and pensions and trying to bring the nation's overworked roads into the 21st century. But in order to exchange the forint for the euro by 2010, according to EU rules the country would have had to cut its budget deficit in half – to less than 3% of gross domestic product – slow down inflation, cut government debt, lower interest rates and keep the currency stable.

Though Hungary looked almost certain to miss that target almost two years after joining the EU, Gyurcsány was re-elected in May 2006 on a platform of fiscal reform. With the resounding defeat of the prime minister's plan to reduce health-care expenditure, the acrimonious collapse of his coalition government and the global financial crisis, Gyurcsány's plans to reduce the deficit to 2.9% and bring inflation down to just over 4% were now obsolete and he and his ministers were back at the drafting board.

Hungary's economy grew at less than 2% in 2007, among the slowest rates in Europe. Unemployment remained a very high 8% nationwide (though less than half that rate in Budapest) and inflation was more than 7%, half of what it was a decade before but up from the previous year's 3.7%. Still, all is not total despair in the land of the Magyar; the country continues to attract foreign direct investment, though at a price. Indeed, Hungary was able to beat Poland and Romania in winning contracts for an €800 million Daimler plant but had to come up with €300 million of the total investment. Foreign companies pick Hungary as a manufacturing base because the workforce is considered flexible, skilled, highly educated and relatively inexpensive.

POPULATION

Just over 92% of the population is ethnically Magyar. Non-Magyar minorities include Germans (2.6%), Serbs and other South Slavs (2%), Slovaks (0.8%) and Romanians (0.7%). The number of Roma is officially put at 1.9% of the population (or just under 200,000 people), but some people believe the figure is twice as high, and members of the Romani community itself put the number at 800,000.

The population density is about 109 people per sq km and just under 65% of the total live in towns or cities. Almost a quarter of the population lives in one of the nation's six largest cities: Budapest (1.67 million), Debrecen (215,000), Miskolc (184,100), Szeged (177,000), Pécs (156,000) and Győr (127,600). More than half of the 3150 communities in Hungary are in Transdanubia.

For the most part, ethnic minorities in Hungary aren't discriminated against and their rights are inscribed in the constitution. Yet this has not stopped the occasional attack on nonwhite foreigners, a rise in anti-Semitism and the widespread discrimination against Roma.

For a list of people who you may or may not have known were Magyar, get hold of *Eminent Hungarians* by Ray Keenoy, a 'light-hearted look' at the subject.

Significantly, almost half as many Magyars (or descendants of ethnic Hungarians) – upwards of five million people – live outside the country's national borders as within them, mostly as a result of the Treaty of Trianon of 1920 (see the boxed text, p32), WWII and the 1956 Uprising. The estimated 1.45 million Hungarians in Transylvania (now Romania) constitute the largest ethnic minority in Europe, and there are another 530,000 Magyars in Slovakia, 293,000 in Serbia, 156,000 in Ukraine, 40,500 in Austria, 16,500 in Croatia, 14,600 in the Czech Republic and 10,000 in Slovenia. Hungarian immigrants to the USA total 1.4 million and there are significant communities in Canada, Australia and Israel.

SPORT

Hungarians enjoy attending sporting matches and watching them on TV as much as they do participating. The most popular spectator sports are football and water polo, though auto and horse racing and even spectator chess have their fans.

Football is far and away the nation's favourite sport, and people still talk about the 'match of the century' at Wembley in 1953 when the Magic Magyars beat England 6–3 – the first time England lost a match at home. There are 16 premier league football teams in Hungary, five of which are based in the capital (see p128).

In water polo, Hungary has dominated the European Championships a dozen times since 1926 and has taken nine gold medals at Olympic Games, so it's worthwhile catching a professional or amateur game of this exciting seven-a-side sport. For details, see p128.

The Formula One Hungarian Grand Prix (p374), *the* sporting event of the year here, takes place just outside Budapest in August.

MEDIA

As in most European countries, printed news has strong political affiliations in Hungary. Almost all of the major broadsheets have left or centre-left leanings, with the exception of the conservative *Magyar Nemzet* (Hungarian Nation).

The most respected publications are the weekly news magazine *Heti Világgazdaság* (World Economy Weekly), known as HVG (pronounced 'ha-gay-vay'), and the former Communist Party mouthpiece *Népszabadság* (People's Freedom). The latter, a daily broadsheet, is now completely independent and had until recently the highest paid circulation of any Hungarian newspaper. It has now been overtaken by *Blikk*, a trashy tabloid that focuses on sport, stars and sex – not necessarily in that order. Specialist publications include the weekly intellectual *Élet és Irodalom* (Life and Literature), the satirical biweekly *Hócipő* (Snowshoe) and the mass-circulation daily *Nemzeti Sport* (National Sport).

Hungary finished 22nd at the 2008 Olympic Games in Beijing with 10 medals (three gold, five silver and two bronze). At the 2004 Olympic Games in Athens and the Games in Sydney in 2000, its athletes picked up exactly the same number of medals: eight gold, six silver and three bronze.

Magyar Televízió (MTV) controls two channels, recently rebranded as M1 and M2. The third public service station, Duna TV, which was launched in 2004, is independent of MTV. The two main commercial channels are TV2, which airs the ever-popular *Megasztár* (a kind of Pop Idol knock-off) and prime-time daily soap *Jóban Rosszban* (In Good Times and Bad), and RTL Klub, with the highly successful Big Brother–like *Való Világ* (Real World), daily soap opera *Barátok Közt* (Among Friends) and *Legyen Ön Is Milliomos* (Be a Millionaire).

The public Magyar Rádió (MR; Hungarian Radio) has three stations. They are named after famous Hungarians: Lajos Kossuth (jazz and news; 107.8FM), the most popular station in the country; Sándor Petőfi (1960s to 1980s music, news and sport; 94.8FM); and Béla Bartók (classical music and news; 105.3FM). Budapest Rádió, the external arm of Hungarian Radio, broadcasts on 88.1FM. Juventus (89.5FM), a music station popular with youngsters, claims the second-highest audience in Hungary. Rádió 88 (95.4FM) is a dance-music station from Szeged – just what students want. Rádió Danubius (103.3FM) is a mixture of popular hits and news, while Tilos Rádió (90.3FM) is an alternative station based in Budapest.

RELIGION

Hungarians tend to have a more pragmatic approach to religion than most of their neighbours; it has even been suggested that this generally sceptical view of matters of faith has led to Hungary's high rate of success in science and mathematics. Except in villages and on the most important holy days (Easter, the Assumption of Mary and Christmas), churches are never full. The Jewish community in Budapest, on the other hand, has seen a great revitalisation in recent years, mostly due to an influx of Orthodox Jews from the USA and Israel.

Of those Hungarians declaring religious affiliation in the most recent census, just under 52% said they were Roman Catholic, 16% Reformed (Calvinist) Protestant and 3% Evangelical (Lutheran) Protestant. There are also small Greek Catholic and Orthodox (2.6%) and other Christian (1%) congregations. Hungary's Jews (not all practicing) number around 100,000, down from a pre-WWII population of nearly eight times that amount. An estimated 80,000 live in Budapest.

ARTS

Hungarian art has been both stunted and spurred on by the pivotal events in the nation's history. King Stephen's conversion to Catholicism brought Romanesque and Gothic art and architecture, while the Turkish occupation nipped most of Hungary's Renaissance in the bud. The Habsburgs opened the doors wide to baroque influences. The arts thrived under the Dual Monarchy, through Trianon and even under fascism. The early days of communism brought the aesthetics of wheat sheaves and muscle-bound steelworkers to a less-than-impressed populace, but much money was spent on music and 'correct art' such as classical theatre.

It would be foolish – if not impossible – to ignore folk art when discussing fine art in Hungary. The two have been inextricably linked for several centuries and have greatly influenced one another. The music of Béla Bartók and the ceramic sculptures of Margit Kovács are deeply rooted in traditional culture. You'll see many fine examples of folk baroque and neoclassical peasant houses throughout Hungary but especially in Southern Transdanubia and around Lake Balaton.

Architecture

You won't find as much Romanesque and Gothic architecture in Hungary as you will in, say, Slovakia or the Czech Republic – the Mongols, Turks and Habsburgs destroyed most of it here – but the Benedictine Abbey Church at Ják (p185) is a fine example of Romanesque architecture, and there are important Gothic churches in Nyirbátor (p363) and Sopron (p174).

Baroque architecture abounds in Hungary; you can see examples in virtually every town in the country. For something on a grand scale, visit the Esterházy Palace at Fertőd (p177) or the Minorite church in Eger (p333).

Distinctly Hungarian architecture didn't come into its own until the mid-19th century, when Mihály Pollack, József Hild and Miklós Ybl were changing the face of Budapest or racing around the country building mansions and cathedrals. The Romantic Eclectic style of Ödön Lechner (Budapest Museum of Applied Arts; p100) and Hungarian Secessionist or Art Nouveau (Reök Palace in Szeged; p266) brought unique architecture to Hungary at the end of the 19th century and the start of the 20th. Art Nouveau fans will find in cities such as Budapest, Szeged and Kecskemét some of the best examples of the style in Europe.

The yellow ochre that became the standard colour for all Habsburg administrative buildings and many churches in the late 18th century and that is ubiquitous throughout Hungary is now called 'Maria Theresa yellow'.

Post-WWII architecture in Hungary is almost completely forgettable. One exception is the work of Imre Makovecz, who developed his own 'organic' style (not always popular locally) using unusual materials like tree trunks and turf. His work is everywhere, but among the best (or strangest) examples are the cultural centres at Sárospatak (p352) and Szigetvár (p308), and the Evangelist church in Siófok (p197).

Painting & Sculpture

For Gothic art, have a look at the 15th-century altarpieces done by various masters at the Christian Museum in Esztergom (p156). The Corpus Christi Chapel in the basilica at Pécs (p298), the Bakócz Chapel in Esztergom Basilica (p154) and the Royal Palace at Visegrád (p150) contain exceptional examples of Renaissance sculpture and masonry.

The finest baroque painters in Hungary were the 18th-century artists Franz Anton Maulbertsch, who did the frescoes in the Church of the Ascension at Sümeg (p212), and István Dorffmeister, whose work can be seen in the sublime murals in the Bishop's Palace in Szombathely (p182). The ornately carved altars in the Minorite church at Nyírbátor (p363) and the Abbey Church in Tihany (p216) are masterpieces of baroque carving.

The saccharine Romantic Nationalist school of heroic paintings, best exemplified by Bertalan Székely (1835–1910) and Gyula Benczúr (1844–1920), gave way to the realism of Mihály Munkácsy (1844–1900), the 'painter of the *puszta*'. The greatest painters from this period were Tivadar Kosztka Csontváry (1853–1919), who has been compared with Van Gogh (see the boxed text, p299), and József Rippl-Rónai (1861–1927), the key exponent of Secessionist painting in Hungary. There are museums dedicated to their work in Pécs (p298) and Kaposvár (p305), respectively.

The dynamic Association of Young Artists (www.c3.hu/fkse), a branch of the Hungarian Artists' National Association, only allows those under 35 to join it and is a showcase for contemporary Hungarian art.

Hungary's favourite artists of the 20th century include Victor Vasarely (1908–97), the so-called father of Op Art who began life as Győző Vásárhelyi but changed his name when he emigrated to Paris in 1930, and the sculptor Amerigo Tot (1909–84). There are museums dedicated to Victor Vasarely in both Pécs (p298) and Budapest (p94). Contemporary painters to keep a look out for include Árpád Müller and the late Endre Szász, who died in 2003 at the age of 77.

FOLK ART

Hungary has one of the richest folk traditions in Europe and, quite apart from its music, this is where the country often has come to the fore in art.

From the beginning of the 18th century, as segments of the Hungarian peasantry became more prosperous, ordinary people tried to make their world more beautiful by painting and decorating objects and clothing. It's important to remember two things when looking at folk art. First, with very few exceptions (such as the 'primitive' paintings in Kecskemét's Hungarian Museum of Naive Artists; p254), only practical objects used daily were decorated. Second, this was not 'court art' or the work of artisans making Chinese cloisonné or Fabergé eggs. It was the work of ordinary people trying to express the simple world around them in a new and different way. Some of it is excellent and occasionally you will spot the work of a genius who probably never ventured beyond his or her village or farm.

Outside museums most folk art in Hungary is largely moribund, though the ethnic Hungarian regions of Transylvania in Romania are a different story. Through isolation or a refusal to let go for economic or aesthetic reasons, however, pockets remain throughout the country. Ignore the central *népművészeti bolt* (folk-art shop) you'll find in most towns: they're mostly full of mass-produced kitsch.

The main centre of cottage weaving has always been the Sárköz region (p285) near Szekszárd in Southern Transdanubia – its distinctive black and red fabric is copied everywhere. More simple homespun material can be found in the Northeast, especially around Tiszahát.

Three groups of people stand out for their embroidery, the acme of Hungarian folk art: the Palóc of the Northern Uplands, especially around the village of Hollókő (p319); the Matyó from Mezőkövesd (p336); and the women of Kalocsa (p257). Also impressive are the waterproof woollen coats called *szűr*, once worn by herders on the Great Plain, which were masterfully embroidered by men using thick, 'furry' yarn.

Though a commercial site, www.folk-art-hungary.com is an excellent introduction and primer to embroidery and other textile folk art by artisans in Hollókő, Kalocsa and Mezőkövesd.

Folk pottery is world-class here and no Hungarian kitchen is complete without a couple of pairs of matched plates or shallow bowls hanging on the walls. The centre of this industry is in the Great Plain towns of Hódmezővásárhely, Karcag and Tiszafüred, though fine examples also come from Transdanubia, especially the Őrség region. There are jugs, pitchers, plates, bowls and cups, but the rarest and most attractive are the *írókázás fazékok* (inscribed pots), usually celebrating a wedding day, or produced in the form of animals or people, such as the *Miskai kancsó* (Miska jugs), not unlike English Toby jugs, from the Tisza River region. Nádudvar near

Hajdúszoboszló on the Great Plain specialises in black pottery – striking items and far superior to the greyish stuff produced at Mohács in Southern Transdanubia.

Objects carved from wood or bone – mangling boards, honey-cake moulds, mirror cases, tobacco holders, salt cellars – were usually the work of herders or farmers idle in winter. The shepherds and swineherds of Somogy County, south of Lake Balaton, and the cowherds of the Hortobágy excelled at this work, and their illustrations of celebrations and local 'Robin Hood' outlaws are always fun to look at.

Most people made and decorated their own furniture in the old days, especially cupboards for the *tiszta szoba* (parlour) and *tulipán ládák* (trousseau chests with tulips painted on them). The oaken chests decorated with geometrical shapes from the Ormánság region of Southern Transdanubia are superior to the run-of-the-mill tulip chests.

One art form that ventures into the realm of fine art is ceiling and wall folk painting. Among the best examples of the former can be found in churches, especially in the Northeast (eg at Tákos), the Northern Uplands (Füzér) and the Ormánság (Drávaiványi). The women of Kalocsa also specialise in colourful wall painting, some of it so overdone as to be garish.

Music

Hungary has produced many of the leading lights in the world of classical music, but one person stands head and shoulders above the rest: Franz (or, in Hungarian, Ferenc) Liszt (1811–86). Liszt established the Academy of Music in Budapest and liked to describe himself as 'part Gypsy'. Some of his works, notably his 20 *Hungarian Rhapsodies,* do in fact echo the traditional music of the Roma.

Franz Liszt was born in the Hungarian village of Doborján (now Raiding in Austria) to a Hungarian father and an Austrian mother, but never learned to speak Hungarian.

Ferenc Erkel (1810–93) is the father of Hungarian opera, and two of his works – the nationalistic *Bánk Bán,* based on József Katona's play of that name, and *László Hunyadi* – are standards at the Hungarian State Opera House.

Imre Kálmán (1882–1953) was Hungary's most celebrated composer of operettas. *The Queen of the Csárdás* and *Countess Marica* are two of his most popular works.

Béla Bartók (1881–1945) and Zoltán Kodály (1882–1967) made the first systematic study of Hungarian folk music, travelling together and recording throughout the Magyar linguistic region in 1906. Both incorporated some of their findings in their music – Bartók in *Bluebeard's Castle,* for example, and Kodály in the *Peacock Variations.*

The most prestigious orchestras in Hungary are the Budapest-based Hungarian National Philharmonic Orchestra and the Budapest Festival Orchestra, which has been voted by the London-based music magazine *Gramophone* as one of the world's top 10 symphonies.

When discussing folk music, it's important to distinguish between 'Gypsy' music and Hungarian folk music. Gypsy music as it is known and heard in Hungarian restaurants from Budapest to Boston is schmaltzy and based on tunes called *verbunkos* played during the Rákóczi independence wars. At least two fiddles, a bass and a cymbalom (a curious stringed instrument played with sticks) are de rigueur. You can hear this *csárda*-style (Hungarian-style restaurant/inn) music at almost any fancy hotel restaurant in the provinces or get hold of a recording by Sándor Lakatos and his band.

Hungarian folk musicians play violins, zithers, hurdy-gurdies, bagpipes and lutes on a five-tone diatonic scale. Watch out for Muzsikás, Marta Sebestyén, Ghymes (a Hungarian folk band from Slovakia), and the Hungarian group

Vujicsics that mixes elements of South Slav music. Another folk musician with eclectic tastes is the Paris-trained Bea Pálya, who combines such sounds as traditional Bulgarian and Indian music with Hungarian folk.

The music of the Csángó people, an ethnic group of Hungarians living in eastern Transylvania and Moldavia, is particularly haunting and is performed during the 10-day Jászberény Summer (p374), which attracts folk aficionados from all over.

Roma – as opposed to Gypsy – music is different altogether, and traditionally sung a cappella. Some modern Roma music groups – Kalyi Jag (Black Fire) from northeastern Hungary, Romano Drom (Gypsy Road) and Romani Rota (Gypsy Wheels) – have added guitars, percussion and even electronics to create a whole new sound.

Pop music is as popular here as anywhere – indeed, Hungary has one of Europe's biggest pop spectacles, the annual Sziget Music Festival (p374). It boasts more than 1000 performances over a week and attracts an audience of up to 385,000 people.

Dance

Groups like the State Folk Ensemble perform dances essentially for tourists throughout the year; visit a *táncház* (dance house; p125) if you prefer authentic folk dance rather than touristy two-stepping. The *táncház* is an excellent way to hear Hungarian folk music and to learn traditional dance, and they're good fun and relatively easy to find, especially in Budapest, where the dance house revival began in the 1970s (although they haven't really spread from there – villagers prefer DVDs, game shows and weekend discos). You'll rarely – if ever – encounter such traditional dances as the *karikázó* (circle dance) and *csárdás* outside the capital.

For times, dates and places of *táncház* meetings and performances in Budapest and elsewhere in Hungary, check out www.tanchaz.hu.

Hungary also has ballet companies based in Budapest, Pécs and Szeged, but the best by far is the Győr Ballet (p168).

Literature

No one could have put it better than the poet Gyula Illyés (1902–83), who wrote: 'The Hungarian language is at one and the same time our softest cradle and our most solid coffin.' The difficulty and subtlety of the Magyar tongue has excluded most outsiders from Hungarian literature for centuries and, though it would be wonderful to be able to read the swashbuckling odes and love poems of Bálint Balassi (1554–94) or Miklós Zrínyi's *Peril of Sziget* (1651) in the original, most people have to make do with their works in translation (see the boxed text, p50).

Sándor Petőfi (1823–49) is Hungary's most celebrated and widely read poet, and a line from his work *National Song* became the rallying cry for the 1848–49 War of Independence. A deeply philosophical play called *The Tragedy of Man* by Imre Madách (1823–64), published a decade after Hungary's defeat in the War of Independence, is still considered the country's greatest classical drama.

Hungary's defeat in 1849 led many writers to look to Romanticism for comfort and inspiration: winners, heroes and knights in shining armour became popular subjects. Petőfi's comrade-in-arms, János Arany (1817–82), whose name is synonymous with impeccable Hungarian, wrote epic poetry (including the *Toldi Trilogy*) and ballads. Another friend of Petőfi, the prolific novelist and playwright Mór Jókai (1825–1904), gave expression to heroism and honesty in such accessible works as *The Man with the Golden Touch* and *Black Diamonds*. Another perennial favourite, Kálmán Mikszáth (1847–1910), wrote satirical tales such as *The Good Palóc People* and *St Peter's Umbrella*, in which he poked fun at the gentry in decline.

The former US president Theodore Roosevelt enjoyed *St Peter's Umbrella* by Kálmán Mikszáth so much that he insisted on visiting the ageing novelist during a European tour in 1910.

Zsigmond Móricz (1879–1942) was a very different type of writer. His works, in the tradition of Émile Zola, examined the harsh reality of peasant life in Hungary in the late 19th century. His contemporary Mihály Babits (1883–1941), poet and editor of the influential literary magazine *Nyugat* (West), made the rejuvenation of Hungarian literature his lifelong work.

Two 20th-century poets are unsurpassed in Hungarian letters. Endre Ady (1877–1919), sometimes described as a successor to Petőfi, was a reformer who ruthlessly attacked Hungarians' growing complacency and materialism, provoking a storm of protest from right-wing nationalists. The work of socialist poet Attila József (1905–37) expressed the alienation felt by individuals in the modern age; his poem *By the Danube* is brilliant even in translation. József ran afoul of both the underground communist movement and the Horthy regime. Tragically, he threw himself under a train near Lake Balaton at the age of 32. A perennial favourite is the late Sándor Márai (1900–89), whose crisp style has encouraged worldwide interest in Hungarian literature.

Hungarian Literature Online (www.hlo.hu) leaves no page unturned in the world of Hungarian books, addressing everyone from writers and editors to translators and publishers, with a useful list of links as well.

Among Hungary's most important contemporary writers are Imre Kertész (1929–), György Konrád (1933–), Péter Nádas (1942–) and Péter Esterházy (1950–). Konrád's *A Feast in the Garden* (1985) is an almost autobiographical account of a Jewish community in a small eastern Hungarian town. *A Book of Memoirs* by Nádas traces the decline of communism, written in the style of Thomas Mann, and has been made into a film. In *The End of a Family Story,* Nádas uses a child narrator as a filter for the adult experience of 1950s communist Hungary. Esterházy's partly autobiographical *Celestial Harmonies* (2000) paints a favourable portrait of the protagonist's father. His later *Revised Edition* (2002) is based on documents revealing his father to have been a government informer during the communist regime.

Novelist and Auschwitz survivor Kertész won the Nobel Prize for Literature in 2002, the first time a Hungarian had gained that distinction. Among his novels available in English are *Fatelessness* (1975), *Detective Story* (1977), *Kaddish for an Unborn Child* (1990) and *Liquidation* (2003). Hungary's foremost female contemporary writer is Magda Szabó (*Katalin Street,* 1969; *The Door,* 1975), who died in 2007 at age 90.

Cinema

Cuts in state funding for films has limited the production of new Hungarian films to under 30 a year, but there are a handful of good (and even great) ones being made in what is still one of the more dynamic film-making countries in the region. For classics, look out for films by Oscar-winning István Szabó *(Sweet Emma, Dear Böbe, The Taste of Sunshine),* Miklós Jancsó *(Outlaws)* and Péter Bacsó *(The Witness, Live Show).* Other favourites are *Simon Mágus,* the surrealistic tale of two magicians and a young woman in Paris, from Ildikó Enyedi, and her *Tender Interface,* about the brain-drain from Hungary after WWII.

In Anthony Minghella's film *The English Patient* (1996), when László Almásy (Ralph Fiennes) plays a Hungarian folk song on the phonograph for Katharine Clifton (Kristin Scott Thomas), it is Marta Sebestyén singing 'Szerelem, Szerelem' (Love, Love).

Péter Timár's *Csinibaba* is a satirical look at life – and film production quality – during communism. *Zimmer Feri,* set on Lake Balaton, pits a young practical joker against a bunch of loud German tourists; the typo in the title is deliberate. Timár's *6:3* takes viewers back to that glorious moment when Hungary defeated England in football (see p43). Gábor Herendi's *Something America* is the comic tale of a film-making team trying to profit from an expatriate Hungarian who pretends to be a rich producer.

Of more recent vintage is Hungarian-American director Nimród Antal's *Kontroll,* a high-speed romantic thriller set almost entirely in the Budapest

HUNGARIAN WRITERS IN ENGLISH

The following is a small selection of classic Hungarian literary works available at English-language bookshops in Budapest (p72).

- *The Tragedy of Man* (Imre Madách, 1861) This lyrical drama, inspired by Milton and Goethe, puts a different spin on human history and examines the limitations of science and technology in dealing with moral issues through the eyes of Adam, Eve and Lucifer.
- *The Man with the Golden Touch* (Mór Jókai, 1872) The *chef d'œuvre* of the so-called Hungarian Dickens is a realistic portrait of the cruel world of finance, which is conquered by a hero with the 'Midas touch', and an attack on the commercialism of modern civilisation.
- *St Peter's Umbrella* (Kálmán Mikszáth, 1895) This delightful novel is a mixture of legend, fairy tale and social satire woven into the upbeat tale of a successful search for happiness.
- *The Paul Street Boys* (Ferenc Molnár, 1906) A turn-of-the-century novel about boys growing up in the tough 8th district, which can be read both as a youth novel and a biting satire on European nationalism.
- *Be Faithful unto Death* (Zsigmond Móricz, 1921) This moving story of a bright and sensitive schoolboy being educated at an old, very established boarding school in Debrecen is a microcosm of Hungary in the aftermath of the Republic of Councils and the Treaty of Trianon.
- *Skylark* (Dezső Kosztolányi, 1924) The story of a spinster living in the back of beyond of provincial Hungary conceals tensions and the purposeless of life; what appears to be provinciality may in fact be wisdom.
- *Journey Around My Skull* (Frigyes Karinthy, 1939) Though it hardly sounds a crowd-pleaser, Karinthy's autobiographical novel describing his descent into illness with a brain tumour and both his and others' reactions to his situation makes for engrossing reading.
- *Embers* (Sándor Márai, 1942) The story of a lifelong grievance that consumed the lives and friendship of two men for more than four decades.

metro in which assorted outcasts, lovers and dreamers commune. If it's unusual you want, try *Hukkle* by György Pálfi, a curious film where a bizarre cacophony of hiccups, belches, buzzing and grunting replaces dialogue. Kornél Mundruczó's recent award-winning *Delta* is the brooding tale of a man's return to his home in Romania's Danube Delta and his complex relationship with his half-sister.

Two films worth seeing that use pivotal events in recent Hungarian history as backdrops are *Children of Glory* by Krisztina Goda, which recounts the 1956 Uprising through the eyes of a player on the Olympic water polo team, and Ferenc Török's *Moszkva Tér,* the comic tale of high-school boys in 1989 oblivious to the important events taking place around them.

Food & Drink

There's a lot that's true and a lot that's not about Hungarian food. It certainly is the bright point among the cuisines of Eastern Europe, but it is decidedly not one of the world's three essential styles of cooking (after French and Chinese) as many here would have you believe. Hungarian cooking has had a lot of outside influences but has changed relatively little over the centuries. And while the cuisine makes great use of paprika, even the spice's hottest variety (called *csípős*) is pretty tame stuff; a taco with salsa or chicken vindaloo will taste a lot more 'fiery' to you.

Hungary's reputation as a food centre dates from the 15th century – apparently there was a lot of tasty cooking being done in Visegrád Castle – and, more importantly, the late 19th and first half of the 20th centuries. During the 'Golden Age' between the promulgation of the Dual Monarchy up to the start of WWII, food became a passion here. The world took note and Hungarian restaurants, complete with imported Gypsy bands, sprouted up in cities around the world. After WWII, during the chilly days of communism, the country's gastronomic reputation lived on, most notably because the food was so bad elsewhere in the region.

A good source for Hungarian recipes and techniques in the kitchen is http://hungarian foodrecipes.blogspot .com, a blog with favourite recipes from Hungary in English.

Although relatively inexpensive by Western standards and served in huge portions, Hungarian food can be heavy and verging on the unhealthy. Meat, sour cream and animal fat abound and, except in season, *saláta* (salad) usually means a plate of pickled vegetables. Things are changing, however, at least in Budapest. A number of vegetarian (or partially meatless) restaurants have opened, more places now offer a wider selection of 'real' vegetarian dishes on their menus and ethnic food is very popular. Even Hungarian food itself is undergoing a long-awaited transformation, with *kortárs magyar konyha* (modern Hungarian cuisine) being served at more and more restaurants.

STAPLES & SPECIALITIES

Bread & Pasta

It is said that Hungarians will eat 'bread with bread' and *kenyér* (leftover bread) has been used to thicken soups and stews since at least the reign of King Matthias Corvinus. *Kifli* (crescent-shaped rolls) have been popular since the Turkish occupation. But, frankly, bread in Hungary is not as memorable as the flour-based *galuska* (dumplings) and *tarhonya* (egg pasta resembling barley) served with such dishes as *pörkölt* (stew), *paprikás* and *tokány* (p52).

Soups

Most Hungarian meals start with *leves* (soup). This is usually something like *gombaleves* (mushroom soup) or *májgombócleves* (tiny liver dumplings in consommé). More substantial fare is beef *gulyásleves* (p52) and *bableves,* a thick bean soup, which are sometimes eaten as a main course. Another favourite is *halászlé* (fisherman's soup), a rich soup of poached carp, fish stock, tomatoes, peppers and paprika.

Meat & Fish

Hungarians eat an astonishing amount of meat, with pork, beef, veal and poultry the most commonly consumed. They can be breaded and fried, baked, turned into some paprika-flavoured concoction or simmered in *lecsó,* a tasty mix of red and green peppers, tomatoes and onions (and one of the few sauces here that does not include paprika).

A typical menu will have up to 10 pork and beef dishes, a couple of fish dishes and usually only one poultry dish. Goose livers and legs and turkey breasts – though not much else of either bird – make it onto most menus. Lamb is rarely eaten here.

Freshwater fish, such as the indigenous *fogas* (great pike-perch) and the younger and smaller *süllő* from Lake Balaton, and *ponty* (carp) from the nation's rivers and streams, is plentiful but is often overcooked.

Paprika

It takes almost six tonnes of fresh peppers to produce one tonne of paprika powder.

Many dishes are seasoned with paprika, a spice as Magyar as King Stephen; indeed, not only is it used in cooking but it also appears on restaurant tables as a condiment. It's generally quite a mild spice and is used predominantly with sour cream or in *rántás*, a heavy roux of pork lard and flour added to cooked vegetables. *Töltött*, vegetables stuffed with meat and/or rice, such as cabbage or peppers, are cooked in *rántás* as well as in tomato sauce or sour cream.

There are four major types of meat dishes that contain paprika. The most famous is *gulyás* (or *gulyásleves*), a thick beef soup cooked with onions, cubed potatoes and paprika, and usually eaten as a main course. *Pörkölt*, or 'stew', is closer to what we call 'goulash'; the addition of sour cream, a reduction in paprika and the use of white meat, such as chicken, makes the dish *paprikás*. *Tokány* is similar to *pörkölt* and *paprikás* except that the meat is usually cut into strips, black pepper is on equal footing with the paprika, and bacon, sausage or mushrooms are added.

Vegetables

Fresh salad is called *vitamin saláta* here and is usually available when lettuce is in season; almost everything else is *savanyúság* (literally 'sourness'), which can be anything from mildly sour-sweet cucumbers and pickled peppers to very acidic sauerkraut.

Boiled or steamed *zöldség* (vegetables), as we know them, are 'English-style' or *angolos zöldség*. The traditional Hungarian way of preparing vegetables is in *főzelék*, where peas, green beans, lentils, marrow or cabbage are fried or boiled and then mixed into a roux with milk. This dish, which is sometimes topped with a few slices of meat, is enjoying a major comeback at 'retro-style' eateries.

The 1971 film *Szindbád* (Sinbad), based on the novel of that name by Gyula Krúdy (1878–1933) and directed by Zoltán Huszárik, features a scene of a diner eating bone marrow on toast, which had the audience spellbound and salivating at a time when such luxuries were at a premium in socialist Hungary.

Desserts

Hungarians love sweets. Intricate pastries such as *dobostorta*, a layered chocolate and cream cake with a caramelised brown-sugar top, and *rétes* (strudel) filled with poppy seeds, cherry preserves or *túró* (curd or cottage cheese), and *piték* (fruit pies) are usually consumed mid-afternoon in a *cukrászda* (cake shop or patisserie). Desserts more commonly found on menus include *Somlói galuska*, a sponge cake with chocolate and whipped cream, and *Gundel palacsinta* (flambéed pancake with chocolate and nuts).

DRINKS

Nonalcoholic Drinks

Most international soft-drink brands are available here, but *ásvány víz* (mineral water) seems to be the most popular libation for teetotallers. Fruit juice is usually a canned or boxed fruit 'drink' with lots of sugar added.

Hungarians drink a tremendous amount of *kávé* (coffee) – as a *fekete* (single black) or a *dupla* (double). *Tejes kávé* (coffee with frothed milk) is actually what we call a cappuccino. *Cappuccino* here is coffee with whipped cream. Decaffeinated coffee is *koffeinmentes kávé*.

TASTY TRAVEL

Hungarians will happily consume *libamáj* (goose liver) and, to a lesser extent, *kacsamáj* (duck liver) whenever the opportunity presents itself, be it cold *zsírjában* (in its own fat), *roston sült* (pan-fried) with apples, or as *pástétom* (pâté), but they generally eschew other forms of offal. In general, the most 'unusual' Hungarian dishes are meatless and quite inviting. Cold fruit soups such as *meggyleves* (sour cherry soup) or *fahéjas-almaleves* (cinnamon apple soup) are a positive delight on a warm summer's evening. And 'odd' dishes such as *makós metélt* (vermicelli topped with poppy seeds) may look bizarre, fall neither in the savoury nor sweet category and stain your teeth for days, but you won't soon forget the taste.

Tea (pronounced *tay*-ah) is not as popular as coffee in Hungary, though *teaház* (tea houses) serving every imaginable type of tea and tisane have become very trendy over the past decade.

Alcoholic Drinks

Drinking is an important part of social life in a country that has produced wine and fruit brandies for thousands of years, and consumption is high.

Hungarians don't clink glasses when drinking beer because that's how the Habsburgs celebrated the execution of Lajos Kossuth, hero of the 1848–49 War of Independence, and his 13 generals at Arad.

BEER

Hungary produces a number of its own beers for national distribution, and the most common three are Dreher, Kőbányai and Arany Ászok, all produced by the same Budapest-based brewery. Some, however, are found more commonly in the vicinity of where they are brewed, such as Borsodi near Miskolc, Szalon in Pécs and Soproni in, of course, Sopron. Bottled and canned Austrian, German and Czech beers are readily available. Locally brewed and imported beer in Hungary is almost always *világos sör* (lager), though there's also Szalon Barna (Szalon Brown), which is stout, and Dreher Bak, a double bock. At a pub, beer is served in a *pohár* (0.3L) or a *korsó* (0.4L or 0.5L).

BRANDY & LIQUEUR

Pálinka is a strong (usually 40% but as high as 50%), uniquely Hungarian brandy or *eau de vie* distilled from a variety of fruits but most commonly from apricots or plums. There are many different types and qualities, but among our favourites are Óbarack, the double-distilled 'Old Apricot', the kind made with *málna* (raspberry) or *kökény* (blackthorn or sloe) and anything with *kóser* (kosher) on the label, which is always a sign of quality.

Hungarian liqueurs are usually unbearably sweet and artificial tasting, though the Zwack brand is good. Zwack also produces Unicum, a bitter aperitif that has been around since 1790.

Habsburg Emperor Joseph II supposedly gave Hungary's most famous herbal liqueur its name when he first tasted it, exclaiming *'Das ist ein Unikum!'* (This is a unique drink!)

WINE

Wine has been made in Hungary for thousands of years and is sold by the glass or bottle everywhere – at food stalls, wine bars, restaurants, supermarkets and 24-hour grocery stores – and usually at reasonable prices. Old-fashioned wine bars ladle it out by the *deci* (decilitre, 0.1L), but if you're seriously into wine, you should visit one of Budapest's wine restaurants, such as Klassz (p118), or speciality wine shops (p130).

When choosing a Hungarian wine, look for the words *minőségi bor* (quality wine) or *különleges minőségű bor* (premium quality wine), Hungary's version of the French quality regulation *appellation controlée*. Generally speaking, the *évjárat* (vintage) has become important only recently; see the boxed text, p55. On a wine label the first word indicates the region, the second the grape variety (eg Villányi Kékfrankos) or the type or brand of wine (eg Tokaji Aszú,

Szekszárdi Bikavér). Other important words that you'll see include: *édes* (sweet), *fehér* (white), *félédes* (semisweet), *félszáraz* (semidry or medium), *pezsgő* (sparkling), *száraz* (dry) and *vörös* (red).

Hungary counts 22 distinct wine-growing areas in four regions: Transdanubia, Balaton, Northern Uplands and Great Plain. They range in size from tiny Somló in Western Transdanubia, to the vast vineyards of the Kunság on the Southern Plain, with its sandy soil nurturing more than a third of all of the vines growing in the country.

The best website for Hungarian wines is www.bortarsasag.hu/en. It appraises vintners and their vintages and lists prices from the Bortársaság (Budapest Wine Society), Hungary's foremost wine club.

Arguably the most distinctive Hungarian red wines come from Villány and Szekszárd in Southern Transdanubia, and the best dry whites are produced around Lake Balaton and in Somló. The reds from Eger and sweet whites from Tokaj are much better known abroad, however.

Tokaj

The volcanic soil, sunny climate and protective mountain barrier of the Tokaj-Hegyalja region in the Northern Uplands make it ideal for growing grapes and making wine.

Tokaj dessert wines are rated according to the number – from three to six – of *puttony* (butts, or baskets for picking) of sweet Aszú grapes added to the base wines. These are grapes infected with so-called noble rot, the *Botrytis cinera* mould that almost turns them into raisins on the vine. Aszú Eszencia, an essence even sweeter than six-*puttony* wine, is added – very judiciously – to improve the wine. Some supermarket six-*puttony* Aszú sells for as little as 6500Ft.

Louis XIV famously called Tokaj 'the wine of kings and the king of wines', while Voltaire wrote that 'this wine could be only given by the boundlessly good God'.

Tokaj also produces less-sweet wines, including dry Szamorodni (an excellent aperitif) and sweet Szamorodni, which is not unlike an Italian *vin santo;* try Disznókő's fine sweet Szamorodni (5050Ft). Of the four grape varieties grown here, Furmint and Hárslevelű (Linden Leaf) are the driest. Some Hungarian wine experts believe Tokaj's future is in dry white wine, with sweet wines just the icing on the cake. They say that dry Furmint, with a flavour recalling apples, has the potential to become the best white wine in the country and that István Szepsy's 2006 vintage (4350Ft) could pass for a top-notch Burgundy.

For Tokaji Aszú, Szepsy is also the name to look out for; he concentrates on both the upscale six-*puttony* variety and the Aszú Eszencia itself. His

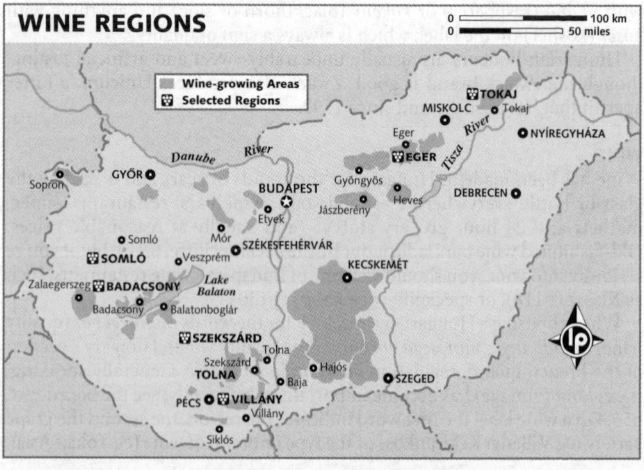

TAKING VINTAGE ADVANTAGE

2000 Very hot summer raises alcohol levels in whites, impairing acids and lowering quality; excellent for reds in Eger, Szekszárd and Villány.
2001 Decent year for whites in general; very good for some top-end reds (eg from Eger and Villány).
2002 No great whites, but the reds are firm and cellar well, depending on the grower.
2003 Very hot year, with a long, very even ripening season. The whites suffer from burned acids and preponderant alcohol; however, the reds are even more promising than in 2000 – full-bodied and big, almost with a California flair.
2004 Inferior year throughout, with aggressive whites and thin reds.
2005 A very wet summer was catastrophic for whites, but the quality of reds certainly beat 2004; no Villány cuvée produced.
2006 Bad start with a cool summer but long, very hot autumn proves excellent for whites and certain reds, putting in deep hues and high tannins. Especially good vintage for late-harvested sweet whites.
2007 Much hotter summer creates more rounded acidity in whites, especially in Tokaj.
2008 Too early to call at the time of writing, but a nice quantity of noble rot looks promising for Tokaj.

2003 six-*puttony* Aszú currently retails for a cool 24,300Ft a bottle. Szepsy Cuvée, aged in stainless steel barrels for a year or two (against the usual five for Tokaji Aszú) was first bottled in 1999 and is a complex, elegant blend comparable to Sauternes. A bottle of his 2006 vintage is 11,700Ft. Other names to watch out for in quality Tokaj wines are Hétszőlő, Degenfeld, Pendits and, for Furmint, Oremus and Béres. Oremus' Mandolás Furmint 2006 (2850Ft) and Béres' Lőcse Furmint 2006 (2650Ft) are both excellent value for money.

Vintage has always played a more important role in Tokaj than elsewhere in Hungary. Though it is said that there is only one truly excellent year each decade, the wines produced in 1972, 1988, 1999, 2000, 2003 and 2006 were all superb, and 1993 was almost as good.

Eger

Flanked by two of the Northern Uplands' most beautiful ranges of hills and on the same latitude as Burgundy, Eger is the home of the celebrated Egri Bikavér (Eger Bull's Blood). By law, Hungarian vintners must spell out the blend of wine on their label; the sole exception is Bikavér, though it's usually Kékfrankos (Blaufränkisch) mixed with other reds, sometimes including Kadarka. One of the few wineries whose blend of Bikavér is known for sure is Tibor Gál's. Its blend is 50% Kékfrankos and 50% Cabernet and his 2005 vintage (2650Ft) is excellent. Another producer of Bikavér to watch out for is István Toth, whose 1999 Bikavér easily compared with any of the 'big' reds from Villány and is said to have set the standard for Bull's Blood in Hungary. Much effort has gone into resuscitating the reputation of Bikavér at home and abroad by creating a new denomination called Egri Bikavér Superior.

The website www.wineportal.hu is excellent for basic and background information on Hungarian wine. It also lists accommodation options in the various wine regions and wine restaurants around the country.

Eger's signature grape is Pinot Noir and connoisseurs think that some of Vilmos Thummerer's vintages have been on par with the *premiers crus* from Burgundy. His Vili Papa Cuvée, a blend of Cabernet Franc, Cabernet Sauvignon and Merlot, is a monumental wine aged in new wood, with fleshy fruit flavours. It's priced from 8850Ft for the 2003 vintage. You'll also find several decent whites in Eger, including Leányka (Little Girl), Olaszrizling (Italian Riesling) and Hárslevelű from Debrő. Single-vineyard wines are also a trend in Eger. A curiosity is Tibor Gál's Viognier 2006 (4950Ft), a delicate floral white from a grape variety once limited to two hectares and now planted on an area five times that size.

Villány

Villány-Siklós, in Hungary's southernmost and warmest region – it is on the same latitude as Bordeaux – is especially noted for red wines: Blauer Portugieser (formerly called Kékoportó), Cabernet Sauvignon and, in particular, Cabernet Franc and Merlot. The region has also been experimenting in Pinot Noir in recent years. Red wines here are almost always big-bodied, Bordeaux-style and high in tannins.

Among the best vintners in Villány is József Bock, whose Royal Cuvée (4500Ft) is a special blend of Cabernet Franc, Pinot Noir and Merlot. Other vintners to watch out for are Márton Mayer and Alajos Wunderlich. Wines to try from this region include Attila Gere's elegant and complex Cabernet Sauvignon (3050Ft) and his Kopár (7950Ft), a blend of Cabernet Sauvignon, Merlot and Cabernet Franc, as well as Ede and Zsolt Tiffán's austere, tannic Blauer Portugieser and Cabernet Franc (3600Ft).

Szekszárd

Mild winters and warm, dry summers combined with favourable loess soil help Szekszárd in Southern Transdanubia to produce some of the best affordable red wines in Hungary. They are not like the big-bodied reds of Villány, but softer and less complex, with a distinct spiciness and are easy to drink. In general they are much better value. An excellent, premium-quality Szekszárd retails for under 3000Ft.

The premier grape here is Kadarka, a late-ripening variety, which is produced in limited quantities. The best Kadarka is made by Ferenc Takler (2300Ft). Kadarka originated in the Balkans – the Bulgarian Gamza grape is a variety of it – and is a traditional ingredient here in making Bikavér, a wine usually associated with Eger. In fact, many wine aficionados in Hungary prefer the Szekszárd variety of 'Bull's Blood'; try the Heimann variety (2250Ft).

The best Merlot (2450Ft) and Kékfrankos (1350Ft) from Szekszárd is produced by Ferenc Vesztergombi, who also makes an excellent Bikavér Reserve (3450Ft). Syrah, Hungary's 'newly discovered' variety of grape is making quite a splash in Szekszárd; try Takler's 2007 vintage (2490Ft). Tamás Dúzsi is acknowledged to be the finest producer of rosé; sample his Kékfrankos Rosé 2007 (1750Ft).

Two excellent sources on Hungarian wines are the rather, err, sober *The Wines of Hungary* by Alex Liddell and the much flashier (and more lightweight) *Hungary: Its Fine Wines & Winemakers* by David Copp. Both books don't just look at the wines but at the whole wine-making process.

Badacsony

The Badacsony region is named after the 400m-high basalt massif that rises like a bread loaf from the Tapolca Basin, along the northwestern shore of Lake Balaton. Wine has been produced here for centuries and the region's signature Olaszrizling, especially that produced by Huba Szeremley (1750Ft) and Ödön Nyári (1530Ft), is among the best dry white wine for everyday drinking that is available in Hungary. It's a straw-blond Welschriesling high in acid that is related to the famous Rhine vintages in name only and is actually French in origin. Drink it young – in fact, the younger, the better. Szeremley's 2000 late harvest Olaszrizling (6480Ft) is almost as sweet as Tokaj.

The area's volcanic soil gives the unique, once-threatened Kéknyelű (Blue Stalk) wine its distinctive mineral taste; it is a complex tipple wine of very low yield that ages well. Szeremley's Kéknyelű (3750Ft) is the only reliably authentic example. A big-name producer of quality white wines (eg Nagykúti Chardonnay 2007; 3390Ft) is Jásdi in the nearby Balaton wine area of Csopak.

Somló

The entire region of Somló is a single volcanic dome and the soil (basalt talus and volcanic tuff) helps to produce wine that is mineral-tasting, almost flinty. The region boasts two indigenous grape varieties: Hárslevelű and

A MATCH MADE IN HEAVEN

The pairing of food with wine is as great an obsession in Hungary as it is in France. Everyone agrees that sweets like strudel go very well indeed with a glass of Tokaji Aszú, but what is less appreciated is the wonderful synergy that this wine enjoys with savoury foods like foie gras and cheeses such as Roquefort, Stilton and Gorgonzola. A bone-dry Olaszrizling from Badacsony is a superb accompaniment to any fish dish, but especially the pike-perch indigenous to nearby Lake Balaton, while dry Furmint goes well with *harcsa* (catfish). Villány Sauvignon Blanc is excellent with creamy and salty goat's cheese.

It would be a shame to 'waste' a big wine like a Vili Papa Cuvée on simple Hungarian dishes like *gulyás* or *pörkölt;* save it for a more complex meat dish. Try Kékfrankos or Szekszárd Kadarka with these simpler dishes. Cream-based dishes stand up well to late-harvest Furmint and pork dishes are nice with new Furmint or any type of red, especially Kékfrankos. Try Hárslevelű with poultry.

Juhfark (Sheep's Tail). Firm acids give 'spine' to this wine, and it reaches its peak at five years old.

Béla Fekete is foremost among the producers of Somlói Hárslevelű and Juhfark (3600Ft); another excellent producer of the latter is Kreinbacher (3600Ft). Imre Györgykovács' Olaszrizling (3390Ft) is a big wine with a taste vaguely reminiscent of burnt almonds. His Hárslevelű (3600Ft) is a brilliant golden wine, with a tart, mineral finish.

CELEBRATIONS

Traditional culture, particularly where it involves food, is not exactly thriving in Hungary, though a popular event for city folk with tenuous ties to the countryside is the *disznótor,* the slaughtering of a pig followed by an orgy of feasting on a special dish called *disznótoros káposzta,* which is stuffed cabbage served with freshly made sausages. Dozens of wine festivals, often commercial events with rock bands and the like, occur across the country during the harvest in September and October. The most important one is the **Budapest International Wine Festival** (www.winefestival.hu), held in the Castle District in September.

WHERE TO EAT & DRINK

An *étterem* is a restaurant with a large selection, sometimes including international dishes. A *vendéglő* or *kisvendéglő* is smaller and is supposed to serve inexpensive regional dishes or 'home cooking', but the name is now 'cute' enough for a lot of large places to use it. An *étkezde* or *kifőzde* is something like a diner, smaller and cheaper than *kisvendéglő* and often with counter seating. The overused term *csárda* originally signified a country inn with a rustic atmosphere, Gypsy music and hearty local dishes. Now any place that strings dried peppers and a couple of painted plates on the wall is one. Most restaurants offer an excellent-value *menü* (set menu) of two or three courses at lunch.

A *bisztró* is a much cheaper sit-down place that is often *önkiszolgáló* (self-service). A *büfé* is cheaper still with a very limited menu. Food stalls, known as *Laci konyha* (literally, 'Larry's kitchen') or *pecsenyesütő* (roast ovens), can be found near markets, parks or train stations. At these you eat while standing at counters.

Other useful words include *élelmiszer* (grocery store), *csemege* (delicatessen) and *piac* (market).

A *kávéház,* literally a 'coffee house' or 'cafe', is the best place to get something hot or nonalcoholic and cold. An *eszpresszó,* along with being a type of coffee, is essentially a coffee house too, but it usually also sells alcoholic drinks and light snacks.

To sample the local brew or vintage, try visiting a *söröző,* which is a pub with *csapolt sör* (draught beer); a *borozó,* which is an establishment (usually a dive) serving wine; or a *pince,* which can be a beer or wine cellar but is usually the latter (also called *bor pince*).

Restaurant menus are often translated into German, English and sometimes French, with mixed degrees of success.

Quick Eats

Many *hentesáru bolt* (butcher shops) have a *büfé* selling boiled or fried *kolbász* (sausage), *virsli* (frankfurters), *hurka* (blood sausage or liverwurst), roast chicken and pickled vegetables. Point to what you want; the staff will weigh it all and hand you a slip of paper with the price. You usually pay at the *pénztár* (cashier) and hand the stamped receipt back to the staff for your food. Here you pay for everything, including a slice of rye bread and a dollop of mustard for your *kolbász.*

Food stalls sell the same sorts of things, as well as fish when located near lakes or rivers. One of the more popular snacks is *lángos,* deep-fried dough with various toppings (usually cheese and sour cream), available at food stalls throughout Hungary. *Pogácsa,* a kind of dry, savoury scone introduced by the Turks, is the preferred snack of beer drinkers.

VEGETARIANS & VEGANS

Such a carnivorous country as Hungary has always been suspicious of non-meat eaters, but things are changing and we've found places even in the provinces that serve good vegetarian meals. Where there are no vegetarian restaurants, you'll have to make do with what's on the regular menu or shop for ingredients in the markets. The selection of fresh vegetables and fruit is not great in the dead of winter, but come spring a cycle of bounty begins: from strawberries and raspberries, through cherries and all the stone fruits to apples, pears and nuts. Large supermarket chains such as Kaiser's, Match and Rothschild usually sell takeaway salads in plastic containers.

Culinaria Hungary by Anikó Gergely et al is a beautifully illustrated, 320-page tome on all things involving Hungarian food, from soup to nuts and more. It is as prized for its recipes as for the history and traditions it contains.

In restaurants, vegetarians can usually order *gombafejek rántva* (fried mushroom caps), pasta and noodle dishes with cheese, such as *túrós csusza* and *sztrapacska,* and any number of types of *főzelék* (creamed vegetables).

Other vegetarian dishes include *gombaleves* (mushroom soup), *gyümölcsleves* (fruit soup), *rántott sajt* (fried cheese) and *sajtos kenyér* (sliced bread with soft cheese). *Bableves* (bean soup) usually – but not always – contains meat. *Palacsinta* (pancakes) may be savoury and made with *sajt* (cheese) or *gomba* (mushrooms), or sweet and prepared with *dió* (nuts) or *mák* (poppy seeds).

EATING WITH KIDS

Children are welcome in most restaurants and snack bars in Hungary, but it's very rare to find a high chair or special children's menu – you'll have to make do with smaller portions of the adult menu. For more information on travelling with children, see p371.

HABITS & CUSTOMS

Most Hungarians are not big eaters of *reggeli* (breakfast), preferring a cup of tea or coffee with a plain bread roll at the kitchen table or on the way to work. *Ebéd* (lunch), eaten at around 1pm, is traditionally the main meal in the countryside and can consist of two or three courses, but this is no longer the case for workers in the cities and towns. *Vacsora* (dinner or supper) is less substantial when eaten at home, often just sliced meats, cheese and pickled vegetables.

COOKING COURSES

For a country with such a sophisticated cuisine, cooking courses are thin on the ground. The best known cookery school dealing with foreigners is **Chefparade** (☎ 1-210 6042; www.chefparade.hu; IX Pāa utca 13) in Budapest, just east of Ferenc körút. Course dates vary – consult the website – but usually run from 10am to 1pm, involve visiting a market and preparing a four-course lunch, and cost €50 per person. Courses at other times and of longer durations can be organised in advance.

EAT YOUR WORDS

For pronunciation guidelines, see p397.

Useful Phrases

I'm hungry/thirsty.
Éhes/szomjas vagyok. — *ay*·hesh/*sawm*·yosh *vo*·dyawk

The menu, please.
Az étlapot, kérem. — az *ayt*·lo·pawt *kay*·rem

Is there an English-language menu?
Van angol nyelvű étlap? — von *on*·gawl *nyel*·vēw *ayt*·lop

What would you recommend?
Mit ajánlana? — *mit o*·yaan·lo·no

I'd like a local speciality.
Valamilyen helyi specialitást szeretnék. — *vo*·lo·mi·yen *he*·yi *shpe*·tsi·o·li·taasht *se*·ret·nayk

I'm (a) vegetarian.
Vegetáriánus vagyok. — *ve*·ge·taa·ri·aa·nush *vo*·dyawk

Do you have vegetarian food?
Vannak önöknél vegetáriánus ételek? — *von*·nok *eu*·neuk·nayl *ve*·ge·taa·ri·aa·nush *ay*·te·lek

I'm allergic to (nuts/peanuts).
Allergiás vagyok a (diófélékre/mogyoróra). — *ol*·ler·gi·aash *vo*·dyawk o (*di*·āw·fay·layk·re/*maw*·dyaw·rāw·ro)

Is service included in the bill?
A kiszolgálás díja benne van a számlában? — o *ki*·sawl·gaa·laash *dee*·ya *ben*·ne von o *saam*·laa·bon

I'd like..., please.
Legyen szíves, hozzon egy... — *le*·dyen *see*·vesh *hawz*·zawn ej...

The quintessential reference in the kitchen is *Gundel's Hungarian Cookbook*, by Károly Gundel, who ran his eponymous restaurant in City Park in Budapest from 1910 until it was nationalised in 1949. It has the advantage of listing all dishes bilingually.

HUNGARY'S TOP TRADITIONAL RESTAURANTS

- Kisbuda Gyöngye, Budapest (p116) – traditional but elegant *fin-de-siècle* restaurant in Óbuda that specialises in goose liver.
- Matróz, Győr (p167) – marketside restaurant with some of the best fish soup west of the Danube.
- Liberté Étterem, Kecskemét (p256) – traditional Hungarian specialities served in a modern, artistic way, with great seating on the main square.
- Kővirág, Köveskál (p210) – beautifully renovated stone cottage in the heart of the Kál Basin, where regional cuisine and local produce are of paramount importance.
- Degenfeld, Tokaj (p351) – try different local wines recommended by the chef to go with each course from a fabulous set menu.
- Fülemüle Csárda, Villány (p294) – a lovely old inn set within a wood northwest of town, with traditional dishes and excellent local wines.

Another… please.
Még (egy)…kérek szépen. mayg (ej)…*kay*·rek *say*·pen
Please bring the bill.
Kérem, hozza a számlát. *kay*·rem *hawz*·zo o *saam*·laat

Food Glossary

BASICS

bors	bawrsh	pepper
cukor	*tsu*·kawr	sugar
cukorral/cukor nélkül	*tsu*·kawr·ol/*tsu*·kawr *nayl*·kewl	with/without sugar
étel	*ay*·tel	food
étlap	*ayt*·lop	menu
gyümölcs	*dyew*·meulch	fruit
hús	hūsh	meat
jéggel/jég nélkül	*yay*·gel/yayg *nayl*·kewl	with/without ice
meleg/forró/hideg	*me*·leg/*fawr*·rāw/*hi*·deg	warm/hot/cold
sajt	*sho*·y·t	cheese
só	shāw	salt
tojás	*taw*·yaash	egg
vaj	*vo*·y	butter
zöldség	*zeuld*·shayg	vegetables

MEAT & FISH (HÚS & HAL)

borjúhús	*bawr*·yū·hūsh	veal
csirke	*chir*·ke	chicken
disznóhús	*dis*·nāw·hūsh	pork
hal	hol	fish
hús	hūsh	meat
marhahús	*mor*·ho·hūsh	beef
pulyka	*pu*·y·ko	turkey

VEGETABLES (ZÖLDSÉG)

gomba	*gawm*·bo	mushroom
káposzta	*kaa*·paws·to	cabbage
karfiol	*kor*·fi·awl	cauliflower
sárgarépa	*shaar*·go·ray·po	carrot
spenót	*shpe*·nāwt	spinach
zöldbab	*zeuld*·bob	string (green) bean
zöldborsó	*zeuld*·bawr·shāw	pea

FRUIT (GYÜMÖLCS)

alma	*ol*·mo	apple
banán	*bo*·naan	banana
cseresznye	*che*·res·nye	(sweet) cherry
eper	e·per	strawberry
körte	*keur*·te	pear
meggy	mejj	sour (Morello) cherry
narancs	*no*·ronch	orange
őszibarack	*ēū*·si·bo·rotsk	peach
sárgabarack	*shaar*·go·bo·rotsk	apricot
szőlő	*sēū*·lēū	grape

NONALCOHOLIC DRINKS

almalé	*ol*·mo·lay	apple juice
ásvány víz	*aash*·vaan'·veez	mineral water

gyümölcslé	*dyew*·meulch lay	fruit juice
narancslé	*no*·ronch·lay	orange juice
tej	*te*·y	milk
üdítőital	*ew*·dee·tēū·i·tal	soft drink
víz	veez	water

ALCOHOLIC DRINKS

barackpálinka	bo·rotsk·*paa*·lin·ko	apricot brandy
barna sör	*bor*·no sheur	dark beer/stout
bor	bawr	wine
csapolt sör	*cho*·polt sheur	draught beer
édes bor	*ay*·desh bawr	sweet wine
fehér bor	*fe*·hayr bawr	white wine
fél barna sör	fayl *bor*·no sheur	dark lager
fröccs	freuch	spritzer (wine soda)
korsó sör	*kawr*·shāw sheur	mug (half-litre) of beer
körtepálinka	*keur*·te·*paa*·lin·ko	pear brandy
pezsgő	*pezh*·geu	champagne/sparkling wine
pohár sör	*paw*·haar sheur	glass (one-third litre) of beer
sör	sheur	beer
szilvapálinka	*sil*·vo·*paa*·lin·ko	plum brandy
világos sör	*vi*·laa·gawsh sheur	lager
vörös bor	*veu*·reush	red wine

APPETISERS (ELŐÉTELEK)

Hortobágyi palacsinta	*hawr*·taw·baa·dyi *po*·lo·chin·to	meat-filled pancakes with paprika sauce
libamájpástétom	*li*·bo·maa·y·paash·tay·tawm	goose-liver pâté
rántott gombafejek	*raan*·tawtt *gom*·bo·fe·y·ek	breaded, fried mushroom caps

SOUPS (LEVESEK)

csontleves	*chont*·le·vesh	consommé
Jókai bableves	*yāw*·kai *bob*·le·vesh	bean soup with meat
meggyleves	*mejj*·le·vesh	cold sour-cherry soup (in summer)
tyúkhúsleves	*tyūk*·hūsh·le·vesh	chicken soup with carrot, kohlrabi, parsley and celery roots

SALADS (SALÁTÁK)

cékla saláta	*tsay*·klo *sho*·laa·to	pickled beetroot salad
ecetes almapaprika	*e*·tse·tesh *ol* mo·*pop*·ri·ko	pickled (apple) peppers
paradicsom saláta	*po*·ro·di·chawm *sho*·laa·to	tomato salad
uborka saláta	*u*·bawr·ko *sho*·laa·to	sliced pickled-cucumber salad
vegyes saláta	*ve*·dyesh *sho*·laa·to	mixed salad of pickles

SIDE DISHES (KÖRETEK)

rizi-bizi	*ri*·zi·*bi*·zi	rice with peas
sült hasábburgonya	shewlt *ho*·saa·bur·gon'	chips (French fries)

READY-MADE DISHES (KÉSZÉTELEK)

csirke paprikás	*chir*·ke *pop*·ri·kaash	chicken paprika
(marha) pörkölt	(*mor*·ho)·*peur*·keult	(beef) stew (many types)
töltött paprika/káposzta	*teul*·teutt *pop*·ri·ko/*kaa*·paws·to	stuffed peppers/cabbage

DISHES MADE TO ORDER (FRISSENSÜLTEK)

Bécsiszelet	*bay*·chi·se·let	Wiener schnitzel
Brassói aprópecsenye	*bra*·shāwy *a*·prāw·*pe*·che·nye	braised pork, Braşov-style
cigánypecsenye	*tsi* gawn·y·*pe*·che·nye	roast pork, Roma-style
csülök	*chew*·leuk	smoked pork knuckle
hagymás rostélyos	*hoj*·maash *rawsh*·tay·yawsh	beef sirloin fried with onions
rántott hátszínszelet	*raan*·tawtt *haat*·seen·se·let	breaded, fried rump steak
rántott pulykamell	*raan*·tawtt *pu*·y·ko·mell	breaded, fried turkey breast
sertésborda	*sher*·taysh·bawr·do	pork chop
sült csirkecomb	shewlt *chir*·ke·tsawmb	roast chicken thigh
sült libacomb	shewlt *li*·bo·tsawmb	roast goose leg

DESSERTS (ÉDESSÉGEK)

dobostorta	*daw*·bawsh·tawr·to	multilayered 'dobos' chocolate and cream cake with caramelised brown-sugar top
Gundel palacsinta	*gun*·del *po*·lo·chin·to	'Gundel' flambéed pancake with chocolate and nuts
rétes	*ray*·tesh	strudel
Somlói galuska	*shawm*·lāw·i *go*·lush·ko	Somló-style sponge cake with chocolate and whipped cream

Environment

THE LAND

The stereotypical view of Hungary as a land of never-ending plains and big skies is pretty much on the money. Over 80% of the country is below 200m and less than 2% over 400m, making it largely a land of flat prairies, or *puszta*, and low-lying hills. Its highest peak, Kékestető (p328), rises to just over 1000m, and the entire country is blessed with more thermal activity than most states. Around 60% of the land comprises fertile plains used primarily for agriculture; only 12% of the country remains in its natural native state.

Catch up on Hungary's latest environmental affairs at www.wwf.hu.

Hungary's kidney-shaped 93,030 sq km – about the same area as Portugal or the US state of Indiana – sits in the very heart of Eastern Europe and occupies much of the Carpathian Basin. Along its 2171km of border are a total of seven countries: Austria, Slovakia, Ukraine, Romania, Serbia, Croatia and Slovenia.

The country has three basic topographies: the low-lying regions of the Great Plain (Nagyalföld) in the east, centre and southeast, and of the Little Plain (Kisalföld) in the northwest, which together account for two-thirds of Hungary's territory; the mountain ranges in the north; and the hilly regions of Transdanubia in the west and southwest.

The Danube (p146) may be the most famous river in the land, but it's not the longest – crossing 596km of Hungarian territory, the Tisza outstrips its rival by 179km. Together, the rivers split the country into three unequal parts, the largest of which covers all of Western and Southern Transdanubia and the Lake Balaton region. Aside from rivers, the country is blessed with well over 1000 lakes, of which the largest by far is Lake Balaton (596 sq km; p194) followed by Lake Tisza (127 sq km; p239). Lake Hévíz (p205), at 4.75 sq km, is the world's second-largest thermal lake.

The mean depth of Balaton, the largest lake in Europe outside Scandinavia, is only 3m, though the lake floor drops to 12m in the Tihany Strait.

Hungary's topographical divisions do not accurately reflect the country's cultural and subtler geographical differences, nor do the 19 administrative *megye* (counties) help travellers much. Instead, Hungary can be divided into eight main regions: Budapest and environs, the Danube Bend, Western Transdanubia, the Lake Balaton region, Southern Transdanubia, the Great Plain, the Northern Uplands and the Northeast.

WILDLIFE

Animals

There are a lot of common European animals in Hungary (deer, hare, wild boar and foxes), as well as some rare species (wild cat, lake bat and Pannonian lizard), but most of the country's wildlife comes from the avian family.

Around 75% of the country's 480 known vertebrates are birds, for the most part waterfowl attracted by the rivers, lakes and wetlands. The rare black stork, a smaller, darker version of its common cousin, also spends time in Hungary on its migration from Africa to Europe. For details on the best places to watch birds in Hungary, see p68.

Birds of Hungary, by Gerard Gorman, is an essential book for anyone interested in bird-watching in the country.

Of a total of 55 mammal species living in Hungary, 14 are endangered. Wolves and lynxes are the largest carnivores on the list; Slovakia sustains stable populations of both, and the occasional individual crosses over the border into the Northern Uplands. The present population of beavers in Hungary hovers at around 450, thanks largely to reintroduction programs over the past decade. Small populations have been established in floodplain forest regions, such as Gemenc (p284) in Southern Transdanubia and Fertő-Hanság National Park (p177) near Sopron.

Plants

Almost a fifth of the country is forested, but only 10% is natural forest. Hungary is home to some 2200 flowering plant species and, because of its topography and transitional climate, many of them are not normally found at this latitude. Much of the flora in the Villány (p293) and Mecsek Hills (p304) of Southern Transdanubia, for example, is usually seen only around the Mediterranean. The salty Hortobágy region (p247) on the Eastern Plain has many plants normally found by the seashore, and the Nyírség area is famous for meadow flowers. The Gemenc Forest (p284) on the Danube near Szekszárd, the Little Balaton (p204) in the centre of Transdanubia and the Tisza River backwater east of Kecskemét are all important wetlands. Most of the trees in the nation's forested areas are deciduous (beech, oak and birch); only a small percentage are fir.

The Nature Guide to the Hortobágy and Tisza River Floodplain makes a grand companion for anyone with an in-depth interest in the flora and fauna of the *puszta*.

Since the 14th century, over 250 new plant species have colonised Hungary, of which almost 70 are considered invasive. Many such plants are perennial herbs that have taken root on the plains, causing some of the native flora to slowly disappear.

NATIONAL PARKS

National parks in Hungary number 10 (up from only five a little over a decade ago), totalling approximately 5% of the country's land. In addition to its national parks, Hungary maintains over 1400 protected areas of national or local significance – of this, only a fraction is highly protected. Such areas range from the entire Tihany peninsula on Lake Balaton (p215) to a clump of ancient oak trees in the tiniest of villages.

Hungary's national parks website, www.nationalpark.hu, provides direct links to the websites of all of the parks scattered throughout the country.

The rules and regulations in most national parks and nature reserves are fairly obvious: no littering, no picking flowers, no collecting insects (eg butterflies), no open fires except in designated areas, no loud noises or music and so on. Bear in mind that the flora and fauna of certain ecosystems – Hortobágy National Park, for example – are very fragile, and you should never stray from marked hiking trails and paths.

Minimise the waste you carry out of protected areas by removing packaging and taking no more food than you need. Don't use detergents or toothpaste in or near watercourses, even if they are biodegradable.

ENVIRONMENTAL ISSUES

In the past 10 years there has been a marked improvement in both the public's awareness of environmental issues and the government's dedication to environmental safety. This has largely been due to the creation of the Ministry of Environment and Water and the introduction of EU regulations.

ONLY IN HUNGARY

Hungary is unique in many ways, none more so than in its domesticated animals. The country's sheep-dog breeds, such as the Puli, Komondor and Kuvasz, have distinct coats of tangled hair that resemble dreadlocks or your household mop. Not to be outdone, the Mangalica pig has its own coat of long, curly tassels and is characterised by very fatty meat. The Racka sheep has a particularly devilish look, with long, spiralled horns, while the Hungarian Grey Cattle is tall and slender and sports long, pointed horns (much like those of the American Long Horn). The Vizsla breed of dog is one of the oldest hunting dogs in the world; with its gold-rust coloured coat and noble stance, it's often mistaken as a Rhodesian Ridgeback.

Catch a close-up glimpse of these animals and more at the Puszta Zoo (p248) on the Great Plain and Salföld Ranch (p210) in the Kál Basin.

HUNGARY'S NATIONAL PARKS

National Park	Features	Activities	Best Time to Visit	Website
Aggtelek (p346)	extensive cave system	caving, cycling, hiking	year-round	www.anp.hu
Balaton Uplands (p204)	marshlands, rolling hills, meadows, volcanic formations	bird-watching, caving, cycling, fishing, hiking	spring, summer, autumn	www.bfnpi.hu
Bükk Hills (p330)	caves, forest	bird-watching, caving, cycling, hiking	spring, summer, autumn	www.bnpi.hu
Danube-Ipoly (p149)	forests, river	bird-watching, caving, cycling, hiking	spring, summer, autumn	www.dinpi.hu
Duna-Drava (p284)	rivers, forests, grassland	bird-watching, canoeing, walking	spring, summer	www.ddnp.hu
Fertő-Hanság (p177)	lakeland, marshes	bird-watching, boating, cycling, hiking	spring, summer, autumn	www.ferto-hansag.hu
Hortobágy (p248)	grasslands, wetlands	hiking, horse riding, scenic flights	spring, summer, autumn	www.hnp.hu
Kiskunság (p257)	grasslands, sand dunes, lakes, marshes	bird-watching, horse riding	spring, summer, autumn	www.knp.hu
Körös-Maros (p276)	wetlands, marshes, grasslands	bird-watching, cycling, hiking	spring, summer, autumn	www.kmnpi.hu
Őrség (p192)	woodlands, meadows	cycling, hiking, horse riding	spring, summer, autumn	onp.nemzetipark.gov.hu

Air pollution has long been a problem due to outdated and inefficient coal-fired power plants and the amount of nitrogen oxide produced by the nation's ancient car fleet. Many of the plants have been shut down in recent years, resulting in the reduction of the country's sulphur dioxide emissions by a third. Additionally, the government has taken the country's cars to task, forcing many polluting vehicles off the road and introducing lead- and sulphur-free petrol.

The Ministry of Environment and Water provides information in English on its activities at www.kvvm.hu.

Hungary produces around 80 million tonnes of waste annually, down from just over 100 million tonnes at the turn of the century. Despite the government's push to place recycling stations across the country and clean up waste landfills, not a great amount of waste is recycled. Only 14.2% of household rubbish is recycled and a further 5.8% is burnt – the rest goes into the ground. Approximately 4000 recycling collection points (600 of which are in Budapest) have been introduced to towns and villages in Hungary.

Of the 1026 freshwater surface bodies identified in Hungary, 579 are classified as being 'at risk' from hazardous substances, mainly from nitrogen and phosphorus used in farming practices. Household discharge also plays its part in the contamination process, as only 56% of all households in Hungary have central plumbing connected to the town supply. The vast majority of Hungary's waterworks are reliant on groundwater: more than 90% of the population is supplied in this way. Fortunately, to date no groundwater sources have been reported as contaminated, but some are graded as potentially at risk.

Log on to www.rec.org to learn about the Regional Environmental Center for Central and Eastern Europe, a Szentendre-based body that is developing a common ecosystem strategy and solving environmental problems in the region.

Almost a quarter of the country is below river flood level, putting thousands of dwellings and over 2000 industrial plants at major risk of flooding. Despite attempting to keep the waters at bay since the 16th century, Hungary still suffers regular flooding: both the Tisza and the Danube have caused severe damage to urban centres and rural pastures almost annually since 2000. Flood control consists of around 4200km of defences, mainly in the form of earth embankments, and 10 emergency flood reservoirs.

Activities

Whether hiking, swimming, horse riding or having a picnic of *gulyás* (beef soup) cooked outdoors in a *bogrács* (a kettle suspended over a fire with a tripod), Hungarians do prize a day's *kirándulás* (outing); and you can, too. The country has plenty more to offer than just admirable architecture and high culture. Bike or boat around an area lake, see if you can spot one of Europe's largest land birds, taste a vintage vino or dip into the famous thermal waters – your adventure awaits.

Water-sport rentals are exclusively available in summer (June through August), the same months that outdoor thermal pools are generally open. Autumn (October in particular) is the best time for watching migratory birds, and biking can be undertaken any month – though August gets hot on the Plains.

THERMAL BATHS

Since Roman times in the 2nd century AD, citizens have enjoyed Hungary's abundant thermal waters. But it was during the 150 years of Turkish domination that spa culture really flourished. Some of the thermal baths you see today, like the Rudas and Király Baths in Budapest (p103) and part of the thermal complex in Eger (p333), date back to the 16th and 17th centuries. Nearly 300 hot springs in Hungary are used for public bathing – in lakes, open-air pools, indoor spas and private hotel baths.

There are more than 3000 thermal springs registered in Hungary.

While 'taking the waters' used to be very serious medical business, the past few years have seen the rise of the aqua park, *elmény fürdo* (experience, or enjoyment bath), with higher entrance prices. Some people still come specifically to treat respiratory, muscular, cardiac or gynaecological maladies with the chemical compounds in the *gyögy fúrdők* (medicinal pools, usually a lovely mustard to mud colour, and up to 38°C). And Hungary's older generation is as committed as ever to maintaining their health (and keeping up with gossip) at the neighbourhood bath house. More and more though, you'll see clear chlorinated waters in organic-shaped pools that bubble, squirt, giggle and spurt at different rhythms and temperatures (24°C to 34°C). The slips and slides in the water-park sections usually cost extra. Food stands selling sour-cream-slathered *lángos* (fried dough) and beer are all but standard at parklike outdoor pools.

The spa at Hajdúszoboszló (p249) is king of recreation, the largest in Hungary (40 hectares), with more than a dozen outdoor pools that have themes, slides, wave action, sunbathing decks and the like – plus an adjacent aqua park. Other noteworthy new-fangled complexes include those at Győr (p166) in the west and Nyíregyháza (p360) in the east.

If you're looking for a more traditional experience, head to the Art Nouveau Gellért Baths, or to the much larger, neobaroque Szechényi Baths, both in Budapest (p103). For something original, float among the water lilies in the thermal lake at Hévíz (p205), near Lake Balaton, or submerge yourself in a cave bath at Miskolctapolca (p345).

The **Hungarian National Tourist Office** (www.hungary.com) puts out a *Spa & Wellness* booklet and has listings online. For more about spas in Budapest, check out www.spasbudapest.com.

WINE TASTING

And oh, what wine it is. Eger's Bull's Blood and Tokaj's sweet dessert wines are recognised worldwide. Lesser known whites and reds come from the Balaton Region (Badacsony) and southern Hungary (Villány, Szekszárd

HOW TO TAKE A BATH

Don't worry, the days of scary ladies in lab coats and treatment rooms that look like antiseptic torture chambers are all but over. Seems like most bath houses that have not been recently refurbished are scheduled to be soon. Not only are there different temperature pools to bathe in, you can sweat it out in the various sauna and steam rooms and, at larger spas, massage and bodywork service menus (from 1400Ft per half-hour) rival any in Western Europe.

Pricing systems differ widely, but in general you enter a thermal complex on a ticket good for at least four hours (from 1400Ft to 3000Ft). Water slides, aqua parks and other 'adventure pools' cost extra; admission is usually reduced after 4pm. Included in the price is clothing storage of some type, mostly lockers. The newest spas give you waterproof electronic watches or key cards that are all-access passes – they open your assigned cabin, they let you charge drinks at the bar, and upon check out they tell the attendant if you owe extra (eg for staying longer or going into the slide area) or get a refund (eg for staying fewer hours than paid). In older spas, you find a locker, get changed beside it and call over the attendant to lock the door and hand you a numbered tag. Note that for theft protection the tag number is not always the same as the one on the locker. At smaller thermal baths, the attendants may not speak English, but a smile, a point to your clothes and a shrug will usually elicit someone's help in explaining the system.

Don't forget to bring your own towel!

and Hajós). Often you can knock on a cellar door and ask to taste a sample (1 decilitre from 100ft), buy a bottle or have your own empty container filled up with cask wine (from 300Ft per litre). The **Hungarian National Tourist Office** (www.hungary.com) puts out a free *Hungary's Wine Regions* map-guide and has listings online. For more on Hungarian wine, see the Food & Drink chapter (p53).

Learn about Hungarian wine regions, varietals and wineries at www.wineportal.hu and www.hungarywines.net.

HORSE RIDING

There's a Hungarian saying that the Magyars were 'created by God to sit on horseback' – just look at any statue of Árpád. There are a huge number of stables and riding schools around the country, though most are more local- than tourist-oriented (English is not always spoken, but German may be). You will find follow-the-leader horse treks up to scenic spots, but the emphasis is usually on lessons. English riding and saddles are the preferred style; you'll need to book ahead.

The nonprofit **Hungarian Equestrian Tourism Association** (MLTSZ; ☎ 1-456 0444; www.equi.hu/eng) classifies stables countrywide. Four- and five-horseshoe properties must have staff members who speak a foreign language. MLTSZ also helps the **Hungarian National Tourist Office** (www.hungary.com) put together the searchable web listings under the 'sports and free time' link and the helpful *Hungary on Horseback* brochure (also online).

Pegazus Tours (☎ 1-317 1644; www.pegazus.hu; V Ferenciek tere 5, Budapest) organises three-night tours (from €350) and seven-night tours (from €850) in Transdanubia, the Great Plain and around Lake Balaton. **Equus Tours** (☎ 1-317 1644; www.equi.hu/equus/eng/; XXVI Özgida ul 32, Budapest) leads seven-night horseback tours (from €900) in the Mátra Hills, the Eastern Plain and Tokaj wine region. Both companies include transfers from Budapest.

Nonius horses, bred at Máta, have been raised in Hungary since 1671.

Not surprisingly, the two places where you can see horsemen ride, herd and perform shows, Hortobágy (p248) and Kiskunság National Park (p257), are also the best places for individual riding. Look, too, for good schools at Orfű (p304), in Southern Transdanubia, and in towns around the Lake Balaton region (p194). Riding a white Lipizzaner horse bred for coach racing (unlike the dancing variety in Vienna) through the wooded hills in Szilvásvárad (p338) is an experience like no other.

BIG BIRD

The gooselike great bustard *(Otis tarda)*, weighing in between 10kg and 16kg (and with a wing span of up to 1.5m), is the heaviest European land bird capable of flying. It attracts quite a lot of attention for Hungary in birding circles. 'Well, it is large, endangered and very localised,' Budapest-based author and expert birding guide Gerard Gorman explains. 'Hungary's population [about 1200 birds] is the largest in Central and Eastern Europe.' The species can be spotted in Kiskunság (p257) and Hortobágy (p248) National Parks, but for such a big bird, individual sightings can be elusive. 'You have to know exactly which fields they frequent, and these change. But that is where a guide comes in.' Case of the missing big bird solved.

BIRD-WATCHING

Hungary is the ornithological crossroads of Europe. Some 380 of the continent's 400-odd species have been sighted here, and a full 250 are resident or regular visitors. The country's indigenous populations of great white egrets (over 2000 nesting pairs), great bustards (about 1200 birds), and red-footed falcons (800 pairs), as well as white-tailed eagles (70 pairs), aquatic warblers (600 singing males) and saker falcons (150 pairs) are among the most important in Europe. And more eastern imperial eagles (80 pairs) nest here than anywhere else in Europe. Spring and autumn are always great for bird-watching (May and October, especially). Huge white storks nesting atop chimneys in eastern Hungary are a striking sight from May through October.

Find out about conservation of the rare imperial eagle at www.imperialeagle.hu.

There are dozens of excellent birding sites in Hungary, but the grassy, saline steppe, large fish ponds and marshes of Hortobágy (p247) are some of the best. Look for red-footed falcons and aquatic warblers, grebes, herons, saker falcons, long-legged buzzards and white-tailed eagles. In October up to 100,000 common cranes and geese stop on the plains as they migrate south.

The wooded hills of Bükk National Park (p330) hold woodpeckers from May to July, imperial eagles and woodland birds; April to June sees the most activity in the reed beds of the shallow, saline Lake Fertő (p177), and autumn brings white-fronted and bean geese. Freshwater lakes like Kis-Balaton (p204), Lake Tisza (p239) and Öreg-tó (p161) are prime sites for wading birds and waterfowl.

For a guided outing, go to the expert Gerard Gorman, author of *The Birds of Hungary* and *Birding in Eastern Europe*. He operates **Probirder** (www.probirder.com), an informational website and guide service out of Budapest. Fixed tours take in the woodland birds of the Bükk Hills, the plains birds near Hortobágy, or both, and last between four and eight days. Tailor-made day trips are also available.

University-based **Saker Tours** (☎ 52-456 744; www.sakertours.com), out of Debrecen, offers bird-watching tours around Hortobágy and in the Zemplén Hills. **Hungarian Bird Tours** (☎ 07 77 457 4204; www.hungarianbirdtours.com) operates similar woodland and plains tours from a base in Eger. For both companies, three-night tours cost around €350, seven-night tours are €900 and it's €150 per day for tailored trips. Transfers from Budapest are usually available.

The **Hungarian Ornithological & Nature Conservation Society** (MME; ☎ 1-275 6247; www.mme.hu) works to protect the nation's feathered friends. Pick up guides, binoculars, clothing and bird-watching accessories at the associated **Birder Shop** (☎ 1-270 2920; XIII Katona József utca 35, Budapest; 🕑 8am-6pm Mon-Fri, 10am-2pm Sat), where proceeds benefit conservation efforts.

CYCLING

Hungary's flat terrain makes it ideal for cycling; more than 2000km worth of trails stretch across the land, and that's not including the thousands more kilometres of country roads. Budapest, Szeged and Kecskemet are among the larger places dedicated to cyclists, but often even smaller towns like Nyíregyháza have dedicated bike lanes. Two Eurovelo routes sponsored by the **European Cycling Federation** (www.ecf.com) cross Hungary. Route 6 travels from Komarom through Győr and Budapest, and south to Croatia (440km). Route 11 for the most part follows the Tisza River through Tokaj and Szeged in eastern Hungary, between Slovakia and Serbia (300km).

Travel the Eurovelo from the Atlantic to the Black Sea – through Hungary – virtually, at www.eurovelo6.org.

The Danube Bend (p139) is among the best areas to explore on two wheels. In the Lake Balaton region (p194) a track circles the entire lake, a new cycle path connects Keszthely and Hévíz, and Balaton Uplands National Park has some particularly scenic rides. You can also cycle 70km around Lake Tisza from Tiszafüred (p239) on the plains.

Local tourist offices are good sources of information about suggested routes, and some routes are posted at **Hunbike** (www.hunbike.hu), an information portal (not all in English) connected to the Hungarian Cyclists' Club. **Frigoria** (www.frigoriakiado.hu) publishes a very useful 1:250,000-scale atlas called *Cycling around Hungary*, which outlines 100 tours, places of interest and service centres listed in several languages. Remember when planning your itinerary that bicycles are banned from motorways as well as national highways 0 to 9, and they must be fitted with lights and reflectors. On certain train lines, bicycles can be transported in special carriages.

Happy Bike (☎ 06 70 507 1363; www.happybike.hu), in association with the Hungarian Cyclists' Club, organises ambitious week-long cycle tours of Lake Balaton, the Danube Bend and the Őrség region (from €450). **Velo-Touring** (☎ 1-319 0571; www.velo-touring.hu), a large cycling travel agency, has a great selection of seven-night trips in all regions, from a senior-friendly Danube Bend tour (€690) to a bike ride between spas on the Great Plain (€750). **Ecotours** (☎ 1-361 0438; www.ecotours.hu) has five- to seven-night cycle trips through Transdanubia, the Zemplén Hills and around Balaton (from €450). Tours have a slight nature focus but they still include diversions such as wine tasting. Transfers from Budapest can be provided.

The Danube Cycleway, by John Higginson, maps the riverfront route along the Danube from Germany through Slovakia and Hungary.

CANOEING & KAYAKING

Some 4000km of waterways meander around this mostly flat country (Hungary is in a basin). Many are navigable by *kajak* (kayak) or *kenu* (canoe) at least from April to September. The most famous long-haul routes course from Rajka to Mohács (386km) on the Danube and from Tiszabecs to Szeged (570km) on the Tisza River. Though much area rowing is done in association with member-only boat clubs, rentals are available at tourist centres such as Tiszafüred (p239) and Tokaj (p349).

Ecotours (☎ 1-361 0438; www.ecotours.hu) leads seven-day Rajka–Mohács Danube River canoe and camping trips for about €500 (tent rental and food extra), as well as shorter Danube Bend and Tisza River trips. The staff includes biologists and national park rangers, who help ensure the experience is eco-friendly. **Kékcápák** (☎ 47-353 227; www.turak.hu) organises four-day trips on the smaller rivers in north and eastern Hungary, with transport from Tokaj included.

Cartographia (www.cartographia.hu) publishes several water-sports maps that are available at bookstores; online river-route maps are posted at http://viziterkep.fw.hu (in Hungarian). The nonprofit **Hungarian Friends of Nature Federation** (MTSZ; ☎ 1-332 7177; www.fsz.bme.hu/mtsz) may also be of assistance.

HIKING

The forests of the Bükk Hills (p330) are the best in Hungary for serious trekkers; much of the national park there is off-limits to cars. The Zemplén Hills (p347) and Mátra Hills (p324), to the east and west, respectively, also offer hiking possibilities.

There are good short hikes in the forests around Visegrád (p152), Esztergom (p153), Badacsony (p207), Kőszeg (p191) and Budapest (p94).

Cartographia (www.cartographia.hu) publishes 30 hiking maps (average scales 1:40,000 and 1:60,000) to the hills, plains and forests of Hungary. On all hiking maps, paths appear as a red line and with a letter, or an abbreviation in Hungarian, indicating the colour-coding of the trail. Colours are painted on trees or the letter of the colour in Hungarian appears on markers: 'K' for *kék* (blue), 'P' for *piros* (red), 'S' for *sárga* (yellow) and 'Z' for *zöld* (green).

András Vojnits' *National Parks of Hungary* provides a short, glossy introduction to the flora, fauna and trails of Hungary's national parks.

The **Hungarian Friends of Nature Federation** (MTSZ; ☎ 1-332 7177; www.fsz.bme.hu/mtsz) can offer advice.

SWIMMING

Swimming is extremely popular in Hungary; lakes and rivers of any size have at least a grassy, if not sandy, *strand* (beach) and wading bathers. Some have changing cabins and food booths, and some managed beaches have locker rooms, restaurants, camping areas, live entertainment – and admission fees. Lake Balaton's southern shore towns, such as Siófok (p197), are prime examples, but you'll even find managed areas on rivers like the Tisza at Szolnok (p235).

Most towns have a covered pool dedicated to athletic training, but far more interesting are the thermal spas (p66). At least a few lanes in these, if not a whole pool, are dedicated to swimming laps, and water aerobics may be offered.

BOATING & WINDSURFING

The sailing centre of Hungary is undoubtedly Lake Balaton (p194). Those qualified can rent sail boats at resorts around the lake, including Siófok and Tihany. You'll find sailboards available for rent at Keszthely, and at Gárdony and Velence town on Lake Velence. On Lake Tisza (p239) you can rent small motor boats for puttering around, as you can in a few other towns along the Tisza River.

CAVING

Locate a hill in Hungary, be it in Budapest or Bükk, and you're likely to find a labyrinthine cavern below. Four hundred caves have been identified in Aggtelek National Park alone. The Baradla Cave (p346) in that park is undoubtedly the country's most famous. This 25km-long cave system spans into Slovakia and has long been on the Unesco World Heritage List. You can not only tour here, but canoe on the river Styx and do some serious spelunking. Other interesting caves include those under the Buda Hills (p105) and in Lillafüred (p343) in the Northern Uplands. Not far away, in Miskolctapolca (p345), you can have the interesting experience of taking a thermal dunk in a cave bath. For more information about the country's caving, contact the **Hungarian Karst and Cave Explorers Society** (MKBT; ☎ 1-201 9493; www.barlang.hu).

FISHING

Hungary's lakes and sluggish rivers are home to pike, perch, carp and other coarse fish. You'll see locals fishing in waterways everywhere, but Lake Balaton (p195) and Tiszafüred (p239) are particularly popular. In order to fish, you need a state fishing licence valid for a year as well as a local one issued for the day, week or year for the area that interests you. You can usually buy them at tackle shops, anglers' clubs and fishing associations. The **National Federation of Hungarian Anglers** (MOHOSZ; ☎ 1-248 2590; www.mohosz.hu; XII Korompai utca 17, Budapest) sells licences and has an excellent website to help sort out permissions and locations. There are few resources for equipment rental though.

Budapest

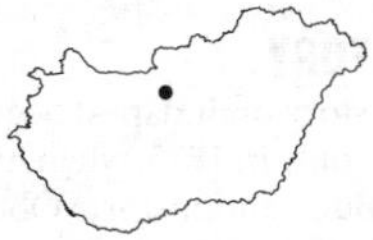

There's no other city in Hungary like Budapest in terms of size and importance. Home to almost 20% of the national population, Hungary's capital (*főváros*, or 'main city') is the administrative, business and cultural centre; everything of importance starts or ends here.

But it is the beauty of Budapest – both natural and manmade – that makes it stand apart. Straddling a gentle curve in the Danube, it is flanked by the Buda Hills on the west bank and what is the start of the Great Plain to the east. Architecturally, it is a gem, with enough baroque, neoclassical, Eclectic and Art Nouveau (Secessionist) to satisfy anyone.

In recent years Budapest has taken on the role of the region's party town, especially in the warmer months when outdoor entertainment areas called *kertek* (literally 'gardens') are heaving with party-makers or during the world-class Sziget Music Festival in August. And you need not venture out for fun: the city's scores of new hostels offer not just some of the best facilities and prices in Europe, but company too.

Budapest does have its 'ugly' side, with organised crime, pollution, international fast-food eateries at every corner and mindless graffiti covering much of all that gorgeous architecture. But come spring (or summer, or a brisk autumn day, or dusk), cross the Danube on foot and see why unique, passionate, vibrant Budapest remains unmissable.

HIGHLIGHTS

- Taking in the views of the Danube and the rest of the city from **Fishermen's Bastion** (p90) on Castle Hill
- Soaking the afternoon away in a thermal bath – Turkish-style (**Rudas**, p103), in an Art Nouveau 'cathedral' (**Gellért**, p103) or in the park (**Széchenyi**, p104)
- Ogling the sinuous curves and asymmetrical forms of the city's incomparable Art Nouveau architecture, such as that of the **Royal Postal Savings Bank** (p97)
- Enjoying a slice of something sweet at a traditional cafe like **Művész** (p121) in Pest or **Auguszt** (p117) in Buda
- Taking in an evening of music at the **Hungarian State Opera House** (p101) or the **Liszt Academy of Music** (p127)
- Sizing up the monumental socialist mistakes on display at **Memento Park** (p136), a well-manicured trash heap of history that now includes Stalin's truncated boots

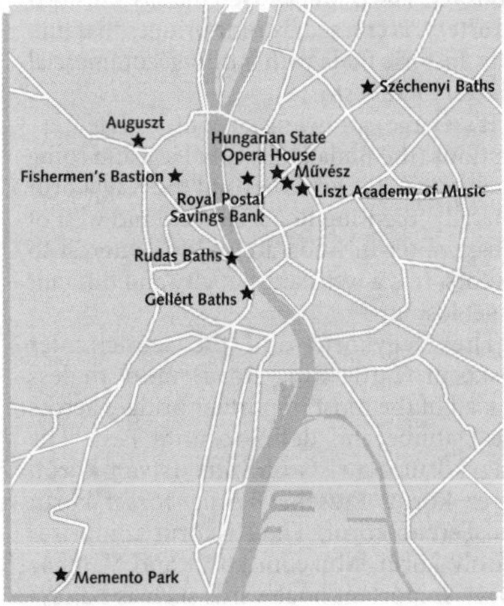

TELEPHONE CODE: 1	POPULATION: 1.67 MILLION	AREA: 525 SQ KM

HISTORY

The story of Budapest begins – strictly speaking – only in 1873, when hilly, largely residential Buda and historic Óbuda on the western bank of the Danube merged with flat, industrial Pest on the eastern side to form what was at first called Pest-Buda.

The Romans had an important colony here called Aquincum until the mid-5th century, when they were forced to flee by the Huns. The Magyars arrived five centuries later, but Buda and Pest were no more than villages until the 12th century, when foreign merchants and tradespeople settled. In the late 13th century King Béla IV built a fortress in Buda, but it was King Charles Robert (Károly Róbert) who moved the court from Visegrád to Buda 50 years later.

The Mongols burned Buda and Pest to the ground in 1241, and thus began a pattern of destruction and rebuilding that would last until the mid-20th century. Under the Turks, the two towns lost most of their populations, and when they were defeated by the Habsburgs in the late 17th century, Buda Castle was in ruins. The 1848–49 revolution, WWII and the 1956 Uprising all took their toll.

ORIENTATION

Budapest lies in the north-central part of Hungary. The Danube River, the city's historical artery, is crossed by nine bridges that link hilly, historic Buda with bustling, commercial and very flat Pest.

It's a large, sprawling city but, with few exceptions (the Buda Hills, City Park and some excursions), the areas beyond the Nagykörút (literally 'Big Ring Road') in Pest and west of Moszkva tér in Buda are of little interest to visitors. It is a well-laid-out city and difficult to get lost in.

The Nagykörút and the semicircular Kiskörút (Little Ring Road) more or less link all of the most important bridges across the Danube and define central Pest. The Nagykörút consists of Szent István körút, Teréz körút, Erzsébet körút, József körút and Ferenc körút. The Kiskörút comprises Károly körút, Múzeum körút and Vámház körút. Important boulevards such as Bajcsy-Zsilinszky út, Andrássy út and Rákóczi út fan out from the ring roads.

Buda is dominated by Castle and Gellért Hills. Important roads on this side are Margit körút (the only part of either ring road to cross the river), Fő utca and Attila utca on either side of Castle Hill, and Hegyalja út and Bartók Béla út running to the west and southwest. Its busiest square is Moszkva tér.

Budapest is divided into 23 *kerület* (districts), which usually also have traditional names, such as Lipótváros (Leopold Town) in district V and Víziváros (Watertown) in district I. The Roman numeral appearing before each street address indicates the district.

Travellers can reach the city centre from Budapest's Ferihegy International Airport, 24km southeast of the city centre, by bus and metro, train, minibus or taxi. For details, see p131.

Maps

The best folding maps of Budapest are Cartographia's 1:22,000 (770Ft) and 1:28,000 (640Ft) ones. There's also a waterproof 1:30,000 map, which costs 1490Ft. If you plan to explore the city thoroughly, the *Budapest Atlas,* also from Cartographia, is indispensable. It comes in the same scale (1:20,000), in two sizes: a smaller format (2190Ft) and a larger one (4300Ft). There is also a 1:25,000 pocket atlas of the Inner Town available for 1400Ft.

Many bookshops, including Libri Könyvpalota (below), stock a wide variety of maps. **Cartographia** (Map p84; ☎ 312 6001; www.cartographia.hu; VI Bajcsy-Zilinszky út 37; 🕑 10am-6pm Mon-Fri; Ⓜ M3 Arany János utca) has its own outlet in Budapest. An even better bet is **Térképkirály** (Map King; Map p84; ☎ 472 0505; www.mapking.hu; VI Bajcsy-Zsilinszky út 23; 🕑 9am-6pm Mon-Fri, to 1pm Sat; Ⓜ M3 Arany János utca), which also has a **Buda branch** (Map pp80-1; ☎ 315 2729; I Margit körút 1; 🕑 9am-6pm Mon-Fri, to 1pm Sat; 🚊 4 or 6).

INFORMATION

Bookshops

Bestsellers (Map p86; ☎ 312 1295; www.bestsellers.hu; V Október 6 utca 11; 🕑 9am-6.30pm Mon-Fri, 10am-5pm Sat, 10am-4pm Sun; Ⓜ M1/2/3 Deák Ferenc tér) Probably the best English-language bookshop in town, with fiction, travel guides and lots of Hungarica, as well as a large selection of newspapers and magazines, and helpful staff.

Írók Boltja (Writers' Bookshop; Map p84; ☎ 322 1645; www.irokboltja.hu, in Hungarian; VI Andrássy út 45; 🕑 10am-7pm Mon-Fri, to 1pm Sat; Ⓜ M1 Oktogon) Excellent for Hungarian authors in translation.

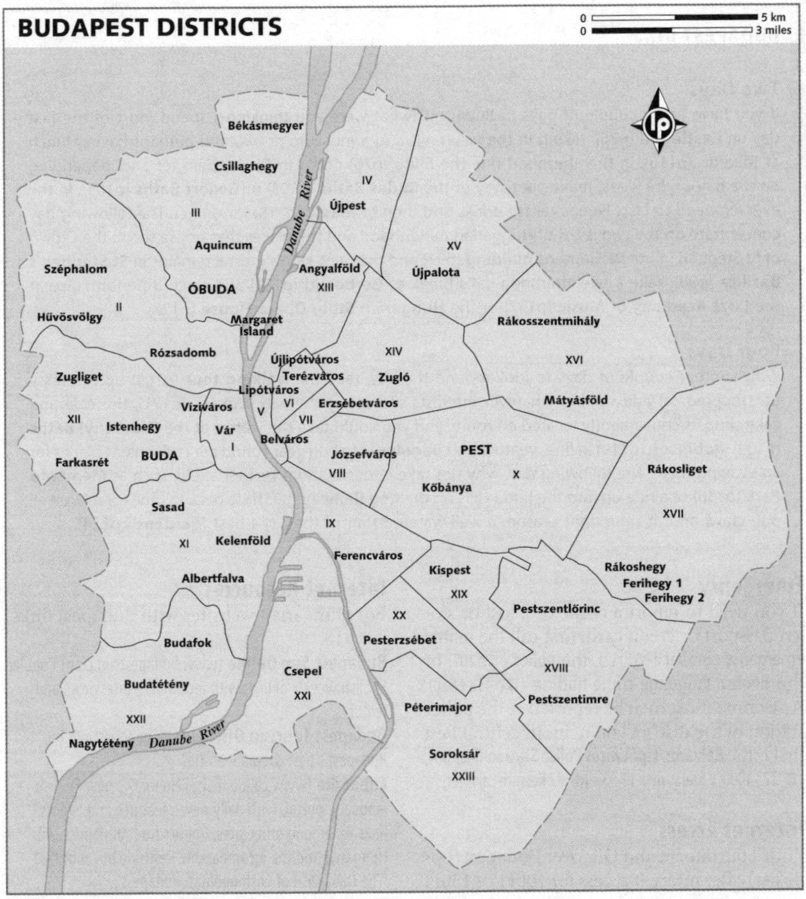

Libri Könyvpalota (Map p84; ☎ 267 4844; VII Rákóczi út 12; 🕒 10am-7.30pm Mon-Fri, to 3pm Sat; Ⓜ M2 Astoria) Spread over two floors, the 'Book Palace' has a selection of English-language novels, art books, guidebooks, maps, music and a cafe on the 1st floor.

Pendragon (Map pp80-1; ☎ 340 4426; XIII Pozsonyi út 21-23; 🕒 10am-6pm Mon-Fri, to 2pm Sat; 🚊 4 or 6) This exclusively English-language bookshop has an excellent selection of books and guides (including many Lonely Planet titles).

Red Bus Bookstore (Map p86; ☎ 337 7453; V Semmelweis utca 14; 🕒 11am-6pm Mon-Fri, 10am-2pm Sat; Ⓜ M1/2/3 Deák Ferenc tér) Below the popular hostel of the same name (p111), this shop has a good selection of used English-language books.

Treehugger Dan's Bookstore (Map p84; ☎ 322 0774; www.treehugger.hu; VI Csengery utca 48; 🕒 10am-7pm Mon-Fri, to 5pm Sat; Ⓜ M1 Oktogon) This new kid on the block has thousands of second-hand English-language books, does trade-ins and serves organic fair-trade coffee. There's also a **branch** (Map p84; ☎ 269 3843; VI Lázár utca 16; 🕒 9.30am-6.30pm Mon-Fri, 10am-4pm Sat & Sun; Ⓜ M1 Opera) at Discover Budapest.

Discount Cards

Budapest Card (☎ 266 0479; www.budapestinfo.hu; per 48/72hr 6500/8000Ft) This card, valid for two or three days, offers free admission to 60 museums and other sights, unlimited travel on all forms of public transport, and discounts on organised tours, on car rental, at thermal baths and at selected shops and restaurants. Available at Tourinform offices, travel agencies, hotels and main metro stations, and online.

BUDAPEST IN...

Two Days

If you have just a couple of days in Budapest (what were you thinking?) spend most of the first day on **Castle Hill** (p76), taking in the views, visiting a museum or two and perhaps having lunch at **Rivalda** (p116). In the afternoon ride the **Sikló** (p76) down to Clark Ádám tér and, depending on the day of the week, make your way to the **Rudas Baths** (p103) or **Gellért Baths** (p103). In the evening head to Liszt Ferenc tér for drinks and then to **Klassz** (p118) for dinner. The following day concentrate on the two icons of Hungarian nationhood and the places that house them: the Crown of St Stephen in the **Parliament building** (p97) and the saint-king's mortal remains in **St Stephen's Basilica** (p98). Take a late-afternoon cake break at **Gerbeaud** (p121) and catch a performance at the **Liszt Academy of Music** (p127) or the **Hungarian State Opera House** (p127).

Four Days

With another couple of days to look around the city, take the **walking tour** (p105) up Andrássy út, stopping off and visiting whatever interests you along the way. **Lukács** (p121), the cafe and cake shop, is conveniently located en route, and you could take the waters at the **Széchenyi Baths** (p104). **Robinson** (p119) in fine weather and **Bagolyvár** (p118) year-round are convenient places for an evening meal. The following day, why not take in destinations further afield, such as **Memento Park** (p136) or a ride up into the Buda Hills on the **Cog Railway** (p95)? Be back in time for a farewell pub crawl or, if it's the right season, a well-watered tour of the city's best **'gardens'** (p124).

Emergency

If you need to report a crime or a lost or stolen passport or credit card, first call the **central emergency number** (☎ 112), the **police** (☎ 107) or the **English-language crime hotline** (☎ 438 8080). Any crime must then be reported at the police station of the district you're in. In central Pest that is the **Belváros-Lipótváros Police Station** (Map p84; ☎ 373 1000; V Szalay utca 11-13; Ⓜ M2 Kossuth Lajos tér).

Internet Access

Both Tourinform and Discover Budapest (opposite) offer internet access for 100Ft or 150Ft per 15 minutes.

Electric Cafe (Map p84; ☎ 413 1803; VII Dohány utca 37; per 30/60min 100/200Ft; 9am-midnight; Ⓜ M2 Blaha Lujza tér) A huge place that's very popular with travellers.

Narancs (Map p84; ☎ 413 6071; VII Akácfa utca 5; per 30/60min 100/200Ft; 9am-1am; Ⓜ M2 Blaha Lujza tér) *Très* charming French-run neighbourhood internet cafe.

Plastic Net (Map p86; ☎ 317 4638; V Szép utca 5; per 30/60min 200/390Ft; 9.30am-11.30pm Mon-Sat, 10am-10pm Sun; Ⓜ M3 Ferenciek tere) A branch of Plastic Web.

Plastic Web (Map p86; ☎ 337 1374; V Irányi utca 1; per 30/60min 200/390Ft; 9.30am-11.30pm; 2) This friendly place is about as central as you'll find in Pest.

Vist@netcafe (Map p84; ☎ 320 4332; XIII Váci út 6; per 1hr 10am-10pm 500Ft, 10pm-10am 400Ft; 24hr; Ⓜ M3 Nyugati pályaudvar) One of the very few internet cafes open round the clock.

Internet Resources

For Hungarian websites with Budapest links, see p18.

Budapest Sun Online (www.budapestsun.com) Popular English weekly online, with local news, interviews and features.

Budapest Tourism Office (www.budapestinfo.hu) Budapest's best overall website.

Caboodle (www.caboodle.hu) Hungary's best English-language portal, with daily news, features and events, links to, among other sites, Politics.hu ('All Politics. All Hungary') and the incomparable Pestiside.hu, subtitled 'The Daily Dish of Cosmopolitan Budapest'.

The Hub (www.thehub.hu) Excellent all-inclusive site on nightlife and culture, including both performances and exhibitions.

Left Luggage

Budapest's three major train stations and two bus stations all have left-luggage offices and/or lockers; see p131 and p130. For information about left luggage at Ferihegy International Airport, see p131.

Medical Services

CLINICS

FirstMed Centers (Map p83; ☎ 224 9090; www.firstmedcenters.com; I Hattyú utca 14, 5th fl; appointments 8am-8pm Mon-Fri, 9am-2pm Sat, urgent care 24hr; Ⓜ M2 Moszkva tér) This modern, private medical clinic has round-the-clock emergency treatment that is as expensive as you'll find in Europe (a basic consultation for under 10/20 minutes costs 15,400/30,900Ft).

S.O.S. Dent (Map p86; ☎ 269 6010, 06 30 383 3333; www.sosdent.hu, in Hungarian; VI Király utca 14; ⏲ 24hr; Ⓜ M1/2/3 Deák Ferenc tér) Consultations at this round-the-clock dental surgery are free, with extractions 7000Ft to 9000Ft, fillings 7000Ft to 11,000Ft and crowns from 40,000Ft.

PHARMACIES

Each of Budapest's 23 districts has a rotating all-night pharmacy; a sign on the door of any pharmacy will help you locate the nearest 24-hour place. Conveniently located pharmacies:

Déli Gyógyszertár (Map p83; ☎ 355 4691; XII Alkotás utca 1/b; ⏲ 8am-8pm Mon-Fri, to 2pm Sat; Ⓜ M2 Déli pályaudvar)

Teréz Patika (Map p84; ☎ 311 4439; VI Teréz körút 41; ⏲ 8am-8pm Mon-Fri, to 2pm Sat; Ⓜ M3 Nyugati pályaudvar)

Money

There are ATMs everywhere in Budapest, including in the train and bus stations, and quite a few foreign-currency exchange machines, too.

K&H bank (Map p86; V Váci utca 40; ⏲ 8am-5pm Mon, to 4pm Tue-Thu, to 3pm Fri; Ⓜ M3 Ferenciek tere) Conveniently located on the main shopping drag; offers fairly good rates.

OTP bank (Map p86; V Deák Ferenc utca 7-9; ⏲ 7.45am-6pm Mon, to 5pm Tue-Thu, to 4pm Fri; Ⓜ M1/2/3 Deák Ferenc tér) The National Savings Bank offers among the best exchange rates for cash and travellers cheques.

Post

Post office Belváros main post office (Map p86; V Petőfi Sándor utca 13-15; ⏲ 8am-8pm Mon-Fri, to 2pm Sat; Ⓜ M1/2/3 Deák Ferenc tér); Keleti train station (Map pp80-1; VIII Kerepesi út 2-6; ⏲ 7am-9pm Mon-Fri, 8am-2pm Sat; Ⓜ M2 Keleti pályaudvar); Nyugati train station (Map p84; VI Teréz körút 51-53; ⏲ 7am-8pm Mon-Fri, 8am-6pm Sat; Ⓜ M3 Nyugati pályaudvar)

Telephone

You can buy SIM cards and rent hand units from mobile-phone outlets throughout the city.

Pannon (Map pp80-1; ☎ 345 8088; www.pannon.hu; II Mammut I, 2nd fl, Lövőház utca 2-6; ⏲ 9am-8pm Mon-Sat, to 6pm Sun; Ⓜ M2 Moszkva tér)

T-Mobile (Map p86; ☎ 266 5723; www.t-mobile.hu; V Petőfi Sándor utca 12; ⏲ 9am-7pm Mon-Fri, 10am-1pm Sat; Ⓜ M3 Ferenciek tere)

Vodafone (Map p84; ☎ 238 7281; www.vodafone.hu; West End City Centre, VI Váci út 1-3, 1st fl; ⏲ 10am-9pm Mon-Sat, to 6pm Sun; Ⓜ Nyugati pályaudvar)

Tourist Information

Tourinform (www.tourinform.hu) Belváros (Map p86; ☎ 438 8080; V Sütő utca 2; ⏲ 8am-8pm; Ⓜ M1/2/3 Deák Ferenc tér); Castle Hill (Map p83; ☎ 488 0475; I Szentháromság tér; ⏲ 9am-7pm May-Oct, 10am-6pm Nov-Apr; 🚌 16, 16A or 116); Oktogon (Map p84; ☎ 322 4098; VI Liszt Ferenc tér 11; ⏲ 10am-6pm Mon-Fri; Ⓜ M1 Oktogon) In addition, there are Tourinform desks in the arrivals sections of Ferihegy International Airport's terminals 1, 2A and 2B.

Travel Agencies

For details on agencies that book private accommodation, see p111.

Discover Budapest (Map p84; ☎ 269 3843; VI Lázár utca 16; ⏲ 9.30am-6.30pm Mon-Fri, 10am-4pm Sat & Sun; Ⓜ M1 Opera) Visit this one-stop shop for helpful tips and advice, accommodation bookings, internet access, and cycling and walking tours with Yellow Zebra Bikes (p108) and Absolute Walking Tours (p108).

Express (Map p84; ☎ 327 7298; www.express-travel.hu; cnr VII Dohány utca 30/a & Kazinczy utca 3/b; ⏲ 8.30am-5pm Mon-Fri, 9am-1pm Sat; Ⓜ M2 Astoria) The main office of this youth- and student-orientated agency can book accommodation in Budapest, particularly hostels and colleges, and sells transport tickets.

Ibusz (Map p86; ☎ 501 4910; www.ibusz.hu; V Ferenciek tere 10; ⏲ 9am-6pm Mon-Fri, to 1pm Sat; Ⓜ M3 Ferenciek tere) The main office of this travel-agency giant changes money, books all types of accommodation and sells transport tickets.

Vista (Map p86; ☎ 429 9999; www.vista.hu, in Hungarian; VI Andrássy út 1; ⏲ 9.30am-6pm Mon-Fri, 10am-2.30pm Sat; Ⓜ M1/2/3 Deák Ferenc tér) Vista is an excellent destination for all your travel needs, both outbound (air tickets, package tours etc) and incoming (room bookings, organised tours, study etc).

Wasteels (Map pp80-1; ☎ 210 2802, 343 3492; www.wasteels.hu; VIII Kerepesi út 2-6; ⏲ 8am-8pm Mon-Fri, to 6pm Sat; Ⓜ M2 Keleti pályaudvar) This agency next to platform 9 at Keleti train station sells Billet International de Jeunesse (BIJ) 26 tickets, which are discounted train tickets available throughout Europe to those under 26 years of age.

DANGERS & ANNOYANCES

No parts of Budapest are 'off limits' to visitors, although some locals now avoid Margaret Island after dark during the low season, and both residents and visitors give the dodgier parts of the VIII and IX districts (areas of prostitution) a wide berth.

Pickpocketing is most common in markets, the Castle District, Váci utca and Hősök tere, near major hotels and on certain popular buses (eg 7) and trams (2, 4, 6, 47 and 49).

Taking a taxi in Budapest can be an expensive and even unpleasant experience. For more information, see p135.

If you've left something on any form of public transport in Budapest, contact the **BKV Lost & Found Office** (Map p84; ☎ 258 4636, 461 6688; VII Akácfa utca 18; 8am-5pm Mon, Tue, Thu & Fri, to 6pm Wed; Ⓜ M2 Blaha Lujza tér).

Scams

Scams involving attractive young women, gullible guys, expensive drinks in nightclubs and a frog-marching to the nearest ATM by gorillas-in-residence have been all the rage in Budapest for well over a decade now, and we get stacks of letters from male readers complaining they've been ripped off (sometimes hundreds, even thousands, of dollars). Guys, please, do us all a favour. If it seems too good to be true, it is. Tourinform distributes a brochure called *Well-informed in Budapest*, with useful tips on avoiding such problems.

SIGHTS

Budapest is an excellent city for touring around (especially on foot), and there are sights around every corner – from a brightly tiled gem of an Art Nouveau building to women fresh in from the countryside hawking their homemade *barack lekvár* (apricot jam). The Castle District in Buda contains a number of museums, both major and minor, but the lion's share is in Pest. Think of Margaret Island as a green buffer between the two – short on things to see as such but a great place for a breather.

Buda

Hilly, leafy and unpolluted, Buda is more than just a pretty face. The area's majestic western side fronting the Danube has some of the city's most important and historical landmarks (eg Castle Hill, the Citadella) and museums (Hungarian National Gallery, Budapest History Museum), and, to the north, the original Roman settlement at Aquincum.

CASTLE HILL

Castle Hill (Várhegy; Map p83), also called the Castle District, is a 1km-long limestone plateau towering 170m above the Danube. It contains Budapest's most important medieval monuments and museums, and is a Unesco World Heritage Site. Below it is a 28km-long network of caves formed by thermal springs, which contain several attractions.

The walled area consists of two distinct but contiguous parts: the Old Town, where commoners once lived, and the Royal Palace, the original site of the castle built in the 13th century by Béla IV and reserved for the nobility.

The easiest way to reach Castle Hill from Pest is to take bus 16 from Deák Ferenc tér to Dísz tér, more or less the centre point between the Old Town and the Royal Palace. Much more fun, though, is to stroll across Széchenyi Chain Bridge and board the **Sikló** (1-way/return ticket adult 800/1400Ft, 3-14yr 500/900Ft; 7.30am-10pm, closed 1st & 3rd Mon of month), a funicular railway built in 1870 that ascends at 48% from Clark Ádám tér to Szent György tér near the Royal Palace.

Alternatively, you can walk up the Király lépcső, the 'Royal Steps' that lead northwest off Clark Ádám tér.

Another option is to take metro M2 to Moszkva tér, go up the stairs in the northeastern part of the square and walk up I Várfok utca to **Vienna Gate**, the medieval entrance to the Old Town rebuilt in 1936 to mark the 250th anniversary of the retaking of the castle from the Turks. Bus 16A follows the same route from the start of Várfok utca.

Royal Palace

The former Royal Palace (Budavári Palota; Map p83) has been razed and rebuilt at least a half-dozen times over the past seven centuries. Béla IV established a royal residence here in the mid-13th century, and subsequent kings added to the structure. The palace was levelled in the battle to rout the Turks in 1686; the Habsburgs rebuilt it, but spent very little time here. Today the Royal Palace contains two important museums as well as the **National Széchenyi Library** (10am-8pm Tue-Sat).

(Continued on page 90)

BUDAPEST & ENVIRONS

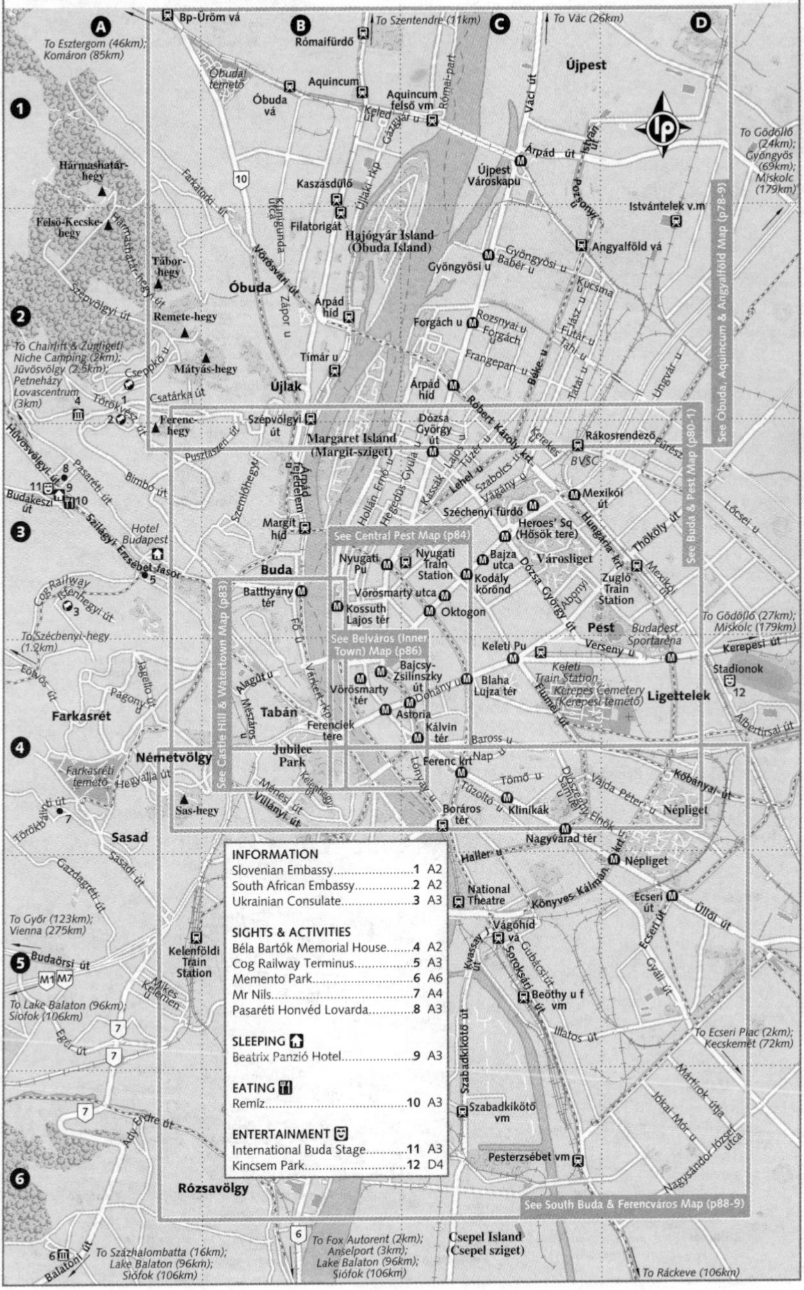

ÓBUDA, AQUINCUM & ANGYALFÖLD

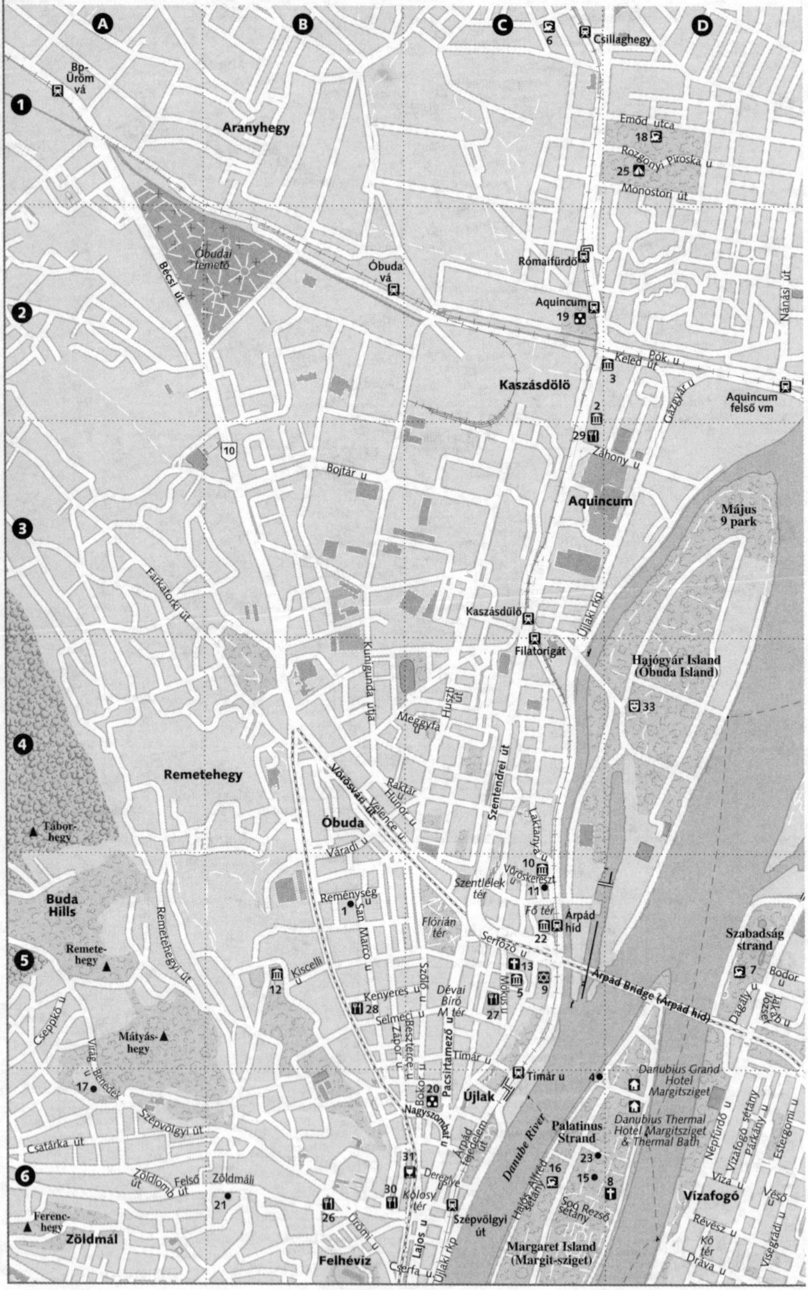

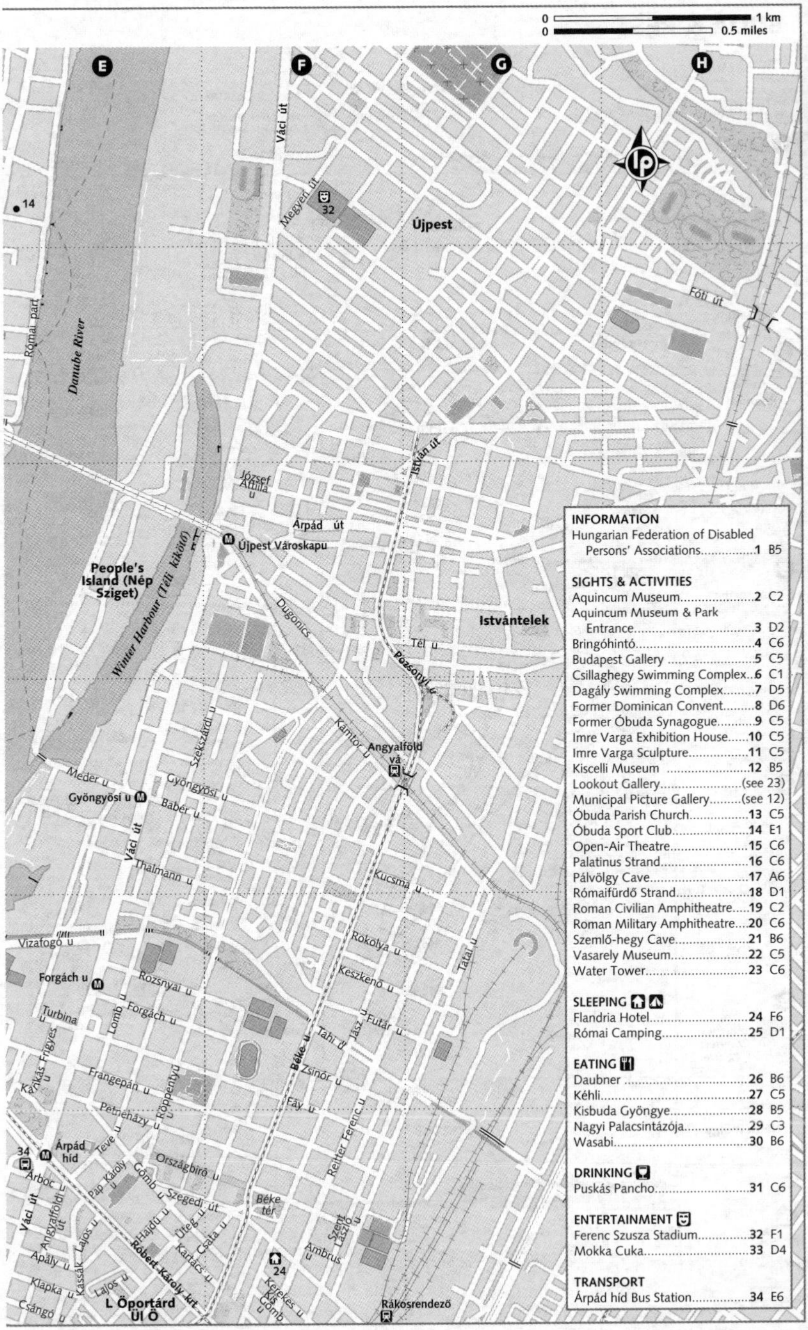

INFORMATION
Hungarian Federation of Disabled Persons' Associations....1 B5

SIGHTS & ACTIVITIES
Aquincum Museum....2 C2
Aquincum Museum & Park Entrance....3 D2
Bringóhintó....4 C6
Budapest Gallery....5 C5
Csillaghegy Swimming Complex....6 C1
Dagály Swimming Complex....7 D5
Former Dominican Convent....8 D6
Former Óbuda Synagogue....9 C5
Imre Varga Exhibition House....10 C5
Imre Varga Sculpture....11 C5
Kiscelli Museum....12 B5
Lookout Gallery....(see 23)
Municipal Picture Gallery....(see 12)
Óbuda Parish Church....13 C5
Óbuda Sport Club....14 E1
Open-Air Theatre....15 C6
Palatinus Strand....16 C6
Pálvölgy Cave....17 A6
Rómaifürdő Strand....18 D1
Roman Civilian Amphitheatre....19 C2
Roman Military Amphitheatre....20 C6
Szemlő-hegy Cave....21 B6
Vasarely Museum....22 C5
Water Tower....23 C6

SLEEPING
Flandria Hotel....24 F6
Római Camping....25 D1

EATING
Daubner....26 B6
Kéhli....27 C5
Kisbuda Gyöngye....28 B5
Nagyi Palacsintázója....29 C3
Wasabi....30 B6

DRINKING
Puskás Pancho....31 C6

ENTERTAINMENT
Ferenc Szusza Stadium....32 F1
Mokka Cuka....33 D4

TRANSPORT
Árpád híd Bus Station....34 E6

BUDA & PEST

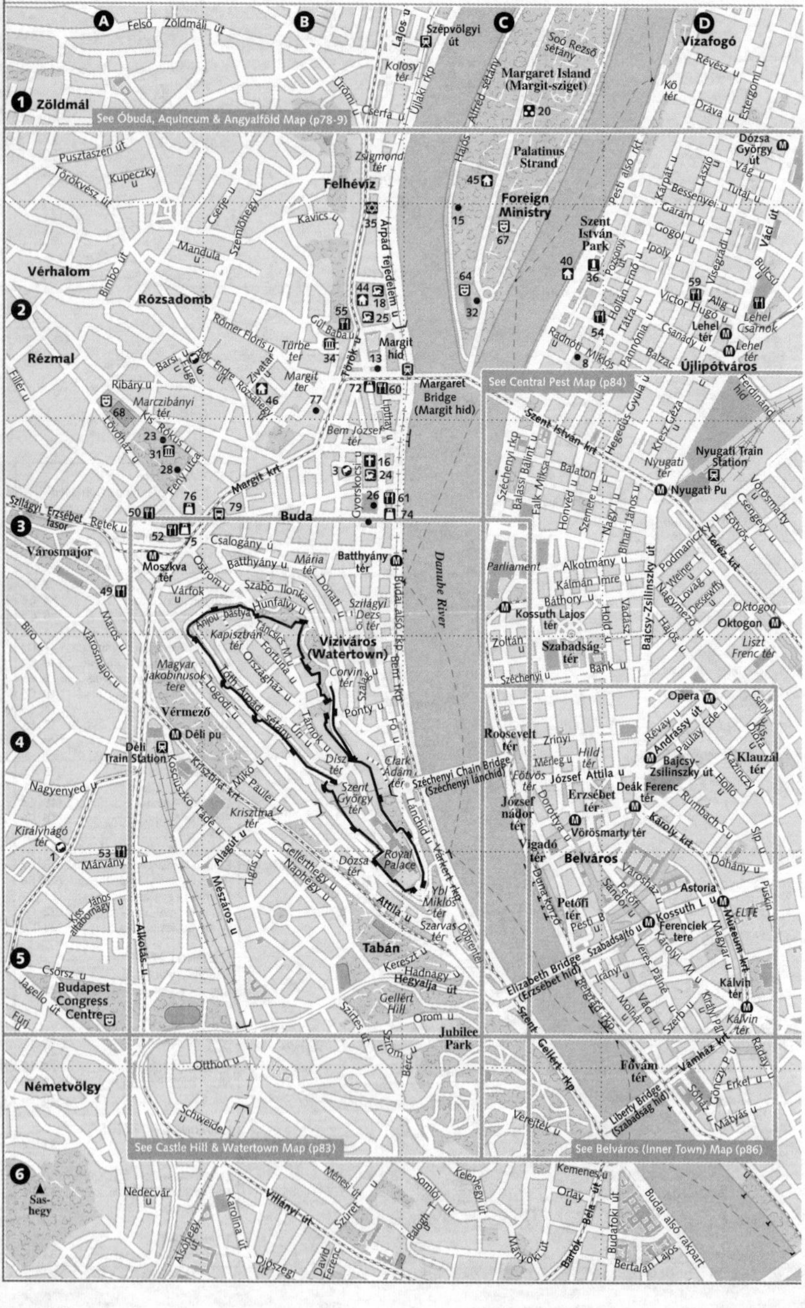
A
B
C
D
1
2
3
4
5
6
Felső Zöldmáli út
Szépvölgyi út
Lajos u
Kolosy tér
Soó Rezső sétány
Margaret Island (Margit-sziget)
Vízafogó
Révész u
Kő tér
Dráva u
Esztergomi u
Zöldmál
See Óbuda, Aquincum & Angyalföld Map (p78-9)
Cserfa u
Újlaki rkp
Ürömi u
Alfréd sétány
20
Pusztaszeri út
Törökvész út
Kupeczky u
Zsigmond tér
Felhévíz
Hajós
Palatinus Strand
Dózsa György út
Vág u
45
Tutaj u
Bessenyei u
Garam u
Cseije u
Szemlőhegy u
Kavics u
35
Árpád fejedelem u
15
Foreign Ministry
67
Pesti alsó rkt
Szent István Park
Gogol u
Ipoly u
Váci út
Mandula u
Vérhalom
Bimbó út
Rózsadomb
44
18
25
55
64
32
40
36
59
Victor Hugó u
Alig u
Bulcsú
Lehel Csarnok
Lehel tér
Római Flóris u
Gül Baba u
Türbe tér
34
Margit hid
13
54
Tátra u
Pannónia u
Csanády u
Balzac
Radnóti Miklós u
8
Újlipótváros
Rézmal
Barsi u
Fuge
6
Ady Endre út
Zivatar u
Rózsahegy
Margit tér
72
60
Margaret Bridge (Margit híd)
See Central Pest Map (p84)
Ferdinánd híd
Ribáry u
68
Marczibányi tér
46
77
Szent István krt
Hegedűs Gyula u
Kresz Géza u
Fillér u
Kis Rókus u
23
31
28
Lövőház u
Fény utca
Bem József tér
Lipthay u
Nyugati Train Station
3
16
24
Széchenyi rkp
Balassi Bálint u
Falk Miksa u
Balaton u
Nyugati tér
Nyugati Pu
Margit krt
76
79
26
61
74
Gyorskocsi u
Honvéd u
Szemere u
Nagy I u
Bihari János u
Vörösmarty u
Szilágyi Erzsébet fasor
Retek u
50
52
75
Buda
Csalogány u
Podmaniczky u
Eötvös u
Városmajor
Moszkva tér
Ostrom u
Batthyány u
Mária tér
Batthyány tér
Danube River
Parliament
Alkotmány u
Teréz krt
Weiner L
Lovag u
Dessewffy u
49
Várfok u
Szabó Ilonka u
Donáti u
Budai alsó rkp
Kálmán Imre u
Báthory u
Kossuth Lajos tér
Anjou bástya
Hunfalvy u
Szilágyi Dezső tér
Vadász u
Hold u
Bajcsy-Zsilinszky út
Nagymező u
Hajós u
Oktogon
Biró u
Maros u
Városmajor u
Kapisztrán tér
Táncsics M u
Fortuna u
Víziváros (Watertown)
Bem rkp
Zoltán u
Szabadság tér
Liszt Ferenc tér
Magyar Jakobinusok tere
Országház u
Corvin tér
Szalag u
Bank u
Széchenyi u
Tóth Árpád sétány
Logodi u
Vérmező
Tárnok u
Úri u
Ponty u
Fő u
Opera
Révay u
Andrássy út
Paulay Ede u
Csányi u
Kis Diófa
Déli pu
Déli Train Station
Dísz tér
Clark Ádám tér
Széchenyi Chain Bridge (Széchenyi lánchíd)
Roosevelt tér
Zrinyi
Mérleg u
Hild tér
Eötvös tér
József Attila u
Bajcsy-Zsilinszky út
Klauzál tér
Kazinczy u
Holló
Nagyenyed u
Kosciuszko
Krisztina krt
Mikó u
Pauler u
Szent György tér
Deák Ferenc tér
József nádor tér
Erzsébet tér
Rumbach S u
Dorottya u
Vörösmarty tér
Károly krt
Királyhágó tér
1
Tóth
Krisztina tér
Alagút u
Lánchíd u
Várkert rkp
Síp
Dohány u
53
Márvány u
Gellérthegy u
Naphegy u
Dózsa tér
Royal Palace
Vigadó tér
Belváros
Duna korzó
Városház u
Sándor
Astoria
Kiss János altábornagy u
Mészáros u
Tigris u
Attila u
Ybl Miklós tér
Petőfi tér
Petőfi Sándor
Pesti B u
Kossuth L u
Ferenciek tere
ELTE
Múzeum krt
Puskin u
Alkotás u
Szarvas tér
Döbrentei
Tabán
Szabadsajtó u
Károlyi M u
Veres Pálné
Magyar u
Kereszt u
Hadnagy u
Hegyalja út
Elizabeth Bridge (Erzsébet híd)
Belgrád rkp
Irányi
Molnár
Váci u
Szerb u
Királyi Pál
Kálvin tér
Csörsz u
Budapest Congress Centre
Jagello út
Fürj
Gellért Hill
Orom u
Jubilee Park
Szent Gellért rkp
Szirtes út
Szirom u
Bérc u
Fővám tér
Vámház krt
Ráday u
Gönczy P u
Sóház u
Erkel u
Németvölgy
Otthon u
Schweidel
Liberty Bridge (Szabadság híd)
Verejték u
Mátyás u
See Castle Hill & Watertown Map (p83)
See Belváros (Inner Town) Map (p86)
Kemenes u
Sas-hegy
Nedecvár u
Ménesi u
Somlói u
Kelenhegyi u
Orlay u
Villányi út
Karolina út
Szüret u
Balogh T u
Bartók Béla út
Budafoki út
Budai alsó rakpart
Alsóhegy u
Diószegi út
David Ferenc
Mányoki út
Bertalan Lajos

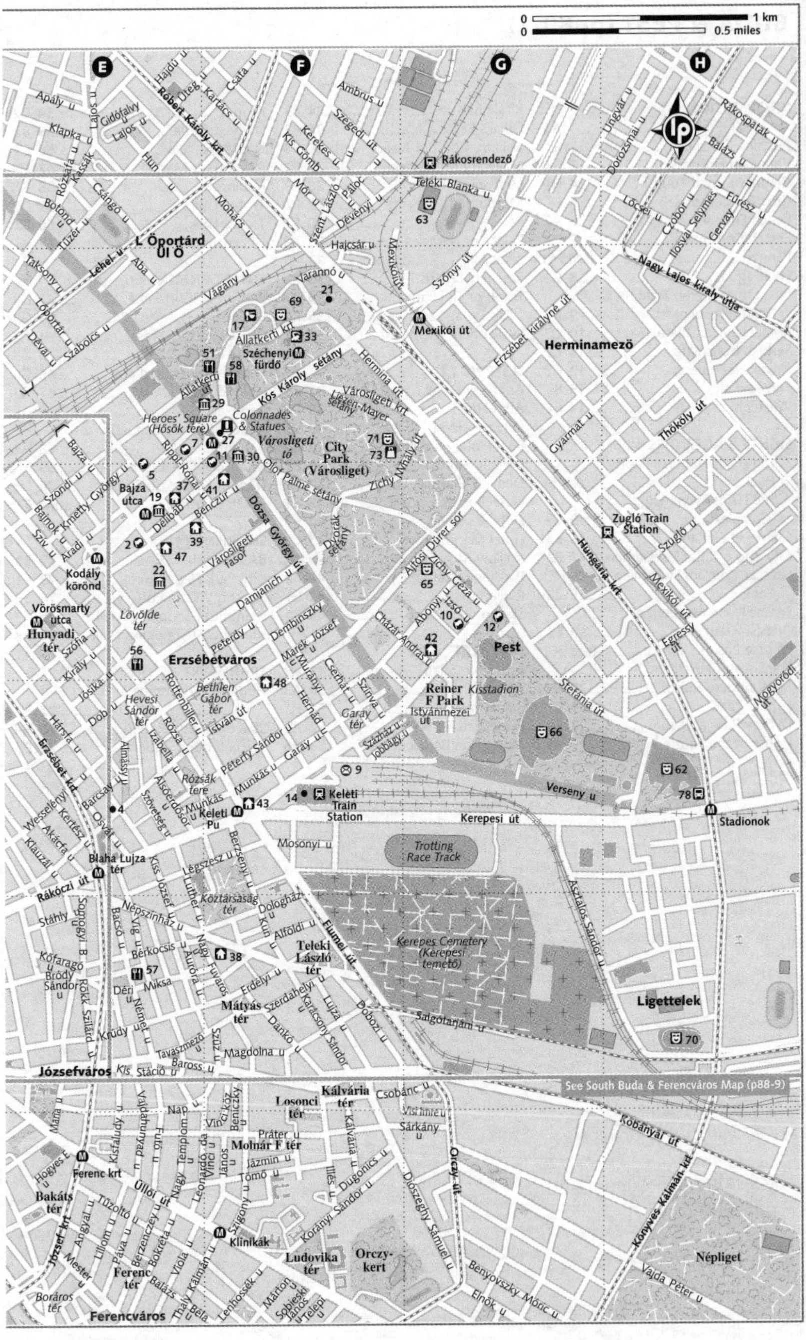
0 1 km
0 0.5 miles
E
F
G
H
Rákosrendező
Teleki Blanka u
Hajcsár u
Mexikói út
Szőnyi út
Vágány u
Varannó u
Állatkerti krt
Széchenyi fürdő
Kós Károly sétány
Hermina út
Városligeti krt
Liezen-Mayer sétány
Heroes' Square (Hősök tere)
Colonnades & Statues
Városligeti tó
City Park (Városliget)
Olof Palme sétány
Zichy Mihály út
Dózsa György út
Bajza utca
Dvořák sétány
Városligeti fasor
Kodály körönd
Vörösmarty utca
Hunyadi tér
Lövölde tér
Erzsébetváros
Bethlen Gábor tér
Hevesi Sándor tér
István út
Garay tér
Reiner F Park
Kisstadion
Istvánmezei út
Pest
Stefánia út
Herminamező
Erzsébet királyné út
Thököly út
Zugló Train Station
Hungária krt
Nagy Lajos király útja
Verseny u
Keleti Train Station
Keleti Pu
Kerepesi út
Stadionok
Trotting Race Track
Blaha Lujza tér
Rákóczi út
Köztársaság tér
Fiumei út
Kerepes Cemetery (Kerepesi temető)
Teleki László tér
Mátyás tér
Salgótarjáni u
Ligettelek
Aszalos Sándor u
Józsefváros
See South Buda & Ferencváros Map (p88-9)
Kálvária tér
Losonci tér
Molnár F tér
Kőbányai út
Ferenc krt
Üllői út
Bakáts tér
Klinikák
Ludovika tér
Orczy-kert
Orczy út
Könyves Kálmán krt
Népliget
Vajda Péter u
Ferenc tér
Boráros tér
Ferencváros
József krt
Erzsébet krt
Lehel u
Róbert Károly krt
Dorozsmai u
Mexikói út
Egressy út
Mogyoródi út
Szugló u
Magdolna u
Baross u
Benyovszky Móric u
Dugonics u
Diószeghy Sámuel u

BUDA & PEST (pp80-1)

INFORMATION

Australian Embassy....1 A5
Austrian Consulate....2 E3
Canadian Embassy....3 B3
Centre of Rural Tourism....4 E4
Croatian Consulate....5 E3
Dutch Embassy....6 A2
French Consulate....7 E2
Pannon....(see 76)
Pendragon....8 C2
Post Office (Keleti Train Station Branch)....9 F4
Romanian Consulate....10 G3
Serbian Consulate....11 F2
Slovakian Embassy....12 G3
Térképkirály....13 B2
Wasteels....14 F4

SIGHTS & ACTIVITIES

Alfréd Hajós National Sports Pool....(see 15)
Alfréd Hajós Swimming Complex....15 C2
Chapel St Florian....16 B3
City Zoo & Botanical Garden....17 F2
Császár-Komjádi Swimming Pool....18 B2
Ferenc Hopp Museum of East Asian Art....19 E3
Fő utca Prison....(see 26)
Franciscan Church and Monastery Ruins....20 C1
Funfair Park....21 F2
György Ráth Museum....22 E3
House of the Future Exhibition..23 A3
Király Baths....24 B3
Lukács Baths....25 B2
Military Court of Justice....26 B3
Millenary Monument....27 F2
Millennium Park....28 A3
Museum of Fine Arts....29 F2
Palace of Art....30 F2
Palace of Miracles....31 A3
Sétacikli....32 C2
Széchenyi Baths....33 F2
Tomb of Gül Baba....34 B2
Újlak Synagogue....35 B2
Wallenberg Memorial....36 C2

SLEEPING

Andrássy Hotel....37 E3
Atlas Hotel....38 F5
Benczúr Hotel....39 E3
Boat Hotel Fortuna....40 C2
Délibáb Hotel....41 F3
Dominik Panzió....42 G3
Hotel Baross....43 F4
Hotel Császár....44 B2
Hotel Margitsziget....45 C1
Mellow Mood Group....(see 43)
Papillon Hotel....46 B2
Radio Inn....47 E3
Star Hotel....48 F4

EATING

Artigiana Gelati....49 A3
Auguszt....50 A3
Bagolyvár....51 F2
Fény Utca Market....52 A3
Mongolian Barbecue....53 A5
Móri....54 C2
Nagyi Kifőzde....55 B2
Napfényes Ízek....56 E3
Rákóczi tér Market....57 E5
Robinson....58 F2
Troféa Grill....59 D2
Troféa Grill....60 B2
Új Lanzhou....61 B3

ENTERTAINMENT

Budapest Sportaréna....62 H4
BVSC....63 G1
Cha Cha Cha Terasz....64 C2
Dürer Kert....65 G3
Ferenc Puskás Stadium....66 G4
Holdudvar....67 C2
Kaméleon....(see 76)
Marczibányi tér Cultural Centre....68 A2
Municipal Great Circus....69 F2
Nándor Hidegkúti Stadium....70 H5
Petőfi Csarnok....71 F2

SHOPPING

BÁV Branch....72 B2
City Park Flea Market....73 F2
Herend Village Pottery....74 B3
Mammut I Shopping Mall....75 A3
Mammut II Shopping Mall....76 A3

TRANSPORT

Hungarian Automobile Club....77 B2
Stadionok Bus Station....78 H4
Széna tér Bus Station....79 B3

CASTLE HILL & WATERTOWN

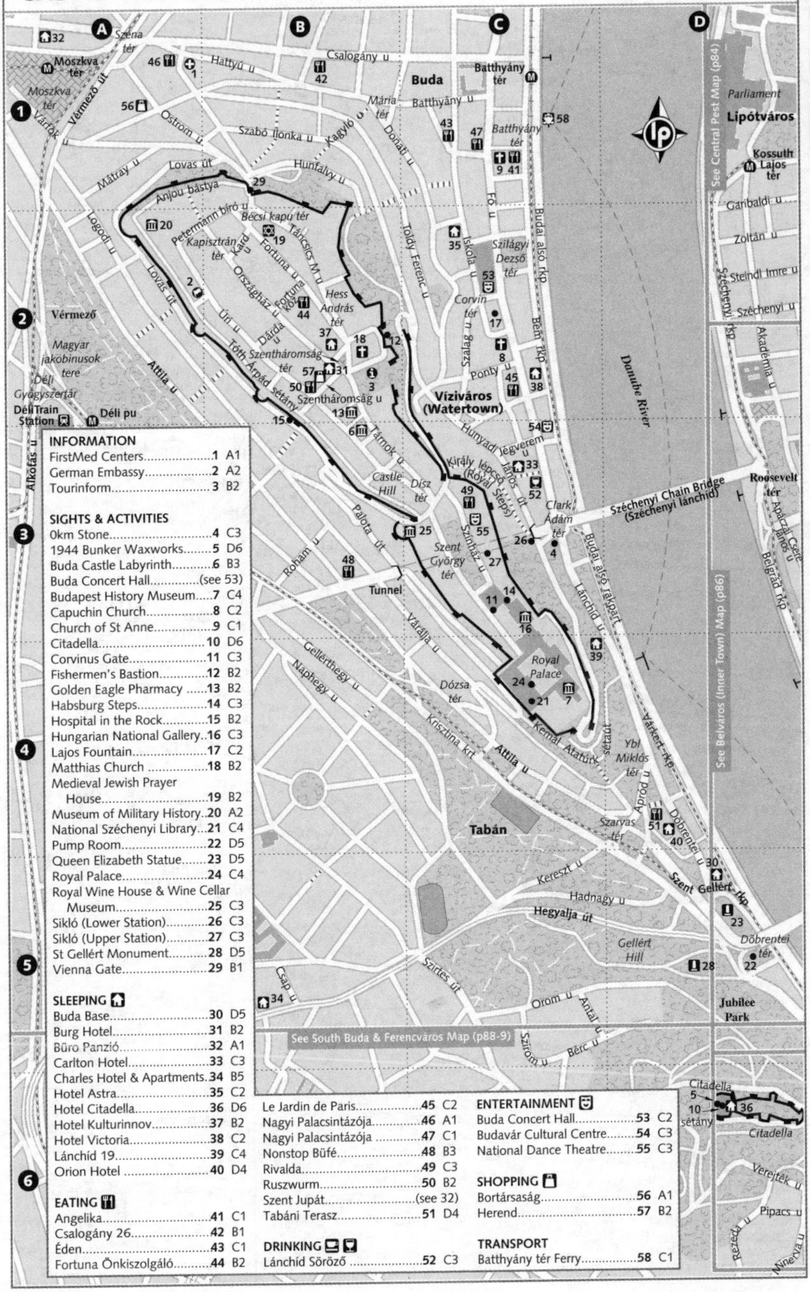

INFORMATION

- FirstMed Centers.................1 A1
- German Embassy..................2 A2
- Tourinform..........................3 B2

SIGHTS & ACTIVITIES

- 0km Stone............................4 C3
- 1944 Bunker Waxworks........5 D6
- Buda Castle Labyrinth..........6 B3
- Buda Concert Hall..............(see 53)
- Budapest History Museum.....7 C4
- Capuchin Church..................8 C2
- Church of St Anne.................9 C1
- Citadella..............................10 D6
- Corvinus Gate.......................11 C3
- Fishermen's Bastion.............12 B2
- Golden Eagle Pharmacy 13 B2
- Habsburg Steps....................14 C3
- Hospital in the Rock............15 B2
- Hungarian National Gallery..16 C3
- Lajos Fountain......................17 C2
- Matthias Church 18 B2
- Medieval Jewish Prayer House............19 B2
- Museum of Military History..20 A2
- National Széchenyi Library...21 C4
- Pump Room..........................22 D5
- Queen Elizabeth Statue.......23 D5
- Royal Palace........................24 C4
- Royal Wine House & Wine Cellar Museum..........25 C3
- Sikló (Lower Station)...........26 C3
- Sikló (Upper Station)...........27 C3
- St Gellért Monument...........28 D5
- Vienna Gate.........................29 B1

SLEEPING

- Buda Base...........................30 D5
- Burg Hotel...........................31 B2
- Bűro Panzió.........................32 A1
- Carlton Hotel.......................33 C3
- Charles Hotel & Apartments..34 B5
- Hotel Astra..........................35 C2
- Hotel Citadella.....................36 D6
- Hotel Kulturinnov................37 B2
- Hotel Victoria.......................38 C2
- Lánchíd 19...........................39 C4
- Orion Hotel 40 D4

EATING

- Angelika..............................41 C1
- Csalogány 26.......................42 B1
- Éden....................................43 C1
- Fortuna Önkiszolgáló..........44 B2
- Le Jardin de Paris................45 C2
- Nagyi Palacsintázója...........46 A1
- Nagyi Palacsintázója 47 C1
- Nonstop Büfé......................48 B3
- Rivalda................................49 C3
- Ruszwurm...........................50 B2
- Szent Jupát.....................(see 32)
- Tabáni Terasz......................51 D4

DRINKING

- Lánchíd Söröző 52 C3

ENTERTAINMENT

- Buda Concert Hall...............53 C2
- Budavár Cultural Centre......54 C3
- National Dance Theatre.......55 C3

SHOPPING

- Bortársaság.........................56 A1
- Herend................................57 B2

TRANSPORT

- Batthyány tér Ferry.............58 C1

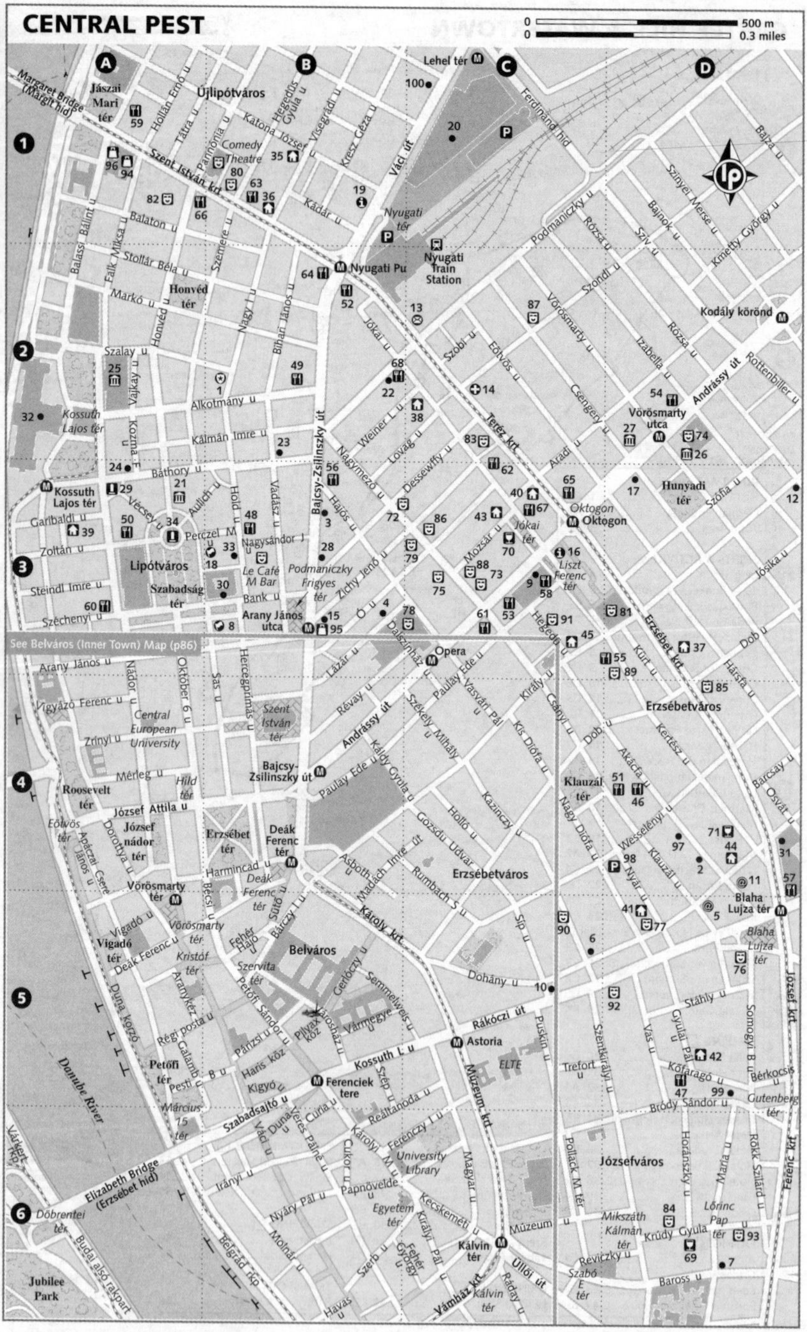
CENTRAL PEST
0 500 m
0 0.3 miles
A
B
C
D
1
2
3
4
5
6
Margaret Bridge (Margit híd)
Jászai Mari tér
Újlipótváros
Comedy Theatre
Szent István krt
Lehel tér
Ferdinánd híd
Váci út
Nyugati tér
Nyugati Pu
Nyugati Train Station
Honvéd tér
Szalay u
Alkotmány u
Kossuth Lajos tér
Kálmán Imre u
Báthory u
Lipótváros
Szabadság tér
Perczel M u
Nagysándor J u
Le Café M Bar
Podmaniczky Frigyes tér
Bank u
Arany János utca
Bajcsy-Zsilinszky út
Teréz krt
Oktogon
Jókai tér
Liszt Ferenc tér
Vörösmarty utca
Andrássy út
Kodály körönd
Hunyadi tér
Erzsébet krt
Erzsébetváros
See Belváros (Inner Town) Map (p86)
Opera
Szent István tér
Central European University
Roosevelt tér
József Attila u
József nádor tér
Erzsébet tér
Deák Ferenc tér
Bajcsy-Zsilinszky út
Vörösmarty tér
Vigadó tér
Kristóf tér
Belváros
Szervita tér
Károly krt
Klauzál tér
Blaha Lujza tér
Dohány u
Rákóczi út
Astoria
ELTE
Múzeum krt
Kossuth L u
Ferenciek tere
Petőfi tér
Március 15 tér
Danube River
Elizabeth Bridge (Erzsébet híd)
Szabadsajtó u
University Library
Egyetem tér
Kálvin tér
Üllői út
Vámház krt
József krt
Józsefváros
Mikszáth Kálmán tér
Lőrinc Pap tér
Szabó E tér
Baross u
Döbrentei tér
Jubilee Park
Gutenberg tér
Ferenc krt
Brody Sándor u

CENTRAL PEST

INFORMATION

Belváros-Lipótváros Police Station 1 B2
BKV Lost & Found Office 2 D4
Cartographia 3 B3
Discover Budapest 4 B3
Electric Cafe 5 D5
Express 6 C5
Hungarian Camping & Caravanning Club 7 D6
Irish Embassy 8 B3
Írók Boltja 9 C3
Libri Könyvpalota 10 C5
Narancs 11 D4
National Federation of Rural & Agrotourism 12 D3
Post Office (Nyugati Train Station Branch) 13 C2
Teréz Patika 14 C2
Térkeépkirály 15 B3
Tourinform 16 C3
Treehugger Dan's Bookstore 17 D3
Treehugger Dan's Bookstore Branch (see 4)
US Embassy 18 B3
Vist@netcafe 19 B1
Vodafone 20 C1

SIGHTS & ACTIVITIES

Bedő House 21 A3
Bike Base 22 B2
Cityrama 23 B2
Debrecen Summer University Branch 24 A3
Ethnography Museum 25 A2
Franz Liszt Memorial Museum 26 D2
House of Terror 27 D2
Hungarian Friends of Nature Federation 28 B3
Hungarian State Opera House (see 78)
Imre Nagy Statue 29 A3
Liszt Academy of Music (see 81)
MNB Visitor Centre (see 30)
National Bank of Hungary 30 B3
New York Palace 31 D4
Parliament 32 A2
Royal Postal Savings Bank 33 B3
Soviet Army Memorial 34 A3
Yellow Zebra Bikes (see 4)

SLEEPING

Aventura Hostel 35 B1
City Ring Hotel 36 B1
Corinthia Grand Hotel Royal 37 D3
Cotton House 38 C2
Garibaldi Guesthouse & Apartments 39 A3
Home-Made Hostel 40 C3
Hostel Marco Polo 41 D5
Hotel Anna 42 D5
Hotel Medosz 43 C3
Soho Hotel 44 D4
Unity Hostel 45 C3

EATING

Art Nouveau Café (see 21)
Bangla Büfé 46 D4
Fülemüle 47 D5
Hold utca Market 48 B3
Hummus Bar 49 B2
Iguana 50 A3
Kádár 51 D4
Kaiser's Supermarket 52 B2
Klassz 53 C3
Lukács 54 D2
M Restaurant 55 D3
Marquis de Salade 56 B3
Match Supermarket 57 D4
Menza 58 C3
Mézes Kuckó 59 A1
Momotaro Ramen 60 A3
Művész 61 C3
Napos Oldal 62 C3
Okay Italia 63 B1
Okay Italia 64 B2
Rothschild Supermarket 65 C3
Szeráj 66 A1
Teaház a Vörös Oroszlánhoz 67 C3
Wasabi 68 B2

DRINKING

Darshan Udvar 69 D6
Kiadó Kocsma 70 C3
Klub Vittula 71 D4

ENTERTAINMENT

Alter Ego 72 B3
Budapest Operetta 73 C3
Budapest Puppet Theatre 74 D2
Café Eklektika 75 C3
Corvintető 76 D5
CoXx Men's Bar 77 D5
Hungarian State Opera House 78 C3
Instant 79 C3
Kino 80 B1
Liszt Academy of Music 81 D3
Morrison's 2 82 A1
Művész 83 C2
Nothing but the Blues 84 D6
Örökmozgó 85 D4
Piaf 86 C3
Pótkulcs 87 C2
Symphony Ticket Office 88 C3
Szimpla 89 D3
Szimpla Kert 90 C5
Tűzraktér 91 C3
Uránia 92 D5
WigWam 2 93 D6

SHOPPING A1

BÁV 94 B3
Haas & Czjzek 95 A1
Szőnyi Antikváriuma 96

TRANSPORT

BKV Office 97 D4
Covered Car Park 98 D4
Kenguru 99 D5
Malév Customer Service Centre 100 C1

BELVÁROS (INNER TOWN)

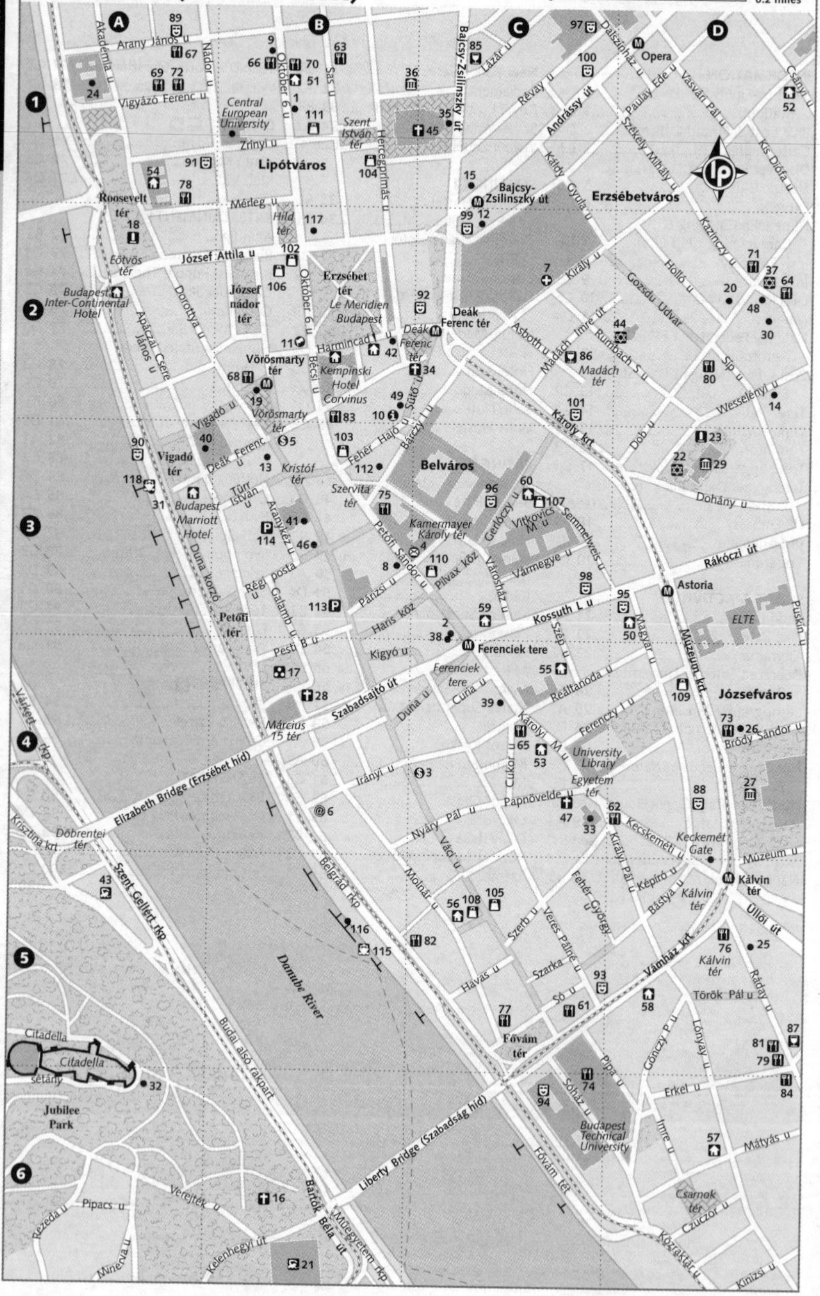

BELVÁROS (INNER TOWN)

INFORMATION

Bestsellers......1 B1
Ibusz......2 C3
K&H Bank......3 C4
Main Post Office......4 C3
OTP Bank......5 B3
Plastic Net......(see 55)
Plastic Web......6 B4
Red Bus Bookstore......(see 60)
S.O.S Dent......7 C2
T-Mobile......8 B3
To-Ma......9 B1
Tourinform (Main Office)......10 B2
UK Embassy......11 B2
Vista......12 C2

SIGHTS & ACTIVITIES

Bank Palace......13 B3
Budapest Bike......14 D2
Budatours......15 C1
Cave Chapel......16 B6
Contra Aquincum......17 B4
Ferenc Deák Statue......18 A2
Free Budapest Tour Departures..19 B2
Fröhlich Cake Shop......20 D2
Gellért Baths......21 B6
Great Synagogue......22 D3
Gresham Palace......(see 54)
Holocaust Memorial......23 D3
Hungarian Academy of Sciences......24 A1
Hungarian Equestrian Tourism Association......25 D5
Hungarian Language School......26 D4
Hungarian National Museum......27 D4
Inner Town Parish Church......28 B4
Jewish Museum......29 D3
Kosher Bakery......30 D2
Legenda......31 A3
Liberty Monument......32 A6
Loránd Eötvös Science University (ELTE)......33 C4
Lutheran Church......34 C2
Maharat PassNave......(see 116)
Mr Nils Tour Departures......35 C1
Museum of Hungarian Trade & Tourism......36 B1
Orthodox Synagogue......37 D2
Párisi Udvar......38 C3
Pegazus Tours......39 C4
Pesti Vigadó......40 A3
Philanthia......41 B3
Program Centrum......42 B2
Rudas Baths......43 A5
Rumbach Sebestyén utca Synagogue......44 D2
St Stephen's Basilica......45 C1
Thonet House......46 B3
University Church......47 C4
Wigmakers......48 D2
Yellow Zebra Bikes......49 B2

SLEEPING

11th Hour Hostel......50 D3
Central Backpack King Hostel......51 B1
Connection Guest House......52 D1
Erzsébet Hotel......53 C4
Four Seasons Gresham Palace Hotel......54 A1
Gingko Hostel......55 C4
Green Bridge Hostel......56 C5
KM Saga Guest Residence......57 D6
KM Saga II Guest Residence......58 D5
Leó Panzió......59 C3
Red Bus Hostel......60 C3

EATING

Bangkok House......61 C5
Café Alibi......62 D4
Café Kör......63 B1
Carmel......64 D2
Centrál Kávéház......65 C4
Első Pesti Rétesház......66 B1
Gastronomia Pomo D'Oro......67 A1
Gerbeaud......68 B2
Govinda......69 A1
Kisharang......70 B1
Köleves......71 D2
Lou Lou......72 A1
Múzeum......73 D4
Nagycsarnok......74 C6
Nagyi Palacsintázója......75 B3
Pata Negra......76 D5
Pireus Rembetiko Taverna......77 C5
Salam Bombay......78 A1
Soul Café......79 D5
Spinoza......80 D2
Teaház a Vörös Oroszlánhoz......81 D5
Trattoria Toscana......82 C5
Vapiano......83 B2
Vörös Postakocsi......84 D6

DRINKING

Box Utca......85 C1
Castro Bisztró......86 C2
Paris,Texas......87 D5

ENTERTAINMENT

Action......88 D4
Aranytíz Cultural Centre......89 A1
Columbus Jazzklub......90 A3
Duna Palota......91 A1
Gödör Klub......92 C2
Jazz Garden......93 C5
Közgáz Klub......94 C6
Living Room......95 D3
Merlin......(see 96)
Merlin Theatre......96 C3
Morrison's Opera......97 C1
Puskin......98 C3
Take 5......99 C2
Ticket Express......100 C1
Ticket Pro......101 C2

SHOPPING

Ajka Kristály......102 B2
BÁV......103 B3
Bortársaság......104 B1
Folkart Centrum......105 C5
Herend......106 B2
Holló Atelier......107 C3
Intuita......108 C5
Központi Antikvárium......109 D4
Magma......110 C3
Mester Pálinka......111 B1

TRANSPORT

Avis......112 B3
Covered Car Park......(see 112)
Covered Car Park......113 B3
Covered Car Park......114 B3
International Ferry Pier......115 B5
Mahart PassNave......116 B5
MÁV-Start Passenger Service Centre......117 B2
Vigadó tér Pier......118 A3

SOUTH BUDA & FERENCVÁROS

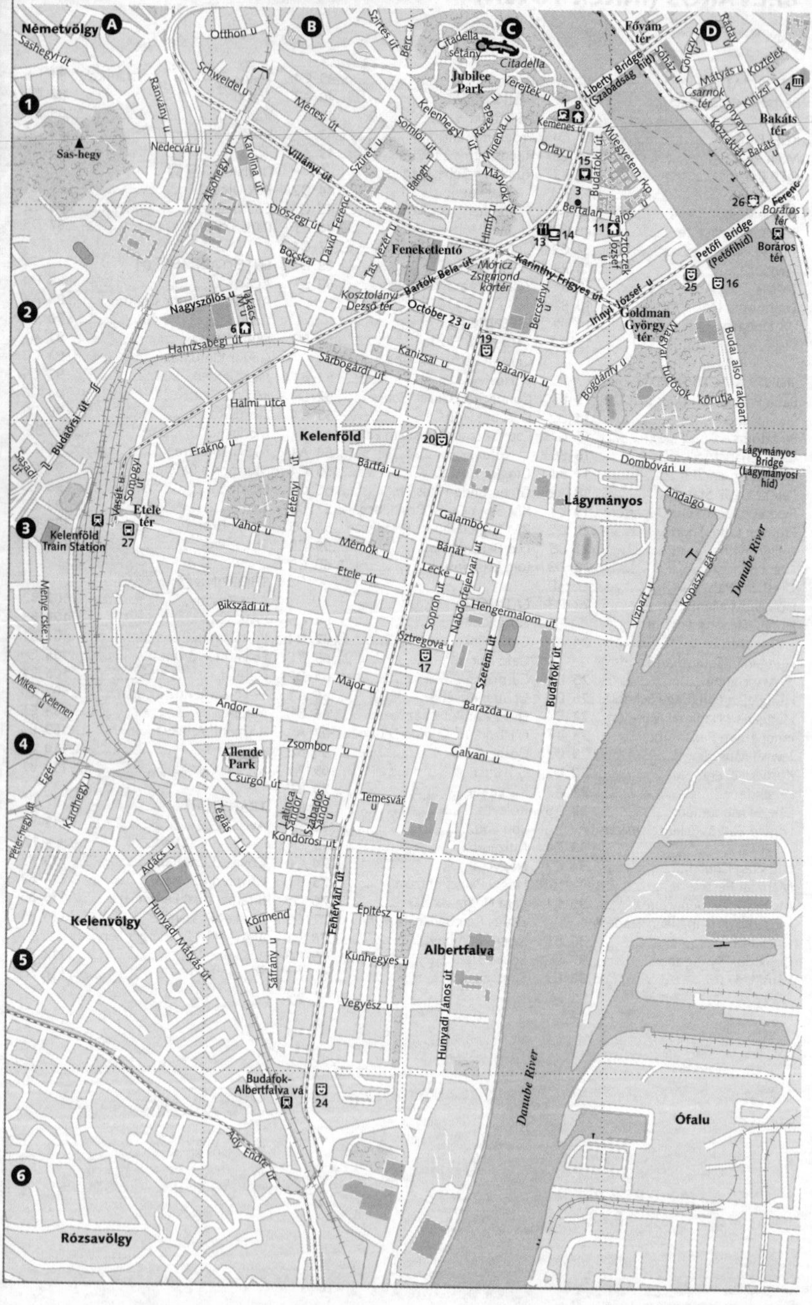

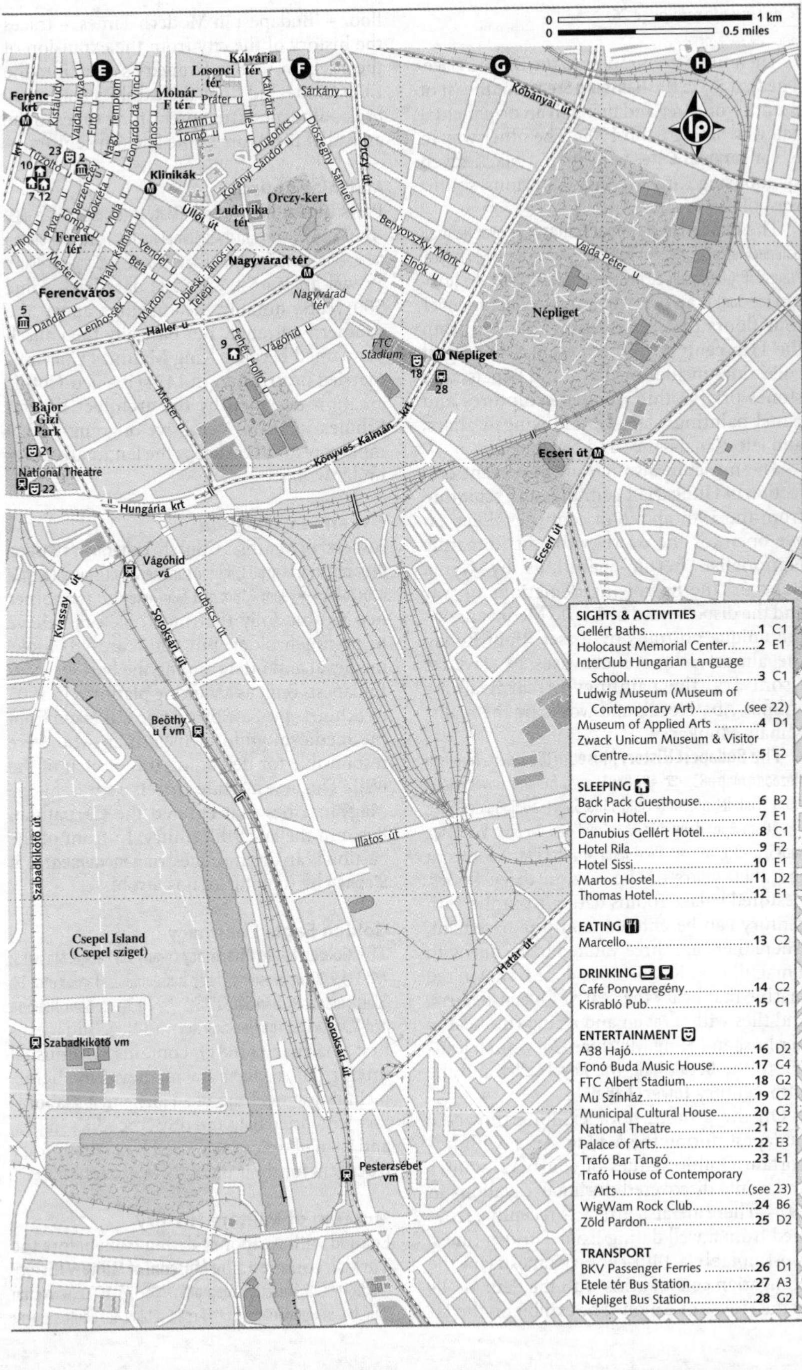
0 1 km
0 0.5 miles
Kálvária tér
Losonci tér
Molnár F tér
Ferenc krt
Klinikák
Ludovika tér
Orczy-kert
Ferenc tér
Ferencváros
Nagyvárad tér
Népliget
FTC Stadium
Bajor Gizi Park
National Theatre
Hungária krt
Könyves Kálmán krt
Kőbányai út
Vajda Péter u
Üllői út
Haller u
Vágóhíd u
Ecseri út
Vágóhíd vá
Beöthy u f vm
Illatos út
Határ út
Soroksári út
Kvassay J út
Gubacsi út
Szabadkikötő út
Szabadkikötő vm
Csepel Island (Csepel sziget)
Pesterzsébet vm
SIGHTS & ACTIVITIES
Gellért Baths 1 C1
Holocaust Memorial Center 2 E1
InterClub Hungarian Language School 3 C1
Ludwig Museum (Museum of Contemporary Art) (see 22)
Museum of Applied Arts 4 D1
Zwack Unicum Museum & Visitor Centre 5 E2
SLEEPING
Back Pack Guesthouse 6 B2
Corvin Hotel 7 E1
Danubius Gellért Hotel 8 C1
Hotel Rila 9 F2
Hotel Sissi 10 E1
Martos Hostel 11 D2
Thomas Hotel 12 E1
EATING
Marcello 13 C2
DRINKING
Café Ponyvaregény 14 C2
Kisrabló Pub 15 C1
ENTERTAINMENT
A38 Hajó 16 D2
Fonó Buda Music House 17 C4
FTC Albert Stadium 18 G2
Mu Színház 19 C2
Municipal Cultural House 20 C3
National Theatre 21 E2
Palace of Arts 22 E3
Trafó Bar Tangó 23 E1
Trafó House of Contemporary Arts (see 23)
WigWam Rock Club 24 B6
Zöld Pardon 25 D2
TRANSPORT
BKV Passenger Ferries 26 D1
Etele tér Bus Station 27 A3
Népliget Bus Station 28 G2

(Continued from page 76)

There are two entrances to the Royal Palace. The first is via the **Habsburg Steps**, southeast of Szent György tér and through an ornamental gateway dating from 1903. The other way in is via **Corvinus Gate**, with its big black raven symbolising King Matthias Corvinus, southwest of the square.

The **Hungarian National Gallery** (Magyar Nemzeti Galéria; Map p83; ☎ 201 9082; www.mng.hu; Royal Palace, Wings A, B, C & D; adult/EU student & child 800/400Ft; ⏰ 10am-6pm Tue-Sun) is an overwhelming collection over four floors that traces Hungarian art from the 11th century to the present. The largest collections include medieval and Renaissance stonework, Gothic wooden sculptures and panel paintings, late-Gothic winged altars, and late-Renaissance and baroque art.

The museum also has an important collection of Hungarian paintings and sculpture from the 19th and 20th centuries. Keep an eye open for the overly wrought Romantic Nationalist 'heroic' paintings by Gyula Benczúr, the harrowing depictions of war and the dispossessed by László Mednyánszky, the unique portraits by József Rippl-Rónai, the almost religious canvases by Tivadar Csontváry, the paintings of carnivals by Vilmos Aba-Novák and works by the realist Mihály Munkácsy.

The **Budapest History Museum** (Budapesti Történeti Múzeum; Map p83; ☎ 487 8801; www.btm.hu; Royal Palace, Wing E; adult/student & child 1100/550Ft, audioguide 850Ft; ⏰ 10am-6pm daily mid-Mar–mid-Sep, to 6pm Wed-Mon mid-Sep–Oct, to 4pm Wed-Mon Nov–mid-Mar) looks at the 2000 years of the city on three floors. Restored palace rooms dating from the 15th century can be entered from the basement, where there are three vaulted halls, one with a magnificent Renaissance door frame in red marble that bears the seal of Queen Beatrix, and tiles with a raven and a ring (the seal of her husband King Matthias Corvinus), leading to the **Gothic Hall**, the **Royal Cellar** and the 14th-century **Tower Chapel**.

On the ground floor exhibits showcase Budapest during the Middle Ages, with important Gothic statues of courtiers, squires and saints discovered during excavations in 1974. There are also artefacts recently recovered from a well dating from Turkish times, most notably a 14th-century tapestry of the Hungarian coat of arms with the fleur-de-lis of the House of Anjou. The exhibit on the 1st floor – 'Budapest in Modern Times' – traces the history of the city from the expulsion of the Turks in 1686 to Hungary's entry into the EU. On the 2nd floor the exhibits reach way back – Budapest from prehistoric times to the arrival of the Avars in the late 6th century.

Matthias Church

Parts of **Matthias Church** (Mátyás-templom; Map p83; ☎ 355 5657; www.matyas-templom.hu; I Szentháromság tér 2; adult/child/family 700/480/1200Ft, audioguide 400Ft; ⏰ 9am-5pm Mon-Sat, 1-5pm Sun) date back some 500 years, notably the carvings above the southern entrance. But basically the church (so named because King Matthias Corvinus married Beatrix here in 1474) is a neo-Gothic creation designed by the architect Frigyes Schulek in 1896. A massive ongoing US$20 million restoration keeps the landmark tower under wraps.

Fishermen's Bastion

Just east of Matthias Church, **Fishermen's Bastion** (Halászbástya; Map p83; during summer adult/student & child 400/200Ft; ⏰ 9am-11pm mid-Mar–mid-Oct) is another neo-Gothic folly that most visitors believe to be much older. But who cares? It looks medieval and offers among the best views in Budapest. Built as a viewing platform in 1905 by Schulek, the bastion's name was taken from the medieval guild of fishermen who were responsible for defending this stretch of the wall. The seven white turrets represent the Magyar tribes that entered the Carpathian Basin in the late 9th century. In front of the bastion is an ornate equestrian **monument to St Stephen** by sculptor Alajos Stróbl.

Golden Eagle Pharmacy

The **Golden Eagle Pharmacy** (Arany Sas Patika; Map p83; ☎ 375 9772; www.semmelweis.museum.hu; I Tárnok utca 18; adult/student & child 500/250Ft; ⏰ 10.30am-6pm Tue-Sun mid-Mar–Oct, to 4pm Tue-Sun Nov–mid-Mar), Budapest's first pharmacy (1681), contains an unusual mixture of displays on medieval medicine, including a mock-up of an alchemist's laboratory with dried bats and tiny crocodiles in jars, and a small 'spice rack' used by 17th-century travellers for their daily fix of elixirs.

Museum of Military History

Loaded with weaponry dating from before the Turkish conquest, the **Museum of Military History** (Hadtörténeti Múzeum; Map p83; ☎ 325 1600; www.hm-him.hu, in Hungarian; I Tóth Árpád sétány 40; adult/student

& child/family 700/350/1400Ft; 10am-6pm Tue-Sun Apr-Sep, to 4pm Tue-Sun Oct-Mar) also does a good job with uniforms, medals, flags and battle-themed fine art. Exhibits focus particularly on the 1848–49 War of Independence and the Hungarian Royal Army under the command of Admiral Miklós Horthy (1918–43). Outside is a mock-up of the electrified fence that once stood between Hungary and Austria.

Buda Castle Labyrinth

In five separate labyrinths, the **Buda Castle Labyrinth** (Budavári Labirintus; Map p83; ☎ 225 0207; www.labirintus.com; I Úri utca 9; adult/child/student/family 1500/600/1100/3400Ft; 9.30am-7.30pm), a 1200m-long cave system located 16m under the Castle District, looks at how the caves have been used since prehistoric times. It's all good fun and a relief from the heat on a hot summer's day (it's always 20°C down here), but it can get pretty scary if you lose your way. After 6pm the visit is by lamp.

Hospital in the Rock

The newly opened **Hospital in the Rock** (Sziklakórház; Map p83; ☎ 06 30 689 8775; www.hospitalintherock.com; I Lovas út 4/c; adult/student & child/family 2000/1000/5000Ft; 10am-7pm Tue-Sun), located in part of the Castle Hill caves, was used extensively during the siege of Budapest during WWII. It contains original medical equipment as well as some 70 wax figures and is visited on a guided half-hour tour. More interesting is the hour-long 'full tour' (3000/1500/7000Ft), which includes a walk through a Cold War–era nuclear bunker.

Royal Wine House & Wine Cellar Museum

The **Royal Wine House & Wine Cellar Museum** (Királyi Borház és Pincemúzeum; Map p83; ☎ 267 1100; www.kiralyiborok.com; I Szent György tér, Nyugati sétány; adult/child 900/500Ft; noon-8pm), a new 1400-sq-m attraction in what once were the royal cellars below Szent György tér, dating back to the 13th century, offers a crash course in Hungarian viticulture in the heart of the Castle District. Tastings cost 1350/1800/2700Ft for three/four/six wines. You can also try various types of Hungarian champagne and *pálinka* (fruit brandy).

Medieval Jewish Prayer House

The **Medieval Jewish Prayer House** (Középkori Zsidó Imaház; Map p83; ☎ 225 7816; I Táncsics Mihály utca 26; adult/child 500/250Ft; 10am-5pm Tue-Sun May-Oct), dating from the late 14th century, contains documents and items linked to the Jewish community of Buda, as well as Gothic stone carvings and tombstones. It's tiny and of only limited interest, even to the faithful.

GELLÉRT HILL & THE TABÁN

Gellért Hill (Gellért-hegy; Map p83), a 235m-high rocky hill southeast of the Castle District, is crowned with a fortress of sorts and the Liberty Monument, Budapest's unofficial symbol. From Gellért Hill, you can't beat the views of the Royal Palace and the Danube. The Tabán (Map p83), the leafy area between Gellért and Castle Hills, is associated with the Serbs, who settled here after fleeing from the Turks in the early 18th century. Later it became known for its restaurants and wine gardens – a kind of Montmartre for Budapest. Most were gone by the turn of the 20th century.

Today, Gellért Hill and the Tabán are given over to private homes, parks and a couple of thermal spas that make good use of the hot springs gushing from deep below, including the **Gellért Baths** (p103) and the renovated **Rudas Baths** (p103). If you don't like getting wet you can try a 'drinking cure' by visiting the **pump room** (ivócsarnok; Map p83; 11am-6pm Mon, Wed & Fri, 7am-2pm Tue & Thu), which is just below the western end of Elizabeth Bridge. A half-litre/litre of the hot smelly water – meant to cure whatever ails you – is just 30/50Ft.

Citadella

The **Citadella** (Map p83; www.citadella.hu; 24hr) is a fortress that never did battle. Built by the Habsburgs after the 1848–49 War of Independence to defend the city from further insurrection, the Citadella was obsolete by the time it was ready (1851) and the political climate had changed. Today the Citadella contains some big guns and dusty displays in the central courtyard, the rather hokey **1944 Bunker Waxworks** (1944 Bunkér Panoptikum; Map p83; ☎ 466 5794; admission 1200Ft; 9am-7pm) inside a bunker used during WWII, and a hotel-cum-hostel (p111).

To reach here from Pest, cross Elizabeth Bridge and take the stairs leading up behind the statue of St Gellért, or cross Liberty Bridge and follow Verejték utca through the park starting at the Cave Chapel. Bus 27 runs almost to the top of the hill from Móricz Zsigmond körtér, southwest of the Danubius Gellért Hotel (and accessible on trams 18, 19, 47 and 49).

Liberty Monument

The Liberty Monument (Szabadság-szobor; Map p86), the lovely lady with the palm frond proclaiming freedom throughout the city, is to the east of the Citadella. Some 14m high, she was raised in 1947 in tribute to the Soviet soldiers who died liberating Budapest in 1945, but the victims' names in Cyrillic letters on the plinth and the statues of the Soviet soldiers were removed in 1992 and sent to Memento Park (p136). Today the monument is dedicated to 'Those who gave up their lives for Hungary's independence, freedom and prosperity'.

Szent Gellért tér

Szent Gellért tér faces **Liberty Bridge** (Szabadság híd; Map pp80–1) and is dominated by the **Danubius Gellért Hotel** (Map pp80–1), an Art Nouveau pile dating to 1918.

The **Cave Chapel** (Sziklakápolna; Map p86; ☎ 385 1529; 9am-8pm), on a small hill directly north of the hotel, was built into a cave in 1926. It was the seat of the Pauline order until 1951, when the priests were arrested and imprisoned by the communists, and the cave sealed off. It was reopened in 1992 and reconsecrated; the main altar with a symbolic fish is made partly of Zsolnay ceramic. Behind the church is the monastery, with its neo-Gothic turrets visible from Liberty Bridge. The chapel is closed to the public during Mass.

Gellért tér can be reached from Pest on bus 7 or tram 47 or 49, and from the Buda side on bus 86 and tram 18 or 19.

Elizabeth Bridge & Statues

Elizabeth Bridge (Erzsébet híd; Map p86) is the gleaming white suspension bridge northeast of Gellért Hill. It enjoys a special place in the hearts of Budapesters, as it was the first newly designed bridge (1964) to open after WWII.

Looking down on Elizabeth Bridge from Gellért Hill is the **St Gellért monument** (Map p83). Gellért was an Italian missionary invited to Hungary by King Stephen to convert the natives. The monument marks the spot where the bishop was hurled to his death in a spiked barrel in 1046 by pagan Hungarians resisting the new faith.

To the north of Elizabeth Bridge and through the underpass is a **Queen Elizabeth statue** (Map p83). As Habsburg empress, Hungarian queen and consort to Franz Joseph, 'Sissi' was much loved by Magyars because, among other things, she learned to speak Hungarian. She was assassinated by an Italian anarchist in Geneva in 1898.

WATERTOWN (VÍZIVÁROS)

Watertown (Víziváros; Map p83 and Map pp80–1) is the narrow area between the Danube and Castle Hill that widens as it approaches Óbuda to the north and Rózsadomb (Rose Hill) to the northwest, spreading as far west as Moszkva tér, one of Buda's most important transport hubs. In the Middle Ages those involved in trades, crafts and fishing lived here. Many of the district's churches were used as mosques under the Turks, and baths were built here, including the **Király Baths** (p103).

You can reach Víziváros on foot from the metro M2 Batthyány tér stop by walking south along the river or via tram 19, which links Batthyány tér with Szent Gellért tér and points beyond. Bus 16 from Deák Ferenc tér stops here on its way to/from Castle Hill and bus 86 links it with Óbuda.

Clark Ádám tér

Clark Ádám tér (Map p83) is named after the 19th-century Scottish engineer who supervised the building of the **Széchenyi Chain Bridge** (Széchenyi lánchíd; Map p83), leading from the square, and who designed the **tunnel** (*alagút;* Map p83) under Castle Hill, which took just eight months to carve out of the limestone in 1853. The bridge was the idea of Count István Széchenyi (see p179), and when it opened in 1849 it was unique for two reasons: it was the first dry link between Buda and Pest; and the aristocracy, previously exempt from all taxation, had to pay the toll just like everybody else. What looks like an elongated concrete doughnut hidden in the bushes to the south is the **0km stone** (Map p83). All Hungarian roads to and from the capital are measured from this spot.

Fő utca

Fő utca (Map p83) is the arrow-straight 'Main Street' running through Víziváros and dates from Roman times. At the former **Capuchin church** (Map p83; I Fő utca 30-32), used as a mosque during the Turkish occupation, you can see the remains of an Islamic-style ogee-arched door and window on the southern side. Around the corner there's the seal of King Matthias Corvinus – a raven with a ring in its beak – and a little square called Corvin tér with the delightful **Lajos Fountain** (Lajos kútja; 1904). The Eclectic-style building on the north side is the **Buda Concert Hall** (p127), which was renovated in 2007.

Batthyány tér (Map p83), a short distance to the northeast, is the centre of Víziváros and the best place to take pictures of the photogenic Parliament building across the river. On the southern side of Batthyány tér is the 18th-century **Church of St Anne** (Szent Ana templom; Map p83; I Batthyány tér 7), with one of the loveliest baroque interiors of any church in Budapest.

A couple of streets north is **Nagy Imre tér** (Map pp80–1), with the former **Military Court of Justice** (Map pp80-1; II Fő utca 70-78) on the northern side. Here Imre Nagy and others were tried and sentenced to death in 1958 (see p35). It was also the site of the notorious **Fő utca prison**, where many victims of the communist regime were incarcerated and tortured.

The **Király Baths** (p103), parts of which date from 1580, are one block to the north. Across pedestrianised Ganz utca is the Greek Catholic **Chapel of St Florian** (Szent Flórián kápolna; Map pp80-1; II Fő utca 88), built in 1760 and dedicated to the patron saint of firefighters.

Millennium Park

Millennium Park (Millenáris Park; Map pp80-1; ☎ 336 4000; www.millenaris.hu; II Kis Rókus utca 16-20; Ⓜ M2 Moszkva tér, 🚊 4 or 6) is an attractive landscaped complex behind the Mammut shopping mall, comprising fountains, ponds, little bridges, a theatre, a gallery and, for kids, the **Palace of Miracles** (Csodák Palotája; Map pp80-1; ☎ 336 4000; www.csodapalota.hu; II Kis Rókus utca 16-20, Bldg D; adult/child/family 1200/1000/3400Ft, with exhibition 1900/1300/4700Ft; 🕑 9am-5pm Mon-Fri, 10am-6pm Sat & Sun). It's an interactive playhouse for children of all ages, with 'smart' toys and puzzles, most of which have a scientific bent. Next door in building B is the **House of the Future Exhibition** (Jövő Háza Kiállítás; Map pp80-1; adult/child/family 1200/1000/3400Ft, with palace 1900/1300/4700Ft; 🕑 9am-5pm Tue-Fri, 10am-6pm Sat & Sun), which hosts some unusual shows for kids. You can also enter the park from Fény utca 20–22 and Lövőház utca 37.

Frankel Leó út

At Bem József tér Fő utca becomes Frankel Leó út, a tree-lined street of antique shops and boutiques. At its northern end is the **Lukács Baths** (p103), which caters to serious bath enthusiasts. A short walk beyond that and tucked away in an apartment block is the **Újlak Synagogue** (Újlaki zsinagóga; Map pp80-1; ☎ 326 1445; II Frankel Leó út 49), built in 1888 on the site of an older prayer house and the only functioning synagogue left in Buda.

Tomb of Gül Baba

The reconstructed **Tomb of Gül Baba** (Gül Baba türbéje; Map pp80-1; ☎ 326 0062; II Türbe tér 1; adult/child/student 500/250/400Ft; 🕑 10am-6pm Mar-Oct, to 4pm Nov-Feb; 🚊 4, 6 or 17) contains the remains of an Ottoman dervish who took part in the capture of Buda in 1541 and is known in Hungary as the 'Father of Roses'. To reach it from Török utca, which runs parallel to Frankel Leó út, walk west along steep, cobbled Gül Baba utca to the set of steps just past house No 16. You can also reach here from Mecset utca 14, which runs north from Margit utca. The tomb is a place of pilgrimage for Turks; remove your shoes before entering.

ÓBUDA

Óbuda is the oldest part of Buda ('ó' means 'ancient' in Hungarian). The Romans settled at Aquincum, north of here (see p23), and when the Magyars arrived they named it Buda, which became Óbuda when the Royal Palace was built on Castle Hill. It's well worth a detour.

You can reach Óbuda on the HÉV commuter train (get off at the Árpád híd stop) from Batthyány tér, which is on the M2 metro line, or on bus 86 from Fő utca and other points along the Danube on the Buda side.

Flórián tér & Surrounds

Flórián tér (Map pp78–9), divided by the Árpád Bridge flyover and encircled by mammoth housing blocks, is not the best introduction to Óbuda, but it remains the district's historic centre.

The yellow baroque **Óbuda Parish Church** (Óbudai plébániatemplom; Map pp78-9; III Lajos utca 168), built in 1749 and dedicated to Sts Peter and Paul, dominates the easternmost side of Flórián tér. There's a lovely rococo pulpit inside. To the southeast, the large neoclassical building beside the Corinthia Aquincum Hotel is the **former Óbuda Synagogue** (Óbudai zsinagóga; Map pp78-9; III Lajos utca 163), dating from 1821. It now houses the sound studios of MTV (Hungarian TV). Opposite is the **Budapest Gallery** (Budapest Galéria; Map pp78-9; ☎ 388 6771; www.budapestgaleria.hu; III Lajos utca 158; adult/child

400/200Ft; ⌚ 10am-6pm Tue-Sun), which hosts some interesting avant-garde exhibitions.

To explore the 2nd-century **Roman Military Amphitheatre** (Római katonai amfiteátrum; Map pp78-9; Pacsirtamező utca), about 800m south of Flórián tér, get off bus 86 at Nagyszombat utca (for HÉV passengers, it's the Tímár utca stop). The amphitheatre could accommodate up to 15,000 people and was larger than the Colosseum in Rome.

Housed in an 18th-century monastery to the southwest of Flórián tér, the **Kiscelli Museum** (Kiscelli Múzeum; Map pp78-9; ☎ 388 8560, 250 0304; www.btm.hu; III Kiscelli utca 108; adult/student & child/family 700/350/1100Ft; ⌚ 10am-6pm Tue-Sun Apr-Oct, to 4pm Nov-Mar; 🚊 17, 🚌 160) contains two excellent sections. The Contemporary City History Collection (Újkori Várostörténeti Gyűjtemény) has a complete 19th-century apothecary moved here from Kálvin tér, a wonderful assembly of ancient signboards advertising shops and other trades, and rooms (both public and private) furnished with Empire, Biedermeier and Art Nouveau furniture and bric-a-brac. The **Municipal Picture Gallery** (Fővárosi Képtár), with its impressive collection of artworks by József Rippl-Rónai, Lajos Tihanyi, István Csók and Béla Czóbel (among others) is upstairs.

Szentlélek tér & Fő tér

Two contiguous squares lying east of Flórián tér – Szentlélek tér (Map pp78–9), a transport hub, and Fő tér (Main Sq; Map pp78–9), a restored square of baroque houses, public buildings and restaurants to the northwest – contain Óbuda's most important museums.

The **Vasarely Museum** (Map pp78-9; ☎ 388 7551; http://vasarely.tvn.hu; III Szentlélek tér 6; adult/student & child 600/300Ft; ⌚ 10am-5.30pm Tue-Sun), housed in the old Zichy Mansion, is devoted to the works of Victor Vasarely (or Győző Vásárhelyi as he was known before he emigrated to Paris in 1930), the late 'Father of Op Art'. The works, especially ones like *Tlinko-F* and *Szerigráfia*, are excellent and fun to watch as they swell and move around the canvas.

The **Imre Varga Exhibition House** (Varga Imre kiállítóháza; Map pp78-9; ☎ 250 0274; III Laktanya utca 7; adult/student & child 500/250Ft; ⌚ 10am-6pm Tue-Sun), part of the Budapest Gallery, includes sculptures, statues, medals and drawings by the octogenarian Varga, one of Hungary's foremost sculptors, who seems to have sat on both sides of the fence politically for decades – sculpting Béla Kun and Lenin as dexterously as he did St Stephen, Béla Bartók and even Imre Nagy (p97). But his work always remains fresh and is never derivative. En route to the museum from Fő tér, you'll pass a Varga **sculpture**: a group of four rather worried-looking women holding umbrellas in the middle of the street.

AQUINCUM

The most complete Roman civilian town in Hungary and now a museum, Aquincum (Map pp78–9) had paved streets and fairly sumptuous single-storey houses with courtyards, fountains and mosaic floors, as well as sophisticated drainage and heating systems. Not all of that is easily apparent today as you walk among the ruins, but you can see its outlines, as well as those of the big public baths, the market, an early Christian church and a temple dedicated to the god Mithra, chief deity of an early religion that competed with Christianity. Across the road to the northwest is the **Roman Civilian Amphitheatre** (Római polgári amfiteátrum; Map pp78-9; Szentendrei út), about half the size of the one reserved for the military.

The new purpose-built **Aquincum Museum** (Aquincumi Múzeum; Map pp78-9; ☎ 250 1650, 430 1081; www.aquincum.hu; III Szentendrei út 139; adult/student & child/family 900/450/1600Ft; ⌚ park 9am-6pm Tue-Sun May-Sep, to 5pm Tue-Sun 15-30 Apr & Oct, museum 10am-6pm Tue-Sun May-Sep, to 5pm Tue-Sun 15-30 Apr & Oct), on the western edge of what remains of this Roman civilian settlement, puts the ruins in perspective, with a vast collection of coins and wall paintings. Look out for the replica of a 3rd-century portable organ called a hydra (and the mosaic illustrating how it was played) and the mock-up of a Roman bath. Most of the big sculptures and stone sarcophagi are outside to the left of the old museum building or behind it in the lapidarium.

You can reach Aquincum on the HÉV (Aquincum stop) or on bus 34 or 106 from Szentlélek tér.

BUDA HILLS

With 'peaks' up to 500m, a comprehensive system of trails and no lack of unusual conveyances to get you around, the Buda Hills (Map p77) are the city's playground and a welcome respite from hot, dusty Pest in summer. If you're planning to do some hiking here, take along Cartographia's 1:25,000 *A Budai-hegység* map (No 6; 990Ft). Apart from the **Béla Bartók Memorial House** (Bartók Béla Emlékház;

Map p77; ☎ 394 2100; www.bartokmuseum.hu; II Csalán út 29; adult/student & child 800/500Ft; 10am-5pm Tue-Sun; 5 or 29), there are few sights here, though you might want to explore one of the hills' pair of caves (p105).

With all the unusual transport options, heading for the hills is more than half the fun. From Moszkva tér metro station on the M2 line in Buda, walk westward along Szilágyi Erzsébet fasor for 10 minutes (or take tram 18 or 56 for two stops) to the circular Hotel Budapest (II Szilágyi Erzsébet fasor 47). Directly opposite is the terminus of the **Cog Railway** (Fogaskerekű vasút; Map p77; ☎ 355 4167; www.bkv.hu; Szilágyi Erzsébet fasor 14-16; admission 1 BKV ticket; 5am-11pm). Built in 1874, the cog climbs 3.6km in 14 minutes three or four times an hour to **Széchenyi-hegy** (427m), one of the prettiest residential areas in Buda.

At Széchenyi-hegy, you can stop for a picnic in the attractive park south of the old-time station or board the narrow-gauge **Children's Railway** (Gyermekvasút; Map p77; ☎ 397 5394; www.gyermekvasut.hu; adult/child 1 stop 450/250Ft, entire line 600/300Ft), two minutes to the south on Hegyhát út. The railway with eight stops was built in 1951 by Pioneers (socialist Scouts) and is now staffed entirely by schoolchildren aged 10 to 14 (the engineer excepted). The little train chugs along for 12km, terminating at Hűvösvölgy. Departure times vary widely depending on the day, week and season (consult the website), but count on one every hour or so between 9am or 10am and 5pm or 6pm. The line is closed on Monday from September to April.

There are walks fanning out from any of the stops along the Children's Railway line, or you can return to Moszkva tér on tram 56 from Hűvösvölgy. A more interesting way down, however, is to get off at **János-hegy**, the fourth stop on the Children's Railway and the highest point (527m) in the hills. About 700m to the east is the **chairlift** (libegő; ☎ 394 3764; adult/child 500/400Ft; 9.30am-5pm mid-May–mid-Sep, 10am-4pm mid-Sep–mid-May), which will take you down to Zugligeti út. From here bus 291 returns to Moszkva tér. Note: the chairlift is closed on the second and fourth Monday of every month.

Margaret Island

Neither Buda nor Pest, 2.5km-long Margaret Island (Margit-sziget; Map pp80–1 and Map pp78–9) in the middle of the Danube was the domain of one religious order or another until the Turks came and turned what was then called the Island of Rabbits into – appropriately enough – a harem. It's been a public park open to everyone since the mid-19th century. Like the Buda Hills, the island is a recreational rather than educational experience.

Cross over to Margaret Island from Pest or Buda via tram 4 or 6. Bus 26 covers the length of the island as it makes the run between Nyugati train station (Nyugati pályaudvar) and Árpád híd bus station. Cars are allowed on Margaret Island from Árpád Bridge only as far as the two big hotels at the northeastern end; the rest is reserved for pedestrians and cyclists.

You can hire a bicycle from one of several stands, including **Sétacikli** (Map pp80-1; ☎ 06 30 966 6453; 3-speed per 30min/hr/day 450/650/1900Ft, pedal coach per hr for 3/5 people 1900/2900Ft; 9am-dusk), which is on the western side just before the athletic stadium as you walk from Margaret Bridge. **Bringóhintó** (Map pp78-9; ☎ 329 2073; www.bringohinto.hu; mountain bike per 30min/hr 590/990Ft, pedal coach for 4 people 1680/2680Ft, inline skates 980/1680Ft; 8am-dusk) rents equipment from the refreshment stand near the Japanese Garden in the northern part of the island.

MEDIEVAL RUINS

The **Franciscan church and monastery ruins** (Ferences templom és kolostor; Map pp80–1) – no more than a tower and a wall dating from the late 13th century – are in the centre of the island. The Habsburg archduke Joseph built a summer residence here when he inherited the island in 1867. It was later converted into a hotel that operated until 1949.

The **former Dominican convent** (Domonkos kolostor; Map pp78–9) lies to the northeast. It was built by Béla IV, whose scribes played an important role in the continuation of Hungarian scholarship. Its most famous resident was Béla's daughter, St Margaret (1242–71). As the story goes, the king vowed that his daughter would commit herself to a life of devotion in a nunnery if the Mongols were driven from Hungary. They were and she did – at nine years of age. Still, she seemed to enjoy it – if we're to believe the *Lives of the Saints* – especially the mortification-of-the-flesh parts. St Margaret, only canonised in 1943, commands something of a cult following in Hungary. A red marble sepulchre cover surrounded by a wrought-iron grille marks her original resting place, and there's a much-visited brick shrine with ex-votives located a short distance to the southeast.

WATER TOWER & OPEN-AIR THEATRE

The octagonal **water tower** (*víztorony*; Map pp78–9), erected in 1911 in the north-central part of the island, rises 66m above the **open-air theatre** (szabadtéri színpad; ☎ 340 4883), which is used for opera, plays and concerts in summer. The tower contains the **Lookout Gallery** (Kilátó Galéria; ☎ 340 4520; adult/child 300/200Ft; 🕑 11am-7pm May-Oct). At the top of the 153 steps is a stunning 360-degree view of the island, Buda and Pest from the cupola terrace.

Pest

While Buda might sometimes feel like a garden, Pest is an urban jungle, with a wealth of architecture, museums, historic buildings and broad boulevards that are unmatched on the other side of the Danube. And while there isn't anything like the Buda Hills here, Pest is not devoid of open green spaces. Indeed, City Park (Map pp80–1) at the end of Andrássy út is the largest park in the city.

BELVÁROS (INNER TOWN)

Belváros (Inner Town; Map p86) is the heart of Pest. The area north of Ferenciek tere is full of flashy boutiques and well-touristed bars and restaurants. The neighbourhood to the south was once rather studenty, quieter and much more local. Now much of it is reserved for pedestrians, and there is no shortage of trendy shops and cafes here, too.

Ferenciek tere, which divides the Inner Town at Szabadsajtó út, is on the M3 metro line and can be reached by bus 7 from Buda or points east in Pest.

Along Váci utca

The best way to see the posher side of the Inner Town is to walk up pedestrianised Váci utca, the capital's premier – and most expensive – shopping street, with designer clothes, expensive jewellery shops, the odd pub and some bookshops for browsing. To gain access from Ferenciek tere, walk through **Párisi Udvar** (Map p86; V Ferenciek tere 5), a gem of a Parisian-style arcade built in 1909, and into tiny Kigyó utca. Váci utca is straight ahead.

Many of the buildings on Váci utca are worth closer inspection, but it's a narrow street and you'll have to crane your neck. **Thonet House** (Map p86; V Váci utca 11/a) is a masterpiece built by Ödön Lechner in 1890, and a florist-cum-gift-shop called **Philanthia** (Map p86; V Váci utca 9) has an original – and very rare – Art Nouveau interior.

Vörösmarty tér & Surrounds

Váci utca ends at Vörösmarty tér (Map p86), a large square of smart shops, galleries, cafes and a smattering of artists who will draw your portrait or caricature.

In the centre is a statue of the 19th-century poet after whom Vörösmarty tér was named. The first station of the little yellow metro line designated the M1 is also in the square, and at the northern end is **Gerbeaud** (p121), Budapest's most famous cafe and cake shop.

South of Vörösmarty tér is the sumptuous **Bank Palace** (Bank Palota; Map p86; Deák utca 5), built in 1915 and the home of the Budapest Stock Exchange for 15 years until 2007. It is now being converted into a shopping gallery called Váci 1. The **Pesti Vigadó** (Map p86; V Vigadó tér 1), the Romantic-style concert hall built in 1865 but badly damaged during WWII, faces the river to the west of Vörösmarty tér. It has now been renovated and its lovely facade cleaned, but the hall still stands empty.

Duna korzó

An easy way to cool down on a warm afternoon (and enjoy views of Castle Hill) is to stroll along the Duna korzó (Map p86), the riverside promenade between Széchenyi Chain Bridge and Elizabeth Bridge and above Belgrád rakpart. It's full of cafes, musicians, handicraft stalls and, at night, prostitutes of every description. It leads into **Petőfi tér** (Map p86), named after the poet of the 1848–49 War of Independence. **Március 15 tér** (Map p86), which marks the date of the outbreak of the revolution, abuts it to the south.

On the eastern side of Március 15 tér, sitting uncomfortably close to the Elizabeth Bridge flyover, is the **Inner Town Parish Church** (Belvárosi Főplébániatemplom; Map p86; V Március 15 tér 2), where a Romanesque church was first built in the 12th century on the grave of St Gellért. It was rebuilt in the 14th and 18th centuries, and you can easily spot Gothic, Renaissance, baroque and even Turkish elements.

In the small park to the north are a few scraggly bits of the Roman fortress called **Contra Aquincum** (Map p86).

Around Egyetem tér

The centre of the Inner Town south of Szabadsajtó út is Egyetem tér (Map p86), a five-minute walk south along Károlyi Mihály utca. The name ('University Sq') refers to the branch of the prestigious **Loránd Eötvös Science University** (ELTE; Map p86; V Egyetem tér 1-3) here. On the northwest side is the **University Church** (Egyetemi templom; V Papnövelde utca 5-7), a lovely baroque structure consecrated in 1742. Over the altar inside is a copy of Poland's much-revered Black Madonna of Częstochowa.

Leafy Kecskeméti utca runs southeast from the square to **Kálvin tér** (Map p86), almost unrecognisable while excavations for the city's fourth metro line continue. **Ráday utca** (Map p86 and Map pp80–1), which leads south from Kálvin tér, is full of cafes, clubs and restaurants. This is where university students and travellers alike entertain themselves.

NORTHERN INNER TOWN

This district, also called Lipótváros (Leopold Town; Map p84 and Map p86) in honour of Archduke Leopold, the grandson of Empress Maria Theresa, is full of offices, government ministries, 19th-century apartment blocks and grand squares.

Roosevelt tér

Roosevelt tér (Map p86; 🚌 16 or 105, 🚊 2 or 2/a), named in 1947 after the long-serving (1933–45) American president, is at the foot of Széchenyi Chain Bridge and offers some of the best views of Castle Hill.

At the southern end of the square is a **Ferenc Deák statue** (Map p86). Deák was the Hungarian minister largely responsible for the Compromise of 1867 (see p31), which brought about the Dual Monarchy of Austria and Hungary. The statues on the western side facing the river portray an Austrian and a Hungarian child holding hands in peaceful bliss.

The Art Nouveau building with the gold tiles to the east is the **Gresham Palace** (Map p86; V Roosevelt tér 5-6), built by an English insurance company in 1907. It now houses the sumptuous **Four Seasons Gresham Palace Hotel** (p115). The **Hungarian Academy of Sciences** (Magyar Tudományos Akadémia; Map p86; V Roosevelt tér 9), founded by Count István Széchenyi, is at the northern end of the square.

Szabadság tér

'Liberty Square' (Map p84; 🚌 15), one of the largest in the city, is a few minutes' walk northeast of Roosevelt tér. In the centre is a **Soviet army memorial** (Map p84), the last of its type still standing in Budapest.

South of the fortresslike **US Embassy** (Map p84; V Szabadság tér 12) is the erstwhile **Royal Postal Savings Bank** (Map p84; V Hold utca 4), a Secessionist extravaganza of colourful tiles and folk motifs built by Ödön Lechner in 1901 and now part of the **National Bank of Hungary** (Magyar Nemzeti Bank; Map p84; V Szabadság tér 8-9) next door. Inside, the **MNB Visitor Centre** (☎ 428 2752; www.lk.mnb.hu; admission free; 🕑 9am-4pm Mon-Wed & Fri, to 6pm Thu) contains an interesting multimedia exhibition on the history of currency and banking in Hungary, but most people come to gawp at the stunning entrance hall and staircase.

Kossuth Lajos tér

Northwest of Szabadság tér is Kossuth Lajos tér, the site of both Budapest's most photographed building and the best museum in the country for traditional arts and crafts. Southeast of the square in Vértanúk tere is an **Imre Nagy statue**. He was the reformist communist prime minister executed in 1958 for his role in the Uprising two years before (see p35). Just around the corner is **Bedő House** (Bedő-ház; Map p84; ☎ 269 4622; www.magyarszecessziohaza.hu; V Honvéd utca 3; adult/student & child 1000/600Ft; 🕑 10am-5pm Mon-Sat), a stunning Art Nouveau apartment block (1903) designed by Emil Vidor. Now a shrine to Hungarian Secessionist interiors, its three floors are crammed with furniture, porcelain, ironwork, paintings and objets d'art.

The Eclectic-style **Parliament** (Országház; Map p84; ☎ 441 4904, 441 4415; V Kossuth Lajos tér 1-3, Gate X; admission free for EU citizens, other adult/student & child 2520/1260Ft; 🕑 8am-6pm Mon & Wed-Fri, to 4pm Sat, to 2pm Sun May-Sep, 8am-4pm Mon & Wed-Sat, to 2pm Sun Oct-Apr; Ⓜ M2 Kossuth Lajos tér), designed by Imre Steindl and completed in 1902, has some 690 sumptuously decorated rooms, but you'll only get to see three on a guided tour of the North Wing: the main staircase and landing, where the **Crown of St Stephen** (see the boxed text, p26), the nation's most important national icon, is on display; the Loge Hall; and the Congress Hall, where the House of Lords of the one-time bicameral assembly sat until 1944. The building is a blend of architectural styles – neo-Gothic, neo-Romanesque, neobaroque – and in sum works very well. You can join a tour in any of eight languages; the English-language ones are at 10am, noon and 2pm (Hungarian tours depart continually). To avoid disappointment, book ahead (in person).

The **Ethnography Museum** (Néprajzi Múzeum; Map p84; ☎ 473 2400; www.neprajz.hu; V Kossuth Lajos tér 12; adult/student & child/family 800/400/1300Ft; ⏰ 10am-6pm Tue-Sun; Ⓜ M2 Kossuth Lajos tér), opposite the Parliament building, offers visitors an easy introduction to traditional Hungarian life, with thousands of displays in 13 rooms on the 1st floor. The mock-ups of peasant houses from the Őrség and Sárköz regions of Western and Southern Transdanubia are well done, and there are some priceless objects collected from Transylvania. On the 2nd floor, most temporary exhibitions deal with cultures further afield: Africa, Asia, Oceania and the Americas.

BAJCSY-ZSILINSZKY ÚT

Bajcsy-Zsilinszky út (Map p84 and Map p86) is the boulevard stretching from central Deák Ferenc tér, the only place in the city where all three metro lines converge, to Nyugati tér, where the Nyugati train station is located. It is named after the author and politician executed by the Germans in 1944.

St Stephen's Basilica

The neoclassical **St Stephen's Basilica** (Szent István Bazilika; Map p86; ☎ 311 0839, 338 2151; V Szent István tér; ⏰ 7am-7pm; Ⓜ M2 Arany János utca), built over the course of half a century, was not completed until 1905. Much of the interruption had to do with the fiasco in 1868 when the dome collapsed during a storm, and the structure had to be demolished and rebuilt. The 'new' **dome** (adult/child 500/400Ft; ⏰ 10am-4.30pm Apr & May, 9.30am-6pm Jun-Aug, 10am-5.30pm Sep & Oct) can be reached by a thigh-strengthening 302 steps (or lift plus 40 steps) and offers some of the best views in the city.

To the right as you enter the basilica is a small **treasury** (kincstár; adult/child 400/300Ft; ⏰ 9am-5pm Apr-Sep, 10am-4pm Oct-Mar) of ecclesiastical objects. Behind the main altar is the basilica's main draw: the **Holy Right Chapel** (Szent Jobb kápolna; ⏰ 9am-4.30pm Mon-Sat, 1-4.30pm Sun Apr-Sep, 10am-4pm Mon-Sat, 1-4.30pm Sun Oct-Mar). It contains the mummified right hand of St Stephen and is an object of great devotion.

Museum of Hungarian Trade & Tourism

A shadow of its former self, when it was based on Castle Hill, the quirky **Museum of Hungarian Trade & Tourism** (Magyar Kereskedelmi és Vendéglátóipari Múzeum; Map p86; ☎ 375 6249; www.mkvm.hu; V Szent István tér 15; adult/child/family 600/300/1200Ft; ⏰ 11am-7pm Wed-Sun) deals almost exclusively in temporary exhibitions and serves as an educational centre for schools and those in the catering and hospitality trade. Only one small room of restaurant items, tableware, advertising and packaging contains remnants of the original collection.

SZENT ISTVÁN KÖRÚT

Szent István körút (Map p84), the northernmost stretch of the Big Ring Road in Pest, runs from Nyugati tér to Margaret Bridge over the Danube. It's an interesting street to stroll along, with many fine Eclectic-style buildings decorated with Atlases, reliefs and other details. Don't hesitate to explore the inner courtyards.

You can reach Jászai Mari tér (Map p84), at the western end of Szent István körút, on tram 4 or 6 from either side of the river, or via tram 2 from the Inner Town in Pest. The eastern end of the boulevard is best reached by metro (M3 Nyugati pályaudvar).

ÚJLIPÓTVÁROS

The area north of Szent István körút is known as Újlipótváros (New Leopold Town; Map pp80–1 and Map p84). It was predominantly upper middle class and Jewish before WWII, and many of the 'safe houses' organised by the Swedish diplomat Raoul Wallenberg (see the boxed text, opposite) during the war were located here. A street named after him two blocks to the north of Szent István körút bears a commemorative plaque, and the **Wallenberg memorial** (Map pp80–1) in his honour was erected in Szent István Park in 1999.

ERZSÉBETVÁROS

The Big Ring Road slices district VII – also called Erzsébetváros (Elizabeth Town; Map p84 and Map p86) – in half between two busy squares: Oktogon and Blaha Lujza tér. The eastern side is rather run-down, with little of interest to travellers except for Keleti train station (Map pp80–1). The western side, bounded by the Little Ring Road, has always been predominantly Jewish, and this was the

RAOUL WALLENBERG: RIGHTEOUS GENTILE

At Yad Vashem, a museum in Jerusalem dedicated to the Holocaust, there is a row of trees called the 'Avenue of the Righteous among Nations'. They represent some of the 21,300-odd gentiles (non-Jews) who either saved Jews during the Holocaust or came to their defence by putting their own lives at risk. Among those so honoured is Raoul Wallenberg, the Swedish diplomat and businessman who rescued as many as 35,000 Hungarian Jews during WWII.

Wallenberg began working in 1936 for a trading firm whose owner was a Hungarian Jew. In July 1944 the Swedish Foreign Ministry, at the request of Jewish and refugee organisations in the USA, sent the 32-year-old Wallenberg on a rescue mission to Budapest as an attaché to the embassy there. By that time almost half a million Jews in Hungary had been sent to Nazi death camps in Germany and Poland.

Wallenberg immediately began issuing Swedish 'protective passports', and set up 'safe houses' flying the flag of Sweden and other neutral countries and bearing signs such as 'Swedish Research Centre', where Jews could seek asylum. He even followed German 'death marches' and deportation trains, distributing food, clothing and passports, and actually freeing some 500 people along the way.

When the Soviet army entered Budapest in January 1945, Wallenberg went to report to the authorities, but in the wartime confusion was arrested for espionage and sent to Moscow. In the early 1950s, responding to reports that Wallenberg had been seen alive in a labour camp, the Soviet Union announced that he had in fact died of a heart attack in 1947. Several reports over the next two decades suggested Wallenberg was still alive, but none were ever confirmed. Many believe Wallenberg was executed by the Soviets, who suspected him of spying for the USA.

Wallenberg has been made an honorary citizen of the USA, Canada, Israel and, most recently (in 2003), the city of Budapest.

ghetto where Jews were forced to live behind wooden fences when the Nazis occupied Hungary in 1944.

Oktogon is on the M1 metro line and Blaha Lujza tér on the M2. You can also reach this area via trams 4 and 6 from both Buda and the rest of Pest.

Liszt Academy of Music

The **Liszt Academy of Music** (Liszt Zeneakadémia; Map p84; ☎ 342 0179; VI Liszt Ferenc tér 8; Ⓜ M2 Oktogon), one block southeast of Oktogon, was built in 1907. It attracts students from all over the world and is one of the top venues for concerts in Budapest. The interior, with large and small concert halls richly embellished with Zsolnay porcelain and frescoes, is worth a look even if you're not attending a performance.

Jewish Quarter

The heart of the old Jewish quarter, **Klauzál tér** (Map p84; tram 4 or 6) and its surrounding streets retain something of a feeling of pre-WWII Budapest. Signs of a continued Jewish presence are everywhere – in a **kosher bakery** (Map p86; Kazinczy utca 28), in the **Frölich cake shop** (Map p86; Dob utca 22), which has old Jewish favourites, and at two **wigmakers** (Map p86; Kazinczy utca 32 & 36).

There are about half a dozen synagogues and prayer houses in the district, which were reserved for different sects and ethnic groups (conservatives, Orthodox, Poles, Sephardics etc). The **Orthodox Synagogue** (Ortodox zsinagóga; Map p86; ☎ 342 1072; VII Kazinczy utca 29-31; admission 800Ft; 🕑 10am-3.30pm Sun-Thu, to noon Fri; tram 4 or 6), which can also be entered from Dob utca 35, was built in 1913. The Moorish **Rumbach Sebestyén utca Synagogue** (Rumbach Sebestyén utcai zsinagóga; Map p86; VII Rumbach Sebestyén utca 11; admission 500Ft; 🕑 10am-5.30pm Mon-Fri, to 2.30pm Sat; Ⓜ M1/2/3 Deák Ferenc tér) was built in 1872 by Austrian Secessionist architect Otto Wagner for the conservatives, but has not been in use since WWII.

The **Great Synagogue** (Nagy zsinagóga; Map p86; ☎ 413 5500; VII Dohány utca 2-8; Ⓜ M2 Astoria) is the largest Jewish house of worship in the world outside New York City and can seat 3000. Built in 1859, the synagogue contains both Romantic-style and Moorish architectural elements. In an annexe of the synagogue is the **Jewish Museum** (Zsidó Múzeum; Map p86; ☎ 342 8949; VII Dohány utca 2; adult/student & child 1600/750Ft; 🕑 10am-6.30pm Mon-Thu, to 2pm Fri, to 5.30pm Sun mid-Apr–Oct, 10am-3pm Mon-Thu, to 2pm Fri, to 4pm Sun Nov–mid-Apr), which contains objects related to religious and everyday life, and an interesting handwritten book of the local Burial Society from the 18th century. The Holocaust Memorial Room relates the events of 1944–45, including the infamous mass murder of doctors and patients at a hospital on XII Maros utca, south of Moszkva tér in Buda.

On the synagogue's north side, the **Holocaust Memorial** (Map p86; opp VII Wesselényi utca 6) stands over the mass graves of those murdered by the Nazis in 1944–45. On the leaves of the metal 'tree of life' are the family names of some of the hundreds of thousands of victims.

Blaha Lujza tér & Rákóczi út

The subway (underpass) below Blaha Lujza tér (Map p84), the square named after a leading 19th-century stage actress, is one of the liveliest in the city, with hustlers, beggars, peasants selling their wares, musicians and, of course, pickpockets. Be on your guard. Just north of the square is the Art Nouveau **New York Palace** (New York Palota; Map p84; VII Erzsébet körút 9-11), erstwhile home of the celebrated **New York Kávéház**, scene of many a literary gathering over the years. The building has been completely restored and is now an over-the-top luxury hotel.

Rákóczi út (Map pp80–1 and Map p84), a busy shopping street, cuts across Blaha Lujza tér and ends at Baross tér and Keleti train station (Keleti pályaudvar; Map pp80–1), built in 1884 and renovated a century later.

JÓZSEFVÁROS & FERENCVÁROS

From Blaha Lujza tér, the Big Ring Road runs through district VIII, which is also called Józsefváros (Joseph Town; Map pp80–1 and Map p84). The western side transforms itself from a neighbourhood of lovely 19th-century town houses and villas around the Little Ring Road to a large student quarter in the IX district. East of the Big Ring Road is the rough-and-tumble district where much of the fighting in October 1956 took place. Today it is being developed at breakneck speed.

The neighbourhood south of Üllői út is Ferencváros (Francis Town; Map pp80–1), home of the city's most popular football team, Ferencvárosi Torna Club (see p128). There is a tremendous amount of building going on in Ferencváros as well.

The Józsefváros and Ferencváros districts are best served by trams 4 and 6.

Hungarian National Museum

The **Hungarian National Museum** (Magyar Nemzeti Múzeum; Map p86; ☎ 338 2122; www.mnm.hu; VIII Múzeum körút 14-16; adult/student & child 1000/500Ft; 10am-6pm Tue-Sun; M M3 Kálvin tér, 47 or 49) contains the nation's most important collection of historical relics in a large neoclassical building purpose-built in 1847. On the 1st floor, exhibits trace the history of the Carpathian Basin from earliest times to the end of the Avar period in the early 9th century, and on the 2nd floor there are exhibits on the Magyar people from the conquest of the Carpathian Basin to the end of communism. In the basement a lapidarium has finds from Roman, medieval and early modern times. Look out for the enormous 3rd-century Roman mosaic from Balácapuszta, near Veszprém; the crimson silk royal coronation robe (or mantle) stitched by nuns in 1031; the reconstructed 3rd-century Roman villa from Pannonia; the treasury room with preconquest gold jewellery; the stunning baroque library; Beethoven's Broadwood piano; and memorabilia from socialist times.

Museum of Applied Arts

The **Museum of Applied Arts** (Iparművészeti Múzeum; Map pp88-9; ☎ 456 5100; IX Üllői út 33-37; adult/student & child/family 800/400/1400Ft; 2-6pm Tue, 10am-6pm Wed & Fri-Sun, 10am-10pm Thu; M M3 Ferenc körút), whose central hall of white marble was supposedly modelled on the Alhambra in southern Spain, owns a king's ransom of Hungarian furniture dating from the 18th and 19th centuries, Art Nouveau and Secessionist artefacts, and objects related to the history of trades and crafts (glass-making, bookbinding, goldsmithing, leatherwork etc), but only a small part of it forms the 400-piece 'Collectors and Treasures' exhibit on the 1st floor. Almost everything else makes up part of one of the four or five temporary exhibitions on display at any given time (a combined ticket for 2500/1250/4500Ft will get you into everything). The building, designed by Ödön Lechner and decorated with Zsolnay ceramic tiles, was completed for the Millenary Exhibition (1896).

Holocaust Memorial Center

The **Holocaust Memorial Center** (Holokauszt Emlékközpont; Map pp88-9; ☎ 455 3322; www.hdke.hu; IX Páva utca 39; adult/student & child 1000Ft/free; 10am-6pm Tue-Sun), housed in a striking modern building in a working-class neighbourhood of Ferencváros, opened in 2004 on the 60th anniversary of the start of the Holocaust in Hungary. Both a museum and an educational foundation, the centre's permanent exhibition traces the rise of anti-Semitism in Hungary from 1938 to the mass deportations to German death camps in 1944–45. In the central courtyard, a sublimely restored synagogue designed by Leopold Baumhorn and completed in 1924 hosts temporary exhibitions on everything from the Anschluss to the genocide of the Roma people during WWII. Outside is an 8m-high wall with the names of the Hungarian victims of the Holocaust.

Ludwig Museum (Museum of Contemporary Art)

Housed in the architecturally controversial Palace of Arts (p127), the **Ludwig Museum** (Kortárs Művészeti Múzeum; Map pp88-9; ☎ 555 3444; www.ludwigmuseum.hu; IX Komor Marcell utca 1; adult/student & child 1200/600Ft; 10am-8pm Tue-Sun; 2 or 24) is Hungary's most important collector and exhibitor of international contemporary art. Works by American, Russian, German and French contemporary artists span the past 50 years, while Hungarian, Czech, Slovakian, Romanian, Polish and Slovenian works date from the 1990s onward. The museum also holds frequent (and cutting-edge) temporary exhibitions.

Zwack Unicum Museum & Visitor Centre

Visit the **Zwack Unicum Museum & Visitor Centre** (Zwack Unicum Múzeum és Látogató Központ; Map pp88-9; ☎ 476 2383; www.zwackunicum.hu; IX Soroksári út 26, enter from Dandár utca; adult/student/senior 1500/850/1250Ft; 10am-6pm Mon-Fri; 2 or 24) if you really can't get enough of Unicum, the thick, brown, bitter aperitif made from 40 herbs and clocking in at 42% alcohol. The museum traces the history of the product since it was first made in 1790 – and supposedly named by Franz Joseph himself.

ANDRÁSSY ÚT & SURROUNDS

Andrássy út (Map pp80–1 and Map p84) starts a short distance northeast of Deák Ferenc tér and stretches for 2.5km, ending at Heroes' Sq (Hősök tere) and the sprawling City Park (Városliget). The best way to see it is on foot (see the Walking Tour, p105).

Hungarian State Opera House

The neo-Renaissance **Hungarian State Opera House** (Magyar Állami Operaház; Map p84; ☎ 332 8197; www.operavisit.hu; VI Andrássy út 22; tour adult/student & child 2600/1400Ft; M M1 Opera) was designed by Miklós Ybl in 1884 and is among the city's most beautiful buildings. If you cannot attend a performance at least join one of the English-language guided tours at 3pm and 4pm. Tickets are available from the souvenir shop inside to the left.

House of Terror

The **House of Terror** (Terror Háza; Map p84; ☎ 374 2600; www.terrorhaza.hu; Andrássy út 60; adult/child 1500/750Ft; 10am-6pm Tue-Fri, to 7.30pm Sat & Sun; M M1 Vörösmarty utca), in what was once the headquarters of the dreaded ÁVH secret police (see p35), focuses on the crimes and atrocities committed by both Hungary's fascist and Stalinist regimes in a permanent exhibition called Double Occupation. But the years after WWII leading up to the 1956 Uprising get the lion's share of the exhibition space (almost three-dozen spaces on three floors). The tank in the central courtyard is a jarring introduction and the wall outside displaying many of the victims' photos speaks volumes. Even more harrowing are the reconstructed prison cells (collectively called the 'gym') and the final Hall of Tears gallery.

Franz Liszt Memorial Museum

The **Franz Liszt Memorial Museum** (Liszt Ferenc Emlékmúzeum; Map p84; ☎ 322 9804; www.lisztmuseum.hu; VI Vörösmarty utca 35; adult/child 600/300Ft; 10am-6pm Mon-Fri, 9am-5pm Sat; M M1 Vörösmarty utca) is situated in the Old Music Academy, where the great composer lived in a 1st-floor apartment for five years until his death in 1886. The four rooms are filled with his pianos (including a tiny glass one), composer's table, portraits and personal effects. Concerts (included in the entry fee) are sometimes held here on Saturdays at 11am.

Asian Art Museums

The **Ferenc Hopp Museum of East Asian Art** (Hopp Ferenc Kelet-Ázsiai Művészeti Múzeum; Map pp80-1; ☎ 322 8476; VI Andrássy út 103; adult/child 600/300Ft; 10am-6pm Tue-Sun; M M1 Bajza utca) is housed in the former villa of its benefactor and namesake. Founded in 1919, the museum's six rooms show an important collection of Chinese and Japanese ceramics, porcelain, textiles and sculpture,

Indonesian *wayang* puppets, Indian statuary, and Lamaist sculpture and scroll paintings from Tibet. The museum's temporary exhibits are shown at the **György Ráth Museum** (Ráth György Múzeum; Map pp80-1; ☎ 342 3916; VI Városligeti fasor 12; adult/child 400/250Ft; ⏰ 10am-6pm Tue-Sun; Ⓜ M1 Bajza utca), housed in an Art Nouveau residence a few minutes' walk southwards down Bajza utca.

HEROES' SQUARE

Andrássy út ends at Heroes' Sq (Hősök tere; Map pp80–1), which effectively forms the entrance to City Park. It is on the M1 metro line (Hősök tere stop).

Millenary Monument

In the centre of the square is the Millenary Monument (Ezeréves emlékmű; Map pp80–1), a 36m-high pillar backed by colonnades to the right and left. Topping the pillar is the Archangel Gabriel holding the Crown of St Stephen and a cross. At the base are Árpád and the six other Magyar chieftains who occupied the Carpathian Basin in the late 9th century.

The 14 statues in the colonnades behind are of rulers and statesmen – from King Stephen on the left to Lajos Kossuth on the right. The reliefs below show a significant scene in the honoured man's life. The four allegorical figures atop are (from left to right) Work and Prosperity, War, Peace and Knowledge and Glory.

Art Museums

The **Museum of Fine Arts** (Szépművészeti Múzeum; Map pp80-1; ☎ 469 7100, 363 2675; www.mfab.hu; XIV Dózsa György út 41; adult/student & child 1200/600Ft; ⏰ 10am-5.30pm Tue, Wed & Fri-Sun, to 10pm Thu), on the northern side of the square, houses the city's outstanding collection of foreign artworks in a building dating from 1906. The Old Masters collection is the most complete, with thousands of works from the Dutch and Flemish, Spanish, Italian, German, French and British schools between the 13th and 18th centuries, including seven paintings by El Greco. Other sections include Egyptian and Greco-Roman artefacts, and 19th- and 20th-century paintings, watercolours, graphics and sculpture, including some important impressionist works. There are usually a couple of excellent temporary exhibitions going on at the same time; a combined ticket for 3200/1600Ft will get you into everything. Free English-language tours of key galleries depart at 11am Tuesday to Saturday, 2pm Tuesday and Friday, and 1pm Wednesday and Thursday.

To the south, the **Palace of Art** (Műcsarnok; Map pp80-1; ☎ 460 7000; www.mucsarnok.hu; XIV Dózsa György út 37; adult/student & child/family 1200/600/1800Ft; ⏰ 10am-6pm Tue, Wed & Fri-Sun, to 8pm Thu), which is among the city's largest exhibition spaces, focuses on contemporary visual arts, with some five to six major exhibitions staged annually. Go for the scrumptious venue alone.

CITY PARK

City Park (Városliget; Map pp80–1) is Pest's green lung, an open space measuring almost a square kilometre that hosted most of the events during Hungary's 1000th anniversary celebrations in 1896. In general, museums lie to the south of XIV Kós Károly sétány, while activities of a less cerebral nature, including the **Municipal Great Circus** (p128) and the **Széchenyi Baths** (p104), are to the north.

City Park is served by the M1 metro (Széchenyi fürdő stop), as well as by trolleybuses 70, 72, 75 and 79.

Transport Museum

The **Transport Museum** (Közlekedési Múzeum; Map pp80-1; ☎ 273 3840; www.km.iif.hu, in Hungarian; XIV Városligeti körút 11; adult/student & child/family 800/400/1600Ft; ⏰ 10am-5pm Tue-Fri, to 6pm Sat & Sun May-Sep, 10am-4pm Tue-Fri, to 5pm Sat & Sun Oct-Apr) is one of the most enjoyable museums in Budapest and a great place for kids. In an old and a new wing there are scale models of ancient trains (some of which run), classic late-19th-century automobiles, sailing boats and lots of those old wooden bicycles called 'bone-shakers'. There are a few hands-on exhibits and lots of show-and-tell from the attendants. Outside are pieces from the original Danube bridges that were retrieved after the bombings of WWII, and a cafe in an old MÁV coach.

City Zoo & Botanical Garden

The large **City Zoo & Botanical Garden** (Városi Állatkert és Növénykert; Map pp80-1; ☎ 273 4900; www.zoobudapest.com; XIV Állatkerti körút 6-12; adult/student & child/family 1690/1190/4800Ft; ⏰ 9am-6.30pm Mon-Thu, to 7pm Fri-Sun May-Aug, 9am-5.30pm Mon-Thu, to 6pm Fri-Sun Apr & Sep, 9am-5pm Mon-Thu, to 5.30pm Fri-Sun Mar & Oct, 9am-4pm Nov-Feb) has a good collection of animals (big cats, hippopotamuses, polar bears, giraffes), but most visitors come for a glimpse of the calves born in recent years to Lulu the white rhino. Away from the beasties, have a look at the Secessionist animal houses built in the early part of the 20th century, such as the Elephant House, with pachyderm heads in beetle-green Zsolnay ceramic, and the Palm House, with an aquarium erected by the Eiffel Company of Paris.

Funfair Park

The **Funfair Park** (Vidámpark; Map pp80-1; ☎ 363 8310; www.vidampark.hu; XIV Állatkerti körút 14-16; adult 3700-3900Ft, child (up to 140cm) 2300-2900Ft; ⏲ 10am-8pm Jul & Aug, 11am-7pm Mon-Fri, 10am-8pm Sat & Sun May, Jun & Sep, noon-6pm Mon-Fri, 10am-7pm Sat & Sun Apr & Oct) is a luna park on 2½ hectares, dating back to the mid-19th century. There are a couple of dozen thrilling rides, including the heart-stopping Ikarus Space Needle, the looping Star roller coaster (alongside a vintage wooden one from 1926) and the Hip-Hop freefall tower, as well as go-karts, dodgem cars, a carousel built in 1906 and the new T-Rex dinosaur attraction.

ACTIVITIES

Budapest is chock-a-block with things to keep you occupied outdoors. From taking the waters and cycling to caving and canoeing, it's all in or within easy access of the capital.

Thermal Baths

Budapest lies on the geological fault separating the Buda Hills from the Great Plain; more than 30,000 cu metres of warm to scalding (21°C to 76°C) mineral water gush forth daily from some 123 thermal springs. As a result, 'taking the waters' at one of the many *gyógyfürdő* (thermal baths) is a real Budapest experience. Some baths date from Turkish times, some are Art Nouveau marvels and others look like they could be film sets for Thomas Mann's *Magic Mountain*.

Almost all the baths now employ a deposit system whereby you are refunded a certain amount (noted in the review) if you stay less than two hours. Most of the baths offer a full range of serious medical treatments, plus more indulgent services such as massage (15/30 minutes 2800/3800Ft) and pedicures (1600Ft to 2000Ft). Specify what you want when buying your ticket.

The procedure at baths is similar to that at swimming pools (see p104), though during the busiest times you may be given a number and will have to wait. Though some of the local spas and baths look a little rough around the edges, they are clean and the water is changed regularly. You might consider taking along a pair of plastic sandals or flip-flops, however. On single-sex days or in same-sex sections, men usually are handed drawstring loincloths and women apronlike garments. You must wear a bathing suit on mixed-sex days; these are available for hire (1000Ft) if you don't have your own.

An excellent source of information is **Budapest Spas and Hot Springs** (www.spasbudapest.com).

Soaking in the Art Nouveau **Gellért Baths** (Gellért Gyógyfürdő; Map p86; ☎ 466 6166; XI Kelenhegyi út 4; admission deposit before/after 5pm 3400/3000Ft; ⏲ 6am-7pm May-Sep, 6am-7pm Mon-Fri, to 5pm Sat & Sun Oct-Apr; tram 18, 19, 47 or 49), open to both men and women in separate sections, has been likened to taking a bath in a cathedral. The eight thermal pools range in temperature from 26°C to 38°C, and the water is good for pains in the joints, arthritis and blood circulation. You get 400Ft back during the day if you leave within two hours.

Built in 1566, the stunningly renovated **Rudas Baths** (Rudas Gyógyfürdő; Map p86; ☎ 356 1322; I Döbrentei tér 9; admission deposit 2400Ft; ⏲ men 6am-8pm Mon & Wed-Fri, women 6am-8pm Tue, mixed 10pm-4am Fri, 6am-5pm & 10pm-4am Sat, 8am-5pm & 10pm-4am Sun; tram 18 or 19, bus 7 or 86) is the most Turkish of all the baths in Budapest, with an octagonal pool, domed cupola with coloured glass and massive columns. During mixed-gender bathing, a bathing costume is compulsory. You get 400Ft back if you leave two hours after you enter.

The four pools at the **Király Baths** (Király Gyógyfürdő; Map pp80-1; ☎ 202 3688; II Fő utca 84; admission deposit 2600Ft; ⏲ men 9am-8pm Tue & Thu-Sat, women 7am-6pm Mon & Wed, mixed 9am-8pm Sun; bus 86), with water temperatures between 26°C and 40°C, are genuine Turkish baths erected in 1570. There is a wonderful skylit central dome, though this place is begging for a renovation. Here you get a whopping 1000/500Ft back if you leave within two/three hours. Note that this bath is something of a gay venue on male-only days. Nothing actually happens, except cruising, but those not into it may feel uncomfortable.

The **Lukács Baths** (Lukács Gyógyfürdő; Map pp80-1; ☎ 326 1695; II Frankel Leó út 25-29; admission deposit locker/cabin 1790/1900Ft; ⏲ 6am-7pm May-Sep, 6am-7pm Mon-Fri, to 5pm Sat & Sun Oct-Apr; tram 17, bus 86), housed in a sprawling, 19th-century complex, is popular with very keen spa aficionados. The thermal baths (temperatures 22°C to 40°C) are mixed and a bathing suit is required. The renovated mud and weight bath, open from 6am to 6pm weekdays and to 4pm on Saturday, welcomes men on Tuesday, Thursday and Saturday, and women on Monday, Wednesday and Friday. You get 400/200Ft back if you leave two/three hours after you enter.

At the northern end of City Park, the **Széchenyi Baths** (Széchenyi Gyógyfürdő; Map pp80-1; ☎ 363 3210; XIV Állatkerti körút 11; admission deposit before/after 5pm 2600/2200Ft; 🕑 6am-10pm; Ⓜ M1 Széchenyi fürdő) is unusual for three reasons: its immense size (a dozen thermal baths and five swimming pools); its bright, clean atmosphere; and its water temperatures (up to 38°C), which really are what the wall plaques say they are. It's open to both men and women at all times, and you get 400Ft back on your daytime entry fee if you leave within two hours.

Cycling

Parts of Budapest, including City and Népliget Parks, Margaret Island and the Buda Hills, are excellent places for cycling. To contact Budapest-based cycling associations for information and advice, see p68.

Frigoria (www.frigoriakiado.hu) publishes a number of useful guides and maps, including the 1:60,000 *Kerékpárral Budapesten* (By Bike in Budapest), available free from tourist offices. If you want something more detailed, pick up its 1:20,000 *Budapest Kerékpáratlasz* (Budapest Bicycle Atlas; 1700Ft).

Long-established and very reliable **Yellow Zebra Bikes** (www.yellowzebrabikes.com; Belváros Map p86; ☎ 266 8777; V Sütő utca 2; per day/24hr 2000/3000Ft; 🕑 10am-6pm Nov-Mar, 8.30am-8pm Apr-Oct; Ⓜ M1/2/3 Deák Ferenc tér; Discover Budapest Map p84; ☎ 269 3843; VI Lázár utca 16; 🕑 9.30am-6.30pm Mon-Fri, 10am-4pm Sat & Sun; Ⓜ M1 Opera) rents out bicycles year-round from outlets just behind the Tourinform office and the Opera House, respectively.

Budapest Bike (Map p86; ☎ 06 30 944 5533; www.budapestbike.hu; VII Wesselényi utca 13; per 6/24hr 2000/3000Ft; 🕑 9am-6pm; 🚊 4 or 6, trolleybus 74) has bikes available year-round. Another outfit is **Bike Base** (Map p84; ☎ 06 70 625 8501; www.bikebase.hu; VI Podmaniczky utca 19; per 1/2/3 days 2000/3500/5000Ft; 🕑 9am-7pm; Ⓜ M3 Nyugati pályaudvar).

For places to rent bicycles on Margaret Island, see p95.

Bicycles can be transported on the HÉV, the Cog Railway and all Mahart boats, but not on the metro, buses or trams.

Swimming

With Hungarians such keen swimmers, it's not surprising that Budapest boasts dozens of pools. They're always excellent places to get in a few laps (if indoor), cool off on a hot summer's day (if outdoor) or watch the posers strut their stuff.

The system at pools is similar to that at the baths, except that rather than a cabin or cubicle you store your gear in lockers. Some new lockers (and cabins in the baths) are 'self-service'; the keys are released when you insert the plastic entry card you receive when you've paid your admission. Otherwise, after you've got changed, call the attendant, who will lock it for you and hand you a numbered tag to tie on your costume. Note: in order to prevent theft, should you lose or misplace the tag, the number is not the same as the one on the locker, so commit the latter to memory. Many pools require the use of a bathing cap, so bring your own or wear the plastic one provided or sold for a nominal fee. Most pools in Budapest rent bathing suits and towels.

Following are the best outdoor and indoor pools in the city. Some are attached to the thermal baths listed on p103.

The indoor pools at the **Gellért Baths** (Gellért Gyógyfürdő; Map p86; ☎ 466 6166; XI Kelenhegyi út 4; admission deposit with locker/cabin 3000/3400Ft, after 5pm May-Sep, after 5pm Mon-Fri & after 2pm Sat & Sun Oct-Apr 3000/2700Ft; 🕑 6am-7pm May-Sep, 6am-7pm Mon-Fri, to 5pm Sat & Sun Oct-Apr; 🚊 18, 19, 47 or 49) are the most beautiful in Budapest. The outdoor pools (open May to September) have a wave machine and nicely landscaped gardens. You get 400Ft back if you stay less than two hours on your daytime ticket.

Use of the three swimming pools at the **Lukács Baths** (Lukács Gyógyfürdő; Map pp80-1; ☎ 326 1695; II Frankel Leó út 25-29; 🕑 6am-7pm May-Sep, 6am-7pm Mon-Fri, to 5pm Sat & Sun Oct-Apr; 🚊 17, 🚌 86) and the three enormous thermal ones at the **Széchenyi Baths** (Széchenyi Gyógyfürdő; Map pp80-1; ☎ 363 3210; XIV Állatkerti körút 11; 🕑 6am-10pm; Ⓜ M1 Széchenyi fürdő) is included in the general admission price (see p103). You can enter the renovated pool at the **Rudas Baths** (Map p86; ☎ 356 1322; I Döbrentei tér 9; admission with locker/cabin 1400/1700Ft; 🕑 6am-6pm Mon-Fri, to 5pm Sat & Sun; 🚊 18 or 19, 🚌 7 or 86) separately without using the thermal bath facilities.

The pools at the **Alfréd Hajós swimming complex** (Map pp80-1; ☎ 450 4214; XIII Margit-sziget; adult/child 1320/790Ft; 🕑 outdoor pools 6am-7pm May-Sep, indoor pools 6am-7pm Mon-Fri, to 5pm Sat & Sun Oct-Apr; 🚊 4 or 6, (bus 26), two indoor and three outdoor, make up the National Sports Pool where the Olympic swimming and water-polo teams train.

The **Császár-Komjádi swimming pool** (Map pp80-1; ☎ 212 2750; II Árpád fejedelem utca 8; adult/child 1320/790Ft; 6am-7pm; tram 17, bus 86) is used by very serious swimmers and fitness freaks, so don't come here for fun and games.

The largest series of pools in the capital, the **Palatinus Strand** (Map pp78-9; ☎ 340 4505; XIII Margit-sziget; adult/child with locker 1500/1300Ft, admission with cabin 1900Ft; 9am-7pm May-Aug; bus 26) on Margaret Island has a total of 11 pools (three with thermal water), wave machines, water slides, kids' pools etc.

The popular **Csillaghegy swimming complex** (Map pp78-9; ☎ 250 1533; III Pusztakúti út 3; adult before/after 4pm 1400/1200Ft, child 1000Ft; 7am-7pm May–mid-Sep, 6am-7pm Mon-Fri, to 4pm Sat, to noon Sun mid-Sep–Apr) north of Óbuda is the oldest open-air baths in Budapest. There are three pools in a 90-hectare terraced park; in winter they are covered by canvas tenting and heated.

The huge **Dagály swimming complex** (Map pp78-9; ☎ 452 4500; XIII Népfürdő utca 36; admission deposit before/after 4pm 1900/1500Ft; outdoor pools 6am-7pm May-Sep, indoor pools 6am-7pm Mon-Fri, to 5pm Sat & Sun Oct-Apr; M M3 Árpád híd, tram 1) has a total of 10 pools, with plenty of grass and shade. If you leave the complex two hours after entering during the day you get 400Ft back.

The outdoor pools at the **Rómaifürdő Strand** (Rómaifürdő Beach; Map pp78-9; ☎ 388 9740; III Rozgonyi Piroska utca 2/a; adult/child with locker Mon-Fri 1500/1000Ft, Sat & Sun 1700/1200Ft; 9am-8pm May-Aug; HÉV Rómaifürdő, bus 34 or 134) are just north of Aquincum.

Caving

Budapest has two caves open for walk-through guided tours (usually in Hungarian).

Pálvölgy Cave (Pálvölgyi-barlang; Map pp78-9; ☎ 325 9505, 336 0760; www.dinpi.hu; II Szépvölgyi út 162/a; adult/child 1100/900Ft; 10am-5pm Tue-Sun; bus 65 from III Kolosy tér in Óbuda) is the second-largest cave in Hungary. Be advised that the 500m route involves climbing some 400 steps and a ladder, so it may not be suitable for children under five. The temperature is a constant 8°C so wear a jacket or jumper. Tours lasting 45 minutes depart hourly from 10.15am to 4.15pm.

A more beautiful cave, with stalactites, stalagmites and weird grapelike formations, is **Szemlő-hegy Cave** (Szemlőhegyi-barlang; Map pp78-9; ☎ 325 6001; www.dinpi.hu; II Pusztaszeri út 35; adult/child 900/700Ft; 10am-4pm Wed-Mon; bus 29 from III Kolosy tér), about 1km southeast of Pálvölgy Cave. The temperature here is 12°C. The tour lasts 35 minutes.

Boating

The best place for canoeing and kayaking in Budapest is on the Danube in Rómaifürdő (Map pp78–9). One very reliable place to rent kayaks and canoes here is **Óbuda Sport Club** (ÓSE; Map pp78-9; ☎ 240 3353; www.ose.hu; III Rozgonyi Piroska utca 28; canoes & kayaks per day from 1500Ft; 8am-6pm May-Sep, 10am-4pm Oct-Apr). To get here take the HÉV suburban line to Rómaifürdő.

Horse Riding

The **Hungarian Equestrian Tourism Association** (MLTSZ; Map p86; ☎ 456 0444; www.equi.hu/eng; IX Ráday utca 8, 1st fl; M M3 Kálvin tér) can provide you with a list of recommended riding schools within striking distance of Budapest, while **Pegazus Tours** (Map p86; ☎ 317 1644; www.pegazus.hu; V Ferenciek tere 5; M M3 Ferenciek tere) can book riding programs (www.ridingtours.hu).

One of the closest riding schools to Budapest is the long-established **Petneházy Lovascentrum** (off Map p77; ☎ 397 5048, 06 20 588 3571; www.petnehazy-lovascentrum.hu; II Feketefej utca 2; 9am-5pm Fri-Sun; bus 63 from Hűvösvölgyi út) at Adyliget near Hűvösvölgy. It offers paddock practice (2500Ft per hour) and open trail riding (4500Ft), as well as pony rides (1500Ft per 15 minutes) for the kiddies and carriage rides (10,000Ft per 30 minutes for eight people). Another place within the city is the **Pasaréti Honvéd Lovarda** (Map p77; ☎ 274 5719; www.honvedlovarda.hu; II Hidász utca 2; lessons per hr 3500-6000Ft; 9am-7pm; bus 5, tram 18 or 56) on the way to the Buda Hills.

WALKING TOUR

This is a fairly easy walk that starts just a little north of Deák Ferenc tér and follows attractive Andrássy út to Heroes' Sq (Hősök tere) and City Park (Városliget). It's not a very long walking tour, demanding about two hours if you just stroll by everything. But there's a tremendous amount to see and do along the way. The little yellow metro (M1) runs just beneath the boulevard, so if you begin to lose your stamina, just go down and jump on.

Andrássy út splits away from Bajcsy-Zsilinszky út some 200m north of Deák Ferenc tér. This section of Andrássy út is lined with plane trees, which make it cool and pleasant on a warm day. The first major sight is the **Hungarian State Opera House** (**1**; p101). The interior, which can be visited on a tour, is especially lovely and sparkles after a total overhaul in the 1980s.

Opposite the Opera House, **Drechsler House** (**2**; VI Andrássy út 25) was designed by Art Nouveau master builder Ödön Lechner in 1882. It once housed the Hungarian State Ballet Institute but has been empty since the late 1990s, awaiting its transformation as a hotel. For something even more magical, walk down Dalszínház utca to the **New Theatre** (**3**; Új Színház; ☎ 351 1406; VI Paulay Ede utca 35), a Secessionist gem (1909) embellished with monkey faces, globes and geometric designs that almost look like an early version of Art Deco.

WALK FACTS

Start Hungarian State Opera House
Finish City Park
Distance 2.6km
Duration Two hours (or more)
Fuel Stop Művész or Lukács cafe

The old-world cafe **Művész** (**4**; p121) is one block up. The next cross street is Nagymező utca, 'the Broadway of Budapest', counting a number of theatres, such as the **Budapest Operetta** (**5**; p127) at No 17 and, just across, the restored **Thália** (**6**; ☎ 331 0500; VI Nagymező utca 22-24).

On the right-hand side of the next block, the so-called **Fashion House** (**7**; Divatcsarnok; VI Andrássy út 39), which was the fanciest emporium in town when it opened as the Grande Parisienne in 1912, contains the ornate Ceremonial Hall (Díszterem) on the mezzanine floor, a room positively dripping with gilt, marquetry and frescoes by Károly Lotz. It is currently being redeveloped as a shopping mall.

Andrássy út meets the Big Ring Road at Oktogon, a busy intersection full of fast-food outlets, shops, cars and pedestrians. Just beyond it, the former secret-police building, which now houses the **House of Terror** (**8**; p101), has a ghastly history; it was here that many activists of whatever political side was out of fashion before and after WWII were taken for interrogation and torture (includ-

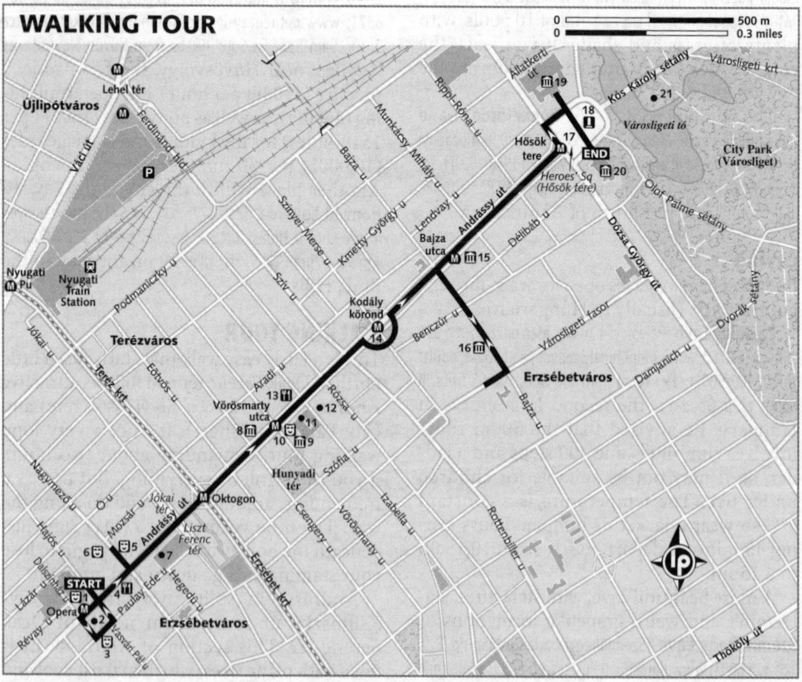

ing Cardinal Mindszenty; see the boxed text, p155). The walls were apparently double the normal thickness to mute the screams. A plaque on the outside reads in part: 'We cannot forget the horror of terror, and the victims will always be remembered.' The **Franz Liszt Memorial Museum** (**9**; p101) is diagonally across the street.

Along the next two blocks you'll pass some very grand buildings: the **Budapest Puppet Theatre** (**10**; p128) at No 69; the **Hungarian University of Fine Arts** (**11**; Magyar Képzőművészeti Egyetem; VI Andrássy út 71), founded in 1871; and the headquarters of **MÁV** (**12**; V Andrássy út 73), the national railway. The posh cafe and cake shop **Lukács** (**13**; p121) is just opposite.

The next square is **Kodály körönd (14)**, one of the most beautiful in the city. Some of the facades of the four neo-Renaissance town houses are at least getting a facelift; the one to the south is being converted into a block of flats.

The last stretch of Andrássy út and the surrounding neighbourhoods are packed with stunning old mansions that are among the most desirable addresses in the city. It's no surprise to see that embassies, like that of France at VI Lendvay utca 27, and even political parties (eg Fidesz-MPP at VI Lendvay utca 28) have moved in.

The **Ferenc Hopp Museum of East Asian Art** (**15**; p101) is at No 103, while the museum's temporary exhibitions are shown at **György Ráth Museum** (**16**; p102), a short distance to the south.

Andrássy út ends at **Heroes' Square** (**17**; Hősök tere; p102), just west of City Park. The city's most flamboyant monument is in the centre and two of its best exhibition spaces are on either side of the square.

The **Millenary Monument** (**18**; Ezeréves emlékmű; p102) in effect defines Heroes' Sq. Beneath the tall column and under a stone slab is an empty coffin representing the unknown insurgents of the 1956 Uprising. To the north of the monument is the **Museum of Fine Arts** (**19**; p102) and its rich collection of Old Masters, while to the south is the ornate **Palace of Art** (**20**; Műcsarnok; p102), which opened in 1896 in time for the city's Millenary Exhibition in City Park.

The M1 Hősök tere metro stop is conveniently just across the square, or you can continue over the footbridge to explore **City Park** (**21**; p102).

COURSES

For details about cooking courses, see p59.

Language

The most prestigious Hungarian-language school in the land, the Debrecen Summer University (p371) has a **Budapest branch** (Map p84; ☎ 320 5751, 06 30 928 6577; www.nyariegyetem.hu/bp; V Báthory utca 4, 2nd fl; Ⓜ M2 Kossuth Lajos tér), with intensive courses lasting three weeks (60 hours) for 78,000Ft and regular evening classes of 60/84 hours for 58,000/79,000Ft.

In addition, the schools below are recommended for either classroom lessons or one-to-one instruction.

Hungarian Language School (Map p86; ☎ 266 2617; www.magyar-iskola.hu; VIII Bródy Sándor utca 4, 1st fl; Ⓜ M3 Kálvin tér)

InterClub Hungarian Language School (Map pp88-9; ☎ 279 0831; www.interclub.hu; XI Bertalan Lajos utca 17; 🚊 47 or 49)

BUDAPEST FOR CHILDREN

Budapest abounds in places that will delight children, and there is always a special child's entry rate (and often a family one) to paying attractions. Group visits to many areas of the city can be designed around a rest stop (or picnic) at, say, City Park, on Margaret Island or along the Danube.

Kids love transport and the city's many unusual forms of conveyance – from the **Cog Railway** (p95) and **Children's Railway** (p95) in the Buda Hills and the **Sikló** (p76) funicular climbing up to Castle Hill, to the trams, trolleybuses and M1 metro – will fascinate and entertain. Specific places to take children include the **Municipal Great Circus** (p128), the **Funfair Park** (p103), the **City Zoo** (p102) and the **Budapest Puppet Theatre** (p128), which still seems to mesmerise young 'uns even in this digital age of computer games. Many kids also love shows in which they can participate, and that's just what the *táncház* (dance house) is all about. Some have afternoon sessions for children, including the **Municipal Cultural House** (p126) and **Budavár Cultural Centre** (p125) in Buda.

More 'educational' (well, hands-on) destinations include the just-for-kids **Palace of Miracles** (p93) and, just next door, the **House of the Future Exhibition** (p93) in Buda's Millennium Park. And don't forget the **Transport Museum** (p102) in City Park.

Among the best playgrounds in town are those on **Margaret Island** (Map pp80–1), about

50m northeast of the fountain at the southern end; on **Hajógyár Island** (Map pp78–9), also called Óbuda Island, about 200m along the main road to the right; and in **Szent István Park** (Map pp80–1).

Lonely Planet's *Travel with Children* by Cathy Lanigan includes all sorts of useful information and advice for those travelling with their little ones.

Babysitting

An ever-growing number of midrange and top-end hotels in Budapest offer babysitting services, although purpose-built casual daycare centres are almost nonexistent. Reputable hotels hire only local qualified sitters. While most can oblige on short notice, try to give the hotel concierge or front-desk staff at least six hours' advance notice.

TOURS

Boat

From late April to late September **Mahart PassNave** (Map p86; ☎ 484 4013; www.mahartpassnave.hu; V Belgrád rakpart) has two-hour cruises along the Danube on the hour from 11am to 7pm and again at 8.30pm and 9.30pm (adult/under 15 years 2900/1490Ft). In the low season, from mid-March to late April and late September to early November, there are between six and eight departures a day, starting at 11am.

Another company running river cruises is **Legenda** (Map p86; ☎ 266 4190; www.legenda.hu; V Vigadó tér, pier No 7), which runs one-/two-hour tours by day (2900/3900Ft) and night tours (4900Ft), with taped commentary in up to 35 languages. Check the website for the schedule.

If you don't give a toss about ever getting your land legs back again, set your sights on the **Power Hour Booze Cruise** (☎ 269 3843; www.powerhourboozecruise.com; adult/student 4500/4000Ft; 🕑 8.30pm Wed May-Sep), which is effectively a one-hour piss-up with nonstop beer for an hour while cruising the Danube. Groups assemble on the steps of the Lutheran church in V Deák Ferenc tér (Map p86).

Bus

Many travel agencies, including **Cityrama** (Map p84; ☎ 302 4382; www.cityrama.hu; V Báthory utca 22) and **Mr Nils** (Map p77; ☎ 302 4567; www.budapestcitytourmrnils.hu; XI Törökbálinti út 28), the latter with departures from V Szent István tér (Map p86), offer three-hour city tours (adult 6500Ft, 12 to 14 years 3000Ft to 3250Ft) with several photo-op stops.

Increasingly popular are the 'hop-on, hop-off' tours run by **Budatours** (Map p86; ☎ 374 7070; www.budatours.hu; VI Andrássy út 2; adult/student & child over 6yr 4000/3000Ft), which depart from V Andrássy út 3 in both open and covered coaches and have 10 different stops. Buses run every half-hour to an hour between 10am and 5.30pm to 7.30pm. Though the ticket is valid for 24 hours, it's a two-hour tour if you just stay on and has taped commentary in 16 different languages. A similar deal is available from **Program Centrum** (Map p86; ☎ 317 7767, 06 20 944 9091; www.programcentrum.hu; V Erzsébet tér 9-10), next to Le Meridien Budapest hotel, though departures are less frequent.

Cycling

Yellow Zebra Bikes (Map p86; ☎ 266 8777; www.yellowzebrabikes.com; V Sütő utca 2; 🕑 10am-6pm Nov-Mar, 8.30am-8pm Apr-Oct; Ⓜ M1/2/3 Deák Ferenc tér) has cycling tours (adult/student 5000/4500Ft) of the city that take in Heroes' Sq, City Park, inner Pest and Castle Hill in 3½ hours. Tours, which include the bike, depart from in front of the Lutheran church in V Deák Ferenc tér (Map p86) at 11am from April to October, with an additional departure at 4pm in July and August. There's also a **branch** (Map p84; ☎ 269 3843; VI Lázár utca 16; 🕑 9.30am-6.30pm Mon-Fri, 10am-4pm Sat & Sun; Ⓜ M1 Opera) at Discover Budapest.

Walking

Run by the same people behind Yellow Zebra Bikes (above), **Absolute Walking Tours** (☎ 266 8777, 269 3843; www.absolutetours.com) has a 3½-hour guided promenade through City Park, central Pest and Castle Hill (adult/student 4000/3500Ft). Tours depart at 9.30am and 1.30pm from April to October and at 10.30am the rest of the year from the steps of the Lutheran church on Deák Ferenc tér (Map p86). It also has some cracker specialist tours, including the Hammer & Sickle Tour (adult/10 to 18 years 7000/3500Ft), the 1956 Revolution Walk (6000/3000Ft) and the Absolute Hungaro Gastro Tour (7000/3500Ft).

Unique (and highly professional) are the walkabouts led by the guides of **Free Budapest Tours** (☎ 06 20 534 5819; www.freebudapesttours.eu), whose name is as descriptive as it is, err, pedestrian. The tours, which take in the Inner Town, the banks of the Danube and the Castle District in 2½ hours, are free of charge, the guides work for tips only (be generous!) and departures are at 10.30am, 2.30pm and 8pm daily from in front of the M1 metro stop in Vörösmarty tér, opposite Gerbeaud (Map p86). An evening thematic tour costs 2500Ft (2000Ft if booked through your hostel) and includes some transport by bus and/or tram.

FESTIVALS & EVENTS

Many festivals and events are held in and around Budapest; look out for the tourist board's annual *Events Calendar* for a complete listing.

January

New Year's Day Concert (www.hungariakoncert.hu) This is an annual event usually held in the Duna Palota on January 1 to herald the new year.

February

Opera Ball (www.operabal.com) This annual, very prestigious event is held usually in the third week of February at the Hungarian State Opera House.

March

Budapest Spring Festival (www.festivalcity.hu) The capital's largest and most important cultural event, with 200 events, takes place for two weeks in late March/early April at five dozen venues across the city.

Budapest Fringe Festival (www.budapestfringe.com) This three-day festival of non-mainstream theatre, music and dance, held in Millennium Park and other venues around town, is a kind of sideshow to the Budapest Spring Festival.

April

National Dance House Festival (www.tanchaztalalkozo.hu/eng) Hungary's biggest *táncház* (p48) is held over two days in early April at the Buda Concert Hall and other venues.

June

Danube Folklore Carnival (www.dunaart.hu) Pan-Hungarian international 10-day carnival of folk, world music and modern dance, held from mid-June in Vörösmarty tér and on Margaret Island.

Bridge Festival (www.festivalcity.hu) Day-long festival of music, dance and street theatre, held on the city's bridges and by the river on or around 21 June to mark the start of summer.

August

Formula One Hungarian Grand Prix (www.hungaroring.hu) Hungary's prime sporting event, held in early August in Magyoród, 24km northeast of the capital.

Sziget Music Festival (www.sziget.hu) Now one of the biggest and most popular music festivals in Europe, held in mid-August on Budapest's Hajógyár (Óbuda) Island.

September

Budapest International Wine Festival (www.winefestival.hu) Hungary's foremost wine-makers introduce their wines in mid-September in the Castle District.

October

Budapest International Marathon (www.budapestmarathon.com) Eastern Europe's most celebrated race goes along the Danube and across its bridges in early October.

November

Budapest Art Fair (www.budapestartfair.hu) Hungary's only forum for representing classical and contemporary fine art and sculpture takes place in late November in the Palace of Art (Műcsarnok) in Heroes' Sq.

December

New Year's Gala & Ball (www.viparts.hu) Gala concert and ball held at the Hungarian State Opera House on 31 December.

SLEEPING

Budget

In Budapest, budget accommodation – hostels, private rooms, *pensions* and camp sites – costs anything under 13,500Ft for a double.

HOSTELS

Hostelling International (HI) cards or their equivalents (see p373) are not required at any hostels in Budapest, but they might bag you a discount of up to 10%. Hostel rates almost always include a simple (Continental) breakfast.

Hostels usually have laundry facilities (around 1500Ft to 2000Ft for a wash and dry), a fully equipped kitchen, storage lockers, a TV lounge with DVDs, no curfew and computers for internet access (almost always free nowadays).

While you can go directly to all of the hostels mentioned here, the travel agency Express (p75) and **Mellow Mood Group** (Map pp80-1; ☎ 343 0748; www.mellowmood.hu; VII Baross tér 15, 3rd fl; Ⓜ M2 Keleti pályaudvar) are the best contacts for budget accommodation information. In fact, the latter, which is affiliated with HI, runs two very central, year-round hostels as well as five that open during summer. You can also make bookings through its **U Tours travel agency** (☎ 343 0748; Keleti train station; 7am-7pm), located near the entrance of the station at the end of platform 6.

Buda

Buda Base (Map p83; ☎ 06 20 543 7481; budabase@gmail.com; I Döbrentei utca 16; dm 3500Ft; 18 or 19, 7 or 86;) Buda hasn't seen anything like the mushrooming of small independent hostels that Pest has recently, but what exists is all quality. Take the Buda Base, a fantastically located hostel by the Danube with 10 beds in a ground-floor dormitory and a loft double with its own bathroom and air-conditioning. You won't soon forget the river view, especially when checking your emails via wi-fi from a bench along the riverside walk. It has two additional apartments available in the same block.

Martos Hostel (Map pp88-9; ☎ 209 4883, 06 30 911 5755; http://hotel.martos.bme.hu; XI Sztoczek József utca 5-7; s/d/tr/q/apt 4000/6000/9000/12,000/15,000Ft, d with shower 8000Ft; 4 or 6;) Though primarily a summer hostel with 200 beds, this student dormitory of the Budapest University of Technology and Economics has about two-dozen beds available year-round. It's reasonably well located, near the Danube, and just a few minutes' walk from Petőfi Bridge.

Pest

Home-Made Hostel (Map p84; ☎ 302 2103; www.homemadehostel.com; VI Teréz körút 22, 1st fl; 8-bed dm €8-15, 6-bed dm €13-17, q per person €14-18, d €40-58; M M1 Oktogon;) This homey, extremely welcoming hostel with 20 beds in four rooms may not deserve inclusion on Unesco's World Heritage List, as its brochure says, but it's unique enough, with recycled tables hanging upside down from the ceiling and old valises under the beds serving as lockers. There's a warmth to this place that will make you want to stay forever, and the old-style kitchen is museum-quality. Maybe it should get that listing.

our pick **Back Pack Guesthouse** (Map pp88-9; ☎ 385 8946; www.backpackbudapest.hu; XI Takács Menyhért utca 33; bed in yurt 2500Ft, large/small dm 3000/3500Ft, d 9000Ft; 7 or 73;) We've always loved this laid-back hostel – Budapest's first! – in a colourfully painted suburban 'villa' in south Buda and we're happy to see more and more hostels are copying its style. The Back Pack is relatively small, with just 50 beds (large dormitories with between seven and 10 beds and small ones with four to five), but the fun (and sleeping bodies in season) spills out into a lovely landscaped garden, with hammocks, a yurt and a Thai-style lounging platform. It's the perfect place for one of the low-cost massages available here. The upbeat attitude of the friendly, much-travelled owner/manager seems to permeate the place, and the welcome is always warm.

Hostel Marco Polo (Map p84; ☎ 413 2555; www.marcopolohostel.com; VII Nyár utca 6; dm 3000-4500Ft, per person s 10,000-18,250Ft, d 6000-8600Ft, tr 5000-6600Ft, q 4500-6000Ft; M M2 Blaha Lujza tér;) The Mellow Mood Group's very central flagship hostel is a swish, powder-blue, 47-room place, with telephones and TVs in all the rooms except the dorms, and a lovely courtyard. Even the five spotless dorms are 'private', with beds separated by lockers and curtains.

11th Hour Hostel (Map p86; ☎ 266 2153; www.11thhourcinemahostel.com; V Magyar utca 11; dm €10-15, tr & q per person from €20; M M2 Astoria;) Just as wonderful as its sister property the Green Bridge Hostel, 11th Hour has half a dozen dorms (six to 12 beds) and two private rooms across three floors in its very own town house. We love the courtyard bar and the low-lit common room with the huge projection screen for watching films.

Gingko Hostel (Map p86; ☎ 266 6107; www.gingko.hu; V Szép utca 5; dm 3500Ft, d/q per person 5500/4500Ft; M M3 Ferenciek tere;) This very green hostel with between 20 and 30 beds in seven big rooms is one of the best-kept in town; the font-of-all-knowledge manager keeps it so clean you could eat off the floor. There are books to share, bikes to rent (2500Ft for 24 hours) and a positively enormous double giving on to Reàltanoda utca.

Unity Hostel (Map p84; ☎ 413 7377; www.unityhostel.com; VI Király utca 60, 3rd fl; dm €12-16, d €36-44; 4 or 6;) This hostel's location in the heart of party town would be draw enough, but add to that a roof terrace with breathtaking views of the Liszt Academy of Music, ceiling fans to cool you down and a resident bearded collie to grab your attention and you've got a winner. There are 24 beds in five rooms over two internal levels – something unique in a Budapest hostel.

Green Bridge Hostel (Map p86; ☎ 266 6922; www.greenbridgehostel.com; V Molnár utca 22-24; dm €12-18, d/

tr/q €50/57/72; M M3 Kálvin tér; ☒ 💻) Few hostels truly stand out in terms of comfort, location and reception, but the five-room Green Bridge has it all – in spades. Bunks are nowhere to be seen, it's on a quiet street just one block in from the Danube and coffee is on offer gratis throughout the day.

Red Bus Hostel (Map p86; ☎ 266 0136; www.redbusbudapest.hu; V Semmelweis utca 14, 1st fl; dm 3900Ft, s & d 9900Ft, tr 13,000Ft; M M1/2/3 Deák Ferenc tér; ☒ 💻) One of the very first truly independent hostels for travellers in Pest, Red Bus is a central and well-managed place, with four large and airy rooms with four to five beds, as well as five private rooms for up to three people. It's a quiet place with a fair number of rules – a full 16 are listed in reception – so don't expect to party here.

Aventura Hostel (Map p84; ☎ 311 1190; www.aventurahostel.com; XIII Visegrádi utca 12, 1st fl; dm €14-21, d €50-60, apt €60-70; M M2 Nyugati pályaudvar, 🚋 4 or 6; ☒ 💻) What has got to be the most chilled hostel in Budapest, with four themed rooms (India, Japan, Africa and – our favourite – Space) and run by two affable ladies, is slightly out of the action in Újlipótváros but easily accessible by public transport. We love the colours and fabrics, the in-house massage and the dorms with loft sleeping.

Central Backpack King Hostel (Map p86; ☎ 06 30 200 7184; www.centralbpk.hu; V Október 6 utca 15, 1st fl; dm €15-19, per person d €27-29, tr €22-24, q €21-23; M M1/2/3 Deák Ferenc tér, 🚌 15 or 115; ☒ 💻) This upbeat place in the heart of the Inner Town has rooms with between seven and nine beds on one floor and another with doubles, triples and quads. There's a small but scrupulously clean kitchen, a large and very bright common room, and views across Október 6 utca to the lovely apartment block at No 16–18, which dates from 1910, where one of Lonely Planet's esteemed authors stays when in town.

PRIVATE ROOMS & APARTMENTS

Private rooms in Budapest generally cost 6000Ft to 7500Ft for a single, 7000Ft to 8500Ft for a double and 9000Ft to 13,000Ft for a small apartment. You might need an indexed city map or atlas (see p72) to find the block where your room is located, though.

Tourinform in Budapest does not arrange private accommodation, but will send you to a travel agency, such as **To-Ma** (Map p86; ☎ 353 0819; www.tomatour.hu; V Október 6 utca 22; 🕑 9am-noon & 1-8pm Mon-Fri, 9am-5pm Sat & Sun; M M1/2/3 Deák Ferenc tér). Among the best places to try for private rooms are Ibusz and Vista (p75) and, in Keleti train station, U Tours (opposite).

PENSIONS & GUEST HOUSES

Budapest has scores of *panzió (pensions)* and guest houses, but most of them are in the outskirts of Pest or in the Buda Hills and not very convenient unless you have your own transport.

Pest

Dominik Panzió (Map pp80-1; ☎ 343 7655; www.dominikpanzio.hu; XIV Cházár András utca 3; s €21-36, d €29-45, tr €39-55, apt €69-100; 🚌 7 or 73; P) Just off Thököly út and located beside a large church, Dominik Panzió is on a leafy street lined with 19th-century villas and just two stops northeast of Keleti train station by bus. The 36 rooms, which could use an upgrade, come with shared bathroom, and there is a five-person apartment available.

Garibaldi Guesthouse & Apartments (Map p84; ☎ 302 3457, 06 30 951 8763; garibaldiguest@hotmail.com; V Garibaldi utca 5, 5th fl; s/d €28/36, apt per person €25-45; M M2 Kossuth Lajos tér) This hostel-cum-guesthouse has five rooms with shared bathroom and kitchen in a flat just around the corner from Parliament. In the same building, the gregarious owner has at least a half-dozen apartments available on several floors and a hostel is being built.

HOTELS

A room in a budget (ie one- or two-star) hotel will cost more than a private room, though the management won't mind if you stay just one night, which can sometimes be a problem when renting a private room.

Buda

Hotel Citadella (Map p83; ☎ 466 5794; www.citadella.hu; XI Citadella sétány; dm 3200Ft, s & d with shared shower/shower/bath 10,500/11,500/12,500Ft; 🚌 27) This hotel in the fortress atop Gellért Hill is pretty threadbare, though the dozen guestrooms are extra large, retain some of their original features and have their own shower (toilets are on the circular corridor). The single dorm room has 14 beds and shared facilities.

Papillon Hotel (Map pp80-1; ☎ 212 4750; www.hotelpapillon.hu; II Rózsahegy utca 3/b; s €31-44, d €41-60, tr €56-75, apt for 3/5 people €72/90; 4 or 6;) One of Buda's best-kept accommodation secrets, this small 20-room hotel in Rózsadomb has a delightful back garden with a small swimming pool, and some rooms have balconies. There are also four apartments available in the same building, one of which boasts a lovely roof terrace.

Hotel Császár (Map pp80-1; ☎ 336 2640; www.csaszarhotel.hu; II Frankel Leó út 35; s €33-45, d €43-59, tr €70-91, ste €99-116; 17, 86;) The huge yellow building in which the 'Emperor' is located was built in the 1850s as a convent, which might explain the size of the 45 cell-like rooms. Request one of the superior rooms, which are larger and look onto the nearby outdoor Olympic-sized pools of the huge Császár-Komjádi swimming complex (p105).

Margaret Island

Hotel Margitsziget (Map pp80-1; ☎ 450 0105; www.hotelmsz.hu; Hajós Alfréd sétány 75, XIII Margit-sziget; s €37-53, d €43-55; 26;) This 11-room budget hotel in the centre of Margaret Island is surrounded by greenery and feels almost like a resort. If you really want to get away from it all on a budget but remain within easy striking distance of the action, choose this place. Rooms 11 to 14 have balconies.

Pest

Flandria Hotel (Map pp78-9; ☎ 350 3181; www.hotelflandria.hu, in Hungarian; XIII Szegedi út 27; s/d/tr/q with washbasin 6200/7500/10,300/11,600Ft, with shower 10,200/12,400/14,100/16,200Ft; 32, 4;) The Flandria is a classic example of a former workers' hostel that has metamorphosed into a budget hotel. Don't expect anything within a couple of light years of luxury, but the 125 guestrooms, which have from one to four beds, TV and refrigerator, are clean, serviceable and very cheap.

Hotel Rila (Map pp88-9; ☎ 323 2999; www.hotelrila.com; IX Fehér Holló utca 2; dm 4000-4500Ft, without bathroom s 7000-9000Ft, d 10,000-13,000Ft, with bathroom s 9000-12,000Ft, d 12,000-15,000Ft, tr 15,000-18,750Ft; M3 Nagyvárad tér, 24;) A former workers' hostel, the 39-room Rila has been spruced up into quite a nice little property. Open year-round, it has both hostel accommodation and rooms for between one and four people (both with and without bathrooms). We like the rustic Hungarian restaurant with old photographs on the walls.

CAMPING

Buda

Római Camping (Map pp78-9; ☎ 388 7167; www.romaicamping.hu; III Szentendrei út 189; camp sites per person/tent/campervan/caravan 1150/3120/3920/5320Ft, 1st-class cabins for 6 people 17,625Ft, 2nd-/3rd-class cabins per person 2930/2115Ft; year-round;) Located in a leafy park north of the city, opposite the popular Rómaifürdő swimming pool complex (p104), this is the city's largest camping ground. To get here, take the HÉV suburban railway from the Batthyány tér metro station in Buda to the Rómaifürdő station, which is almost opposite the site.

Zugligeti Niche Camping (off Map p77; ☎ 200 8346; www.campingniche.hu; XII Zugligeti út 101; camp sites per person/small tent/big tent/campervan 1800/1500/2000/3200Ft; year-round; 291;) This is a small camp site in the Buda Hills for 200 campers, located at the bottom station of the chairlift.

Midrange

Budapest is not bereft of midrange options altogether, but they are not as plentiful as in Western European cities. Midrange – usually *pensions*, guest houses and hotels – means anything between 13,500Ft and 30,000Ft for a double during any season.

BUDA

Büro Panzió (Map p83; ☎ 212 2929; www.buropanzio.hu; II Dékán utca 3, 1st fl; s €42-50, d €56-64, tr €72-76, q €82-92; M2 Moszkva tér;) A *pension* just a block off the northern side of Moszkva tér, this place looks basic from the outside but its 10 small rooms are comfortable and have TV and telephone.

Charles Hotel & Apartments (Map p83; ☎ 212 9169; www.charleshotel.hu; I Hegyalja út 23; standard studio s & d €45-65, tr €60-80, deluxe studio s & d €60-80, tr €75-95, apt €75-155; 8, 112 or 178;) On the Buda side and somewhat on the beaten track (a train line runs right past it), the Charles has 70 'studios' (larger-than-average rooms) with tiny kitchens and weary-looking furniture as well as two-room apartments. It also has bikes for rent for 2000Ft per day.

Beatrix Panzió Hotel (Map p77; ☎ 275 0550; www.beatrixhotel.hu; II Széher út 3; s €50-60, d €60-70, tr €70-80, apt €80-210; 29, 18 or 56;) Up in the Buda Hills but easily accessible by public transport, this is an attractive, award-winning *pension* with 18 rooms and four apartments. Surrounding the property is a lovely garden with fishpond, sun terraces and a grill;

you might even organise a barbecue during your stay.

Hotel Kulturinnov (Map p83; ☎ 224 8102; www.mka.hu; I Szentháromság tér 6; s/d/tr €60/75/100; 🚌 16, 16A or 116) A 16-room hotel in the former Finance Ministry, a neo-Gothic structure dating back to 1904, the Kulturinnov can't be beat for location and price in the Castle District. The guestrooms, though clean and with private bathrooms, are not as nice as the public areas seem to promise.

Hotel Astra (Map p83; ☎ 214 1906; www.hotelastra.hu; I Vám utca 6; s €65-97, d €75-112, ste €129-139; Ⓜ M2 Batthyány tér, 🚌 86; ☒ ❄ 💻) Tucked away in a small street west of Fő utca and just below the Castle District is this hotel-cum-guest house in a centuries-old town house. It has nine double rooms and three suites, one of which has a strange niche illustrated with a mosque and is probably a *mihrab* (Muslim prayer nook) dating back to the Turkish occupation.

Carlton Hotel (Map p83; ☎ 224 0999; www.carltonhotel.hu; I Apor Péter utca 3; s €75-95, d €85-110, tr €100-130; 🚌 86; Ⓟ ❄ 💻) This 95-room hotel at the foot of Castle Hill and at the end of a narrow cul-de-sac in Víziváros is a good choice if you plan to divide your time equally between Pest and Buda. A half-dozen of the rooms lead into a small courtyard garden.

Orion Hotel (Map p83; ☎ 356 8583; www.bestwestern-ce.com/orion; I Döbrentei utca 13; s €75-95, d €95-125, ste €160; 🚋 18 or 19; ☒ ❄ 💻) Hidden away in the Tabán district, this is a cosy place with a relaxed atmosphere and within easy walking distance of the Castle District. The 30 rooms are bright and of a good size, and there's a small sauna for guests' use.

Hotel Victoria (Map p83; ☎ 457 8080; www.victoria.hu; I Bem rakpart 11; s €79-117, d €86-123; 🚌 86, 🚋 19; Ⓟ ☒ ❄ 💻) This rather elegant hotel has 27 comfortable and spacious rooms with larger-than-life views of Parliament and the Danube. Despite its small size it gets special mention for its friendly service and facilities, including the recently renovated rooms of the 19th-century Jenő Hubay Music Hall, attached to and accessible from the hotel and now serving as a small theatre and series of function rooms.

Burg Hotel (Map p83; ☎ 212 0269; www.burghotelbudapest.com; I Szentháromság tér 7-8; s €85-105, d €99-115, ste €109-134; 🚌 16, 16A or 116; ☒ ❄ 💻) This small hotel with all the mod cons is in the Castle District, just opposite Matthias Church. The 26 partly refurbished rooms look fresher but are not much more than just ordinary. But, as they say, location is everything and midrange options are as scarce as hen's teeth on Castle Hill.

PEST

KM Saga Guest Residence (Map p86; ☎ 217 1934; www.km-saga.hu; IX Lónyay utca 17, 3rd fl; s €42-63, d €55-82; 🚌 15 or 115, 🚋 47 or 49; ❄ 💻) This unique place has five themed rooms, an eclectic mix of 19th-century furnishings and a hospitable, multilingual, Hungarian-American owner. It's essentially a gay B&B, but everyone is welcome. **KM Saga II Guest Residence** (Map p86; ☎ 217 1934; IX Vámház körút 11, 6th fl; Ⓜ M2 Kálvin tér; ❄ 💻) is somewhat more modern but less atmospheric, and has three rooms and an 82-sq-m apartment.

Connection Guest House (Map p86; ☎ 267 7104; www.connectionguesthouse.com; VII Király utca 41; s €45-60, d €50-73; Ⓜ M1 Opera; ☒ 💻) This very central gay *pension* above a leafy courtyard attracts a young crowd due to its proximity to nightlife venues. Three of the seven rooms share facilities on the corridor, and rooms 6 and 7 face partially pedestrianised Király utca.

Hotel Medosz (Map p84; ☎ 353 1700; www.medoszhotel.hu; VI Jókai tér 9; s €49-59, d €59-69, tr €69-79, ste €89-100; Ⓜ M1 Oktogon) One of the most central midrange hotels in Pest, the Medosz is just opposite the restaurants and bars of Liszt Ferenc tér. The 68 rooms are well worn but were slated for a revamp at the time of writing. Each has a private bathroom and satellite TV; the best rooms are in the main block, not in the labyrinthine wings.

Leó Panzió (Map p86; ☎ 266 9041; www.leopanzio.hu; V Kossuth Lajos utca 2/a, 2nd fl; s €49-79, d €76-99; Ⓜ M3 Ferenciek tere) This place with a lion theme would be a 'find' just on the strength of its central location, but when you factor in the low cost, this B&B is the king of the jungle. A dozen of its 14 immaculate rooms look down on busy Kossuth Lajos utca, but they all have double-glazing and are quiet. The other two rooms face the rather dark internal courtyard.

Atlas Hotel (Map pp80-1; ☎ 299 0256; www.atlashotel.hu; VIII Népszínház utca 39-41; s €50-68, d €58-88, tr €75-120, q €92-152; 🚋 28 or 37; Ⓟ ☒ ❄ 💻) This enormous place, spread over eight floors in less-than-salubrious district VIII, has 102 standard (though comfortable) renovated singles, doubles, triples and quads as well as another three dozen superior doubles. It is said that you'll always find a room at the Atlas, which may (or may not) be a recommendation.

Thomas Hotel (Map pp88-9; ☎ 218 5505; www.hotels.hu/hotelthomas; IX Liliom utca 44; s €55-65, d €75-95; M M3 Ferenc körút; P) A brightly coloured place in an odd location, this hotel has 43 rooms and is a real bargain for its location in *still* up-and-coming Ferencváros. Some rooms have balconies looking onto an inner courtyard. The kid in the logo is the owner as a young 'un.

Boat Hotel Fortuna (Map pp80-1; ☎ 288 8100; www.fortunahajo.hu; XIII Szent István Park, Pesti alsó rakpart; with bathroom s €55-80, d €65-100, tr €80-120, with washbasin s €20-25, d €30-35, tr €40-47; trolleybus 76) Sleeping on a one-time river ferry anchored in the Danube that goes nowhere may not be everyone's idea of a good time, but it's a unique experience. This 'boatel' has 42 single and double air-conditioned rooms with shower and toilet at water level, and 14 rooms with two or three beds and washbasin below deck that are not so nice and almost feel like old-fashioned hostel accommodation.

Délibáb Hotel (Map pp80-1; ☎ 342 9301; www.hoteldelibab.hu; VI Délibáb utca 35; s €57-71, d €68-83, tr €85-100; M M1 Hősök tere; P) The 34-room 'Mirage' is housed in what was once a Jewish orphanage across from Hősök tere and City Park. It is pretty bare-bones as it still awaits its overdue renovation by the Mellow Mood Group. Ask for one of the nine rooms that face the quiet courtyard to the rear, as the rest look onto busy Dózsa György út.

Benczúr Hotel (Map pp80-1; ☎ 479 5662; www.hotelbenczur.hu; VI Benczúr utca 35; s €60-76, d €75-92, tr €90-111; M M1 Bajza utca; P) This rather faded place done up in creams and oranges has 161 serviceable rooms over seven floors, of which about 65 have been renovated in recent years. Some of these look down on a leafy garden. The hotel is just minutes away from Andrássy út, Heroes' Sq and City Park.

Hotel Baross (Map pp80-1; ☎ 461 3010; www.barosshotel.hu; VII Baross tér 15, 4th-6th fl; s €60-82, d €74-98, tr €90-114, q €100-136; M M2 Keleti pályaudvar) The flagship hotel of the Mellow Mood Group, the Hotel Baross is a comfortable, 49-room caravanserai conveniently located directly opposite Keleti train station. The very blue inner courtyard is a delight, and reception, which is on the 5th floor, is clean and bright, with a dramatic central staircase.

Corvin Hotel (Map pp88-9; ☎ 218 6566; www.corvinhotelbudapest.hu; IX Angyal utca 31; s €60-85, d €75-99, tr €90-110, apt €105-129; M M3 Ferenc körút; P) Close to the Danube, this purpose-built hotel in Ferencváros has 47 very comfortable rooms with all the mod cons and secure parking in a covered garage. The bright and airy breakfast room is a real plus.

Star Hotel (Map pp80-1; ☎ 479 0420; www.starhotel.hu; VII István út 14; s €60-85, d €75-95, tr €85-120, q €100-140; trolleybus 74 or 79) An addition to the Mellow Mood Group's stable is this brightly coloured midrange hotel just a few minutes' walk north of Keleti train station. The ground-floor lobby is quite spacious and a popular meeting place for travellers; most of the guestrooms are doubles spread over four floors.

City Ring Hotel (Map p84; ☎ 340 5450; www.cityhotels.hu; XIII Szent István körút 22; s €61-89, d €69-108, tr €89-134; M M3 Nyugati pályaudvar) This small, almost motel-like place with 39 rooms is on two floors of a *fin-de-siècle* building but you'd never know that from the inside looking out. Some of the rooms gaze down onto the busy ring road, others onto an attractive and very quiet courtyard.

Radio Inn (Map pp80-1; ☎ 342 8347; www.radioinn.hu; VI Benczúr utca 19; s/d €65/78, apt €80-120; M M1 Bajza utca) Just off leafy Andrássy út, this place is a real find. It has 23 large one-bedroom apartments with bathroom and kitchen, 10 with two bedrooms and one with three bedrooms, measuring between 44 and 60 sq m, all spread over five floors. The garden courtyard is a delight; try to get a room with a small balcony.

Hotel Anna (Map p84; ☎ 327 2000; www.annahotel.hu; VIII Gyulai Pál utca; s €66-98, d €82-125, ste €88-149; M M3 Blaha Lujza tér, 7 or 78) Run by the same people who own Fülemüle (p118) and just across the street, Anna has 42 fairly basic rooms but feels twice that size as they are strewn over three floors of two 18th-century buildings surrounding an enormous courtyard and garden. It doesn't offer the greatest value for money in town, but rooms are quieter than the grave and the location is great.

Cotton House (Map p84; ☎ 354 2600; www.cottonhouse.hu; Jókai utca 26; s & d €70-150; 4 or 6) This 23-room guest house has a jazz/speakeasy theme that gets a bit tired after a while – though the old radios and vintage telephones actually work. Prices vary widely depending on the season and whether there's a shower, tub or Jacuzzi in the bathroom.

Erzsébet Hotel (Map p86; ☎ 889 3700; www.danubiusgroup.com/erzsebet; V Károlyi Mihály utca 11-15; s €72-102, d €84-114; M M2 Ferenciek tere;) One of Budapest's first independent hotels, the Erzsébet is in a very good location in the centre of the university district and within easy walking distance of the pubs and bars of Ráday utca. The 123 guestrooms – mostly twins – spread across eight floors are small and dark, with generic hotel furniture, but are comfortable enough.

Hotel Sissi (Map pp88-9; ☎ 215 0082; www.hotelsissi.hu; IX Angyal utca 33; s €90-130, d €100-140, ste €150-180; M M3 Ferenc körút; P) Named in honour of Elizabeth, the Habsburg empress, Hungarian queen and consort of Franz Joseph, who was much beloved by Hungarians, the Hotel Sissi is decorated in a minimalist-cum-elegant sort of style, and the 44 guestrooms spread over six floors are of a good size. Some rooms look onto a back garden.

Top End

Double-room rates at top-end hotels start at around 30,000Ft. From there the sky's the limit.

BUDA

Danubius Gellért Hotel (Map pp88-9; ☎ 889 5500; www.danubiusgroup.com/gellert; XI Szent Gellért tér 1; s €67-110, d €135-216, ste €233-268; 18, 19, 47 or 49; P) Budapest's *grande dame* is a 234-room, four-star hotel with loads of character. The gorgeous thermal baths are free for guests, but overall its other facilities are forgettable. Prices depend on which way your room faces and what sort of bathroom it has.

our pick **Lánchíd 19** (Map p83; ☎ 419 1900; www.lanchid19hotel.hu; I Lánchíd utca 19; s €120-175, d €140-225, ste €300-400; 86, 19;) We've visited, inspected and stayed in lots of hotels in our time, but this new boutique number facing the Danube has the 'wow' factor in spades. And it's not just us who think so. The Lánchíd 19 won the European Hotel Design Award for Best Architecture in 2008 and, watching its facade form pictures as special sensors reflect and follow the movement of the Danube, we can't but agree. Each of the 45 rooms and three 'panoramic' suites is different, with distinctive artwork and a unique chair ('can you *sit* on that?!?') designed by students at art college. And you can't lose with the views: to the front it's the Danube and to the back Buda Castle.

PEST

Soho Hotel (Map p84; ☎ 872 8292, 06 20 779 6341; www.sohohotel.hu; VII Dohány utca 64; s €99-125, d €109-135, ste €169-199; M M2 Blaha Lujza tér, 4 or 6;) This delightfully stylish boutique hotel with 68 rooms and six suites has opened just opposite the New York Palace (p100) and we know which one feels more like the Big Apple. We love the lobby bar in eye-popping reds, blues and lime greens, the nonallergenic rooms with bamboo matting on the walls and parquet floors, and the music/film theme throughout (check out the portraits of Bono, George Michael and Marilyn).

Andrássy Hotel (Map pp80-1; ☎ 462 2100; www.andrassyhotel.com; VI Andrássy út 111; s & d €135-235, ste from €245; M M1 Hősök tere; P) This stunning, five-star hotel just off leafy Andrássy út (enter from Munkácsy Mihály utca 5–7) has 70 tastefully decorated rooms (almost half of which have balconies). The lobby and ground-floor restaurant look fresher, as do many of the guestrooms since their recent renovation. The use in many rooms of etched glass and mirrors as well as wrought iron is inspired.

Corinthia Grand Hotel Royal (Map p84; ☎ 479 4000; www.corinthia.hu; VII Erzsébet körút 43-49; s & d €179-280, ste from €310; 4 or 6; P) Decades in the remaking, the one-time Royal Hotel on the Big Ring Road is now a very grand 414-room, five-star hotel. Its lobby – a double atrium with a massive marble staircase – is among the most impressive in the capital, and the restored Royal Spa, dating back to 1886 but now as modern as tomorrow, is truly the 'legend reborn' we've all been waiting for.

Four Seasons Gresham Palace Hotel (Map p86; ☎ 268 6000; www.fourseasons.com/budapest; V Roosevelt tér 5-6; s €305-850, d €340-885, ste from €1090; M M1 Vörösmarty tér, 16; P) This magnificent 179-room hotel was created out of the long-derelict Art Nouveau Gresham Palace (1907) and a lot of angst and hard work. No expense was spared to piece back together the palace's Zsolnay tiles, famous wrought-iron Peacock Gates and splendid mosaics, and the hotel is truly worthy of its name. You want face and got the dosh? This is simply the best hotel in town.

EATING

Very roughly, a two-course sit-down meal for one person with a glass of wine or beer for under 3000Ft in Budapest is 'cheap', while a 'moderate' meal will cost up to 6500Ft. There's a big jump to an 'expensive' meal (6500Ft to 10,000Ft), and 'very expensive' is anything above that.

Most restaurants are open from 10am or 11am to 11pm or midnight; if there are no times listed under a particular review, you can expect the place to be open between those hours. It's always best to arrive by 9pm or 10pm at the latest, though, to ensure being served. It is advisable to book tables at medium-priced to expensive restaurants, especially at the weekend.

Buda

HUNGARIAN RESTAURANTS

Szent Jupát (Map p83; ☎ 212 2923; II Dékán utca 3; mains 1490-3380Ft; noon-2am Sun-Thu, to 4am Fri & Sat; M M2 Moszkva tér) This is the classic late-night choice for solid Hungarian fare – consider splitting a dish with a friend – and there's half a dozen vegetarian choices, too. It's just north of Moszkva tér and opposite the Fény utca market (enter from II Retek utca 16), so it's within easy striking distance of both Buda and Pest.

Kisbuda Gyöngye (Map pp78-9; ☎ 368 6402; III Kenyeres utca 34; mains 1880-4680Ft; noon-midnight Mon-Sat; 160 or 260, 17) This is a traditional and very elegant Hungarian restaurant in Óbuda; the antique-cluttered dining room and attentive service manage to create a *fin-de-siècle* atmosphere. Try the excellent goose liver speciality plate with a glass of Tokaj (3380Ft) or a pedestrian dish such as *csirke paprikás* (chicken paprika; 2680Ft).

Kéhli (Map pp78-9; ☎ 368 0613; III Mókus utca 22; mains 1990-6290Ft; noon-11.30pm; HÉV Árpád híd) A rustic but stylish place in Óbuda, Kéhli has some of the best traditional Hungarian food in town. In fact, one of Hungary's best-loved writers, the novelist Gyula Krúdy (1878–1933), who lived in nearby Dugovits Titusz tér and whose statue greets you outside the restaurant, moonlighted as a restaurant critic and enjoyed Kéhli's bone marrow on toast (990Ft as an entrée) so much that he included it in one of his novels.

Tabáni Terasz (Map p83; ☎ 201 1086; I Apród utca 10; mains 2600-4900Ft; noon-midnight; 86) This delightful terrace and cellar restaurant at the foot of Castle Hill is a somewhat modern take on Hungarian cuisine, with less calorific dishes and an excellent wine selection. The candlelit cellar is a delight in winter. Set lunch is a snip at under €6.

INTERNATIONAL RESTAURANTS

Remíz (Map p77; ☎ 394 1896; II Budakeszi út 5; mains 2220-4560Ft; 22, 56) Next to a *remíz* (tram depot) in the Buda Hills, this virtual institution remains popular for its reliable food (try the grilled dishes, especially the ribs; 2180Ft to 2980Ft), prices and verdant garden terrace.

Csalogány 26 (Map p83; ☎ 201 7892; I Csalogány utca 26; mains 2800-4000Ft; noon-3pm & 7pm-midnight Tue-Sat; M M2 Batthyány tér) Judged by Hungary's most respected food guide to be the best restaurant in Budapest (the chef comes from Lou Lou, p119), this new institution with the unimaginative name and decor turns its attention to its superb food. Try the tenderloin of Mangalica (a kind of pork) with puy lentils (2800Ft) or the Australian lamb shoulder with polenta (4000Ft). A two-/three-course set lunch is 1200/1400Ft.

Rivalda (Map p83; ☎ 489 0236; I Színház utca 5-9; mains 3100-5600Ft; 11.30am-11.30pm; 16, 16A or 116) A cafe-restaurant offering international favourites in a former convent next to the National Dance Theatre, Rivalda has a thespian theme, delightful garden courtyard and excellent service. This remains one of the very few places we'd choose to visit in the generally touristy and expensive Castle District.

FRENCH RESTAURANTS

Le Jardin de Paris (Map p83; ☎ 201 0047; II Fő utca 20; mains 2200-4700Ft; noon-midnight; 86) A regular haunt of staff from the French Institute across the road (who should know their *cuisine française*), 'The Parisian Garden' is in a wonderful old town house abutting an ancient castle wall with interesting reliefs on the facade. The back garden is a delight in the warmer months. Set lunch is 1500Ft.

ITALIAN RESTAURANTS

Marcello (Map pp88-9; ☎ 466 6231; XI Bartók Béla út 40; pizza 850-980Ft, pasta 1080-1550Ft, mains 2000Ft; noon-10pm Mon-Sat; 47 or 49) Popular with students from the nearby university since it opened almost two decades ago, this father-and-son-owned eatery has good Italian fare at affordable prices. The salad bar (large/small 980/680Ft) is great value and the lasagne (1200Ft) is legendary in these parts.

ASIAN RESTAURANTS

Új Lanzhou (Map pp80-1; ☎ 201 9247; II Fő utca 71; rice & noodle dishes 1290-1690Ft, mains 1190-3290Ft; noon-11pm; 86) A lot of people think this is the most authentic Chinese restaurant in Budapest. We're still out to lunch on the matter but we like the hot-and-sour soup (320Ft), the relatively large choice of vegetarian dishes and the stylish surrounds.

Mongolian Barbecue (Map pp80-1; ☎ 212 1859; XII Márvány utca 19/a; buffet before 5pm 2990Ft, after 5pm & Sat & Sun 4990Ft; noon-5pm & 6pm-midnight; 105, 61) This is one of those predictable all-you-can-eat, pseudo-Asian places, but this one includes as much beer, wine and sangria you can sink for the price. In summer, seating is also available in an attractive, tree-filled courtyard.

Wasabi (Map pp78-9; ☎ 430 1056; III Szépvölgyi út 15; lunch Mon-Fri 3990Ft, Sat & Sun 4990Ft, dinner 4990Ft; 86) This sushi restaurant with a central conveyor belt has more than five-dozen items to choose from and the decor is dark, minimalist and very cool. There's also a central **Pest branch** (Map p84; ☎ 374 0008; VI Podmaniczky utca 21; M M3 Nyugati pályaudvar).

VEGETARIAN RESTAURANTS

Éden (Map p83; ☎ 06 20 337 7575; I Iskola utca 31; mains 790-990Ft; 8am-9pm Mon-Thu, to 6pm Fri, 11am-9pm Sun; 86) In a new location in an old town house dating to 1811, just below Castle Hill, this self-service place offers stodgy but healthy vegetarian platters and ragouts. Seating is in the main dining room on the ground floor or, in warmer months, in the atrium courtyard.

CAFES & TEA HOUSES

Budapest has always been as famous as Vienna for its cafes, cake shops and cafe culture; at the start of the 20th century the city counted more than 500 cafes, but by the collapse of communism in 1989 there were scarcely a dozen left. The majority of the traditional cafes are in Pest, but Buda still lays claim to a handful.

Ruszwurm (Map p83; ☎ 375 5284; I Szentháromság utca 7; cakes 200-550Ft; 10am-7pm; 16, 16A or 116) This is the perfect place for coffee and cakes in the Castle District, though it can get pretty crowded. It's almost always impossible to get a seat.

Daubner (Map pp78-9; ☎ 335 2253; II Szépvölgyi út 50; cakes 250-450Ft; 9am-7pm Tue-Sun; 65) It may seem quite a journey for your Sachertorte, and you can only stand and nibble on the hoof here, but Daubner gets rave reviews from locals and expats alike as the best cake shop in town.

Angelika (Map p83; ☎ 225 1653; I Batthyány tér 7; cakes 320-390Ft; 9am-midnight Mon-Sat, to 11pm Sun; M M2 Batthyány tér) Angelika is a charming cafe attached to an 18th-century church, with a raised terrace. The more substantial food (salads 1390Ft to 2290Ft, sandwiches 1190Ft to 1390Ft) is just so-so; come here for the cakes and the views across the square to the Danube.

Auguszt (Map pp80-1; ☎ 316 3817; II Fény utca 8, 1st fl; cakes 350-450Ft; 10am-6pm Tue-Fri, 9am-6pm Sat; M M2 Moszkva tér) Tucked away on the 1st floor of a building behind the Fény utca market and Mammut shopping mall, this is the original Auguszt cafe (there are two newer branches) and only sells its own cakes, pastries and biscuits.

QUICK EATS

International fast-food places are a dime a dozen in Budapest, but old-style self-service restaurants, the mainstay of both white- and blue-collar workers in the old regime, are disappearing fast. As everywhere else, pizzerias are on an upward spiral.

Artigiana Gelati (Map pp80-1; ☎ 212 2439; XII Csaba utca 8; per scoop 220Ft; 10.30am-7.30pm Tue-Sun; M M2 Moszkva tér) Readers tells us that this place sells the best shop-made ice cream and sorbet in town, and with choices like fig, pomegranate and gorgonzola-walnut, they're also the most unusual.

Nagyi Palacsintázója (Granny's Palacsinta Place; 24hr; Buda Map p83; ☎ 201 5321; I Hattyú utca 16; set menus 760-950Ft; M M2 Moszkva tér; Buda Map p83; ☎ 212 4866; I Batthyány tér 5; M M2 Batthyány tér; Óbuda Map pp78-9; ☎ 212 4866; III Záhony utca 2; 34 or 106; Pest Map p86; ☎ 411 0721; V Petőfi Sándor tér 17-19; M M1/2/3 Deák Ferenc tér) This place, with branches in Buda, Óbuda and Pest, serves Hungarian pancakes or crêpes – both the savoury (240Ft to 620Ft) and sweet (130Ft to 640Ft) varieties – round the clock and is always packed.

Fortuna Önkiszolgáló (Fortuna Self-Service Restaurant; Map p83; ☎ 375 2401; I Fortuna utca 4; mains 700-950Ft; 11.30am-2.30pm Mon-Fri; 16, 16A or 116) You'll find cheap and quick weekday lunches in a place you'd least expect it – the Castle District – at this very basic but clean and cheerful self-service restaurant. Reach it via the stairs on the left side as you enter the Fortuna Passage.

Nagyi Kifözde (Map pp80-1; ☎ 326 2060; Frankel Leó út 36; mains 990-1100Ft; 11.30am-5pm; 4, 6 or 17) Our favourite new homestyle eatery serving Hungarian comfort food in Buda is 'Granny's Canteen', just opposite the Lukács Baths (p103). It's worth a visit for the decor alone.

MARKETS & SELF-CATERING

Budapest counts some 20 large food markets, with the lion's share of them in Pest. **Fény utca market** (Fény utcai piac; Map pp80-1; II Fény utca; 6am-6pm Mon-Fri, to 2pm Sat; M M2 Moszkva tér), one of the largest in Buda, is just next to the Mammut shopping mall.

'Nonstop' (ie 24-hour) shops selling everything from cheese and cold cuts to cigarettes and beer abound in Buda. One conveniently located option is **Nonstop Büfé** (Map p83; I Attila utca 57; 24hr; 5), which also serves prepared foods round the clock.

Pest

HUNGARIAN RESTAURANTS

Köleves (Map p86; 322 1011, 06 20 213 5999; cnr Kazinczy utca 35 & Dob utca 26; mains 1280-3680Ft; noon-midnight; 4 or 6, trolleybus 74) Always buzzy and lots of fun, 'Stone Soup' attracts a young crowd with its delicious matzo-ball soup (large/small 960/670Ft), tapas, lively decor and reasonable prices. It's a great place to try Hungarian food for the first time.

M Restaurant (Map p84; 322 3108; VII Kertész utca 48; mains 1500-2600Ft; 6pm-midnight; 4 or 6) What started life a few years back as a simple little place looking more *menza* than Menza (below) has evolved into a stylish place (love those walls lined with brown paper, and the graphics) with an ever-changing menu of Hungarian dishes with a French twist. The atmosphere is so chilled it's almost comatose.

Menza (Map p84; 413 1482; VI Liszt Ferenc tér 2; mains 1890-2490Ft; 10am-1am; 4 or 6) This stylish Hungarian restaurant on Budapest's liveliest square takes its name from the Hungarian for a drab school canteen – something it is anything but. Book a table: it's always packed with diners who come for its simply but perfectly cooked Hungarian classics with a modern twist, and the chilled atmosphere. Weekday two-course set lunches are 890Ft.

Vörös Postakocsi (Map p86; 217 6756; IX Ráday 15; mains 1900-4000Ft; 11.30am-midnight; 15 or 115) What was for more than three decades a more-than-forgettable eatery serving Hungarian stodge has turned into a trendy retro-style Hungarian restaurant with a lively Gypsy band. If you want a take on how modern Hungarians think they used to eat when times were tougher (and less health-conscious), visit the 'Red Postal Coach'.

Fülemüle (Map p84; 266 7947; VIII Kőfaragó utca 5; mains 1900-4800Ft; noon-10pm Sun-Thu, to 11pm Fri & Sat; 7 or 78) This quaint Hungarian restaurant, which looks like time stood still just before WWII, is quite a find in deepest Józsefváros and well worth the search. Dishes mingle Hungarian and international tastes with some old-style Jewish favourites.

Múzeum (Map p86; 267 0375; VIII Múzeum körút 12; soups 900-1100Ft, mains 2800-5400Ft; noon-midnight Mon-Sat; 47 or 49) This is the place to come if you like to dine in old-world style, with a piano softly tinkling in the background. It's a cafe-restaurant that is still going strong after 125 years at the same location near the National Museum. The goose-liver parfait (3900Ft) is to die for, and there's a good selection of Hungarian wines.

Bagolyvár (Map pp80-1; 468 3110; XIV Állatkerti út 2; mains 2850-4250Ft; noon-11pm; M M1 Hősök tere) With reworked Hungarian classics that make it a winner, the 'Owl's Castle' attracts the Budapest cognoscenti, who leave its sister restaurant, Gundel, next door to the expense-account brigade. It's staffed entirely by women – in the kitchen, at table and front of house.

INTERNATIONAL RESTAURANTS

Café Kör (Map p86; 311 0053; V Sas utca 17; salads 910-1590Ft, mains 1560-4190Ft; 10am-10pm Mon-Sat; M M3 Arany János utca, 15) Just behind St Stephen's Basilica, the 'Circle Café' is a great place for a light meal at any time, including late breakfast till noon. Salads, desserts and daily specials are usually very good.

Café Alibi (Map p86; 317 4209; V Egyetem tér 4; sandwiches 990-1250Ft, salads 1190-1490Ft; 8am-9pm Mon-Wed, to 10pm Thu-Sat, 9am-9pm Sun; M M3 Ferenciek tere) This cafe-restaurant in the heart of Student Land also does more substantial mains (1290Ft to 1590Ft) and even the occasional set dinner paired with Hungarian wines (8990Ft), but we come here for late breakfast (till noon), snacks (650Ft to 1190Ft) and light meals.

our pick **Klassz** (Map p84; 413 1545; www.klassz.eu; VI Andrássy út 41; mains 1490-3490Ft; 11.30am-11pm Mon-Sat, to 6pm Sun; M M1 Oktogon) Probably our favourite restaurant in Budapest at the moment, Klassz is mostly about wine – Hungarian to be precise – and here you can order by the 10cL measure from an ever-changing list of up to four-dozen wines to sip and compare. You can also buy a bottle to take away from the in-house wine shop. Unusually for a wine restaurant, the food is of a very high standard and the cooking uniformly excellent, with foie gras in its various avatars and native Mangalica pork permanent fixtures on the menu. There are also more unusual dishes (for Hungary, at least), such as Burgundy-style leg of rabbit and lamb trotters with vegetable ragout, playing cameo roles. We love the big bright dining room on two levels and the homely floral wallpaper. We don't love having to wait for a table – reservations are not accepted – but we will, again and again.

Soul Café (Map p86; ☎ 217 6986; IX Ráday utca 11-13; mains 1990-4390Ft; ⏰ noon-11.30pm; Ⓜ M3 Kálvin tér) One of the better choices along a street heaving with so-so restaurants and iffy, attitudy cafes, the Soul has inventive Continental food and decor and a great terrace on both sides of the street.

Marquis de Salade (Map p84; ☎ 302 4086; VI Hajós utca 43; mains 2400-3400Ft; ⏰ noon-midnight; Ⓜ M3 Arany János utca, trolleybus 72 or 73) This basement restaurant is a strange hybrid of a place, with dishes from Russia and Azerbaijan as well as Hungary. There are lots of quality vegetarian choices, too.

Troféa Grill (Map pp80-1; ☎ 270 0366; XIII Visegrádi utca 50/a; lunch/dinner Mon-Thu 2999/3999Ft, lunch & dinner Fri-Sun 4299Ft; ⏰ noon-midnight Mon-Fri, 11.30am-midnight Sat, 11.30am-9pm Sun; Ⓜ M3 Lehel tér) This is the place to head when you really could eat a horse (which might be on one of the tables). It's an enormous buffet of more than 100 cold and hot dishes over which diners swarm like bees while being observed by the cooks from their kitchen. There's also a **Buda branch** (Map pp80-1; ☎ 438 9090; I Margit körút 2; lunch Mon-Fri 3399Ft, Sat & Sun 4999Ft, dinner Mon-Thu 4499Ft, Fri-Sun 4999Ft; 🚊 4 or 6), where the opening times are the same but the prices a bit higher.

Robinson (Map pp80-1; ☎ 422 0222; XIV Városligeti-tó; mains 3290-5990Ft; ⏰ noon-4pm & 6pm-midnight; Ⓜ M1 Hősök tere) Located in leafy City Park, Robinson is the place to secure a table on the lakeside terrace on a warm summer's evening. Starters include sliced goose liver (3290Ft) and grilled duck liver on ginger toast (2890Ft), and mains feature *fogas* (Balaton pike-perch; 3990Ft), grilled tuna and smoked duck breast cooked on lava stones.

FRENCH RESTAURANTS

Lou Lou (Map p86; ☎ 312 4505; V Vigyázó Ferenc utca 4; mains 2300-6400Ft; ⏰ noon-3pm & 7-11pm Mon, 11am-3pm & 6pm-midnight Tue-Fri, 7-11pm Sat; 🚌 15, 🚊 2) One of the most popular places with expatriate *français* in Budapest and supposedly chasing a Michelin star, this lovely bistro with its signature antique rocking horse has excellent daily specials. Try the smoked duck breast (4400Ft) or the scrumptious grilled scallops (6400Ft).

ITALIAN RESTAURANTS

Vapiano (Map p86; ☎ 411 0864; V Bécsi utca 5; salads & starters 650-1750Ft, pizza & pasta 1200-1950Ft; Ⓜ M1 Vörösmarty utca) A very welcome addition to the Inner Town is this pizza and pasta bar where everything is prepared on site. You'll be in and out in no time but the taste will certainly linger.

Okay Italia (Map p84; ☎ 349 2991; XIII Szent István körút 20; pizza 1590-2050Ft, pasta 1190-1980Ft, mains 1890-3310Ft; ⏰ 11am-midnight Mon-Fri, noon-midnight Sat & Sun; 🚊 4 or 6) This is a perennially popular place run by Italians. There's a full range of dishes but most people come for the pasta and pizza. A much classier (and more expensive) **Pest branch** (Map p84; ☎ 332 6960; V Nyugati tér 6; mains 1990-3490Ft; Ⓜ M3 Nyugati pályaudvar) is up the ring road opposite the Nyugati train station.

Trattoria Toscana (Map p86; ☎ 327 0045; V Belgrád rakpart 13; pasta & pizza 1650-3890Ft, mains 2390-4590Ft; ⏰ noon-midnight; 🚌 15, 🚊 2) Very close to the Danube, this trattoria serves rustic and very authentic Tuscan and other Italian food, including *pasta e fagioli* (890Ft), a hearty soup of beans and fresh pasta, and a wonderful Tuscan farmer's platter (2350Ft) of prepared meats.

Gastronomia Pomo D'Oro (Map p86; ☎ 374 0288; V Arany János utca 9; mains 1830-3090Ft; ⏰ 9am-10pm Mon-Sat; 🚌 15, 🚊 2) Next door to a much more extravagant (and expensive) trattoria bearing the same name, this Italian delicatessen/caterer has a small dining area on the 1st floor, where you can choose from a small selection of dishes or sample cheese and prepared meats by the 100g measure (490Ft to 890Ft).

GREEK & MIDDLE EASTERN RESTAURANTS

Pireus Rembetiko Taverna (Map p86; ☎ 266 0292; V Fővám tér 2-3; starters & snacks 390-2990Ft, mains 1890-4990Ft; ⏰ noon-midnight; 🚊 47 or 49) Overlooking the Nagycsarnok (Great Market) at the foot of Liberty Bridge, this place serves reasonably priced and pretty authentic Greek fare. *Rembetiko* is a folk-music school and a style of traditional Greek music, but what you'll hear here is canned.

SPANISH & MEXICAN RESTAURANTS

Pata Negra (Map p86; ☎ 215 5616; IX Kálvin tér 8; tapas 350-790Ft, plates 750-2200Ft; 11am-midnight Mon-Wed, to 1am Thu-Sat, noon-midnight Sun; M M3 Kálvin tér) The 'Black Foot' (it's a kind of ham) is a lovely Spanish tapas bar and restaurant at the (almost) top of trendy Ráday utca; the floor tiles and ceiling fans really help create a mood *a la valenciana*. There's good cheese and an excellent wine selection, too.

Iguana (Map p84; ☎ 331 4352; V Zoltán utca 16; mains 1390-3990Ft; 11.30am-12.30am; M M2 Kossuth Lajos tér, 15) Iguana serves decent-enough Mexican food (not a difficult task in this *cantina* desert), but it's hard to say whether the pull is the chilli (1390Ft to 2290Ft), the enchilada and burrito combination *platos* (plates; 1990Ft to 2390Ft), the fajitas (2390Ft to 3390Ft) or the frenetic and boozy 'we-party-every-night' atmosphere.

JEWISH & KOSHER RESTAURANTS

Spinoza (Map p86; ☎ 413 7488; VII Dob utca 15; mains 1690-2490Ft; 47 or 49) This very attractive cafe-restaurant in the Jewish district has become a personal favourite, both for meals and as a chill-out zone. The venue includes an art gallery and theatre, where concerts by the Pannónia Klezmer Band (see p126) and other events take place from September to May, along with a restaurant and coffee house. The food is mostly Hungarian/Jewish nonkosher comfort food. Remember: the play's the thing.

Carmel (Map p86; ☎ 322 1834; VII Kazinczy utca 31; mains 2500-4800Ft; noon-11pm Sun-Fri; trolleybus 74) With kosher restaurants at a premium in Budapest, the Carmel's metamorphosis into a bona-fide glatt kosher eatery is more than welcome. Try any of its authentic Ashkenazi specialities, such as gefilte fish (1700Ft), matzo-ball soup (1000Ft), chopped chicken liver (2500Ft) and a *cholent* (bean-based stew with beef brisket; 3000Ft) almost as good as the one Aunt Goldie used to make. There's live klezmer (Jewish folk music; 2000Ft) at 7.30pm on Thursday evening.

ASIAN RESTAURANTS

Bangla Büfé (Map p84; ☎ 266 3674, 06 30 480 6279; Akácfa utca 40; mains 790-1190Ft; noon-11pm Sat-Thu, 2.30-11pm Fri; 4 or 6, trolleybus 74) This place, started up by a Bangladeshi expatriate, has as authentic samosas (390Ft), biriani (790Ft to 1050Ft) and dhal (490Ft) as you'll find in Budapest.

Momotaro Ramen (Map p84; ☎ 269 3802, 06 30 999 5102; V Széchenyi utca 16; soups 450Ft, noodles & dumplings 800-1800Ft, mains 1500-3600Ft; 11am-10pm; 15, 2) This is a favourite pit stop for noodles – especially the soup variety – and dumplings when *pálinka* was a-flowing the night before. But it's also good for more substantial dishes.

Bangkok House (Map p86; ☎ 266 0584; V Só utca 3; mains 1950-3550Ft; noon-11pm; 47 or 49) Bangkok House is done up in kitsch, Asian-esque decor that recalls takeaway places around the world. The Thai- and Laotian-inspired dishes are acceptable, though, and service all but seamless. A lunch menu (1300Ft to 1500Ft) is available from noon to 4pm.

Salam Bombay (Map p86; ☎ 411 1252; V Mérleg utca 6; mains 2190-3990Ft; noon-3pm & 6-11pm; 15, 2) If you hanker after a fix of authentic curry or tandoori in a bright, upbeat environment, look no further than this attractive eatery just east of Roosevelt tér. Don't believe us? Even staffers at the Indian embassy are said to come here regularly. As would be expected, there's a large choice of vegetarian dishes (950Ft to 1990Ft).

VEGETARIAN RESTAURANTS

Govinda (Map p86; ☎ 269 1625; V Vigyázó Ferenc utca 4; dishes 230-490Ft; 11.30am-8pm Mon-Fri, noon-9pm Sat; 15, 2) This basement restaurant northeast of the Széchenyi Chain Bridge serves wholesome salads, soups and desserts as well as a daily set-menu plate (large/small 1850/1550Ft). It's also a centre for yoga and alternative health remedies.

Napos Oldal (Map p84; ☎ 354 0048; VI Jókai utca 7-8; dishes 260-380Ft; 11am-9pm Mon-Fri, 10am-1.30pm Sat; 4 or 6, M M1 Oktogon) This tiny cafe-restaurant inside a health-food shop on the 'Sunny Side' of the street serves up shop-made salads, pastries and hot soups.

Napfényes Ízek (Map pp80-1; ☎ 351 5649; VII Rózsa utca 39; mains 1390-1890Ft; 10am-10.30pm Mon-Fri, noon-10.30pm Sat & Sun; trolleybus 73 or 76, M M1 Kodály körönd) 'Sunny Tastes' is a bit out of the way (unless you're staying near Andrássy út), but the wholesome food and the speciality cakes are worth the trip. Set lunches are a bargain at 600Ft to 1100Ft.

CAFES & TEA HOUSES

Along with traditional cafes in Pest, a new breed of cafe has emerged on the scene – all polished chrome, halogen lighting and straight lines. Leafy VI Liszt Ferenc tér is surrounded by these hip cafes, and there are a few on IX Ráday utca and V Szent István tér behind St Stephen's Basilica. Tea houses, too, have made a big splash in Budapest in recent years.

Első Pesti Rétesház (Map p86; ☎ 428 0134; V Október 6 utca 22; strudel 240-290Ft; 9am-11pm Mon-Fri, 11am-11pm Sat & Sun; M M1/2/3 Deák Ferenc tér, 15 or 115) It may be a bit overdone (think Magyar Disneyland, with olde-worlde counters, painted plates on the walls and curios embedded in Plexiglass washbasins), but the 'First Strudel House of Pest' is just the place to taste this Hungarian stretched pastry filled with apple, cheese, poppy seeds or sour cherry.

Art Nouveau Café (Map p84; ☎ 269 4622, 06 30 685 5153; V Honvéd utca 3; cakes 290-370Ft; 8am-6pm Mon-Fri, 9am-6pm Sat; M M2 Kossuth Lajos tér) This small but comfortable cafe on the ground floor of delightful Bedő House (p97) is made for fans of the Secessionist style.

Centrál Kávéház (Map p86; ☎ 266 2110; V Károlyi Mihály utca 9; cakes 390-800Ft; 8am-midnight; M M3 Ferenciek tere) This *grande dame* is still jostling to reclaim her title as *the* place to sit and look intellectual in Pest after reopening a few years ago following extensive renovations. It serves meals as well as lighter fare, such as sandwiches (1000Ft) and omelettes (from 1490Ft).

Gerbeaud (Map p86; ☎ 429 9000; V Vörösmarty tér 7-8; cakes 410-1150Ft; 9am-9pm; M M1 Vörösmarty tér) Founded in 1858, Gerbeaud has been the most fashionable meeting place for the city's elite since 1870. Along with exquisitely prepared cakes and pastries, it serves Continental breakfast (2950Ft) and sandwiches (1550Ft to 2950Ft).

Lukács (Map p84; ☎ 373 0407; VI Andrássy út 70; cakes 450-1250Ft; 8.30am-8pm Mon-Fri, 9am-8pm Sat, 9.30am-8pm Sun; M M1 Vörösmarty utca) This cafe is dressed up in the finest of divine decadence – all mirrors and gold – with soft piano music in the background. The selection of cakes is excellent but expensive; the chief *pâtissier* is French.

Művész (Map p84; ☎ 352 1337; VI Andrássy út 29; cakes 490-790Ft; 9am-midnight Sun-Wed, to 1am Thu-Sat; M M1 Opera) Almost opposite the State Opera House, this is an interesting place to people-watch (especially from the terrace). It's been here since 1898.

Teaház a Vörös Oroszlánhoz (Map p84; ☎ 269 0579; VI Jókai tér 8; teas 490-790Ft; 11am-11pm Mon-Sat, 3-11pm Sun; M M1 Oktogon) This serene place with a mouthful of a name (it means 'Tea House at the Sign of the Red Lion') is quite a serious tea house just north of Liszt Ferenc tér. There's also a **Ráday utca branch** (Map p86; ☎ 215 2101; IX Ráday utca 9), which keeps the same hours.

QUICK EATS

Middle Eastern fast food is as popular in Budapest as Indian is in London and Chinese in New York, and there are lots of choices.

Szeráj (Map p84; ☎ 311 6690; XIII Szent István körút 13; dishes 450-1400Ft; 9am-4am Mon-Thu, to 5am Fri & Sat, to 2am Sun; 4 or 6) A very inexpensive self-service Turkish place for *lahmacun* (Turkish pizza; 450Ft), felafel (900Ft) and kebabs (700Ft), with up to a dozen varieties on offer.

Hummus Bar (Map p84; ☎ 302 1385, 06 70 932 8029; V Alkotmány utca 20; dishes 500-1500Ft, 11am-10pm Mon-Sat, noon-10pm Sun; M M2 Kossuth Lajos tér) If you're looking for vegetarian food on the, err, hoof, this is the place to go for mashed chickpeas blended with sesame-seed paste, oil and lemon juice. Have it *au naturel* on pita or in a dish with accompaniments like mushrooms or felafel.

Little restaurants called *étkezdék*, canteens not unlike British 'cafs' that serve simple but very tasty Hungarian dishes, are sprinkled throughout Pest. Some of the better ones include the following.

Móri (Map pp80-1; ☎ 349 8390; XIII Pozsonyi út 39; dishes 520-1350Ft; 10am-5pm Mon-Thu, to 3pm Fri; trolleybus 75 or 76) Probably the most popular of its type, with some of the best home-cooked food in Budapest.

Kisharang (Map p86; ☎ 269 3861; V Október 6 utca 17; mains 540-1250Ft; 11.30am-8pm Mon-Fri, to 4.30pm Sat & Sun; 15 or 115) The centrally located 'Little Bell' is popular with students and staff of the nearby Central European University.

Kádár (Map p84; ☎ 321 3622; X Klauzál tér 9; mains 950-1800Ft; 11.30am-3.30pm Tue-Sat; 4 or 6) In the Jewish area, it attracts punters with its ever-changing menu.

MARKETS & SELF-CATERING

Most of Budapest's 20-odd food markets are in Pest. The vast majority are closed on Sunday, and Monday is always very quiet. Two of the better ones are the **Rákóczi tér market** (Map pp80-1; VIII Rákóczi tér 8; 6am-4pm Mon, to 6pm Tue-Fri, to 1pm Sat; 4 or 6) and the smaller **Hold utca market** (Map p84; V Hold utca 11; 6am-5pm Mon, 6.30am-6pm Tue-Fri, 6.30am-2pm Sat; M3 Arany János utca) near V Szabadság tér.

Nagycsarnok (Great Market; Map p86; IX Vámház körút 1-3; 6am-5pm Mon, to 6pm Tue-Fri, to 2pm Sat; 47 or 49) This is Budapest's biggest market, though it has become a tourist magnet ever since its renovation for the Millecentenary celebrations in 1996. Still, plenty of locals head here for fruit, vegetables, deli items, fish and meat.

Mézes Kuckó (Map p84; XIII Jászai Mari tér 4; 10am-6pm Mon-Fri year-round, 9am-1pm Sat Oct-May; 4 or 6) The 'Honey Nook' is the place to go if you've got the urge for something sweet; its nut and honey cookies (200Ft per 10 decagrams) are to die for. A colourfully decorated *mézeskalács* (honey cake) in the shape of a heart (400Ft to 750Ft) makes a lovely gift.

Large supermarkets, including the following three, are everywhere in Pest.

Kaiser's Supermarket (Map p84; VI Nyugati tér 1-2; 7am-8pm Mon-Fri, to 4pm Sat, 8am-1pm Sun; M3 Nyugati pályaudvar) Opposite Nyugati train station.

Match Supermarket (Map p84; VIII Rákóczi út; 6am-9pm Mon-Fri, 7am-8pm Sat, 7am-3pm Sun; M3 Blaha Lujza tér) On the north side of Blaha Lujza tér.

Rothschild Supermarket (Map p84; VI Teréz körút 19; 24hr; 4 or 6) Open round-the-clock near Oktogon.

DRINKING

Budapest – particularly Pest – is loaded with pubs and bars and there are enough to satisfy all tastes. In summer the preferred drinking venues are the outdoor *kertek* (see the boxed text, p124).

Buda

Café Ponyvaregény (Map pp88-9; 209 5255; XI Bercsényi utca 5; 10am-midnight Mon-Sat, 2-10pm Sun; 18, 19, 47 or 49) A cafe where we like to drink into the not-so-wee hours, the 'Pulp Fiction' is a wonderful and atmospheric place with old books, *fin-de-siècle* fringed lampshades and a chilled clientele.

Lánchíd Söröző (Map p83; 214 3144; I Fő utca 4; 11am-1am; 86, 19) The 'Chain Bridge Pub' has a wonderful retro feel to it, with old Hungarian movie posters and advertisements on the walls, and red-checked cloths on the tables. Friendly service, too.

Kisrabló Pub (Map pp88-9; 209 1588; XI Zenta utca 3; 11am-2am Mon-Sat; 18, 19, 47 or 49) Close to the Budapest University of Technology and Economics (BMGE), this pub is not surprisingly very popular with students. But don't be misled: it's an attractive and well-run place.

Puskás Pancho (Map pp78-9; 333 5656; III Bécsi út 56; 11.30am-midnight; 17) Buda's first 'sports pub' is just one of seven bars and restaurants in the enormous Symbol complex in Óbuda. Should you tire of the place, the world's your oyster.

Pest

Kiadó Kocsma (Map p84; 331 1955; VI Jókai tér 3; 10am-2am Mon-Fri, noon-2am Sat & Sun; M2 Oktogon) The 'Pub for Rent' on two levels is a great place for a swift pint and a quick bite (salads and pasta dishes 1000Ft to 1500Ft). It's a stone's throw physically (but light years in attitude and presentation) from VI Liszt Ferenc tér.

Castro Bisztró (Map p86; 215 0814; VII Madách tér 3; 11am-midnight Mon-Thu, to 1am Fri, noon-1am Sat, 2pm-midnight Sun; M1/2/3 Deák Ferenc tér) Now in a new location just off the Little Ring Road, this eclectic place has a mixed clientele and Serbian finger food such as *čevapčiči* (spicy meatballs; 900Ft to 1800Ft) and tasty *pljeskavica* (meat patties; 1200Ft). There is wi-fi throughout and the same chilled vibe it had when it was located on IX Ráday utca.

Klub Vittula (Map p84; 06 20 527 7069; http://klubvittula.blogspot.com; VII Kertész utca 4; 6pm-dawn Sep-Jun; M2 Blaha Lujza tér) This is a great though very smoky underground (in both senses) bar just off the Big Ring Road, with international performances, cutting-edge DJs and some cheap Slovakian beer.

Paris, Texas (Map p86; 218 0570; IX Ráday utca 22; noon-3am; M3 Kálvin tér) One of the original bars on the Ráday utca nightlife strip, this place has a coffee-house feel to it, with old sepia-tinted photos on the walls and pool tables downstairs. The cocktails are recommended.

Darshan Udvar (Map p84; 266 5541; VIII Krúdy utca 7; 11am-midnight; 4 or 6) This cavernous complex with bar, restaurant and vegetarian cafe, and decor that combines Eastern flair with a hippy vibe, is an easy escape from the bars of VI Liszt Ferenc tér and the dull sophistication of IX Ráday utca.

Box Utca (Map p86; ☎ 354 1444; VI Bajcsy-Zsilinszky út 21; noon-midnight Sun-Thu, to 2am Fri & Sat; M M2 Astoria) This swish new sports bar and restaurant (think 'ring' not 'gift' when you say 'box' – it's owned by local pugilist István 'Ko-Ko' Kovács) has screens a-plenty for all events and a lovely streetside terrace open in the warmer months.

ENTERTAINMENT

For a city of its size, Budapest has a huge choice of things to do and places to go after dark – from opera and (participatory) folk dancing to live jazz and pulsating clubs with some of the best DJs in the region. It's usually not difficult getting tickets or getting in; the hard part is deciding what to do.

Your best source of information in English for what's on in the city is the freebie **Budapest Funzine** (www.funzine.hu), published every other Thursday and available at hotels, bars, cinemas and wherever tourists congregate. More comprehensive but in Hungarian only is the freebie **PestiEst** (www.est.hu, in Hungarian) and the ultra-thorough **Pesti Műsor** (Budapest Program; www.pestimusor.hu, in Hungarian; 295Ft), with everything from clubs and films to art exhibits and classical music. Both appear every Thursday. Other freebies include the vastly inferior monthly **Budapest Life** (www.budapestlife.hu) and the English- and German-language *Programme Magazine in Hungary/in Ungarn*. The free *Koncert Kalendárium*, published monthly (bimonthly in summer), has more serious offerings: classical concerts, opera, dance and the like. A hip little publication with all sorts of insider's tips is the *Budapest City Spy Map*. It's available free at pubs and bars.

For general websites that include lots of information on Budapest nightlife, see p74. For info on clubs, parties, music, DJs and so on check out www.budacast.hu, http://english.mashkulture.net and www.mykunk.com.

Booking Agencies

Some of the most useful booking agencies in Budapest include those listed here. You can book almost anything online at www.jegymester.hu and www.kulturinfo.hu.

Ticket Express (Map p86; ☎ information 312 0000, bookings ☎ 06 30 303 0999; www.tex.hu; VI Andrássy út 18; 10am-6.30pm Mon-Fri, to 3pm Sat; M M1 Opera) The largest ticket-office network in the city, with dozens of outlets.

Ticket Pro (Map p86; ☎ 555 5155; www.ticketpro.hu; VII Károly körút 9; 9am-9pm Mon-Fri, 10am-2pm Sat; M M1/2/3 Deák Ferenc tér) This is a smaller, more personable agency, with tickets to plays and shows, concerts and sporting events.

Symphony Ticket Office (Szimfonikus Jegyiroda; Map p84; ☎ 302 3841; VI Nagymező utca 19; 10am-6pm Mon-Fri, to 2pm Sat; M M1 Opera) Come here for tickets to the philharmonic and other classical-music concerts.

Nightclubs

Not all clubs and music bars in Budapest levy a cover charge, but those that do will ask for between 1000Ft and 2500Ft at the door. The trendier (and trashier) places usually let women in for free.

Merlin (Map p86; ☎ 317 9338, 266 0904; www.merlinbudapest.org; V Gerlóczy utca 4; 10am-midnight Sun-Thu, to 5am Fri & Sat; M M1/2/3 Deák Ferenc tér, tram 47 or 49) This venue is one of those something-for-everyone kind of places, with everything from jazz and breakbeat to techno and house. It is most visitors' first port of call in Bp.

Trafó Bár Tangó (Map pp88-9; ☎ 456 2053, 06 20 414 0322; www.trafo.hu; IX Liliom utca 41; 6pm-4am; M M3 Ferenc körút) One of the hottest venues in town, this club in the basement of the Trafó House of Contemporary Arts (p127) attracts arty (ie less booze, more smoke) types and their cohorts and features some of the best DJs in town.

Morrison's 2 (Map p84; ☎ 374 3329; V Honvéd utca 40; 5pm-4am Mon-Sat; tram 4 or 6) Far and away Budapest's biggest party venue, this cavernous cellar club attracts a younger crowd with its four dance floors, half a dozen bars (including one in a covered courtyard) and enormous games room upstairs. Live bands play from 9pm to 11pm during the week. The No 2's daddy is the much smaller and more sedate **Morrison's Opera** (Map p86; ☎ 269 4060; VI Révay utca 25; 7pm-4am Mon-Sat; M M1 Opera), a music pub with a signature red telephone booth all the way from Londontown.

Instant (Map p84; ☎ 06 30 830 8747; www.instant.co.hu; VI Nagymező utca 38; 1pm-3am; M M1 Opera, trolleybus 70 or 78) Love, love, love this new 'rubble bar' on Pest's most vibrant nightlife strip and so do all our friends. It's got four bars on two levels with bopping, relaxing and chilling. If you want a taste of things to come and can't wait till lunchtime, head for the ground-floor **coffee shop** (8am-10pm).

ATTENDING THE GARDENS

During Budapest's long and hot summers, so-called *kertek*, literally 'gardens' but in Budapest any outdoor spot that has been converted into an entertainment zone (including courtyards and any available stretch along the river), and *romkocsmák* (ruin bars) that rise phoenixlike from abandoned buildings empty out even the most popular indoor bars and clubs. The venues (and their locations) can change from year to year and a definitive list is usually not available until spring; the best single source of information is **Caboodle** (www.caboodle.hu). Some of the more popular ones in recent years:

Cha Cha Cha Terasz (Map pp80-1; ☎ 06 70 554 0670; www.chachacha.hu; XIII Margit-sziget; 🕑 4pm-late; 🚌 26, 🚋 4 or 6) In the stadium at the southern tip of Margaret Island, Cha Cha Cha Terasz is an attitude-free venue, with eclectic party music and dance space.

Corvintető (Map p84; ☎ 461 0007; VIII Blaha Lujza tér 1-2; www.corvinteto.com; 🕑 6pm-5am; Ⓜ M2 Blaha Lujza tér) This 'underground garden above the city' is on the rooftop of the erstwhile Corvin department store and has excellent concerts. Enter from Somogyi Béla utca and take the goods lift to the top floor.

Dürer Kert (Map pp80-1; ☎ 789 4444; www.durerkert.hu, in Hungarian; XIV Ajtósi Dürer sor 19-21; 🕑 4pm-5am; 🚋 1, trolleybus 74 or 75) Very relaxed open space on the southeastern edge of City Park; boasts some of the best DJs on the 'garden' circuit.

Holdudvar (Map pp80-1; ☎ 236 0155; www.holdudvar.net; XIII Margit-sziget; 🕑 10am-5am; 🚋 4 or 6) Another popular 'garden club' on Margaret Island, with a relaxed atmosphere but fairly predictable music.

Mokka Cuka (Map pp78-9; ☎ 242 1707; www.mokkacuka.com; III Hajógyár-sziget; 🕑 5pm-5am Wed-Sun; HÉV Filatorigát) On the island that attracts the capital's beautiful people and hosts the astonishingly successful Sziget Music Festival (p109) in August, Mokka Cuka is a leading outdoor underground venue showcasing indie DJs.

Szimpla Kert (Map p84; ☎ 352 4198; www.szimpla.hu; VII Kazinczy 14; 🕑 noon-3am; trolleybus 74) One of the capital's first *kertek*, Szimpla has now winterised (sort of) and opens year-round.

Zöld Pardon (Map pp88-9; ☎ 279 1880; www.zp.hu; XI Goldman György tér 6; 🕑 9am-6am; 🚋 4 or 6) What bills itself as the 'world's longest summer festival' is a rocker's paradise in Buda, just south of Petőfi Bridge.

Piaf (Map p84; ☎ 312 3823; www.piafklub.hu; VI Nagymező utca 25; 🕑 10pm-6am Sun-Thu, to 7am Fri & Sat; Ⓜ M1 Opera, trolleybus 70 or 78) Piaf is the place to go when everything else slows down. There's dancing and action well into the new day. Most of the action and characters – including some professionals – are in the smoky cavern below.

Tűzraktér (Map p84; ☎ 06 70 321 3536; www.tuzrakter.hu; VI Hegedű utca 3; 🕑 3pm-2am; 🚋 4 or 6) Now in a new but equally 'distressed' location, this independent community turns werewolf by night with DJs, concerts and parties.

Közgáz Klub (Map p86; ☎ 215 4359, 06 30 999 9644; www.kozgazklub.hu; IX Fővám tér 8; 🕑 10pm-5am Tue-Sat; 🚋 47 or 49) With few frills and cheap covers, this never-cool club at the Economics University is the pick-up venue of choice for many a student. Don't hang about if the karaoke kicks in, though.

Gay & Lesbian Venues

Alter Ego (Map p84; ☎ 06 70 345 4302; www.alteregoclub.hu; VI Dessewffy utca 33; 🕑 10pm-5am Fri & Sat; Ⓜ M3 Nyugati pályaudvar, 🚋 4 or 6) Budapest's premier gay club, with the chicest (think attitude) crowd and the best dance music.

Action (Map p86; ☎ 266 9148; www.action.gay.hu; V Magyar utca 42; 🕑 9pm-4am; Ⓜ M3 Kálvin tér) Action is where to head if you want just that (though there's a strip show at midnight that may distract). Take the usual precautions and write home occasionally.

CoXx Men's Bar (Map p84; ☎ 344 4884; www.coxx.hu; VII Dohány utca 38; 🕑 9pm-4am Sun-Thu, to 5am Fri & Sat; 🚌 7) Probably the cruisiest game in town, this boldly named meat rack has a long, brick-lined cellar bar and some significant play areas in the back. You might soon find yourself 'behind bars' in more ways than one.

Le Cafe M Bar (Map p84; ☎ 312 1436; www.mysterybar.hu; V Nagysándor József utca 3; 🕑 4pm-4am Mon-Fri, 6pm-4am Sat & Sun; Ⓜ M3 Arany János utca) Our favourite (err, the only) neighbourhood gay bar in Budapest has supercool decor, friendly staff and internet access (300/500Ft per half-/full hour) for a little cruising while cruising.

There are no specific girl bars in Budapest, though the following might be useful:

Café Eklektika (Map p84; ☎ 266 1226; VI Nagymező utca 30; 🕑 noon-midnight; Ⓜ M1 Opera, trolleybus 70 or 78) This lesbian-owned cafe and restaurant in stunning new digs on Budapest's own Broadway is a great place for lunch – the buffet is a mere 990Ft – and a little LGBT information-gathering.

Candy (☎ 06 70 330 0919; www.candybudapest.hu) Check this site for lesbian parties held at different venues monthly.

Living Room (Map p86; ☎ 06 30 992 9932; www.livingroom.hu; V Kossuth Lajos utca 17; 10pm-5am; M M2 Astoria) Lesbian parties are usually held here on the last Saturday of each month.

Live Music

ROCK & POP

Gödör Klub (Map p86; ☎ 06 20 943 5464; www.godorklub.hu; V Erzsébet tér; 9am-late; M M1/2/3 Deák Ferenc tér) The 'Pit', a city-sponsored cultural centre in the old bus bays below Erzsébet tér in central Pest, is a real mixed bag, offering everything from folk to world music but especially rock and pop.

A38 Hajó (A38 Ship; Map pp88-9; ☎ 464 3940; www.a38.hu; XI Pázmány Péter sétány; 11am-4pm, terraces 4pm-4am Tue-Sat; 4 or 6) Moored on the Buda side just south of Petőfi Bridge, the A38 is a decommissioned Ukrainian stone hauler from 1968 that has been recycled as a major live-music venue. It's so cool it's hot in summer and the hold, well, rocks throughout the year.

WigWam Rock Club (Map pp88-9; ☎ 208 5569; www.wigwamrockclub.hu, in Hungarian; XI Fehérvári út 202; 9pm-5am; 41) This place is one of the best of its kind in Hungary, and hosts some big-name Hungarian rock and blues bands on Friday and Saturday in deepest south Buda. There's a new branch called **WigWam 2** (Map p84; ☎ 06 70 346 2472, VIII Krúdy Gyula utca 17; 6pm-2am Mon-Wed, to 4am Thu-Sat; 4 or 6) that unfortunately keeps the tacky 'cowboy and injun' theme (dead or) alive.

Szimpla (Map p84; ☎ 321 9119; VII Kertész utca 48; 10am-2am Mon-Fri, noon-2am Sat, noon-midnight Sun; 4 or 6) This distressed-looking, very unflashy place remains one of the most popular drinking venues south of VI Liszt Ferenc tér. There's live music Tuesday to Thursday evenings.

Budapest Sportaréna (Map pp80-1; ☎ 422 2600; www.budapestarena.hu; XIV Stefánia út 2; M M2 Stadionok) This purpose-built 12,500-seat arena, named after local pugilist László Papp, is where big local and international acts entertain.

Petőfi Csarnok (Map pp80-1; ☎ 363 3730; www.petoficsarnok.hu; XIV Zichy Mihály út 14; M M1 Széchenyi fürdő, trolleybus 72 or 74) In the southeast corner of City Park, Budapest's main youth centre is the venue for smaller rock concerts as the hall is intimate enough to get really close to the performers.

JAZZ & BLUES

Columbus Jazzklub (Map p86; ☎ 266 9013; www.majazz.hu; V Pesti alsó rakpart at Lánchíd bridgehead; 4pm-midnight; 2) This place, located on a boat moored in the Danube, just off the northern end of V Vigadó tér, has transformed itself from 'just another Irish pub' to a jazz club of note, with big-name local and international bands and home to the Society of Hungarian Jazz Artists. Music starts at 8pm daily.

Take 5 (Map p86; ☎ 06 30 986 8856; www.take5.hu; VI Paulay Ede utca 2; 6pm-2am Wed-Sun; M M1/2/3 Deák Ferenc tér, 47 or 49) This newcomer in the basement of Vista travel agency (p75) takes its jazz very seriously indeed, delivering class acts – both local and international – nightly. Move up to the front; the sound is better closer to the stage.

Jazz Garden (Map p86; ☎ 266 7364; www.jazzgarden.hu; V Veres Pálné utca 44/a; 6pm-1am Sun, Mon, Wed & Thu, to 2am Fri & Sat; 47 or 49) A sophisticated venue with traditional, vocal and Latin jazz, and odd decor: a faux cellar 'garden' with street lamps and a night 'sky' bedecked with blinking stars. Book a table (starters 1680Ft to 2650Ft, mains 2680Ft to 4180Ft) in the dining room; music starts at 9.30pm.

our pick **Nothing but the Blues** (Map p84; ☎ 784 7793, 06 20 404 0304; www.bluespub.hu; VIII Krúdy Gyula utca 6; 11am-11.30pm Mon-Thu, to 4am Fri & Sat, to midnight Sun; 47 or 49) The oldest blues venue in town, NBB has been wailing for more than 15 years now and is under new management. The name may be accurate Thursday to Saturday from 8pm, when there's always a live strummer or some such, but acts vary the rest of the week. Still, it's always good fun, with a warm welcome and a friendly crowd. Jamming is on Sunday afternoon and open mic on Monday night. Grab the in-house 'beer guitar' and give it a shot. Massive approval means a free brew (if not a recording contract). Food is a bit all over the shop – traditional Hungarian specialities, Thai bits and bobs, and what it claims to be the best burger (from 1200Ft) in town.

FOLK & TRADITIONAL

Authentic *táncház*, literally 'dance house' but really folk-music workshops, are held at various locations throughout the week, but less

PANNÓNIA KLEZMER BAND

Formed in 1997, the Budapest-based Pannónia Klezmer Band (www.pannoniaklezmer.hu) suffered a severe blow 10 years later when their much-loved founder and leader Ferenc Gyula Zsákai died unexpectedly. The band, made up of three men and three women ranging in age from 18 to 40, decided to play on, making their own sound. Their most recent CD is *Best of Pannónia Klezmer Band*.

A rather delicate question, but we thought klezmer bands were the last bastion of boys-only clubs. Hey, it's a modern world. Where are you from?

OK, already. Here comes another... Non-Jews playing klezmer? How does that work? Well, that's simple. We're musicians and it's music. Music is music is music. Klezmer is not easy but we like challenges and we get the opportunity to play it here [at Spinoza, p120]. Of course no band can live on just one kind of music.

Then why klezmer? Because it's fun and it's for everyone. And klezmer is a kind of feeling. Everyone says that about all kinds of music, but it's true.

Is klezmer like anything else? Are there influences? Klezmer and Gypsy music are very close now. Jewish and Gypsy musicians played together for the first time in the same concentration camps and influenced each other greatly. Nowadays people are looking for new sounds, so most modern klezmer bands mix in several different types of music – jazz, folk, Gypsy, even techno! It's all improvisation, anyway.

And the instruments? What are the must-haves? The violin and clarinet dominate and you can't do much that's modern without piano and drums. We've added tuba and vocals.

Vocals? Klezmer is mainly instrumental music but there are songs in Yiddish too – ballads and pieces for special occasions like 'Mazel Tov' at weddings. The 'king of klezmer' Giora Feidman plays the clarinet, but he's also one of the greatest male klezmer vocalists in the world. Our singer happens to be female, which restricts our playing at some Jewish events. Orthodox Jews can listen to a male vocalist but not a female one, you see. Male klezmer vocalists are very hard to find in Budapest.

And the fan base? Where's that going? Seems to keep growing. When we played at a *táncház* (dance house) recently we won a new group of fans with klezmer music. Klezmer is very popular right now among non-Jewish people.

frequently in summer. Times and venues often change; consult one of the publications on p123, and expect to pay 500Ft to 1000Ft. Very useful listings can be found on the **Dance House Guild** (www.tanchaz.hu, in Hungarian) and **Folkrádió** (www.folkradio.hu) websites. The former also lists bands playing other types of traditional music, such as *klezmer* (Jewish folk music). Two of the best are the Budapest Klezmer Band (www.budapestklezmer.hu) and the Pannónia Klezmer Band (www.pannoniaklezmer.hu; see the boxed text, above).

Aranytíz Cultural Centre (Aranytíz Művelődési Központ; Map p86; ☎ 354 3400; www.aranytiz.hu, in Hungarian; V Arany János utca 10; 🚌 15) At this cultural centre in the northern Inner Town the wonderful Kalamajka Táncház has programs from 8.30pm on Saturday that run till about midnight.

Pótkulcs (Map p84; ☎ 269 1050; www.potkulcs.hu; VI Csengery utca 65/b; M M3 Nyugati pályaudvar) The terrific little venue called the 'Spare Key' has a varied menu of music most nights, including dance house at 8pm every Tuesday.

Fonó Buda Music House (Fonó Budai Zeneház; Map pp88-9; ☎ 206 5300; www.fono.hu; XI Sztregova utca 3; 🚊 41) This place has *táncház* programs several times a week at 8pm or just after. Consult its website.

In addition, three city cultural houses in Buda have frequent folk programs:

Municipal Cultural House (Fővárosi Művelődési Háza; Map pp88-9; ☎ 203 3868; www.fmhnet.hu, in Hungarian; XI Fehérvári út 47; 🚊 41) There's folk music here every Friday and on the first and third Mondays of the month at 7pm. There's also a children's dance house hosted by the incomparable Muzsikás every Tuesday from 5pm.

Marczibányi tér Cultural Centre (Marczibányi téri Művelődési Központ; Map pp80-1; ☎ 212 2820; www.marczi.hu, in Hungarian; II Marczibányi tér 5/a; 🚊 4 or 6) Offers Hungarian, Moldavian and Slovakian dance and music every Wednesday, and *táncház* every second Saturday from 8pm.

Budavár Cultural Centre (Budavári Művelődési Háza; Map p83; ☎ 201 0234; www.bem6.hu; Bem rakpart 6; 🚌 86) This cultural centre just below Buda Castle has frequent programs for children, including the excellent Fakutya Táncház every third Saturday afternoon.

CLASSICAL

The monthly freebie **Koncert Kalendárium** (www.koncertkalendarium.hu) lists all the concerts in Budapest. The main concert halls are the 1700-seat National Concert Hall (Nemzeti Hangversenyterem) and the smaller 450-seat Festival Theatre (Fesztivál Színház) at the **Palace of Arts** (Művészetek Palotája; Map pp88-9; ☎ information 555 3000, bookings 555 3301; www.mupa.hu; IX Komor Marcell utca; tickets 600-7900Ft; 🕑 ticket office 10am-6pm Mon-Fri, 11am-7pm Sat & Sun; 🚊 2), and the stunning **Liszt Academy of Music** (Liszt Zeneakadémia; Map p84; ☎ information 462 4636, bookings 342 0179; www.zeneakademia.hu; VI Liszt Ferenc tér 8; tickets 500-6000Ft; 🕑 ticket office 2-8pm; Ⓜ M2 Oktogon).

The **Duna Palota** (Map p86; ☎ 235 5500; V Zrínyi utca 5; tickets adult 6400-8100Ft, student 5600-7200Ft; 🚌 15) hosts light classical music concerts at 8pm on Saturday from May to October.

Opera

Hungarian State Opera House (Magyar Állami Operaház; Map p84; ☎ information 331 2550, bookings 353 0170; www.opera.hu; VI Andrássy út 22; tickets 300-16,900Ft; 🕑 ticket office 11am-7pm Mon-Sat, 11am-1pm & 4-7pm Sun; Ⓜ M1 Opera) The opera house should be visited at least once – to admire the incredibly rich decoration inside as much as to view a performance and hear the perfect acoustics.

Budapest Operetta (Budapesti Operettszínház; Map p84; ☎ information 472 2030, bookings 312 4866; www.operettszinhaz.hu; VI Nagymező utca 17; tickets 950-15,000Ft; 🕑 ticket office 10am-7pm Mon-Fri, 1-7pm Sat & Sun; Ⓜ M1 Opera) This theatre presents operettas – always a riot, especially campy ones like *A Csádáskirálynő* (The Queen of the Csárdás) by Imre Kálmán.

Dance

CLASSICAL

The **Hungarian National Ballet** (www.opera.hu) company is based at the Hungarian State Opera House (above), though it occasionally performs at the **National Dance Theatre** (Nemzeti Táncszínház; Map p83; ☎ information 201 4407, bookings 375 8649; www.nemzetitancszinhaz.hu; I Színház utca 1-3; tickets 650-4500Ft; 🕑 ticket office 1-6pm; 🚌 16, 16A or 116) in the Castle District, as does the excellent contemporary troupe, the **Budapest Dance Theatre** (www.budapestdancetheatre.hu).

There are several other excellent options for modern dance fans, including **Mu Színház** (Map pp88-9; ☎ 209 4014, 466 4627; www.mu.hu; XI Kőrösy József utca 17; tickets 1500-2000Ft; 🚊 4) in south Buda, where virtually everyone involved in Hungarian dance got their start. The **Trafó House of Contemporary Arts** (Trafó Kortárs Művészetek Háza; Map pp88-9; ☎ 215 1600; www.trafo.hu; IX Liliom utca 41; tickets 500-3000Ft; Ⓜ M3 Ferenc körút) presents the cream of the crop of dance, including a good pull of international acts.

FOLK

The 30 artistes of the Hungarian State Folk Ensemble (Magyar Állami Népi Együttes) perform at the **Buda Concert Hall** (Budai Vigadó; Map p83; ☎ 201 3766; I Corvin tér 8; 🚌 86, 🚊 19) in Buda on Tuesday and Thursday from May to early October, with occasional performances during the rest of the year. The Rajkó Folk Ensemble (Rajkó Népi Együttes) stages folk-dance performances at the Duna Palota (left) on Friday and Sunday, while the Duna Folk Ensemble (Duna Népi Együttes) dances at the Duna Palota on Monday and Wednesday. The 1½-hour programs begin at 8pm, and tickets cost 3300Ft to 5600Ft for adults and 3000Ft to 5100Ft for students. For information and bookings contact **Hungaria Koncert** (☎ 317 1377, 317 2754; www.ticket.info.hu).

Theatre

Merlin Theatre (Map p86; ☎ 317 9338, 266 4632; www.merlinszinhaz.hu; V Gerlóczy utca 4; tickets 1500-2500Ft; Ⓜ M1/2/3 Deák Ferenc tér, 🚊 47 or 49) This international theatre stages numerous plays in English, often performed by local troupe Scallabouche, Budapest's only alternative British theatre company. It's usually pretty serious stuff, with little scenery and few props.

International Buda Stage (IBS; Map p77; ☎ 391 2525; www.ibsszinpad.hu; II Tárogató út 2-4; tickets 1500-2800Ft; 🚌 29, 🚊 18 or 56) Further afield on the way to the Buda Hills, the IBS is a more recent arrival than the Merlin Theatre, with occasional performances – often comedies – in English.

National Theatre (Nemzeti Színház; Map pp88-9; ☎ information 476 6800, bookings 476 6868; www.nemzetiszinhaz.hu; IX Bajor Gizi park 1; tickets 1000-3800Ft; 🕑 ticket office 10am-6pm Mon-Fri, 2-6pm Sat & Sun; 🚊 2) This rather eclectic venue is the place to go if you want to brave a play in Hungarian or just check out the bizarre architecture. The theatre was built in 2002 according to the designs of Mária Siklós.

Budapest Puppet Theatre (Budapest Bábszínház; Map p84; ☎ information 342 2702, 321 5200; www.budapest-babszinhaz.hu; VI Andrássy út 69; tickets 800-2700Ft; Ⓜ M1 Vörösmarty utca) The puppet theatre, which usually doesn't require fluency in Hungarian, presents shows designed for children at 10am or 10.30am and 3pm. Consult the theatre's website for program schedules.

Cinemas

A couple of dozen cinemas screen English-language films with Hungarian subtitles. Consult the listings in the *Budapest Sun* newspaper or *Budapest Funzine* freebie. *Pesti Est* and *Pesti Műsor* have more complete listings, but in Hungarian only. Tickets cost anywhere from 500Ft to 1100Ft.

Kino (Map p84; ☎ 349 2773; XIII Szent István körút 16; 🚊 4 or 6) Formerly the seminal Szindbád, this newly renovated cinema shows good Hungarian and foreign films with subtitles.

Művész (Map p84; ☎ 332 6726; www.artmozi.hu; VI Teréz körút 30; Ⓜ M1 Oktogon, 🚊 4 or 6) Shows artsy and cult films.

Örökmozgó (Map p84; ☎ 342 2167; VII Erzsébet körút 39; 🚊 4 or 6) Part of the Hungarian Film Institute (www.filmintezet.hu), this cinema (whose name vaguely translates as 'moving picture') screens an excellent assortment of foreign classic films in their original languages.

Puskin (Map p86; ☎ 429 6080; V Kossuth Lajos utca 18; 🚌 7) Screens a mix of art-house and popular releases.

Uránia (Map p84; ☎ 486 3413; VIII Rákóczi út 21; 🚌 7) This Art Deco/neo-Moorish extravaganza is a tarted-up film palace. It has an excellent cafe overlooking Rákóczi út.

Circus

Municipal Great Circus (Fővárosi Nagycirkusz; Map pp80-1; ☎ 343 8300; www.circus.hu; XIV Állatkerti körút 7; adult 1500-2400Ft, child 1200-2000Ft; Ⓜ M1 Széchenyi fürdő) Europe's only permanent big top has everything one would expect from a circus, including acrobats, dare devils on horseback and ice shows in season. Performances are at 3pm Wednesday to Sunday, with additional shows at 11am and 7pm on Saturday and at 11am on Sunday.

Sport

WATER POLO

The **Hungarian Water Polo Association** (MVLSZ; ☎ 412 0041; www.waterpolo.hu, in Hungarian) is based at the Alfréd Hajós swimming complex (p104) on Margaret Island. Matches take place here and at two other pools: the Császár-Komjádi swimming pool (p104) in Buda and the **BVSC** (Map pp80-1; ☎ 251 3888; XIV Szőnyi út 2; trolleybus 74 or 74A) in Pest from September to May. If you want to see a match or watch the lads in training in summer, call the MVLSZ for times and dates, or get someone to check schedules for you in the daily *Nemzeti Sport* (National Sport; 115Ft).

FOOTBALL

Once on top of the heap of European football – the national team's defeat of the England team both at Wembley (6–3) in 1953 and at home (7–1) the following year is still talked about as if the winning goals were scored yesterday – Hungary has failed to qualify for any major tournament since 1986. The national team plays at **Ferenc Puskás Stadium** (Map pp80-1; ☎ 471 4100; XIV Istvánmezei út 1-3; Ⓜ M3 Stadionok), the erstwhile 'People's Stadium', which accommodates almost 70,000 fans.

There are five premier-league football teams in Budapest out of a total of 16 nationwide, including the two best: Újpest, which plays at far-flung **Ferenc Szusza Stadium** (Map pp78-9; ☎ 369 7333; IV Megyeri út 13; 🚌 96 or 196), accommodating 13,500 fans; and MTK, based at **Nándor Hidegkúti Stadium** (Map pp80-1; ☎ 219 0300; VIII Salgótarjáni utca 12-14; 🚊 1), which accommodates 12,700 spectators. But no club has dominated Budapest football over the years like Ferencváros Torna Club (FTC), the country's loudest and brashest team. You either love the Fradi boys in green and white or you hate 'em. Watch them play at **FTC Albert Stadium** (Map pp88-9; ☎ 215 6025; IX Üllői út 129; Ⓜ M3 Népliget), which has space for 18,000 raucous spectators. Check *Nemzeti Sport* for game schedules.

HORSE RACING

The descendants of the nomadic Magyars are keen on horse racing. **Kincsem Park** (Map p77; ☎ 433 0520; www.kincsempark.com; X Albertirsai út 2; Ⓜ M2 Pillangó utca) is the place to go for both *ügető* (trotting) and *galopp* (flat racing). Schedules can change, but in general three trotting meetings of 10 to 11 races take place from 2pm to 9pm on Saturday, and flat racing from 10.30am to 4pm on Sunday between May and November. The biggest event of the year is Ügetőszilveszter, a vastly popular trotting race that attracts all ages on the afternoon of New Year's Eve.

SHOPPING

Budapest is a great place to satisfy that urge to buy, and you'll find all the products described in the Directory (p378) in full supply here. But some people consider the city's flea markets their highlight – not just as places to indulge their vice, but as the consummate Budapest experience. Shops are generally open from 9am or 10am to 6pm during the week and till 1pm on Saturday.

Antiquarian

Szőnyi Antikváriuma (Map p84; ☎ 311 6431; www.szonyi.hu; V Szent István körút 3; 4 or 6) This long-established antiquarian bookshop has, in addition to books, an excellent selection of antique prints and maps (look in the drawers).

Központi Antikvárium (Map p86; ☎ 317 3514; V Múzeum körút 13-15; 10am-6.30pm Mon-Fri, to 2pm Sat; M M3 Kálvin tér) For antique and second-hand books in Hungarian, German and English try the 'Central Antiquarian', which was established in 1885 and is the largest antique bookshop in Budapest.

Flea Markets & Second-Hand Shops

Ecseri Piac (off Map p77; ☎ 282 9563; XIX Nagykőrösi út 156; 8am-4pm Mon-Fri, 6am-3pm Sat, 8am-1pm Sun) This is one of the biggest flea markets in Central Europe, selling everything from antique jewellery and Soviet army watches to Fred Astaire–style top hats. Saturday is said to be the best day to go; dealers get here early for diamonds amid the rust. Take bus 54 from Boráros tér in Pest or, for a quicker journey, the red-numbered express bus 84E, 89E or 94E from the Határ út stop on the M3 metro line and get off at the Fiume utca stop. Then follow the crowds over the pedestrian bridge.

City Park flea market (Városligeti bolhapiac; Map pp80-1; ☎ 363 3730, 251 7266; www.bolhapiac.com; XIV Zichy Mihály utca 14; 7am-2pm Sat & Sun; 1, trolleybus 72 or 74) This is a huge outdoor flea market – a kind of Hungarian boot or garage sale – held next to the Petőfi Csarnok (p125) in City Park. The usual stuff is on offer – from old records and draperies to candles, honey and herbs. Sunday is the better day.

If you don't have time to get to the Ecseri or City Park flea markets, check out any of the branches of **BÁV** (Bizományi Kereskedőház és Záloghitel; ☎ 325 2600; www.bav.hu; 10am-6pm Mon-Fri, to 1pm or 2pm Sat), essentially a chain of pawn and second-hand shops with many branches around town. Try the **V Bécsi utca branch** (Map p86; ☎ 429 3020; V Bécsi utca 1-3; M M1/2/3 Deák Ferenc tér) for knick-knacks, porcelain, glassware and artwork; the **XIII Szent István körút branch** (Map p84; ☎ 473 0666; XIII Szent István körút 3; 4 or 6) for chinaware, textiles and furniture; and the **II Margit körút branch** (Map pp80-1; ☎ 315 0417; II Margit körút 4 & II Frankel Leó út 13; 4 or 6) for jewellery, lamps and fine porcelain.

Gifts & Souvenirs

Holló Atelier (Map p86; ☎ 317 8103; V Vitkovics Mihály utca 12; 10am-6pm Mon-Fri, to 2pm Sat; M M1/2/3 Deák Ferenc tér) This place sells attractive folk art with a modern look and remains a personal favourite place to shop for gifts and gewgaws.

Intuita (Map p86; ☎ 266 5864; V Váci utca 67; 11am-6pm; M M1/2/3 Deák Ferenc tér, 15 or 115) You're not about to find painted eggs and *pálinka* here, but modern Hungarian crafted items such as hand-blown glass, jewellery, ceramics and bound books.

Magma (Map p86; ☎ 235 0277; www.magma.hu; V Petőfi Sándor utca 11; 10am-5pm Mon-Fri, to 3pm Sat; M M3 Ferenciek tere) This showroom in the centre of the Inner Town focuses on Hungarian design and designers exclusively – with everything from glassware and porcelain to textiles and furniture.

Folkart Centrum (Népművészet; Map p86; ☎ 318 4697; V Váci utca 58; 10am-7pm; M M1/2/3 Deák Ferenc tér, 15 or 115) This is a large shop where everything Magyar – whether made here or in China – is available, from embroidered waistcoats and tablecloths to painted eggs and plates. The staff are very helpful and will advise.

Glassware & Porcelain

Herend (Map p86; ☎ 317 2622; www.herend.com; V József nádor tér 11; 10am-6pm Mon-Fri, to 2pm Sat; M M1 Vörösmarty tér) For both contemporary and traditional fine porcelain, there is no place like Herend. There's also a **Castle Hill branch** (Map p83; ☎ 225 1050; I Szentháromság utca 5; 10am-6pm daily Apr-Oct, 10am-6pm Mon-Fri, to 2pm Sat & Sun Nov-Mar; 16, 16A or 116).

Herend Village Pottery (Map pp80-1; ☎ 356 7899; II Bem rakpart 37; 9am-5pm Tue-Fri, to noon Sat; M M2 Batthyány tér) This shop stocks hard-wearing pottery and dishes decorated with bold fruit patterns, an unusual alternative to what some might describe as rather prissy Herend flatware.

Haas & Czjzek (Map p84; ☎ 311 4094; www.porcelan.hu; VI Bajcsy-Zsilinszky út 23; 10am-7pm Mon-Fri, to

3pm Sat; M M3 Arany János utca) Just up from Deák Ferenc tér, this chinaware and crystal shop sells Herend and Zsolnay, as well as more affordable Hungarian-made Hollóháza and Alföldi porcelain.

Ajka Kristály (Map p86; ☎ 317 8133; www.ajka-crystal.hu; V József Attila utca 7; M M1/2/3 Deák Ferenc tér) Established in 1878, Ajka has Hungarian-made lead-crystal pieces and stemware. Most of it is very old-fashioned, but there are some more contemporary pieces.

Wine & Spirits

Bortársaság (Map p83; ☎ 212 2569; www.bortarsasag.hu; I Batthyány utca 59; 10am-8pm Mon-Fri, to 6pm Sat; M M2 Moszkva tér) What was once called the Budapest Wine Society has five retail outlets with an exceptional selection of fine Hungarian wines. No one, but no one, knows Hungarian wines like these guys do. Central for Pest is the **Basilica branch** (Map p86; ☎ 328 0341; V Szent István tér 3; noon-8pm Mon-Fri, 10am-4pm Sat; M M2 Arany János utca).

Mester Pálinka (Map p86; ☎ 374 0388; www.mesterpalinkak.hu, in Hungarian; V Zrínyi utca 18; 10am-6pm Mon-Fri, to 2pm Sat; M M2 Arany János utca) If you're into Hungarian *pálinka*, the exquisite brandy flavoured with everything from apricot and sour cherry to (be still, our heart) raspberry and sloe, choose this new shop that stocks scores of varieties. Service is helpful, advice sound.

GETTING THERE & AWAY

Air

The main **Malév Customer Service Centre** (Map p84; ☎ 235 3888, 24hr information & reservations 06 40 212 121; www.malev.hu; XIII Váci út 26; 9am-6pm Mon, to 5pm Tue-Fri, to 4pm Sat; M M3 Nyugati pályaudvar) is 100m northwest of Nyugati train station. Malév also has ticket-issuing desks in Ferihegy International Airport's **Terminal 2A** (☎ 296 7831) and **Terminal 2B** (☎ 296 7554). For contact telephone numbers and websites of other carriers with offices in the capital, see p382.

Boat

Hydrofoils to Bratislava and Vienna run by **Mahart PassNave** (Map p86; ☎ 484 4005; www.mahartpassnave.hu; V Belgrád rakpart; 9.15am-6pm) arrive at and depart from the **International Ferry Pier** (Nemzetközi hajóállomás; Map p86; V Belgrád rakpart). For more information, see p387.

From early April to late October Mahart PassNave also runs excursion boats on the Danube from Budapest to Szentendre, and between early May and late September hydrofoils from Budapest to Vác, Visegrád, Nagymoros and Esztergom. Boats usually leave from the **Vigadó tér Pier** (Map p86; ☎ 318 1223; M M1 Vörösmarty tér), off V Vigadó tér on the Pest side, and sometimes pick up and discharge passengers from the ferry stop at I Batthyány tér (Map p83) on the Buda side, which is on the M2 metro line.

Bus

All international buses and some – but not all – domestic ones (especially to/from north and north-central Hungary) arrive at and depart from **Népliget bus station** (Map pp88-9; ☎ 219 8000; IX Üllői út 131; M M3 Népliget) in Pest. The **international ticket office** (6am-6pm Mon-Fri, to 4pm Sat & Sun) is upstairs. **Eurolines** (☎ 219 8063; www.eurolines.com) is represented here, as is its Hungarian associate **Volánbusz** (☎ 382 0888; www.volanbusz.hu). There's a **left-luggage office** (6am-9pm) downstairs that charges 280Ft per piece per day.

Stadionok bus station (Map pp80-1; ☎ 220 6227; XIV Hungária körút 48-52; M M3 Stadionok) generally serves cities and towns to the east of Budapest. The **ticket office** (6am-6pm Mon-Fri, to 4pm Sat & Sun) and the **left-luggage office** (per piece 280Ft; 6am-7pm) are on the ground floor. Buses to southwest Hungary use **Etele tér bus station** (Map pp88-9; ☎ 382 0888; XI Etele tér; 6am-6pm; red-numbered express 7E, 19 or 49) in Buda.

Árpád híd bus station (Map pp78-9; ☎ 412 2597; XIII Árboc utca 1-3; ticket office 6am-6pm Mon-Fri, to 4pm Sat & Sun; M M3 Árpád híd), on the Pest side of Árpád Bridge, is the place to catch buses for the Danube Bend and parts of the Northern Uplands (eg Balassagyarmat, Szécsény, Salgótarján). The small **Széna tér bus station** (Map pp80-1; ☎ 201 3688; I Széna tér 1/a; ticket office 6am-6pm Mon-Fri, to 4pm Sat & Sun; M M3 Moszkva tér) in Buda handles some traffic to and from the Pilis Hills and towns northwest of the capital, with a half-dozen departures to Esztergom as an alternative to the Árpád híd bus station.

Car & Motorcycle

All the international car-rental firms have offices in Budapest, but don't expect many bargains. An Opel Corsa or Suzuki Swift from **Avis** (Map p86; ☎ 318 4158; www.avis.hu; V Szervita tér 8; 7am-6pm Mon-Sat, 8am-6pm Sun; M M1/2/3 Deák Ferenc tér), for example, costs €59/369 per day/week, with unlimited kilometres, collision damage waiver (CDW) and theft protection (TP) insurance. The same car and insurance with 800km costs from €165 for a three-day weekend.

One of the cheapest and most reliable outfits for renting cars is **Anselport** (off Map p77; ☎ 362 6080, 06 20 945 0279; www.anselport.hu; XXII V utca 22; 9am-6pm; 213 or 214) in south Buda. Its Suzuki Swift costs between €19 and €34 per day, including unlimited mileage and insurance, depending on the length of the rental (one day to four weeks). Another good bet is **Fox Autorent** (off Map p77; ☎ 382 9000; www.foxautorent.com; XXII Nagytétényi út 48-50; 8am-6pm; 213 or 214), which charges from €38 to €49 per day (€265 per week) for a Smart car and €39 to €50 (€271) for a Fiat Punto (kilometres and insurance included).

Assistance and/or advice for motorists is available from the **Hungarian Automobile Club** (Magyar Autóklub; Map pp80-1; ☎ 345 1800; www.autoklub.hu, in Hungarian; II Rómer Flóris utca 4/a; 4 or 6), off Margit körút near Margaret Bridge. Motorists anywhere in Hungary can call the automobile club on ☎ 188 for assistance.

For information on traffic and public road conditions in the capital, ring **Főinform** (☎ 317 1173; 7am-7pm).

Hitching

The ride service **Kenguru** (Map p84; ☎ 266 5837, 06 20 421 3450; www.kenguru.hu; VIII Kőfaragó utca 15; 10am-2pm Mon-Fri) matches up drivers and riders for a fee – mostly to points abroad. Sample destinations and approximate one-way fares include Amsterdam (15,300Ft), London (17,000Ft), Munich (8100Ft), Paris (16,000Ft), Prague (6100Ft) and Vienna (3500Ft).

Train

Budapest has three main train stations. Most international and all trains to/from the west go via **Keleti train station** (Eastern train station; Map pp80-1; VIII Kerepesi út 2-6; M M3 Keleti pályaudvar). Trains to certain destinations in the east (eg Romania) leave from **Nyugati train station** (Western train station; Map p84; VI Teréz körút 55-57; M M3 Nyugati pályaudvar), while **Déli train station** (Southern train station; Map p83; I Krisztina körút 37; M M2 Déli pályaudvar) handles trains to some destinations in the south (eg Osijek in Croatia and Sarajevo in Bosnia). These are not hard-and-fast rules, so always make sure you check which station your train leaves from when you buy a ticket. The handful of secondary train stations are of little importance to long-distance travellers. Occasionally, though, a through train will stop at **Kelenföldi train station** (Kelenföld train station; Map pp88-9; XI Etele tér 5-7; 19 or 49) in southern Buda. For 24-hour information on international train services ring ☎ 06 40 494 949 (☎ +36-1 371 9449 from abroad) or visit www.mav.hu.

The train stations are generally pretty dismal places, with unsavoury-looking characters hanging about day and night, but all have some amenities. The left-luggage office at **Keleti train station** (24hr) is next to platform 6. At **Nyugati train station** (6.30am-midnight) it's beside the information and ticketing hall, and at **Déli train station** (3.30am-midnight) it's next to platform 1. They charge 150/300Ft for a normal/large piece for six hours and 300/600Ft per 24-hour day. You'll also find post offices and grocery stores that are open late. All three stations are on metro lines and night buses serve them when the metro is closed.

You can buy tickets directly from the train stations in Budapest, but the queues are often long, passengers are in a hurry and sales staff are not the most patient in the city. It's easier at the **MÁV-Start passenger service centre** (Map p86; ☎ 512 7921, 512 7922; www.mav-start.hu; V József Attila utca 16; M M1/2/3 Deák Ferenc tér).

For more information on international train travel, see p384.

GETTING AROUND

To/From the Airport

Budapest's **Ferihegy International Airport** (☎ 296 9696, flight info 296 7000; www.bud.hu), 24km southeast of the city centre, has two modern terminals designated 2A and 2B side by side and within easy walking distance of one another, and an older one (Terminal 1) about 5km to the west. For information on which airlines use which terminal, see p382. Terminal 2B has an **OTP bank** (5.30-10pm) and an ATM, six car-rental desks, a hotel booking office and travel agency, and a **left-luggage office** (24hr).

A company called **Zóna Taxi** (☎ 365 5555; www.zonataxi.eu) now has the monopoly on picking up taxi passengers at the airport. You might pay a little more than in the past – fares to most locations in Pest are 5100Ft and in Buda 5300Ft to 5700Ft – but at least you know you won't be ripped off. Of course, you can take any taxi to the airport and several companies have a flat, discounted fare to/from Ferihegy. **Buda Taxi** (☎ 233 3333; www.budataxi.hu) charges 4600Ft between the airport and Pest, and 5100Ft between Ferihegy and Buda.

The **Budapest Airport Minibusz** (☎ 296 8555; www.airportshuttle.hu) ferries passengers in nine-seat vans from all three of the airport's terminals directly to their hotel, hostel or residence (one way/return 2990/4990Ft). Tickets are available at a clearly marked desk in the arrivals hall, though you may have to wait while the van fills up. You need to book your journey *to* the airport 12 hours in advance, but remember that, with up to eight pick-ups en route, this can be a nerve-wracking way to go if you're running late.

The cheapest (and most time-consuming) way to get into the city centre from Terminals 2A and 2B is to take city bus 200 (270Ft, or 350Ft on the bus) – look for the stop on the footpath between Terminals 2A and 2B – which terminates at the Kőbánya-Kispest metro station. From there, take the M3 metro into the city centre. The total cost is 540Ft to 620Ft. Bus 93 runs from Terminal 1 to Kőbánya-Kispest metro station.

Trains now link Terminal 1 *only* with Nyugati station. They run between one and six times an hour between 4am and 11pm and cost 300Ft (or 520Ft if you board the hourly IC train). The journey takes just 20 minutes.

Bicycle

More and more cyclists are seen on the streets and avenues of Budapest these days, taking advantage of the city's growing network of bike paths. At present, dedicated lanes total 180km, including the path along Andrássy út, though you'll often find yourself fighting for space with pedestrians on them. The main roads in the city might be a bit too busy to allow enjoyable cycling, but the side streets are fine and there are some areas (eg City Park, Margaret Island) where cycling is positively ideal. For ideas on where to cycle and information on where to rent bikes, see p104.

Boat

Between mid-April and mid-October, passenger ferries run by **BKV** (Budapest Transport Company; ☎ 461 6500, 258 4636; www.bkv.hu) depart from IX Boráros tér (Map pp88–9), just north of Petőfi Bridge, between five and seven times daily and head for III Pünkösdfürdő in Óbuda, a 2¼-hour trip with 14 stops along the way. Tickets (adult/child 900/450Ft from end to end, or between 250/150Ft and 600/300Ft for intermediate stops) are sold on board. The ferry stop closest to the Castle District is I Batthyány tér (Map p83), and Vigadó tér is not far from the pier just west of Vörösmarty tér (Map p86). Transporting a bicycle costs 700Ft.

For information on river cruises, see p108.

Car & Motorcycle

Though it's not so bad at night, driving in Budapest during the day can be a nightmare: ongoing road works reduce traffic to a snail's pace; there are more serious accidents than fender-benders; and parking spots are near impossible to find in some neighbourhoods. The public transport system is good and cheap. Use it.

Parking costs 120Ft to 300Ft per hour on the street (up to 600Ft on Castle Hill), generally between 8am and 6pm Monday to Friday and 8am and noon on Saturday. There are 24-hour covered car parks charging from 370Ft to 680Ft per hour at V Váci utca 25 (below the Millennium Center; Map p86), at V Szervita tér 8 (Map p86), where you'll find Avis, at V Aranykéz utca 4–6 (Map p86) in the Inner Town, and at VII Nyár utca 20 (Map p84).

Illegally parked cars are not normally towed in Budapest these days but clamped. If you are trying to trace a vehicle you believe has been towed (this usually only happens during demonstrations), ring ☎ 267 4673. To have a boot removed, which will cost you between 7200Ft and 14,400Ft, ring ☎ 06 80 220 220 or 06 80 330 330.

Drink-driving is taken very seriously in Hungary; for details see p376.

Public Transport

Budapest has a safe, efficient and inexpensive public transport system that is now being upgraded and will never have you waiting more than five or 10 minutes for any conveyance. There are five types of vehicle in general use: metro trains on three (and soon to be four) city lines, green HÉV trains on four suburban lines, blue buses, yellow trams and red trolleybuses. All are run by **BKV** (Budapest Transport Company; ☎ 461 6500, 258 4636; www.bkv.hu). Anyone planning to travel extensively by public transport in Budapest should invest in the invaluable *Budapesti Közlekedési Térképe* (Budapest Public Transport Map; 500Ft), available at most metro ticket booths. You might also try BKV's route planner at http://utvonal.bkv.hu.

BUDAPEST METRO & RAIL ROUTES

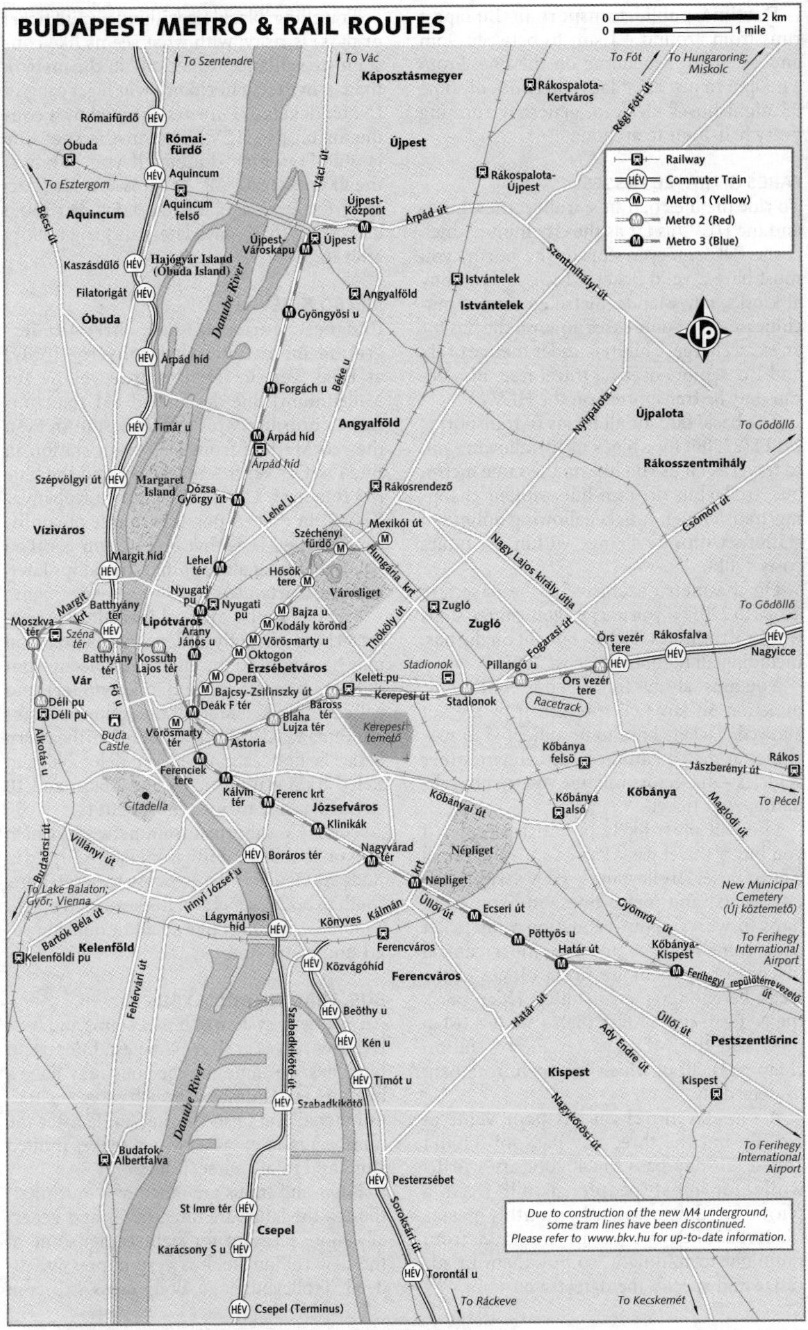

Daytime public transport in Budapest runs from around 4.15am to between 9pm and 11.30pm, depending on the line. From 11.30pm to just after 4am a network of some 35 night buses kicks in, generally running every half-hour to an hour.

FARES & TRAVEL PASSES

To ride the metro, trams, trolleybuses, buses and the HÉV (as far as the city limits, which is the Békásmegyer stop to the north) you must have a valid ticket, which you can buy at kiosks, newsstands, metro entrances, machines and, in some cases now, on the bus for an extra charge. Children under the age of six and EU seniors over 65 travel free. Bicycles can only be transported on the HÉV.

The basic fare for all forms of transport is 270Ft (2350Ft for a block of 10), allowing you to travel as far as you like on the same metro, bus, trolleybus or tram line *without* changing/transferring. A ticket allowing unlimited stations with one change within 1½ hours costs 420Ft.

On the metro exclusively, the base fare drops to 220Ft if you are just going three stops within 30 minutes. Tickets bought on the bus, including all night buses, cost 350Ft.

You must always travel in one continuous direction on any ticket; return trips are not allowed. Tickets have to be validated in machines at metro entrances and aboard other vehicles – inspectors will fine you for not validating your ticket.

Life will most likely be much simpler if you buy a travel pass. Passes are valid on all trams, buses, trolleybuses, HÉV (within the city limits) and metro lines, and you don't have to worry about validating your ticket each time you get on. The most central places to buy them are ticket offices at the Deák Ferenc tér metro station (Map p86), the Nyugati pályaudvar metro station (Map p84) and the Moszkva tér metro station (Map p83), all of which are open from 6am to 8pm daily.

A one-day travel card is poor value at 1550Ft, but the three-day pass for 3400Ft and seven-day pass for 4000Ft are worthwhile for most people. You'll need a photo for the fortnightly/monthly passes (5300/8250Ft). All passes are valid from midnight to midnight, so buy them in advance and specify the date(s) you want.

Travelling 'black' (ie without a valid ticket or pass) is risky; with what seems like constant surveillance (especially in the metro), there's an excellent chance you'll get caught. (Note: tickets are *always* checked by a conductor on the HÉV.) The on-the-spot fine is 6000Ft, which doubles if you pay it at the **BKV office** (Map p84; ☎ 461 6800; VII Akácfa utca 22; 🕑 6am-8pm Mon-Fri, 8am-1.45pm Sat; Ⓜ M2 Blaha Lujza tér) up to 30 days later, and is 24,000Ft after that.

METRO & HÉV

Budapest currently has three underground metro lines that converge (only) at Deák Ferenc tér: the little yellow (or Millennium) line designated M1 that runs from Vörösmarty tér to Mexikoi út in Pest; the red M2 line from Déli train station in Buda to Örs vezér tere in Pest; and the blue M3 line from Újpest-Központ to Kőbánya-Kispest in Pest. A possible source of confusion on the M1 is that one station is called Vörösmarty tér and another, five stops later, is Vörösmarty utca.

The city's long-awaited **M4 metro line** (www.metro4.hu) is currently under construction (you may have noticed the enormous pits in front of Keleti train station and in Kálvin tér), and will run from Kelenföldi train station in southern Buda to XIV Bosnyák tér in northeastern Pest. The first section, between Kelenföldi and Keleti train stations, covering 7.5km and 10 stations, is due to open in late 2011.

The HÉV suburban train network, which runs on four lines (north from Batthyány tér in Buda via Óbuda and Aquincum to Szentendre, south to both Csepel and Ráckeve, and east to Gödöllő), is almost like an additional aboveground metro line.

BUS, TRAM & TROLLEYBUS

An extensive system of buses, trams and trolleybuses serves greater Budapest. On certain bus lines the same number bus may have a black or a red number. In such cases, the red-numbered one (also bearing an 'E' after the number) is an express, which makes limited stops and is, of course, faster.

Buses and trams are much of a muchness, though the latter are often faster and generally more pleasant for sightseeing; some of the new rolling stock is very impressive indeed. Trolleybuses go along cross streets in central Pest and are of limited use to most visitors, with the sole exception of the ones to City and Népliget Parks.

Following are bus routes (shown with blue lines on Budapest maps) you might find useful:

No 7 Cuts across a large swathe of central Pest from XIV Bosnyák tér and down VII Rákóczi út, before crossing Elizabeth Bridge to Kelenföldi train station in southern Buda.
No 86 Runs the length of Buda from XI Kosztolányi Dezső tér to Óbuda.
No 105 Goes from V Deák Ferenc tér to XII Apor Vilmos tér in central Buda.
No 115 Takes in most of the Inner Town from IX Boráros tér to XIII Lehel tér north of Nyugati train station.
Night bus 906 Follows the tram 6 route along the Big Ring Road.
Night bus 907 Traces an enormously long route from Örs vezér tere M2 metro stop in Pest to Kelenföldi train station in Buda.

Important tram lines (always marked with red lines on a Budapest map, while a broken red line signifies a trolleybus):

No 2 Scenic tram that travels along the Pest side of the Danube from V Jászai Mari tér to IX Boráros tér and beyond.
Nos 4 & 6 Extremely useful trams that start at XI Fehérvári út and XI Móricz Zsigmond körtér in south Buda, respectively, and follow the entire length of the Big Ring Road in Pest before terminating at II Moszkva tér in Buda.
No 18 Runs from southern Buda along XI Bartók Béla út, through the Tabán to II Moszkva tér, before carrying on into the Buda Hills.
No 19 Covers part of the same route as No 18, but then runs along the Buda side of the Danube to I Batthyány tér.
Nos 47 & 49 Link V Deák Ferenc tér in Pest with points in southern Buda via the Little Ring Road.
No 61 Connects XI Móricz Zsigmond körtér with Déli train station and II Moszkva tér in Buda.

Taxi

Taxis in Budapest remain very cheap by European standards, but with such an excellent public transport network available, you don't really have to use them very often. We've heard from many readers who were grossly overcharged and even threatened by taxi drivers in Budapest, so taking a taxi in this city should be approached with caution. However, the reputable firms we've listed below have caught on to the concept of customer service and take complaints very seriously indeed nowadays.

Avoid at all costs (operative word) taxis with no name on the door and only a removable taxi light box on the roof; these are just guys with cars and the ones most likely to rip you off. Never get into a taxi that does not have a yellow licence plate and an identification badge displayed on the dashboard (as required by law), the logo of one of the reputable taxi firms on the side doors and a table of fares clearly visible on the right-side back door.

Not all taxi meters are set at the same rates, and some are much more expensive than others, but there are price ceilings under which taxi companies are free to manoeuvre. From 6am to 10pm the highest flag-fall fee that can be legally charged is 300Ft, the per-kilometre charge 240Ft and the waiting fee 60Ft. From 10pm to 6am the equivalent fees are 420/336/84Ft.

Budapest residents – local or foreign – rarely flag down taxis in the street. They almost always ring for them, and fares are actually cheaper if you book over the phone. Make sure you know the number of the landline phone you're calling from, as that's how they establish your address (though you can, of course, call from a mobile phone, too).

Following are the telephone numbers and websites of a half-dozen reputable taxi firms:

Buda (☎ 233 3333; www.budataxi.hu)
City (☎ 211 1111; www.citytaxi.hu)
Fő (☎ 222 2222; www.fotaxi.hu)
Rádió (☎ 377 7777; www.radiotaxi.hu)
Taxi 4 (☎ 444 4444; www.taxi4.hu)
Tele 5 (☎ 355 5555; www.tele5taxi.hu)

AROUND BUDAPEST

Hungary is not huge; a good deal of the rest of the country is 'around Budapest', and many of the towns and cities on the Danube Bend and in Transdanubia, the Northern Uplands and even the Great Plain are relatively easy day trips from the capital. You can be in Szentendre (19km) in half an hour, for example, and Gyöngyös, the gateway to the bucolic Mátra Hills, is only 80km to the east. Here are several easy day or even half-day trips from the capital.

MEMENTO PARK

A truly mind-blowing excursion is a visit to **Memento Park** (Map p77; ☎ 424 7500; www.mementopark.hu; cnr XXII Balatoni út 16-18; adult/student & child 1500/1000Ft; 10am-dusk), 10km southwest of the city centre. Called Statue Park until a recent sprucing up and an injection of government funds, since 1993 it's been home to almost four-dozen statues, busts and plaques of Lenin, Marx, Béla Kun and 'heroic' workers that have ended up on rubbish heaps in other former socialist countries. Ogle at the socialist realism and try to imagine that at least four of these monstrous monuments were erected as recently as the late 1980s; a few of them, including the Béla Kun memorial of our 'hero' in a crowd by sculptor Imre Varga (p94), were still in place when one Lonely Planet author moved to Budapest in early 1992. New attractions here are the replicated remains of Stalin's boots, all that was left after a crowd pulled the enormous statue down from its plinth on XIV Dózsa György út during the 1956 Uprising, and an exhibition centre in an old barracks with displays on the events of 1956, the changes since 1989 and a documentary film with rare footage of secret agents collecting information on 'subversives'.

To reach this socialist Disneyland, take tram 19 from I Batthyány tér in Buda, tram 47 or 49 from V Deák Ferenc tér in Pest or bus 7 or 173 from V Ferenciek tere in Pest to XI Kosztolány Dezsö tér in southern Buda, then board city bus 150 (270Ft, 25 minutes, 8km, every 20 to 30 minutes) for the park.

An easier (though more expensive) way to go is via the park's direct bus (with park admission adult/child return 3950/2450Ft), which departs from in front of the Le Meridien Budapest hotel on Deák Ferenc tér at 11am year-round, with an extra departure at 3pm in July and August.

SZÁZHALOMBATTA

☎ 23 / pop 18,600

Some 28km southwest of Budapest in the unattractive settlement of Százhalombatta, site of a huge heat and power plant (and Hungary's leading energy centre), is **Archaeological Park** (Régészeti Park; ☎ 350 537; www.matricamuzeum.hu; Poroszlai Ildikó utca 1; adult/child/family 780/360/2280Ft; 10am-6pm Tue-Sun Apr-Oct), the only open-air prehistoric museum in Hungary and the country's most important Hallstatt site (see the boxed text, below). The 6-hectare park sits in the middle of some of the more than 120 Iron Age burial mounds – Százhalombatta means '100 Mounds' – in the area and is still undergoing excavation. There are about 10 reconstructed Bronze and Iron Age settlements, including replicas of pottery, cooking utensils, musical instruments and clothing. The highlight of the park is the 2700-year-old oak-timber burial mound No 115, measuring 7m in height, which houses an incredibly detailed 5.5-sq-m burial chamber rebuilt from archaeological finds and floor plans. A 20-minute multimedia presentation in English, Hungarian and German briefly delves into the history of the Bronze and Iron Age in Central Europe, before moving on to the burial process and a step-by-step explanation of the reconstruction of the burial crypt.

The **Matrica Museum** (☎ 354 591; www.matricamuzeum.hu; Gesztenyés út 1-3; adult/child/family 780/360/2280Ft; 10am-5pm Tue-Sun), part of the Archaeological Park but closer to town, traces the history of the settlement from prehistoric

HALLSTATT IN HUNGARY

Hallstatt is the name of a village in the Salzkammergut region of Austria where objects characteristic of the early Iron Age (from about 800 to 500 BC) were found in the 19th century. Today it's used generically for the late Bronze and early Iron Age cultures that developed in Central and Western Europe from about 1200 to 450 BC.

Parts of western Hungary, including Százhalombatta, were settled during this period. Tumuli (burial mounds) and forts have yielded axes, body armour, jewellery and especially dishes, mugs, cups and other utensils that are often richly decorated. Some of these finds are now on display at the Matrica Museum (above).

Hallstatt art is very geometric, and typical motifs include birds and figures arranged in pairs. It was not until the advent of the late Iron Age La Tène culture (450 to 390 BC) of the European Celts that S-shapes, spirals and round patterns developed.

times till today. A ticket to both the park and the museum costs 1200/600/3000Ft per adult/child/family.

Some 300m northeast of the museum en route to the park, the **Harcsa Csárda** (☎ 354 926; Dunafüredi út 1; mains 1450-3900Ft; 🕑 11.30am-11pm Mon-Thu, to midnight Fri & Sat, noon-8pm Sun) is an old-style inn serving generous grilled and fish dishes, including its signature *harcsa halászlé* (catfish soup; 1350Ft).

Getting There & Away

Over two dozen daily trains leaving Budapest's Déli train station for Pécs via Kelenföldi station stop at Százhalombatta (450Ft, 40 minutes, 28km, every 20 minutes); the last train returns at 10.25pm. An infrequent bus links the Százhalombatta train station with the park; the last one leaves for the station at around 4pm.

Buses bound for Százhalombatta (375Ft, 40 minutes, 25km, half-hourly) leave frequently throughout the day from the bus station on IX Etele tér next to Kelenföldi train station in southern Buda.

RÁCKEVE

☎ 24 / pop 9780

The attractions of this town on the southeastern end of Csepel, the long island in the Danube south of Budapest, are its pretty riverside park and *strand,* a colourful Gothic Serbian Orthodox church – *rác* is the old Hungarian word for 'Serb' – and the former Savoya Mansion, now a lovely hotel. **Tourinform** (☎ 429 747; www.tourinform.rackeve.hu; Eötvös Károly utca 11; 🕑 9am-5pm Mon-Sat mid-Jun–mid-Sep, 8am-5pm Mon-Fri mid-Sep–mid-Jun) is in the centre of town, due west of the Árpád Bridge over the Danube.

Sights

SAVOYA MANSION

About 600m south of the HÉV station is the **Savoya Mansion** (Savoyai-kastély; ☎ 485 253; www.savoyai.hu; Kossuth Lajos utca 95), now a 30-room hotel facing the Ráckeve-Danube River branch. The domed manse with two wings was finished in 1722 in the baroque style for Prince Eugene of Savoya, who drove out the last of the Turkish occupiers from Hungary at the Battle of Zenta in 1697, by an Austrian architect who would later go on to design Schönbrunn Palace in Vienna. The mansion was completely renovated and turned into a pricey hotel and conference centre in 1982.

SERBIAN ORTHODOX CHURCH

From Hősök tere in the centre of town you can't miss the blue clock tower of the **Serbian Orthodox Church** (Görög-keleti szerb templom; Viola utca 1; adult/child 400/200Ft; 🕑 10am-noon & 2-5pm Tue-Sat, 2-5pm Sun) to the southeast. The late-Gothic church was originally built in 1487 by Serbs who fled their town of Keve ahead of the invading Turks, and many street signs in the neighbourhood are in Serbian. It was enlarged with two Renaissance side chapels in the following century. The free-standing clock tower was added in 1758.

The walls and ceiling of the church interior are covered with colourful frescoes painted by a Serbian master from Albania between 1765 and 1771. The walls depict scenes from the Old and New Testaments and a panoply of saints; they were meant to teach the Bible to illiterate parishioners. The first section of the nave is reserved for women; the part beyond the separating wall is for men. Only the priest and his servers enter the sanctuary beyond the iconostasis, the richly carved and gilded gate covered in icons.

ÁRPÁD MUSEUM

This small **museum** (☎ 519 035; Kossuth Lajos utca 34; adult/child 400/200Ft; 🕑 10am-6pm Tue-Sun Apr-Sep, 1-5pm Tue-Sun Oct-Mar), about 500m south of the mansion, has exhibits focusing on the Danube, with an emphasis on water mills of various types, along with a lot of old photographs.

Eating

Cadran (☎ 485 470; Hősök tere 1; pizza 590-1190Ft, Mexican dishes 990-2590Ft; 🕑 10am-10pm Mon-Sat, 12.30-10pm Sun) A popular eatery and pub in the centre of town, facing the river and Árpád Bridge, Cadran is recommended for a lunch stop before or after visiting the nearby Serbian church. There's outside seating in a back courtyard.

Savoyai Kastély (☎ 424 189; Kossuth Lajos utca 95; mains 1800-5000Ft; 🕑 noon-10pm) The Savoya Mansion's cellar restaurant is one of the better eateries in Ráckeve and offers an easy way to have a good look at the mansion's interior without actually staying here.

Getting There & Away

The easiest way to reach Ráckeve is on the HÉV suburban train (720Ft, 70 minutes, 40km, half-hourly), departing from the Vágóhíd HÉV terminus in district IX on the Pest side. You can reach that train station from the Inner Town on tram 2 or from Keleti train station on tram 24. The last HÉV train back to Budapest leaves Ráckeve just after 10pm.

GÖDÖLLŐ

☎ 28 / pop 34,300

Just 30km northeast of the Inner Town and easily accessible on the HÉV, Gödöllő (pronounced – roughly – *good*-duh-ler) is an easy day trip from the capital. The main draw here is the Gödöllő Royal Palace, which rivalled Esterházy Palace at Fertőd in Western Transdanubia (p177) in splendour and size when it was completed in the 1760s, and is the largest baroque manor house in Hungary. But the town itself, full of lovely baroque buildings and monuments and host to a couple of important annual music festivals, is worth the trip.

Tourinform (☎ 415 402; www.godollotourinform.hu; 10am-6pm Tue-Sun Apr-Oct, to 5pm Tue-Sun Nov-Mar) has an office just inside the entrance to the palace, but you'll do better directing any query to the ticket office.

Sights

Gödöllő Royal Palace (Gödöllői Királyi Kastély; ☎ 410 124; www.kiralyikastely.hu; Szabadság tér 1; adult/student & child/family 1800/900/3800Ft; 10am-6pm Apr-Oct, 11am-2.30pm Mon, 10am-5pm Tue-Sun Nov-Mar) was designed by Antal Mayerhoffer for Count Antal Grassalkovich (1694–1771), confidante of Empress Maria Theresa, in 1741. After the formation of the Dual Monarchy, the palace was enlarged as a summer retreat for Emperor Franz Joseph, and soon became the favoured residence of his consort, the much-beloved Habsburg empress and Hungarian queen, Elizabeth (1837–98), affectionately known as Sissi. Between WWI and WWII the regent, Admiral Miklós Horthy, also used it as a summer residence, but after the communists took control part of the mansion was used as a barracks for Soviet and Hungarian troops and as an old people's home. The rest was left to decay.

Partial renovation of the mansion began in the 1990s, and today more than two-dozen rooms are open to the public as the Palace Museum on the ground and 1st floors. The rooms have been restored (too thoroughly in some instances) to the period when the imperial couple were in residence, and on the 1st floor Franz Joseph's suites, done up in 'manly' greys and maroons, and Sissi's violet-coloured private apartments are impressive, if not as evocative of the past as the rooms at the Esterházy Palace. On the 1st floor, check out in particular the **Ceremonial Hall**, all gold tracery, stucco and chandeliers, where chamber-music concerts are held throughout the year but especially in October during the Liszt and International Harp Festivals; the **Queen's Reception Room**, with a Romantic-style oil painting of Sissi patriotically repairing the coronation robe of King Stephen with needle and thread; and the **Grassalkovich Era exhibition**, which offers an in-depth look at the palace before the royal couple moved in.

A number of other recently opened rooms and buildings can be visited on a guided tour only at extra cost, including the **Baroque Theatre** (adult/student & child 1200/600Ft) in the southern wing. A combined ticket offering entry to the **Royal Hill Pavilion** in the park, built in the 1760s, the **Royal Baths** as well as the museum and the theatre costs 3300/1650Ft for adults/students and children.

Eating

Pizza Palazzo (☎ 420 688; Szabadság tér 2; pizza 830-1110Ft, pasta 1190-1450Ft) This popular pizzeria with some more substantial pasta dishes is attached to the Szabadság tér HÉV station.

Szélkakas (☎ 423 119; Bajcsy-Zsilinszky utca 27; mains 1300-2250Ft; 11.30am-11pm Sun-Thu, to midnight Fri & Sat) The 'Weathervane' is a charming eatery in a neighbourhood of 18th-century farmhouses about 500m north of the Szabadság tér HÉV stop. The partially covered garden is a delight in the warmer months.

Getting There & Away

HÉV trains from Örs vezér tere, at the terminus of the M2 metro, link Budapest with Gödöllő (570Ft, 45 minutes, 26km, hourly) throughout the day. Make sure you get off at the Szabadság tér stop, which is the third from the last stop. The last train leaves this stop for Budapest just before 10.45pm.

In addition, buses from Stadionok bus station in Budapest also serve Gödöllő (450Ft, 45 minutes, 28km, hourly). The last bus back is just before 7.30pm Monday to Friday (shortly after 8pm on Saturday and Sunday). The bus station is due east of the Szabadság tér HÉV station, next to the 1960s-style cultural centre.

Danube Bend

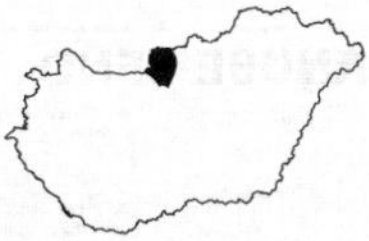

The Danube Bend is pint-sized compared to many of Hungary's regions, but what it lacks in size it makes up for with an overabundance of natural beauty and a venerable wealth of human endeavour.

The region's name is highly literal, for the mighty river does indeed bend. With the unrelenting mass of the Börzsöny Hills on its north bank and the Pilis Hills to the south, the Danube is forced into a handful of tight, bunched curves, creating the country's prettiest stretch of the river. A boat trip here is a must, for there is no other way to truly appreciate Hungary's dustless highway, or see it in all its guises. The forested hills that rise on each side of the Danube are attractions in their own right; together they make up the Danube-Ipoly National Park, and nature lovers will find hiking paths aplenty.

Four towns on the banks of the Danube vie for visitors' attention. Szentendre, for centuries a community open to new settlers, unorthodox religions, and artists, is today a tourist hotspot with cobbled streets and a profusion of church spires. Further round the bend is tiny Visegrád, once the seat of Hungary's kings and queens and today home to Renaissance-palace ruins and a forbidding hilltop castle. Esztergom, for so many years the Pope's 'eyes and ears' in Hungary, is now a sleepy town with the biggest basilica this side of the Balkans, while Vác is a lovely spot with a laid-back attitude and a macabre crypt of mummies.

All this, and all within easy reach of the capital. Sometimes size really doesn't matter.

HIGHLIGHTS

- Strolling the cobbled back streets of **Szentendre** (p141), where life remains untouched by the town's mass tourism
- Making a day of it on the Danube, cruising from town to town by **ferry** or **hydrofoil** (p140)
- Discovering the forgotten Renaissance splendour of the royal enclaves at **Visegrád** (p149)
- Climbing Castle Hill in Esztergom to explore the nooks and crannies of the town's massive **basilica** (p154)
- Picking a path for a pleasurable hike through the green hills of **Börzsöny** (p149) or **Pilis** (p152)

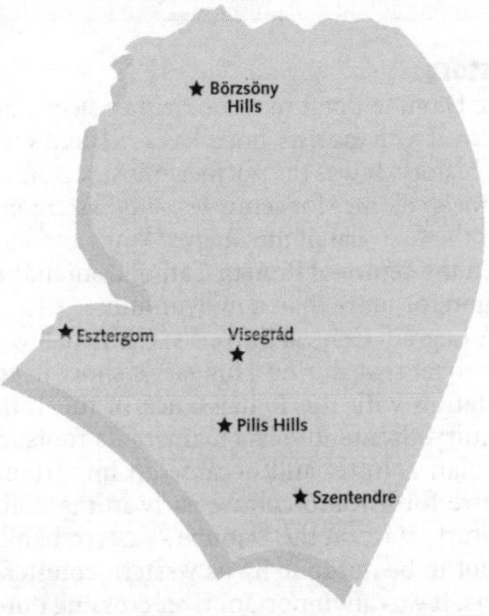

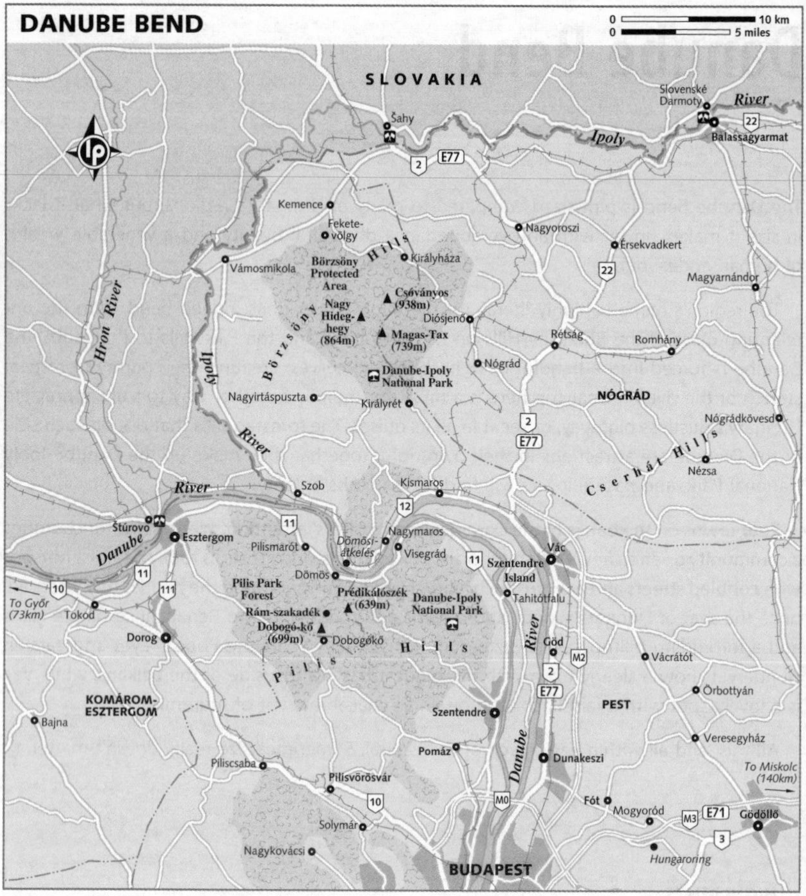

History

The Danube Bend may look either sleepy or overrun with tourists, but it has a rich and varied history. It was the northernmost region of Rome's colonies for centuries, and Esztergom was the first seat of the Magyar kings and has been the centre of Roman Catholicism in the region for more than a millennium.

Visegrád, Central Europe's 'Camelot', was the royal seat during Hungary's short-lived flirtation with the Renaissance in the 15th century. Szentendre has many of its roots in Serbian culture, and became an important centre for art and culture early in the 20th century. Vác, on the Danube's eastern bank, is not to be outdone by its western counterparts. It was an important river crossing during Roman times and King Stephen himself thought the town valuable enough to establish an episcopate here in the 11th century.

Getting There & Around

Being so close to Budapest, the Danube Bend has good connections to the rest of Hungary. Regular buses serve towns on the western bank of the Danube, but trains only go as far as Szentendre with a separate line running to Esztergom; the eastern bank has the luxury of excellent bus and train links. The river itself is a perfect highway, and regular boats ferry tourists to and from Budapest over the summer months.

From May to September, one daily **Mahart** (www.mahartpassnave.hu) ferry departs Budapest's

Vigadó tér at 10.30am bound for Szentendre (one way/return 1490/2235Ft, 80 minutes), returning at 5pm; the service dwindles to weekends only in April and October. In July and August the service is increased to two sailings a day, the second one at 2.30pm and returning at 7pm. Additionally, from May to August a daily 9am ferry leaves Budapest, calling in at Szentendre (10.40am) and Visegrád (one way/return 1590/2385Ft, 12.30pm), before returning from Visegrád at 4.30pm. The service dwindles to weekends only in April, Friday in September, and Friday to Sunday in October.

Hydrofoils travel from Budapest to Visegrád (one way/return 2690/3990Ft, one hour), Vác (one way/return 1990/2990Ft, 40 minutes) and Esztergom (one way/return 3290/4990Ft, 1½ hours) on Friday, Saturday and Sunday from June to August and on weekends in May and September; sailings leave at 9.30am and return at 5pm from Esztergom, 5.30pm from Visegrád and 5.45pm from Vác.

Lastly, there are daily ferries at 8am from Budapest to Vác (one way/return 1490/2235Ft, two hours 20 minutes, returns at 6.45pm), Visegrád (one way/return 1590/2385Ft, 3½ hours, returns at 6pm), and Esztergom (one way/return 1990/2985Ft, 5½ hours, returns at 4.30pm) between June and August. Services decrease to Friday, Saturday and Sunday in May and weekends only in September.

SZENTENDRE

☎ 26 / pop 24,000

Szentendre is a town that has changed little in appearance since the 18th century. For some this is a blessing, for others a curse; its cobblestone alleyways and skyline of church spires are indeed something special, but the hoards of tourists jostling you as you attempt to appreciate the scene can at times simply be too much. Either way you look at it, Szentendre is worth visiting – however brief – and if its architecture doesn't impress, its plethora of art museums and galleries should. Note that Szentendre is best avoided on weekends in summer, and between November and mid-March much of the town shuts down on weekdays.

History

Like most towns along the Danube Bend, Szentendre was home first to the Celts and then the Romans, who built an important border fortress here called Wolf's Castle (Ulcisia Castra). The Magyars arrived late in the 9th century and established a colony here and by the 14th century Szentendre was a prosperous estate under the supervision of the royal castle at Visegrád.

It was about this time that the first wave of Serbian Orthodox Christians came from the south in advance of the Turks, but the Turkish occupation of Hungary over the ensuing centuries brought the town's peaceful co-existence to an end, and by the end of the 17th century the town was deserted. Though Hungary was liberated from the Ottomans soon afterwards, fighting continued in the Balkans and a second wave of Serbs, together with Greeks, Dalmatians and others, fled to Szentendre. Believing they would return home, but enjoying complete religious freedom under the relatively benevolent rule of the Habsburgs (a right denied to Hungary's Protestants at the time), half a dozen Orthodox clans each built their own churches and gave the town its unique Balkan feel.

Szentendre's delightful location began to attract day trippers and painters from Budapest early last century; an artists colony was established here in the 1920s. The town has been known for its art and artists ever since.

Orientation

The HÉV commuter train and bus stations lie side by side south of the town centre at the start of Dunakanyar körút (Danube Bend Ring Road). From here it's a short walk north along Kossuth Lajos utca and Dumtsa Jenő utca to Fő tér, the heart of Szentendre. The Duna korzó promenade along the Danube and the ferry to Szentendre Island are a few minutes' walk east and northeast, respectively, of Fő tér. The Mahart ferry pier (Czóbel Béla sétány) is about a kilometre northeast, off Duna korzó.

Information

New Cultural Centre of Szentendre (www.szentendreprogram.hu) Provides loads of online information.
OTP bank (Dumtsa Jenő utca 6) Has a change machine and ATM.
Post office (Kossuth Lajos utca 23-25)
Silver Blue (Dunakanyar Körút 14; per hr 400Ft; 🕒 10am-8pm Mon-Sat) Small internet cafe close to the train and bus stations.
Tourinform (☎ 317 965; szentendre@tourinform.hu; Dumtsa Jenő utca 22; 🕒 9.30am-4.30pm Mon-Fri year-round, 10am-2pm Sat & Sun mid-Mar–Oct) Helpful centre with stacks of information.

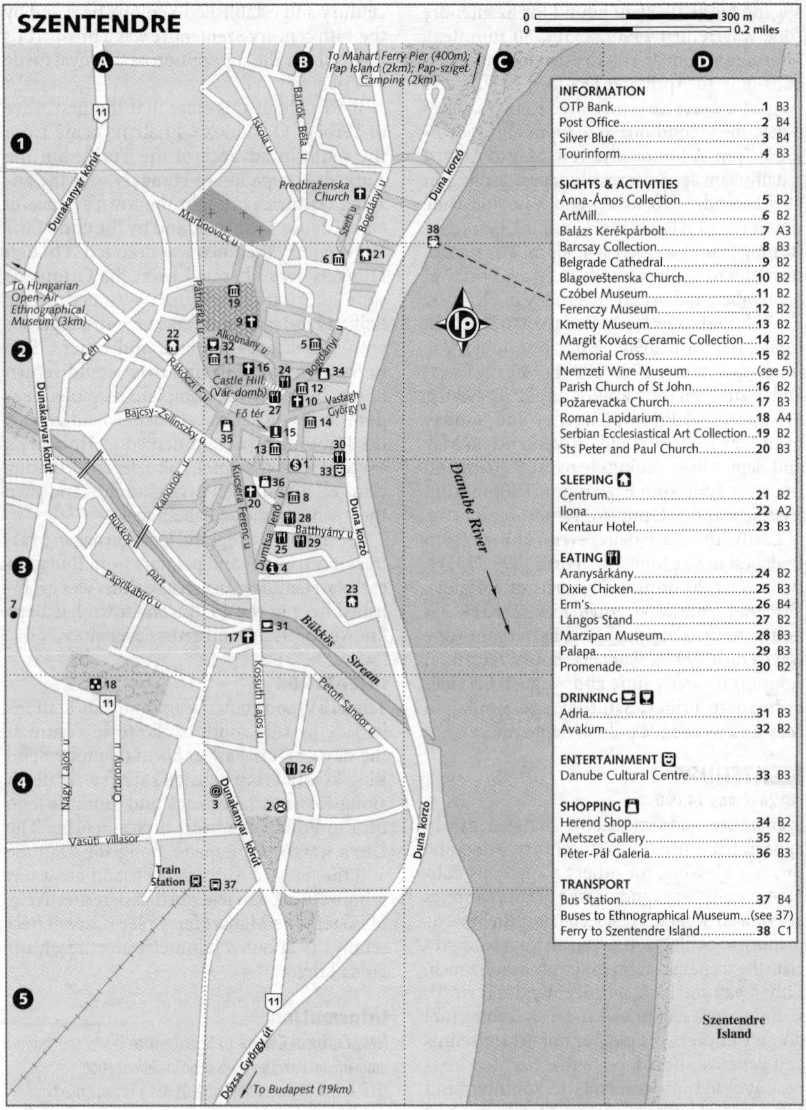

Sights

INNER TOWN

A good starting point on your tour of Szentendre is the **Požarevačka Church** (☎ 310 554; Kossuth Lajos utca 1; admission 200Ft; by appointment), which you'll pass on the way from the stations. Dedicated in 1763, this Serbian Orthodox church has a lovely iconostasis dating from 1742.

To the north, the **Sts Peter and Paul Church** (Péter-Pál utca 6; admission free; 10am-4pm Tue-Sun) began life as the Čiprovačka Orthodox Church in 1753, but was later taken over by Dalmatian Catholics. Its simple interior is dominated by a gigantic crucifixion icon hanging above the altar. The **Barcsay Collection** (Barcsay Gyüjtemény; Dumtsa Jenő utca 10; adult/child 400/200Ft; 9am-5pm

Wed-Sun mid-Mar–Sep, 1-5pm Wed-Sun Oct–mid-Mar), to the east, contains the work of one of the founders of Szentendre's art colony, Jenő Barcsay (1900–88).

Moving onto Fő tér, the colourful heart of Szentendre surrounded by 18th- and 19th-century burghers' houses, you'll find the **Memorial Cross** (1763), an iron cross decorated with icons on a marble base. The **Kmetty Museum** (☎ 310 790; Fő tér 21) on the southwestern side of the square normally displays the work of the cubist János Kmetty (1889–1975), but was closed at the time of research due to technical reasons; check with Tourinform for more information.

The square's highlight is the **Blagoveštenska Church** (☎ 310 554; Fő tér; admission 250Ft; 10am-5pm Tue-Sun), built in 1754. The church, with fine baroque and rococo elements, hardly looks 'eastern' from the outside, but the inside gives the game away. The small but powerful nave is lined with an ornate iconostasis and elaborate 18th-century furnishings. It is a sight to behold.

The **Ferenczy Museum** (☎ 310 790; Fő tér 6; adult/child 400/200Ft; 9am-5pm Wed-Sun mid-Mar–Sep, 1-5pm Wed-Sun Oct–mid-Mar) next to the Blagoveštenska Church is devoted to Károly Ferenczy (1862–1917), the father of plein-air painting in Hungary, and his three children: a painter, a sculptor and a weaver.

Descending Görög utca and turning right onto Vastagh György utca, you'll reach the **Margit Kovács Ceramic Collection** (Kovács Margit Kerámiagyűjtemény; ☎ 310 244; Vastagh György utca 1; adult/child 700/350Ft; 10am-6pm) in an 18th-century salt house. Kovács (1902–77) was a ceramicist who combined Hungarian folk, religious and modern themes to create Gothic-like figures. Some of Kovács' works are overly sentimental, but many are very powerful, especially the later ones in which mortality is a central theme.

Castle Hill (Vár-domb), which can be reached via Váralja lépcső, the narrow steps between Fő tér 8 and 9, was the site of a fortress in the Middle Ages. All that's left of it today is the walled **Parish Church of St John** (Templom tér; admission free), from where you get splendid views of the town. Unfortunately the church entrance (which is early Gothic) is often locked, but you can peer through the bars at the frescoes that were painted by members of the artists colony in the 1930s. Also on Castle Hill is the **Czóbel Museum** (☎ 310 790; Templom tér 1; adult/child 400/200Ft; 10am-6pm Wed-Sun), which contains the works of the impressionist Béla Czóbel (1883–1976), a friend of Pablo Picasso and student of Henri Matisse.

Just north of Castle Hill you'll notice the red tower of **Belgrade Cathedral** (Belgrád Székesegyház; Alkotmány utca; admission incl art collection 500Ft; 10am-4pm Fri-Sun Jan & Feb, 10am-6pm Tue-Sun May-Sep, 10am-4pm Tue-Sun Oct-Dec), completed in 1764 and seat of the Serbian Orthodox bishop in Hungary. One of the church buildings beside it now contains the **Serbian Ecclesiastical Art Collection** (Szerb Egyházművészeti Gyüjtemény; ☎ 312 399; Pátriárka utca 5; adult/child 500/250Ft; 10am-4pm Fri-Sun Jan & Feb, to 6pm Tue-Sun Mar-Sep, to 4pm Tue-Sun Oct-Dec), a treasure-trove of icons, vestments and other sacred objects in precious metals. A 14th-century glass painting of the crucifixion is the oldest item on display; a 'cotton icon' of the life of Christ from the 18th century is unusual. Take a look at the defaced portrait of Christ upstairs on the right-hand wall. The story goes that a drunken *kuruc* (anti-Habsburg) mercenary slashed it and, told the next morning what he had done, drowned himself in the Danube.

Bogdányi utca, Szentendre's busiest pedestrian street, leads north from Fő tér, where you'll find the excellent **Anna-Ámos Collection** (☎ 310 790; Bogdányi utca 10-12; adult/child 400/200Ft; 10am-6pm Wed-Fri & Sun Apr-Oct), displaying the symbolist paintings of husband-and-wife team Margit Anna and Imre Ámos. Next door the **Nemzeti Wine Museum** (Nemzeti Bormúzeum; ☎ 317 054; Bogdányi utca 10; admission 200Ft, 5/9 tastings 1500/2200Ft; 10am-10pm) traces the development of winemaking in Hungary and charges quite a bit more to sample various vintages.

Housed in a 19th-century industrial complex at the northern end of Bogdányi utca is the **ArtMill** (MűvészetMalom; ☎ 301 701; Bogdányi utca 32; adult/child 1000/500Ft; 10am-6pm), Szentendre's bid to recapture its past as a serious centre for artists and the arts. Its extensive exhibition space is used for paintings, sculpture, graphics and applied arts, and its grounds are possibly the quietest spot in the touristy centre.

A field on busy Dunakanyar körút was the site of the Roman fort Ulcisia Castra in the 2nd century, and excavations are currently underway to unearth what remains. A few of the finds are on display at the **Roman Lapidarium** (Dunakanyar körút 1; admission free; 9am-4pm Mon-Thu, to noon Fri) near the site, and amateur archaeologists can visit the dig from 10am to 11am Tuesday and Thursday if field work is taking place.

HUNGARIAN OPEN-AIR ETHNOGRAPHICAL MUSEUM

The collection of buildings at this **museum** (Magyar Szabadtéri Néprajzi Múzeum; ☎ 502 500; www.skanzen.hu; Sztaravodai út; adult/student 1000/500Ft, on festival days 1400/700Ft; 9am-5pm Tue-Sun late Mar-Oct), about 3km northwest of the centre, is Hungary's most ambitious *skanzen* (open-air museum). Highlights include the Calvinist church and 'skirted' belfry from the Erdőhát region of the Northeast, the German 'long house' from Harka outside Sopron, the curious heart-shaped gravestones from the Buda Hills and the lovely whitewashed facade of the thatched house from Sükösd on the Great Plain. Craftspeople and artisans do their thing on random days from Easter to early December (generally on Sundays and holidays), and the museum hosts festivals throughout the season.

See Getting Around (opposite) for information on buses to the museum.

Activities

Pap Island (Pap-sziget), 2km north of the centre, is Szentendre's playground and has a grassy *strand* (beach) for sunbathing, a **swimming pool** (adult/child 700/350Ft; 8am-7pm May-Sep), and **tennis courts** and **rowing boats** for hire.

Bicycles can be rented from **Balázs Kerékpárbolt** (☎ 312 111; Elód utca 2/a; 1 hr/day 500/3000Ft; 10am-6.30pm Mon-Fri, 9am-2pm Sat); take the hourly ferry across to Szentendre Island to enjoy kilometres of uncrowded cycling paths.

Sleeping

With Budapest so close, there's no point overnighting here unless you plan to push on to the rest of the Danube Bend. There are, however, a few worthwhile options. Contact Tourinform for private rooms.

Pap-sziget Camping (☎ 310 697; www.pap-sziget.hu; camp sites per adult/child/tent 1000/600/2920Ft, bungalows 8200-12,000Ft; May–mid-Oct;) This big, leafy camping site takes up most of Pap Island, some 2km north of Szentendre. Motel and *pension* rooms (from 5800Ft) are very basic, as are the bungalows; facilities include a small supermarket, a snack bar and a restaurant. See Getting Around (opposite) for information on getting here by bus.

Ilona (☎ 313 599; www.ilonapanzio.hu; Rákóczi Ferenc utca 11; s/d 5500/7700Ft) A spiffy little *pension*, with plenty going for it: superb central location, locked parking, inner courtyard for breakfast and rooms in very good nick (although on the small side).

Centrum (☎ 302 500; www.hotelcentrum.hu; Bogdányi utca 15; s/d from 11,380/13,500Ft) Centrum resides in a beautifully renovated house, that is indeed central. It's a stone's throw from the Danube and rooms are bright, large and filled with antique furniture. Breakfast is optional.

Kentaur Hotel (☎ 312 125; www.hotels.hu/kentaur; Marx tér 3; s/d 11,700/14,500Ft;) After receiving a recent makeover, Kentaur hotel is a fine choice close to the action. Rooms are neat and tidy, and staff are eager to please.

Eating & Drinking

Palapa (☎ 302 418; Batthyány utca 4; mains 1500-3000Ft; 5pm-midnight Mon-Fri, noon-midnight Sat & Sun) This colourful Mexican restaurant, which serves all the Mexican favourites, is the perfect place for a change from heavy Hungarian fare. Live music is occasionally featured, and the summer garden quickly fills up with revellers.

Promenade (☎ 312 626; Futó utca 4; mains 1700-3000Ft) Vaulted ceilings, whitewashed walls and a wonderful terrace overlooking the Danube are all highlights of this, one of Szentendre's best restaurants. The menu makes a nice change from heavy Hungarian, featuring 'wellness' dishes such as turkey strips with mozzarella cheese and salad.

our pick **Erm's** (☎ 303 388; Kossuth Lajos utca 22; mains around 2000Ft) Erm's is an unpretentious spot that welcomes guests with a smorgasbord of Hungarian specialities, and even some vegetarian choices. Its brick walls are covered in early 20th-century memorabilia, and the simple wooden tables dressed in lacy cloth are reminiscent of yesteryear. You can hear live jazz on weekends.

Aranysárkány (Golden Dragon; ☎ 301 479; Alkotmány utca 1/a; mains 2400-3600Ft) Fashionable Aranysárkány is still playing up the fact that Laura Bush dined here, but it doesn't need to considering such fine ingredients as Angus steak and salmon fillets are used in its dishes.

Adria (☎ 06 20 448 8993; Kossuth Lajos utca 4; coffee 200-500Ft) This funky little spot by the canal has a cosy interior bedecked in bright colours and a tree-shaded terrace. Expect soulful music served alongside your choice of coffee, tea and cake.

Avakum (☎ 500 145; Alkotmány utca 14) Dive into this place, a cellar bar near Castle Hill, to escape the tourist hordes and rehydrate.

Marzipan Museum (☎ 311 931; Dumtsa Jenő utca 12; 🕑 10am-7pm May-Oct, to 6pm Nov-Apr) This is a good place to stop for cake and ice cream, and kids will love the marzipan creations inside the museum (adult/child 400/250Ft).

For a quick bite to eat, try the food stalls at the bus and HÉV stations, the small **lángos stand** (Váralja lépcső; lángos from 240Ft) halfway up the steep steps from Fő tér to Castle Hill or **Dixie Chicken** (Dumtsa Jenő utca 16; burgers from 240Ft), a standard fast-food joint with the added bonus of a salad bar.

Entertainment

Danube Cultural Centre (☎ 312 657; Duna korzó 11/a) This centre stages theatrical performances, concerts and folk dance gatherings and can tell you what's on elsewhere in Szentendre.

Shopping

Szentendre is a shopper's town – from souvenir embroidery to the latest fashions – and although prices are at Budapest levels, not everything you see is available in the capital.

Péter-Pál Galeria (☎ 311 182; Péter-Pál utca 1; 🕑 10am-6pm Thu-Sun) For local art and fine jewellery, try this place.

Metszet Gallery (☎ 312 577; Fő tér 14; 🕑 11am-6pm Tue-Sun) This shop has wonderful old engravings, prints and a handful of maps.

Herend Shop (☎ 505 288; Bogdányi út 1; 🕑 10am-6pm) If you don't make it to Herend (p226), you can pick up an expensive piece of porcelain here.

Getting There & Away

BOAT

See p140 for more information on getting to and from Szentendre by boat.

BUS

Buses from Budapest's Árpád híd station, which is on the blue metro line, run to Szentendre at least once an hour throughout the day (250Ft, 30 minutes, 16km). Onward service to Visegrád (375Ft, 45 minutes, 25km, hourly) and Esztergom (750Ft, 1½ hours, 50km, hourly) is frequent.

TRAIN

The easiest way to reach Szentendre from Budapest is to catch the HÉV suburban train from Batthyány tér in Buda (370Ft, 40 minutes, every 10 to 20 minutes). Remember that a yellow city bus/metro ticket is good only as far as the Békásmegyer stop; you'll have to pay extra to get to Szentendre. Also, many HÉV trains run only as far as Békásmegyer, where you must cross the platform to board the train for Szentendre. The last train leaves Szentendre for Budapest at around 11pm.

Getting Around

Any bus heading north on Rte 11 to Visegrád and Esztergom will stop near Pap-sziget Camping (opposite); ring the bell after you pass the Danubius hotel at Ady Endre utca 28 on the left. Between 14 and 17 buses daily leave bus stop 7 (located at the town's bus station) for the Hungarian Open-Air Ethnographical Museum.

Ferries run hourly to Szentendre Island (5am to 7.30pm daily from March to October) and cost 250/100/250Ft one way for an adult/child/bicycle.

You can also book a **taxi** (☎ 341 341) in town.

VÁC

☎ 27 / pop 33,300

Lying on the eastern side of the river, Vác is the odd one out in the Danube Bend, but its locals don't seem to care. And it's no surprise, for this unpretentious town with a resonant history has plenty to keep people enthralled, from its collection of baroque town houses to its vault of 18th-century mummies. Plus it has one distinct advantage over its west-bank counterparts – glorious sunsets over the Börzsöny Hills, reflected in the Danube.

History

Unlike most Hungarian towns, Vác can prove its ancient origins without putting a spade into the ground: Uvcenum – the town's Latin name – is mentioned in Ptolemy's 2nd-century *Geographia* as a river crossing on an important road. King Stephen established an episcopate here in the 11th century, and within 300 years Vác was rich and powerful enough for its silver mark to become the realm's legal tender. The town's medieval centre and Gothic cathedral were destroyed during the Turkish occupation; reconstruction under several bishops in the 18th century gave Vác its present baroque appearance.

No more than a sleepy provincial centre in the middle of the 19th century, Vác was the first Hungarian town to be linked with Pest by train (in 1846), but development didn't really come until after WWII. Sadly, for many older Hungarians the name Vác conjures up a single frightening image: the notorious prison on Köztársaság út, where political prisoners were incarcerated and tortured both before the war under the rightist regime of Miklós Horthy and in the 1950s under the communists. Today you'd scarcely be aware of it as you enjoy the breezes along the embankment of the Danube, a more prominent feature here than in the Bend's other towns.

Orientation

The train station is at the northeastern end of Széchenyi utca, the bus station is a short walk southwest of the train station. Following Széchenyi utca toward the river for about 500m will take you across the ring road (Dr Csányi László körút) and down to Március 15 tér, the main square. The Mahart ferry pier is at the northern end of Liszt Ferenc sétány; the car and passenger ferry pier to Szentendre Island is just south of it.

Information

Main post office (Posta Park 2) Off Görgey Artúr utca.
Matrix (Rév köz; per hr 280Ft; ⌚ 9am-1pm Mon-Fri) Small internet cafe.
OTP Bank (Dunakanyar shopping centre, Széchenyi utca)
Tourinform (☎ 316 160; www.tourinformvac.hu; Március 15 tér 17; ⌚ 10am-7pm Mon-Fri, to 2pm Sat mid-Jun–Aug, 9am-5pm Mon-Fri, 10am-noon Sat Sep–mid-Jun) Overlooking the main square.
Town website (www.vac.hu)

Sights

Március 15 tér has the most colourful buildings in Vác. In 2006 the square itself gained the outline of St Michael Church, a medieval house of worship constructed in the early 14th-century. Only the church's **crypt** (Március 15 tér; admission 240Ft; ⌚ 9am-5pm May-Sep) remains, which contains a brief history of the church and town in the Middle Ages.

Dominating the square is the **Dominican church** (Fehérek temploma; ☎ 305 988; Március 15 tér 19; admission free); its interior is richly baroque, but the doors are normally locked outside services. Also worthy of note is another baroque masterpiece, the **Town Hall** (Március 15 tér 11) dating from 1764. Note the seals held by the two figures on the gable – they represent Hungary and Bishop Kristóf Migazzi, the driving force behind Vác's reconstruction more than 200 years ago. The building next door at No 9 has been a hospital since the 18th century. Opposite is the **former Bishop's Palace** (Március 15 tér 6), parts of which belong to the oldest building in Vác. Next door, the **Vác Diocesan Museum** (☎ 319 494; Március 15 tér 4; adult/child 500/200Ft; ⌚ 2-6pm Wed-Fri, 10am-6pm Sat & Sun) displays a tiny portion of the wealth the Catholic Church amassed in Vác over the centuries.

THE DUSTLESS HIGHWAY

No other river in Europe is as evocative, or important, as the Danube. It has been immortalised in legends, tales, songs, paintings, and movies through the ages, and has played an essential role in the cultural and economic life of millions of people since the earliest human populations settled along its banks.

Originating in Germany's Black Forest, the river cuts an unrelenting path through – or along the border of – 10 countries and, after 2800km, empties itself into the Black Sea in Romania. It is second only in length to the Volga in Europe (although, at 6400km, the Amazon dwarfs both), and contrary to popular belief, is green-brown rather than blue. Around 2400km of its length is navigable, making it a major transport route across the continent.

Even though only 12% of the river's length is located in the country, Hungary is vastly affected by the Danube. The entire country lies within the Danube river basin, and being so flat, it is highly prone to flooding. As early as the 16th century, large dyke systems were built for flood protection, but it's hard to stop water running where it wants to – as recently as 2006 the river burst its banks, threatening to fill Budapest's metro system and putting the homes of 32,000 people in danger.

Despite the potential danger, the river is beloved, so much so that it's been designated its own day. On 29 June every year cities along the river host festivals, family events and conferences in honour of the mighty Danube. If you'd like to join in, check www.danubeday.org for more information.

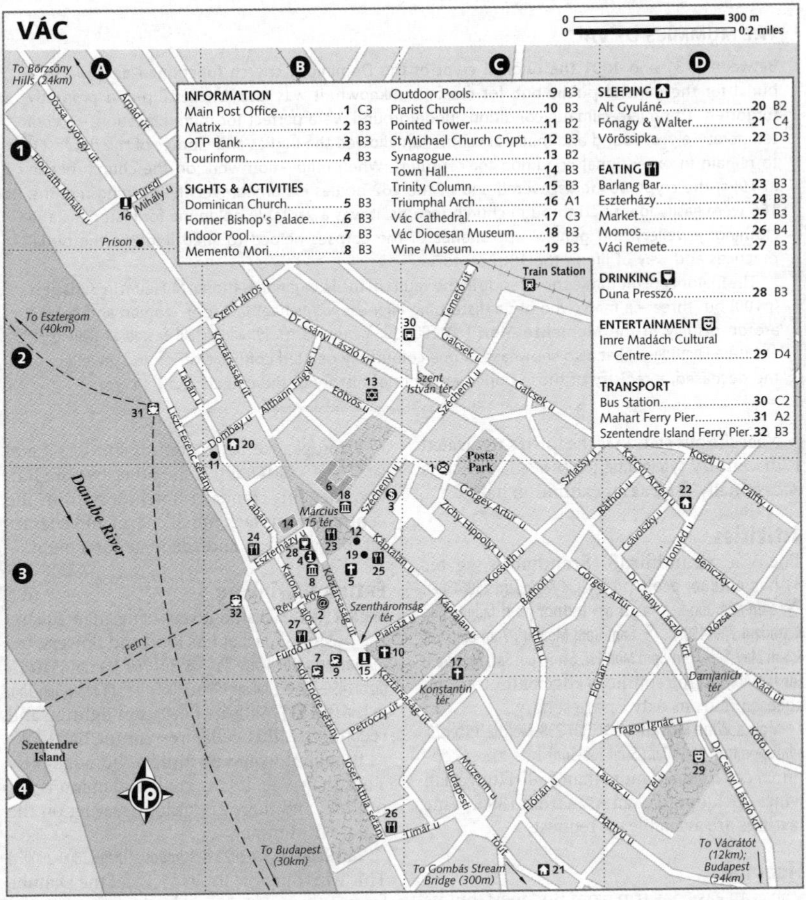

North of the main square is the **Triumphal Arch** (Diadalív-kapu; Dózsa György út), the only such structure in Hungary. It was built by Bishop Migazzi in honour of a visit by Empress Maria Theresa and her husband Francis of Lorraine (both pictured in the arch's oval reliefs) in 1764. From here, dip down one of the narrow side streets (such as Molnár utca) to the west for a stroll along the Danube. The **old city walls** and Gothic **Pointed Tower** (now a private home) are near Liszt Ferenc sétány 12.

If you climb up Fürdő utca near the pool complex, you'll reach tiny Szentháromság tér and its renovated **Trinity Column** (1755). The twin-spired **Piarist church** (Piarista templom; admission free; ⌚ during services), completed in 1741, with a stark white interior and marble altar, is to the east across the square.

Tree-lined Konstantin tér to the southeast is dominated by colossal **Vác Cathedral** (Váci székesegyház; admission free; ⌚ 10am-noon & 1.30-5pm Mon-Sat, 7.30am-7pm Sun), which dates from 1775 and was one of the first examples of neoclassical architecture in Hungary. This imposing grey church was designed by French architect Isidore Canevale, but the frescoes on the vaulted dome and the altarpiece are by the celebrated Franz Anton Maulbertsch and are worth a look.

If you continue walking south along Budapesti főút, you'll reach the small stone **Gombás Stream Bridge** (Gombás-patak hídja; 1757), lined with statues of seven saints – Vác's modest response to Charles Bridge in Prague.

THE MUMMIES OF VÁC

Between 1731 and 1801 the original crypt of the Dominican church functioned as a place of burial for the general public but, for reasons unknown, it was later bricked up and promptly forgotten. The micro-climatic conditions underground were perfect for mummification – a cool temperature year-round and minimal ventilation allowed the bodies and clothes of the deceased to remain in exceptional condition for centuries. When renovation work on the church began in 1994, the crypt was rediscovered and of the 262 bodies exhumed over the ensuing months, 166 were easily identified through church records. It was a veritable goldmine for historians; the clothing, jewellery and general appearance of the corpses helped to shed light on the burial practices and way of life in the 18th century.

The majority of mummies now reside in the vaults of the Hungarian National Museum in Budapest (p100) but three – a man (who has a disturbing likeness to Michael Jackson), woman and baby – are on display in the **Memento Mori** (☎ 500 750; Március 15 tér 19; adult/child & student 800/400Ft; 🕑 10am-6pm Tue-Sun). It also showcases some colourfully painted coffins, clothes and jewellery of the deceased, a registry of those buried and a brief history of the church and its crypt.

Near the bus station is the town's renovated 19th-century **synagogue** (Eötvös utca 5), which is occasionally used as an exhibition hall.

Activities

The Vác Strandfürdő (Szentháromság tér 3) has **outdoor pools** (adult/child & student 750/450Ft; 🕑 6am-8pm Jun-Sep) and an **indoor pool** (adult/child & student 750/450Ft; 🕑 6am-8pm Mon-Fri, 7am-8pm Sat & Sun May-Sep, 6am-8pm Mon-Fri, 6am-7pm Sat, 7am-5pm Sun Oct-Apr) on the southern edge of the 'beach', accessible from Ady Endre sétány.

Vác's **Wine Museum** (☎ 307 238; Március 15 tér 20; admission free; 🕑 10am-5pm Tue-Sun) has an exceptional collection of more than 2500 Hungarian wines, including Tokaji Aszú from 1880. Wine tastings are available on request.

Sleeping

Vác is an easy day trip from Budapest, but its accommodation options aren't bad either.

Alt Gyuláné (☎ 316 860; altvendeghaz@invitel.hu; Tabán utca 25; s/d without bath 5000/12,000Ft; ☒ ☒) Staying at this small *pension* is like staying with nice relatives. The owners are more than happy to while away the hours chatting, and the breakfast will keep you going all day. Rooms are kitschy but very cosy, and there's a fully equipped kitchen and private garden for guests.

Fónagy & Walter (☎ 310 682; www.fonagy.hu; Budapesti főút 36; r 8500Ft) Fónagy & Walter is another *pension* from the 'homely' mould – rooms are lovingly prepared, the hosts love to sit and talk, the wine selection from the private cellar is outstanding and the outdoor grill may be fired up just for you.

Vörössipka (☎ 501 055; okktart@netelek.hu; Honvéd utca 14; s/d 9000/14,000Ft) If the other two are full, consider this standard hotel away from the centre. Rooms lack much charm and character, but are clean and adequate for a night.

Eating & Drinking

Market (Káptalan utca) Southeast of the main square, the bustling market has food and flowers.

Barlang Bar (Cave Bar; ☎ 501 760; Március 15 tér 12; pizzas 490-1840Ft, mains 1000-2800Ft; 🕑 to 11pm Sun-Thu, to 1am Fri & Sat) With its florescent lighting and red booths, this cellar restaurant/bar looks as though it would be more at home in New York than Vác. Its international menu is appealing, and there is outdoor seating on the square in summer.

Váci Remete (☎ 302 199; Fürdő utca; mains 1800-2600Ft) This wins our vote for its views of the Danube from its terrace, top-notch wine selection and fine spread of Hungarian specialities.

Duna Presszó (☎ 310 569; Március 15 tér 13) Duna is the quintessential cafe: dark-wood furniture, chandeliers, excellent cake and ice cream, and the occasional drunk. It's good for coffee during the day and something stronger at night.

Also worth a look:

Eszterházy (Eszterházy utca; ice cream 100Ft; 🕑 9am-8pm) Perfect spot for refreshments on your stroll along the Danube.

Momos (Tímár utca 9; mains 1500-2500Ft) Huge terrace overlooking parkland and the river; excellent for fish and anything from the grill.

Entertainment

Imre Madách Cultural Centre (☎ 316 411; Dr Csányi László körút 63) This circular centre can help you with what's on in Vác, such as theatre, concerts and kid's shows.

Concerts are occasionally held in Vác Cathedral, the Dominican church and the former Bishop's Palace.

Getting There & Away

BOAT

Car ferries (1200/400/400/330Ft per car/bicycle/adult/child, hourly 6am to 8pm) cross over to Szentendre Island; a bridge connects the island's west bank with the mainland at Tahitótfalu. From there, hourly buses run to Szentendre. See p140 for more information.

BUS

Catch buses from Vác to the following destinations.

Destination	Price	Duration	Km	Frequency
Balassagyarmat	675Ft	1¼hr	45	8 daily
Budapest	450Ft	45-55min	30	half-hourly
Diósjenő	375Ft	50min	25	up to 9 Mon-Sat
Nógrád	300Ft	30min	20	up to 9 Mon-Sat
Salgótarján	1500Ft	2½hr	95	3 daily
Vácrátót	250Ft	30min	14	hourly

TRAIN

Once a month in April, May, June and July **MÁV Nostalgia** (☎ 1-269 5242; www.mavnosztalgia.hu; 1 way adult/child 1900/1290Ft) runs a *nosztalgiavonat* (vintage steam train) from Nyugati station in Budapest (departing at 9.40am) to Szob (two hours) via Vác (10.40am) and Nagymaros-Visegrád; the train returns to Vac at 5pm. But verify this service and schedule with MÁV Nostalgia, or check its website, before making plans.

Other train connections to Vác include the following destinations.

Destination	Price	Duration	Km	Frequency
Balassagyarmat	1050Ft	2hr	70	11 daily
Budapest	525Ft	40min	34	half-hourly
Vácrátót	200Ft	12min	10	hourly

AROUND VÁC

Börzsöny Hills

These hills begin the series of six ranges that make up Hungary's Northern Uplands, and – along with the Pilis Hills (p152) on the opposite bank of the Danube – form Hungary's 600-sq-km **Danube-Ipoly National Park**. There's very good hiking, but make sure you get hold of Cartographia's 1:40,000 map *A Börzsöny* (No 5; 950Ft), which is available at **Tourinform** (p146) in Vác.

Nógrád, with the ruins of a hilltop castle dating from the 12th century, could be considered the gateway to the Börzsöny. Diósjenő, 6km north, is a good base for exploring the hills and has a few accommodation options, including **Diósjenő Camping** (☎ 35-364 134; www.patakpart.hu; camp site per person/tent 1000/800Ft, 2-person bungalows 5000Ft; May-Sep). It's rather disorganised, but staff are welcoming, some camping spots have tree shade and bungalows have cookers and bathrooms. From here you can strike out west along marked trails to **Nady Hideg-hegy** (864m) or **Magas-Tax** (739m). The Börzsöny's highest peak, **Csóványos** (938m), lies to the west of Diósjenő and is a much more difficult climb.

If you're under your own steam, take the beautiful restricted road from Diósjenő to Kemence via Királyháza; it follows the Kemence Stream almost the entire way – a great place for a cool dip or a picnic in summer. Just before you reach Kemence, there is a turn-off south to the beautiful **Fekete-völgy** (Black Valley), and **Feketevölgy Pension** (☎ 27-365 153; www.feketevolgy.hu, in Hungarian; s/d from 7000/14,000Ft;), a peaceful oasis set well back in the forest. Otherwise, head onto Kemence, a nondescript town with a few *pensions* and restaurants, internet access and an ATM.

The southern end of the Börzsöny is bereft of any tourist infrastructure, aside from the ecofriendly **Szent Orbán** (☎ 27-378 034; www.szentorban.hu; r 17,600-68,700Ft;) in the heart of the forest at tiny **Nagyirtáspuszta**. This huge log villa has an array of exceptionally cosy rooms, along with a wellness centre, fine restaurant, bowling alley and plenty of outdoor activities. There's no public transport to the hotel and it often caters to conferences, so call ahead rather than turn up on the doorstep.

Hourly trains travelling north out of Vác pass through Nógrád (375Ft, 40 minutes, 24km) and Diósjenő (400Ft, 48 minutes, 29km); both can also be reached by bus from Vác.

VISEGRÁD

☎ 26 / pop 1710

Of the four main towns on the Danube Bend, Visegrád (from the Slavic words for 'high castle') has the most history. While much of it has crumbled to dust over the centuries, reminders of its grand past can still be seen in its Renaissance palace and accompanying citadel.

History

The Romans built a border fortress on Sibrik Hill just a little north of the present castle in the 4th century, and it was still being used by Slovak settlers 600 years later. After the Mongol invasion in 1241, King Béla IV began work on a lower castle by the river and then on the hilltop citadel. Less than a century later, King Charles Robert of Anjou, whose claim to the local throne was being fiercely contested in Buda, moved the royal household to Visegrád and had the lower castle converted into a palace.

For almost 200 years, Visegrád was Hungary's 'other' (often summer) capital and an important diplomatic centre. But Visegrád's real golden age came during the reign of King Matthias Corvinus (r 1458–90) and Queen Beatrix, who had Italian Renaissance craftsmen rebuild the Gothic palace. The sheer size of the residence, and its stonework, fountains and hanging gardens were the talk of 15th-century Europe.

The destruction of Visegrád came with the Turks and later in 1702, when the Habsburgs blew up the citadel to prevent Hungarian independence fighters from using it as a base. All trace of the palace was lost until the 1930s, when archaeologists, following descriptions in literary sources, uncovered the ruins.

Orientation

The Mahart ferry pier, just south of the city gate and opposite the Vár hotel, is one of two stops where buses from Szentendre or Budapest will drop you off. To the right of the Vár hotel are steps to Salamon-torony utca, which go to the lower castle and the citadel. There are also bus stops near the village centre, and the car ferry is about 1km south on Rte 11.

Information

OTP ATM (Fő utca) A short stroll from the Catholic church.
Post office (Fő utca 77; ⏲ 8am-4pm Mon-Fri)
Town website (www.visegrad.hu) Provides general information on Visegrád.
Visegrád Tours (☎ 398 160; www.visegradtours.hu; Rév utca 15; ⏲ 8am-5.30pm) The only place with information on the town.

Sights

A logical place to start a tour of Visegrád is down by the river. The main attraction here is the **Royal Palace** (Visegrádi királyi palota; ☎ 398 026; Fő utca 23; adult/child/family 1000/500/2300Ft; ⏲ 9am-5pm Tue-Sun), situated not far south of the Mahart ferry pier.

Once featuring a massive 350 rooms, the palace today is a shadow of its former self and only a small section has been reconstructed; the rest has been overrun with weeds and still lies in ruin. The handful of rooms that can be visited – the royal suites – are centred on the Court of Honour and its **Hercules Fountain**, a replica of the original Renaissance piece. Moving from room to room, you'll discover more reconstructions and replicas: a cold and clammy royal bedchamber from the 1400s, a warmer kitchen, and the **Lion Fountain**, famed for its red marble. Also of note is the petite **St George's Chapel** (1366), but once again, it's not the original. The history of the palace and its reconstruction, along with architectural finds, including richly carved stones dating from the 14th century, is told in the **King Mathias Museum**, occupying one of the rooms.

If you walk back to the ferry pier and north up Salamon-torony utca, the first thing you'll see is the 13th-century **Solomon's Tower** (☎ 398 026; adult/child & student 600/300Ft; ⏲ 9am-5pm Tue-Sun May-Sep), a stocky, hexagonal keep with walls up to 8m thick. Once used to control river traffic, it now houses many of the precious objects unearthed at the Royal Palace, such as the original pieces of the Hercules and Lion fountains.

Medieval shows are held in the grounds of the palace and Solomon's tower over the summer months.

North of the tower, a trail marked 'Fellegvár' turns southeast at a fork and leads up to **Visegrád Citadel** (☎ 398 101; adult/child & student 1400/700Ft; ⏲ 9.30am-5.30pm daily mid-Mar–mid-Oct, 9.30am-5.30pm Sat & Sun mid-Oct–mid-Mar), sitting atop a 350m hill and surrounded by moats hewn from solid rock. Completed in 1259, the citadel was the repository for the Hungarian crown jewels until 1440, when Elizabeth of Luxembourg, the daughter of King Sigismund, stole them with the help of her lady-in-waiting and hurried off to Székesfehérvár to have her infant son László crowned king. (The crown was returned to the citadel in 1464 and held

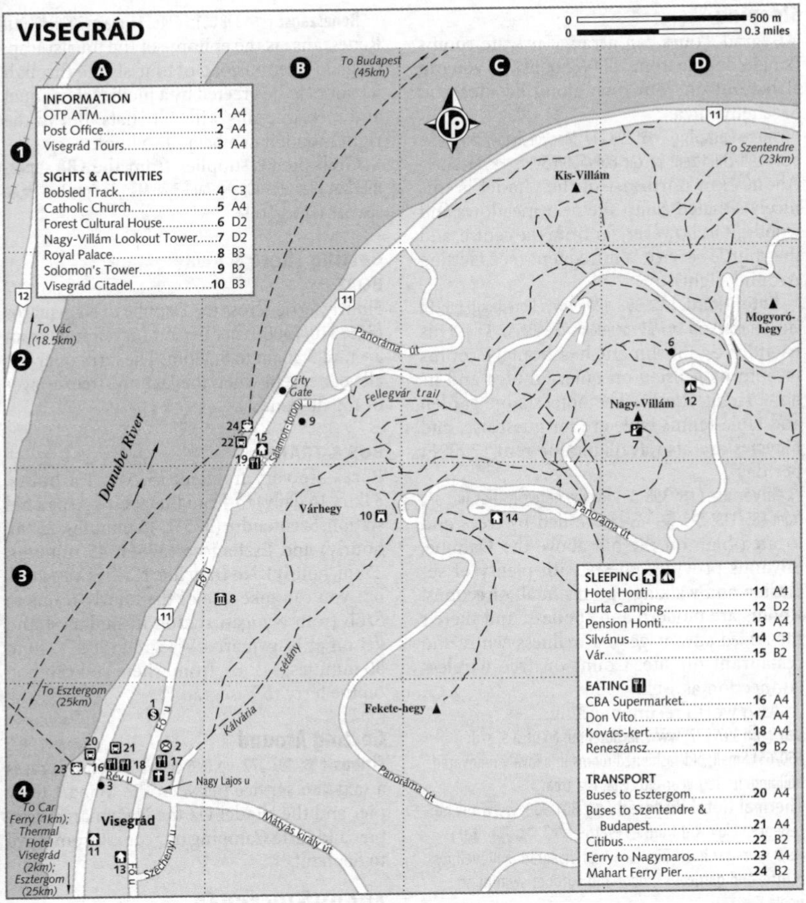

here – under a stronger lock, no doubt – until the Turkish invasion.)

There's a small pictorial exhibit in the residential rooms on the west side of the citadel and two smaller displays near the east gate: one on hunting and falconry, the other on traditional occupations in the region (stone-cutting, charcoal-burning, beekeeping and fishing). However, the real highlight is just walking along the ramparts of this eyrie, admiring the views of the Börzsöny Hills and the Danube, which are arguably the best in the region.

If you're walking to the citadel from the village centre, Kálvária sétány, a trail beginning from behind the 18th-century **Catholic church** (Fő tér), is less steep than the trail from Solomon's Tower. You can also reach it by minibus (p152).

Activities

There are some easy **walks** and **hikes** in the immediate vicinity of Visegrád Citadel – to the 377m-high **Nagy-Villám Lookout Tower**, for example. Across from Jurta Camping is the sod-and-wood **Forest Cultural House** designed by Imre Makovecz; it caters to visiting school groups only.

A 750m **bobsled track** (bob-pálya; ☎ 397 397; adult/child 350/280Ft; 9am-6pm Mon-Fri, to 7pm Sat & Sun Apr-Sep, 11am-4pm Oct-Mar), on which you wend your way down a metal chute while sitting on a felt-bottomed cart, is on the hillside below the lookout.

Sleeping

Visegrád Tours can arrange private rooms (single/double from 5000/8500Ft), or you can strike out on your own along Fő utca and Széchenyi utca.

Jurta Camping (☎ 398 217; Mogyoróhegy; camp sites per adult/child/tent or car 800/500/650Ft; ⏰ May-Sep) About 2km northeast of the citadel is this nicely situated camp site near meadows and woods. It is, however, far from the centre, and the shuttle service is infrequent (see Getting Around, right).

Hotel Honti (☎ 398 120; www.hotelhonti.hu; Fő utca 66; hotel s/d €45/65, pension s/d €40/55; 💻) This friendly establishment has homely rooms in both its *pension* on quiet Fő utca and its hotel facing Rte 11. The hotel's large garden and table-tennis table are for guest use, and bicycles are also available for rent (2000Ft per day).

Silvánus (☎ 398 311; www.hotelsilvanus.hu; s/d from €85/118; ⊠ 🍴) Surrounded by trees and located high on the hill above the Danube, Silvánus provides guests with plenty of seclusion and walking options in all directions. Rooms are modern and spotless, and there's the added advantage of a wellness centre and restaurant on site. Count on free wireless connection as well.

Also worth recommending:

Vár (☎ 397 522; www.varhotel.hu; Fő utca 9; s/d €50/65) Small, old-fashioned rooms in a lovely renovated building. Its 100-year-old cellar is a treat.

Thermal Hotel Visegrád (☎ 801 900; www.thv.hu; Lepence völgy; s/d from €119/169; ⊠ ❄ 💻 🍴) New four-star hotel 2km south of Visegrád. Full wellness centre, and gorgeous indoor and outdoor swimming pools.

Eating

Don Vito (☎ 397 230; Fő utca 83; pizzas from 900Ft, mains 1500-3000Ft) Don Vito is quite a classy joint for such a small town. Its collection of gangster memorabilia is impressive (and we're not talking about Snoop Dog here), as is its selection of top-shelf liquor. The list of pizzas is long, and lo-and-behold, there are even vegetarian mains to choose from.

Kovács-kert (Rév utca 4; mains 1300-2500Ft) A clean and neat restaurant close to the Nagymaros ferry. The large menu covers a fine array of Hungarian standards and its terrace seating is a welcome relief in the warmer summer months.

Reneszánsz (☎ 398 081; Fő utca 11; mains 2000-4000Ft) Reneszánsz is the epitome of the tourist trap: busload after busload of tourists file through its doors to be greeted by a medieval banquet and men in tights with silly hats. But in the right mood, it can be quite a hoot.

Grab picnic supplies from the **CBA supermarket** (Rév utca 10; ⏰ 7am-3pm Mon, to 6pm Tue-Fri, to 1pm Sat, to noon Sun).

Getting There & Away

BOAT

Hourly ferries cross the Danube to Nagymaros (375/310/1300Ft per person/bicycle/car) from around 5.30am to 8.30pm. The ferry operates all year except when the Danube freezes over or fog descends.

BUS & TRAIN

Buses are very frequent (525Ft, 1¼ hours, 34km, 16 daily) to/from Budapest's Árpád híd station, Szentendre (375Ft, 45 minutes, 25km, hourly) and Esztergom (375Ft, 45 minutes, 25km, hourly). No train line reaches Visegrád, but you can take one of the hourly trains to Szob from Nyugati station in Budapest and get off at Nagymaros-Visegrád (900Ft, 40 to 50 minutes, 51km), from where you can hop on the ferry to Visegrád.

Getting Around

Citibus (☎ 397 372; up to 6 people 2500Ft) operates a taxi van service between the Mahart ferry pier and the citadel via the Nagymaros ferry pier and Jurta Camping on request from April to September.

AROUND VISEGRÁD

Pilis Hills

Directly to the south and southwest of Visegrád are the Pilis Hills, an area of rolling ranges blanketed in oak and beech woods. Once the private hunting grounds of Matthias Corvinus, the hills are now Budapest's outdoor playground, criss-crossed by a lot more hiking trails (including Hungary's first, laid in 1869) than roads. The entire region, which covers 250 sq km, falls within the scope of the **Danube-Ipoly National Park**; the Börzsöny Hills (p149), north of the Danube, make up the rest of the park.

A good starting point for exploring the hills is **Dobogó-kő** (699m), the region's largest settlement. From here, marked trails head off to various vantage points in the park, including

Prédikálószék (Pulpit Seat), a 639m crag for experienced hikers and climbers only, and **Rám-szakadék** (Rám Precipice), from where you can descend to Dömös, 6km southwest of Visegrád, in around three hours. Some of the best bird-watching in western Hungary is in these hills. *A Pilis és a Visegrádi-helység*, the 1:40,000 Pilis and Visegrád Hills map (No 16; 950Ft) from Cartographia, outlines the many hiking possibilities for the entire area.

Dobogókő has an **excursion centre** (variable) and a smattering of accommodation and eating options, including **Pilis Hotel** (26-347 504; Téry Ödön utca 1; s/d/tr/apt from 5000/10,000/15,000/9000Ft;), a dated communist-era haunt with fading rooms and fabulous views. Alternatively, try the more personal **Platán Panzió** (26-347 680; www.platanpanzio.hu; Téry Ödön utca 15; s/d 6500/9500Ft) close by.

Transport to Dobogókő is limited; up to four buses daily travel to/from Esztergom (300Ft, 40 minutes, 20km), and up to nine Monday to Friday (and one on weekends) to/from the HÉV station in Pomáz (300Ft, 30 minutes, 19km), two stops before Szentendre.

ESZTERGOM

33 / pop 29,800

It's easy to see the attraction of Esztergom, even from miles away. The city's massive basilica, sitting high above the town and Danube River, is an incredible sight, rising out of what seems like nowhere in a rural stretch of country. But Esztergom's attraction runs deeper than the domed structure: the country's first king, St Stephen, was born here in 975; it was a royal seat from the late 10th to the mid-13th centuries; and it has been the seat of Roman Catholicism in Hungary for more than 1000 years. As a result, Esztergom has both great spiritual and temporal significance for Hungarians.

History

Vár-hegy (Castle Hill), towering over the city centre, was the site of the Roman settlement of Solva Mansio in the 1st century, and it is thought that Marcus Aurelius finished his *Meditations* in a camp nearby during the second half of the 2nd century.

Prince Géza chose Esztergom as his capital, and his son Vajk (later Stephen) was crowned king here in 1000. Stephen founded one of the country's two archbishoprics at Esztergom and built a basilica, bits of which can be seen in the Castle Museum.

Esztergom lost its political significance when King Béla IV moved the capital to Buda after the Mongol invasion in 1241. It remained the ecclesiastical seat, however, vying with the royal court for power and influence. But Esztergom's capture by the Turks in 1543 interrupted the church's activities, and the city's archbishop fled to Nagyszombat (now Trnava in Slovakia) to the northwest.

The church did not reestablish its base in this 'Hungarian Rome' until the early 19th century. It was then that Esztergom went on a building spree that transformed it into a city of late baroque and, in particular, neoclassical buildings.

Orientation

Esztergom lies on a high point above a slight curve of the Danube across from the Slovakian city of Štúrovo, to which it is linked by the Mária Valéria Bridge. The centre of Esztergom today is Rákóczi tér, a few steps east of the Little Danube (Kis-Duna), the tributary that branches off to form Primate Island (Prímás-sziget). From the square Bajcsy-Zsilinszky utca leads northwest to Castle Hill. To the southwest of Rákóczi tér is Széchenyi tér, the town centre in the Middle Ages and site of the rococo town hall.

Esztergom's bus station (Simor János utca) is beyond the street market, 700m south of Rákóczi tér. The train station (Bem József tér) is another 1.2km further south. Mahart boats dock at the pier just south of Mária Valéria Bridge on Primate Island.

Information

Atek Computers (501 320; atekcomp@axelero.hu; Bajcsy-Zsilinszky utca 5; per hr 500Ft; 8.30am-5pm Mon-Fri, to noon Sat) Computer shop in small courtyard with internet access on two machines.

Cathedralis Tours (520 260; Bajcsy- Zsilinszky utca 26; 9am-noon, 1-4pm Mon-Fri) Useful for information and private rooms.

City website (www.esztergom.hu) Hungarian only, but with English-language links.

Gran Tours (502 001; grantours@freemail.hu; Széchenyi tér 25; 8am-5pm Mon-Fri, 9am-noon Sat Jun-Aug, 8am-4pm Mon-Fri Sep-May) Visitor centre run by the city of Esztergom; unfortunately stocks very little information.

OTP bank (Rákóczi tér 2-4) Has a 24hr ATM.

Post office (Arany János utca 2) Enter from Széchenyi tér.

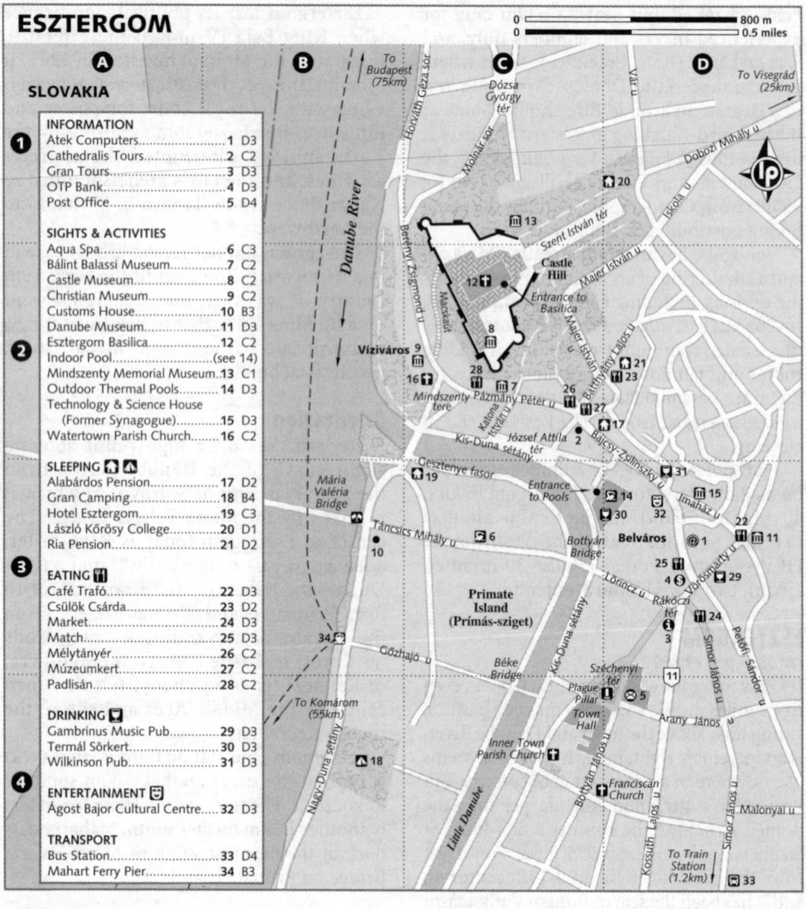

Sights

ESZTERGOM BASILICA

The **basilica** (Bazilika; ☎ 411 895; www.bazilika-esztergom.hu; Szent István tér 1; admission free; 🕑 6am-6pm), the largest church in Hungary, is on Castle Hill, and its 72m-high central dome can be seen for many kilometres around. The building of the present neoclassical church was begun in 1822 on the site of its 12th-century counterpart destroyed by the Turks. József Hild, who designed the cathedral at Eger, was involved in the final stages, and the basilica was consecrated in 1856 with a sung Mass composed by Franz Liszt.

The grey church is colossal (117m long and 47m wide) and rather bleak inside, but it does a grand job of inspiring awe. Its highlight is the red-and-white marble **Bakócz Chapel** on the south side, which is a splendid example of Italian Renaissance stone-carving and sculpture. It was commissioned by Archbishop Tamás Bakócz who, having failed in his bid for the papacy, launched a crusade that turned into the peasant uprising under György Dózsa in 1514 (see p27). The chapel escaped most – though not all – of the Turks' axes; notice the smashed-in faces of Gabriel and other angels above the altar. It was dismantled into 1600 separate pieces and then reassembled in its present location in 1823. The copy of Titian's *Assumption* over the church's main altar is said to be the world's largest painting on a single canvas.

On the northwest side of the church is the entrance to the basilica's **treasury** (kincstár; ☎ 402 354; adult/child/family 600/300/1500Ft; 🕑 9am-4.30pm daily Mar-Oct, 11am-3.30pm Sat & Sun Nov & Dec), an Aladdin's cave of vestments and religious plates in gold and silver and studded with jewels. It is the richest ecclesiastical collection in Hungary and contains Byzantine, Hungarian and Italian objects of sublime workmanship and great artistic merit.

The door to the right as you enter the basilica leads to the **crypt** (altemplom; admission 150Ft; 🕑 9am-4.45pm), a series of eerie vaults with tombs guarded by monoliths representing Mourning and Eternity. Among those at rest here are János Vitéz, Esztergom's enlightened Renaissance archbishop, and József Mindszenty, the conservative primate who opposed the former regime (see the boxed text, below). It's worth making the tortuous climb up to the **cupola** (admission 250Ft; 🕑 9am-5pm) for the outstanding views over the city; the stairs leading up to it are to the left of the crypt entrance.

CASTLE MUSEUM

The **Castle Museum** (Vármúzeum; ☎ 500 136; Szent István tér 1; adult/child/family 800/400/1500Ft; 🕑 10am-6pm Tue-Sun Apr-Oct, to 4pm Tue-Sun Nov-Mar) at the southern end of Castle Hill is housed in the former Royal Palace, which was built mostly by French architects under Béla III (r 1172–96) during Esztergom's golden age. Most of the palace was destroyed by the Turks and today the structure is a combination of modern brick work and medieval stone masonry.

The museum concentrates on archaeological finds from the town and its surrounding area, the majority of which is pottery dating from the 11th century onwards. Other points of interest include some of the basilica's original ornate capitals and a fantastic view across the Danube to Slovakia. Outside are 15 enormous church bells from around the country that are no longer in use.

OTHER SIGHTS

Below Castle Hill on the banks of the Little Danube is **Víziváros**, the colourful 'Watertown' district of pastel town houses, churches and museums. The fastest way to get there is to walk down steep Macskaút, which can be accessed from just behind the basilica.

The **Bálint Balassi Museum** (☎ 412 584; Pázmány Péter utca 13; adult/child & student 200/100Ft; 🕑 9am-5pm Tue-Sun), in an 18th-century baroque building, has a small collection of black-and-white photos of the excavations of the castle.

Just north of the Italianate **Watertown Parish Church** (Víziváros plébániatemplom; 1738),

CARDINAL MINDSZENTY

Born József Pehm in 1892 in the village of Csehimindszent near Szombathely, Mindszenty was politically active from the time of his ordination in 1915. Imprisoned under the short-lived regime of communist Béla Kun in 1919 and again when the fascist Arrow Cross came to power in 1944, Mindszenty was made archbishop of Esztergom – and thus primate of Hungary – in 1945, and cardinal the following year.

In 1948, when he refused to secularise Hungary's Roman Catholic schools under the new communist regime, Mindszenty was arrested, tortured and sentenced to life imprisonment for treason. Released during the 1956 Uprising, he took refuge in the US Embassy on Szabadság tér when the communists returned to power. He remained there until September 1971.

As relations between the Kádár regime and the Holy See began to improve in the late 1960s, the Vatican made several requests for the cardinal to leave Hungary, which he refused to do. Following the intervention of US President Richard Nixon, Mindszenty left for Vienna, where he continued to criticise the Vatican's relations with the regime in Hungary. He retired in 1974 and died the following year. But as he had vowed not to return to his homeland until the last Soviet soldier had left Hungarian soil, Mindszenty's remains were not returned until May 1991. This was actually several weeks before the last soldier had been repatriated.

If you want to know more about one of Hungary's most controversial figures, visit the **Mindszenty Memorial Museum** (Mindszenty Emlékmúzeum; ☎ 403 162; Szent István tér 4; adult/child 400/200Ft; 🕑 9am-5pm Wed-Sun May-Dec), northeast of the basilica, which displays a handful of his personal items and has a short film on his life and times.

which is vaguely reminiscent of the glorious Minorite church in Eger, is the former Bishop's Palace. Today it houses the **Christian Museum** (Keresztény Múzeum; ☎ 413 880; www.christianmuseum.hu; Mindszenty tere 2; adult/child & student 700/350Ft; 🕑 10am-6pm Wed-Sun May-Oct, 11am-3pm Tue-Sun Nov, Dec, Mar & Apr) – the finest collection of medieval religious art in Hungary. Established by Archbishop János Simor in 1875, it contains Hungarian Gothic triptychs and altarpieces; later works by German, Dutch and Italian masters; tapestries; and what is arguably the most beautiful object in the nation: the sublime *Holy Sepulchre of Garamszentbenedek* (1480), a sort of wheeled cart in the shape of a cathedral, with richly carved figures of the 12 Apostles and Roman soldiers guarding Christ's tomb. The sepulchre was used during Easter Week processions and was painstakingly restored in the 1970s.

Be sure to see Tamás Kolozsvári's Calvary altar panel (1427), which was influenced by Italian art; the late Gothic *Christ's Passion* (1506) by 'Master M S'; the gruesome *Martyrdom of the Three Apostles* (1490) by the so-called Master of the Martyr Apostles; and the *Temptation of St Anthony* (1530) by Jan Wellens de Cock, with its druglike visions of devils and temptresses. Audio guides are available for 500Ft, and guided tours in English and German for 5000Ft.

Cross the bridge south of Watertown Parish Church and around 100m further south is the **Mária Valéria Bridge**, connecting Esztergom with the Slovakian city of Štúrovo. Destroyed during WWII, the bridge only reopened in 2002. The bridge's original **Customs House** (Vámház) now houses a currency exchange booth.

The so-called **Technology & Science House** (Technika és Tudomány Háza; Imaház utca 4) built in 1888, once served as a synagogue for Esztergom's Jewish community, the oldest in Hungary, and now contains a regional government office. It was designed in Moorish Romantic style by Lipót Baumhorn, and is today in excellent condition. Close by is the **Danube Museum** (Duna Múzeum; ☎ 500 250; www.dunamuzeum.hu; Kölcsey utca 2; adult/child 500/250Ft; 🕑 10am-5pm Wed-Mon May-Oct, to 4pm Wed-Mon Nov-Apr), with displays on – you guessed it – Hungary's mightiest river and life on it. With all the hands-on exhibits, it's a great place for kids.

Activities

Just east of the Little Danube are **outdoor thermal pools** (☎ 312 249; Kis-Duna sétány 1; adult/child 1100/800Ft; 🕑 9am-7pm Mon-Sat, 8am-7pm Sun May-Sep) and stretches of grass 'beach'. You can use the **indoor pool** (🕑 6am-7pm Tue-Fri, to 6pm Sat, 8am-4pm Sun) throughout the year.

At the northern end of Primate Island is Esztergom's new **Aqua Spa** (☎ 511 100; www.aquasziget.hu, in Hungarian; Táncsics Mihály utca 5; adult/child 2650/1300Ft; 🕑 10am-8pm Mon-Fri, 9am-9pm Sat, 9am-8pm Sun), with a plethora of indoor and outdoor pools, along with a full wellness centre and curly waterslide.

Sleeping

BUDGET

Contact Gran Tours or Cathedralis Tours about private rooms (3000Ft to 4000Ft per person) or apartments (9000Ft to 14,000Ft).

Gran Camping (☎ 402 513; www.grancamping-fortanex.hu; Nagy-Duna sétány 3; camp sites per adult/child/tent/tent & car 1500/750/1000/1600Ft, dm 1900Ft, d/tr pension 8500/9500Ft, bungalows 12,000-16,000Ft; 🕑 May-Sep; 🏊) Small but centrally located on Primate Island, this camping ground has space for 500 souls in various forms of accommodation, as well as a good-sized swimming pool. It also has a hostel with dormitory accommodation.

László Kőrösy College (☎ 400 005; kolesz@korosi-koll.sulinet.hu; Szent István tér 6; dm with/without bathroom 3800/2000Ft; 🕑 Jul & Aug) This school dormitory just a stone's throw from the basilica opens its doors during the college's summer break.

MIDRANGE

Alabárdos Pension (☎ 312 640; Bajcsy-Zsilinszky utca 49; s/d 7500/11,500Ft; ⊠) Alabárdos isn't flashy but it does provide neat, tidy and sizeable accommodation. The breakfast is big, as is the friendly guard dog.

Ria Pension (☎ 313 115; www.riapanzio.com; Batthyány Lajos utca 11-13; s/d 9000/12,000Ft) This family-run place in a converted town house just down from the basilica has quiet, cosy rooms, a small sauna and fitness centre, and bicycles to rent.

Hotel Esztergom (☎ 412 555; www.hotel-esztergom.hu; Nagy-Duna sétány; s/d 15,000/16,000Ft; ⊠ 💻 🏊) Hotel Esztergom is fairly uninspiring, but it occupies a leafy spot on Primate Island and has modern guestrooms, a restaurant and a roof terrace. There's a sports centre with a tennis court, and guests can use a nearby swimming pool.

Eating

Múzeumkert (☎ 403 775; Batthyány Lajos utca 1; cakes 200-400Ft; 9am-midnight Apr-Oct, 9am-10pm Nov-Mar) This modern cocktail lounge near the basilica happens to serve some of the best cakes and pastries in Esztergom.

Café Trafó (☎ 403 980; Vörösmarty utca 15; coffee 200-500Ft; 7am-11pm) This little cafe housed in a glass box opposite the Danube Museum thankfully has plenty of tree shade and a large terrace for hot summer days. It's a wonderful place to take a breather, sit back and relax.

Mélytányér (☎ 412 534; Pázmány Péter utca 1; mains 950-2800Ft) This simple eatery on the edge of the Víziváros has a wild array of pork, fish, and poultry dishes cooked the Hungarian way. Football fans will appreciate the large collection of team scarves.

our pick **Padlisán** (☎ 311 212; Pázmány Péter utca 21; mains 1500-3000Ft) With a sheer rock face topped by a castle bastion as its courtyard backdrop, Padlisán surely has the most dramatic setting of any restaurant in Esztergom. Thankfully its menu doesn't let the show down either, featuring modern Hungarian dishes (the perch in red-wine sauce is divine) and imaginative salads. Get here early in case they run out of the popular stuff.

Csülök Csárda (☎ 412 420; Batthyány Lajos utca 9; mains 1800-3900Ft) The 'Pork Knuckle Inn' – guess the speciality here – is a charming eatery that is popular with visitors and locals alike. It serves up good home cooking (try the bean soup) and the portions are huge. Highly recommended.

Self-caterers can head to **Match** (Bajcsy-Zsilinszky utca; 6.30am-8pm Mon-Fri, to 6pm Sat, 8am-noon Sun), next to the OTP bank, and the small town **market** (Simor János utca).

Drinking

Termál Sörkert (Kis-Duna sétány; 9am-10pm May–mid-Oct) The 'Thermal Beer Garden' in the outdoor thermal pool grounds is a great place to be on a balmy summer evening, when its outdoor seating area is jam-packed with people trying to be heard over the music.

Wilkinson Pub (Bajcsy-Zsilinszky utca 25-27) This friendly pub overlooking busy Bajcsy-Zsilinszky utca attracts a student/grungy crowd with cheap beer and a party vibe.

Gambrinus Music Pub (Vörösmarty utca 3; 1pm-1am Mon-Thu, to 2am Fri, 3pm-2am Sat, 3pm-midnight Sun) If you want to kick your heels up, head for this popular pub-bar with a retro Hungarian look (curios and 'antiqued' stuff) and canned music.

Entertainment

For up-to-date information about what's on, check the listings in the biweekly freebie *Komárom-Esztergomi Est*.

Organ concerts take place in the basilica over summer, the Esztergom Chroniclers sometimes perform ancient Hungarian music at the Castle Museum, and a bunch of concerts and plays are held in the town from mid-July to mid-August. Check with Gran Tours (p153), the **Ágost Bajor Cultural Centre** (☎ 313 888; Bajcsy-Zsilinszky utca 4) or visit www.egomkultur.hu (in Hungarian).

Getting There & Away

BUS

Esztergom has excellent bus connections, including to the following destinations.

Destination	Price	Duration	Km	Frequency
Balatonfüred	2540Ft	4hr	165	1 daily at 5am
Budapest	675Ft	70min-2hr	45	half-hourly
Dobogókő	300Ft	40min	20	up to 4 daily
Komárom	900Ft	1½hr	60	up to 5 daily
Szentendre	750Ft	1½hr	50	hourly
Tata	900Ft	1hr 40min	54	hourly
Veszprém	2290Ft	3½hr	145	3 daily
Visegrád	375Ft	45min	25	hourly

TRAIN

To get to Western Transdanubia and points beyond from Esztergom, take a train to Komárom.

Destination	Price	Duration	Km	Frequency
Budapest	900Ft	1½hr	53	hourly
Komárom	900Ft	1½hr	53	4 daily

Western Transdanubia

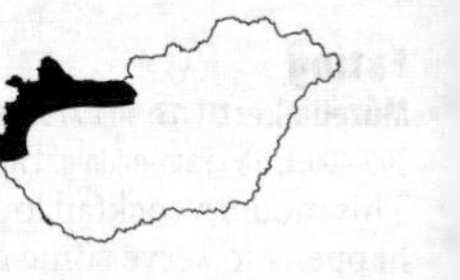

A visit to Western Transdanubia is a boon for anyone wishing to see remnants of Hungary's Roman legacy, medieval heritage and baroque splendour.

This swathe of land bordering Austria, Slovenia and Slovakia was more fortunate than its neighbours to the south and east, largely avoiding the Ottoman destruction wrought on the country in the 16th and 17th centuries. Its seminal towns – Sopron, Kőszeg and Győr – all managed to save their medieval centres from total devastation, and exploring their cobbled streets and hidden courtyards is a magical experience. These same towns, along with a handful of tiny settlements like Fertöd, also house a cornucopia of baroque architecture, something rare in much of Hungary.

Equally rewarding are reminders of Roman settlement. Szombathely, the former Roman capital of Upper Pannonia, has a rich collection of ruins, and Sopron coughs up its fair share of the Italians' enduring handiwork. Even the Romanesque period has its say in these parts – the Benedictine Abbey Church of Ják is among the finest examples of 13th-century architecture in the country.

Not to be overlooked is the region's natural beauty. Őrség, for many centuries the nation's sentry in the far southwest, is an untouched rural paradise, where pristine forests, rolling farmland and folk traditions are protected under the blanket of national park status. Further north the Fertő-Hanság National Park, a wetland/lakeland area beloved for its birdlife and cycling and walking opportunities, spills over into Austria.

HIGHLIGHTS

- Exploring **Pannonhalma Abbey** (p169), a deserved Unesco World Heritage Site
- Wandering the Inner Town of **Sopron** (p171), a district unchanged for centuries
- Calling in at **Ják** (p185) to admire the Romanesque handiwork of the town's abbey church
- Stopping for coffee and cake at Kőszeg's **Jurisics tér** (p189), arguably Hungary's finest medieval centre
- Hiking in the **Őrség National Park** (p192), a region of unspoilt rural beauty where three countries meet

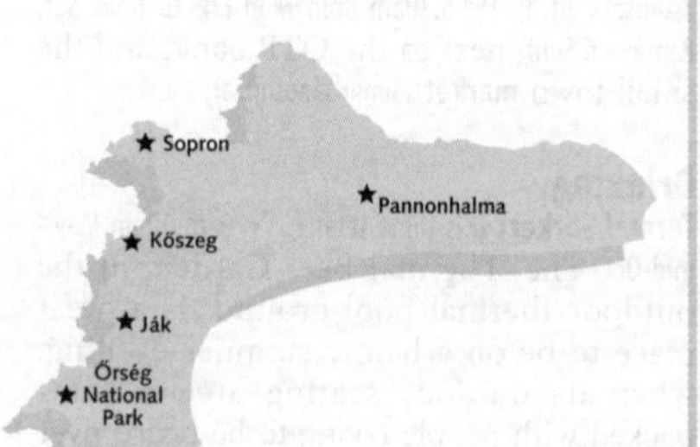

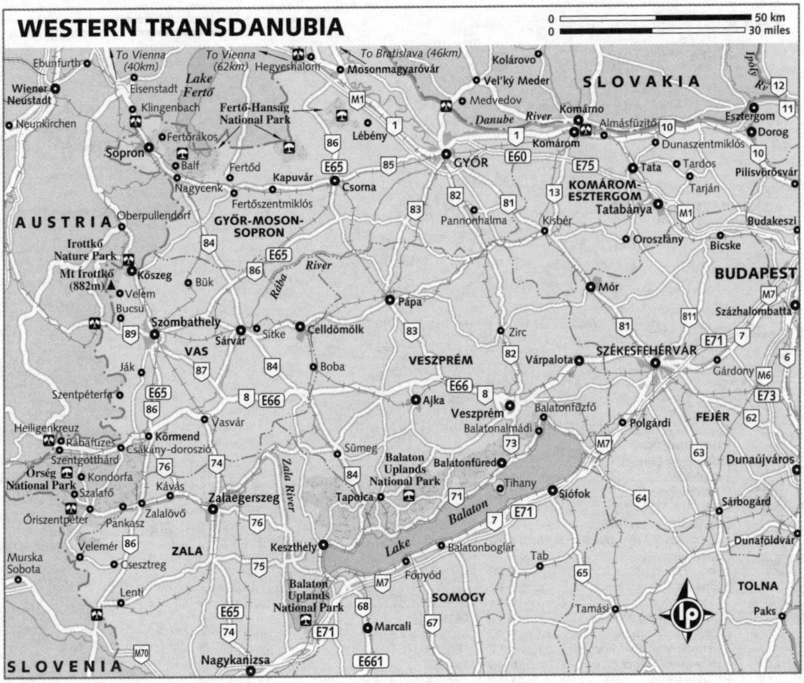

History

The Danube River was the limit of Roman expansion in what is now Hungary, and most of today's Western Transdanubia formed the province of Pannonia Superior, or 'Upper Pannonia'. The Romans built some of their most important military and civilian towns here, including Arrabona (Győr), Scarbantia (Sopron), Savaria (Szombathely), Adflexum (Mosonmagyaróvár) and Brigetio (Komárom). Because of their positions on the trade route from northern Europe to the Adriatic Sea and Byzantium, and the influx of such ethnic groups as Germans and Slovaks, these towns prospered in the Middle Ages. Episcopates were established, castles were built and many of the towns were granted special royal privileges.

A large part of Western Transdanubia remained in the hands of the Habsburgs during the Turkish occupation, and it was thus spared the ruination suffered in the south and on the Great Plain. As a result, some of the best examples of Romanesque and Gothic architecture in the country can be found here. Because of Vienna's authority and influence throughout the 16th and 17th centuries, Western Transdanubia received Hungary's first baroque churches and civic buildings.

TATA

☎34 / pop 24,100

There is no escaping water in Tata (German: Totis), a small, historical town in the northeast of Western Transdanubia. Its urban centre, complete with proud castle and smattering of neoclassical mansions, is squeezed between two lakes – one big, one small – from which canals drain in all directions.

Along Tata's eastern horizon lies a long stretch of wooded hills that only add to the town's aesthetic appeal; they make a fine destination for a day's hiking.

History

Tata's Öregvár (Old Castle), perched on a rock at the northern end of a large lake, has been the focus of the town since the 14th century. It was a favourite residence of King Sigismund, who added a palace to it in the early 15th century, and his

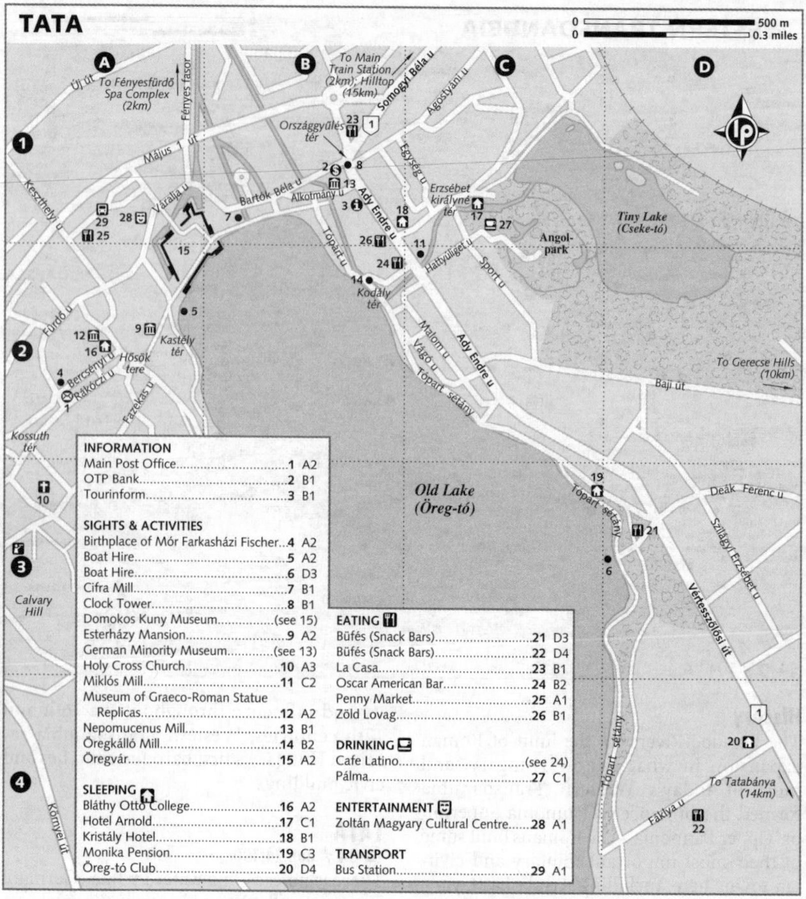

daughter, Elizabeth of Luxembourg, tarried here in 1440 with the purloined crown of St Stephen, en route to Székesfehérvár, where her newly born son would be crowned king. King Matthias Corvinus turned Tata into a royal hunting reserve attached to Visegrád, and his successor, Vladislav (Úlászló) II, convened the diet here to escape from plague-ravaged Buda at the turn of the 16th century. The castle was badly damaged by the Turks in 1683, and the town did not begin its recovery until it was acquired by a branch of the aristocratic Esterházy family in the 18th century. They retained the services of Moravian-born architect Jakab Fellner, who designed most of Tata's fine baroque buildings.

Orientation

Tata's bustling main street (Ady Endre utca), a section of busy Rte 1, separates larger Öreg-tó (Old Lake) from Cseke-tó (Tiny Lake). The bus station is 200m northwest of the castle on Május 1 út. The main train station is 1.5km north of the city centre.

Information

Main post office (Kossuth tér 19; 8am-7pm Mon-Fri)

OTP bank (Ady Endre utca 1-3) Has an exchange machine and ATM.

Tourinform (586 045; tata@tourinform.hu; Ady Endre utca 9; 9am-5pm Mon-Fri, 10am-7pm Sat & Sun Jul & Aug, 8am-4pm Mon-Fri Sep-Jun) Central, with very helpful staff.

Sights

ÖREGVÁR

The sturdy remains of the medieval **Öregvár** (Old Castle) – one of four original towers and a palace wing – were rebuilt in neo-Gothic style at the end of the 19th century to mark a visit by Emperor Franz Joseph. Today they house the **Domokos Kuny Museum** (☎ 381 251; adult/senior & student 600/300Ft; 🕑 10am-6pm Tue-Sun mid-Apr–mid-Oct, 10am-2pm Wed-Fri, to 4pm Sat & Sun mid-Oct–mid-Apr). On the ground floor are a mishmash of archaeological finds from nearby Roman settlements, bits of the 12th-century Benedictine monastery near Oroszlány and contemporary drawings of the castle in its heyday. The 'Life in the Old Castle' exhibit on the 1st floor is interesting; don't miss the cathedral-like green-tiled Gothic stove that takes pride of place in the **Knights' Hall**. Material on the 2nd floor examines the work of a dozen 18th-century artisans, including Kuny, a master ceramicist. Tata porcelain was well known for centuries (the crayfish, once abundant in the lake, was a common motif) and the craft indirectly led to the foundation of the porcelain factory at Herend near Veszprém.

MILLS

In former days Tata had so many mills controlling the flow of water into nearby canals that it was known as the 'town of mills'. Today a handful of the mills still stand, but none are in working order, all are in private hands and most are falling down.

Just east of the castle is the 16th-century **Cifra Mill** (Cifra-malom; Váralja utca 3), interesting only for its red marble window frames and five rapidly deteriorating water wheels lying against the eastern outside wall of the mill. Further around the eastern side of the lake are two more mills of interest, the crumbling, yellow **Öregkálló Mill** (Tópart sétány) and the **Miklós Mill** (Ady Endre utca 26), which until recently housed a bar.

Of all the mills the **Nepomucenus Mill** (Alkotmány utca 1), built in 1758, is the most interesting, for it now houses the **German Minority Museum** (Német Nemzetiségi Múzeum; ☎ 381 251; adult/child & student 200/100Ft; 🕑 10am-6pm Thu Apr–mid-Oct, at other times by appointment only). Like Pécs and Székesfehérvár, Tata was predominantly German-speaking for centuries, and the exhibition ('Living Together for 1100 Years') explores all aspects of the German experience in Hungary.

OTHER SIGHTS

Walking southwest from the castle for a few minutes through leafy Kastély tér to Hősök tere, you'll pass the Zopf-style former **Eszterházy Mansion** (Eszterházy Kastély; ☎ 708 106; Kastel tér; adult/student & child 400/200Ft; 🕑 10am-6pm Wed-Sun May-Sep). Designed by Jakab Fellner in 1764 and used as a hospital for many years, it has now been restored and hosts temporary exhibitions. In the renovated Romantic-style former synagogue is the **Museum of Graeco-Roman Statue Replicas** (Görög-Római Szobormásolatok Múzeuma; ☎ 381 251; Hősök tere 7; adult/student & child 200/100Ft; 🕑 10am-6pm Tue-Sun Apr-Oct). Here you'll find displays of plaster copies of stone sculptures that lined the walkways of Cseke-tó in the 19th century. At Bercsényi utca 1, just before you enter Kossuth tér, is the **birthplace of Mór Farkasházi Fischer**, founder of the Herend porcelain factory (see the boxed text, p228) and Tata's most famous son. Dominating the square is another of Fellner's works, the 18th-century **Holy Cross Church** (Szent Kereszt-templom), also called the Great Church. Inside you'll find modern ceiling frescoes and simple walls, for the baroque period that is.

Cseke-tó, surrounded by the protected 200-hectare **Angolpark**, built in 1780 and Hungary's first 'English park', is a relaxing place for a walk or a day of fishing. The park itself, which was established in 1783 by the Eszterházy family, contains an open-air theatre and 18th-century folly ruins built using Roman stones.

The octagonal wooden **clock tower** (óratorony; Országgyűlés tér) is a lot older than it looks. Designed by Fellner in 1763, it once housed the town's tiny prison.

Activities

Öreg-tó, a 'Wetland of International Importance' and protected by the Ramsar Convention, attracts a considerable number and variety of waterfowl. It's a pleasure to stroll its banks and spot avian life. The lake also has **boats** (☎ 487 441; adult/child 500/400Ft; 🕑 Jun-Aug), which depart from the pier just southwest of the castle and on the eastern shore of the lake. **Fishing** in the smaller Cseke-tó is also possible; check with Tourinform about the availability of fishing licences (3000Ft per day).

There is good **hiking** to be had in the Gerecse Hills east of Tata. To get a head start on the crowd, catch a bus to Tardos, Tarján or Dunaszentmiklós, but before setting off pick up Cartographia's 1:40,000-scale map of the area called *Gerecse Turistatérkép* (No 10; 990Ft), which has hiking trails marked.

The **Fényesfürdő** (☎ 588 144; www.fenyesfurdo.hu; Fényes fasor; adult/child & student 850/550Ft, after 5pm 500/300Ft; 9am-7pm May–mid-Sep) spa complex and camping ground north of the city centre has thermal spas and several huge pools.

Sleeping

BUDGET

Öreg-tó Club (☎ 383 496; www.tatacamping.hu; Fáklya utca 2; camp sites per tent/adult/child 480/750/480Ft, bungalows per person 1440Ft, apt 8820Ft, hotel r 7800Ft; P) All the accommodation options here are fairly unexciting, but they're cheap and only a short walk to the lake and its surrounding woods.

Bláthy Otto College (☎ 586 563; Hősök tere 9; dm 2500Ft; Jul & Aug) This small college only a minute's walk from the castle has simple yet clean rooms available over the summer months.

MIDRANGE

Monika Pension (☎ 383 208; www.hotels.hu/monikapanzio; Tópart sétány 9; r 9630Ft;) Monika is not the most modern *pension,* but it's right on the big lake (ask for a room with balcony) and the price is right. If it's full, there are another couple of places close by with much the same standard.

our pick Hilltop (☎ 550 440; www.hilltop.eu; Neszmély; s/d/tr 11,900/13,900/15,900Ft;) Hilltop has a lot going for it. Not only does it have expansive views of Slovakia and a 30km stretch of the Danube River, but it's located in the middle of the vineyards from which it makes its very own wine. Rooms are accordingly tasteful and modern, and the restaurant on-site serves regional and seasonal specialities along with local reds and whites. Hilltop is best reached with your own transport; find it 15km northeast of Tata just past the tiny village of Dunaszentmiklós.

Hotel Arnold (☎ 588 028; www.hotels.hu/arnold; Erzsébet királyné tér 8; s/d/tr 12,800/14,800/17,800Ft;) In an older building on the edge of Angolpark just metres from the small lake, this lovely hotel occupies a tranquil spot away from the town centre. Rooms are comfortable and stylish and tranquil, and the buffet breakfast is an extra 1600Ft.

TOP END

Kristály Hotel (☎ 383 577; www.hktata.hu; Ady Endre utca 22; s 13,800-15,500Ft, d 18,700-21,000Ft;) This beautifully appointed hotel on the main drag has been lovingly renovated and it now wins first prize in Tata's 'best in show' competition. Rooms are tastefully designed and come with little surprises, such as fresh fruit and flowers, and the restaurant is well recommended.

Eating & Drinking

Büfés (snack bars) line Fáklya utca near Öreg-tó Club and along Deák Ferenc utca near the pier where you can rent boats.

Penny Market (Május 1 út) Self-caterers can pick up supplies here, located beside the bus station.

Zöld Lovag (Green Knight; ☎ 481 681; Ady Endre utca 17; mains 1200-2700Ft) This courtyard eatery is another one of those 'medieval-style' restaurants, with colourful banners, large rough-hewn tables and chairs, a menu in Old Hungarian script and men in tights. But the food ain't half bad at this particular one.

Oscar American Bar (☎ 588 040; Ady Endre utca 29; mains 1200-3800Ft) Hollywood features strongly in the decor of this modern bar-restaurant on busy Ady Endre utca. Shots of bygone film stars line the walls, and seats are named after celluloid greats. The large menu features the likes of big beef steaks and tortillas snacks, and the long, high bar is perfect for highballs come sundown.

La Casa (☎ 06 70 252 2884; Országgyülés tér 3; mains around 1500Ft) La Casa is a tidy little eatery with a huge terrace and a Mediterranean vibe. The menu is a tad heavy on meat choices, but you can't go wrong with one of the six pancake desserts available.

Pálma (☎ 586 553; Angolkert; coffee 260Ft; 10am-5pm) Housed in the former palm house of the English garden, this beautiful cafe, with its chandeliers, high ceilings, columns, shaded terrace and uninterrupted views of the park, is the most elegant spot in town for coffee or something stronger.

Cafe Latino (☎ 655 065; Ady Endre utca 33) This modern cocktail bar next door to Oscar is the pick of the crop for an evening drink. Expect the occasional live concerts on weekends.

Entertainment

Zoltán Magyary Cultural Centre (☎ 380 811; Váralja utca 4), between the castle and the bus station, can provide you with brochures and up-to-date information on what's going on. Also consult the listings in the biweekly freebie *Komárom-Esztergomi Est,* which includes Tata.

Getting There & Away

BUS

Main centres, such as Győr (1200Ft, 1½ hours, 72km, three daily Monday to Saturday), Budapest (12007Ft, 1¼ hours, 77km, one daily) and Esztergom (900Ft, one hour and 40 minutes, 54km, hourly), are connected to Tata. Alternatively, catch a bus to Tatabánya (250Ft, 24 minutes, 11km, half-hourly), which has better connections.

There are regular departures to Tarján (525Ft, one hour, 31km, six daily) in the Gerecse Hills and Oroszlány (525Ft, one hour, 32km, hourly), which is the gateway to the Vértes Hills.

TRAIN

Tata has excellent links with Budapest (1200Ft, around one hour, 74km, hourly) and Győr (900Ft, 50 minutes, 57km, hourly). There are direct trains to Sopron (2250Ft, two to 2½ hours, 142km, four daily) and Szombathely (2540Ft, three hours, 174km, two daily), but you usually have to change at Győr. If you're travelling by train to Esztergom (900Ft, at least two hours, 51km, up to six daily with change), you must change at Almásfüzitő. To get to Slovakia, take the train to Komárom (300Ft, 12 to 17 minutes, 20km, half-hourly) and walk across the border.

Getting Around

Bus 1 links the main train station with the bus station and Kossuth tér. Bus 3 will take you to Fényesfürdő; bus 5 gets you close to Fáklya utca. For a local taxi call ☎ 489 808.

GYŐR

☎ 96 / pop 127,600

Not many tourists make the effort to stop at Győr (German: Raab), which is all the more reason to visit. This large city with the funny name (pronounced jyeur) is a surprisingly splendid place, with a medieval heart hidden behind a commercial façade. Additionally, its central Basilica holds one of Hungary's most precious gold artefacts, the Herm of László, and spread across the town is a gathering of intriguing private art collections.

History

Situated in the heart of the so-called Little Plain, or Kisalföld, at the meeting point of the Mosoni-Danube and Rába Rivers, Győr was settled first by the Celts and then by the Romans, who called it Arrabona. The Avars came here, too, and built a circular fort (called a *gyűrű,* from which the town took its name) before the arrival of the Magyars.

King Stephen established a bishopric at Győr in the 11th century, and 200 years later the town was granted a royal charter, allowing it to levy taxes on goods passing through.

A castle was built here in the 16th century and, being surrounded by water, was an easily defended outpost between Turkish-held Hungary and Vienna, the seat of the Habsburg Empire, until late in the century. When the Ottomans captured Győr, they were able to hold on to it for only four years and were evicted in 1598. For that reason Győr is known as the 'dear guard', watching over the nation through the centuries.

Orientation

Győr's train station lies south of Soldier Park (Honvéd liget) on Révai Miklós utca. To reach the bus station in Hunyadi utca on the other side of the train line, go through the underpass east of the main entrance. Baross Gábor utca leads to the Belváros, the historic Inner Town, and the rivers run to the north and northwest.

Information

City website (www.gyor.hu) The city's official website, aimed at tourists and business people alike.

Mandala (☎ 319 729; Sarkantyú köz 7; per hr 300Ft; 🕑 10am-10pm Mon-Thu, 10am-11pm Fri & Sat, 2-9pm Sun) This small tea house has internet access on one computer.

OTP bank (Baross Gábor utca 16; 🕑 7.45am-4.30pm Mon, to 3.30pm Tue-Thu, to 2pm Fri)

Post office Main branch (Bajcsy-Zsilinszky út 46; 🕑 8am-6pm Mon-Fri); Post office branch (Révai Miklós utca 8) The main branch is opposite the Győr National Theatre; the train station branch is south of the colossal city hall.

Tourinform (☎ 311 771; www.gyortourism.hu; Árpád út 32; 🕑 9am-6pm Mon-Fri, to 7pm Sat & Sun Jun-Aug, 9am-5pm Mon-Fri, to 1pm Sat Sep-May) Kiosk office, just north of the county hall, with helpful staff and plenty of informative brochures.

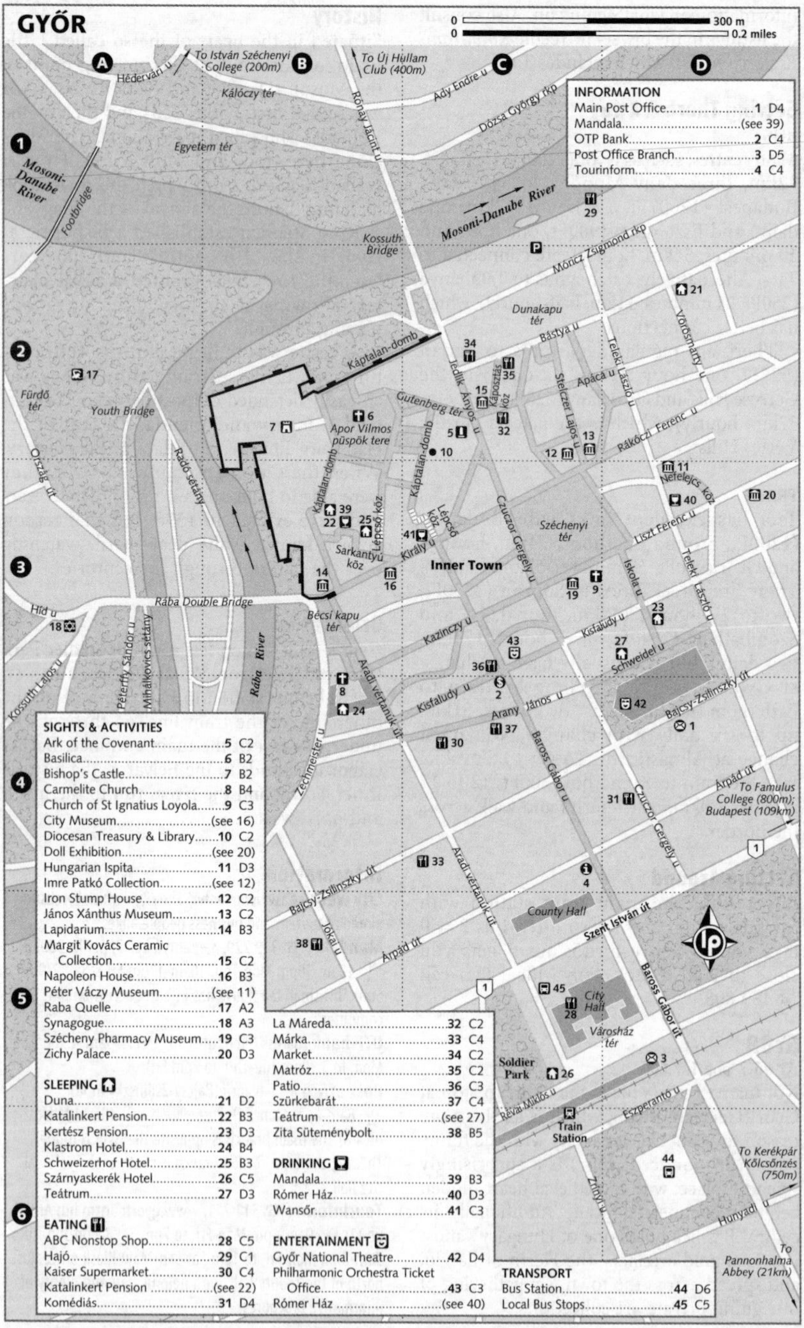
GYŐR
0 300 m
0 0.2 miles
To István Széchenyi College (200m)
To Új Hullam Club (400m)
Hédervári u
Kálóczy tér
Ady Endre u
Dózsa György rkp
Egyetem tér
Rónay Jácint u
Mosoni-Danube River
Footbridge
Kossuth Bridge
Móricz Zsigmond rkp
Dunakapu tér
Bástya u
Káptalan-domb
Fürdő tér
Youth Bridge
Radó sétány
Gutenberg tér
Apor Vilmos püspök tere
Jedlik Ányos u
Kaposztás köz
Stelczer Lajos u
Apáca u
Teleki László u
Vörösmarty u
Rákóczi Ferenc u
Nefelejcs köz
Ország út
Káptalan-domb
Lépcső köz
Király u
Sarkantyú köz
Inner Town
Széchenyi tér
Czuczor Gergely u
Liszt Ferenc u
Iskola u
Híd u
Rába Double Bridge
Bécsi kapu tér
Kazinczy u
Kisfaludy u
Schweidel u
Kossuth Lajos u
Péterfy Sándor u
Mihálkovics sétány
Rába River
Aradi vértanúk út
Kisfaludy u
Arany János u
Bajcsy-Zsilinszky út
Zechmeister u
Baross Gábor u
Árpád út
To Famulus College (800m); Budapest (109km)
Bajcsy-Zsilinszky út
Jókai u
County Hall
Szent István út
Árpád út
City Hall
Városház tér
Soldier Park
Révai Miklós u
Eszperantó u
Train Station
Zrínyi u
To Kerékpár Kölcsönzés (750m)
Hunyadi u
To Pannonhalma Abbey (21km)
INFORMATION
Main Post Office 1 D4
Mandala (see 39)
OTP Bank 2 C4
Post Office Branch 3 D5
Tourinform 4 C4
SIGHTS & ACTIVITIES
Ark of the Covenant 5 C2
Basilica 6 B2
Bishop's Castle 7 B2
Carmelite Church 8 B4
Church of St Ignatius Loyola 9 C3
City Museum (see 16)
Diocesan Treasury & Library 10 C2
Doll Exhibition (see 20)
Hungarian Ispita 11 D3
Imre Patkó Collection (see 12)
Iron Stump House 12 C2
János Xánthus Museum 13 C2
Lapidarium 14 B3
Margit Kovács Ceramic Collection 15 C2
Napoleon House 16 B3
Péter Váczy Museum (see 11)
Raba Quelle 17 A2
Synagogue 18 A3
Szécheny Pharmacy Museum 19 C3
Zichy Palace 20 D3
SLEEPING
Duna 21 D2
Katalinkert Pension 22 B3
Kertész Pension 23 D3
Klastrom Hotel 24 B4
Schweizerhof Hotel 25 B3
Szárnyaskerék Hotel 26 C5
Teátrum 27 D3
EATING
ABC Nonstop Shop 28 C5
Hajó 29 C1
Kaiser Supermarket 30 C4
Katalinkert Pension (see 22)
Komédiás 31 D4
La Máreda 32 C2
Márka 33 C4
Market 34 C2
Matróz 35 C2
Patio 36 C3
Szürkebarát 37 C4
Teátrum (see 27)
Zita Süteménybolt 38 B5
DRINKING
Mandala 39 B3
Római Ház 40 D3
Wansőr 41 C3
ENTERTAINMENT
Győr National Theatre 42 D4
Philharmonic Orchestra Ticket Office 43 C3
Római Ház (see 40)
TRANSPORT
Bus Station 44 D6
Local Bus Stops 45 C5

Sights

KÁPTALAN-DOMB

A fine place to start a tour of Győr is on Chapter Hill (Káptalan-domb). This, the oldest part of the city, is criss-crossed with quiet cobbled streets and tight alleyways and dominated by the **Basilica** (Bazilika; admission free; 8am-noon & 2-6pm), whose foundations date back to the 11th century. Over the ensuing centuries the religious centre of Győr gained an amalgam of styles – Romanesque apses (have a look from the outside), a neoclassical facade, and a Gothic chapel riding piggyback on the south side. But most of what you see inside, including the stunning frescoes by Franz Anton Maulbertsch, the main altar, the bishop's throne and the pews hewn from Dalmatian oak, is baroque and dates from the 17th and 18th centuries.

Despite the attractive mishmash of architecture, the real highlight here is the **Herm of László**, an incredible, and priceless, goldwork dating from the early 15th century. Housed in the Gothic **Hédervár y Chapel**, the herm is a bust reliquary of one of Hungary's earliest king-saints (r 1077–95) and a spectacular piece of metalwork. On 27 June it is taken from its resting place and paraded around the city.

If you're looking for miracles, though, move to the north aisle and the **Weeping Icon of Mary**, an altarpiece brought from Galway by the Irish Bishop of Clonfert in 1649, who had been sent packing by Oliver Cromwell. Some 40 years later – on St Patrick's Day no less – it began to cry tears of blood and is still a pilgrimage site.

Not far east of the Basilica is the **Diocesan Treasury and Library** (Egyházmegyei kincstár és könyvtár; ☎ 525 090; adult/senior & student/family 700/400/1500Ft; 10am-4pm Tue-Sun Mar-Oct), one of the richest in Hungary and labelled in English. Of particular value are the Gothic chalices and Renaissance mitre embroidered with pearls, but stealing the show is the precious library, containing almost 70,000 volumes printed before 1850.

On the opposite side of the Basilica to the treasury rises the remnants of the **Bishop's Castle** (Püspökvár), a fortresslike structure with parts dating from the 13th century; it's currently closed to the public. The foundations of an 11th-century Romanesque chapel are on its south side. A quick stroll down Kaptalan-domb brings you to the **Lapidarium** (☎ 310 588; Bécsi kapu tér 5; adult/senior & student 550/300Ft; 10am-6pm Tue-Sun Apr-Oct), a rich collection of Roman and medieval bits and pieces (the majority of which is stone remains); it is a branch of the János Xánthus Museum.

AROUND KÁPTALAN-DOMB

Descending narrow Gutenberg tér to the east of the Basilica, you'll pass the outstanding **Ark of the Covenant** (Frigyszekrény szobor; Jedlik Ányos utca), a large statue dating from 1731. Local tradition has it that King Charles (Károly) III erected the ark, the city's finest baroque monument, to appease the angry people of Győr after one of his soldiers accidentally knocked a monstrance containing the Blessed Sacrament out of the bishop's hands during a religious procession. Just opposite the ark but entered from Káposztás köz 8 is the **Margit Kovács Ceramic Collection** (Kovács Margit kerámiagyűjtemény; ☎ 326 739; Apáca utca 1; adult/senior & student 550/300Ft; 10am-6pm Tue-Sun), a branch of the City Art Museum devoted to the celebrated ceramicist Margit Kovács (1902–77), who was born in Győr. Many of her works deal with rural and family life and have touches of folk art to them, but her best pieces are located in Szentendre (p143).

Baroque Bécsi kapu tér (Viennese Gate Sq), to the south of Káptalan-domb, is dominated by the **Carmelite church**. Built in 1725, the church is suitably baroque, but the interior is too dark to fully appreciate its intricate ornamentation. On the north and northwest side of the square and cutting it off from the river are the fortifications built in the 16th century to stop the Turkish onslaught, and a bastion that has served as a prison, a chapel, a shop and, until recently, even a restaurant.

SZÉCHENYI TÉR

A couple of blocks southeast of Káptalan-domb is enormous Széchenyi tér, which was the town's marketplace in the Middle Ages. On the south side, the Jesuit and later Benedictine **Church of St Ignatius Loyola** dates from 1641. The 17th-century white-stucco side chapels and the ceiling frescoes painted by the Viennese baroque artist Paul Troger in 1744 are worth a look. Next door, the **Szécheny Pharmacy Museum** (Szécheny Patikamúzeum; ☎ 320 954; Széchenyi tér 9; admission free; 7.40am-4pm Mon-Fri) was established by the Jesuits in 1654 and is a fully operational baroque institution. You can inspect the rococo vaulted ceiling and its fabulous frescoes with religious and herbal themes while buying aspirin.

On the north side of the square is the main branch of the **János Xánthus Museum** (☎ 310 588; Széchenyi tér 5; adult/senior & student 650/300Ft; ⌚ 10am-6pm Tue-Sun Apr-Sep, 1-5pm Tue-Sun Oct-Mar). Its historical exhibits include stamps, coins and antique furniture, but unfortunately it's all fairly ho-hum. Next door, the **Imre Patkó Collection** (☎ 310 588; Széchenyi tér 5; adult/senior & student 550/300Ft; ⌚ 10am-6pm Tue-Sun Apr-Sep, 1-5pm Tue-Sun Oct-Mar) is the most international of Győr's museums. It contains an intriguing collection of 20th-century fine art on the first two floors, while the 3rd floor is devoted to objects collected by the journalist and art historian Imre Patkó during his travels in India, Tibet, Vietnam and west Africa. The museum is located in the 17th-century **Iron Stump House** (Vastuskós Ház), a former caravanserai entered from Stelczer Lajos utca that still sports the log into which itinerant artisans would drive a nail to mark their visit.

OTHER SIGHTS

To the east of Széchenyi tér is the late Renaissance **Hungarian Ispita** (Magyar Ispita; 3 Nefelejcs köz), once a charity hospital, which now houses the **Péter Váczy Museum** (☎ 318 141; adult/senior & student 550/300Ft; ⌚ 10am-6pm Tue-Sun). Váczy, a history professor and avid antiques collector, managed to assemble quite an eclectic assortment of pieces, from Greek and Roman relics to Chinese terracotta figures, all of which are on display.

In the stunning **Zichy Palace** (Zichy palota; Liszt Ferenc utca 20) is the **Doll Exhibition** (Baba Kiállítás; ☎ 320 289; admission free; ⌚ 8am-3.30pm Mon-Thu, 8am-1pm Fri, noon-6pm Sat), consisting of some 72 19th-century dolls and furniture. It's worth a visit just to see the 18th-century baroque palace, which is also used sometimes for concerts and plays.

Across the Rába River the richly decorated octagonal cupola, galleries and tabernacle of the city's erstwhile **synagogue** (☎ 322 695; Kossuth Lajos utca 5; adult/child 600/300Ft; ⌚ 10am-6pm Wed-Sun), built in 1870, poke above the tree line. The former Jewish house of worship now plays host to the private collection of János Vasilesu, consisting of so-so contemporary pieces, but the true star here is the beautifully restored interior. Next door is the city's music academy, which occasionally holds concerts in the synagogue.

> **NAPOLEONIC PAUSE**
>
> Known only to pedants and Lonely Planet guidebook writers is the 'footnote fact' that Napoleon actually spent a night in Hungary – at Király utca 4, due east of Bécsi kapu tér, on 31 August 1809. The building is now called **Napoleon House** (Napoleon-ház), appropriately enough, and contains a branch of the **City Museum** (⌚ 10am-6pm Tue-Sun). And why did NB choose Győr to make his grand entrée into Hungary? Apparently the city was near a battle site and an inscription on the Arc de Triomphe in Paris recalls *'la bataille de Raab'*.

Activities

On the left bank of the Rába River is **Raba Quelle** (☎ 514 900; www.gyortermal.hu; Fürdő tér 1; adult/child & student per day 1950/1350Ft, per 3hr 1550/1100Ft; ⌚ thermal baths 9am-8.30pm Sun-Thu, to 9pm Fri & Sat, covered pool 6am-8pm Mon-Sat year-round, open-air pool 8am-8pm May-Aug), Győr's complex of thermal baths, pools, and fitness and wellness centres, offering every treatment imaginable.

The city produces a map of the surrounding area with over a dozen **cycle paths** marked. Pick up a copy at Tourinform and hire a bicycle from **Kerékpár Kölcsönzés** (☎ 335 567; Corvin utca 44; per day 1500Ft; ⌚ noon-5pm Mon-Sat, 10am-1pm Sun).

Festivals & Events

The prestigious **Hungarian Dance Festival** (www.hungariandancefestival.hu) is held biannually in Győr in late June.

Sleeping

Tourinform can provide you with a list of accommodation options, but won't arrange anything for you.

BUDGET

Szárnyaskerék Hotel (☎ 314 629; Révai Miklós utca 5; s/d without bathroom 2700/5400Ft, with bathroom 3800/7600Ft) Dilapidated is a good word to describe the 'Winged Wheel', but it does have two redeeming features – it's cheap as chips and it's within stumbling distance of the train and bus stations.

Student accommodation abounds in Győr. The following are open year-round:

Famulus College (☎ 547 723; www.hotelfamulus.hu; Budai út 4-6; dm 3100Ft;) New building east of the city centre, with modern rooms and a selection of singles and doubles (from €60).

István Széchenyi College (☎ 503 447; Hédervári út 3; dm 3100Ft) Dormitory accommodation at this huge school north of the city centre.

MIDRANGE

Unusually for a Hungarian city, Győr is full of small private *pensions* (guest houses). Very central and in some of the city's most colourful old buildings, they're very good value but seldom have lifts.

Duna (☎ 329 084; www.hotelspaar.hu; Vörösmarty utca 5; s/d/tr 6500/8500/10,400Ft) A sister *pension* of Teátrum's, the powder-blue Duna is more old fashioned than its sibling, with standard furniture in rooms and a collection of antique furniture in some common areas.

Kertész Pension (☎ 317 461; www.kertesz-panzio.hu; Iskola utca 11; s/d/tr/q 7000/11,000/14,000/16,000Ft) The 'Gardener' has very simple rooms, but it's well located in central Győr and staff couldn't be more friendly.

Katalinkert Pension (☎ 542 088; katalinkert@t-online.hu; Sarkantyú köz 3; s/d 7100/9900Ft) Tucked away on a tiny alleyway in the medieval heart of Győr, Katalinkert offers wonderful privacy in the thick of things. The large rooms, with whitewashed walls, clean wooden floors and pot plants, are perfect for those looking for a degree of comfort without breaking the bank.

Teátrum (☎ 310 640; www.teatrum.hu; Schweidel utca 7; s/d/tr 9500/12,500/15,000Ft) Teátrum is arguably the best choice in town, with warm, cosy guestrooms featuring plenty of natural wood, a very central location and a highly recommended restaurant on the ground floor.

TOP END

Klastrom Hotel (☎ 516 910; www.klastrom.hu; Zechmeister utca 1; s/d/tr 14,700/18,700/21,400Ft;) This delightful three-star hotel occupies a 300-year-old Carmelite convent south of Bécsi kapu tér. Rooms are charming and bright, and extras include a sauna, solarium, pub with a vaulted ceiling, and a restaurant with seating in a leafy and peaceful inner garden. The best rooms face the courtyard.

Schweizerhof Hotel (☎ 329 171; www.schweizerhof.hu; Sarkantyú köz 11-13; s 16,800Ft, d 18,300-21,800Ft;) This is Győr's finest top-end hotel and about as plush as you'll find here. Rooms are individually decorated but each is large enough to have lounge chairs and sport sparkling bathrooms. There's a wellness centre, wine cellar, and quality restaurant and bar within the hotel.

Eating

RESTAURANTS & CAFES

Zita Süteménybolt (☎ 323 180; Jókai utca 6/a; cakes 60-200Ft; 10am-5pm) What was once a hole-in-the-wall serving homemade cakes has turned into a flash little cake shop – serving homemade cakes. Join the cue at the window, take a pew inside, or plonk down on the back terrace and enjoy.

Hajó (☎ 337 700; Móricz Zsigmond rakpart 3; pizzas 500-1700Ft) For the novel experience of dining on the Mosoni-Danube River, try this pizza restaurant filling an atmospheric old riverboat.

Szürkebarát (☎ 311 548; Arany János utca 20; mains 900-3000Ft; 9am-10pm Mon-Fri, to 4pm Sat) A decent wine cellar-restaurant in a small courtyard, where you'll also find a small kiosk selling very popular ice cream for 150Ft per scoop. If you've missed breakfast or you're looking for a cheap, filling lunch menu (700Ft), this is a good place to come.

Patio (☎ 310 096; Baross Gábor utca 12; mains 1000-2000Ft) Patio has an above-average restaurant serving Hungarian cuisine, but it's overshadowed by the cakes and marzipan creations in its cafe. We dare anyone to walk by without salivating at the calorie bombs in the window.

our pick **Matróz** (☎ 336 208; Dunakapu tér 3; mains 1080-1700Ft) This marketside restaurant may serve poultry and meat dishes, but avoid them like the plague. Not because they're bad, but because Matróz makes the best damn fish dishes around. Over 20 fish specialities are on offer, from warming carp soup to delicate pike-perch fillets. The handsome vaulted brick cellar, complete with dark-blue tiled oven and nautical memorabilia, completes this wonderful little eatery.

La Maréda (☎ 510 982; Apáca utca 4; mains 1350-3000Ft) La Maréda wears the fancy pants in Győr's restaurant scene. Its small but selective menu focuses on gourmet dishes, such as duck breast with apples and honey and mushroom ragout with camembert, along with seasonal specialities. A cheaper and less extravagant bistro resides next door.

Komédiás (☎ 527 217; Czuczor Gergely utca 30; mains 1500-2600Ft; 11am-midnight Mon-Sat) A very upscale cellar eatery decorated in postmodern greys and blacks, the 'Comedian' caters to a firm local following with a thoroughly Hungarian menu. It has courtyard seating, which is a delight in the warmer months, and there are good-value set menus (670Ft and 950Ft).

Both **Teátrum** (☎ 310 640; www.teatrum.hu; Schweidel utca 7; mains 1000-2500Ft) and **Katalinkert Pension** (☎ 542 088; katalinkert@t-online.hu; Sarkantyú köz 3; mains 1000-2500Ft) have reputable restaurants.

QUICK EATS & SELF-CATERING

Márka (☎ 320 800; Bajcsy-Zsilinszky út 30; dishes 300-600Ft; 11am-5pm Mon-Sat) Márka is good for anyone looking for a filling meal on a tight budget. The cafeteria-style surroundings aren't particularly appetising but the crowd doesn't seem to mind.

Market (Dunakapu tér; 7am-1pm Wed & Sat) A very small but colourful open-air market is held near the river.

Shops selling foodstuffs and sundries:

ABC nonstop shop (Révai Miklós utca; 24hr) In the train station's underground pass.

Kaiser supermarket (Arany János utca 16; 7.30am-7pm Mon, 6.30am-7pm Tue-Fri, 6.30am-3pm Sat, 8am-1pm Sun)

Drinking

Rómer Ház (☎ 550 850; www.romerhaz.eu; Teleki László utca 21) The bar on the ground floor of this independent art centre accepts all and has a sweet inner courtyard for late-night drinking in summer.

Mandala (☎ 319 729; Sarkantyú köz 7; 10am-10pm Mon-Thu, 10am-11pm Fri & Sat, 2-9pm Sun) This small tea house has more tea varieties on offer than some Hungarian towns. Choose your poison and relax in what can only be described as a chilled environment with good – almost spiritual – vibes.

Wansör (☎ 314 856; Lépcső köz) Mix up a night on the tiles with pizza slices at Wansör, a cellar pub that attracts a jovial crowd, with occasional live music and inexpensive drinks.

Entertainment

A good source of information for what's on in Győr is the free fortnightly magazine *Győri Est*.

Győr National Theatre (Győri Nemzeti Színház; ☎ 520 600, ticket office 520 611; www.gyoriszinhaz.hu, in Hungarian; Czuczor Gergely utca 7; 10am-1pm Mon, 10am-1pm & 2-6pm Tue-Fri) This is a modern, technically advanced though rather unattractive structure covered in Op Art tiles by the promoter of the style, Victor Vasarely. The celebrated **Győr Ballet** (www.gyoribalett.hu), the city's opera company and the **philharmonic orchestra** (☎ ticket office 326 323; Kisfaludy utca 25; 10am-noon & 1-4pm Mon-Thu, 10am-3pm Fri) all perform here.

Rómer Ház (☎ 550 850; www.romerhaz.wu; László Teleki utca 21) Rómer Ház is a one-stop shop for entertainment, featuring an independent cinema upstairs and regular live concerts and clubbing down in the dungeon.

Új Hullám Club (☎ 313 373; Hédervári utca 24) One of the bigger clubs in town, with a Moroccan-themed restaurant. It's open Monday to Saturday.

Getting There & Away

BUS

Buses travel to the following destinations from Győr.

Destination	Price	Duration	Km	Frequency
Balatonfüred	1500Ft	2½hr	100	6 daily
Budapest	2040Ft	1hr 50min	128	up to 11 daily
Esztergom	1770Ft	2½hr	102	1-2 daily
Keszthely	2040Ft	3¼hr	136	4 daily
Pannonhalma	375Ft	30min	21	half-hourly
Pápa	750Ft	1hr	48	hourly
Pécs	3440Ft	4½-5hr	254	2 daily
Sümeg	1500Ft	2¼hr	96	3 daily
Székesfehérvár	1500Ft	1¾hr	95	6 daily
Szombathely	1770Ft	2½hr	110	3-5 daily
Tapolca	1770Ft	2½hr	106	2-3 daily
Tata	900Ft	1½hr	58	up to 4 daily
Veszprém	1350Ft	2hr	86	9 daily

TRAIN

Győr is the main train junction after Budapest. It has convenient connections with Budapest (2040Ft, 1½ to two hours, 131km, half-hourly) and Vienna (2750Ft, 1½ hours, 119km, 10 daily) via Hegyeshalom. Trains to Ebenfurth in Austria via Sopron are run by GySEV, which isn't part of the MÁV system; they are less frequent.

You can also reach Szombathely (2245Ft, 1½ to two hours, 117km, seven daily) by train via Celldömölk or Csorna and the gateway to the Balaton region, Veszprém (1200Ft, two to three hours, 79km, three daily), via Pannonhalma and Zirc. If heading for Slovakia, change trains at Komárom (600Ft, 30 minutes, 37km, hourly).

WESTERN TRANSDANUBIA

Getting Around

Most local buses stop beside the city hall on Városház tér.

Parking is difficult (and costly) in Győr and the one-way system very confusing for the uninitiated. Avoid driving in the city if at all possible. Local taxis are available on ☎ 444 444.

PANNONHALMA

☎ 96 / pop 3850

High on a hill 21km southeast of Győr in the small village of Pannonhalma stands one of Hungary's celebrated Unesco World Heritage Sites, the 1000-year-old Benedictine abbey. In a country filled with religious sites, nothing comes close to it in terms of architectural splendour and historical significance, and visitors to Western Transdanubia would be wise to take the time and effort to include it in their itinerary.

History

The monastery was founded by monks from Venice and Prague in 996 with the assistance of Prince Géza. The Benedictines were considered a militant order, and Géza's son, King Stephen, used them to help convert the Magyars to Christianity.

The abbey and associated buildings have been razed, rebuilt and restored many times over the centuries; it escaped damage during the Turkish occupation when it was used as a mosque. As a result, the complex is a patchwork of architectural styles.

Orientation

Pannonhalma is dominated by Castle Hill (Várhegy) and the abbey. Most buses from Győr stop in the village centre; from here follow Váralja up to the abbey. About four or five buses continue up the eastern side of the hill and stop at the abbey's main entrance.

The train station is a few kilometres west of the village off Petőfi utca in the direction of Rte 82.

Information

Main post office (Dózsa György utca 7; 🕒 8am-4pm Mon-Fri) Also does foreign exchange.

OTP ATM At the abbey ticket office.

Tourinform (☎/fax 471 733; pannonhalma@tourinform.hu; Petőfi utca 25; 🕒 9am-4pm Mon-Fri) Inconveniently located about 600m south of Szabadság tér at the Ferenc Kazinczy Cultural Centre.

Sights

PANNONHALMA ABBEY

Not even the power of Stalin could shut down the **Pannonhalma Abbey** (Pannonhalmi főapátság; ☎ 570 191; www.bences.hu; Vár utca 1; Hungarian tour adult/student/family 1700/800/3800Ft, foreign-language tour 2400/1500/6000Ft; 🕒 9am-4pm Tue-Sun Apr & Oct–mid-Nov, 9am-4pm May, 9am-5pm Jun-Sep, 10am-3pm Tue-Sun mid-Nov–Mar), and today it still functions as a monastery. Additionally, it runs one of the best secondary schools in the country, founded in 1802.

After buying your ticket at the reception building opposite the car park and watching a 15-minute film about life in the monastic community, follow the overhead walkway to the central courtyard, where the tour begins. In the centre you'll see a statue of the first abbot, Asztrik, who brought the crown of King Stephen to Hungary from Rome, and a relief of King Stephen himself presenting his son Imre to the tutor Bishop Gellért. To the north are dramatic views of the Kisalföld, while looming behind you are the abbey's modern wings and a neoclassical clock tower built in the early 19th century.

The entrance to **St Martin's Basilica** (Szent Márton-bazilika), built early in the 12th century, is through the **Porta Speciosa**. This arched doorway in red limestone was recarved in the mid-19th century by the Stornos, a controversial family of restorers who imposed 19th-century Romantic notions of Romanesque and Gothic architecture on ancient buildings (see p173); it is beautiful despite the butchery. The fresco above the doorway by Ferenc Storno depicts the church's patron, St Martin of Tours, giving half his cloak to a crouching beggar. Look down to the right below the columns and you'll see what is probably the oldest graffiti in Hungary: 'Benedict Padary was here in 1578', in Latin.

As you walk along the **cloister** arcade, you'll notice the little faces carved in stone on the wall. They represent human emotions and vices, such as wrath, greed and conceit, and are meant to remind monks of the baseness and transitory nature of human existence. In the cloister garden a Gothic sundial offers a sobering thought: 'Una Vestrum, Ultima Mea' (One of you will be my last).

The most beautiful part of the abbey is the neoclassical **abbey library** (*főapátság könyvtára*) built in 1836 by János Packh, who was involved in designing the Esztergom Basilica (p154). It contains some 300,000 volumes – many of them priceless historical records – making it the largest private library in Hungary. But the rarest and most important document is in the abbey archives. It is the Deed of Foundation of the Abbey Church of Tihany and dates from 1055. It is written in Latin, but also contains about 50 Hungarian place names, making it the earliest surviving example of written Hungarian. The library's interior may look like marble, but it is actually wood made to look like the more expensive stone. An ingenious system of mirrors within the skylights reflects and redirects natural light throughout the room.

The **art gallery** *(képtár)* off the library contains works by Dutch, Italian and Austrian masters from the 16th to 18th centuries. The oldest work, however, goes back to 1350.

Because it still functions as a monastery, the abbey must be visited with a guide. Tours in Hungarian (with foreign-language text) go on the hour throughout the year; English and German tours leave at 11.20am and 1.20pm, with an extra tour at 3.20pm from June to September. Between October and March, foreign-language tours must be booked in advance.

OTHER SIGHTS

Up until 1945, the abbey and its monks had a long, fruitful history of wine-making. The communist takeover managed to destroy 1000 years of abbey viticulture, but since the early 1990s the monks have been hard at work reviving it. Their efforts can be seen at the **Abbey Winery** (☎ 570 191; www.apatsagipinceszet.hu; tours 500Ft, with 3/5 wine tastings 1400/2200Ft), where tours of the press house and wine storage facilities are available throughout the year between 10am and 7pm, by prior arrangement only.

If you've time to kill waiting for your tour to begin, a visit to the **Glass Gallery** (☎ 470 318; www.hefterlaszlo.hu; Tóthegy utca 11/a; adult/senior & student 350/250Ft; ⏰ 10am-5pm Tue-Sun) makes a rewarding filler. Located 120m below the abbey, the gallery features the colourful and striking glassworks by Hefter László and other artists.

Festivals & Events

Six **organ and choral concerts** (adult/student 1700/800Ft) are scheduled between the end of March and December in the basilica – always at the same time, 3.30pm, and on the same dates: Easter Monday, Whit Monday, St Stephen's Day (20 August), National Day (23 October) and 26 December (also at 1.30pm). See www.bences.hu for details.

Sleeping, Eating & Drinking

Família (☎ 570 592; http://w3.enternet.hu/familiap; Béke utca 61; s/d/tr/q 4400/6800/8700/11,600Ft; ⊠) It's hard to find a more friendly and hospitable *pension* than Família. Some rooms come with a balcony, and there's a small garden, kitchen and lounge available for guests' use. It's located just off Rte 82 as you enter the town from the north.

Pannon (☎ 470 041; www.hotelpannon.hu; Hunyadi út 7/c; s/d/tr/q 7800/9700/12,000/13,900Ft) This relatively large guest house is more functional than familial, but its rooms are clean and quiet, and some come with a small terrace. Plus it's only a short walk to the abbey from here and the restaurant on-site (mains 1000Ft to 2500Ft) serves typically hearty Hungarian food.

Szent Márton (☎ 470 793; Vár utca 1; mains 1100-2600Ft; ⏰ 9am-5pm Tue-Fri, to 6pm Sat & Sun) Below the abbey and at the back of the car park, Szent Márton has a snack bar, pub and gift shop, as well as an uninspiring restaurant. But it is handy to the abbey.

Kolostor (☎ 470 012; Szabadság tér 1; mains 1500-3000Ft; ⏰ 10am-10pm Tue-Sat, 11am-9pm Sun & Mon) In a historic building in the village centre, this place has rustic charm, traditional farming implements lining the walls and a very large, sunny terrace at the rear.

While in town try some of the wine from the nearby Pannonhalma-Sokoróalja region, which produces some excellent white wines, notably Rieslings. The abbey's vineyard produces some 300,000 bottles annually from vines planted only in 2001. A good place to start is **Borbirodalom** (Wine Empire; ☎ 471 240; www.borbirodalom.hu; Szabadság tér 27; ⏰ 11am-7pm), a wine cellar and restaurant in the heart of the village. It has an extensive selection available for tasting (four/seven wines 1400/2000Ft) as well as buying.

Getting There & Away

There are frequent buses to/from Győr (375Ft, 30 minutes, 21km, half-hourly). Buses from Győr leave as early as 5.10am (5.50am on weekends) for Pannonhalma and return as late as 10pm (8.45pm on weekends).

Pannonhalma can be reached from Veszprém (900Ft, 1½ to 2½ hours, 58km, three daily), but more frequently from Győr (375Ft, 30 minutes, 21km, nine daily).

SOPRON

☎ 99 / pop 56,400

It's true – most visitors to Sopron (German: Ödenburg) are Austrians seeking inexpensive dental work and cheap hair cuts. But most Austrians are missing the point. For this westerly Hungarian city, with its intact medieval Inner Town (Belváros) and wooded backdrop, is so much more than simply a place to save some euros. A stroll through its quiet back streets, lined with Gothic churches and baroque town houses, is a real delight, and once you're done with that, you can opt for a glass or two of the local wine, or head out of town and enjoy nature's offerings.

History

Sopron has had more wars, difficult decisions and political rulings thrust upon it than most other Hungarian cities. Indeed as recently as 1921 its citizens had to vote whether to stay in Austria's Bürgenland as a result of the Trianon Treaty (see the boxed text, p32) or be reannexed by Hungary. They resoundingly chose the latter, which explains the little knot of Hungarian territory that juts into Austria.

First to arrive in the area were the Celts, then came the Romans, who lived in a settlement called Scarbantia (now Sopron's Inner Town) between the 1st and 4th centuries. The Germans, Avars, Slavs and the Magyars followed in succession. In medieval times Sopron was ideally situated for trade along the so-called Amber Route from the Baltic Sea to the Adriatic and Byzantium. By the 1300s, after a century of struggle between the Hungarians and the Austrians for hegemony over the city, Sopron had been made a royal free town – its mixed population able to pursue their trades without pressure from feudal landlords. Thus a strong middle class of artisans and merchants emerged here, and their wealth contributed to making Sopron a centre of science and education.

Neither the Mongols nor Turks were able to penetrate the heart of Sopron, which is why so many old buildings still stand. But damage during WWII was extensive – the area saw much restoration work done in the 1960s.

Orientation

The medieval Inner Town, shaped like a horseshoe, contains almost everything of interest, though there are a few worthy sights across the narrow Ikva Stream to the northeast, just beyond the city walls. The Lővér Hills start about 4km southwest of the city. Várkerület and Ógabona tér form a ring around the Inner Town, roughly following the city's Roman and medieval walls.

Sopron train station is on Állomás utca, about 800m south of the Inner Town. Sopron-Déli train station, through which trains to/from Szombathely also pass, is to the northwest of Sopron train station. The bus station is just northwest of the Inner Town on Lackner Kristóf utca.

Information

City website (www.sopron.hu, in Hungarian) Attractive and easy to use, with practical and background info.

OTP bank (Várkerület 96/a)

Post office Main branch (Széchenyi tér 7-8); Post office branch (Várkerület 37; ⌚ 8am-4pm Mon-Fri) The main branch is south of the Inner Town, while the secondary branch is within the Inner Town.

Tourinform Main branch (☎ 517 560; sopron@tourinform.hu; Ferenc Liszt Conference & Cultural Centre, Liszt Ferenc utca 1; ⌚ 9am-6pm Mon-Fri, to 7pm Sat & Sun mid-Jun–Aug, 9am-5pm Mon-Fri, to noon Sat Sep–mid-Jun); Tourinform branch (☎ 505 438; Deák tér 45; ⌚ 9am-5pm Mon-Fri, 9am-noon Sat Apr-Oct) Both branches offer free internet access and a plethora of information on Sopron and the surrounding area.

Sights

INNER TOWN

For a complete overview of Sopron climb the 200 steps of the narrow circular staircase to the top of the 60m-high **firewatch tower** (tűztorony; ☎ 311 327; Fő tér; adult/senior & student 700/350Ft; ⌚ 10am-8pm May-Aug, 10am-6pm Tue-Sun Apr, Sep & Oct) at the northern end of Fő tér. Standing at its summit, the city, the Lővér Hills to the southwest, the Austrian Alps to the west and the entire Inner Town are perfectly laid out before you.

The tower, from which trumpeters would warn of fire, mark the hour (now done by chimes and tinny music) and greet visitors to the city in the Middle Ages, is a true architectural hybrid. The 2m-thick square base, built on a Roman gate, dates from the 12th century, and the cylindrical middle and arcaded balcony from the 16th century. The

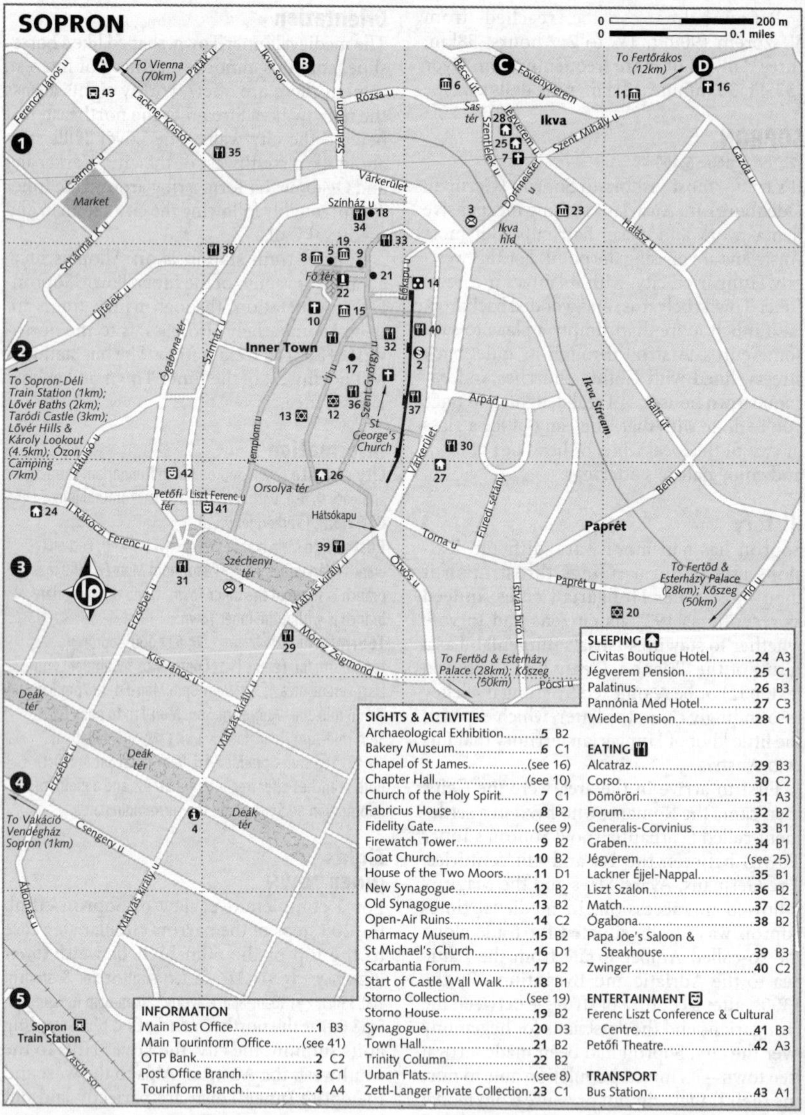

SIGHTS & ACTIVITIES
Archaeological Exhibition.........5 B2
Bakery Museum.........6 C1
Chapel of St James.........(see 16)
Chapter Hall.........(see 10)
Church of the Holy Spirit.........7 C1
Fabricius House.........8 B2
Fidelity Gate.........(see 9)
Firewatch Tower.........9 B2
Goat Church.........10 B2
House of the Two Moors.........11 D1
New Synagogue.........12 B2
Old Synagogue.........13 B2
Open-Air Ruins.........14 C2
Pharmacy Museum.........15 B2
St Michael's Church.........16 D1
Scarbantia Forum.........17 B2
Start of Castle Wall Walk.........18 B1
Storno Collection.........(see 19)
Storno House.........19 B2
Synagogue.........20 D3
Town Hall.........21 B2
Trinity Column.........22 B2
Urban Flats.........(see 8)
Zettl-Langer Private Collection.........23 C1

INFORMATION
Main Post Office.........1 B3
Main Tourinform Office.........(see 41)
OTP Bank.........2 C2
Post Office Branch.........3 C1
Tourinform Branch.........4 A4

SLEEPING
Civitas Boutique Hotel.........24 A3
Jégverem Pension.........25 C1
Palatinus.........26 B3
Pannónia Med Hotel.........27 C3
Wieden Pension.........28 C1

EATING
Alcatraz.........29 B3
Corso.........30 C2
Dömörőri.........31 A3
Forum.........32 B2
Generalis-Corvinius.........33 B1
Graben.........34 B1
Jégverem.........(see 25)
Lackner Éjjel-Nappal.........35 B1
Liszt Szalon.........36 B2
Match.........37 C2
Ógabona.........38 B2
Papa Joe's Saloon & Steakhouse.........39 B3
Zwinger.........40 C2

ENTERTAINMENT
Ferenc Liszt Conference & Cultural Centre.........41 B3
Petőfi Theatre.........42 A3

TRANSPORT
Bus Station.........43 A1

baroque spire was added in 1681. **Fidelity Gate** at the bottom of the tower shows 'Hungaria' receiving the *civitas fidelissima* (Latin for 'the most loyal citizenry') of Sopron. It was erected in 1922 after that crucial referendum.

From the firewatch tower it's only a short stroll to Fő tér, the graceful heart of the Inner Town. At its focal point is the tall **Trinity Column** (1701), among the finest examples of a 'plague pillar' in Hungary. Dominating the southern side of the square is the **Goat Church** (Kecsketemplom; Templom utca 1; admission free; 8am-9pm mid-Apr–Sep, 8am-6pm Oct–mid-Apr), which collected its strange name from the heraldic animal of its chief benefactor, the Gaissel family. Originally built in the late 13th century, the church has an overall

Gothic look, but there were many additions made over the ensuing centuries, including a mostly baroque interior. The highlight inside is the red marble pulpit in the centre of the south aisle, which dates from the 15th century. Better yet is the church's **Chapter Hall**, located off the main nave. Part of a 14th-century Benedictine monastery, it has fading frescoes and grotesque stone carvings – mainly animals with human heads – representing the deadly sins of humankind.

Housed in a Gothic building close to the Goat Church is the **Pharmacy Museum** (Patikamúzeum; ☎ 311 327; Fő tér 2; adult/senior & student 400/200Ft; 🕑 10am-6pm Tue-Sun Apr-Sep, 10am-2pm Tue-Sun Oct-Mar), housing an assortment of ancient pharmaceutical tools, cures and books. Look for oddities such as the amulet to ward off the evil eye and the hat against epilepsy.

Facing off against the Goat Church are two buildings of historical importance to the town, the **Fabricius House** (Fő tér 6) and **Storno House** (Fő tér 8). The baroque Fabricius House was built on Roman foundations and houses an **archaeological exhibition** (adult/senior & student 700/350Ft; 🕑 10am-6pm Tue-Sun Apr-Sep, 10am-2pm Tue-Sun Oct-Mar) covering Celtic, Roman and Hungarian periods of history on its lower floors, but more intriguing are the Scarbantia-era statues reconstructed from fragments found in the area (including enormous statues of Juno, Jupiter and Minerva), located in the cellar. On the upper floors are further historical displays, this time in the form of **urban flats** (polgári lakások; ☎ 311 327; adult/senior & student 700/350Ft; 🕑 10am-6pm Tue-Sun Apr-Sep, 2-6pm Tue-Sun Oct-Mar), with rooms devoted to domestic life in Sopron in the 17th and 18th centuries. Only the antique furniture here will spark most people's interests.

On the 1st floor of Storno House, built in 1417, there's a so-so exhibit on Sopron's more recent history, but on the floor above is the wonderful **Storno Collection** (Storno Gyűjtemény; ☎ 311 327; adult/senior & student 1000/500Ft; 🕑 10am-6pm Tue-Sun Apr-Sep, 2-6pm Tue-Sun Oct-Mar), which belonged to a 19th-century Swiss-Italian family of restorers whose recarving of Romanesque and Gothic monuments throughout Transdanubia is frowned upon today. To their credit, the much-maligned Stornos did rescue many altarpieces and church furnishings from oblivion, and their house is a Gothic treasure-trove. Highlights include the beautiful enclosed balcony with leaded windows and frescoes, leather chairs with designs depicting Mephisto with his dragons, and door frames made from pews taken from 15th-century St George's Church on Szent György utca. Franz Liszt played a number of concerts in this house in the mid-19th century.

Solid reminders of Sopron's Roman past – in the form of reconstructed Roman walls and outlines of 2nd-century buildings – can be found at the **open-air ruins** (admission free; 🕑 24hr) behind the city's town hall. From here it's possible to climb onto the city's medieval defensive walls for a quick stroll. Roman fanatics who still need a fix can then head to the **Scarbantia Forum** (☎ 321 804; Új utca 1; adult/senior & student 300/150Ft; 🕑 8am-4pm Mon-Fri, 10am-5pm Sat & Sun), an original Roman-era marketplace discovered under – and accessible through – the Uniqa block.

For centuries Sopron, like many towns in central Europe, was home to a substantial Jewish population. Új utca, known as Zsidó utca (Jewish St) until the Jews were evicted from Sopron in 1526, has two remnants of the community's existence – the **Old Synagogue** (Ó Zsinagóga; ☎ 311 327; Új utca 22; adult/senior & student 600/300Ft; 🕑 10am-6pm Tue-Sun May-Oct) and the **New Synagogue** (Új Zsinagóga; Új utca 11). Both were built in the 14th century and are unique in Hungary. The Old Synagogue, now a museum, contains two rooms, one for each sex (note the women's windows along the west wall). The main room contains a medieval 'holy of holies', with geometric designs and trees carved in stone, and some ugly new stained-glass windows. The inscriptions on the walls date from 1490. There's a reconstructed *mikvah* (ritual bath) in the courtyard. The New Synagogue, which once formed part of a private house and offices, was renovated with EU funds but is closed to the public.

OTHER SIGHTS

Just north of Fő tér is another concentration of Sopron sights. The first you'll come across is the **Zettl-Langer Private Collection** (Zettl-Langer Magángyűjtemény; ☎ 311 136; Balfi út 11; admission 500Ft; 🕑 10am-noon Tue-Sun Apr-Oct, 10am-noon Fri-Sun Nov-Jan & Mar), which contains a menagerie of antique ceramics, paintings, furniture, books and weapons. Much of it dates from the Biedermeier period, but there some pieces from an earlier age.

Heading northwards again, on Dorfmeister utca, you'll come across the 15th-century **Church of the Holy Spirit** (Szentlélek-templom).

Its interior is rather dark, but if you time your visit for midday, you'll be able catch a glimpse of some fine wall and ceiling frescoes. Further north again at Szent Mihály utca 9 is the **House of the Two Moors** (Két mór ház). It was fashioned from two 17th-century peasant houses and is guarded by two large statues, which are now painted politically correct white.

At the top of the hill, along Szent Mihály utca, is **St Michael's Church** (Szent Mihály-templom), built between the 13th and 15th centuries, and behind it to the south is the little Romanesque-Gothic **Chapel of St James** (Szent Jakab-kápolna), the oldest structure in Sopron and originally an ossuary. Not much escaped the Stornos' handiwork when they 'renovated' St Michael's – they even added the spire. Check out the lovely polychrome Stations of the Cross (1892) in the churchyard and the large number of tombstones with German family names.

If you return to the House of the Two Moors and walk west along Fövényverem utca, you'll soon reach Bécsi út and the **Bakery Museum** (Pékmúzeum; ☎ 311 327; Bécsi út 5; adult/senior & student 400/200Ft; ⌚ 2-6pm Tue-Sun Apr-Sep), a fantastic reminder of a bygone era. It's actually the completely restored home, bakery and shop of a successful 19th-century bread and pastry-maker named Weissbeck, and contains some interesting gadgets and work-saving devices.

Further evidence of Sopron's Jewish past can be seen at the crumbling **synagogue** (Paprét utca 14) east of the Inner Town. A plaque tells passers-by that '1640 martyrs' were taken from here to Auschwitz on 5 July 1944.

Activities

Avid cyclists should pick up a copy of the brochure *Cycling Around Sopron* from Tourinform, which lists eight tours – between 10km and 130km – that explore the surrounding countryside. Many people head for the Fertő-Hanság National Park – see p177 for more details. Tourinform's southern branch rents bicycles for 1000/1500Ft per four hours/one day.

Alternatively, there's plenty of hiking options in the Lővér Hills (p176); the pamphlet *Green Sopron*, also available from Tourinform, suggests a number of walks in the hills, along with horse-riding and sailing possibilities nearby.

Festivals & Events

Sopron is a musical town, and the highlights of the season are the **Spring Days** in late March, the **Sopron Festival Weeks** from mid-June to mid-July and the **International Choir Festival** in early July. Tickets to the various events are available from the ticket office in the Ferenc Liszt Conference and Cultural Centre.

Sleeping

Tourinform can supply you with a complete list of accommodation in the town.

BUDGET

Ózon Camping (☎ 331 144; Erdei Malom köz 3; camp sites per large tent/small tent/adult/child 1800/1000/1500/900Ft; ⌚ mid-Apr–mid-Oct; 🏊) This delightful camping ground with 60 sites has everything you could want, from fridges and washing machines to a pool and other sports facilities. It's set in a leafy valley about 4.5km west of the Inner Town (take bus 3) in the green of the Lővér Hills.

Vakáció Vendégház Sopron (☎ 338 502; www.vakacio-vendeghazak.hu; Ady Endre út 31; dm 2800Ft; ⊠) This big yellow dot on Sopron's accommodation horizon offers backpackers a cheap and cheerful bed not far west of the Inner Town. Rooms are clean and furnished with two to 10 beds; bus 10 will drop you off right outside the door.

MIDRANGE

Jégverem Pension (☎ 510 113; www.jegverem.hu; Jégverem utca 1; s/d 6900/8900Ft) This is an excellent and central bet, with five suitelike rooms in an 18th-century ice cellar in the Ikva district. Staff are exceptionally accommodating, and the restaurant comes highly recommended whether you're staying here or not.

Palatinus (☎ 523 816; www.palatinussopron.com; Új utca 23; s/d from 6900/9900Ft, apt 13,900Ft; ⊠) If it's important to have a medieval scene and the peace of the Inner Town outside your window, then bunk down at Palatinus. Its location on cobbled Új utca is hard to beat, and while rooms could do with modernising, they're large and suitably accommodating.

Wieden Pension (☎ 523 222; www.wieden.hu; Sas tér 13; s/d/tr from 7700/10,900/12,900Ft, apt from 11,900Ft; ⊠) Sopron's loveliest *pension* is located in an attractive old town house within easy walking distance of the Inner Town. Rooms are spacious, bright and coloured in peaceful hues, and bigger apartments are also an option. Wi-fi connection is available.

TOP END

Pannónia Med Hotel (☎ 312 180; www.pannoniahotel.com; Várkerület 75; s/d 18,900/20,900Ft, ste 31,900Ft;) Sopron's plush century-old hotel is now part of the Best Western stable. Thankfully rooms have been renovated in the right places – namely bathrooms, windows and carpets – but there's still a taste of yesteryear grandeur in its antique-furnished suites. On the 1st floor you'll find the very green (as in the colour) wellness centre, with pool, sauna and gym.

Civitas Boutique Hotel (☎ 788 228; www.civitashotel.com; s/d from €40/63, apt from €80;) The latest edition to Sopron's accommodation scene is the Civitas, a thoroughly modern hotel within easy striking distance of the Inner Town. It's the most fashionable spot to overnight, with rooms featuring smart and simple furniture, flat-screen TV and wi-fi connection. There's not a lot of character, but that may come with time.

Eating

For a town with such a tourist pull, Sopron's eating options may leave you disappointed. There are a couple of spots that will satisfy hungry souls, however.

RESTAURANTS

Corso (☎ 340 990; 1st fl, Várkerület 73; mains 1000-2500Ft; 11am-10pm Mon-Fri, 11am-4pm Sun) Corso is a run-of-the-mill restaurant with dated furniture and above-average Hungarian fare. Its two-course set menus (from 690Ft) are a real bargain as well; find it in the Korona shopping arcade next to the Pannónia Med Hotel.

Generális-Corvinus (☎ 505 035; Fő tér 7-8; pizza 700-1700Ft, mains 1000-2700Ft) This large restaurant is in reality two places – one serving decent Hungarian cuisine and guarded by a very camp General, the other dishing up pizzas under the gaze of a black crow. In the summer months its tables on the Inner Town's main square are *the* place to dine.

Jégverem (☎ 510 113; Jégverem utca 1; mains 1000-3000Ft) This rustic *pension* restaurant, whose slogan is 'The Restaurant for Guzzle-guts' (we think they mean 'greedy-guts'), serves a huge selection of reasonably priced Hungarian dishes, some of them quite inventive, in portions that are enormous even by Hungarian standards (where available, order half-portions). The central table – with glass top – sits directly above the 18th-century ice cellar.

Forum (☎ 340 231; Szent György utca 3; mains 1200-2490Ft) This popular spot is great in the warmer months when tables spread out into a courtyard between two Inner Town streets. It serves the whole range, but we'd stick to pizza (690Ft to 1390Ft), pasta dishes (890Ft to 1590Ft) and/or the self-serve salad bar (small/large 450/590Ft).

Graben (☎ 340 256; Várkerület 8; mains 1290-2500Ft; 8am-10pm) Located in a cosy cellar near the old city walls, Graben is more upmarket than most restaurants in town and offers traditional Hungarian dishes as well as local cuisine with a modern twist. In summer its terrace spreads itself out over an inner courtyard.

Papa Joe's Saloon & Steak House (☎ 340 933; Várkerület 108; mains around 2000Ft; 11am-midnight Sun-Wed, to 2am Thu-Sat) Like so many Hungarian towns, Sopron has at least one Wild-West themed pub-restaurant, and Papa Joe's it is. It's rather kitsch inside, but it does a fine steak (per 200g from 900Ft) and passable Tex-Mex (1300Ft to 1800Ft) if you're looking for a diet change.

CAFES

Zwinger (☎ 340 287; Várkerület 92; cakes 200Ft; 8am-7pm) Sidling up to the old city walls down a narrow alleyway is Zwinger, a cute cafe your grandma would just love. It's pink, purple and flowery decor may not be to everyone's liking, but its winter garden and homemade cakes make it a place worth stopping at.

Dömöröri (☎ 506 623; Széchenyi tér 13; ice cream per scoop 150Ft, cakes from 250Ft; 7am-9pm Mon-Thu, 7am-10pm Fri & Sat, 8am-9pm Sun) There is no need to look any further than Dömöröri for the best ice cream in Sopron. Take your place at the back of the queue and wait patiently like everyone else.

Liszt Szalon (☎ 323 407; Szent György utca 12; coffee 450Ft; 10am-10pm) This very stylish and mature cafe attracts locals and newcomers alike with a huge array of teas and coffee and two distinct areas – one with low, comfy couches and the other featuring upright chairs and tables for bad backs. Occasional classical concerts are held here, too.

QUICK EATS & SELF-CATERING

Alcatraz (Mátyás Király utca 1; gyros 500-700Ft, pizza slices 200-400Ft; 10am-9pm Sun & Mon, to 11pm Tue-Thu, to 1am Fri & Sat) Nothing like the prison, but modern Alcatraz is an island of quick eats, such as pizza, sandwiches and gyros, in a town with very few such places. Sit down or take-away available.

Self-catering is easy in Sopron, with a number of supermarkets scattered around the centre, including **Match** (Várkerület 100-102; 6.30am-7pm Mon-Fri, to 3pm Sat). Outside normal shopping hours, there are two shops open round the clock within staring distance of one another:

Ógabona (Ógabona tér 12; 24hr) Essentially a tobacconist and drinks shop.

Lackner Éjjel-Nappal (Lackner Kristóf utca 2; 24hr) The usual necessities available here.

Drinking

The Sopron region is noted for its red wines, especially Kékfrankos and Merlot. Many – but not all by any means – are cheap and high in acid and tannin, so watch your intake if you don't want a massive *macskajaj* ('cat's wail' – Hungarian for 'hangover') the next day.

There are a number of small wine cellars scattered around the city where you can try the local drop, but if you want to go right to the source, pick up the pamphlet *A Soproni Bor Útja* (The Sopron Wine Rd) from Tourinform, which lists vintners throughout the region. Only a handful reside in the city; most are located on its outskirts.

Entertainment

For more up-to-date entertainment listings on Sopron, get hold of the freebie biweekly *Soproni Est* or go direct to the city's Tourinform offices.

Ferenc Liszt Conference and Cultural Centre (☎ 517 500, ticket office 517 517; www.prokultura.hu; Liszt Ferenc utca 1; 9am-5pm Mon-Fri, to noon Sat) This beautifully renovated venue facing Széchenyi tér contains a theatre, concert hall, Tourinform office, casino and restaurant, and hosts some of the most important music and other cultural events in Sopron.

Petőfi Theatre (☎ 517 517; www.prokultura.hu; Petőfi tér 1) This beautiful theatre with National Romantic–style mosaics on the front facade is Sopron's leading theatre.

Getting There & Away

BUS

Buses travel to the following destinations from Sopron. There are also buses to Munich (12,000Ft, seven hours, 496km) and Stuttgart (16,000Ft, 10½ hours, 728km) on Thursday (8.05pm) and Sunday (9.05pm).

Destination	Price	Duration	Km	Frequency
Balatonfüred	2540Ft	4hr	178	2 daily
Budapest	3010Ft	3¾hr	217	2 daily
Fertőd	450Ft	45min	28	hourly
Győr	1350Ft	2hr	90	7 daily
Keszthely	2290Ft	3¼hr	143	1 daily
Kőszeg	900Ft	1hr 20min	59	6 daily
Nagycenk	250Ft	20min	15	half-hourly
Pécs	3830Ft	6hr	300	1 daily
Sárvár	1050Ft	1½hr	62	3 daily
Sümeg	1770Ft	2½-3½hr	112	3 daily
Szombathely	1200Ft	2hr	76	up to 7 daily
Tapolca	2540Ft	4hr	170	1 daily
Veszprém	2290Ft	3½hr	155	3 daily

TRAIN

There are express trains to Budapest (3390Ft, 2¾ hours, 216km, eight daily) via Győr and Csorna. Local trains run to Szombathely (1050Ft, 1¼ hours, 62km, hourly) and Wiener Neustadt in Austria (2400Ft, 40 minutes, 34km, hourly), where you change for Vienna (3850Ft, 1¼ hours, 84km, up to nine daily). There are also direct trains to Vienna's Südbahnhof (3750Ft, 1¼ hours, 84km, up to 15 daily).

Getting Around

Buses 1 and 2, from the bus and train stations, circle the Inner Town. For the Vakáció Vendégház Sopron hostel, take bus 10 from the bus station; for Ózon Camping, catch bus 3. You can call a local taxi on ☎ 555 555 or ☎ 333 333.

AROUND SOPRON

Lővér Hills

This range of 300m- to 400m-high foothills of the Austrian Alps, some 5km south and southwest of the city centre, is Sopron's playground. It's a great place for hiking and walking, but is not without bitter memories, for it was here that partisans and Jews were executed by Nazis and the fascist Hungarian Arrow Cross during WWII. You can climb to the top of **Károly Lookout** (Károly kilátótorony; ☎ 313 080; adult/child & student 250/150Ft; 9am-8pm May-Aug, 9am-7pm Sep, 9am-6pm Apr & Oct, 9am-5pm Mar, 9am-4pm Nov-Feb Tue-Sun) on the hill (394m) west of the Lővér hotel; walk to **Taródi Castle** (Csalogány köz 8; adult/student 500/300Ft; variable), a 'self-built private castle' owned by the obsessed Taródi family and a pack-rat's delight; or visit the **Lővér Baths** (☎ 510 964; Lővér körút 82; adult/child per day 800/470Ft, half-day 520/350Ft; covered pools 6am-8pm

Mon-Fri, 9am-8pm Sat & Sun year-round, sauna & solarium 2-7.30pm Mon-Fri, 10am-7pm Sat & Sun year-round, outside pools 9am-8pm late May–mid-Sep).

The hills are a 15- to 20-minute walk from the city centre, otherwise bus 2 from the Inner Town can save you the leg work.

Fertő-Hanság National Park

The flat expanse of the **Fertő-Hanság National Park** (www.ferto-hansag.hu) begins almost at Sopron's easterly border. Made up of reedy marshland and a slither of Lake Fertő (most of the lake lies in Austrian territory), the park is a paradise for birds, and therefore bird lovers. White egrets, godwits, great crested grebes and 50,000 wild geese – among many others – use the park as refuge, particularly during the migration months in spring and autumn. Due to its gently undulating landscape, Fertő-Hanság is also a favourite of cyclists – the *Fertő-Shore Cyclists Guide* booklet, available from Sopron's Tourinform offices (p171), details a number of cycle paths through the region.

By public transport, the best way to reach the park is to catch a bus to Fertőrákos (250Ft, 25 minutes, 14km, hourly) or Balf (bus 14), both of which are located within the park's borders.

FERTŐD

☎ 99 / pop 3400

The tiny town of Fertőd, 27km east of Sopron, was put on the map in the mid-18th century when a proud Miklós Esterházy proclaimed that 'Anything the [Habsburg] emperor can afford, I can afford too'. The aristocrat went about constructing one of the largest and most opulent summer palaces in central Europe and the fruits of his endeavours can be visited today.

History

Much has been written about the Esterházy Palace and many hyperbolic monikers bestowed upon it (the 'Hungarian Versailles' is the most common). But the fact remains that this baroque and rococo structure – its architects unknown except for the Austrian Melchior Hefele – is the most beautiful palace in Hungary. While the rooms are for the most part bare, history is very much alive here. Many of the works of composer Franz Joseph Haydn (a 30-year resident of the palace) were first performed in the Concert Hall, including the *Farewell Symphony*. In the Chinoiserie Rooms Empress Maria Theresa attended a masked ball in 1773, and in the French Garden Miklós 'the Splendour Lover' threw some of the greatest parties of all time for friends like Goethe, complete with fireworks and tens of thousands of Chinese lanterns.

After a century and a half of neglect (it was used as stables in the 19th century and a hospital during WWII), the palace has been partially restored to its former glory and renovations are continuing.

Orientation

Esterházy Palace and its gardens on Joseph Haydn utca dominate the town; the town centre is 700m to the west. Most buses stop close to the town centre. Fertőszéplak train station is 1.5km to the west again, but is of little use to most travellers. The train station at Fertőszentmiklós (on the Sopron–Győr line) is 4km to the south.

Information

OTP bank (Fő utca 7; 7.45am-noon Mon, Wed, Fri, 8am-noon & 12.30-3pm Tue & Thu)
Post office (Fő utca 6; 8am-4pm Mon-Fri)
Tourinform (☎ 537 140; fertotaj@tourinform.hu; Joseph Hayden utca 2; 9am-5pm Mon-Fri, 10am-6pm Sat & Sun mid-Mar–Oct, variable Nov–mid-Mar) Next to Esterházy Palace ticket office.

Sights & Activities

There's nothing else to see in Fertőd aside from the **Esterházy Palace** (☎ 537 640; Joseph Haydn utca 2; Palace Museum tour adult/senior & student 1500/750Ft, Great Palace tour 2500/2000Ft; 10am-6pm Tue-Sun mid-Mar–Oct, 10am-4pm Fri-Sun Nov–mid-Mar), but what a sight it is. It can only be visited with a guide, but armed with a fact sheet in English (available from the ticket office), try to lag behind and explore the rooms away from the crowds.

When originally completed, the horseshoe-shaped palace boasted 126 rooms, a separate opera house, a hermitage (complete with a real-live cranky old man in a sack cloth who wanted to be left alone), temples to Diana and Venus, a Chinese dance house, a puppet theatre and a 250-hectare garden laid out in the French manner. Today only 23 rooms are open to the public; the rest of the huge complex houses a hotel and a secondary school.

As you approach the main entrance to the so-called **Courtyard of Honour**, notice the ornamental wrought-iron gate, a masterpiece of the rococo. The Palace Museum tour (one hour) passes through all the main rooms, including several rooms decorated in the pseudo-Chinese style that was all the rage in the late 18th century; the pillared **Sala Terrena**, which served as the summer dining room, with its floor of cool Carrara marble and Miklós Esterházy's monogram in floral frescoes on the ceiling; and the **Prince's Bed Chamber**, with paintings of Amor. On the 1st floor are more sumptuous baroque and rococo salons as well as the lavish **Concert Hall** and **Ceremonial Hall**, which lead on to one another. There's also an exhibit dedicated to the life and times of Haydn. The Great Palace tour (two hours; advance booking essential) also includes the stable block and estate office, but it's only for hardcore fans of baroque opulence.

The apartment where Haydn lived, off and on, from 1761 to 1790 in the west wing of the baroque **Music House** (Muzsikaház; Madach sétány 1), southwest of the palace, now contains the **Joseph Haydn Memorial Hall** (Joseph Haydn Emlékszoba; ☎ 370 934; adult/senior & student 300/150Ft; ⏲ 9am-5pm Mon-Fri May-Aug) on the 1st floor, a veritable temple to the great Austrian composer.

Festivals & Events

Two major musical events at the palace are the **Haydn Festival of the Budapest Strings** in July and the more established **Haydn Festival** in late August/early September. For information and tickets on both check www.ticketportal.hu or www.interticket.hu.

Sleeping

Fertőd is an easy day trip from Sopron, but if you want to overnight, there are a couple of options.

Kastély (☎ 537 640; eszterhaza@t-online.hu; Joseph Haydn utca 2; d/tr/apt 8000/16,000/18,000Ft) If you've ever wanted to stay in a palace, then this is your option. Rooms are nothing exceptional, but they are located on the 2nd floor of the palace's east wing.

Bagatelle (d 36,000ft) If you have the cash, opt for this separate pavilion in the park and arboretum behind the palace with four apartments.

Also recommended:

Rábensteiner Panzió (☎ 371 651; www.rabensteiner.hu; Fő utca 10-12; s/d 8000/11,800Ft) Spick and span rooms.

Dori Hotel & Camping (☎ 370 838; www.dorihotel.hu; Pomogyi út 1; camp sites per tent/adult/child/car €2.50/2.90/2.30/2.50, s/d/tr bungalows €26.70/37.60/48.90, s/d/tr hotel rooms €30/46/60) A large complex just 100m north of the palace with plenty of basic accommodation options. It also rents bicycles (per day 1500Ft) for exploring the surrounding parkland.

Eating

Two very convenient restaurants for a bite to eat are both located in Grenadier House, the former living quarters of the grenadier guards opposite the palace.

Gránátos (☎ 370 944; Joseph Haydn utca 1; mains 1000-1900Ft; ⏲ 9am-10pm) Split between a relaxed cafe area and more formal restaurant.

Kastélykert (☎ 349 418; Joseph Haydn utca 1; mains 1200-1900Ft; ⏲ 10am-10pm) Offers a good-value set menu (11500Ft) available throughout the day.

Coop (Fő utca 5; ⏲ 5.15am-4pm Mon, 5.15am-6pm Tue-Fri, 6am-1pm Sat, 8-11am Sun) A branch of the ubiquitous supermarket chain, next to the OTP bank.

Getting There & Away

Frequent bus services serve Sopron (450Ft, 45 minutes, 28km, hourly), and there are services to Győr (900Ft, 1¾ hours, 57km, two to four daily).

Trains link Fertőszentmiklós to the south of Fertőd with Sopron (375Ft, 20 minutes, 24km, up to 12 daily) and Győr (1050Ft, one hour, 61km, up to 11 daily).

NAGYCENK

☎ 99 / pop 1860

Only 14km west of Fertőd and the Esterházy Palace, but light years away in spirit, lies Nagycenk, site of the ancestral mansion of the Széchenyi clan. No two houses – or families – could have been more different than these. While the privileged, often frivolous Esterházys held court in their imperial palace, the Széchenyis – democrats and reformers all – went about their work in a sombre neoclassical manor house that aptly reflected their temperament and sense of purpose. The mansion has been completely renovated and part of it has been turned into a superb museum dedicated to the family. It's a must for those who want to understand Hungarian history and put things in perspective.

History

The Széchenyi family's public-spiritedness started with patriarch Ferenc, who donated his entire collection of books and objets d'art to the state in 1802, laying the foundations for the National Library now named in his honour. But it was his son, István (1791–1860), who made the greatest impact of any Hungarian on the economic and cultural development of the nation. For more information, see the boxed text, below.

Orientation

The train station is near the town centre, southwest of the Széchenyi mansion, not far from the neo-Romanesque St Stephen's Church, designed by Miklós Ybl in 1864, and the Széchenyi family's mausoleum. The bus from Sopron stops close to the mansion's main gate.

Sights

The entrance to the **Széchenyi Memorial Museum** (Széchenyi Emlékmúzeum; ☎ 360 023; www.nagycenk.hu; Kiscenki utca 3; adult/senior & student 600/300Ft; 10am-6pm Tue-Sun Apr-Oct, 10am-5pm Tue-Sun Nov & Dec, 10am-4pm Tue-Sun Jan-Mar) is in the mansion through the Sala Terrena – it's almost austere compared with the similarly named hall at the Esterházy Palace in Fertőd. There's a taped commentary in several languages (including English) in each room; just press the button.

The rooms on the museum's ground floor, furnished with period pieces, trace the Széchenyi family and their political development, from typical baroque aristocrats in the 18th century to key players in the 1848–49 War of Independence and István's involvement in the ill-fated government of Lajos Batthyány. A sweeping baroque staircase leads to the exhibits on the 1st floor – a veritable temple to István's many accomplishments – from Budapest's Chain Bridge and the Danube and Tisza Rivers' engineering works, to steamboat and rail transport. There's also an interesting exhibition on Hungarian coinage.

It is fitting that the mansion of a railway developer like István Széchenyi is near an open-air **Locomotive Outdoor Museum** (Mozdony Skanzen; admission free; 24hr), with steam engines that were still in use on main lines as late as 1950. You can actually ride a

THE GREATEST HUNGARIAN

The contributions of Count István Széchenyi were enormous and extremely varied. In his seminal 1830 work *Hitel* (meaning 'credit' and based on *hit* or 'trust'), he advocated sweeping economic reforms and the abolition of serfdom (he himself had distributed the bulk of his property to landless peasants two years earlier).

The Chain Bridge, the design of which Széchenyi helped push through Parliament, was the first link between Buda and Pest, and for the first time everyone, nobles included, had to pay a toll to use it.

Széchenyi was instrumental in straightening the serpentine Tisza River, which rescued half of Hungary's arable land from flooding and erosion, and his work made the Danube navigable as far as the Iron Gates in Romania.

He arranged the financing for Hungary's first train lines (from Budapest to Vác in the north and Szolnok in the east, and west to what is now Wiener Neustadt in Austria), and launched the first steam transport on the Danube and Lake Balaton.

A lover of all things English, Széchenyi got the upper classes interested in horse racing with the express purpose of improving breeding stock for farming.

A large financial contribution made by Széchenyi led to the establishment of the nation's prestigious Academy of Science.

Széchenyi became part of Lajos Batthyány's revolutionary government in 1848, but political squabbling and open conflict with Vienna caused him to lose control and he suffered a nervous breakdown. Despite a decade of convalescence in an asylum, Széchenyi never fully recovered and tragically took his own life in 1860.

For all his accomplishments, Széchenyi's contemporary and fellow reformer, Lajos Kossuth, called him 'the greatest Hungarian'. This dynamic but troubled visionary retains that accolade to this day.

narrow-gauge train for 6km to Fertőboz and back (one way/return adult 320/6400Ft, child 320/160Ft). Departures leave on weekends only between April and early October from the Kastély train station at Nagycenk at 10.35am, 12.15pm, 2pm, 3.37pm and 5.30pm. All except the last turn around at Fertőboz in less than half an hour for the return trip to Kastély. There are also shorter trips to Barátság (3km, 9.45am and 4.50pm), which cost the same.

A 2.6km **row of linden trees** opposite the mansion's main gate, planted by István's grandmother in 1754, leads to a **hermitage**. Like the Esterházys, the Széchenyi family had a resident loner who, in this case, was expected to earn his keep by ringing the chapel bell and tending the garden.

The **Széchenyi Mausoleum** (☎ 360 059; Széchenyi tér; adult/senior & student 300/200Ft; ⏰ 10am-6pm Tue-Sun May-Oct), the final resting place of István and other family members and a great place of pilgrimage for Hungarians, is in the village cemetery across the road from St Stephen's Church.

Sleeping & Eating

ourpick **Kastély** (☎ 360 061; www.szechenyikastelyszallo.hu; Kiscenki utca 3; s/d/tr 12,600/16,800/21,600Ft, apt from 24,000Ft; ⊠) In the west wing of the mansion, this beautifully appointed inn offers large rooms with a touch of old-school charm. If you can afford it, opt for room No 106 or 107, which are large suites with period furniture and restful views of the 6-hectare garden. Rates include entrance to the museum. The splendid dining room (mains 1700Ft to 4000Ft; open 7am to 10pm) at the Kastély is highly rated by all and sundry, and its outdoor tables in the hotel's splendid courtyard are the only place to dine in summer.

Getting There & Away

Nagycenk is accessible from Sopron (250Ft, 20 minutes, 15km, half-hourly) by frequent bus. The village is on the train line linking Sopron (250Ft, 14 minutes, 12km, up to a dozen daily) and Szombathely (750Ft, one hour, 50 minutes, up to 13 daily).

If you time it right, you can reach Nagycenk by the narrow-gauge train. Take the bus from Sopron to Fertőboz and board the train for Kastély at 10.35am or at 12.15pm, 2pm or 3.37pm.

SZOMBATHELY

☎ 94 / pop 80,200

Bustling Szombathely (German: Steinamanger) is often overlooked by travellers who normally only take a glance at the place as they zip past, heading for Kőszeg or Lake Balaton. Yet a day, or at least a few hours, spent here will bring its just rewards, for Szombathely has more Roman ruins than most Hungarians towns and a handful of absorbing museums.

History

Szombathely got an earlier start than most. In AD 43 the Romans established a trade settlement called Savaria here on the lucrative Amber Route. By the start of the 2nd century it was important enough to be named capital of Upper Pannonia. Over the next few centuries Savaria prospered and Christianity arrived; Martin of Tours, the patron saint of France, was born here in 316. But attacks by Huns, Longobards and Avars weakened its defences, and in 455 an earthquake reduced the town to rubble.

Szombathely began to develop again in the early Middle Ages, but the Mongols, then the Turks and the Habsburgs put a stop to that. It was not until 1777, when János Szily was appointed Szombathely's first bishop, that the city really began to flourish economically and culturally. The building of the train line to Graz brought further trade. In 1945 Allied bombers levelled much of the town, which has since been largely rebuilt.

Orientation

Szombathely is made up of narrow streets and squares, with the centre at enormous Fő tér. To the west are Berzsenyi Dániel tér and Mindszenty József tér, the administrative and ecclesiastical centres of the city respectively. The train station is on Éhen Gyula tér, about 1km northeast of Mártírok tere at the end of Széll Kálmán út. The bus station is on Petőfi Sándor utca, northwest of Fő tér.

Information

City website (www.szombathely.hu, in Hungarian) Has lots of practical and background information.
Internet Club (Széchenyi István utca 1; per hr 500Ft) Small internet cafe open daily.
Post office (Kossuth Lajos utca 18)
OTP bank (Király utca 10)
Tourinform (☎ 514 451; szombathely@tourinform.hu; Király utca 1/a; ⏰ 9am-5pm Mon-Fri mid-Sep–mid-Jun,

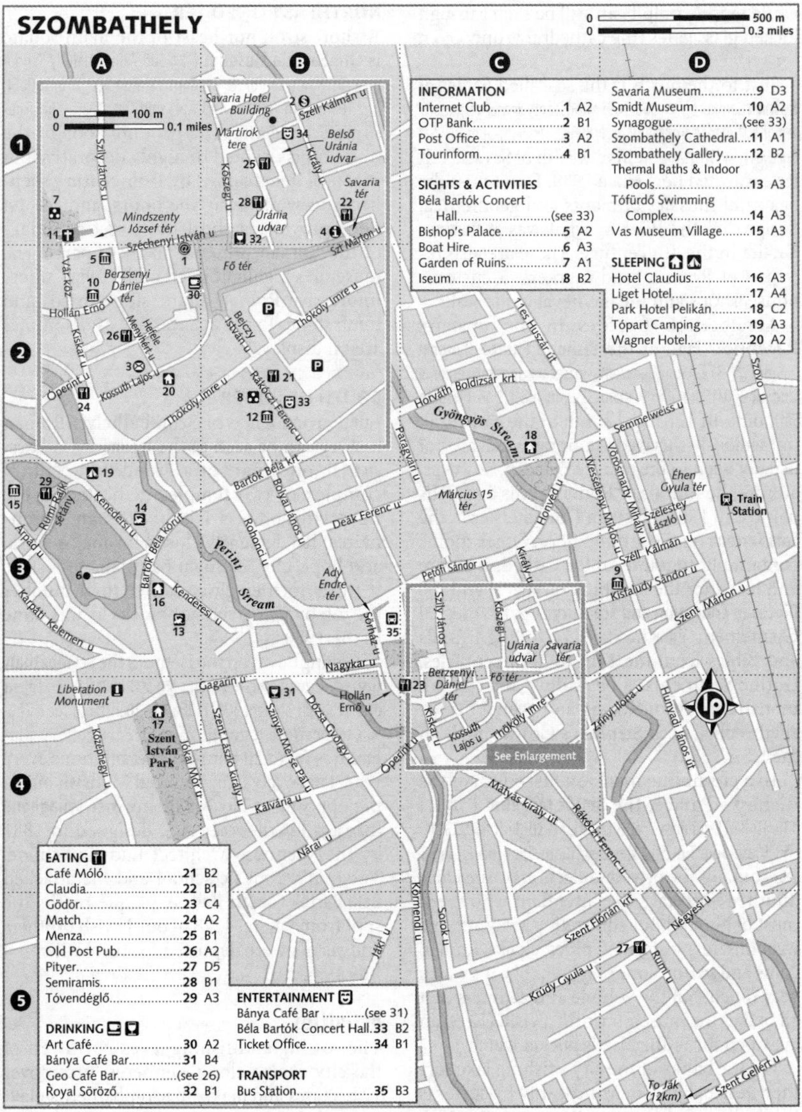

9am-6pm Mon-Fri, 10am-6pm Sat & Sun mid-Jun–mid-Sep) At the eastern end of Fő tér.

Sights

WEST OF FŐ TÉR

A cluster of fine attractions lie within sight of Mindszenty József tér, including the Zopf-style **Szombathely Cathedral** (Szombathelyi Székeshegyház; Mindszenty József tér; admission free), which dominates the quiet square. Built in 1797, it once featured stuccowork and frescoes by Franz Anton Maulbertsch and was supported by grand marble columns. Unfortunately allied bombing in the final days of WWII did not spare the cathedral, but a couple of Maulbertsch originals and a glorious red-and-white marble pulpit can still be seen through locked glass gates (the cathedral is only open for services).

Just to the north is the so-called **Garden of Ruins** (Romkert; ☎ 313 369; Mindszenty József tér; adult/senior & student/family 400/200F/800Ft; 9am-5pm Tue-Sat Apr-Nov), which contains a wealth of Savaria relics excavated here since 1938. Don't miss the beautiful mosaics of plants and geometrical designs on the floor of what was **St Quirinus Basilica** in the 4th century. There are also remains of Roman road markers, a customs house, shops and the medieval castle walls.

Maulbertsch frescoes in the upstairs Reception Hall at the **Bishop's Palace** (Püspöki palota; ☎ 312 056; Mindszenty József tér 1; adult/senior & student 300/150Ft; 9.30am-3.30pm Tue-Fri, to 11.30am Sat), built in 1783 and south of the cathedral, miraculously survived the air raids, but are not usually open to the public. You can, however, admire the murals of Roman ruins and gods painted in 1784 by István Dorffmeister in the **Sala Terrena** on the ground floor. Other rooms contain photographs of the cathedral before and just after the bombing of WWII and the **Diocesan Collection and Treasury** (Egyházmegyei Gyüjtemény és Kincstár), including missals and Bibles from the 14th to 18th centuries, Gothic vestments, a beautiful 15th-century monstrance from Kőszeg and even a bejewelled replica of St Stephen's Crown made in the USA.

In a crumbling mansion just south of the Bishop's Palace, the **Smidt Museum** (☎ 311 038; Hollán Ernő utca 2; adult/senior & student 460/230Ft; 10am-5pm Tue-Sun Mar-Dec, 10am-5pm Tue-Fri Jan & Feb) contains the private collection of one Lajos Smidt, a hospital superintendent who spent most of his adult life squirreling away antique weapons, furniture, fans, pipes, clocks, Roman coins and so on. None of it looks like it's worth very much, but the volume and zaniness of it all makes the museum worth a visit. (Keep an eye open for Franz Liszt's pocket watch.)

On the banks of the city's fishing lake further west again from Mindszenty József tér is the **Vas Museum Village** (Vasi Múzeumfalu; ☎ 311 004; Árpád út 30; adult/senior & student/family 500/250/1000Ft; 9am-5pm Tue-Sun mid-Mar–mid-Sep). This open-air museum contains over 40 18th- and 19th-century farmhouses *(porták)* moved here from more than two dozen villages in the Őrség region. The most interesting of these are the Croatian, German and 'fenced' houses.

NORTHEAST OF FŐ TÉR

A short stroll northeast of the main square is the **Savaria Museum** (☎ 500 720; Kisfaludy Sándor utca 9; adult/senior & student/family 500/250/1000Ft; 10am-5pm Tue-Sat mid-Apr–mid-Oct, 10am-5pm Tue-Fri mid-Oct–mid-Apr). The ground floor of the museum is devoted to highly decorative but practical items carved by 19th-century shepherds to while away the hours, and the 1st floor provides a short but sweet summary of the Roman presence in these parts. The museum's highlight is left of the cellar, where impressive Roman altars, stone torsos and tomb stones found at Savaria excavation sites are on display.

SOUTH OF FŐ TÉR

Further evidence of Szombathely's Roman history can be seen at the **Iseum** (Rákóczi Ferenc utca 12), once part of a grand 2nd-century complex of two temples dedicated to the Egyptian goddess Isis by Roman legionnaires. It's currently closed for major work, and hopefully the town has plans to restore it to its former glory rather than butcher the job by using cement blocks as was done in the 1950s.

Gazing down on the Iseum is the **Szombathely Gallery** (Szombathelyi Képtar; ☎ 508 800; Rákóczi Ferenc utca 12; adult/student 300/150Ft; 10am-5pm Tue & Thu-Sun, to 7pm Wed), a grand modern art gallery that features up to 20 temporary exhibitions every year. The lovely twin-towered Moorish building opposite at No 3 is the former **synagogue** (zsinagóga; Rákóczi Ferenc utca 3), designed in 1881 by the Viennese architect Ludwig Schöne. Today it's a music school and the attached **Béla Bartók Concert Hall**. A plaque marks the spot from where '4228 of our Jewish brothers and sisters were deported to Auschwitz on 4 July 1944'.

Activities

The rowing and fishing lakes northwest of the city centre along Kenderesi utca cover 12 hectares and make up Szombathely's playground; **boats** (rowing/pedal boat per hr 760/900Ft; 1-8pm Apr-Sep) can be hired from the western side of the little island in the middle. The huge **Tófürdő swimming complex** (☎ 505 689; Kenederesi utca 2; adult/child 900/700Ft; 9am-8pm May-Sep) close by has huge pools and a bunch of slides for both big and small kids. The city's **thermal baths and indoor pools** (☎ 314 336;

Bartók Béla körút 41; adult/child 900/600Ft; thermal baths 9am-7pm May-Sep, swimming pool 2-9.30pm Mon, 6am-9.30pm Tue-Fri, 9am-6pm Sat & Sun year-round) are just to the south. Admission is cheaper the later you enter.

There is also plenty of **hiking**, **cycling** and **horse riding** to be had in and around Szombathely. For more information, pick up a copy of the helpful *Green Tourism* brochure from Tourinform.

Sleeping

Tourinform has a list of private rooms and student hostels (dorm bed from approximately 3000Ft), with beds available over summer.

Tópart Camping (509 038; Kenederesi utca 6; camp sites per tent/adult/child 600/800/400Ft, d/q bungalows 7000/16,500Ft; May-Sep;) Northwest of the city centre, near the lakes and swimming complex, this camping ground is spacious, friendly and family orientated. Bus 27 runs from the bus station along Bartók Béla körút, from where the camp is only a short walk.

Liget Hotel (509 323; www.hotels.hu/liget_szombathely; Szent István Park 15; s/d with shower 5490/7490Ft, with bath 7490/9490Ft) Liget is a hotel that is functional at best, with very basic rooms and average service. It is, however, quite cheap and is convenient to the lakes and the museum village.

Wagner Hotel (322 208; www.hotelwagner.hu; Kossuth Lajos utca 15; s/d from 11,000/17,500Ft, apt from 21,500Ft;) A lovely hotel very close to the heart of Szombathely. It has a sunny inner courtyard, and while rooms are small, they're quite comfortable and have all the mod cons.

Hotel Claudius (313 760; www.claudiushotel.hu; Bartók Béla körút 39; s/d €58/70, ste from €94;) It may look like an eyesore from the outside, but this former Soviet monstrosity is a stunner from the inside. Public spaces have been thoroughly modernised and are now coloured in pleasing shades of purple and brown, while rooms are sizeable, cosy and come with balcony. There's also a decent restaurant on-site.

Park Hotel Pelikán (513 800; www.hotelpelikan.hu; Deák Ferenc utca 5; s 22,000-26,000Ft, d 25,500-33,200Ft;) This highly professional four-star hotel occupies a former orphanage and children's hospital, and retains many of the building's original features. Rooms may be small but their high ceilings distract you from the fact, and there's a full fitness centre and a lovely indoor pool on the ground floor.

Eating

RESTAURANTS

Café Móló (509 200; Rákóczi Ferenc utca 1-3; pizza 900-1490Ft, mains 1000-2500Ft) With images of Asia adorning its walls, a spacious, modern interior and huge terrace, Móló is a refreshing change to stuffy cellar restaurants. Pick from the huge selection of pizzas and enjoy the upbeat vibe.

Gödör (510 078; Hollán Ernő utca 12; mains 1000-2000Ft; 11am-11pm Mon-Thu, to midnight Fri & Sat, to 3pm Sun) This restaurant-cum-wine cellar is affiliated with the Jégverem (p175) in Sopron and as such caters to 'greedy-guts' types. Portions are massive, dishes relatively authentic and prices reasonable. It really is a lovely spot, but best enjoyed in winter.

Old Post Pub (510 530; Hefele Menyhért utca 2; mains 1500-2200Ft) This new kid on the block is a bright, clean eatery with more old-fashioned beer mugs than there are Zsa Zsa Gabor exes (OK, maybe not quite that many). There are a number of beers on tap, a mixed international menu with the likes of grilled meat and chilli-based dishes, and a small summer terrace.

Pityer (508 010; Rumi út 18; mains 1500-3000Ft) It may be out of the way but Pityer is worth making the 1.5km trip southwest of Fő tér for its excellent fish dishes (over a dozen) and all round traditional feel. Portions are large and the surrounds are quite atmospheric.

Tóvendéglő (900 700; Rumi Rajki sétány 1; mains 1590-3000Ft) With a view overlooking the city's small lake from its terraced patio, modern Tóvendéglő has the finest location of any eatery in Szombathely. With dishes like grilled black cod, duck liver with grilled apples and honey, and Hungarian beef stew with dumplings on the menu, it has the best choice of dishes, too.

CAFES

Claudia (313 375; Savaria tér 1; ice cream from 100Ft; 9am-10pm Mon-Sat, 2-10pm Sun) Claudia is a genteel cafe with old-fashioned ideas, where you can sit on a coffee for hours and watch the world go by. It has excellent cakes and ice cream, and in summer its tables spill out onto the pavement.

Semiramis (Király utca 7; coffees 250-550Ft; 🕑 7am-6pm Mon-Fri, 8am-1pm Sat) Tiny Semiramis easily fits the bill of a downtown Manhattan cafe, with great coffee and snacks and quick service.

QUICK EATS & SELF-CATERING

Menza (☎ 511 348; Mártírok tere 5/b; meals 500-700Ft; 🕑 7.30am-5pm Mon-Fri, to 2pm Sat) There is no better place in town for decent filling meals at cheap prices than this modern take on a workers' (or student) canteen.

Match (cnr Óperint utca & Kiskar utca; 🕑 6am-7pm Mon-Fri, to 2pm Sat) A huge central branch of the popular supermarket chain.

Drinking

Geo Café Bar (☎ 333 322; Hefele Menyhért utca 2; 🕑 8am-11pm Mon-Wed, 8am-1am Thu & Fri, 9am-2am Sat, 11am-1pm Sun) This sleek new bar has a split personality – chilled cafe serving excellent coffee and light snacks during the day and exclusive cocktail bar after dark. Grab a comfy couch and join in.

Bánya Café Bar (☎ 321 123; Szinyei Merse Pál utca; 🕑 10am-11pm Mon-Wed, 10am-midnight Thu, 10am-2am Fri, 4pm-2am Sat) This impressive basement (*bánya* means 'mine'), a former workers' pub, has been dragged into the 21st century and wouldn't look out of place in London.

Royal Söröző (☎ 339 727; Fő tér 16; 🕑 8.30am-midnight Sun-Thu, to 1am Fri & Sat) With tables on the main square, popular Royal is a grand place for people watching. It doesn't do bad food and service either, and there's internet access as well (per hour 600Ft).

Art Café (☎ 310 661; Fő tér 10; 🕑 8am-11pm Mon-Sat, 9am-11pm Sun) This sedate cafe-pub on the main square attracts watchers and talkers, not party people. Come here for a quiet drink and a slow time.

Entertainment

An excellent source of information is the free biweekly entertainment guide *Szombathelyi Est*. For tickets to most events head to the **ticket office** (☎ 318 738; Király utca 11; 🕑 10am-6pm Mon-Fri), just south of the old Savaria Hotel. Enter from Mártírok tere.

Szombathely has devoted a lot of attention to music ever since Bishop Szily engaged the services of full-time musicians to perform at church functions – not services. Important venues include the **Béla Bartók Concert Hall** (☎ 313 747; Rákóczi Ferenc utca 3), attached to the former synagogue, where the Savaria Symphony Orchestra performs throughout the year; the **AGORA Szalon** (☎ 509 641; Fő tér 10); and the ugly **AGORA** (☎ 312 666; www.agorasavaria.hu, in Hungarian; Március 15 tér 5) dating from the 1960s.

Bánya Café Bar (☎ 321 123; Szinyei Merse Pál utca; 🕑 10am-11pm Mon-Wed, 10am-midnight Thu, 10am-2am Fri, 4pm-2am Sat) Clubs are rare in Szombathely, but if you're hankering for a big night out on Friday or Saturday head to Bánya.

Getting There & Away

BUS

In general the bus service isn't so good to/from Szombathely, though there are hourly departures to Ják (250Ft, 21 minutes, 14km) and Kőszeg (375Ft, 37 minutes, 22km). Buses also depart Szombathely for the following destinations.

Destination	Price	Duration	Km	Frequency
Budapest	3230Ft	3½-5½hr	240	3 daily
Győr	1770Ft	2½hr	110	3-5 daily
Kaposvár	2780Ft	3½-4½hr	188	3 daily
Keszthely	1350Ft	2¼hr	90	2 daily
Pécs	3640Ft	4½-5½hr	261	3 daily
Sárvár	525Ft	1hr	35	hourly
Sopron	1200Ft	2hr	76	up to 7 daily
Sümeg	1200Ft	1½-2hr	73	up to 4 daily
Veszprém	1770Ft	2½-3hr	117	2-3 daily

TRAIN

Some trains to Budapest (from 3230Ft, three to four hours, 236km, 13 daily) go via Veszprém and Székesfehérvár. Győr (from 1770Ft, 1½ to two hours, 103km, eight daily) is served by express train (via Celldömölk), as is Pécs (from 3440Ft, four hours, 250km, four daily). There are local trains to Kőszeg (300Ft, 27 minutes, 18km, up to 14 daily), Sopron (1050Ft, 1¼ hours, 62km, up to 13 daily) and Körmend (450Ft, 34 minutes, 26km, up to 15 daily). There are also direct trains to/from Graz (5000Ft, 2½ to three hours, 136km, two daily).

Getting Around

Szombathely is simple to negotiate on foot, but bus 27 will take you from the train station to the Vas Museum Village, lakes, Tópart Camping and the Liget Hotel. You can also call a taxi on ☎ 322 222.

AROUND SZOMBATHELY

Ják

☎ 94 / pop 2470

The tiny settlement of Ják is home to the finest examples of Romanesque architecture, the **Benedictine Abbey Church** (Bencés apátsági templom; ☎ 356 217; adult/senior & student 300/150Ft; 8am-5pm May-Aug, 9am-5pm Sep-Apr). The two-towered structure was begun as a family church in 1214 by Márton Nagy and dedicated to St George four decades later in 1256. Somehow the partially completed church escaped destruction during the Mongol invasion, but it was badly damaged during the Turkish occupation. The church has had many restorations, the most important three being in the mid-17th century, between 1896 and 1904 (when most of the statues in its portal were recut or replaced, rose stained-glass windows added and earlier baroque additions removed) and from 1992 to 1996 for Hungary's millecentenary celebrations.

The church's feature that draws the most attention is its magnificent **portal** on the west side. Carved in geometric patterns 12 layers deep and featuring carved stone statues of Christ and his Apostles, the portal is an exceptional piece of art and not to be missed. If you think it looks in great condition because of its age, it's because renovations were completed in 1996 in time for Hungary's millennium celebrations.

Facing the portal is the tiny clover-leaf **Chapel of St James** (Szent Jakab-kápolna) topped with an onion dome. It was built around 1260 as a parish church, since the main church was monastic. Note the paschal lamb (symbolising Christ) over the main entrance, and the baroque altar and frescoes inside.

In stark contrast to the baroque flourishes of St James, the **interior** of the abbey church is rather simple and plain, with few added extras. However, this seems to work to its advantage, for its single nave and three aisles have a much more graceful and personal feel than most Hungarian Gothic churches. To the west and below the towers is a gallery reserved for the benefactor and his family. The rose-and-blue frescoes on the wall between the vaulting and the arches below could very well be of Márton Nagy and his progeny.

Buses from Szombathely (250Ft, 21 minutes, 14km, hourly) are frequent and will drop you off in Szabadság tér. From Ják you can return to Szombathely or continue on to Körmend (300Ft, 32 minutes, 20km, two Monday to Saturday) and make connections there.

SÁRVÁR

☎ 95 / pop 15,300

The small town of Sárvár, 27km east of Szombathely on the Rába River, is popular for the 44°C thermal waters, discovered in the 1960s during exploratory drilling for oil, that lie below its urban centre. These soothing waters have been channelled into a modern spa complex, and people from Austria and Hungary flock here to avail of their healing powers.

Not everyone visits Sárvár for the hot water, however. Some want a glimpse of the castle where a certain 18th-century countess developed a taste for blood – literally (see the boxed text, p188).

History

Sárvár has experienced some good and some very bad times over the past 500 years or so. During the Reformation Sárvár's fortified castle was a centre of Calvinist culture and scholarship, and its owners, the Nádasdy family, were a respected dynasty in statecraft and military leadership. In 1537 Tamás Nádasdy set up a press that published the first two printed books in Hungarian – a Magyar grammar in Latin and a translation of the New Testament. Ferenc Nádasdy II, dubbed the 'Black Captain', fought heroically against the Turks, and his grandson Ferenc III, a lord chief justice, created one of the greatest libraries and private art collections in central Europe.

But everything began to go pear-shaped at the start of the 17th century. It seems that while the Black Captain was away at war, his wife Erzsébet Báthory, as mad as a hatter and bloodthirsty to boot, was up to no good. Then Ferenc III's involvement in a plot led by Ferenc Wesselényi to overthrow the Habsburgs was exposed. He was beheaded in Vienna in 1671.

Orientation

Sárvár's train station is on Selyemgyár utca. To reach the town centre, walk south along Hunyadi János utca and turn east on Batthyány Lajos utca, which leads to Kossuth tér and the castle. Rákóczi Ferenc utca leads southeast to Vadkert utca and the spa complex. The bus station is at the western end of Batthyány Lajos utca.

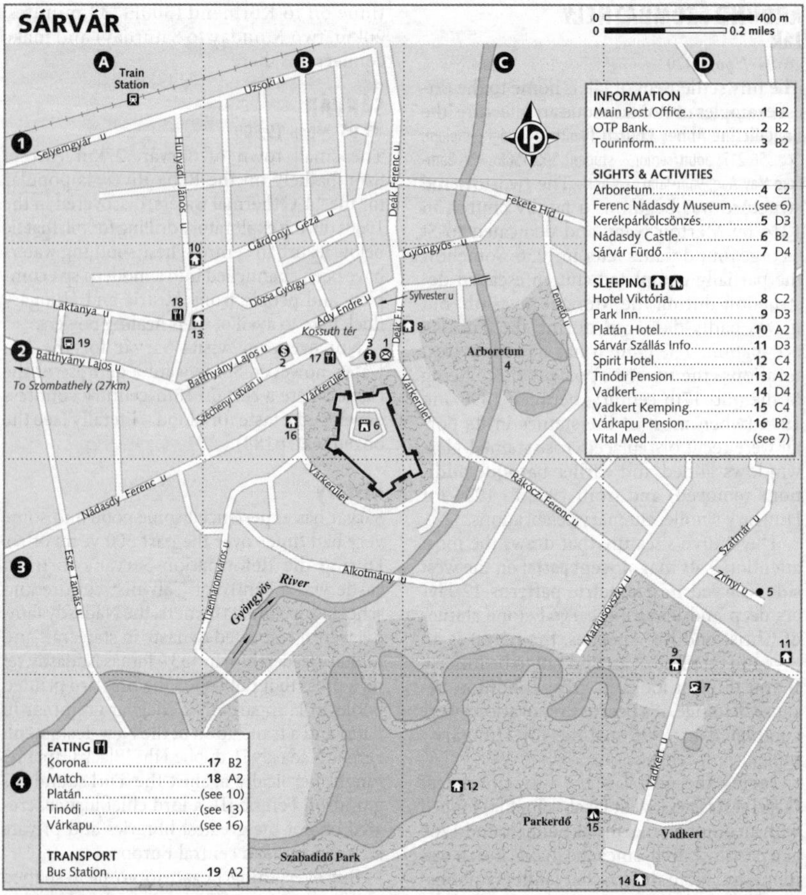

Information

Main post office (Várkerület 32)

OTP bank (Batthyány Lajos utca 2) ATM and exchange machine.

Tourinform (☎ 520 178; sarvar@tourinform.hu; Várkerület 33; ⏰ 9am-4pm Jul & Aug, 9am-4pm Mon-Fri Sep-Jun) This tourist office is almost opposite the castle entrance.

Sights

NÁDASDY CASTLE

The entrance to the **Ferenc Nádasdy Museum** (☎ 320 158; Várkerület 1; adult/senior & student/family 600/300/900Ft; ⏰ 8am-5pm Tue-Sun) in the pentagonal Nádasdy Castle is across a brick footbridge from Kossuth tér and through the gate of a 14th-century tower. Parts of the castle date from the 13th century, but most of it is 16th-century Renaissance and in good condition despite Erzsébet Báthory's shenanigans and all the plundering by the Habsburgs. As punishment for the Nádasdy family's involvement in the rebellion of 1670, their estate was confiscated by the Austrian crown and the castle's contents – including much of the library – were taken to Vienna. As a result, many of the furnishings, tapestries and objets d'art you see in the museum's three wings today were collected from other sources.

One thing the Habsburgs could not take with them was the magnificent ceiling fresco in the **Knight's Hall**, picturing Hungarians – the Black Captain included – battling the Turks at Tata, Székesfehérvár, Győr, Pápa, Kanizsa and Buda. They were painted by Hans Rudolf Miller in the mid-17th century. The biblical scenes on the walls, depicting Samson and Delilah, David and Goliath, Mordechai and Esther, and so on, were painted in 1769 by István Dorffmeister. There's a particularly beautiful 16th-century cabinet of gilded wood and marble to the right of the hall as you enter.

The museum also has one of the nation's best collections of weapons and armour, and almost an entire wing is given over to the Hussars, a regiment of which was named after the Nádasdy family. The uniforms, all buttons, ribbons and fancy epaulettes, would do a Gilbert and Sullivan operetta proud.

Among the exhibits about the castle and Sárvár is the printing press established here, and some of the then inflammatory Calvinist tracts it published. One work in Hungarian, entitled *The Pope Is Not the Pope – That's That* and dated 1603, was later vandalised by a Counter-Reformationist who defiantly wrote 'Lutheran scandal' across it in Latin.

A superb (and priceless) collection of some 60 antique Hungarian maps donated by a UK-based expatriate Hungarian in 1986 and called 'Carta Hungarica' is on exhibit in a room at the end of the west wing.

The 9-hectare **arboretum** (Várkerület 30/a; adult/child 200/100Ft; 8am-7pm Apr–mid-Oct, 8am-5pm mid-Oct–Mar), east of the castle and bisected by the Gyöngyös River, a tributary of the Rába River, was planted by the Nádasdys' successors, the royal Wittelsbach family of Bavaria (the castle's last royal occupant was Ludwig III, who died in exile in 1921). You could do worse than take a stroll through its green acres.

Activities

A huge and very modern spa and wellness complex southeast of the castle, **Sárvár Fürdő** (523 600; www.sarvarfurdo.hu; Vadkert utca 1; adult/6-16yr 1950/1100Ft, adult after 5/8pm 1200/700Ft; thermal baths 8am-10pm year-round, outdoor pools 8am-dusk May-Oct) has indoor and outdoor thermal and swimming pools, several types of sauna, a wellness and fitness centre, and comprehensive medical facilities with all kinds of treatments. The summer entrance to the open-air pools is just south of the main entrance.

Horse riding (per hr 3000Ft) and **coach rides** (up to 3 people 4500Ft) are possible at the Vadkert inn (right). Bicycles can be hired from **Kerékpárkölcsönzés** (06 30 292 3259; Zrínyi utca 19) for 1500Ft per day.

Sleeping

BUDGET

Vadkert (320 045; www.vadkertfogado.hu; Vadkert utca; camp sites per tent/adult/child 700/650/500Ft, s/d 8500/9800Ft) This inn south of the spa exudes a simple country charm despite being so close to the city. It began life as a 19th-century royal hunting lodge and now offers homey rooms with a minimum of clutter. Its camping ground is quite basic and has little tree cover.

Sárvár Szállás Info (06 30 911 3942; www.sarvarszallasinfo.hu; Rákóczi Ferenc utca 43; r from 3000Ft) This office lists all manner of private accommodation, from rooms to whole houses, in and around Sárvár. It's a good, cheap alternative to the city's *pensions* and hotels.

MIDRANGE

Várkapu Pension (326 475; Várkerület 5; s/d 6700/8900Ft) As close to the castle as you can get without actually staying there, the 'Castle Gate' is central and friendly, with clean and accommodating rooms. It also has a sauna and a great restaurant.

Tinódi Pension (323 606; www.tinodifogado.hu; Hunyadi János utca 11; s/d/tr from 7100/8800/12,500Ft) As long as you're not too tall or don't mind banging your head occasionally on the sloping roof, the attic rooms at this tidy *pension* are quite lovely, featuring plenty of natural finish and large beds.

Hotel Viktória (320 525; www.hotel-viktoria.hu; Deák Ferenc utca 6; s/d/ste 9500/13,400/13,800Ft) Once a Romantic-style synagogue built in 1850, Viktória is now a peachy pastel hotel on a quiet central street. Its sunny rooms are complemented by even sunnier balconies.

TOP END

our pick **Spirit Hotel** (889 500; www.spirithotel.hu; Vadkert utca 5; s €140, d from €200, ste from €350) With its smooth lines and slick look, the new five-star Spirit Hotel looks seriously out of place in little Sárvár. Inside, the plush, contemporary interior is dazzling, with open logwood fireplaces, mosaic-tiled floors, a silver-service restaurant and a spacey bar. Rooms are coloured in soft autumn tones and have that interior-designer look and feel to them. Activities abound, and there's a full thermal spa and wellness centre offering every treatment imaginable. Check its website for regular specials.

THE BLOOD COUNTESS

It was the scandal of the 17th century. On the night of 29 December 1610 the Lord Palatine of Hungary, Count György Thurzó, raided the castle at Csejta (now Čachtice in western Slovakia) and caught Countess Erzsébet Báthory literally red-handed – or so he and history would later claim. Covered in blood and screaming like a demon, the widow of the celebrated Black Captain was in the process of eating (as in chomp, chomp) one of her servant girls.

Yet another one, or so it would seem… By the time Thurzó had finished collecting evidence from household staff and the townspeople at Čachtice and Sárvár, some 300 depositions had been given, accusing the countess of torturing, mutilating, murdering and – worst of all – disposing of the bodies of more than 600 girls and young women without so much as a Christian burial.

The case of the so-called Blood Countess has continued to grab the imagination of everyone from writers (Erzsébet is believed to have been the model for Bram Stoker's *Dracula*) and musicians (remember the Goth group Bathory?) to film-makers and fetishists over the centuries, and some pretty crazy theories as to why she did it have emerged. Some say she considered the blood of young maidens to be an *elixir vitae* and bathed in it to stay young. Others claim she suffered from acute iron deficiency and just had to have those red corpuscles. Still others point to the high incidence of lunacy in the two much intermarried branches of the Báthory dynasty. Most likely, however, Erzsébet Báthory was the victim of a conspiracy.

When the Black Captain died in 1604, his widow inherited all of his estates – properties coveted by both Thurzó and Erzsébet's son-in-law Miklós Zrínyi, the poet and great-grandson of the hero of Szigetvár (see p308), who themselves were linked by marriage. Worse, the election of the countess' nephew Gábor Báthory as prince of Transylvania, a vassal state under Ottoman rule, threatened to unite the two Báthory families and strengthen the principality's position. It was in the interest of the Palatine – and the Habsburgs – to get this matriarch of the Báthory family out of the way.

Gábor was murdered in 1613 and the 'Báthory faction' in Hungary ceased to be a threat. The case against the Blood Countess never came to trial, and she remained interned 'between stones' (ie in a sealed chamber) at the castle until she died in 1614 at the age of 54.

Was Erzsébet as bloodthirsty as history has made her out to be? Did she really bite great chunks out of the girls' necks and breasts and mutilate their genitals? Much of the villagers' testimony does appear to be consistent, but to form your own conclusions read Tony Thorne's well-researched *Countess Dracula: The Life and Times of Elisabeth Bathory.*

Other top-end choices:

Park Inn (☎ 530 100; www.parkinnsarvar.hu; Vadkert utca 4; s/d from €80/95; ⊠) Bright, bubbly, modern and connected to the Sárvár Fürdő by a covered walkway.

Vital Med (☎ 523 700; www.vitalmedhotel.hu; Vadkert utca 1; s/d €75/118; ⊠) Hotel of the Sárvár Fürdő.

Eating

Eating options are largely restricted to *pensions* and hotel restaurants.

Match (Hunyadi János 16) Large supermarket around the corner from the bus station.

Korona (☎ 320 542; Kossuth tér 3; ice cream from 120Ft, cakes 160Ft; 9am-8pm) Overlooking the central square next to the town hall is the finest cafe in town, where in summer people line up for a scoop of ice cream or spend a lazy afternoon sipping coffee on the outdoor seating.

Várkapu (☎ 320 045; Várkerület 5; mains 1000-2500Ft; 8.30am-10pm Sun-Thu, to 11pm Fri & Sat) The pick of the crop in Sárvár; we especially like the Hungarian and international menu that changes with the seasons and the good selection of Hungarian wines. There are restful views of the castle and surrounding park, and a bargain lunch menu (700Ft to 1000Ft).

Tinódi (☎ 323 606; Hunyadi János utca 11; mains 1000-2500Ft; 8am-10pm) A *pension* eatery worthy of mention. This one features a bare-bones interior on the 1st floor and a hearty midday menu (700Ft) that will keep you going well into the evening. In summer patrons take over the sunny inner courtyard.

Platán (☎ 320 623; Hunyadi János utca 23; mains 1000-2800Ft) It's a little further from the town centre, but that doesn't seem to bother the lunchtime diners who head to this *csárda* (Hungarian-style inn or restaurant) for the two-course daily menu (700Ft to 1000Ft) of Hungarian cuisine. There's also a well-stocked bar, a summer terrace and a bright cafe.

Getting There & Away

BUS

Buses from Sárvár go to the following destinations.

Destination	Price	Duration	Km	Frequency
Budapest	3230Ft	3hr	221	1-2 daily
Győr	1500Ft	2hr	96	2 daily
Keszthely	1200Ft	1½-2hr	75	1-2 daily
Pápa	750Ft	1½hr	50	up to 3 daily
Pécs	3230Ft	4½hr	224	1 daily
Sopron	1050Ft	1¼hr	62	2-3 daily
Sümeg	600Ft	1hr	40	up to 5 daily
Szombathely	525Ft	1hr	35	hourly
Veszprém	1200Ft	1½hr	77	2 daily

TRAIN

Sárvár is on the train line linking Szombathely (375Ft, 21 minutes, 24km, hourly) with Veszprém (1500Ft, 1½ to two hours, 100km), Székesfehérvár (2290Ft, two to 2½ hours, 145km) and Budapest (from 3010Ft, 3½ hours, 212km) up to eight times daily.

KŐSZEG

☎ 94 / pop 12,000

The tranquil town of Kőszeg (German: Güns) is sometimes called 'the nation's jewellery box', and as you pass under the pseudo-Gothic Heroes' Gate into Jurisics tér, you'll see why. What opens up before you is a treasure-trove of colourful Gothic, Renaissance and baroque buildings that together make up one of the most delightful squares in Hungary. At the same time the nearby Kőszeg Hills, which include Mt Írottkő (882m), the highest point in Transdanubia, and the Írottkő Nature Park, offer endless possibilities for outdoor activities.

Orientation

Kőszeg's historic district, the Inner Town, is ringed by the Várkör, which follows the old castle walls. The city's bus 'station' is a half-dozen stands on Liszt Ferenc utca, a few minutes' walk to the southeast. The train station is on Alsó körút, about 1.5km in the same direction.

Information

Fehér (☎ 360 034; cnr Várkör & Kiss János utca; 8am-9pm) Small bar with internet access for guests.

Írottkő Nature Park information centre (☎ 563 121; www.naturpark.hu; Rajnis József út 7; 8am-6pm Mon-Fri, 9am-1pm Sat mid-Apr–Oct, 8am-5pm Mon-Fri mid-Oct–mid-Apr) Shares space with Tourinform.

Main post office (Várkör 65)

OTP bank (Kossuth Lajos utca 8; 7.45am-5pm Mon & Wed, to 3pm Tue-Thu, to 12.30pm Fri)

Tourinform (☎ 563 120; koszeg@tourinform.hu; Rajnis József út 7; 8am-6pm Mon-Fri, 9am-1pm Sat mid-Apr–Oct, 8am-5pm Mon-Fri mid-Oct–mid-Apr) Deals out brochures on the town and its surrounds.

Town website (www.koszeg.hu) Provides a great deal of online information in a variety of languages.

Sights

Heroes' Gate (Hősök kapuja), leading into Jurisics tér, was erected in 1932 (when these nostalgic portals were all the rage in Hungary) to mark the 400th anniversary of Suleiman's withdrawal. Attached is the **General's House** (Tábornokház; ☎ 360 240; Jurisics tér 6; adult/senior & student 400/200Ft; 10am-5pm Tue-Fri, to 1pm Sat mid-Mar–Sep), a small museum with an average collection of folk art and local history pieces from the area. It does, however, provide access to the top of Heroes' Gate, which makes paying the entrance fee worth it.

Almost all the buildings in Jurisics tér are interesting. The red-and-yellow **Town Hall** (Városháza; Jurisics tér 8), a mixture of Gothic, Renaissance, baroque and neoclassical styles, has oval paintings on its facade of worldly and heavenly worthies. The **Renaissance house** (Jurisics tér 7), built in 1668, is adorned with graffiti etched into the stucco. A few doors down is the **Golden Unicorn Pharmacy Museum** (Arany Egyszarvú Patikamúzeum; ☎ 360 337; Jurisics tér 11; adult/senior & student 400/200Ft; 10am-5pm Tue-Sun Apr-Nov), which contains some exceptional 18th-century oak furniture, and plenty of drugs in old jars.

In the centre of Jurisics tér a statue of the Virgin Mary (1739) and the town fountain (1766) adjoin two fine churches. The Gothic **Church of St James** (Szent Jakab-templom), built in 1407, is to the north and contains very faded 15th-century frescoes on the east wall (ie to the right of the main altar) of a giant St Christopher carrying the Christ Child, Mary Misericordia sheltering supplicants under a massive cloak, and the Three Magi bearing their gifts of gold, frankincense and myrrh. The altars and oaken pews are masterpieces of baroque woodcarving, and Miklós Jurisics and two of his children are buried in the crypt. The baroque **Church of St Henry** (Szent Imre-templom) with the tall steeple is dark and austere inside, but it does contain a few art treasures.

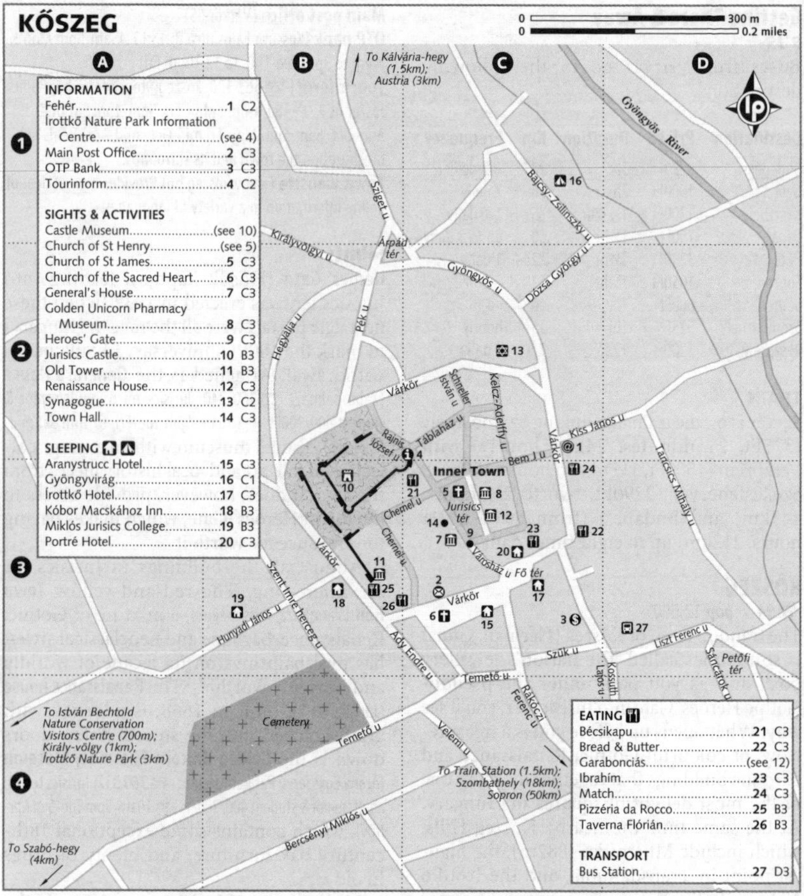

Not far north of Jurisics tér is the town's squat **Jurisics Castle** (☎ 360 113; Rajnis József utca 9; adult/child/family 1000/700/2500Ft; ⌚ 10am-6pm Tue-Sun Apr-Oct, 10am-5pm Tue-Sun Nov-Mar). Originally built in the mid-13th century, but reconstructed several times (most recently in 1962), the four-towered fortress is now a hotchpotch of Renaissance arcades, Gothic windows and baroque interiors. Inside is a museum with static exhibits on the history of Kőszeg from the 14th century (with the events of 1532 taking up most of the space; see the boxed text, opposite) and on local wine production. Among the latter is the curious *Szőlő jővésnek könyve* (Arrival of the Grape Book), a kind of gardener's logbook of grape shoot and bud sketches begun in 1740 and updated annually on St George's Day (23 April). You can climb two of the towers for views over the town.

Walking south along narrow Chernel utca, with its elegant baroque facades and saw-toothed rooftops (which allowed the defenders a better shot at the enemy), you'll pass the remains of the ancient **castle walls** and the so-called **Old Tower** (Öreg Zwinger; ☎ 360 240; Chernel utca 16; adult/senior & child 300/150Ft; ⌚ 10am-1.30pm Fri-Sun), an 11th-century corner bastion, which houses a small wine museum.

The neo-Gothic **Church of the Sacred Heart** (Jézus Szíve-templom; Fő tér), built in 1894, has refreshingly different geometric frescoes reminiscent of those in Matthias Church in Budapest (p76), a spire that can be seen from anywhere in the town and those 'midday' bells at 11am. The circular **synagogue** (zsinagóga; Várkör 38), built in 1859, with its strange neo-Gothic towers, once served one of the oldest Jewish communities in Hungary, but now sits abandoned and in decay to the northeast of Jurisics tér.

Activities

Walking up to the baroque chapel on 394m-high **Kálvária-hegy** (Calvary Hill) northwest of the town centre, or to the vineyards of **Király-völgy** (Royal Valley) west of Jurisics Castle, is a very pleasant way to spend a few hours. You can also follow Temető utca southwest and then south up to 458m-high **Szabó-hegy** (Tailor's Hill). Tourinform has a brochure with easy walks in the area called *Kőszeg-Hegyaljai Séták* (Kőszeg Upland Paths), but a copy of Cartographia's 1:40,000-scale *Kőszegi-hegység* (Kőszeg Hills; No 13; 700Ft) map will prove more useful if you plan to do adventurous hiking or visit the **Írottkő Nature Park** to the west. Alternatively, stop by the **István Bechtold Nature Conservation Visitors Centre** (☎ 563 174; Hunyadi János utca; 10am-5pm Tue-Sun May-Oct, 10am-4pm Tue-Fri Nov-Apr) and arrange a guided walk in the protected landscape.

Sleeping

BUDGET

Gyöngyvirág (☎ 360 454; www.gyongyviragpanzio.hu; Bajcsy-Zsilinszky utca 6; camp sites per tent/adult/child/car 500/750/350/400Ft, s/d/tr/q with washbasin 5000/6000/7500/9500Ft, s/d with shower 6500/7500Ft) The 'Lily of the Valley' caters to budget travellers with a standard guest house with stripped-back rooms, and a tiny camping ground with no tree cover that backs onto the Gyöngyös River. It's at most a 10-minute walk to the town centre.

Miklós Jurisics College (☎ 361 404; Hunyadi János utca 10; dm 3000Ft) This enormous college west of the Inner Town has over 100 beds in dormitory accommodation available in July and August.

Kóbor Macskához Inn (☎ 362 273; Várkör 100; d/tr 6900/8900Ft) Just west of the Inner Town, 'At the Sign of the Stray Cat' is a basic inn with relatively simple yet large rooms and a downstairs bar that can sometimes be noisy.

Aranystrucc Hotel (☎ 360 323; www.aranystrucc.hu; Várkör 124; s/d 6200/9400Ft) The 'Golden Ostrich' is a worn, though wonderfully atmospheric, hotel in the heart of Kőszeg. Of all the rooms in this 18th-century building, No 7 is the best choice – it's the biggest and has balcony views over the main square (Fő tér).

MIDRANGE

Portré Hotel (☎ 363 170; www.portre.com; Fő tér 7; s/d 7300/12,000Ft; 💻) This positive stunner of a boutique hotel offers a half-dozen individually decorated rooms on Fő tér. Try and get a room on the 1st floor, as those on the 2nd floor have dormer windows.

Írottkő Hotel (☎ 360 373; www.hotelirottko.hu; Fő tér 4; s/d/tr 12,000/17,000/20,500Ft; 💻) Kőszeg's main hotel. Although unappealing from the outside, it's large, central and caters to business types with vaguely interesting rooms and a full wellness centre in the basement.

Eating & Drinking

Match (Várkör 20; 6am-6.30pm Mon-Fri, 6am-1pm Sat) A very central branch of the supermarket chain.

Ibrahim (☎ 360 854; Fő tér 17; ice cream from 100Ft; 8am-10pm) For ice cream don't go past this place; what looks like half the population of Kőszeg queuing outside can't be wrong.

Pizzéria da Rocco (☎ 362 379; Várkör 55; pizza 600-2200Ft) With its huge garden within the old castle walls, da Rocco is a coveted address and great for a pizza or indeed just a drink.

FOR WHOM THE BELL TOLLS

Kőszeg has played pivotal roles in the nation's defence over the centuries. The best-known story is the storming of the town's castle by Suleiman the Magnificent's troops in August 1532, which sounds all too familiar but has a surprise ending. Miklós Jurisics' 'army' of fewer than 50 soldiers and the town militia held the fortress for 25 days against 100,000 Turks. An accord was reached when Jurisics allowed the Turks to run up their flag over the castle in a symbolic declaration of victory provided they left town immediately thereafter. The Turks kept their part of the bargain (packing their bags at 11am on 30 August), and Vienna was spared the treatment that would befall Buda nine years later. To this day church bells in Kőszeg peal an hour before noon to mark the withdrawal.

DIY: ZALA COUNTRY

Travelling from Őrség region to Lake Balaton you'll soon notice an explosion of tiny villages beginning with Zala; in fact every second place seems to begin with the word. You've arrived in Zala country – or county to be correct – one of the smallest in Western Transdanubia. It gained its name from the Zala River, a fast flowing tributary that snakes its way through the countryside and eventually empties into Kis-Balaton (p204).

The region's main town is Zalaegerszeg (no surprise there), a sizeable place with a couple of impressive open-air museums, but the real reason for diverging from the well-trodden path is to experience rural bliss in the Göcsej and Hetés hills. Lying to the west of Zalaegerszeg, these gentle rolling ranges are covered in Adler (*éger* in Hungarian) forests and the occasional farmer's field; they offer ample opportunities for hiking, cycling and berry picking. Folk traditions are alive and well here, too, and villages such as Kávás, Zalalövő and Csesztreg still contain original 18th-century farmers houses.

For more information, call in at **Tourinform** (☎ 92 316 160; zalaegerszeg@tourinform.hu; Széchenyi tér 4-6; ⏰ 9am-5pm Mon-Fri) in Zalaegerszeg, or go online to www.zalatourism.hu.

Bécsikapu (☎ 563 122; Rajnis József utca 5; mains 1000-3300Ft) Almost opposite the Church of St James, this is a pleasant *csárda* with a back garden looking towards the castle. There are plenty of fish dishes to choose from, but the wild boar goulash is the true winner here.

Taverna Flórián (☎ 563 072; Várkör 59; mains 2000-4290Ft; ⏰ 11.30am-2.30pm & 7-10pm Wed-Sun) For fine dining, head here for quality Mediterranean food in beautiful cellarlike surroundings or a sunny inner courtyard setting. The pasta dishes (730Ft to 2650Ft) are particularly recommended.

Bread & Butter (☎ 561 604; Várkör 10; coffee 250-500Ft) A funky little cafe with comfy booths and a large street-side pagoda. Its coffee and cakes are hard to beat in Kőszeg.

Garabonciás (☎ 360 050; Jurisics tér 7; coffee 350-500Ft; ⏰ noon-10pm Mon-Sat, 5-10pm Sun) Amazingly, this simple yet pleasant cafe is the only eating/drinking establishment on Fő tér. It's a fab spot to enjoy a coffee and the medieval surrounds.

Getting There & Away

Bus departures are frequent to Sopron (900Ft, one hour 20 minutes, 59km, six daily) and Szombathely (375Ft, 37 minutes, 22km, hourly). Kőszeg is at the end of an 18km railway spur from Szombathely (300Ft, 35 minutes, 21km, hourly).

ŐRSÉG REGION

Unspoilt nature and pure rural essence are the biggest drawcards of Őrség, Hungary's westernmost region, where it converges with Austria and Slovenia in forest and farmland. Much of this area falls within the borders of a national park, and it's best explored by foot, bicycle or on horseback. For those looking for somewhere to get away from it all, it's hard to find a better place in Magyarország than here.

Information

Pick up information on the park and region from the local **Tourinform** (☎ 548 034; orseg@tourinform.hu; Siskaszer 26/a; ⏰ 9am-5pm Mon-Fri, 10am-7pm Sat & Sun mid-Jun–Aug, 10am-4pm Mon-Fri Sep–mid-Jun) in Őriszentpéter at the turn-off to Szalafő. There's an ATM in the centre of Őriszentpéter.

Őrség National Park

Much of the region forms the boundaries of the 440-sq-km **Őrség National Park** (http://onp.nemzetipark.gov.hu), which borders both Austria and Slovenia. The park's **information centre** (☎ 548 034; onp.nemzetipark.gov.hu; Siskaszer 26/a; ⏰ 9am-5pm Mon-Fri, 10am-7pm Sat & Sun mid-Jun–Aug, 10am-4pm Mon-Fri Sep–mid-Jun) is housed in the same building as Tourinform. The park itself is a green belt of dense woods, peaceful meadows, rolling hills and slow streams, which makes it a grand place for hiking, cycling and horse riding. Tourinform can provide information on all of these activities. There are marked hiking trails that link many of Őrség's villages, including Őriszentpéter, Szalafő, Velemér and Pankasz. Cartographia's 1:60,000-scale map *Őrség, Göcsej* (No 21; 950Ft) is a good reference for hikers.

Őriszentpéter

☎94 / pop 1280

Őriszentpéter, the centre of the Őrség region, is a pretty village of timber and thatch-roofed houses and large gardens. Its most interesting sight, a remarkably well-preserved 13th-century **Romanesque church** (Templomszer 15; Mass 8.30am Sun), is an easy 2km walk northwest of the village centre on the road to Szalafő. On the southern extension of the church is a wonderful carved portal and small fragments of 15th-century frescoes. On the north side, a set of wooden steps leads to the choir – the door at the top may be open during the day, so try your luck. The writings on the internal south walls, dating from the 17th century, are Bible verses in Hungarian, and the 18th-century altarpiece was painted by a student of Franz Anton Maulbertsch.

Szalafő

☎94 / pop 235

Energetic travellers may want to continue another 4km or so along Templomszer, past arcaded old peasant houses and abandoned crank wells to Szalafő, the oldest settlement in the Őrség. In Szalafő-Pityerszer, 2km west of the village, is the **Open-Air Ethnographical Museum** (Szabadtéri Néprajzi Múzeum; ☎06 30 467 7022; adult/senior & student/family 400/200/800Ft; 10am-6pm May-Aug, 10am-6pm Tue-Sun Apr, Sep & Oct), the grandiose name given to a mini-*skanzen* (open-air museum displaying village architecture) of three folk compounds of 10 houses, storerooms and outbuildings unique to the Őrség. Built around a central courtyard, the houses are very cute and have large overhangs, which allowed neighbours to chat when it rained – a frequent occurrence in this very wet region. The **Calvinist church** in the village centre has frescoes from the 16th century.

Sleeping & Eating

Tourinform has a comprehensive list of private accommodation in the park (for around 3000Ft per person). If the sleeping options following are full, the sizeable town of Szentgotthárd, on the northwestern edge of the park, also has a few hotels and *pensions*.

Domino (☎428 115; Siskaszer 5/a; bungalows d/tr/q 7000/9000/11,500Ft) This place has five lovely little bungalows complete with kitchen and private bathroom. It's at the northern end of Őriszentpéter away from what little action there is, but it's only a 15-minute walk to Bognár.

our pick Vadkörte (☎429 031; www.vadkorte.hu, in Hungarian; Alvég 7; s/d/tr 6600/11,200/15,000Ft, apt from 12,600Ft; ☒) In the heart of the park at tiny Kondorfa is this sweet country inn, with characterful rooms upstairs and large, well-equipped apartments in a house next door. Many of the rooms have furnished antique beds and cupboards featuring folk-art flourishes, but the bathrooms are all quite modern. The ground-floor restaurant (mains 1000Ft to 2400Ft) is appropriately kitschy and serves a mix of regional Hungarian and Austrian cuisine, alongside seasonal specialities. Turn up in autumn for wild meats and pumpkin, in spring for asparagus and from August to October for wild berries. Bicycles are available for hire for 1500Ft per day.

Bognár (☎428 027; Kovácsszer 96; mains 850-2500Ft; 7am-9pm) About 500m up the hill, north of the bus station on the road to Csákánydoroszió, this large country guest house is the best choice for food in Őriszentpéter.

Getting There & Around

It's best to have your own transport to explore the region, as buses are very infrequent. Őriszentpéter (and sometimes Szalafő) can be reached by bus from Körmend (600Ft, one hour, 37km, three daily), Kőszeg (1350Ft, two hours, 87km, one daily) and Szentgotthárd (375Ft, one hour, 25km, up to four daily); there are also buses between Őriszentpéter, Szalafő (200Ft, six to nine minutes, 5.6km, up to two daily) and Kondorfa (200Ft, 11 to 15 minutes, 7.5km, up to four daily).

Lake Balaton Region

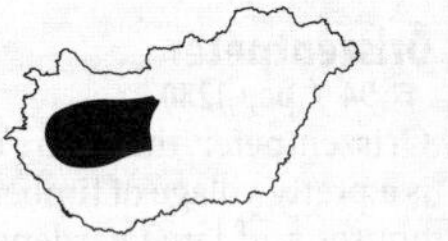

Europe's largest expanse of fresh water is the 'Hungarian Sea', a vast lake covering 600 sq km. People flock here to enjoy the obvious – swimming, sailing, sun worshipping, fishing and unwinding. Yet the region's attraction extends far beyond the obvious.

Take the southern shore. Most of it is a forgettable tangle of tacky resorts popular with families, for here the water is at its shallowest and safest (the lake's depth averages only 3m). Yet Siófok stands head and shoulders above it all, a centre for hedonism whose reputation is beginning to make serious waves on Europe's summer party pond. It will please anyone with a penchant for dance beats by night and beach bumming by day.

The northern shore is the yin to the southern's yang. Here the pace of life is more gentle and refined, and the forested hills of the Balaton Uplands National Park create a wonderful backdrop. Historical towns, such as Keszthely, Balatonfüred and Veszprém, dot the landscape, and Europe's largest thermal lake at Hévíz is close at hand. Tihany, a unique peninsula cutting the lake almost in half, is home to an important historical church, while the hilltop fortress at Sümeg provides commanding views. Badacsony draws crowds with its lakeside location, robust white wines and cultivated slopes.

But still the best thing about the Lake Balaton region is the lake itself. Spend some time here and before you know it you'll have fallen under its spell, like so many artists and holidaymakers have over the centuries.

HIGHLIGHTS

- Wondering how tiny **Sümeg** (p212) came to have such a striking hilltop fortress, let alone such impressive frescoes in its Church of the Ascension
- Taking a dip in the healing waters of the world's second-largest thermal lake at **Hévíz** (p205)
- Wandering the wild peninsula and poking around in the Abbey Church at **Tihany** (p215)
- Sailing, swimming, fishing and cycling in the **Lake Balaton region** (opposite)
- Discovering the **Kál Basin** (p210), a region of unspoilt beauty in the heart of a national park

History

The area around Lake Balaton was settled as early as the Iron Age and the Romans, who called the lake Pelso, built a fort at Valcum (now Fenékpuszta), south of Keszthely, in the 2nd century AD. Throughout the Great Migrations (see p23), Lake Balaton was a reliable source of water, fish, reeds for thatch and ice in winter. The early Magyars found the lake a natural defence line, and many churches, monasteries and villages were built in the vicinity. In the 16th century the lake served as the divide between the Turks, who occupied the southern shore, and the Habsburgs to the northwest. Before the Ottomans were pushed back they had already crossed the lake and razed many of the towns and border castles in the northern hills. Croats, Germans and Slovaks resettled the area in the 18th century, and the subsequent building booms gave towns such as Sümeg, Veszprém and Keszthely their baroque appearance.

Balatonfüred and Hévíz developed early as resorts for the wealthy, but it wasn't until the late 19th century that landowners, their vines destroyed by phylloxera lice, began building summer homes to rent out to the burgeoning middle classes. The arrival of the southern railway in 1861 and the northern line in 1909 increased the tourist influx, and by the 1920s resorts on both shores welcomed some 50,000 holiday-makers each summer. Just before the outbreak of WWII that number had increased fourfold. After the war, the communist government expropriated private villas and built new holiday homes for trade unions. Many of these have been turned into hotels in recent years, greatly increasing the accommodation options.

Activities

The main pursuits for visitors at Lake Balaton – apart from **swimming**, of course – are **boating** (p70) and **fishing** (p70). Motor boats running on fuel are banned entirely, so 'boating' here means sailing, rowing and windsurfing. Fishing is good – the indigenous *fogas* (pike-perch) and the young version, *süllő*, being the prized catch – and edible *harcsa* (catfish) and *ponty* (carp) are in abundance.

Licences are required to fish on the lake – ask at the various Tourinform offices on the lake for places to purchase them. It's also possible to procure one from the **National Federation of Hungarian Anglers** (MOHOSZ; ☎ 1-248 2590; www.mohosz.hu; XII Korompai utca 17) in Budapest.

One of the big events of the year at the lake is the **Cross-Balaton Swimming Race** from Révfülöp to Balatonboglár in late July.

Lake cruises are a popular pastime over the summer months (July and August). Cruises usually last one hour (adult/child 1250/625Ft) or 1½ hours (1400/700Ft) and leave from all points on the lake. There are also themed cruises for kids, along with sunset tours and grill parties. Check www.balatonihajozas.hu for more details.

With the recent completion of the 210km designated bike path around the lake, **cycling** (p68) has become an attractive activity. Additionally, most towns on the lake's shores have at least one bike rental agent operating over the summer months. If you plan to do a bit of cycling, pick up a copy of *Két keréken a Balatonnál* (Cycling around the Balaton), a free map available from Tourinform offices that details the round-the-lake path, along with 13 other cycle routes in the Balaton area.

Getting There & Away

Trains to Lake Balaton usually leave from Déli or Kelenföld train stations in Budapest, and buses from Népliget bus station. If you're travelling north or south from the lake to towns in Western or Southern Transdanubia, buses are usually preferable to trains.

Getting Around

Railway service on both the northern and southern sides of the lake is fairly frequent. A better way to see the lake up close, though, is on a ferry run by the **Balaton Shipping Co** (Balatoni Hajózási Rt; ☎ 84-310 050; www.balatonihajozas.hu; Krúdy sétány 2, Siófok). Ferries operate on the Siófok–Balatonfüred–Tihany–Balatonföldvár route, and from Fonyód to the Badacsony, up to four times daily from April to May and September to October, with many more frequent sailings from June to August. From late May to early September, ferries ply the lake from Balatonkenese to Keszthely and Révfülöp to Balatonboglár. There is also a regular car ferry between Tihanyi-rév and Szántódi-rév (from early March to late November). There are no passenger services on the lake in winter, ie from November to March.

Adults pay 930Ft for distances of one to 10km, 1280Ft for 11km to 20km and 1430Ft

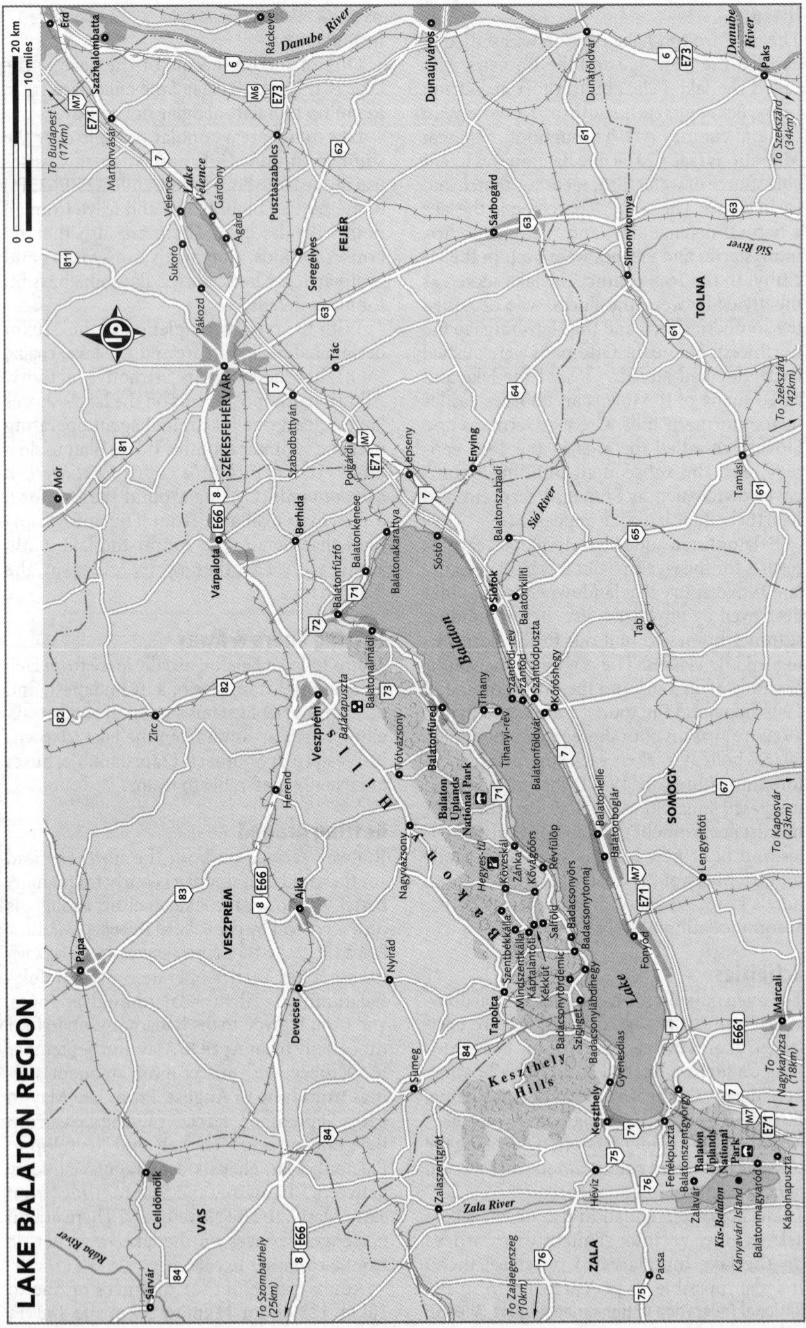
LAKE BALATON REGION
0 20 km
0 10 miles
Érd
Százhalombatta
Ráckeve
Danube River
Dunaújváros
Dunaföldvár
Paks
To Budapest (17km)
Martonvásár
Velence
Lake Velence
Gárdony
Agárd
Sukoró
Pákozd
Pusztaszabolcs
Seregélyes
FEJÉR
Sárbogárd
Simontornya
Sió River
TOLNA
To Szekszárd (34km)
To Szekszárd (42km)
Tamási
Tác
SZÉKESFEHÉRVÁR
Szabadbattyán
Polgárdi
Lepseny
Enying
Mór
Berhida
Várpalota
Balatonfűzfő
Balatonkenese
Balatonakarattya
Sóstó
Balatonszabadi
Siófok
Balatonkiliti
Tab
Lake Balaton
Balatonalmádi
Balácapuszta
Veszprém
Zirc
Herend
Tótvázsony
Balatonfüred
Tihany
Tihanyi-rév
Szántódi-rév
Szántód
Szántódpuszta
Kőröshegy
Balatonföldvár
Balatonlelle
Balatonboglár
SOMOGY
To Kaposvár (23km)
Lengyeltóti
Bakony Hills
Balaton Uplands National Park
Hegyes-tű
Nagyvázsony
Zánka
Köveskál
Kővágóörs
Révfülöp
Szentbékkálla
Mindszentkálla
Káptalantóti
Kékkút
Salföld
Badacsonyörs
Badacsonytomaj
Badacsony
Badacsonylábdihegy
Badacsonytördemic
Szigliget
Gyenesdias
Tapolca
Fonyód
Marcali
To Nagykanizsa (18km)
Keszthely Hills
Keszthely
Hévíz
Fenékpuszta
Balatonszentgyörgy
Zalavár
Balatonmagyaród
Kápolnapuszta
Kis-Balaton
Kányavári Island
Zala River
Pacsa
ZALA
To Zalaegerszeg (10km)
VESZPRÉM
Ajka
Pápa
Nyirád
Devecser
Sümeg
Zalaszentgrót
Celldömölk
VAS
Sárvár
Rába River
To Szombathely (25km)
E66
E71
E73
E661
M6
M7
LAKE BALATON REGION

for 21km to 70km. Children pay half-price, and return fares are marginally less than double the one-way fare. Bicycle transportation costs 770/900Ft one way/return.

Car ferries charge 480/415/200/710/1360Ft per adult/child/bicycle/motorcycle/car.

SIÓFOK

☎ 84 / pop 23,900

Siófok is officially known as 'Hungary's summer capital' – unofficially it's called 'Hungary's Ibiza'. Come July and August, nowhere else in the country parties as hard or stays up as late as this lakeside resort, which attracts an ever-increasing number of international DJs and their avid followers. Outside the summer months Siófok returns to relative normality, and is largely indistinguishable from the other resorts on the southern shore.

Orientation

Greater Siófok stretches for some 17km, as far as the resort of Balatonvilágos (once reserved exclusively for communist honchos) to the east and Balatonszéplak to the west. The dividing line between the so-called Aranypart, or Gold Coast, in the east, where most of the big hotels are, and the less-developed Silver Coast (Ezüstpart) to the west is the lake-draining Sió Canal, which runs in a southeasterly direction to the Danube River.

Szabadság tér, the centre of Siófok, is to the east of the canal and about 500m southeast of the ferry pier. The bus and train stations are in Millennium Park just off Fő utca, the main drag.

DISCOUNT CARDS

The **Balaton Card** (2700Ft) is a useful purchase if you intend to spend some time at the lake. Valid for one year, it provides discounts of anything between 10% and 100% on selected hotels, restaurants, museums, attractions, special events, sports-equipment rental, beach entry and public transport (including boat services). Cards are sold at all Tourinform offices; check www.balatoncard.com for online information.

In addition, various towns on the lake have their own discount cards; they are mentioned throughout the chapter.

Information

Main post office (Fő utca 186)

OTP bank (Szabadság tér 10/a) Has a currency-exchange machine and ATM.

Tourinform (☎ 310 117; tourinform@siofokportal.hu; Szabadság tér; ⏰ 8am-7pm Mon-Fri, 10am-7pm Sat & Sun mid-Jun–mid-Sep, 8am-4pm Mon-Fri, 9am-noon Sat mid-Sep–mid-Jun) Based in the old *víztorony* (water tower); very knowledgeable about Siófok.

Town website (www.siofok.hu) Info on the town.

Sights

There's not a whole lot to see of cultural or historical importance in a place where hedonism rules the roost. The **canal locks** system, which was partly built by the Romans in AD 292 and used extensively by the Turks in the 16th and 17th centuries, can be seen from Krúdy sétány, the walkway near the ferry pier, or Baross Bridge to the south. Nearby are the headquarters of the Hungarian navy. The tower on the western tip of the canal entrance is the **weather observatory** (Vitorlás utca) of the National Meteorological Service (Országos Meteorológiai Szolgálat).

If you walk north on narrow Hock János köz, you'll reach the **Imre Kálmán Museum** (☎ 311 287; Kálmán Imre sétány 5; adult/child 300/150Ft; ⏰ 9am-5pm Tue-Sun Apr-Oct, to 4pm Tue-Sun Nov-Mar). It is devoted to the life and works of the composer of popular operettas, Imre Kálmán, who was born in Siófok in 1882.

East of Szabadság tér in Oulu Park, Hungary's maverick architect Imre Makovecz strikes with his winged and 'masked' **Evangelist church** (Evangélikus templom; ⏰ services 10am Sun), which bears a strong resemblance to an Indonesian *garuda* (mythical bird).

For an overview of the town and lake beyond, climb the wooden **Water Tower** (☎ 310 117; Szabadság tér; adult/child 200/100Ft; ⏰ 8am-7pm Mon-Fri, 10am-7pm Sat & Sun mid-Jun–mid-Sep, 8am-4pm Mon-Fri, 9am-noon Sat mid-Sep–mid-Jun). It currently houses Tourinform and was built in 1912.

Activities

Nagy Strand (adult/child 750/500Ft; ⏰ varies), Siófok's 'Big Beach', takes centre stage on Petőfi sétány; there's often free concerts here on summer evenings. There are many more 'managed' **swimming** areas along the Gold and Silver Coasts that cost around the same as Nagy Strand.

There are **rowing** and **sailing boats** for hire at various locations along the lake, including the

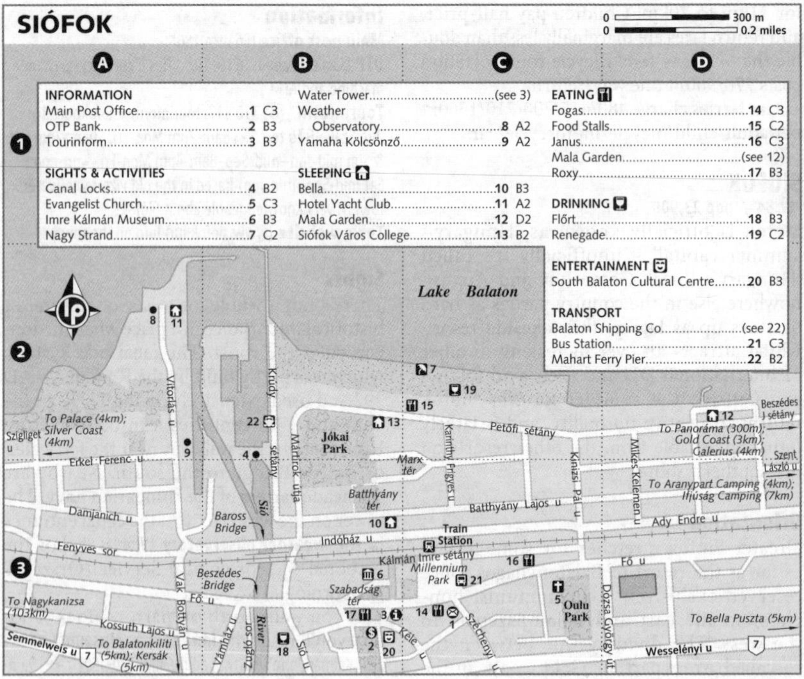

Nagy Strand. **Lake cruises** run from late May to mid-September, generally daily at 10am, 11.30am, 1pm, 2.30pm, 4pm and 5.30pm. There are additional cruises at 11am, 2pm and 4pm daily from late April to late May.

Siófok's newest attraction, **Galerius** (☎ 506 580; www.galerius-furdo.hu, in Hungarian; Szent László utca 183; swimming pools adult/child 2000/1300Ft, sauna & swimming pools adult 2300Ft; 🕑 9am-9pm), is located 4km east of downtown Siófok. It offers a plethora of indoor thermal pools, saunas and massages.

A good way to see the town is on two wheels. **Yamaha Kölcsönző** (☎ 06 20 945 1279; Vitorlás utca; 🕑 mid-May–mid-Oct), on the canal's western bank, hires bicycles for 1500Ft per day and mopeds for 4000Ft.

Horse riding is another popular pastime in these parts; **Kersák** (☎ 322 819; Töltényi utca 2/b) in nearby Balatonkiliti has lessons for €10 per hour, as does **Bella Puszta** (☎ 352 698; www.bellapuszta.hu; Verebes dűlő 14-18) east of Siófok centre.

Sleeping

Siófok is one of the few places on the lake where you will have trouble finding accommodation from late July to August – during this time it is worth booking ahead. Also note that many small establishments only open during this time. Prices quoted here are for July and August.

Tourinform can help find you a private room (€12 to €20 per person) and an apartment for slightly more. Singles are rare and those staying only one or two nights are generally unwelcome; if you want to do it alone, check for *'Zimmer frei'* signs along Erkel Ferenc utca and Damjanich utca on the Silver Coast, and Petőfi sétány and Beszédes József sétány on the Gold Coast.

BUDGET

There are over two-dozen camp sites on Balaton's southern shore, and Siófok has nine, most with bungalows sleeping up to four people. They are open from May to September; the highest rates apply during most of July and August.

Ifjúság Camping (☎ 352 571; www.balatontourist.hu; Pusztatorony tér 1; camp sites 1350Ft, bungalows 2600-7500Ft; 🕑 late Apr–mid-Sep) This place in Sóstó, 7km east of Siófok between tiny 'Salt Lake' and Lake Balaton, is good for fishing, swimming and taking it easy. Choose shady camp sites or simple wooden cabins with shared facilities that sleep two to four people.

Aranypart Camping (☎ 353 399; www.balatontourist.hu; Szent László utca 183-185; camp sites 1800Ft, bungalows 5100-14,000Ft; late Apr–mid-Sep) Around 4km east of the centre in Balatonszabadi is this camping ground with its own beach and restaurant. Bungalows are basically small, well-kept apartments, and there is some tree cover for camping.

Siófok Város College (☎ 312 244; www.siofokvaroskollegiuma.sulinet.hu; Petőfi sétány 1; dm 2530Ft) Situated close to the action in central Siófok, it's hard to beat this college accommodation for price and location. Rooms are very basic, and with all that partying going on at the nearby beach don't expect to get much sleep. There are a handful of rooms available year-round.

MIDRANGE

Bella (☎ 510 078; www.siofokbella.hu; Batthyány Lajos utca 14/a; r 11,500-29,500Ft) Occupying one half of a large villa, Bella provides its guests with modern, compact apartments that have kitchens and balconies, and is on a quiet street within easy walking distance of the beach. Rates are substantially cheaper outside July and August.

Hotel Yacht Club (☎ 311 161; www.hotel-yachtclub.hu; Vitorlás utca 14; s/d €58/92) Overlooking the harbour is this excellent little hotel, with cosy rooms, some of which sport balconies overlooking the lake. Its new wellness centre has whirlpools, saunas and a private sunbathing terrace. Bicycles can be rented.

Panoráma (☎ 311 638; www.panoramahotel-siofok.hu; Beszédes József sétány 80; s/d/apt €76/95/166) It doesn't look like much from the outside, but Panoráma comes up trumps where it counts. Rooms are well designed and modern, and most come with a small, private balcony. Its newly fitted wellness centre features an array of saunas and even a cave-bath, and there is a reasonable restaurant on-site.

TOP END

our pick **Mala Garden** (☎ 506 687; www.malagarden.hu; Petőfi sétány 15/a; r 18,900-26,900Ft) Most of Siófok's accommodation options pale in comparison to this gorgeous boutique hotel. It's all very reminiscent of Bali, with Indonesian art lining the walls, a small, manicured flower garden at the rear of the hotel, and a quality restaurant serving Asian cuisine downstairs. Rooms are immaculate and bedecked in pleasing shades of orange, brown and red, and there are enough pillows for a group pillow fight. All in all, Mala Garden does a wonderful job of creating a tranquil setting.

Eating

Jaunus (☎ 312 546; Fő utca 93; coffee 250-500Ft; mid-Mar–Oct) Take a break in the cafe of the newly renovated Janus Hotel. Its lovely conservatory features wrought-iron furniture reminiscent of yesteryear, and the cake selection is extensive.

Roxy (☎ 506 573; Szabadság tér; mains 990-3000Ft) This pseudo-rustic restaurant-pub on busy Szabadság tér attracts diners with its wide range of international cuisine and surprisingly imaginative Hungarian mains. Don't arrive too late in the evening or you'll be hard pressed to find a table.

Fogas (☎ 311 405; Fő utca 184; mains 1000-2500Ft; Mar-Oct) Locals swear by Fogas for its fish dishes, and the large selection is indeed hard to beat. However, aside from the sunny conservatory, Fogas' decor is fairly uninspiring.

our pick **Mala Garden** (☎ 506 687; Petőfi sétány 15/a; mains 1400-4000Ft) It's taken a while, but Siófok finally has a top-class international eatery. Carrying on the theme of the hotel in which it's located, the restaurant's menu features plenty of Asian influences, including delectable Thai noodles, spicy Thai vegetable soups, and the best chicken *tikka masala* in provincial Hungary. The global cuisine doesn't stop there though – Uruguay steaks, sea bass, goose liver and homemade pastas are just some of the myriad choices. Pick a wicker chair or comfy couch indoors, or a terrace table near the lake, and enjoy.

For quick eats, attack one of a bunch of **food stalls** (Petőfi sétány) by the Nagy Strand.

Drinking & Entertainment

South Balaton Cultural Centre (☎ 311 855; Fő tér 2) Siófok's main cultural venue stages concerts, dance performances and plays.

Siófok is the region's club central. In the summer months the best of the town's bars are located on Nagy Strand; up to four free concerts a week are also held here in July and August.

The turnover rate of bars and clubs is high, but the following manage to attract punters year after year:

Flőrt (☎ 06 20 333 3303; www.flort.hu; Sió utca 4) Well-established club with trippy light shows, carnival girls and queues. DJs perform here once a month outside the high season.

Palace (☎ 351 295; www.palace.hu; Deák Ferenc utca 2) Hugely popular club on the Silver Coast, with Hungarian DJs on Friday and their international counterparts on Saturday. Accessible by free bus from outside Tourinform between 9pm and 5am daily from May to mid-September.

Renegade (☎ 06 20 317 3304; Petőfi sétány 9) Wild pub near the beach where table-top dancing and live music are commonplace.

Getting There & Away

BOAT

Between April to June and September to October, four daily Mahart ferries run between Siófok and Balatonfüred, two of which carry on to Tihany. Up to eight ferries follow the same route in July and August. See also Getting Around (p195) for more details about other routes and frequencies for ferry services.

BUS

Buses serve a lot of destinations from Siófok, but compared with train connections, they're not very frequent.

Destination	Price	Duration	Km	Frequency
Budapest	1770Ft	1½-2½hr	108	5 daily
Hévíz	1350Ft	1¾-2hr	86	up to 3 daily
Kaposvár	1350Ft	2hr	85	10 Mon-Sat
Keszthely	1200Ft	1¾hr	78	up to 3 daily
Pécs	2040Ft	3hr	133	3-6 daily
Szekszárd	1500Ft	2¼hr	97	8 daily
Veszprém	750Ft	1¼hr	48	7 daily

TRAIN

Trains to Nagykanizsa pass through all of the resorts on the southern edge of the lake. The following destinations can be reached by train from Siófok.

Destination	Price	Duration	Km	Frequency
Budapest	1770Ft	2hr	115	8 daily
Kaposvár	1500Ft	3½hr	100	4 daily
Nagykanizsa	1770Ft	2hr	106	14 daily
Székesfehérvár	750Ft	40-60min	48	hourly

Getting Around

Leaving from the bus station, just outside the train station, buses 1 and 2 run to the Silver Coast and Gold Coast, respectively. There are also **taxis** (☎ 317 713) around town; Tourinform can also order one for you.

KESZTHELY

☎ 83 / pop 21,400

At the very western end of Lake Balaton sits Keszthely, a city of grand town houses that exudes a gentle ambience far removed from the tourist hot spots on the lake. Its small, shallow beaches are well suited to families, and there are enough accommodation options to suit most holiday-makers. Of its handful of museums and historical buildings, nothing tops the Festetics Palace, a lavish baroque home fit for royalty.

History

The Romans built a fort at Valcum (now Fenékpuszta), around 5km to the south, and their road north to the colonies at Sopron and Szombathely is today's Kossuth Lajos utca. The town's former fortified monastery and Franciscan church on Fő tér were strong enough to repel the Turks in the 16th century.

In the middle of the 18th century, Keszthely and its surrounds (including Hévíz) came into the possession of the Festetics family, who were progressives and reformers very much in the tradition of the Széchenyis. In fact, Count György Festetics (1755–1819), who founded Europe's first agricultural college, the Georgikon, here in 1797, was an uncle of István Széchenyi.

Orientation

The centre of town is Fő tér, from where Kossuth Lajos utca, lined with colourful old houses, runs to the north (pedestrian only) and south. The bus and train stations are opposite one another near the lake at the end of Mártírok útja. From the stations, follow Mártírok útja up the hill, then turn north into Kossuth Lajos utca to reach the centre. The ferry docks at a stone pier not far east of the train and bus stations.

Information

Main post office (Kossuth Lajos utca 46-48)

OTP bank (Kossuth Lajos utca 38) Has an ATM and exchange machine.

Tourinform (☎ 314 144; keszthely@tourinform.hu; Kossuth Lajos utca 28; 🕑 9am-8pm Mon-Fri, to 6pm Sat mid-Jun–mid-Sep, 9am-5pm Mon-Fri, to 12.30pm Sat mid-Sep–mid-Jun) An excellent source of information on Keszthely and the entire Balaton area. Provides free maps of the town and has expensive internet access (600Ft per 30 minutes).

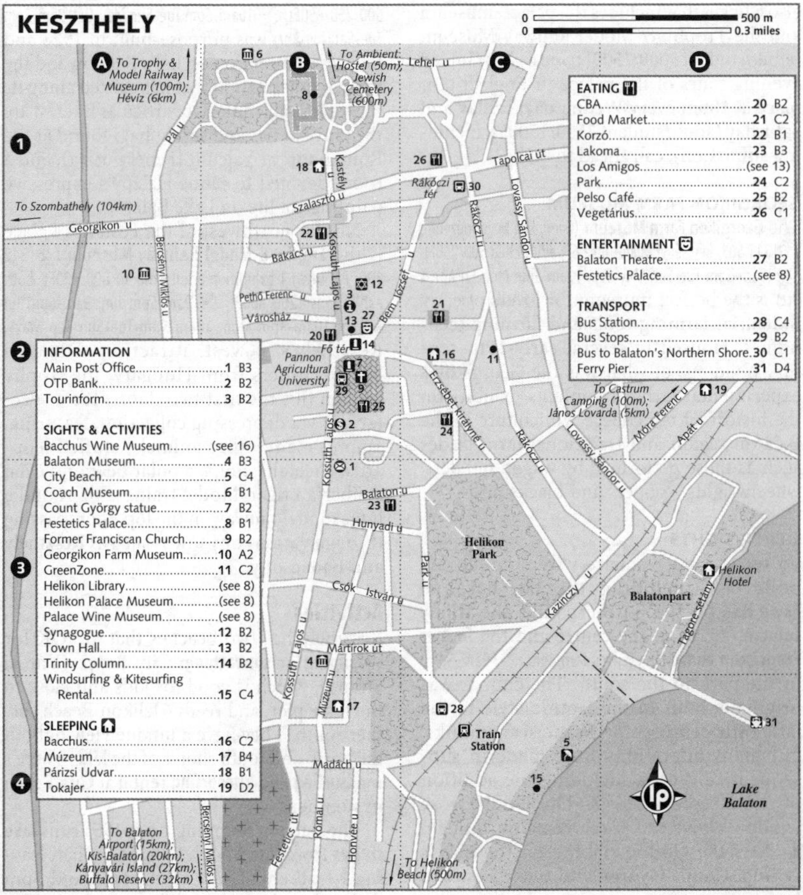

Sights

FESTETICS PALACE

The **Festetics Palace** (Festetics kastély; ☎ 312 190; Kastély utca 1; adult/student 1650/800Ft; 🕑 9am-6pm Jul-Aug, 10am-4pm Mon, to 5pm Tue-Sun Sep-Jun), built in 1745 and extended 150 years later, contains 100 rooms in two sprawling wings. The 19th-century northern wing houses a music school, city library and conference centre; the **Helikon Palace Museum** (Helikon Kastélymúzeum) and the palace's greatest treasure, the renowned **Helikon Library** (Helikon Könyvtár) are in the baroque south wing.

The museum's rooms (about a dozen in all, each in a different colour scheme) are full of portraits, bric-a-brac and furniture, much of it brought from England by Mary Hamilton, a duchess who married one of the Festetics men in the 1860s. The library is known for its 100,000-volume collection, but just as impressive is the golden oak shelving and furniture carved in 1801 by local craftsman János Kerbl. Also worth noting are the Louis XIV Salon with its stunning marquetry, the rococo music room and the private chapel (1804). If you want to get the most out of your visit, pick up an audio guide (500Ft) from the ticket desk.

Behind the palace in a separate building is the **Coach Museum** (adult/student 800/400Ft; 🕑 9am-6pm Jul-Aug, 10am-4pm Mon, to 5pm Tue-Sun Sep-Jun), which is filled with coaches and sleighs fit for royalty. To visit both the palace and coach museum costs 2000/1000Ft per adult/child; there is also a ticket that includes the palace, museum and the Trophy & Model Railway Museum (adult/student 3000/1500Ft; see right). Guided evening tours of the palace in English take place at 10pm every Wednesday, Friday and Saturday (adult/student 2500/1500Ft, including admission); call ahead to book.

GEORGIKON FARM MUSEUM

The **Georgikon Farm Museum** (Georgikon Majormúzeum; ☎ 311 563; Bercsényi Miklós utca 67; adult/child 500/250Ft; ⏰ 10am-5pm Tue-Sun May-Sep, 10am-5pm Mon-Fri Apr & Oct) is the perfect museum for lovers of early industrial farming tools and farming techniques. Housed in several early-19th-century buildings of what was the Georgikon's experimental farm, it contains exhibits on the history of the college, viniculture in the Balaton region and traditional farm trades such as those performed by wagon builders, wheelwrights, coopers and blacksmiths.

OTHER SIGHTS

Fő tér is a busy square with some lovely buildings, including the late-baroque **Town Hall** on the northern side, the **Trinity Column** (1770) in the centre and the **former Franciscan church** (Ferences templom; ⏰ 9am-6pm) in the park to the south. The church was originally built in the Gothic style in the late 14th century for Franciscan monks, but many alterations were made in subsequent centuries, including the addition of the steeple in 1898. The Gothic rose window above the porch remains, though, as does the Gothic ribbing on the nave's ceiling. Count György and other Festetics family members are buried in the crypt below. The Count is further honoured by a larger-than-life **statue** of the great man in front of the church.

Before WWII Keszthely's Jewish community numbered 1000; at the end of the war it had dropped to 170. Today at most 50 Jews live in the town and attend services at the **synagogue** (Kossuth Lajos utca 22), located behind the Pethö House. It's not possible to visit the interior outside of service times, but you can wander the peaceful Bible Garden at the rear from 5pm to 6pm on Friday. Further evidence of the town's Jewish community can be found at the largely forgotten **Jewish cemetery** (Goldmark karoly utca 33; ⏰ 10am-4pm Sun-Fri), north of the palace.

The **Balaton Museum** (☎ 312 351; www.balatonimuzeum.hu; Múzeum utca 2; adult/child/family 500/250/850Ft; ⏰ 10am-6pm Tue-Sun May-Oct, 9am-5pm Tue-Sat Nov-Apr) was purpose-built in 1928 and focuses its attention on Lake Balaton and the human inhabitation that has existed along its shores for millennia. Of particular interest are the gravestones and sarcophagi found at the Roman fort at Valcum (Fenékpuszta), and a room devoted to János Halápy's expressive paintings of life on Lake Balaton.

Not far northwest of the Festetics Palace is the **Trophy & Model Railway Museum** (☎ 312 190; Pál utca; 1 exhibition adult/student 800/400Ft, both exhibitions 1200/600Ft; ⏰ 9am-5pm Jun, 9am-6pm Jul & Aug, 10am-3pm Mon, 10am-5pm Tue-Sun Sep-May), Keszthely's newest attraction. Donated by six hunters from Hungary, the trophy section fills the first two floors. It's a spectacular yet depressing collection, featuring, among many other animals, stuffed leopards, cheetahs, lions, a polar bear and even a Siberian tiger. Model trains whiz round a huge model railway on the top floor, passing through various tiny towns such as Keszthely and Badacsony.

Activities

Keszthely has two beaches that are OK for **swimming** or **sunbathing**: City Beach (Városi Strand), which is good for kids and close to the ferry pier, and reedy Helikon Beach further south. They have a unique view of both the north and south shores of the lake. There's **windsurfing** and **kitesurfing** rental at City Beach in summer.

The Balaton Shipping Co (p195) runs **lake cruises** from late March to late October, leaving Keszthely pier at 11am, 1pm and 3pm daily. There is an extra sailing at 5pm in May and September, and hourly sailings in July and August.

There are several horse-riding schools in the area, including **János Lovarda** in Sömögye-dűlő, northeast of Keszthely; ask at Tourinform for directions as it doesn't have a phone.

The 210km Balaton cycle path passes through Keszthely, and there is a 4km path that connects the town with Hévíz. Rent bicycles from **GreenZone** (☎ 315 463; Rákóczi utca 15; 3hr/1 day 800/2000Ft; ⏰ 9am-6pm Mon-Fri, to 1pm Sat).

For wine tastings, try the **Bacchus Wine Museum** (☎ 510 450; Erzsébet királyné utca 18; admission free, 6 wines 2200Ft; ⏰ 11am-11pm) or the **Palace Wine Museum** (☎ 312 190; Kastély utca 1; admission 600Ft, guided tour with wine tastings 2500Ft; ⏰ 9am-6pm Jul-Aug, 10am-4pm Mon, to 5pm Tue-Sun Sep-Jun).

Festivals & Events

The biggest annual cultural event in Keszthely is the **Balaton Festival**, featuring music and street theatre, held throughout May.

Sleeping

Tourinform can help find private rooms (from 3000Ft per person), otherwise, strike out on your own (particularly along Móra Ferenc utca) and keep an eye out for signs saying *'szoba kiadó'* or *'Zimmer frei'* (Hungarian and German, respectively, for 'room for rent').

BUDGET

Castrum Camping (☎ 312 120; www.castrum-group.hu; Móra Ferenc utca 48; camp sites per adult/child/tent 1200/900/1800Ft; Apr-Oct;) Northeast of the bus and train stations, this large camping ground is green and spacious, but it seems to prefer caravans to tents. Unfortunately you have to cross the railway tracks to reach the lake.

Ambient Hostel (☎ 06 30 460 3536; www.hostel-accommodation.fw.hu; Sopron utca 10; dm from 2900Ft, d 6800Ft;) Only a short walk north of the palace ground is this new hostel. It has basic, cheap dorm rooms, each of which comes with its own ensuite bathroom. Ambient also has a colourful, modern roadside cafe, and laundry service is available from 3pm to 5pm from Monday to Friday.

Múzeum (☎ 313 182; Múzeum utca 3; s/d 4000/8000Ft) Ignore the effervescent smell of stale air and dog on entering – rooms in this cute yellow cottage are well-aired and very clean, and the whole place has a homey feel. It's an easy walk to the bus and train stations.

MIDRANGE

Párizsi Udvar (☎ 311 202; parizsiudvar@freemail.hu; Kastély utca 5; d/tr/apt 9400/11,400/15,000Ft) There's no closer accommodation to Festetics Palace than Párizsi Udvar. Rooms are a little too big to be cosy, but they're well kept and face onto a sunny inner courtyard (a corner of which is taken over by a daytime restaurant).

Tokajer (☎ 319 875; www.pensiontokajer.hu; Apát utca 21; s/d €33/50, apt from €58;) Spread over four buildings in a quiet area of town, Tokajer has slightly dated rooms, but they're still in good condition and some have a balcony and kitchen. Added extras include three pools, free use of bicycles and the fitness room, and a mini wellness centre.

Bacchus (☎ 510 450; www.bacchushotel.hu; Erzsébet királyné utca 18; s/d/apt 12,300/16,500/24,800Ft) Bacchus' central position and immaculate rooms make it a popular choice with travellers. Equally pleasing is its atmospheric cellar, which is divided between a fine restaurant and a wine museum (opposite).

Eating & Drinking

Pelso Café (☎ 315 415; Fő tér; coffee & cake from 290Ft, cocktails around 900Ft; 9am-9pm) This modern two-level cafe at the southern end of the main square does decent coffee and cake, has a selection of teas from around the world, and attracts both young and old. However, it has no Hungarian beer.

Korzó (☎ 311 785; Kossuth Lajos utca 7; cakes around 350Ft) Korzó is one of the few cafes worthy of your attention on pedestrian Kossuth Lajos utca. It's a simple place with street seating, but the cakes are divine and the music thankfully not too intrusive.

Vegetárius (☎ 311 023; Rákóczi tér 3; mains 460-1000Ft; 11am-4pm Mon-Fri) It may have changed its name, but this small vegetarian restaurant down the hill from the palace has buckets of good energy and healthy pickings during the midweek lunch-hour rush. Daily menus go for anything between 460Ft and 920Ft.

Lakoma (☎ 313 129; Balaton utca 9; mains 1000-2600Ft) With a good vegetarian and fish selection (for Hungarian-restaurant standards), grill/roast specialities and a back garden that transforms itself into a leafy dining area in the summer months, it's hard to go wrong with Lakoma.

Park (☎ 311 654; Vörösmarty utca 1/a; mains 1500-3100Ft) The orange decor might be too much for sensitive folk and the service can be a little haphazard, but Park does some damn fine Hungarian cuisine. If you're a party of two, you can't go wrong with the grilled platter, and if you can fit in a Drunken Monk, the house dessert, at the end, you're doing better than us.

Los Amigos (☎ 312 137; Fő tér 2; mains 1900-3000Ft) Give your digestive system a break from Hungarian and try Los Amigos. Its menu is filled with Mexican classics, and vegetarian choices abound. If your meal doesn't have the crispy topping you desire, they'll bring out a piping hot iron to do the job, and there are 16 varieties of tequila to wash it all down.

Keszthely's lively **food market** (7am-2pm Mon-Sat) combines the best and worst of

Hungary's markets, with homemade honey and jam alongside T-shirts with Native Indians on Harleys. Even if you don't need a supermarket, take a look at the beautiful stained-glass windows of the **CBA** (Kossuth Lajos utca 35) on the main street.

Entertainment

The biweekly *ZalaEst* booklet, available from Tourinform, is a good source of information on entertainment activities in Keszthely.

Balaton Theatre (☎ 515 230; www.balatonszinhaz.hu, in Hungarian; Fő tér 3) Glean information on the town's cultural events and catch the latest in performances at this theatre on the main square.

Festetics Palace (Festetics kastély; ☎ 312 190; Kastély utca 1) Operetta concerts are held every Thursday at 8pm (tickets from 5750Ft) throughout the year in the music hall of the palace.

Getting There & Away

AIR

Balaton Airport (SOB; ☎ 83-354 256; www.flybalaton.hu), 15km southwest of Keszthely at Sármellék, receives Ryanair flights from Dusseldorf, Frankfurt and London Standsted. There is no public transport between the airport and Keszthely, but transfers can be arranged with **FlyBalaton Airport Transfer** (☎ 554 055; www.balatonairporttransfer.com; 1 way/return €6/10).

BUS

Keszthely is well served by buses. Some, including those to Hévíz, Nagykanizsa and Sümeg, can be boarded at the bus stops in front of the Franciscan church on Fő tér. Catch buses to the lake's northern shore (Badacsony, Nagyvázsony and Tapolca) along Tapolcai út.

Destination	Price	Duration	Km	Frequency
Badacsony	450Ft	35min	27	8 daily
Budapest	2780Ft	2½-4hr	190	7 daily
Hévíz	200Ft	15min	8	half-hourly
Nagykanizsa	900Ft	1½hr	52	6 daily
Pécs	2290Ft	3½hr	152	up to 4 daily
Sümeg	525Ft	50min	31	hourly
Tapolca	450Ft	35-60min	28	hourly
Veszprém	1200Ft	1¾hr	77	hourly

TRAIN

From late June to late August, **MÁV Nostalgia** (www.mavnosztalgia.hu) runs a vintage steam-train from Keszthely to Badacsonytomaj (one way 1170Ft, 1¾ hours) at 9.50am every Tuesday, Thursday and Saturday, returning at 2.53pm. Verify this service on the website before making plans.

Keszthely has train links to the following destinations.

Destination	Price	Duration	Km	Frequency
Badacsony	600Ft	1hr	39	8 daily (change at Tapolca required)
Budapest	2780Ft	3½-4hr	190	6 daily
Székesfehérvár	2040Ft	2¾hr	123	7 daily
Szombathely	2040Ft	2hr	126	2 daily
Tapolca	375Ft	30min	25	hourly

Getting Around

Buses run from the train and bus stations to the Franciscan church on Fő tér, but unless there's one waiting on your arrival it's just as easy to walk. You can also make a booking for a **taxi** (☎ 333 666).

AROUND KESZTHELY

Around 20km southwest of Keszthely is **Kis-Balaton** (Little Balaton), a small lake far removed from the hustle and bustle of its bigger cousin. The lake and the marshes that spread eastwards from it are a haven for bird life, and both fall under the protection of the **Balaton Uplands National Park** (Felvidéki Nemzeti Park; www.bfnpi.hu). The **Kis-Balaton House** (☎ 87-710 002; 9am-noon, 1-6pm Tue-Sun Mar-Oct), in the village of Zalavár near the northern end of the lake, has information on the area.

Tiny **Kányavári Island** (parking per hr/day 200/600Ft), near the lake's eastern edge and accessible via a wooden footbridge, is one of the better spots to view avian life; there are bird-watching towers and picnic tables scattered its length and breadth. At the southern end of Kis-Balaton is a **Buffalo Reserve** (☎ 87-555 291; adult/child/student 500/200/400Ft; 9am-6pm), which is home to some 200 water buffalo; the best time to visit is late afternoon, when the buffalo gather near the reserve headquarters. The reserve is 3km south of Balatonmagyaród.

Despite there being hourly buses from Keszthely to Zalavár (300Ft, 30 to 45 minutes, 18km) and two to Balatonmagyaród from Monday to Saturday (450Ft, 30 to 45 minutes, 26km), you're better off exploring the region under your own steam.

HÉVÍZ

☎ 83 / pop 4500

Hévíz is the most famous of Hungary's spa towns, and rightly so, for it is home to Gyógy-tó, Europe's largest thermal lake. It could be argued that Hévíz is the slowest town in the country, partly because the average visitor age is well over 60, but mostly because it's impossible to move quickly after a dip in the lake's therapeutic waters. A day here is essential for anyone visiting the Lake Balaton region.

Orientation

The centre of Hévíz is Park Wood (Parkerdő) and its thermal lake. The bus station (on Deák tér) is a few steps from the northern entrance to the lake; the town's small commercial centre lies to the west of the bus station. Kossuth Lajos utca, where most of the big hotels are located, forms the western boundary of Park Wood.

Information

Caffe Machiato (Széchenyi utca 7; 8am-10pm) Internet access (per hour 300Ft) and bike rental (two hours/one day 1000/1900Ft).

OTP bank (Erzsébet királynő utca 7) Has an ATM and money-exchange machine.

Post office (Kossuth Lajos utca 4)

Tourinform (☎ 540 131; Rákóczi utca 2; 9am-6pm Mon-Fri, 10am-7pm Sat & Sun mid-Jun–Aug, 9am-5pm Mon-Fri, 10am-4pm Sat May–mid-Jun, Sep & Oct, 9am-4pm Mon-Fri, 10am-3pm Sat Dec-Apr) Friendly and informed, it provides free maps and brochures.

Activities

The **Thermal Lake** (Gyógy-tó; ☎ 501 700; www.spaheviz.hu; 3hr/5hr/whole day 1900/2500/2900Ft, rubber-ring hire 500Ft, cabin hire 1200Ft; 8am-7pm Jun-Aug, 8am-6pm May & Sep, 8am-5pm Apr & Oct, 8.30am-4pm Mar & Nov, 9am-4pm Dec-Feb) is an astonishing sight: a surface of 4.4 hectares in the Park Wood, covered for most of the year in pink and white lotuses. The source is a spring spouting from a crater some 40m below ground that disgorges up to 80 million litres of warm water a day, renewing itself every 48 hours or so. The surface temperature averages 33°C and never drops below 22°C in winter, allowing bathing throughout the year, even when there's ice on the fir trees of Park Wood.

A covered bridge leads to the thermal lake's newly renovated *fin-de-siècle* **central pavilion**, which contains a small buffet, sun chairs, showers, changing rooms and steps down into the lake. Catwalks and piers fan out from the central pavilion to sun decks and a second pavilion where massage treatments are offered. You can swim protected beneath the pavilions and piers or swim out into the lake and rest on wooden planks secured to the lake's bottom. There are some piers along the shore for sunbathing as well.

If you're looking for treatments, head to the **indoor spa** (☎ 501 700; www.spaheviz.hu; Park utca; 7am-7pm), which offers every kind of thermal remedy imaginable.

Sleeping

Hévíz has an abundance of sleeping options, and the list grows longer every year. Most hotels have specials for stays of one week or more, and the rates vary depending on the season. Tourinform can provide you with a list of private rooms and apartments in town (€20 to €25 per double), and can also help you find something suitable. You'll see signs reading *'Zimmer frei'* and *'szoba kiadó'* (meaning 'room for rent') along Kossuth Lajos utca, Zrínyi utca and Vörösmarty utca, where you can make your own deals directly.

Castrum Camping (☎ 343 198; www.castrum-group.hu; Tó-part; camp sites per adult/child/tent 1250/1000/1800Ft; pension s/d 7250/10,750Ft; year-round) Only a short walk from the lake is this very green and very large camp site, with a range of accommodation options and Fort Knox–like security. Bicycles can be rented for 200/1000Ft per hour/day.

Villa Fortuna (☎ 343 179; www.fortunavilla.hu; Fortuna utca 1; s/d 9350/12,100Ft, apt from 14,300Ft; ⊠ 💻 🅿) On the hill above Hévíz central is yellow Fortuna, a bright, new villa with large, colourful rooms overlooking the town. Staff are professional and helpful, and there is a spa and sauna for guest use. The buffet breakfast is extra (1100Ft), but it will keep you going all day long.

Hotel Sante (☎ 540 133; www.hotelsante.eu; Nyírfa utca 1; s/d 11,000/16,000Ft; ⊠ 💻 🅿) Like Fortuna, Sante is a new generation of *pension* in Hévíz, where quality and service are (finally) seen as important. The turreted villa features modern, spacious rooms with a touch of class to them, and there is a small wellness centre on-site.

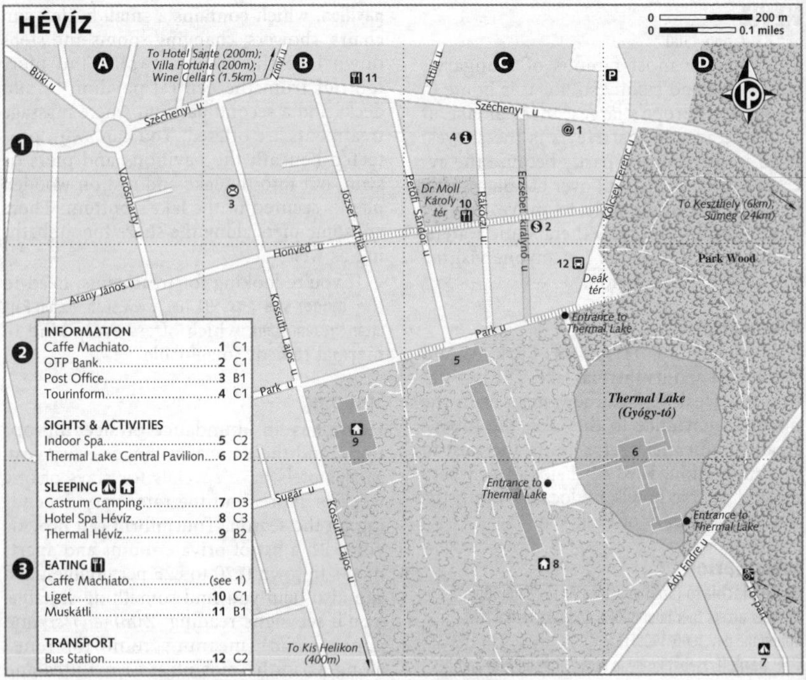

Kis Helikon (☎ 340 754; www.kishelikonhotel.hu; Kossuth Lajos utca 72; s/d €47/74) Kis Helikon is an attractive stone villa with large, modern rooms, some with balcony and separate lounge. The hotel has an above-average restaurant and its own wellness centre. Prices include breakfast.

Thermal Hévíz (☎ 889 400; heviz.reservation@danubiushotels.com; Kossuth Lajos utca 9-11; s €71-93, d €114-158;) From the outside it looks like it should be put down, but this old communist-era eyesore doesn't appear anywhere near as bad from the inside. Its 200-odd rooms are in good condition and it has indoor and outdoor pools, a sauna, a solarium, a gym and tennis courts.

Hotel Spa Hévíz (☎ 501 708; www.spaheviz.hu; Dr Schulhof Vilmos sétány 1; s/d €72/122;) Spa Hévíz is a recovery zone located in the Park Wood and within sight of the thermal lake. The rooms have been recently renovated to bring them into the 21st century, and some come with a balcony. Entry to the lake is included in the price, and you can also sooth those aching bones in the hotel's sauna and Jacuzzi.

Eating & Drinking

Considering its tourist pull, eating options in Hévíz are limited. In the centre of town, **Muskátli** (☎ 341 475; Széchenyi utca 30; mains 1300-2500Ft) does a good job of fish dishes and has a pretty roadside terrace, while **Liget** (Dr Moll Károly tér; pizza & mains 1200-2000Ft), which has hardly changed for years, serves standard Hungarian fare on its grand terrace.

Alternatively, you could avoid the centre and walk 15 to 20 minutes north to the town's vineyards and its cluster of **wine cellars** (Zrínyi utca). These simple eateries serve local wines and simple, tasty Hungarian food – a combination guaranteed to deliver a full stomach and light head. Many only open from 2pm or 3pm till 10pm and close from October to May.

Caffe Machiato (Széchenyi utca 7; 8am-10pm) is a modern cafe and cocktail bar that attracts a regular crowd under the age of 50.

Getting There & Away

Hévíz isn't on a train line, but buses travel east to Keszthely (200Ft, 15 minutes, 8km) almost every half-hour from stand 3 at the bus station. Buses also service the following destinations.

Destination	Price	Duration	Km	Frequency
Badacsony	525Ft	45min	35	6 daily
Balatonfüred	1200Ft	1½hr	75	7 daily
Budapest	3010Ft	2¾-4½hr	205	5 daily
Sopron	2040Ft	2½-3hr	129	1-2 daily
Sümeg	450Ft	35-55min	27	hourly
Veszprém	1500Ft	2hr	96	8 daily

A 4km bicycle path connects Hévíz with Keszthely, beginning near the southern entrance to the thermal lake. Bicycles can be rented from Caffe Machiato (p205) and Castrum Camping (p205).

BADACSONY

☎ 87 / pop 2250

Badacsony is a conglomeration of four towns: Badacsonylábdihegy, Badacsonyörs, Badacsonytördemic and Badacsonytomaj. But when Hungarians say Badacsony, they usually mean the little resort at the Badacsony train station, near the ferry pier southwest of Badacsonytomaj.

The area has been blessed by nature – it has the lake for swimming and boating, is backed by forested hills for walking and hiking, and has soil perfectly suited for wine production. It also has a laid-back feel and development has been slow to pick up here, making it just dandy for a couple of days of relaxation.

Orientation

Rte 71, the main road along the lake's northern shore, runs through Badacsony as Balatoni út; this is where the bus lets you off. The ferry pier is on the eastern side of this road; almost everything else is to the west. Above the village, several *pensions* and houses with private accommodation ring the base of the hill on Római út, which debouches into Balatoni út at Badacsonytomaj, a few kilometres to the northeast. Szegedi Róza utca branches off to the north from Római út and runs through the vineyards to the Kisfaludy House restaurant (p209) and the base of the hill.

Information

Miditourist (☎ 431 028; www.miditourist.hu) Egry sétány (Egry sétány 3; 🕑 9am-6pm May–mid-Oct); Park utca branch (Park utca 53; 🕑 8am-10pm May–mid-Oct) The main office in the centre of the village also exchanges money and provides internet access (per hr 500Ft).

OTP ATM (Park utca 4) Beside Tourinform.

Post office (Park utca 3; 🕑 8am-noon & 12.30-4pm Mon-Fri) Will exchange foreign currency.

Tourinform (☎ 431 046; badacsonytomaj@tourinform.hu; Park utca 6; 🕑 9am-7pm mid-Jun–mid-Sep, to 3pm Mon-Fri mid-Sep–mid-Jun) Informed staff with details on the region.

Town website (www.badacsony.com) Provides online details of activities and services in the region.

Sights & Activities

Most people either hit the beach or head for the hills, but on rainy days neither may be worthwhile. When it's wet consider visiting the town's two museums. The first, the **József Egry Museum** (☎ 431 044; Egry sétány 12; adult/child 500/250Ft; 🕑 10am-8pm Jul-Aug, to 4pm Tue-Sun May-Jun & Sep-Oct) is down by the lake and devoted to the Balaton region's leading painter. Many of Egry's (1883–1951) works powerfully capture the essence of village and fishing life on the lake through the use of strong, dark colours.

The second museum is located on the vine-covered slopes above Badacsony. The **Róza Szegedi House** (☎ 430 906; Szegedi Róza utca; adult/child 500/250Ft; 🕑 10am-6pm Tue-Sun May-Sep) belonged to the actress wife of the poet Sándor Kisfaludy from Sümeg and contains a tiny literature museum. Wine by the glass and bottle is for sale, but the grand views are free.

The dramatic slopes and vineyards above the town centre are sprinkled with little wine-press houses and 'folk baroque' cottages. Further up is the flat-topped forested massif which can be seen for miles around. Both make excellent destinations for walking tours, and if you'd like to get a running start on your hike, catch one of the open 4WDs marked 'Badacsony-hegy járat' (one way per person 750Ft). The driver will drop you off at the Kisfaludy House restaurant (p209), where a large map of the marked trails is posted by the car park. Or you might arm yourself in advance with a copy of Cartographia's *A Balaton* 1:40,000 topographical map (No 41; 990Ft).

Several paths lead to lookouts – at 437m, **Kisfaludy Lookout** (Kisfaludy kilátó) is the highest – and to neighbouring hills like **Gulács-hegy** (393m) and **Szentgyörgy-hegy** (415m) to the north. The landscape includes abandoned quarries and basalt towers that resemble organ pipes; of these, **Stone Gate** (Kőkapu) is the most dramatic. Several of the trails take you past **Rose Rock** (Rózsakő). A plaque explains an unusual tradition: 'If a lad and a lass sit here together with their backs to the lake, they will be married in a year.' Good luck – or regrets (as the case may be).

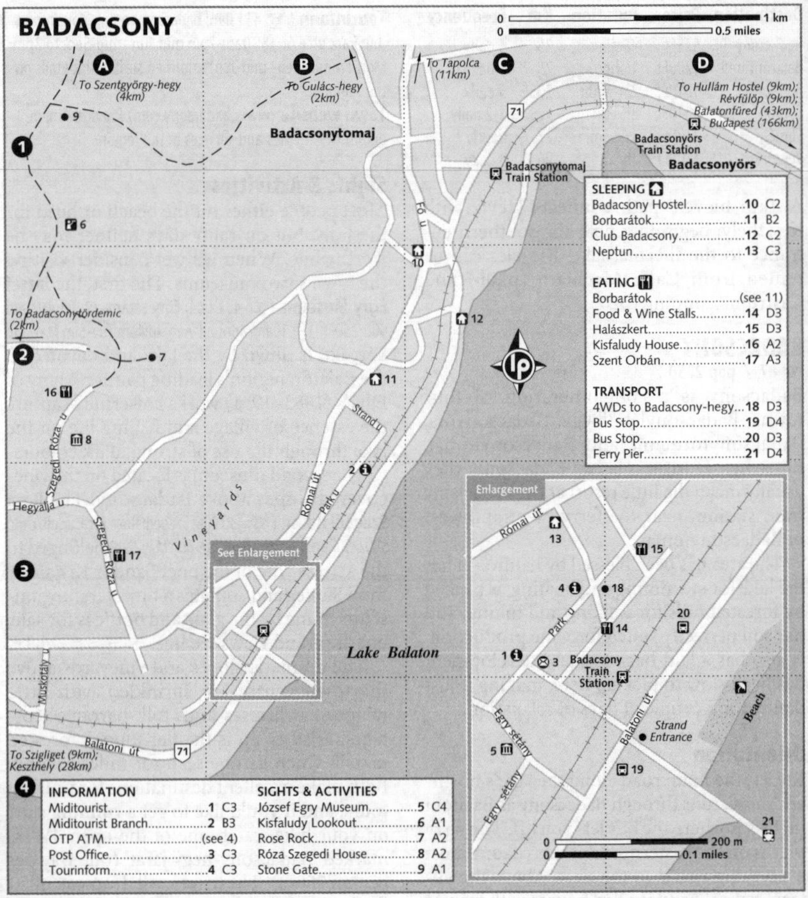

The postage-stamp-sized **beach** (adult/child 400/250Ft; May-Sep) is reedy; you would do better to head a few kilometres northeast to Badacsonytomaj or Badacsonyörs for a swim.

Lake cruises, run by the Balaton Shipping Co (p195), leave from Badacsony's pier at 4.30pm Tuesday, Thursday, Saturday and Sunday, and at 7.30pm Wednesday in July and August.

Sleeping

Miditourist has a list of private rooms for the entire Badacsony area, as does Tourinform; expect to pay anything between €20 and €30 per double. It generally costs more for stays of less than three nights. If you want to strike out on your own, there are places along Római út and Park utca and among the vineyards.

Note that much of Badacsony's accommodation opens weekends only from November to April – some close entirely over the winter period.

Badacsony Hostel (471 057; badacsonyfogado@t-online.hu; Római út 1; dm/d 2700/5400Ft;) Once the ugly duckling of Badacsony, this hostel has grown up and become a very pleasant spot to crash. Rooms are still quite bare-boned but they're clean and highly adequate, and there's a relaxing cafe downstairs run by very helpful staff. In summer, take advantage of the private garden at the rear.

our pick Hullám Hostel (☎ 463 089; www.balatonhostel.hu; Füredi út 6; dm/s/d €14/32/44; ⏱ mid-Mar–Sep; ☒ 💻) With a decidedly laid-back air, young staff happy to share a drink and a tale, and bright colours splashed across its basic rooms, Hullám appeals to those looking for a fun yet relaxed time. The newly renovated house at the rear, with three attic rooms, private terrace and separate bathroom, is perfect for families, and the secluded garden is inviting for all. Staff organise a film festival in mid-July, regular barbecues and parties, and can provide information on self-guided bicycle tours of the Kál Basin and lake. Facilities include bicycles for hire (four hours/one day 1500/2500Ft), laundry (1500Ft per load), internet access (250Ft per hour) and kitchen. Hullám is located 9km east of Badacsony in the township of Révfülöp.

Borbarátok (☎ 471 597; www.borbaratok.hu; Római út 78; s/d 6000/8500Ft) Rooms at this *pension* are above its restaurant and a little on the small side, but they have a semblance of charm, and some come with antique furniture. It's a short walk to the lake and there's the advantage of an extensive wine cellar.

Neptun (☎ 431 293; www.borbaratok.hu; Római út 156; s/d 8500/12,000Ft) This very central town house has basic rooms, some of which have views of the lake. Its large garden turns into a restaurant in summer, where breakfast can be taken (1200Ft).

Club Badacsony (☎ 471 040; www.badacsonyhotel.hu; Balatoni út 14; r €50-127; 🅟) Club Badacsony is regarded as an exclusive hotel in these parts, largely due to its private beach, small wellness centre and large restaurant. It is, however, starting to become quite dated, but it's a fine option if you're planning on staying in one place your entire holiday.

Eating

Halászkert (☎ 431 054; Park utca 5; mains 1000-2500Ft) If you can't make it up the hill and are looking for a range of fish dishes to choose from, head here. It may be crowded and touristy at times, but the food is top-rate.

> **BADACSONY CARD**
>
> The Badacsony Card, available free to guests at the region's hotels and *pensions*, provides discounts at restaurants, wine shops and bathing spots along the coast.

Borbarátok (☎ 471 597; Római út 78; mains 1500-2500Ft) A lively bar and restaurant where the food is served on wooden plates (adds to the flavour perhaps?). It's a good place to try a glass of Badacsony's premier white wines, Kéknyelű (Blue Stalk) or Szürkebarát (Pinot Gris).

Szent Orbán (☎ 431 382; Szegedi Róza utca 22; mains 1500-3000Ft) A combination of restaurant and wine tavern in the vineyards above Badacsony, Szent Orbán is a fine destination for anyone looking to sample above-par local produce alongside regional cuisine. The views from its vine-laced terrace are extensive, and it's not such a long stumble back down to the lake afterwards.

Kisfaludy House (☎ 431 016; Szegedi Róza utca 87; mains 1500-3000Ft; ⏱ to midnight Apr–mid-Oct) Perched high on the hill overlooking the vineyards and the lake is Kisfaludy House, a charming stone cottage built in 1798 that was once a press house of the Kisfaludy family. The food quality has slipped somewhat in the past few years, but the views are still as impressive as ever.

Food stalls with picnic tables dispensing sausage, fish soup, *lángos* (deep-fried dough) and *gyros* (meat skewers) line the pedestrian walkway between the train station and Park utca, and are intermingled with **wine stalls** (per glass 100Ft, per litre 500-700Ft) serving cheap plonk.

Getting There & Away

Up to eight buses connect Badacsony with Keszthely (450Ft, 35 minutes, 27km) daily; seven travel to Balatonfüred (675Ft, 50 minutes, 44km) and six to Hévíz (525Ft, 45 minutes, 35km). At least three daily go to Tapolca (300Ft, 30 minutes, 16km) and Veszprém (1050Ft, 1½ hours, 62km), and one to Budapest (2540Ft, three hours, 170km).

Badacsony is on the train line linking all the towns on Lake Balaton's northern shore with Budapest (2540Ft, 3½ hours, 170km, five daily). Révfülöp (250Ft, 17 minutes, 13km, 10 daily) and Tapolca (250Ft, 20 minutes, 14km, hourly) are easily reached by train; to get to Keszthely (600Ft, one hour, 39km) you must change at Tapolca.

See the Keszthely section (p204) for information on the MÁV Nostalgia steam-train service between the two towns, and p195 for details on passenger ferries that call at Badacsony.

THE KÁL BASIN

Only a few kilometres north of the lake in the heart of the Balaton Uplands National Park is a tiny pocket of rural paradise where time stands still. Of all the spots close to Lake Balaton, there is no better place to escape the hubbub of the lake and relax.

For such a small place (it covers around 120sq km), Kál Basin (Káli-medence) offers more variety than entire regions. Protected by forested hills and rocky basalt outcrops, it has a mild climate that has attracted settlers for centuries. Their endeavours can be seen in the form of crumbling ruins, forgotten monasteries and disused water mills. Vineyards cling to gently undulating hills, and much of the land is either farmed or home to horse studs. Of its handful of small villages, **Salföld** is the most interesting architecturally; its streets are lined with beautifully restored cottages with whitewashed walls and shingled roofs.

Geographically, the basin is unusual. Sandstone is commonplace here, and fields of boulders can be seen in the so-called **Seas of Stones** near the villages of Salföld, Kővágóörs and Szentbékkálla – look for the **swinging rock** at the latter. **Hegyes-tű** (Pointed Needle), at the eastern border of the basin, is a dramatic basalt formation, featuring 20m-high rock columns.

Preservation of Hungary's rural past is important to the locals. Many farmers only farm or grow organic produce native to the country, such as at **Kecskefarm** (☎ 87-707 601), 4km west of Kékkút village on the road to Tapolca; pick up Mangalica sausage and freshly made goat's cheese here. It, along with other farms, sells its wares at a Sunday morning **market** on the outskirts of Káptalantóti. At the **Salföld Ranch** (Salföld Major; ☎ 87-702 857; Salföld; shows adult/child 2600/2000Ft, zoo adult/child 450/200Ft; 🕑 8am-8pm Apr-Oct, to 5pm Nov-Mar) you can see cowboys ride 'five-in-hand', head out on horse treks (2500Ft per hour), and take a peek at Mangalica pigs and Racka sheep.

Surprisingly few hotels and *pensions* are located in the basin, but what you do find is generally top-notch.

our pick **Kővirág** (☎ 06 20 568 4724; www.kovirag.hu, in Hungarian; Fő út 9/a, Köveskál; s/d 6900/13,800Ft), in the back alleys of Köveskál, is a real gem. Its handful of apartments are housed in lovingly restored 19th-century cottages, which are in turn filled with folk-art furniture you normally see in museums. Each has a lounge, clay oven and small patio. Its restaurant is next door, in another of the basin's distinct stone cottages. Here you can dine on exceptional regional and seasonal cuisine, made using local produce, and sample wines from the surrounding vineyards.

The basin is best approached from Tapolca or Révfülöp and can be tackled as a day trip from either – as long as you have your own transport. Buses are infrequent but thankfully the basin is small enough to explore by bicycle. Pick up a bike, along with information on the basin, from Hullám Hostel (p209).

LAKE BALATON REGION

TAPOLCA

☎ 87 / pop 17,400

Despite being only 14km northwest of Badacsony, Tapolca is far removed from the touristy atmosphere of the resorts lining the Balaton. It's a good spot to bring the kids, who can run riot around the two small lakes at the centre of the town, or head underground to explore the Lake Cave. It's also a major transport hub, with buses and trains heading in all directions.

History

Tapolca has always been an important crossroads; under the Romans both the road between Rome and Aquincum and the road that linked Savaria (Szombathely) and Arrabona (Győr) passed through here. The Romans were followed by the Avars and, in turn, by the Slavs, who called the area Topulcha, from the Slavic root word for 'hot springs'. Tapolca's original source of wealth was wine – a legacy of the Romans – but it only really appeared on the map when the Bakony bauxite mining company set up its headquarters here.

Orientation

Tapolca's main thoroughfare is Deák Ferenc utca, which runs west from Hősök tere, where the bus station is located, and east to Fő tér, just north of Mill Lake. The train station is on Dózsa György út, about 1.2km southwest of the centre.

Information

OTP bank (Fő tér 2) Has an ATM and money-exchange machine.
Post office (Deák Ferenc utca 19)
Tourinform (☎ 510 777; tapolca@tourinform.hu; Fő tér 17; 9am-5pm Mon-Fri, to noon Sat mid-May–Aug, to 4pm Mon-Fri Sep–mid-May) Just north of Mill Lake.
Town website (www.tapolca.hu) Good introduction to the town and its sights.

Sights

MILL LAKE

Mill Lake (Malom-tó), just south of Fő tér, is reached through the gateway at No 8 or by walking south along Arany János utca. A small footbridge divides it in two: to the north is the **Big Lake** (Nagy-tó), which is about the size of a large pond, and to the south the **Little Lake** (Kis-tó). Created in the 18th century to power a water mill, the lake has been artificially fed since the nearby bauxite mine lowered the level of the water. But it remains a picturesque area, with pastel-coloured houses reflected in the water of the Big Lake, and a church and museum near the Little Lake. In the centre are the slowly turning blades of the mill house, which is now the Gabriella hotel (right).

The 18th-century baroque **Catholic church** (services only) on Templom-domb is rather dark and gloomy, but it does have a Gothic sanctuary. The vague outline of Tapolca's **medieval castle**, destroyed during the Turkish occupation, can be seen to the southwest. Nearby is the small **City Museum** (☎ 413 415; Templom-domb 15; adult/child 200/100Ft; noon-4pm Mon-Fri mid-Apr–mid-Oct), which has dusty displays on the town's history.

LAKE CAVE

Tapolca's second big attraction, the **Lake Cave** (Tavasbarlang; ☎ 412 579; Kisfaludy utca 3; adult/child/student 1000/700/850Ft; 9am-7pm Jul & Aug, 10am-5pm mid-Mar–Jun, Sep & Oct) is a short distance to the northeast. At only 250m long, it's a rather tiny cave, but over two-thirds of it lies under water (which has returned since mining ended here in 1990). Visitors can explore the underground lake using self-propelled boats.

Activities

There's a **thermal spa** and **open-air swimming pool** (Sümegi út; adult/child 750/500Ft; 10am-8pm Mon-Fri, 9am-8pm Sat & Sun May-Sep) a good 2km northwest of the centre; look for it tucked in behind Tapolca's sports centre.

Sleeping & Eating

There's no need to overnight in Tapolca with the lake and its attractions so close, but if you find yourself stuck, check in with Tourinform for private rooms.

Gabriella (☎ 511 070; www.hotelgabriella.hu; Batsányi tér 7; s 7400-9800Ft, d 9800-14,800Ft, mains 1600-3500Ft;) Occupying the town's original mill house, Gabriella proudly stands on the edge of both lakes. Its large, modern rooms feature plenty of natural wood and look directly onto one of the town's peaceful waterways. Its restaurant is also a delight, with tables on the footbridge in warm weather and attentive service.

Pelion (☎ 513 100; www.hotelpelion.hunguesthotels.com; Köztársaság tér 10; s/d from €125/166;) This huge all-in-one wellness/thermal hotel is the cream of the crop in Tapolca. There's every possible treatment available, including its very own humidity cave. Rooms here are modern and comfy, and designed for a good night's sleep.

Pepinó (☎ 414 133; Kisfaludy utca 9; pizza from 600Ft) If you're looking for a quick, cheap, filling meal after paddling around on the cave's lake, consider grabbing a pizza on Pepinó's streetside terrace.

Getting There & Away

BUS

Tapolca is a major transport hub.

Destination	Price	Duration	Km	Frequency
Badacsonytomaj	300Ft	30min	16	at least 3 daily
Balatonfüred	900Ft	1½hr	55	2 daily
Budapest	2540Ft	3½hr	162	5 daily
Keszthely	450Ft	35-60min	28	hourly
Nagyvázsony	450Ft	35min	28	10 daily
Pápa	900Ft	1½-2hr	59	3 daily
Sümeg	525Ft	40-60min	31	hourly
Székesfehérvár	1500Ft	2hr	94	4 daily
Veszprém	750Ft	1-1½hr	49	hourly

TRAIN

Tapolca is the main terminus for the train line linking most of the towns along Lake Balaton's northern shore with Székesfehérvár (1770Ft, 2¾ hours, 117km, 10 daily) and Budapest (from 2780Ft, three to 4½ hours, 184km, seven daily). The train line also heads northwest to Sümeg (300Ft, 25 minutes, 20km, 12 daily) and Celldömölk (900Ft, one hour, 56km, 11 daily), from where frequent trains continue on to Szombathely (1770Ft, two to three hours, 101km) in western Hungary.

SÜMEG

☎ 87 / pop 6680

Sümeg may be small in size but it's big on attractions. The first is obvious as the town swings into view – a rocky, basalt hill topped by a proud castle with commanding views of the surrounding countryside. The others are a little harder to find, hidden in the back streets. A studied search will bring great rewards though, including the best baroque frescoes in the country.

History

Sümeg was on the map as early as the 13th century, when an important border fortress was built by King Béla IV in the aftermath of the Mongol invasion. The castle was strengthened several times during the next three centuries, repelling the Turks but falling to the Habsburg forces, which torched it in 1713.

Sümeg's golden age came later in the 18th century, when the all-powerful bishops of Veszprém took up residence here and commissioned some of the town's fine baroque buildings.

Orientation

Kossuth Lajos utca is the main street running north–south through Sümeg. The bus station is on Béke tér, a continuation of Kossuth Lajos utca south of the town centre. The train station is a 10-minute walk northwest, at the end of Darnay Kálmán utca.

Information

OTP bank (Kossuth Lajos utca 17) Has a currency-exchange machine and ATM.

Post office (Kossuth Lajos utca 1)

Tourinform (☎ 550 275; sumeg@tourinform.hu; Kossuth Lajos utca 15; 🕓 9am-5pm Jun-Aug, 8am-4pm Mon-Fri Sep-May) Small office with a few brochures; it can organise private rooms.

Sights

SÜMEG CASTLE

Sitting on a 270m-high cone of limestone above the town – a rare substance in this region of basalt – is this imposing **castle** (☎ 352 737; adult/child 1000/500Ft; 🕓 9am-6pm May-Sep, to 4pm Oct-Apr). It fell into ruin after the Austrians abandoned it early in the 18th century, but was restored in the 1960s. Today it is the largest and best preserved castle in all of Transdanubia and well worth the climb for the views east to the Bakony Hills and south to the Keszthely Hills. There's a small **Castle Museum** (Vármúzeum) of weapons, armour and castle furnishings in the 13th-century Old Tower (Öregtorony); pony rides and archery in the castle courtyard; a snack bar; and a restaurant. Medieval tournaments and feasts within the castle walls are organised throughout the year. You can still see bits of the **old town walls** below the castle at the northern end of Kossuth Lajos utca (Nos 13 to 33). A 16th-century tower is now the living room of the house at No 31.

Reach the castle by climbing Vak Bottyán utca, which is lined with lovely baroque *kúriak* (mansions), from Szent István tér and then following Városdal utca past the **Castle Stables** (Váristálló; Városdal utca 5), which now house a riding school (see p214). The castle is also accessible from the northeast via Rte 84 and by getting a ride in a jeep (one way/return 400/700Ft) from the parking lot at the end of Városdal utca.

CHURCH OF THE ASCENSION

The castle may dominate the town, but for many people it is not Sümeg's most important sight. For them that distinction is reserved for the **Church of the Ascension** (☎ church office 352 003; Szent Imre tér; admission free; 🕓 9am-5pm Mon-Fri, 11am-noon & 5-6pm Sat & Sun May-Sep, 9am-noon & 1-5pm Mon-Fri, services only Sat & Sun Mar, Apr, Oct, Nov). Architecturally, the building (1756) is unexceptional. But step inside and marvel at what has been called the 'Sistine Chapel of the rococo'.

That's perhaps an overstatement, but it's true that Franz Anton Maulbertsch's frescoes (1757–58) are the most beautiful baroque examples in Hungary and by far the prolific painter's best work. Despite now needing a good clean, the frescoes, whose subjects are taken from the Old and New Testaments, are still brilliant expressions of light and shadow. Pay special attention to the Crucifixion scene in Golgotha on the northern wall in the nave; the Adoration of the Three Kings, with its caricature of a Moor opposite Golgotha; the Gate of Hell, across the aisle under the organ loft on the western side under the porch; and the altarpiece of Christ ascending airily to the clouds. Maulbertsch managed to include himself in a couple of his works, most clearly among the shepherds in the first fresco on

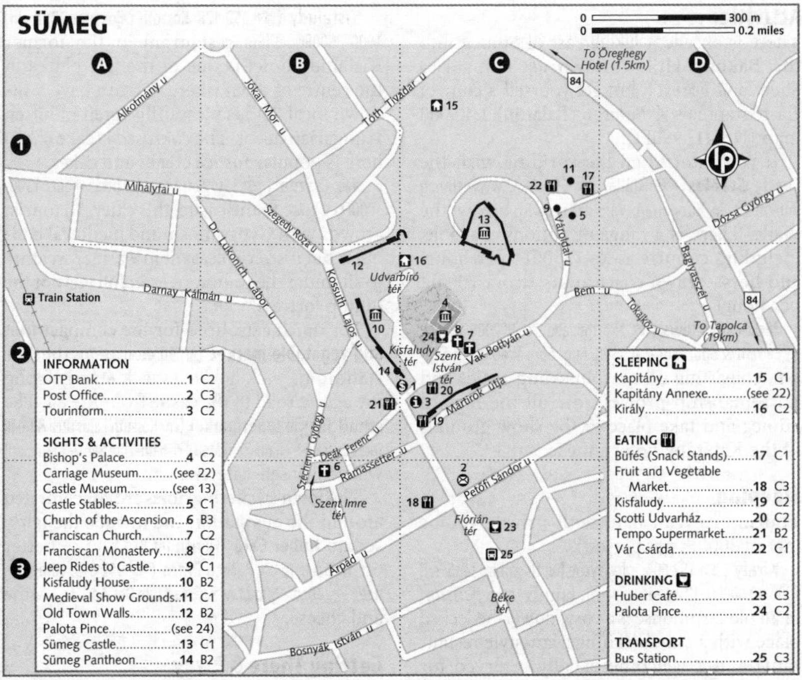

the southern wall (he's the one holding the round cheeses and hamming it up for the audience). The commissioner of the frescoes, Márton Padányi Bíró, bishop of Veszprém, is shown on the western wall near the organ. Drop a coin in the machine to illuminate the frescoes and to view them at their best.

OTHER SIGHTS

The Church of the Ascension steals the limelight from the 17th-century **Franciscan church** (Ferences templom; Szent István tér 7; admission free; 7am-6pm), which has modern frescoes, a beautifully carved baroque altar and a pietà that has attracted pilgrims for 300 years. Don't miss the ornate pulpit with the eerie dismembered hand grasping a crucifix. The baroque **Franciscan monastery** (Ferences kolostor; Szent István tér 7; admission free; 11.30am-3pm), built in 1657, is next door, but there's not a lot to see.

The former **Bishop's Palace** (Püspöki palota; ☎ 550 277; Szent István tér 8-10; adult/child 400/200Ft; 10am-6pm Wed-Sun May-Sep, 8am-4pm Mon-Fri Oct-Apr) was a grand residence when completed in 1755, but now it needs some TLC. It still sports some wonderful baroque flourishes, including two Atlases holding up the balcony at the entrance and the copper rain-spouts in the shape of sea monsters, and the renovated ground floor currently hosts temporary art exhibitions. The highlight, though, is the palace cellar, which is in perfect order – it now houses **Palota Pince** (☎ 352 643; admission free; 10am-9pm May-Sep, variable Oct-Apr), an atmospheric wine cellar with original wine barrels and a huge selection of wines from around the country.

Kisfaludy House (Kisfaludy szülőháza; ☎ 06 30 491 9719; Kisfaludy tér 4; adult/child 400/200Ft; 10am-6pm May-Sep, 8am-4pm Mon-Fri Oct-Apr) is the birthplace of Sándor Kisfaludy (1772–1844), the Romantic 'poet of the Balaton'. Together with a history of his life and work, the museum contains further exhibits on Sümeg Castle and the area's geology. Outside, along a wall is the **Sümeg Pantheon** of local sons and daughters who made good.

The small **Carriage Museum** (Városoldal utca; adult/child 200/100Ft; 9am-5pm Tue-Sun), next to the Kapitány hotel's annexe, has well-restored horse carriages and a small array of medieval weapons and armour.

Activities

There is excellent **hiking** east of Sümeg into the Bakony Hills (known as 'Hungary's Sherwood Forest'), but get yourself a copy of Cartographia's *A Balaton* (Balaton) 1:40,000 map (No 41; 990Ft).

If you want to go horse riding, visit the **Castle Stables** (Váristálló; ☎ 550 087; www.sumeg.hu/capari, in Hungarian; Váraldal utca 5) below the castle. There is a range of options available, including country rides (3500Ft per hour) and horse-drawn coach tours (from 7000Ft per hour).

Medieval shows (☎ 550 166; adult/child 2000/1000Ft; 11am & 6pm Mon-Sat Jul & Aug, 5pm Wed & Sat Sep-Jun), consisting of swashbuckling antics and horsemanship prowess, are all the rage in Sümeg and take place in the show grounds of the Kapitány hotel annexe.

Sleeping

Tourinform can help with private rooms (about 3000Ft per person).

Király (☎ 352 605; info@tyche.hu; Udvarbíró tér 5; s/d 5000/10,000Ft) This six-room, family-run *pension* in an old farmhouse is a cosy, flower-bedecked place with a *csárda* (Hungarian-style restaurant) and a welcome usually reserved for friends and family. At the time of writing, rooms were undergoing renovation.

Öreghegy Hotel (☎ 350 501; www.oreghegyhotel.hu; Karolina utca vége; s/d 7000/14,000Ft) This small hotel borders woods and vineyards about 1.5km north of the town centre. Views of the castle and surrounding plains are fabulous, and rooms are large, airy and stylish in their simplicity. A bar and restaurant are also on-site.

Kapitány (☎ 352 598; www.hotelkapitany.hu; Tóth Tivadar utca 19; r from 12,000Ft;) A modern hotel with well-appointed rooms, some of which have fabulous views of the castle. There's plenty of added extras, including a sauna, tennis court, horse riding, a wine cellar and a full wellness centre. It also has an annexe near the Carriage Museum.

Eating & Drinking

Eating and drinking are very limited in Sümeg.

Scotti Udvarház (☎ 350 997; Szent István tér 1; pizza from 880Ft, mains 1000-2000Ft) Scotti accommodates busloads of tourists but at least its menu features some unusual dishes, such as rabbit with garlic and cocks-balls goulash. Its huge inner courtyard is another drawcard.

Kisfaludy (☎ 352 128; Kossuth Lajos utca 13; mains 1000-2500Ft) This restaurant at the former Kisfaludy hotel is one of the few places in the centre of town where you can have a sit-down meal, and is pleasantly bereft of kitsch Hungarian decor. The *cukrászda* (cake shop) here is popular for ice cream and cakes.

Vár Csárda (☎ 350 924; Váraldal utca; mains 1500-3000Ft) Close to the castle, this caters to tourist crowds with Gypsy music and medieval banquets but it's very pleasant in warmer weather to sit under the walnut trees in full view of the hilltop fortress.

For quick eats, head for the compact **fruit and vegetable market** (Árpád utca) near the bus station, or pick a *büfé* (snack stand) along the access road to the castle from Rte 84. The small **Tempo supermarket** (cnr Kossuth Lajos utca & Deák Ferenc utca; 6am-7pm Mon-Fri, 6am-2pm Sat, 7-11am Sun) will satisfy self-caterers.

The town's watering holes are concentrated around the bus station and include the fairly sedate **Huber Café** (Flórián tér 8). You're better off heading to **Palota Pince** (☎ 352 643; admission free; 10am-9pm May-Sep, variable Oct-Apr) for wine and cheese.

Getting There & Away

Buses leave Sümeg hourly each day for Hévíz (450Ft, 35 to 55 minutes, 27km), Keszthely (525Ft, 50 minutes, 31km) and Tapolca (525Ft, 40 to 60 minutes, 31km); departures to Pápa (900Ft, 1¼ hours, 51km) and Veszprém (1050Ft, two hours, 68km) are also frequent. Other buses go to Budapest (3830Ft, four hours, 184km, four daily), Győr (1500Ft, 2¼ hours, 99km, five daily) and Sopron (1770Ft, 2½-3½ hours, 107km, three daily).

Sümeg is on the train line linking Tapolca (300Ft, 25 minutes, 20km, 12 daily) and Celldömölk (600Ft, 45 minutes, 36km, nine daily), from where frequent trains continue on to Szombathely (1350Ft, two hours, 81km). For Budapest (3010Ft, four to five hours, 204km) and other points to the east and west along the northern shore of Lake Balaton, change at Tapolca.

NAGYVÁZSONY

☎ 88 / pop 1830

The sleepy town of Nagyvázsony, only 15km north of the lake, makes for a pleasant day trip. Its centrepiece is the remnants of a 15th-century castle, which is complemented by a couple of small but worthwhile museums.

LAKE BALATON REGION

Orientation & Information

In the town centre you'll find Nagyvázsony's three bus stops, a **post office** (Kinizsi utca 59), a 24-hour ATM and a small food store.

Sights

VÁZSONYKŐ CASTLE

This **castle** (☎ 264 786; Vár utca; adult/child 500/300Ft; 🕑 9am-5pm May-Sep, 10am-5pm Apr & Oct), on a gentle slope north of the tiny town centre, is little more than a ruin these days, but in the early 15th century it was home to the influential Vezsenyi family. In 1462 it was presented to General Pál Kinizsi by King Matthias Corvinus in gratitude for the brave general's military successes against the Turks, and became an important border fortress during the occupation.

The castle is essentially a rectangle with a horseshoe-shaped barbican. The 30m-high, six-storey keep is reached via a bridge over the dry moat. A large crack runs from the top of the tower to the bottom, but it must be secure enough: the upper rooms contain the **Kinizsi Castle Museum** (Kinizsi Vármúzeum), while the lower room displays dummies torturing one another. Part of General Kinizsi's red-marble sarcophagus sits in the centre of the restored chapel and there's a collection of archaeological finds in the crypt.

OTHER SIGHTS

Most of Nagyvázsony's other sights are within easy walking distance of the castle.

Directly opposite the castle is the **Post Office Museum** (Postmúzeum; ☎ 264 300; Temető utca 3; adult/child 200/100Ft; 🕑 10am-6pm Tue-Sun Apr–mid-Oct), which is a lot more interesting than it sounds. Nagyvázsony was an important stop along the postal route between Budapest and Graz in the 19th century (horses were changed here), and the museum does a good job of retelling the town's story. There's also a particularly good section on the history of the telephone in Hungary, beginning with the installation of the first switchboard in Budapest in 1890.

Next to the museum is an 18th-century **Evangelist church** with whitewashed walls and a free-standing belfry, while not far away is a small **Open-Air Folk Museum** (Szabadtéri Néprajzi Múzeum; ☎ 264 724; Bercsényi utca 21; adult/child 300/150Ft; 🕑 10am-5pm Tue-Sun May-Sep) at a farmhouse dating from 1825. It was once the home of a coppersmith, and his workshop remains.

The **Church of St Stephen** (Szent István templom; Rákóczi utca), at the main road linking Veszprém with Tapolca, was built by General Kinizsi in 1481 on the site of an earlier chapel. Most of the interior, including the richly carved main altar, is baroque.

Sleeping & Eating

Vázsonykő (☎ 264 289; Sörház utca 2; s/d/tr 5500/7500/8500Ft, mains 1150-1550Ft) This friendly *pension* is only a short walk from the castle. Rooms are large but in poor order, but it's the only accommodation option available over the winter months. The restaurant is pleasant enough and has a big terrace.

Malomkő (☎ 264 165; www.malomko.hu; Kinizsi utca 47-49; s/d 6500/9000Ft; 🕑 Apr-Oct; 🅿) Malomkő is the liveliest and flashiest accommodation in town, with spacious rooms (some with kitchen) filled with natural-wood furniture and plenty of light. The ground floor is given over to a simple but satisfying restaurant that often hosts bands on weekends.

Vár Csárda (Temető utca 5; mains 1000-2500Ft; 🕑 10am-6pm Jun-Sep) In the summer months there is no better place than this thatched cottage for a snack or larger Hungarian meal. Its large garden looks directly onto the castle.

Getting There & Away

At least 10 buses per day link Nagyvázsony with Veszprém (375Ft, 30 minutes, 22km) and Tapolca (450Ft, 35 minutes, 28km).

TIHANY

☎ 87 / pop 1460

The place with the greatest historical significance on Lake Balaton is Tihany, a peninsula jutting 5km into the Balaton. Activity here is centred on the tiny town of the same name, which is home to the celebrated Abbey Church. In the height of summer the church attracts so many people it's hard to find space to breathe, let alone find a free space for lunch. Juxtaposing this claustrophobic vibe is the peninsula itself – a nature reserve of hills and marshy meadows – that has an isolated, almost wild feel to it.

Tihany Peninsula is a popular recreational area with beaches on its eastern and western coasts and a big resort complex on its southern tip. The waters of the so-called Tihany Well, off the southern end of the peninsula, are the deepest – and coldest – in the lake, reaching an unprecedented 12m in some parts.

History

There was a Roman settlement in the area, but Tihany first appeared on the map in 1055, when King Andrew I (r 1046–60), a son of King Stephen's great nemesis, Vászoly, founded a Benedictine monastery here. The Deed of Foundation of the Abbey Church of Tihany, now in the archives of the Pannonhalma Abbey (p169), is one of the earliest known documents bearing any Hungarian words – some 50 place names within a mostly Latin text. It's a linguistic treasure in a country where, until the 19th century, the vernacular in its written form was spurned – particularly in schools – in favour of the more 'cultured' Latin and German.

In 1267 a fortress was built around the church and was able to keep the Turks at bay when they arrived 300 years later. But the castle was demolished by Habsburg forces in 1702 and all you'll see today are ruins.

Orientation

Tihany village, perched on an 80m-high plateau along the peninsula's eastern coast, is accessible by two roads when you turn south off Rte 71. The Inner Harbour (Belső kikötő), where ferries to/from Balatonfüred and Siófok dock, is below the village. Tihany Port (Tihanyi-rév), to the southwest at the tip of the peninsula, is Tihany's recreational area. From here, car ferries run to Szántódi-rév and passenger ferries to Balatonföldvár.

Two inland basins on the peninsula are fed by rain and ground water. The Inner Lake (Belső-tó) is almost in the centre of the peninsula and visible from the village, while the Outer Lake (Külső-tó), to the northwest, has almost completely dried up and is now a tangle of reeds. Both basins attract considerable bird life.

Information

Kakas Csárda (☎ 448 541; Batthyány utca 1; ⏲ 11am-10pm) Restaurant with internet access (per hour 500Ft).
Post office (Kossuth Lajos utca 37; ⏲ 8am-4pm Mon-Fri) Has an exchange bureau.
Tihany Tourist (☎ 448 481; www.tihanytourist.hu; Kossuth Lajos utca 11; ⏲ 9am-5pm May-Sep, 9am-4pm Apr & Oct) Organises accommodation and local tours.
Tourinform (☎ 448 804; tihany@tourinform.hu; Kossuth Lajos utca 20; ⏲ 9am-7pm Mon-Fri, 10am-6pm Sat & Sun mid-Jun–mid-Sep, 9am-5pm Mon-Fri, 10am-4pm Sat mid-Apr–mid-Jun & mid-Sep–end Sep, 10am-4pm Mon-Fri Oct–mid-Apr)
Town website (www.tihany.hu) Digital information on the town and its surrounds.

Sights

ABBEY CHURCH

This twin-spired and ochre-coloured **church** (☎ 538 200; Kossuth Lajos utca; adult/child 700/300Ft, tours in English & German 8000Ft; ⏲ 9am-6pm May-Sep, 10am-5pm Apr & Oct, 10am-3pm Nov-Mar) is the dominating feature in the small village of Tihany and should not be missed.

Built in 1754 on the site of King Andrew's church, this impressive house of God contains fantastic altars, pulpits and screens carved between 1753 and 1779 by an Austrian lay brother named Sebastian Stuhlhof, all baroque-rococo masterpieces in their own right.

Upon entering the main nave, turn your back to the sumptuous main altar and the Abbot's throne and look right to the side altar dedicated to Mary. The large angel kneeling on the right supposedly represents Stuhlhof's fiancée, a fisherman's daughter who died in her youth. On the Altar of the Sacred Heart across the aisle, a pelican (Christ) nurtures its young (the faithful) with its own blood. The besotted figures atop the pulpit beside it are four doctors of the Roman Catholic church:

HUNGARY'S SPRING SNOW

Hungary is not a country known for its blankets of snow, particularly in spring, but from May to June, that all changes. During this time, *nyárfa* (poplar trees) give up their pollen to the four winds, which carry it to every nook and cranny imaginable. The Balaton area is particularly bad, and the fluffy white substance lines gutters, covers footpaths, and pools in courtyards. As every hay-fever sufferer knows, poplar pollen is about as bad as it gets, so if you suffer from this annoying condition be sure to bring something to counteract its strong effect (or be prepared to buy something quick), because a severe case of runny nose, itchy eyes and sinus congestion can wreak havoc on a well-earned holiday. For more information on health issues in Hungary, consult the Health chapter (p394).

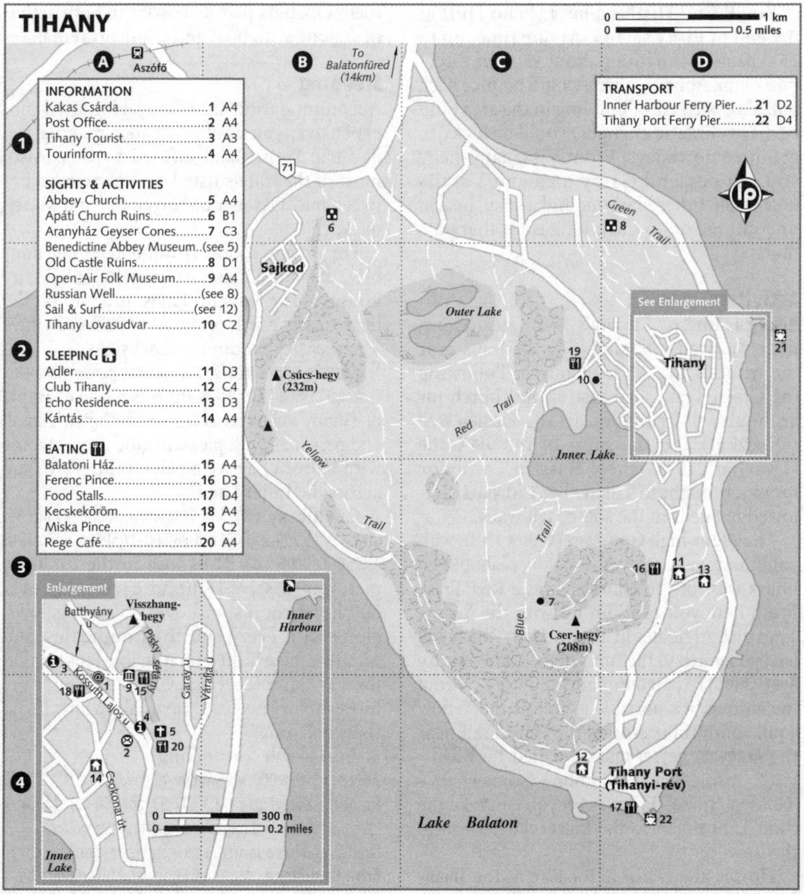

Sts Ambrose, Gregory, Jerome and Augustine. The next two altars on the right- and left-hand sides are dedicated to Benedict and his twin sister, Scholastica; the last pair, a baptismal font and the Lourdes Altar, date from 1896 and 1900, respectively.

Stuhlhof also carved the magnificent choir rail above the porch and the organ with all the cherubs. The frescoes on the ceilings by Bertalan Székely, Lajos Deák-Ébner and Károly Lotz were painted in 1889, when the church was restored.

The remains of King Andrew I lie in a limestone sarcophagus in the atmospheric Romanesque **crypt**. The spiral swordlike cross on the cover is similar to ones used by 11th-century Hungarian kings.

The **Benedictine Abbey Museum** (Bencés Apátsági Múzeum; admission incl with church entry fee; 9am-6pm May-Sep, 10am-5pm Apr & Oct, 10am-3pm Nov-Mar), next door to the Abbey Church in the former Benedictine monastery, is entered from the crypt. It contains exhibits on Lake Balaton, liturgical vestments, religious artefacts, a handful of manuscripts and a history of King Andrew.

OTHER SIGHTS

Pisky sétány, a promenade running along the ridge north from the church to Visszhang-hegy, passes a cluster of folk houses with thick thatch roofs that have been turned into a small **Open-Air Folk Museum** (Szabadtéri Néprajzi Múzeum; ☎ 538 022; adult/child 350/250Ft; 10am-6pm May-Sep).

You'll find **Visszhang-hegy** (Echo Hill) at the end of Pisky sétány. At one time, up to 15 syllables of anything shouted in the direction of the Abbey Church would bounce back but, alas, because of building in the area (and perhaps climatic changes) you'll be lucky to get three nowadays. From Visszhang-hegy you can descend Garay utca and Váralja utca to the Inner Harbour and a small beach, or continue on to the hiking trails that pass this way.

Activities

Hiking is one of Tihany's main attractions; there's a good map outlining the trails near the front of the Abbey Church. Following the Green Trail northeast of the church for an hour will bring you to the **Russian Well** (Oroszkút) and the ruins of the **Old Castle** (Óvár) at 219m, where Russian Orthodox monks, brought to Tihany by Andrew I, hollowed out cells in the soft basalt walls.

The 232m-high **Csúcs-hegy** (Csúcs Hill), with panoramic views of Lake Balaton, is about two hours west of the church via the Red Trail. From here you can join up with the Yellow Trail that originates in Tihany Port, which will lead you north to the ruins of the 13th-century **Apáti Church** (Ápáti templom) and Rte 71. From the church, it's possible to follow the Yellow Trail south till it crosses the Blue Trail near the **Aranyház geyser cones**, formed by warm-water springs and resembling (somewhat) a 'Golden Horse'. From here, you can take the Blue Trail north to the **Inner Lake** and on to the town centre.

Horses are available for hire at the **Tihany Lovasudvar** (☎ 06 30 275 3293; Kiserdőtelepi utca 10; 1hr ride 3000Ft), just north of the Inner Lake. In an hour you can circumnavigate the Inner Lake, trot to the top of Cser-hegy, and return to Lovasudvar.

As the lake bottom drops away quicker here than in other parts of the lake, Tihany's **beaches** are an inviting option. The stretches on the eastern side are the most accessible, which also means they're the most popular, but if you're looking to escape the crowds head to **Sajkod** at the peninsula's northwestern point. A small track leads south from this small settlement to a secluded beach; with Tihany's hills as a backdrop, it's one of the most peaceful spots to while away the day.

Sail & Surf (☎ 06 30 227 8927; www.wind99.com), a sailing and windsurfing centre at Club Tihany (below), offers private lessons in both activities, along with boat and windsurf rental.

Sleeping

Accommodation in Tihany is limited and expensive; you could consider making it a day trip from Balatonfüred by bus. Also, most of the hotels listed here are closed between mid-October or November and March or April.

For private rooms (from 6000Ft per double), consult Tihany Tourist (p216). Many houses along Kossuth Lajos utca and on the little streets north of the Abbey Church have *'Zimmer frei'* (room for rent) signs.

Kántás (☎ 448 072; www.kantas-panzio-tihany.hu; Csokonai út 49; r 11,000Ft) Kántás is a fine example of Tihany's cheaper accommodation; it's small and personal, with pleasant attic rooms (some with balcony) above a restaurant. Views are across the Inner Lake.

Club Tihany (☎ 538 564; www.clubtihany.hu; Rév utca 3; s 15,750-24,000Ft, d 26,500-37,500Ft, bungalows 13,250-32,000Ft; 🅿 ⛶) Close to the car-ferry pier, this massive 13-hectare resort has over 300 hotel rooms and over 150 bungalows, along with every sporting, munching and quaffing possibility imaginable. Its bungalows are simple affairs, while the rooms are more luxurious and have lake views from their balconies.

Also worth considering:

Adler (☎ 538 000; www.adler-tihany.hu; Felsőkopaszhegyi utca 1/a; r €41-52, apt €68-95; ⛶ 🅿) Large, whitewashed rooms with balconies; good for families and has a Jacuzzi, sauna and restaurant.

Echo Residence (☎ 448 043; www.echoresidence.hu; Felsőkopaszhegyi utca 35; ste €140-326; ⊠ ⛶ 🅿) Boutique hotel featuring luxury suites with views of Lake Balaton. All come with small kitchen and lounge, and some have their own sauna.

Eating

Like the hotels, most restaurants are closed between mid-October or November and March or April.

Rege Café (☎ 448 280; Kossuth Lajos utca 22; coffee from 460Ft; 🕑 10am-6pm) From its high vantage point near the Benedictine Abbey Museum, this modern cafe has an unsurpassed panoramic view of the Balaton. On a sunny day, there is no better place to enjoy coffee, cake and the sparkling lake.

Balatoni Ház (☎ 448 608; Pisky sétány; mains 1000-3000Ft) With fabulous views of the lake from its enormous terrace, this thatched-cottage restaurant attracts the attention of many passersby. Its welcoming staff and Hungarian menu, featuring touches of Italian cuisine, manage to convince them to stay put.

our pick **Ferenc Pince** (☎ 448 575; Cser-hegy 9; mains from 1500Ft; ⌚ noon-11pm Wed-Mon) Ferenc is both a wine- and food-lover's dream; not only does its chef cook up a Hungarian storm in the kitchen, but some of Tihany's best wine is served by the very people who produce the stuff. During the day, its open terrace offers expansive views of the lake, while at night the hypnotic twinkling lights of the southern shore are in full view from its cosy thatched-roof house. Ferenc Pince is just under 2km south of the Abbey Church.

Miska Pince (☎ 06 30 929 7350; Kiserdőtelepi utca; mains 1500-2830Ft) Miska Pince is a cute thatch-roof cottage down near the banks of the Inner Lake. It serves big portions of Hungarian cuisine, and its secluded, sunny terrace is just the place to escape the madding crowds up near the church.

Kecskeköröm (Fossil Shell; Kossuth Lajos utca 19; mains 1500-3000Ft) Kecskeköröm has its fair share of Hungarian kitsch but it's not done in an insulting way. It's a fine central option and has a menu filled with solid Hungarian fare.

Cheap food stalls greet passengers to-ing and fro-ing across the lake at Tihany Port.

Getting There & Away

Buses cover the 14km from Balatonfüred's bus and train station to and from Tihany at least 13 times daily (250Ft, 30 minutes). The bus stops at both ferry landings before climbing to Tihany village.

The Balaton passenger ferries from Siófok, Balatonfüred and elsewhere stop at Tihany from early April to early October. Catch them at the Inner Harbour ferry pier or at Tihanyi-rév. From early March to late November the car ferry takes 10 minutes to cross the narrow stretch of water between Tihanyi-rév and Szántódi-rév, and departs every 40 minutes to an hour.

BALATONFÜRED

☎ 87 / pop 13,000

Balatonfüred is not only the oldest resort on the Balaton's northern shore, it's also the most fashionable. In former days the wealthy and famous built large villas on its tree-lined streets, and their architectural legacy can still be seen today. More recently, the lake frontage received a massive makeover, and now sports the most stylish marina on the lake.

The town is also known for the thermal waters of its world-famous heart hospital.

History

The thermal water here, rich in carbonic acid, have been used as a cure for stomach ailments for centuries, but its other curative properties were only discovered by scientific analysis in the late 18th century. Balatonfüred was immediately declared a spa with its own chief physician in residence.

Balatonfüred's golden age was in the 19th century, especially the first half, when political and cultural leaders of the Reform Era (roughly 1825–48) gathered here in the summer. Balatonfüred was also the site chosen by István Széchenyi to launch the lake's first steamship *Kisfaludy* in 1846.

By 1900 Balatonfüred was a popular place for increasingly wealthy middle-class families to escape Budapest's heat. Wives would base themselves here all summer along with their children while husbands would board the 'bull trains' in Budapest at the weekend. It is a sign of the times that even Balatonfüred has begun to modernise itself in the last couple of years.

Orientation

Balatonfüred has two distinct districts: the lakeside resort area and the commercial centre in the older part of town around Szent István tér to the northwest. Almost everything to see and do is down by the water.

The train and bus stations are on Dobó István utca, about a kilometre northwest of Vitorlás tér, where the ferry pier is located. The quickest way to get to the lake from either station is to walk east on Horváth Mihály utca and then southeast on Jókai Mór utca.

Information

OTP bank (Petőfi Sándor utca 8) With 24-hour ATM.
Post office (Zsigmond utca 14; ⌚ 8am-4pm Mon-Fri)
Tourinform (☎ 580 480; balatonfured@tourinform.hu; Kisfaludy utca 1; ⌚ 9am-7pm Mon-Fri, to 6pm Sat, to 1pm Sun Jul & Aug, to 5pm Mon-Fri, to 1pm Sat Jun & Sep, to 4pm Mon-Fri Oct-May) Well-stocked tourist office run by helpful staff.
Town website (www.balatonfured.hu) Online information in a number of languages.

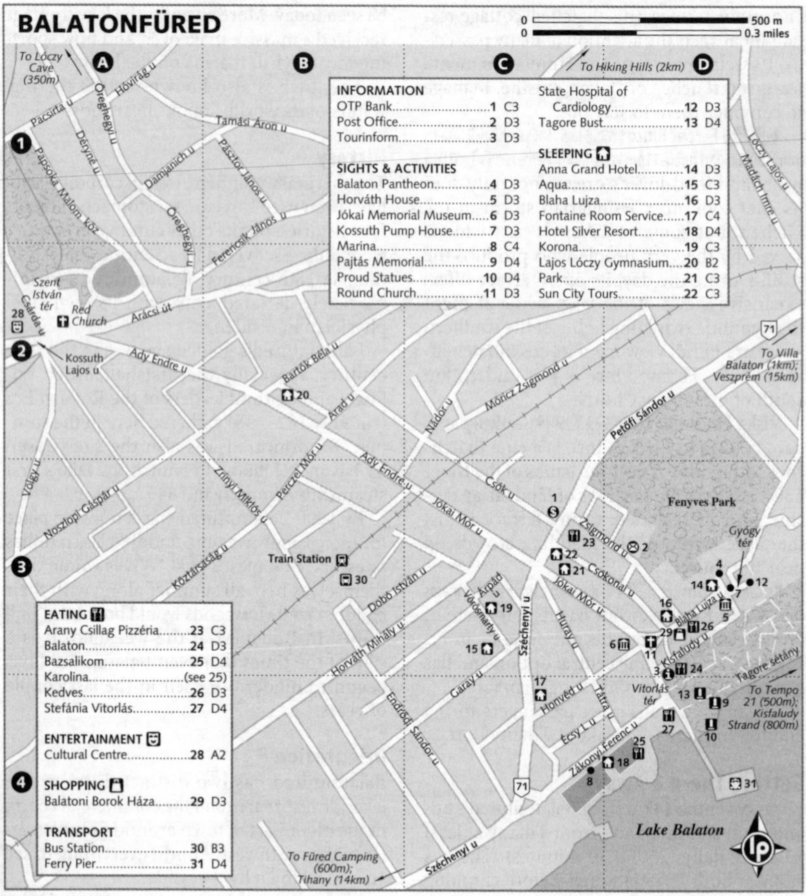

Sights

A stroll along Balatonfüred's tree-shaded streets close to the lake quickly reveals the town's wealth of 19th-century villas. At the junction of Honvéd utca and Jókai Mór utca, one such architectural delight houses the **Jókai Memorial Museum** (Jókai Emlékmúzeum; ☎ 343 426; Honvéd utca 1). For many years the prolific writer used it as his summer villa, and now it's filled with family memorabilia and period furniture. At the time of writing it was closed for renovation; check with Tourinform for more details.

Across the street from the museum is the tiny neoclassical **Round Church** (Kerek templom; ☎ 343 029; Blaha Lujza utca 1; admission free; services only), completed in 1846. The *Crucifixion* (1891) by János Vaszary sits above the altar on the western wall and is the most notable thing inside.

Walking down Blaha Lujza utca, past the villa (now a hotel) at No 4 where 19th-century actress-singer Lujza Blaha spent her summers from 1893 to 1916, will bring you to Gyógy tér and the heart of the spa. In the centre of this leafy square, **Kossuth Pump House** (1853) dispenses slightly sulphuric, but drinkable, thermal water. This is as close as you'll get to the hot spring. Although Balatonfüred is a major spa, the mineral baths are reserved for patients of the **State Hospital of Cardiology** (Országos Szívkórház; Gyógy tér 2), which put Balatonfüred on the map. On the northern side of the square is the **Balaton Pantheon**, with memorial plaques from those who took the cure at the hospital.

From Gyógy tér it's only a quick saunter down to the lake promenade, Tagore sétány. This leafy stretch hides a number of statues, including a **bust** of Nobel Prize–winning poet Rabindranath Tagore in front of a lime tree that he planted in 1926 to mark his recovery from illness after treatment here. Diagonally opposite and closer to the lake is a disturbing **memorial** of a hand stretching out of the water in memory of those who drowned in the lake when the *Pajtás* boat sank in 1954. Additionally, two very **proud statues** – one a fisherman, the other a boatman – stand guard over the harbour entrance.

Sprawled the length of Zákonyi Ferenc utca is Balatonfüred's biggest development in years, a sparkling new **marina**. Stylish cafes, fashionable restaurants, boutique shops and the Hotel Silver Resort now reside where once simple food stalls and dry docks stood.

The late baroque **Horváth House** (Gyógy tér 3), for many years a hotel, was the site of the first **Anna Ball** in 1825, but now the Anna Grand Hotel (see p222) hosts the event. The ball is held on 26 July (the name-day for Anna) and tickets go for anywhere between 15,000Ft and 50,000Ft.

Activities

Balatonfüred has three **public beaches**, of which **Kisfaludy Strand** (Aranyhíd sétány; adult/child per day 375/275Ft, per week 2250/1410Ft; ⌚ 8am-6pm mid-May–mid-Sep) to the east of Tagore sétány is the best.

Popular **lake cruises** by the Balaton Shipping Co (p195) leave Balatonfüred at 10am, noon, 2pm, 4pm and 5.30pm daily between late May and mid-September.

Rent bicycles from **Tempo 21** (☎ 06 20 924 4995; Deák Ferenc utca 56; 1hr/day 350/2400Ft; ⌚ 9am-7pm mid-May–mid-Sep), located at the eastern end of the promenade.

Consider walking or cycling to **Lóczy Cave** (Lóczy-barlang; Öreghegyi utca; adult/child 400/200Ft; ⌚ 10am-6pm Tue-Sun May–mid-Sep), north of the old town centre. Around 40m of cave is accessible to the public, and the highlight inside is the thick layers of limestone. There's also good **hiking** in the three hills with the names Tamás (Thomas), Sándor (Alexander) and Péter (Peter) to the northeast.

DISCOUNTS ON THE LAKE

If you're overnight in Balatonfüred, ask the staff at your hotel or *pension* about the free Füred Card, which offers between 5% and 50% discount on various sights, activities and restaurants in the town.

Sleeping

Prices fluctuate throughout the year and usually peak between early July and late August. As elsewhere around Lake Balaton, private room prices are rather inflated. **Sun City Tours** (☎ 06 30 947 2679; Csokonai utca 1) can help with finding you a place, as can **Fontaine Room Service** (☎ 343 673; Honvéd utca 11). There are lots of houses with rooms for rent on the streets north of Kisfaludy Strand.

BUDGET

Füred Camping (☎ 580 241; fured@balatontourist.hu; Széchenyi utca 24; camp sites per adult/child/tent 1600/1200/5500Ft, bungalow from 17,000Ft, caravan 23,000Ft; ⌚ mid-Apr-early Oct) This, the largest camping ground on the lake, can accommodate 3500 people. Most bungalows sleep up to four people, and the camp ground has direct access to the lake.

Lajos Lóczy Gymnasium (☎ 343 428; Bartók Béla utca 4; dm 3000Ft) This school turns into dorm accommodation over the summer months, and is more than handy to the train and bus stations.

MIDRANGE

Villa Balaton (☎ 06 30 223 6453; www.villabalaton.hu; Deák Ferenc utca 38; s/d 6000/12,000Ft) The large, bright upstairs rooms of this pastel-yellow villa uphill from the lake are available for rent. Each has its own balcony overlooking a sunny garden and grape vines, and guests can make use of a well-equipped kitchen and grill area.

Blaha Lujza (☎ 581 210; www.hotelblaha.hu; Blaha Lujza utca 4; s/d from €37/50) This small hotel is one of the loveliest to stay in. Its rooms are a little compact but very comfy, and it was the summer home of the much loved 19th-century actress-singer from 1893 to 1916.

Park (☎ 788 223; www.parkhotel.hu; Jókai Mór utca 24; s/d 12,000/14,000Ft; 🅿) A massive villa away from the lake houses this old-world hotel, where you'll find huge rooms (some with balcony) with a touch of class. The private garden is a plus, and rates include half-board (ie breakfast and dinner included).

A huddle of attractive *pensions* can be found close to the bus and train stations:

Aqua (☎ 342 813; www.ah1.hu; Garay utca 2; s/d 9500/11,200Ft) Dependable *pension* with friendly staff and wi-fi throughout.

Korona (☎ 343 278; www.koronapanzio.hu; Vörösmarty utca 4; s/d/tr/apt €39/52/66/56) Homely decor bordering on kitsch; big, bright rooms.

TOP END

Hotel Silver Resort (☎ 583 001; www.silverresort.hu; Zákonyi Ferenc utca 4; r/ste from €77/114;) Overlooking the lake is the new four-star Silver Resort, which sports small, modern rooms bedecked in calming shades of brown. The more expensive variety have balconies, and suites are great for families. The wellness centre, which is free for guests, has a fitness centre, whirlpool and Finnish sauna.

Anna Grand Hotel (☎ 342 044; www.annagrandhotel.eu; Gyógy tér 1; s/d 25,000/35,000Ft;) In a former life the Anna Grand was the town's sanatorium, but in recent years it has been transformed into a luxurious hotel. Choose from rooms with either period antiques or modern furnishings, and views of the hotel's peaceful inner courtyard or tree-shaded Gyógy tér. Activities are plentiful for a hotel of this size, and include a wellness centre, bowling alley and climbing wall.

Eating & Drinking

Kedves (Blaha Lujza utca 7; coffee 250-450Ft) Join fans of Lujza Blaha and take coffee and cake at the cafe where the famous actress used to while away the hours. It's also appealing for its location, away from the madding crowds.

Arany Csillag Pizzéria (☎ 482 116; Zsigmond utca 1; mains 1000-2500Ft) A convivial pizzeria away from the flashy waterfront, Arany Csillag caters to both couples and small groups who are happy to eat, chat and drink till closing. Italian flavours fill the menu, and its small terrace fills up quickly in summer.

Balaton (☎ 481 319; Kisfaludy utca 5; mains 1000-3000Ft) This cool, leafy oasis amid all the hubbub is set back from the lake in the shaded park area. It serves generous portions and, like so many restaurants in town, has an extensive fish selection.

Stefánia Vitorlás (☎ 343 407; Tagore sétány 1; mains 1500-3000Ft) This enormous wooden villa sits right on the lake's edge at the foot of the town's pier. Watch the yachts sail in and out of the harbour from the terrace while munching on Hungarian cuisine and sipping local wine.

Bazsalikom (☎ 06 30 538 0690; Zákonyi Ferenc sétány 4; mains 1500-3000Ft) Taking pride of place on the new marina's waterfront is Bazsalikom, a restaurant that combines both fine dining and a relaxed atmosphere. Pasta and pizza are the mainstays of the menu, but better yet are the daily blackboard specials that employ seasonal ingredients. The lounges facing the lake are perfect for an afternoon cocktail.

our pick **Karolina** (☎ 583 098; Zákonyi Ferenc sétány 4; coffee 250-500Ft) Karolina is a sophisticated cafe/bar that does an excellent job of serving fresh coffee, aromatic teas and quality local wines. The interior, with its Art Nouveau wall hangings and subtle lighting, has a certain decadent – yet inviting – air about it, while the terrace area with sofas couldn't be more laid-back.

Entertainment

Cultural centre (☎ 481 187; Kossuth Lajos utca 3) The staff at this centre near Szent István tér can tell you what's on, such as musical performances and theatre productions.

Shopping

Balatoni Borok Háza (☎ 580 660; Blaha Lujza utca 5) Purchase the wines of 26 vintners from the Balaton's northeast at this well-informed wine house. Look for Italian Riesling, the best of the region. Wine tastings can also be organised.

Getting There & Away

BOAT

From April to June and September to October, at least four daily Balaton Shipping Co ferries (p195) link Balatonfüred with Siófok and Tihany. Up to seven daily ferries serve these ports from July to August.

BUS

Bus connections from Balatonfüred include the following destinations.

Destination	Price	Duration	Km	Frequency
Budapest	2040Ft	2-3hr	136	4 daily
Győr	1500Ft	2½hr	100	6 daily
Keszthely	1050Ft	1-1½hr	67	7 daily
Székesfehérvár	1050Ft	1½hr	69	7 daily
Tihany	250Ft	30min	14	at least 13 daily
Veszprém	375Ft	40min	20	half-hourly

TRAIN

Trains travel from Balatonfüred to the following destinations.

LAKE BALATON REGION

Destination	Price	Duration	Km	Frequency
Badacsony	600Ft	1	38	12 daily
Budapest	2040Ft	2½	132	3 daily
Székesfehérvár	1050Ft	1½	65	12 daily
Tapolca	900Ft	1¼	52	12 daily

Getting Around

You can reach Vitorlás tér and the lake from the train and bus stations on buses 1, 1/a and 2; bus 1 continues on to Füred Camping.

You can also book a local **taxi** (☎ 444 444).

VESZPRÉM

☎ 88 / pop 61,100

Spreading over five hills between the northern and southern ranges of the Bakony Hills, Veszprém has one of the most dramatic locations in the Lake Balaton region. The walled castle district, atop a plateau, is a living museum of baroque art and architecture. It's a delight to stroll along the windy Castle Hill district's single street, admiring the embarrassment of fine churches. As the townspeople say, 'Either the wind is blowing or the bells are ringing in Veszprém'.

History

The Romans did not settle in what is now Veszprém but 8km to the southwest at Balácapuszta, where important archaeological finds have been made. Prince Géza, King Stephen's father, founded a bishopric in Veszprém late in the 10th century, and the city grew as a religious, administrative and educational centre (the university was established in the 13th century). It also became a favourite residence of Hungary's queens.

The castle at Veszprém was blown up by the Habsburgs in 1702, and lost most of its medieval buildings during the Rákóczi war of independence (1703–11) shortly thereafter. But this cleared the way for Veszprém's golden age, when the city's bishops and rich landlords built most of what you see today. The church's iron grip on Veszprém prevented it from developing commercially, however, and it was bypassed by the main railway line in the 19th century.

Orientation

The bus station (on Piac tér) is a few minutes' walk northeast from Kossuth Lajos utca, a pedestrian street of shops and banks. If you turn north at the end of Kossuth Lajos utca at Szabadság tér, and walk along Rákóczi utca, you'll soon reach the entrance to Castle Hill (Vár-hegy) at Óváros tér.

The train station is 4km north of the bus station at the end of Jutasi út.

Information

City website (www.veszprem.hu)

Daiquiri (Kossuth Lajos utca; per hr 300Ft; ⏰ 9am-10pm Mon-Thu, to midnight Fri & Sat, 2-10pm Sun) Bar on the 1st floor of the Cserhát shopping complex with internet access.

OTP bank (Óváros tér 25) Has an ATM.

Post office (Kossuth Lajos utca 19)

Tourinform (☎ 404 548; www.veszpreminfo.hu; Vár utca 4; ⏰ 9am-7pm Mon-Fri, 10am-4pm Sat & Sun May, Jun & Sep, 9am-7pm Mon-Fri, 10am-8pm Sat & Sun Jul & Aug, 9am-5pm Mon-Fri Oct-Apr) Extremely helpful information office with plenty of brochures on Veszprém and its surrounds.

Sights

CASTLE HILL

Any tour of Veszprém should begin in Óváros tér, the medieval market place at the foot of Castle Hill. Of the many fine 18th-century buildings in the square, the most interesting is the late-baroque **Pósa House** (Óváros tér 3), built in 1793 and now a bank. Others include the former **customs house** (Óváros tér 7) and **town hall** (Óváros tér 9). Fans of the *fin de siècle* will appreciate the pale yellow facade and Art Nouveau flourishes of the **Chinese House** (Óváros tér 22).

As you begin to ascend Castle Hill and its sole street, Vár utca, you'll pass through **Heroes' Gate** (Hősök kapuja), an entrance built in 1936 from the stones of a 15th-century castle gate.

To your left is the 48m-high **firewatch tower** (tűztorony; ☎ 425 204; Vár utca 9; adult/child/family 300/200/600Ft; ⏰ 10am-5pm mid-Mar–Apr, to 6pm May-Oct), which, like the one in Sopron, is an architectural hybrid of Gothic, baroque and neoclassical styles. You can climb to the top for excellent views of the rocky hill and the Bakony Hills.

Squeezed between two town houses further up Vár utca is the extremely rich **Piarist church** (Piarista templom; ☎ 426 088; Vár utca 12; admission free; ⏰ 10am-5pm Tue-Sun May–mid-Oct), which was built in 1836 in neoclassical style. Only a couple of doors along is the U-shaped **Bishop's Palace** (Püspöki palota; ☎ 426 088; Vár utca 16; adult/child 500/250Ft; ⏰ 10am-5pm Tue-Sun May–mid-Oct), designed by Jakab Fellner of Tata in the mid-18th century. It is thoroughly baroque inside

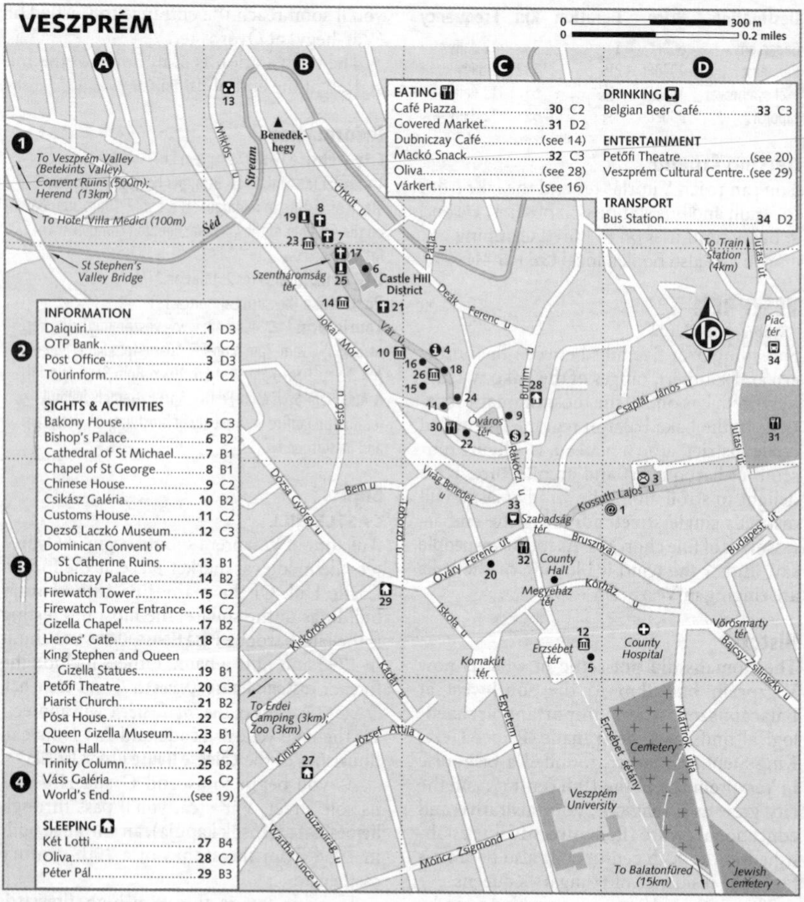

and out, and stands on the site where the queen's residence stood in the Middle Ages. The Palace faces Szentháromság tér, named for the **Trinity Column** (1751) in the centre.

Next to the Bishop's Palace is the early Gothic **Gizella Chapel** (Gizella-kápolna; ☎ 426 088; Vár utca 18; adult/child 200/100Ft; ⌚ 10am-5pm Tue-Sun May–mid-Oct), named after Gizella, the wife of King Stephen, who was crowned near here early in the 11th century. The chapel was discovered when the Bishop's Palace was being built in the mid-18th century. Inside the chapel are valuable Byzantine-influenced, 13th-century frescoes of the Apostles. The **Queen Gizella Museum** (☎ 426 088; Vár utca 35; adult/child 300/150Ft; ⌚ 10am-5pm May–mid-Oct) of religious art is slightly north of the chapel.

Parts of the dark and austere **Cathedral of St Michael** (Székesegyház; ☎ 328 038; Vár utca 18-20; admission free; ⌚ 10am-5pm May–mid-Oct) date from the beginning of the 11th century, but the cathedral has been rebuilt many times since then – the early Gothic crypt is original, though. Vibrant stained-glass windows back the church's modest altar, and little of the nave's high walls are left bare of intricate designs. Beside the cathedral, the octagonal foundation of the 13th-century **Chapel of St George** (Szent György kápolna; ☎ 426 088; Vár utca; adult/child 200/100Ft; ⌚ 10am-5pm Tue-Sun May-Oct) sits under an ugly concrete dome.

From the rampart known as **World's End**, at the end of Vár utca, you can gaze north to craggy Benedek-hegy (Benedict

Hill) and the Séd Stream, and west to the concrete viaduct (now St Stephen's Valley Bridge) over the Betekints Valley. In Margit tér, below the bridge, are the ruins of the medieval **Dominican Convent of St Catherine**, and to the west is what little remains of the 11th-century **Veszprém Valley (Betekints Valley) Convent**, whose erstwhile cloistered residents are said to have stitched Gizella's crimson silk coronation robe in 1031. The **King Stephen and Queen Gizella statues** at World's End were erected in 1938 to mark the 900th anniversary of King Stephen's death (see the boxed text, p227).

Vár utca is home to a number of art galleries specialising in 20th-century contemporary pieces from Hungary and abroad, including the **Váss Galéria** (☎ 561 310; www.vasscollection.hu, in Hungarian; Vár utca 7; adult/child 500/300Ft; 🕑 10am-6pm mid-Apr–mid-Oct, to 5pm Tue-Sun mid-Oct–mid-Apr), the **Csikász Galéria** (☎ 425 204; Vár utca 17; adult/child 250/150Ft; 🕑 10am-6pm May-Oct, to 5pm Mon-Sat Nov-Apr) and the newly renovated **Dubniczay Palace** (☎ 560 507; www.carllaszlocollection.hu; Vár utca 29; adult/student 800/400Ft; 🕑 10am-6pm Tue-Sun).

DEZSŐ LACZKÓ MUSEUM

The **Dezső Laczkó Museum** (Bakony Museum; ☎ 564 310; Erzsébet sétány 1; adult/child 600/300Ft, includes entrance to Bakony House; 🕑 10am-6pm Tue-Sun mid-May–mid-Oct, noon-4pm Tue-Sun mid-Oct–mid-Mar) is south of Megyeház tér. It has archaeological exhibits (the emphasis is on the Roman settlement at Balácapuszta), a large collection of Hungarian, German and Slovak folk costumes and superb wooden carvings, including objects made by the famed outlaws of the Bakony Hills in the 18th and 19th centuries. Next to the main museum is **Bakony House** (Bakonyi ház; ☎ 564 330; adult/child 250/125Ft; 🕑 10am-6pm Tue-Sun mid-May–mid-Oct), a copy of an 18th-century thatched peasant dwelling in the village of Öcs, southwest of Veszprém. It has the usual three rooms found in Hungarian peasant homes, and the complete *kamra* (workshop) of a flask-maker has been set up. Its roof suffered fire damage in May 2008, so what you see today is very new.

PETŐFI THEATRE

Take a peek inside the **Petőfi Theatre** (☎ 424 235; www.petofiszinhaz.hu, in Hungarian; Óváry Ferenc út 2) even if you're not attending a performance. Designed by István Medgyaszay in 1908, this pink, grey and burgundy building is a gem of Hungarian Art Nouveau architecture. It's also important structurally, as the theatre was the first building in the country to be made entirely of reinforced concrete. The large round stained-glass window entitled *The Magic of Folk Art* by Sándor Nagy is exceptional. See p226 for show information.

Festivals & Events

The free **Veszprém Festival**, held at the beginning of August, attracts some big international names in jazz and classical music. You'll find stages set up across town.

Sleeping

Tourinform organises private rooms for 3000Ft to 5000Ft per person.

Erdei Camping (☎ 326 751; Kittenberger utca 14; camp sites per adult/child/tent 1000/500/1000Ft, bungalows 10,000Ft; 🕑 mid-Apr–mid-Oct) This small camping ground is a fair way west of town, which is great if you're looking for some peace and quiet, but you'll need your own transport. It's surrounded by fields and woods, and is next to the zoo.

Péter Pál (☎ 328 091; www.peterpal.hu, in Hungarian; Dózsa György utca 3; s/d 6440/8480Ft; ⊠) Péter Pál is a lovely little *pension* bordering on boutique class. It has a fine choice of simple yet stylish rooms, a lovely garden, above-average restaurant and very friendly and helpful staff.

Két Lotti (☎ 566 520; www.ketlotti.hu; József Attila utca 21; s/d 9600/11,600Ft; ⊠) A peaceful and relaxing stay is almost always guaranteed at Két Lotti, a boutique villa-*pension* west of the centre. Rooms are spacious and tastefully decorated in calming hues, and there's a large, manicured garden to enjoy. Additionally, guests can use the sauna and arrange massages on-site.

Oliva (☎ 403 875; www.oliva.hu; Buhim utca 14-16; s/d 17,860/20,220Ft; ⊠ 💻) This exquisite little *pension* is located in a beautifully restored town house just below Castle Hill. Rooms are modern, spacious and furnished with pseudo-antiques, and its restaurant is first rate.

Hotel Villa Medici (☎ 590 070; www.villamedici.hu; Kittenberg utca 11; r/ste from 23,800/34,500Ft; ⊠ 🏊) Tucked away in a secluded valley between two of Veszprém's hills is the four-star Villa Medici. Rooms are fine but a tad dated, but there are plenty of added luxuries such as sauna, indoor pool, sculptured garden, English-style pub, wine cellar and quality restaurant.

Eating & Drinking

Covered market (Piac tér) This large market, where you can buy food among other things, is south of the bus station.

Mackó Snack (Szabadság tér; burgers & pizza from 300Ft; 8am-5pm Mon-Fri) Join students and workers on the run at lunchtime for Mackó's quick snacks and pizzas, or stay put and dig into the healthy salad bar in non-smoking surroundings.

our pick **Oliva** (☎ 403 875; Buhim utca 14-16; mains 1000-3000Ft) Subdued lighting and vaulted ceilings help make Oliva an intimate setting for a romantic evening. The menu changes with the seasons, but regularly features Hungarian specialities cooked with care. A substantial wine selection supplements the menu, and in summer the restaurant's huge outdoor patio often features live bands.

Café Piazza (☎ 444 445; Óváros tér 4; mains from 1200Ft; 8.30am-10pm) With seating on pretty Óváros tér and plentiful lunchtime specials, Café Piazza attracts workers and tourists by the droves. Also good for a coffee or something stronger.

Várkert (☎ 560 468; Vár utca 17; mains 1400-2800Ft) Newly renovated and bubbling with energy, Várkert is a welcome addition to Veszprém's dining scene. Its menu features unusual dishes, such as wild game ragout and rabbit stew, alongside imaginative Hungarian specialities. There's live music most evenings, and its sunny inner courtyard is an attraction in its own right over summer.

Dubniczay Café (☎ 560 507; Vár utca 29; coffee 300Ft; 10am-6pm) Hidden behind the austere facade of the Dubniczay Palace is this inviting cafe, with a sunny terrace looking west across the rooftops of the city.

Belgian Beer Café (☎ 444 900; Szabadság tér 5) Why Belgian beer is such a hit in Hungary when the amber liquid north of the border is a far better option is anyone's guess, but no matter, this place attracts punters by the dozen with its convivial, relaxed atmosphere and huge terrace overlooking Petőfi Theatre.

Entertainment

Veszprém Cultural Centre (☎ 429 111; Dózsa György utca 2) This is where the city's symphony orchestra is based.

Petőfi Theatre (☎ 424 235; www.petofiszinhaz.hu, in Hungarian; Óváry Ferenc út 2; box office 11am-6pm Mon-Fri) This theatre is magnificent and stages both plays and concerts; tickets are available from the box office in the theatre. See also p225.

Getting There & Away

BUS

Connections with Veszprém are excellent.

Destination	Price	Duration	Km	Frequency
Balatonfüred	375Ft	40min	20	half-hourly
Budapest	1770Ft	2¼hr	112	hourly
Győr	1350Ft	2hr	86	9 daily
Herend	375Ft	20min	21	half-hourly
Keszthely	1200Ft	1¾hr	77	hourly
Nagyvázsony	375Ft	30min	22	10 daily
Pápa	750Ft	1¼hr	50	hourly
Siófok	750Ft	1¼hr	48	7 daily
Sümeg	1050Ft	2hr	68	up to 18 daily
Székesfehérvár	675Ft	55min	45	half-hourly
Tapolca	750Ft	1-1½hr	49	hourly

TRAIN

For destinations along the northern and southern shores of Lake Balaton, a change at Székesfehérvár is required. Direct connections include the following destinations:

Destination	Price	Duration	Km	Frequency
Budapest	1770Ft	2hr	112	6 daily
Győr	1200Ft	2-3hr	79	3 daily
Pannonhalma	900Ft	1¾hr	58	4 daily
Székesfehérvár	675Ft	40-55min	45	16 daily
Szombathely	2040Ft	2hr	124	12 daily

Getting Around

Buses 1, 2 and 4 run from the train and bus stations to Szabadság tér. You can also book a local **taxi** (☎ 444 444).

HERBEND

☎ 88 / pop 3560

The porcelain factory at **Herend** (www.herend.hu), 13km west of Veszprém, has been producing Hungary's finest handpainted chinaware for over 180 years. There's not a lot to see in this dusty one-horse village, and prices at the outlet don't seem any cheaper than elsewhere in Hungary, but the **Porcelánium** (☎ 523 190; www.herend.com; Kossuth Lajos utca 140; adult/child/family factory & museum 1700/800/3600Ft; 9am-5pm mid-Apr–Oct, 9.30am-4pm Tue-Sat Feb–mid-Apr & Nov–mid-Dec) is worth the trip. Guided tours, in Hungarian, English, German or Spanish, leave every 15 minutes and walk visitors through a museum that displays the most prized pieces of the rich Herend collection, and a mini-factory, where you can witness first-hand how ugly clumps of clay become delicate porcelain. It's

REACH OUT & TOUCH

It could have been a chapter from a Mills & Boon novel for the macabre. It was 1996. Millecentenary celebrations honouring the arrival of the Magyars in the Carpathian Basin in 896 were underway in Hungary. People were in the mood to mark dates and one of those people was the archbishop of Veszprém.

He knew that it had been in Veszprém that the future king, Stephen, and a Bavarian princess, Gizella, were married in 996. Just suppose, he thought, that the bishop of the Bavarian city of Passau, where Gizella's remains had been resting these nine centuries, agreed to send her hand to Hungary. The Holy Dexter, St Stephen's revered right hand, could be brought down from the Basilica in Budapest and they could… Well, the mind boggled.

All parties agreed (the bishop of Passau even threw in Gizella's arm bone) and the date was set. In the square in front of the Cathedral of St Michael in Veszprém, the hands were laid together and – 1000 years to the day of the wedding – coyly touched in marital bliss once again.

The world did not change as we know it that fine spring morning – tram 2 raced along the Danube in Budapest, Mr Kovács dished out steaming *lángos* from his stall somewhere along Lake Balaton, and schoolchildren in Sárospatak recited their *ábécé*. But all true Magyars knew, deep in their hearts, that all was right with the world.

a five-minute walk northeast from the bus station. Labels are in four languages, including English, which makes it easy to follow the developments and changes in patterns and tastes (see the boxed text, p228), and there's a short film tracing the history of Herend porcelain.

The complex has a **shop** (🕑 same hours as Porcelánium) selling antique pieces; otherwise scout around the few shops close to the Porcelánium for new pieces.

Should you feel hungry, Porcelánium has an upmarket cafe called **Apicius** (set menus 2700-5700Ft; 🕑 9am-6pm mid-Apr–Oct, to 5pm Tue-Sat Feb–mid-Apr & Nov–mid-Dec), otherwise you'll have to make do with the handful of food stalls close to the Porcelánium complex.

Getting There & Away

You can reach Herend by bus from Veszprém at least every 30 minutes (375Ft, 20 minutes, 21km); other destinations include Sümeg (900Ft, 1½ hours, 52km, eight daily) and Balatonfüred (600Ft, one hour, 37km, two daily). Six trains run through Herend daily from Veszprém (250Ft, 12 minutes, 14km) on their way to Szombathely.

PÁPA

☎ 89 / pop 33,180

The small town of Pápa will be of interest to anyone with a bent for Calvinism or the art of dyeing. It was once called the 'Athens of Transdanubia' largely because of its Calvinist school, and its blue dyeing museum still has machines in working order.

History

Religious tolerance has been a hallmark of Pápa for centuries. Protestantism gained ground swiftly in the area in the 16th century and during the late Middle Ages Pápa was the third most important Protestant stronghold in Transdanubia after Sopron and Sárvár.

Pápa flourished after liberation from the Turks, with Bishop Károly Esterházy overseeing the construction of many of its fine baroque buildings; his family effectively owned the town from 1648 to after WWII. His brother Ferenc encouraged trade by allowing Jews to settle in Pápa and by the end of the 19th century Pápa had one of the largest Jewish populations in Hungary.

Orientation

Pápa's central square is Fő tér, which is dominated by the town's large parish church. Kastély-park is just north of the square, and the bus station, on Szabadság utca, is a short distance to the east. Fő utca and pedestrian Kossuth Lajos utca are the town's main drags; both run south from Fő tér. The train station (Béke tér) is north of the centre at the end of Esterházy Károly utca.

Information

Main post office (Kossuth Lajos utca 29)
OTP bank (Fő tér 22) Has an ATM.
Tourinform (☎ 311 535; papa@tourinform.hu; Kossuth Lajos utca 18; 🕑 9am-5pm Mon-Fri) Stocks some information on the town.

LAKE BALATON REGION

HEREND PORCELAIN

A terracotta factory, set up at Herend in 1826, began producing porcelain 13 years later under Mór Farkasházi Fischer of Tata in Western Transdanubia.

Initially it specialised in copying and replacing the nobles' broken chinaware settings imported from Asia. You'll see some pretty kooky 19th-century interpretations of Japanese art and Chinese faces on display in the Porcelánium (p226). But the factory soon began producing its own patterns; many, like the 'Rothschild bird' and 'petites roses', were inspired by Meissen and Sèvres designs from Germany and France. The Victoria pattern of butterflies and wild flowers of the Bakony was designed for Queen Victoria after she admired a display of Herend pieces at the Great Exhibition in London in 1851.

To avoid bankruptcy in the 1870s, the Herend factory began mass production; tastes ran from kitschy pastoral and hunting scenes to the ever-popular animal sculptures with the distinctive scalelike triangle patterns. In 1992 three-quarters of the factory was purchased by its 1500 workers and became one of the first companies in Hungary privatised through an employee stock-ownership plan. The state owns the other quarter.

Sights

It's hard to avoid the **Great Church** (Nagytemplom; Fő tér; admission free; 9am-6pm) in the centre of Pápa. Built by Jacob Fellner in 1786 and dedicated to St Stephen, it contains wonderful yet fading ceiling frescoes (1781–82) of St Stephen's life and martyrdom by Franz Anton Maulbertsch and Hubert Mauer. Its bland, grey walls are rather depressing, though.

Behind the church at the entrance to Kastélypark sits the former **Esterházy Palace** (Esterházy kastély; ☎ 313 584; admission free; 9am-5pm Tue-Sun). The huge U-shaped building, built in 1784 on the foundations of an older castle, doesn't appear to have been renovated much since its construction, and now houses a rarely open regional museum, a music school and a library. Russian soldiers were billeted here as late as 1990.

South of Fő tér lies many of Pápa's other sights. First up is the **Calvinist Church History Museum** (Református Egyháztörténeti Múzeum; ☎ 342 240; Fő utca 6; adult/child 200/100Ft; 8am-4pm Tue-Fri May-Oct), which may not sound like a crowd-pleaser but it does have a lovely collection of simple wooden altars. Further south is the **Calvinist College Library** (☎ 324 420; Március 15 tér 9; adult/child 500/300Ft; 8am-4pm Tue-Fri, 9am-5pm Sat & Sun), where some 75,000 valuable tomes are kept.

Arguably the most popular museum in Pápa is the **Blue Dyeing Museum** (Kékfestő Múzeum; ☎ 324 390; Március 15 tér 12; adult/child 500/250Ft; 9am-5pm Tue-Sun Apr-Oct, to 4pm Tue-Sat Nov-Mar). It showcases a method of colouring cotton fabric deep blue that was a famous Pápa export throughout Hungary. The museum is housed in a factory that stopped operating in 1956, but the machines remain in perfect working order. Demonstrations are sometimes held and there's an interesting display of samples and old photographs.

The streets running west off Kossuth Lajos utca are particularly rich architecturally, especially along **Korvin utca** – check out the Gothic, baroque and rococo gems at Nos 4, 9, 7 and 13, most of which are now offices. To the south, the **Great Synagogue** (Nagyzsinagóga; Petőfi Sándor utca 24-26), a romantic structure built in 1846 with some 100,000 bricks donated by the Esterházy family, sadly barely stands.

Sleeping & Eating

There's no need to stay in Pápa overnight with such regular bus connections to more lively places, but if you're stuck head for central **Arany Griff** (☎ 312 000; www.hotelaranygriff.hu; Fő tér 15; s/d from 10,600/12,600Ft, mains 1600-2800Ft). Rooms here are comfy yet dated, but there are excellent views of the Great Church across Fő tér. Its restaurant on the ground floor does surprisingly good Hungarian dishes and a handful of healthy salads. Parking is available here.

Getting There & Away

BUS

Pápa has good bus connections.

Destination	Price	Duration	Km	Frequency
Balatonfüred	1050Ft	1¾hr	63	2 daily
Budapest	2540Ft	4hr	170	3 daily
Győr	750Ft	1hr	48	hourly
Keszthely	1200Ft	2¼hr	80	6 daily
Sümeg	900Ft	1¼hr	51	5 daily
Tapolca	900Ft	1½-2hr	59	3 daily
Veszprém	750Ft	1¼hr	50	hourly

TRAIN

Pápa is on the rail line linking Győr (750Ft, one hour, 47km, hourly) with Celldömölk, from where you can change for Szombathely (1050Ft, one to two hours, 70km, hourly).

SZÉKESFEHÉRVÁR

☎ 22 / pop 101,500

From the outside, Székesfehérvár (*sake*-kesh-fehair-vahr) looks like just another big city, but dig a little deeper and you find a settlement with a rich history. Roman ruins fill the centre of this bustling metropolis, and it is traditionally known as the place where the Magyar chieftain Árpád first set up camp, making it the oldest town in Hungary. Despite this, Székesfehérvár attracts few visitors, making it all that more appealing.

History

As early as the 1st century, the Romans had a settlement at Gorsium near Tác. When Árpád arrived late in the 9th century, the surrounding marshes and the Sárvíz River offered protection – the same reason Prince Géza built his castle here less than 100 years later. But it was King Stephen I who raised the status of Székesfehérvár by building a fortified basilica in what he called Alba Regia. Hungary's kings (and some of its queens) would be crowned and buried here for the next 500 years. In fact, the city's name means 'Seat of the White Castle', as it was the royal capital and white was the king's colour.

With Visegrád, Esztergom and Buda, Székesfehérvár served as an alternative royal capital for centuries, and it was here in 1222 that King Andrew II was forced by his mercenaries to sign the Golden Bull, an early bill of rights. The Turks captured Székesfehérvár in 1543 and used the basilica to store gunpowder. It exploded during a siege in 1601; when the Turks left in 1688, the town, the basilica and the royal tombs were in ruins.

The arrival of the railway in the 1860s turned the city into a transport hub. WWII left much of the city in ruins (though the historic centre was left more or less intact), but this opened the way for postwar industrial development.

Orientation

Városház tér and Koronázó tér form the core of the old town. Pedestrian Fő utca – what the Romans called Vicus Magnus – runs north from here. The train station is a 15-minute walk southeast and can be reached via József Attila utca and its continuation, Deák Ferenc utca. The bus station is near the market, just outside the old town's western wall.

Information

City website (www.szekesfehervar.hu) Online information about the city.

Hiemer Internet Café (Városház tér; per hr 360Ft; 🕑 9am-10pm) Next door to Tourinform.

Main post office (Kossuth Lajos utca 16)

OTP bank (Fő utca 7) Has an ATM.

Tourinform (☎ 537 261; tourinform@szekesfehervar.hu; Városház tér; 🕑 9am-6pm Mon-Fri, to 4pm Sat, to 2pm Sun mid-May–mid-Sep, to 5pm Mon-Fri mid-Sep–mid-May) Not particularly useful, aside from picking up a few brochures.

Sights

ST STEPHEN'S CATHEDRAL & ST ANNE'S CHAPEL

St Stephen's Cathedral (Szent István székesegyház; Géza nagyfejedelem tér; admission free; 🕑 services only), just off Arany János utca, was constructed in 1470, but what you see today is essentially an 18th-century baroque church. The interior, featuring an enormous high altar and light ceiling frescoes by Johannes Cymbal, is ornate but not overbearing. On the paving stones in front of the cathedral are foundation outlines of an earlier (perhaps 10th century) church. The bent and tortured wooden crucifix on the northern wall is dedicated to the victims of the 1956 Uprising.

Just north of the cathedral is **St Anne's Chapel** (Szent Anna kápolna; Arany János utca; admission free; 🕑 services only) built around the same time, with additions (the tower, for example) made some centuries later. The Turks used the chapel as a place of worship; you can still see the remains of a painting from that era.

VÁROSHÁZ TÉR, KORONÁZÓ TÉR & AROUND

Arany János utca debouches into Városház tér and Koronázó tér. Each square sports an unusual monument – the former the **broken bell** (1995) lying on its side, dedicated to the victims of WWII; and the latter the **National Orb** (Országalma – which means 'national apple' in Hungarian), dedicated to King Stephen. On Városház tér is the **Franciscan church** (Ferences templom; admission free; 🕑 services only), built in 1745. Its high altar is complemented by no less than six side altars, all of which are impressive in their own right.

The most imposing building on Koronázó tér is the Zopf-style **Bishop's Palace** (Püspöki palota), built with the rubble from the medieval basilica and royal burial chapels in 1801. The basilica and chapels stood to the east, in what is now the **Garden of Ruins** (Romkert; ☎ 315 583; adult/child/family 600/300/1350Ft; ⏰ 9am-5pm Tue-Sun Apr-Oct). The site is sacred to Hungarians – about 30 of their kings and queens were crowned here and 15 were buried here. The white marble sarcophagus in the chamber to the right as you enter the main gate is thought to contain the remains of Géza, Stephen or his young son, Imre. Decorative stonework from the basilica and royal tombs lines the walls of the loggia, and in the garden are the **cathedral and Coronation Church foundations**. Most of it can be seen from the raised **viewing platform** (Koronázó tér), saving you the entrance fee.

FŐ UTCA & AROUND

North of the town centre, the **Black Eagle** (Fekete Sas; ☎ 315 583; Fő utca 5; adult/child 400/200Ft; ⏰ 10am-6pm Tue-Sun) is a pharmacy set up by the Jesuits in 1758, and by the looks of the beautiful rococo furnishings on display, it hasn't changed a bit since then. Just to the west, on Oskola utca, the **István Csók Gallery** (☎ 314 106; Bartók Béla tér 1; adult/child 400/200Ft; ⏰ 10am-7pm Mon-Fri, to 6pm Sat & Sun) has a good collection of 19th- and 20th-century Hungarian art.

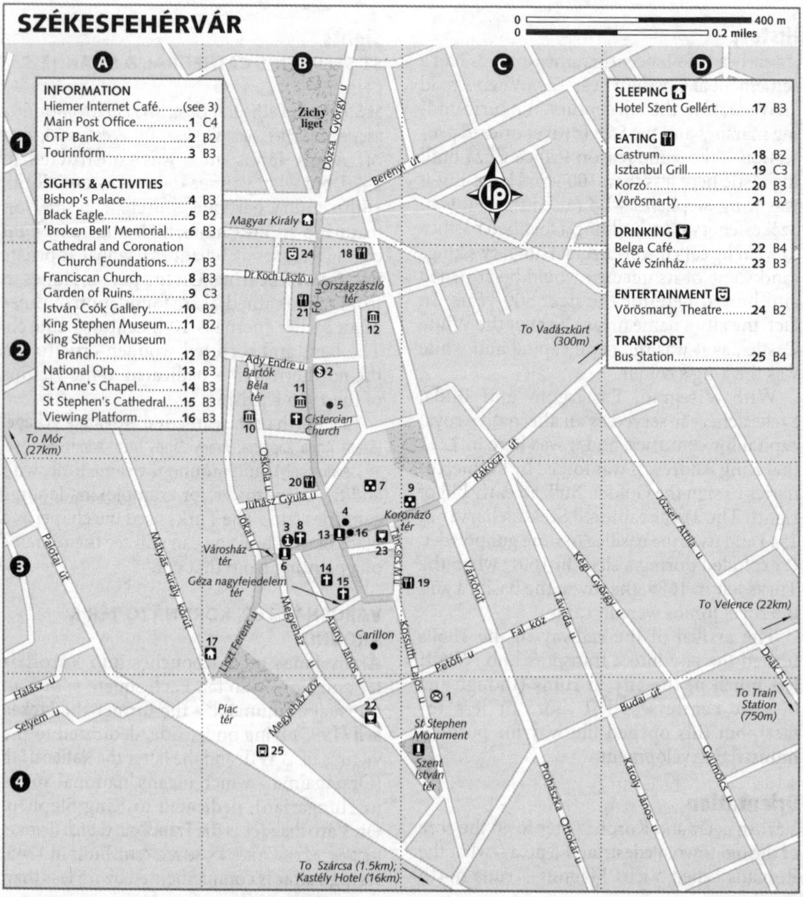

The **King Stephen Museum** (István Király Múzeum; ☎ 315 583; Fő utca 6; adult/child 400/200Ft; 🕑 10am-4pm Tue-Sun May-Sep, to 2pm Tue-Sun Oct-Apr) has a large collection of Roman pottery (some of it from Gorsium), an interesting folk-carving display and an exhibit covering 1000 years of Székesfehérvár history. The **museum branch** (Országzászló tér 3; 🕑 2-6pm Tue-Sun May-Oct, to 4pm Tue-Sun Nov-Apr) has temporary exhibits.

Sleeping

Check with Tourinform for college accommodation in July and August for between 3000Ft and 5000Ft per person.

Hotel Szent Gellért (☎ 510 810; www.hotels.hu/szentgellert; Mátyás király körút 1; dm without bathroom 3400-4400Ft, dm with bathroom 3900-4900Ft, s/d 11,900/14,700Ft) This central option has bare-bone dormitories with wooden bunks and cupboards for storage, along with spacious rooms with fridges and a smattering of charm. Breakfast is an extra 300Ft.

Vadászkürt (☎ 507 515; www.jagerhorn.hu; Berényi út 1; r/apt 9000/12,000Ft; ⊠ ⁜ ▣) This *pension* caters to business travellers and has lifeless rooms, but they're modern and clean, and there is a small wellness centre on-site. It's about a 15-minute walk to the centre from here.

Kastély Hotel (☎ 447 030; www.kastelyhotel-seregelyes.hu; Kastély utca 1; s/d 17,960/19,240Ft, apt from 28,640Ft; ▣) Some 16km southeast of town at Seregélyes is this stately home, surrounded by 22 hectares of manicured parkland. Originally the Zichy family's country manor (1821), it now houses a hotel, complete with frescoed dining hall, tennis court and sauna. Rooms are tasteful but not luxurious, however, you're paying for ambience, not over-the-top luxury.

Szárcsa (☎ 325 700; www.szarcsa.com; Szárcsa utca 1; s/d 20,000/25,000Ft; ⁜ ▣) This is a fair distance south from the town centre but it's worth the trip. Each of its nine rooms are individually decorated with antique furniture and the entire effect is one of a giant doll's house. There's a quality restaurant here, too.

Eating & Drinking

Along with the restaurants listed here, the eatery at Szárcsa (above) is worth dining at. The wine to try in these parts is Ezerjó from Mór, 27km to the northwest in the Vértes Hills. It's an acidic, greenish-white tipple that is light and fairly pleasant.

Vörösmarty (Fő utca 6; ice cream 120Ft; 🕑 9am-9pm) This is an ice cream and cake shop that keeps the crowds satisfied with sweet delights throughout the year.

Isztanbul Grill (Táncsics Mihály utca 6; kebabs from 400Ft; 🕑 11am-10pm Mon-Sat) Stop in at this bright little eatery for cheap, filling kebabs. A fresh salad bar caters to non-meat eaters.

Korzó (☎ 312 674; Fő utca 2; mains 1500-2500Ft) With its pole position providing views the length of Fő utca, Korzó is the pick of the restaurants in the heart of Székesfehérvár. Its menu is filled with hefty Hungarian cuisine and its terrace is perfect for enjoying a sunny day.

Castrum (☎ 505 720; Várkörút 3; mains 2000-4390Ft) This medieval-themed cellar restaurant isn't the cheapest but the portions are big enough for two. Choose from the likes of leg of venison or duck on a spit and stuff yourself to bursting point. In the summer months the restaurant spills out onto tree-shaded Országzászló tér.

Kávé Színház (Coffee Theatre; ☎ 310 923; Táncsics Mihály utca 1) This 1st-floor cafe is great for a quiet drink, day or night. Its huge terrace overlooks Koronázó tér and the Garden of Ruins, and its warm red interior is complemented by posters from the 1920s. Enter from Vasvári Pál utca.

Belga Café (☎ 507 585; Szent István tér 14; 🕑 10am-midnight) This grown-up cafe with a grown-up crowd occupies a quiet corner south of the centre. Pull up a pew in the wood interior or grab a seat on the small streetside terrace and enjoy the array of Belgian beers on offer.

Entertainment

For information on what's on, check the free bi-weekly *Fehérvári Est* magazine.

Vörösmarty Theatre (☎ 327 056; Fő utca 8) This theatre, near the former Magyar Király hotel, has recently experienced a complete overhaul, so expect cultural performances against a grand backdrop.

Getting There & Away

BUS

There are buses to the following destinations.

Destination	Price	Duration	Km	Frequency
Balatonfüred	1050Ft	1½hr	69	7 daily
Budapest	1050Ft	1¼hr	68	hourly
Keszthely	2040Ft	2¾hr	123	7 daily
Mór	375Ft	35min	22	half-hourly
Siófok	675Ft	50min	44	5 daily
Sümeg	1770Ft	2½-3hr	116	3 daily
Szekszárd	1770Ft	2hr	104	7 daily
Tapolca	1500Ft	2hr	94	4 daily
Veszprém	675Ft	55min	45	half-hourly

TRAIN

The town is a main train junction and you can reach most destinations in Transdanubia from here. One line splits at Szabadbattyán (10km to the south), leading to Lake Balaton's northern shore and Tapolca on one side of the lake, and to the southern shore and Nagykanizsa on the other.

Destination	Price	Duration	Km	Frequency
Budapest	1050Ft	1½hr	67	half-hourly
Mór	450Ft	31min	29	6 daily
Szombathely	2540Ft	2½-4hr	169	7 daily
Veszprém	675Ft	40-55min	45	16 daily

Getting Around

Bus 12/a runs close to Szárcsa Hotel. You can also book local **taxis** (☎ 222 222).

AROUND SZÉKESFEHÉRVÁR

To the east of Székesfehérvár is **Velence**, the third-largest lake in Hungary at 10.5km long and 26 sq km in size. It's a far more subdued lake than Balaton, and with an average depth of under 2m, it's ideal for families. Almost a third of the lake's surface is covered in reeds, making it a good place to observe birdlife.Other activities here include swimming, boating, windsurfing, water skiing and fishing.

Most of the action is concentrated in the towns of **Gárdony** and **Agárd** on the south side of the lake, and in **Velence** to the northeast, including 10 camp sites and a plethora of hotels and *pensions*. For more information, try your luck at Székesfehérvár's Tourinform or log on to www.velence.hu.

Great Plain

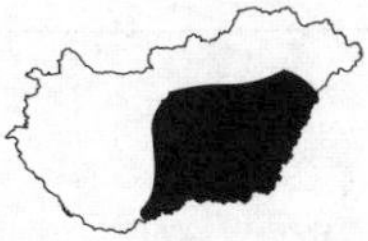

Like the Outback for Australians or the Old West for Americans, the Nagy Alföld (Great Plain) holds a romantic appeal for most Magyars. The image of shepherds guiding their flocks with moplike Puli dogs and cowboys riding five-in-hand across the prairies comes as much from imagination (and the nation's poetry and painting) as it does from history. The Great Plain covers some 45,000 sq km east and southeast of Budapest, encompassing half the nation's territory, but only about a third of the population. At times the unending fields with sporadic tree stands can feel numbingly monotonous and be uncomfortably hot. But there's no arguing the spellbinding potential of big-sky country, especially around Hortobágy and Kiskunság National Parks.

Not as one-dimensional as it might seem, the Great Plain is also home to cities of graceful architecture, winding rivers and easygoing afternoons. Szeged is a centre for art and Art Nouveau gems, while its neighbour Kecskemét is a small city packing a big architectural punch. Further east, day-trip opportunities abound from Debrecen, Hungary's second city. With terrific bird-watching, a huge thermal bath resort, and horse riding and horse shows to seek out, it should be easy to create your own memories of the plain.

HIGHLIGHTS

- Sampling the namesake meat-filled pancakes with paprika sauce in a hundred-year-old inn after horse riding or bird-watching in **Hortobágy** (p247)
- Spending the day taking pictures of the Art Nouveau palaces in culture-filled **Szeged** (p263)
- Attending a street festival on the pretty pedestrian squares of **Kecskemét** (p252)
- Feeling the earth shake as a Hungarian cowboy rides by 'five-in-hand' at the *puszta* horse show in **Bugac** (p257)
- Soaking in the thermal baths beneath the only castle on the plain, at **Gyula** (p276), near the Romanian border

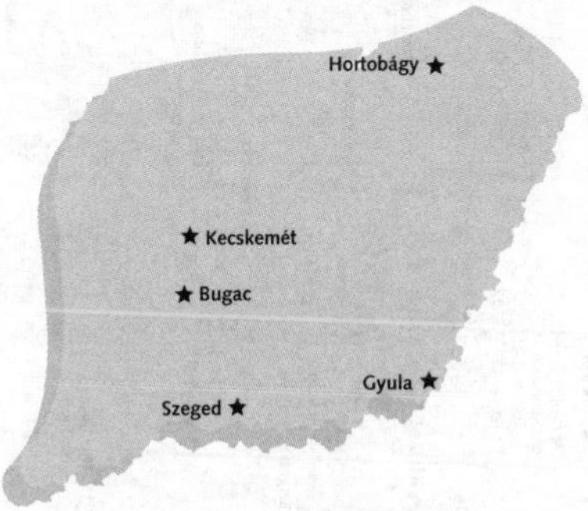

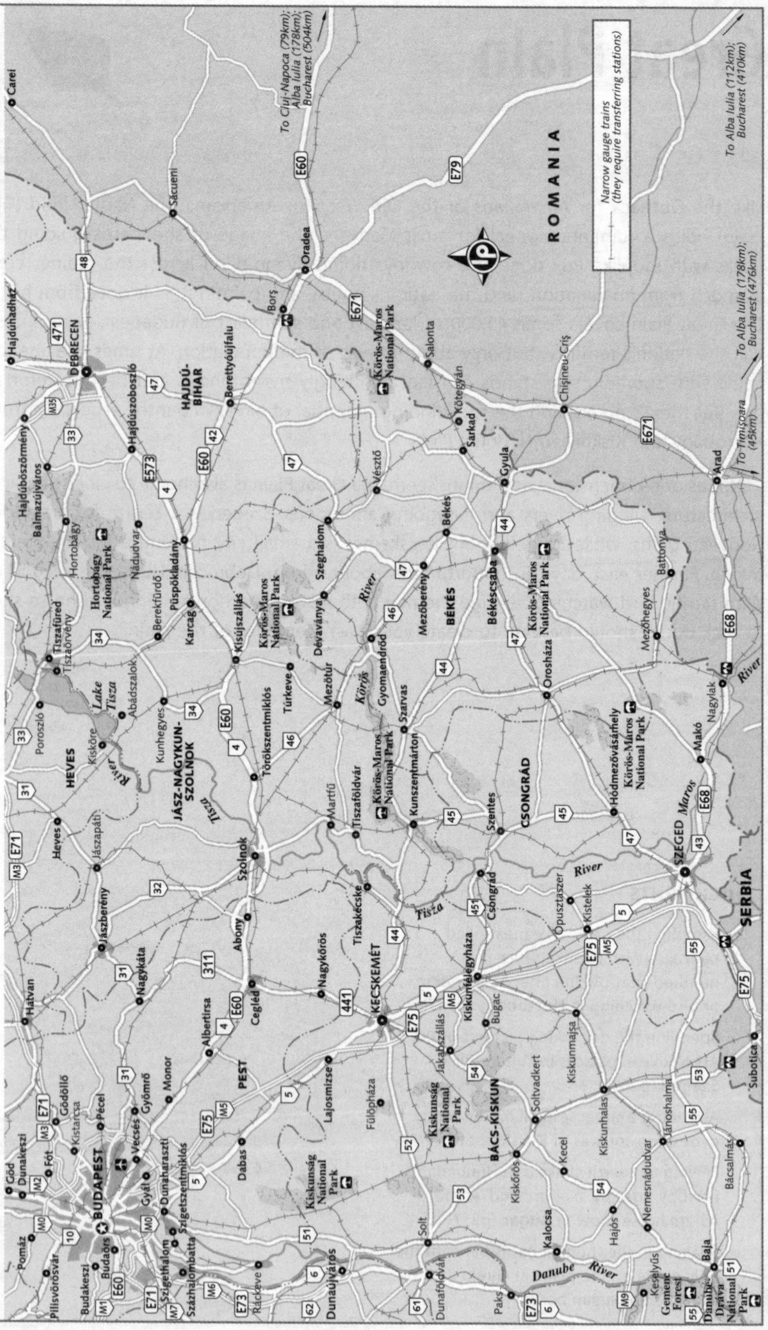
GREAT PLAIN
0 40 km
0 20 miles
ROMANIA
SERBIA
Narrow gauge trains (they require transferring stations)
To Cluj-Napoca (79km); Alba Iulia (178km); Bucharest (504km)
To Alba Iulia (112km); Bucharest (410km)
To Alba Iulia (178km); Bucharest (476km)
To Timişoara (45km)
HEVES
JÁSZ-NAGYKUN-SZOLNOK
HAJDÚ-BIHAR
PEST
BÉKÉS
CSONGRÁD
BÁCS-KISKUN
BUDAPEST
DEBRECEN
KECSKEMÉT
SZEGED
Carei
Săcueni
Oradea
Borş
Salonta
Chişineu-Criş
Arad
Hajdúhadház
Hajdúböszörmény
Hajdúszoboszló
Berettyóújfalu
Balmazújváros
Hortobágy
Hortobágy National Park
Nádudvar
Püspökladány
Berekfürdő
Karcag
Kisújszállás
Tiszafüred
Tiszaörvény
Poroszló
Lake Tisza
Abádszalok
Kisköre
Kunhegyes
Heves
Jászapáti
Jászberény
Hatvan
Nagykáta
Szolnok
Abony
Cegléd
Albertirsa
Monor
Gyömrő
Pécel
Gödöllő
Kistarcsa
Fót
Göd
Dunakeszi
Pomáz
Pilisvörösvár
Budakeszi
Budaörs
Gyál
Vecsés
Dunaharaszti
Szigetszentmiklós
Szigethalom
Százhalombatta
Ráckeve
Dunaújváros
Dabas
Lajosmizse
Nagykőrös
Tiszakécske
Törökszentmiklós
Túrkeve
Mezőtúr
Dévaványa
Szeghalom
Vésztő
Sarkad
Kötegyán
Gyula
Békés
Békéscsaba
Mezőberény
Gyomaendrőd
Szarvas
Kunszentmárton
Tiszaföldvár
Martfű
Szentes
Csongrád
Orosháza
Battonya
Mezőhegyes
Nagylak
Makó
Hódmezővásárhely
Kistelek
Ópusztaszer
Kiskunfélegyháza
Bugac
Jakabszállás
Fülöpháza
Kiskunmajsa
Kiskunhalas
Soltvadkert
Kiskőrös
Kecel
Solt
Dunaföldvár
Paks
Kalocsa
Hajós
Nemesnádudvar
Jánoshalma
Bácsalmás
Subotica
Baja
Kiskunság National Park
Körös-Maros National Park
Gemenc Forest
Duna-Dráva National Park
Danube River
Tisza River
Körös River
Maros River

History

Five hundred years ago the region was not a steppe but forest land at the constant mercy of the flooding Tisza and Danube Rivers. The Turks felled most of the trees, destroying the protective cover and releasing the topsoil to the winds; villagers fled north or to the market towns and *khas* (towns under the sultan's jurisdiction). The region had become the *puszta* ('wild' or 'uninhabited' lands), home to shepherds, fisher folk, runaway serfs and outlaws. You'll find few fortifications outside Gyula on the Great Plain; the Turks required they be destroyed as part of the agreement of retreat. In the 19th century regulation of the rivers dried up the marshes and allowed for methodical irrigation, paving the way for intensive agriculture, particularly on the Southern Plain, but flooding does still occur.

CENTRAL PLAIN

The Central Plain, the smallest of the Great Plain's divisions, stretches eastward from Budapest to the Tisza River and encompasses the likes of Szolnok and Jászberény, river towns of little importance to most travellers even though the latter holds a historical gem. The biggest attraction in the region is Lake Tisza, Hungary's second-largest and a water-lover's paradise.

SZOLNOK

☎56 / pop 75,000

The Tisza River, and the park and thermal spa across it from the old town, hold Szolnok's limited, laid-back appeal. Otherwise, besides a couple of old buildings and a decent museum, much of the stretched-out modern city is not pretty. Walking distances between city services and island hotels can be daunting on hot summer days – take a taxi.

History

A 'deed of gift' issued by King Géza I makes mention of Szolnok, then called Zounok, as early as 1075, and it has remained the most important settlement in the Central Plain ever since.

Szolnok has had its share of troubles: it was laid to waste more than a dozen times over the centuries. The last disaster came in 1944, when Allied bombing all but flattened the city and the retreating German troops blew up the bridge over the Tisza.

Orientation

Szolnok is situated on the confluence of the Tisza and narrow Zagyva Rivers. Its main street, Kossuth Lajos út, runs roughly east–west a few blocks north of the Tisza. Across the Tisza Bridge (Tisza híd) is the city's recreational area (Tiszaliget), which has the best of the city's accommodation, as well as the thermal spa.

The city's busy train station is 2km west of the city centre at the end of Baross Gábor út. The closer bus station is on Ady Endre utca, a few minutes' walk north of Kossuth Lajos út, off Ságvarí körút.

Information

Ibusz (☎ 423 602; Jászkürt út 1; ⌚ 8am-5pm Mon-Fri, to noon Sat) Travel agent, and handles private rooms and apartments.

Main post office (☎ 341 301; Baross Gábor út 14)

Matrix (☎ 06 30 606 3666; Baross Gábor út 40; per 15min 100Ft; ⌚ 8am-midnight Mon-Fri, 1pm-midnight Sat) Internet cafe.

OTP bank (☎ 420 033; Szapáry út 31) Has an ATM.

Tourinform (☎ 424 704; www.tiszainform.com; Ságvári körút 4; ⌚ 8am-6pm Mon-Fri Jul-Aug, to 4pm Mon-Fri Sep-Jun) Small office just south of the bus station.

Sights & Activities

Other than strolling along the riverfront, or kicking back on a restaurant terrace, the town's thermal baths are the place to be on a lovely summer afternoon. You can 'take the waters' at the **Liget Thermal Spa** (☎ 379 701; www.szolnokfurdok.hu; Tiszaligeti sétány; adult/child 900/600Ft; ⌚ 6am-8pm Mon-Fri, 10am-8pm Sat & Sun), where different temperature pools are arranged in a grassy park and sun worshippers loll about from June through August. Year-round you can frequent the indoor pools, fitness room and saunas (which cost 1000Ft extra).

Across the river, dip into the mock Turkish indoor pools at the **Hotel Tisza Thermal Baths** (☎ 422 104; Verseghy Park 2; adult/child 1200/600Ft; ⌚ 7.30am-6pm Mon-Fri May-Sep, 7.30am-4pm Sun-Wed, to 8pm Thu, to 10pm Fri & Sat Oct-Apr). From there you can walk along the riverbank through a flower-filled park to the **Szolnok Gallery** (☎ 378 023; Templom utca 2; adult/child 500/200Ft; ⌚ 9am-5pm Tue-Sun), which shows works by contemporary artists from the region. The building

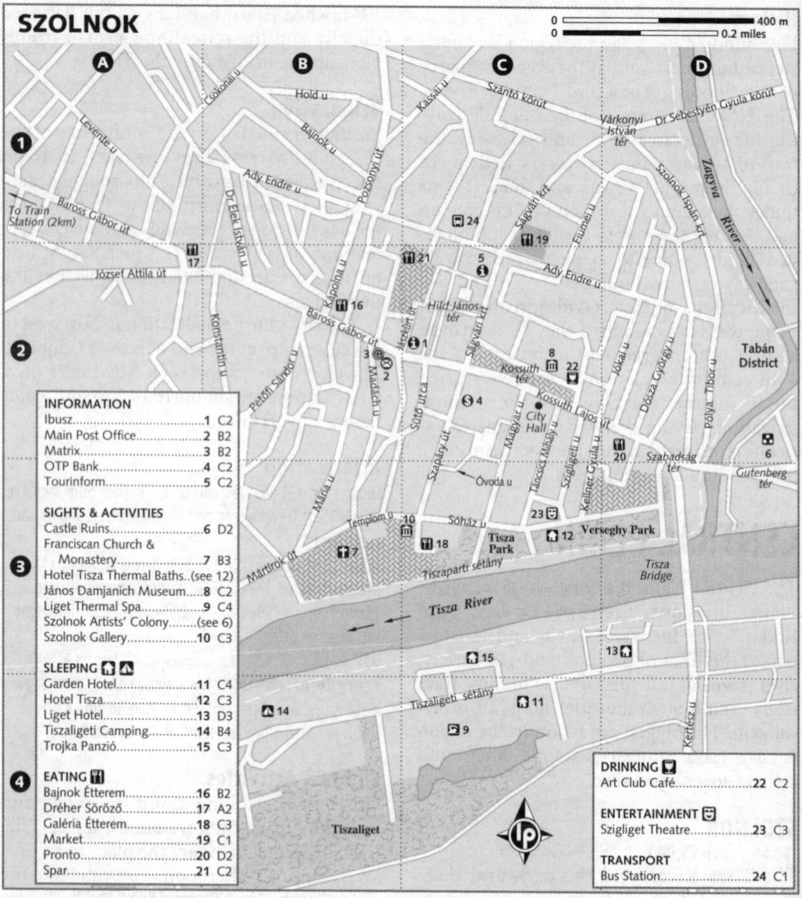

itself – a Romantic-style synagogue designed by Lipót Baumhorn in 1898 – is stunning. (Baumhorn also did the glorious temples in Szeged and Gyöngyös.) West of the gallery are the baroque **Franciscan church and monastery** (Templom utca 8) completed in 1757 – the city's oldest buildings.

The town's **János Damjanich Museum** (☎ 421 602; Kossuth tér 4; adult/child 1000/500Ft; ⌚ 9am-5pm Tue-Sun) is divided into three sections: archaeological finds from the Bronze Age and Roman times; an extensive ethnographical collection; and exhibits relating to Szolnok's history, especially the local artists' colony.

Like so many fortresses on the Great Plain, Szolnok Castle was blown to bits by the Habsburgs in 1710, and the rubble was later used to rebuild the city centre. What little is left of the **castle ruins** – just a bit of wall – can be seen near Gutenberg tér, across the Zagyva River. The park is also the site of **Szolnok Artists' Colony** (Szolnoki Művésztelep; ☎ 230 605; Gutenberg tér 12), founded in 1902 and once counting among its members the realist painters Adolf Fényes, István Nagy and László Mednyánszky. Fronting the Zagyva northeast of Szabadság tér is the **Tabán district**, with the last remaining peasant houses in Szolnok.

Sleeping

Tiszaligeti Camping (☎ 424 403; http://tiszaligetimotel.hu; Tiszaligeti sétány 34; camp sites per person/tent/car 900/800/400Ft, motel s/d 4000/8000Ft; ⌚ camping May-Sep) Tucked into the quiet far corner of Tiszaliget, this tree-shaded, 2-hectare camping ground is a good place to pitch your tent. The motel complex looks more like an army barracks than anything else. There's an on-site restaurant, and bike hire is available.

Trojka Panzió (☎ 514 600; www.trojka.hu; Tiszaligeti sétány 5; s/d 6000/8000Ft) Is there a musty smell to the all-wood rooms or is it just the aquarium and plant menagerie on the 2nd-floor landing? No matter – the rate is right, and the rambling old guest house is just across the road from the thermal spa.

Liget Hotel (☎ 515 043; www.ligethotelszolnok.hu; Tiszaligeti sétány 1; s/d incl breakfast 8600/14,000Ft) Pine laminate floors and built-in nightstands give this streamlined hotel a clean and simple look. Each of the bright rooms has floor-to-ceiling windows and a private balcony with a partial river view. Free wi-fi.

Hotel Tisza (☎ 510 850; www.hoteltisza.hu; Verseghy Park 2; s/d incl breakfast 11,000/14,700Ft;) Rooms at Szolnok's fancy old-world hotel (built in 1928) are more old-fashioned than antique, but weekend specials often include reduced rates and admission to the hotel's thermal bath.

Garden Hotel (☎ 520 530; www.gardenhotel.hu; Tiszaligeti sétány 4; s/d incl breakfast 18,600/24,200Ft) Wandering up the lush green lawn, you might be tempted to stop at the terrace restaurant before you even get to your sumptuous room. Why not – you have plenty of time to enjoy the sunny yellow facade and garden setting before heading off to the thermal baths next door.

Eating & Drinking

Pronto (Kossuth Lajos út 6; pizzas & salads 400-800Ft; closed Sun) This clean and simple shopfront churns out pizzas and salads by the truckload for hungry locals on the run.

Dréher Söröző (☎ 424 706; Baross Gábor út 52; mains 900-1400Ft) Fill up on hearty food like bean soup and *csölök pörkölt* (pig knuckle stew) at this simple pub. Dréher being the obvious draught beer of choice.

Bajnok Étterem (☎ 421 809; Baross Gabor út 2; mains 1100-2000Ft) What Hungarian speciality can't you try? Goose liver pâte, fish soup, *borjú paprikas* (veal in a creamy paprika sauce), *Gundel palacsinta* (flambéed pancake with chocolate and nuts) for dessert; they're all here. You also get a choice of three dining rooms: a ground-floor courtyard, a cellar pub or a more formal restaurant.

Galéria Étterem (☎ 378 358; Szapáry út 1; mains 1800-2250Ft) With dishes like walnut-encrusted hen stuffed with camembert and blueberries, Galéria rates as the most creative restaurant in Szolnok. The flower-art garnishes are edible.

Art Club Café (Kossuth tér 2; 9am-midnight) Kick back with the city's creative types at this bohemian cafe.

The outdoor terraces at both the **Hotel Tisza** (☎ 510 850; www.hoteltisza.hu; Verseghy Park 2; mains 1500-2500Ft) and **Garden Hotel** (☎ 520 530; www.gardenhotel.hu; Tiszaligeti sétány 4; mains 1800-2600Ft) restaurants are pleasant, upscale places to sup, but the latter has much better food.

Pick up fruits, vegetables and flowers at the colourful outdoor **market** (Ady Endre utca 11; 6am-2pm); the **Spar** (Szolnok Plaza) supermarket is off Kossuth Lajos út.

Entertainment

Ask at Tourinform about concerts at the Franciscan church and Béla Bartók Chamber Choir performances.

Szigliget Theatre (Szigligeti színház; ☎ 342 633; Tisza Park 1) This pretty provincial theatre was at the forefront of drama when it became the first in Eastern Europe to stage *Dr Zhivago* (1988) – pretty daring stuff at the time. The operettas and musicals are arrestingly visual enough for non-Hungarian speakers.

Getting There & Away

Szolnok has excellent east–west, main-line train connections. But going north or south, it's more direct to take a bus to Jászberény (950Ft, 1¼ hours, 55km, eight daily), Kecskemét (1050Ft, 1¾ hours, 65km, seven daily), Szeged (2040Ft, three hours, 135km, seven daily) and Tiszafüred (1200Ft, two hours, 70km, three daily); more buses run on some weekdays.

Dozens of trains travel daily to/from Budapest (1500Ft, 1¾ hours, 100km), Debrecen (2050Ft, 1½ hours, 120km), Nyíregyháza (2540Ft, two hours, 170km) and points in between.

Getting Around

From the train station, buses 7 and 8 stop at Szabadság tér before continuing over the river to Tiszaliget.

JÁSZBERÉNY

☎ 57 / pop 27,200

Today Jászberény is a sleepy town of tree-lined streets and quiet squares, but as early as the 13th century it was the main political, administrative

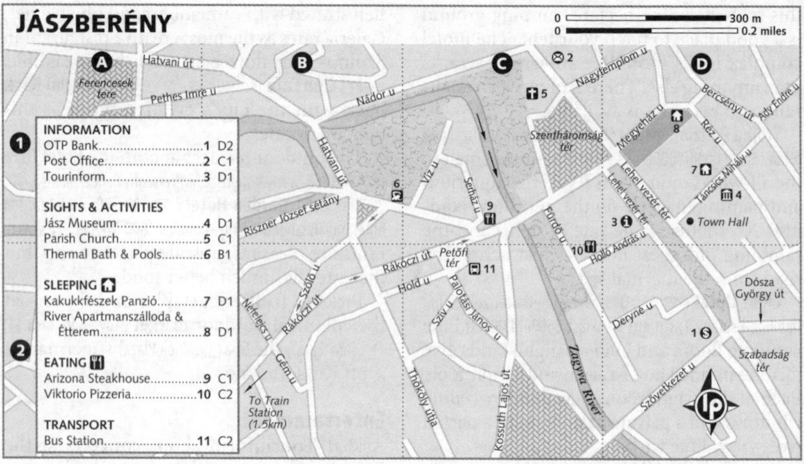

and economic centre of the Jazygians, an obscure pastoral people of Persian origin brought in by King Béla IV (r 1235–70) to strengthen his position. Its biggest (if only) drawcard has always been the Lehel Horn, an ancient, almost magical ivory piece, for centuries the Jazygian chief's symbol of power.

Orientation

The main street is a long 'square' (Lehel vezér tér), which runs almost parallel to the narrow 'city branch' of the Zagyva River. The bus station, on Petőfi tér, is two blocks to the west across the Zagyva River, while the train station is 1.5km southwest at the end of Rákóczi út.

Information

OTP bank (Lehel vezér tér 28) With ATM.

Post office (Lehel vezér tér 8)

Tourinform (☎ 406 439; www.jaszbereny.hu; Lehel vezér tér 33; 🕑 8am-5pm Mon-Fri, 9am-1pm Sat Jun-Sep, 8am-4.30pm Mon-Fri Oct-May)

Sights & Activities

The **Jász Museum** (☎ 412 753; Táncsics Mihály utca 5; adult/child 260/150Ft; 🕑 9am-5pm Tue-Sun), housed in what was once the Jazygian military headquarters, runs the gamut of Jász culture and life – from costumes and woodcarving to language and homelife. But all aisles lead to the **Lehel Horn**, a richly carved ivory piece with birds, battle scenes and anatomically correct satyrs. Legend has it that Magyar leader Lehel (or Lél) was taken captive in the Battle of Augsburg (AD 955) against the united German armies and, just before being executed, tricked the king into giving him his horn as a last request. Lehel bludgeoned the king with the horn, killing him instantly. The fact that early chronicles depict a different horn and that the Jászberény horn doesn't get linked to legend until the 14th century doesn't deter from the national interest.

Have a look at the fading ceiling frescoes inside the Roman Catholic **Parish Church** (Szentháromság tér 4; admission free); the church's nave was designed in 1774 by András Mayerhoffer and József Jung, two masters of baroque architecture.

Like most towns on the plains, Jászberény has a **Thermal Bath & Pools** (☎ 412 108; Hatvani út 5; adult/child 700/500Ft; 🕑 9am-6pm, outdoor pools May-Sep only), with two big outdoor pools and several, not terribly modern, indoor ones.

Sleeping & Eating

Unfortunately the only time you can try regional Jász cooking, like *nagy haluska leves* (large-dumpling soup), is during the **Csángó Festival** (www.csangofesztival.hu), held on the second weekend in August.

Kakukkfészek Panzió (☎ 412 345; Táncsics Mihály utca 8; s/d without bathroom 4000/6000Ft) Mismatched furniture and bedding may befit a 'Cuckoo's Nest', but the owners are supremely friendly and have created a homey atmosphere.

River Apartmanszálloda & Étterem (☎ 407 500; club.river@gmail.com; Lehel vezér tér 15; apt 15,000-18,000Ft; ⊠) Inside one long shopping arcade building, opened in 2008, you can eat a full, modern Hungarian meal (mains 1200Ft to 1800Ft) in a stylish restaurant (smoked ham in a cheese-wine sauce, anyone?), dine out during the evening (6pm to 10pm) on the grill terrace, bowl a few rounds at the arcade and then retire to one of two apartments on the upper floor. Both have full kitchens and separate bedrooms with contemporary furnishings.

Viktorio Pizzeria (☎ 411 053; Holló András utca; pizzas 400-1000Ft, mains 500-1000Ft) On a peaceful street just around the corner from the main square, this simple pizzeria has an incredible 45 pizza choices. Magyar varieties include those topped with pork stew or liver and bacon.

Arizona Steakhouse (cnr Rákóczi út & Serház utca; steaks 2000-3000Ft) A rare breed in these parts, American-style steaks are served at a rustic restaurant decked out in Wild West gear.

Getting There & Away

Buses are most convenient to Budapest (1200Ft, 1¾ hours, 80km, nine daily), Szolnok (900Ft, 1¼ hours, 55km, six daily) and Kecskemét (1200Ft, two hours, 85km, seven daily).

Jászberény lies approximately halfway between Hatvan (450Ft, 30 minutes, 26km, hourly) and Szolnok (650Ft, 45 minutes, 42km, hourly) on a spur train line. These two cities are on Hungary's two main train lines, and have frequent direct links to Budapest and other major cities.

Getting Around

Bus 4 connects the train station with the bus station, from where you can walk to the town centre.

TISZAFÜRED

☎ 59 / pop 14,000

Bird-watching, boating, kayaking, canoeing… This may not be the 'Lake Balaton of the Great Plain' as tourist brochures say, but Lake Tisza (Tisza-tó) offers outdoors enthusiasts a quiet, laid-back alternative. Few visitors came to town before the 1980s, when they dammed the Tisza River and opened more than 127 sq km of lakes to holidaymakers. Tiszafüred, on the northeastern edge, is recreation central. Bungalows, camping grounds and eateries line the shore; the small town core has little more to offer than a few restaurants.

Orientation

From the bus and train stations, opposite one another on Vasút utca, walk 10 or 15 minutes west and then southwest to the beach and camping grounds (via Vasút utca, Poroszlói út and Fürdő út). To reach the town centre, follow Baross Gábor utca and then Fő út south for about 1km.

Information

Horgász Camping (Kasthély út; per hr 300Ft; 🕑 8am-10pm) Internet access at camping ground office.
OTP bank (Piac út 3) Behind Fő út.
Post office (Fő út 14)
Tourinform (☎ 511 123; tiszafured@tourinform.hu; Fürdő út 21; 🕑 8am-6pm Jun-Sep, 8am-4pm Mon-Fri Oct-May) Has good cycling maps.

Sights

Tiszafüred is essentially an activity town, but there are a couple of small sights, including the **Pál Kiss Museum** (☎ 352 106; Tariczky sétány 6; adult/child 260/130Ft; 🕑 9am-noon & 1-5pm Wed-Sat). Housed in a beautiful old manor (1840) south of the city's thermal baths, its collection is given over to the everyday lives of Tisza fisher folk and the work of local potters.

The area east of Szőlősi út is a veritable patchwork of traditional houses, with thatched roofs and orderly little flower and vegetable gardens. Ceramic artist **Nagyné Török Zsóka** (☎ 353 538; Szőlősi út 21; 🕑 8am-5pm Mon-Fri) has her studio in one of them. The **Gáspár Nyúzó House** (Nyúzó Gáspár Fazekas Tájház; Malom utca 12; adult/child 200/150Ft; 🕑 9am-noon & 2-5pm Wed-Sun May-Oct) is a former potter's residence and contains antique potting wheels, drying racks, furniture and plates in pale primary colours and patterns of stars, and birds and flowers unique to the region.

Activities

Swimming and sunbathing on the narrow lake's sandy strip are popular activities; the **beach** area is ringed by food stands and a changing pavilion. To the west is a series of **boat rental stands** (🕑 10am-8pm Jun-Aug), where you can get outfitted with a canoe (per hour 700Ft), paddle boat (per hour 1000Ft), one-person kayak (per hour 600Ft) or 5HP motor boat (per hour 3600Ft).

The expanse west and north of the water connected to Tiszafüred's shore is protected as part of the **Tisza-tavi Bird Reserve** (Tisza-tavi Madárrezervátum; www.tisza-to.hu), a division of Hortobágy National

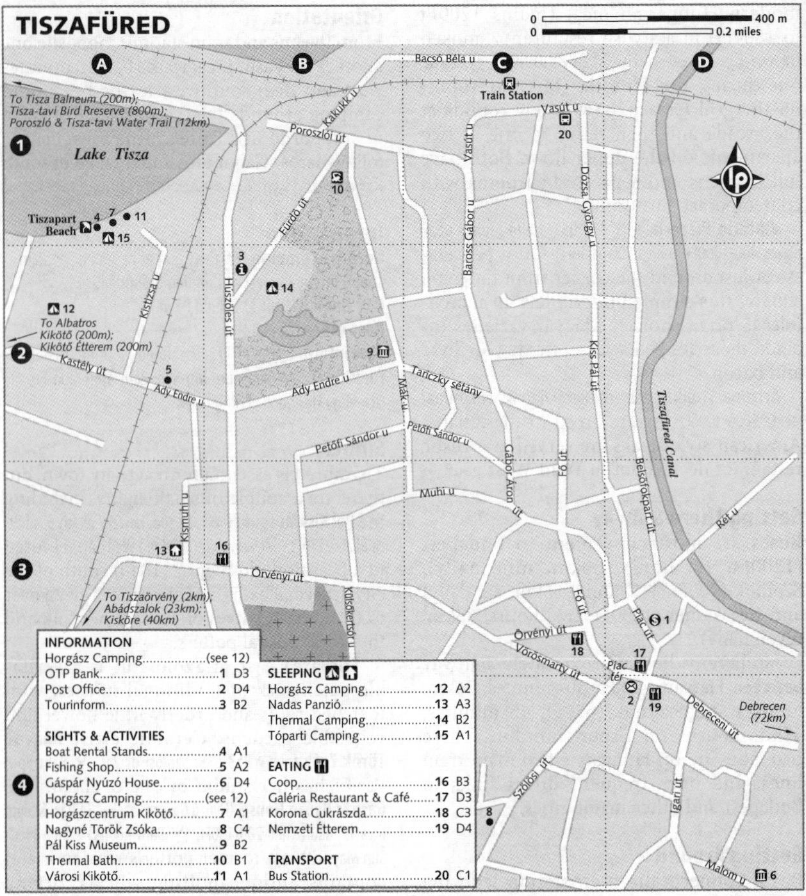

Park. More than 200 birds breed in the area; following one of the outlined water routes by kayak or canoe is a great way to see them. Ask for a route map when you rent a boat, as certain areas are off-limits, especially during breeding season from February through May.

To go into the park by motor boat, you'll need a guide. In addition to boat rental, **Városi Kikötő** (☎ 06 20 916 2589; www.varosikikoto.hu, in Hungarian; Gát sétány 1) and **Horgászcentrum Kikötő** (☎ 06 30 965 9824; www.horgaszcentrum.hu, in Hungarian; Tiszapart) offer guided fishing and nature trips from around 7500Ft. The **Fishing Shop** (Horgász Bolt; Ady Endre utca 35) sells reels, lures and permits.

If the lake is too cold for you, Tiszafüred's **Thermal Bath** (☎ 352 366; Poroszlói út; adult/child 900/650Ft; 🕑 8am-7pm May-Sep) has four open-air pools, as well as a sauna and a wide range of spa services.

Those looking for adventure away from water can most likely rent a bicycle (per day 1500Ft) from their lodging or at **Horgász Camping** (☎ 351 220; Kasthély út; 🕑 8am-10pm). The towns along the east side of the lake are all cycling friendly, joined by a bike path following the lake shore. From Tiszafüred to Kisköre is a rather flat 40km. This segment of trail is part of the Eurovelo 11 bike track, signposted in mid-2008 in Hungary. You could circuit the lake by continuing north along the waterfront trail to Poroszló and crossing back via Hwy 33 (38km). For more on stops, see opposite.

Sleeping

Horgász Camping (☎ 351 220; www.hotels.hu/horgcamp; Kasthély út; camp sites per person/tent 700/600Ft, d/tr 5200/7600Ft, bungalows with/without bathroom 6000/9000Ft; Apr-Oct;) This 600-site camping ground, a stone's throw from the beach, has plenty of amenities: bike and kayak rental, volleyball court, full restaurant and internet access. Some of the bungalows are well worn. 'Apartment' cabins (per two people 8500Ft, with private bathroom and full kitchen) are newest; ask for units M1 through M4.

Albatros Kikötő (☎ 06 30 234 5108; www.albatroszkikoto.hu, in Hungarian; Bán Zsigmond út 67; camp sites 1250Ft, bungalows without bathroom 9000Ft) Being primarily a long-established marina, Albatros gives you a few advantages: the closest camping option to the water, and on-site boat rental and tour arrangement. The tributary locale is quiet and shady, too. Showers cost 200Ft extra.

our pick **Nadas Panzió** (☎ 511 401; www.nadaspanzio.hu; Kismuhi utca 2; s/d/apt 6000/8000/7500Ft;) A purpose-built *panzió* (guest house) made for recreation. Here you can bubble in the Jacuzzi, take a dip in the pool, sweat in the sauna, play billiards or tennis, or just watch your kids romp on the playground while you picnic at a garden table. Staff rent out bikes and boats, and arrange nature tours of waterways in the area. The rough-hewn beams and wooden doors make rooms feel rustic, but wi-fi and minifridges come standard. Apartments have full kitchens – or you're welcome to cook in the outdoor oven. So many choices, so little time.

Tisza Balneum (☎ 886 200; www.balneum.hu; Húszöles út 27; r incl breakfast 27,000-30,000Ft;) Flat-screen TVs hang on the walls of the Zen minimalist guestrooms, where wicker, wood and natural linens provide a perfect complement to the lake view off the balcony. A private thermal spring supplies the water for one outdoor and two indoor pools; a private harbour offers boat rentals and trips. Tiszafüred has gone four-star.

Other options:

Thermal Camping (☎ 352 911; www.thermalcampingeng.shp.hu; Húszöles út 2; camp sites per person/tent 1000/850Ft, dm 4500Ft, bungalows 10,800Ft, mobile homes 13,800Ft) Near Thermal Bath; two-bedroom mobile homes added as an option in 2008.

Tóparti Camping (☎ 351 606; Tiszapart; camp sites per person/tent 300/500Ft, bungalows 6500Ft; May-Sep) Step out the gate onto the beach.

Eating

The five different food stands around the beach area are mini self-service restaurants selling fried fish and pork cutlets, various soups and stews, sausages, starches and the all-important beer, to be eaten at covered picnic tables. Most camping grounds have an OK restaurant or snack bar attached.

Korona Cukrászda (Örvényi út 41; cakes 350-450Ft; 9am-8pm) Cakes and pastries and ice creams – oh my. A cool treat from Korona provides a lovely respite from summer heat.

Nemzeti Étterem (☎ 352 349; Fő út 8; mains 1000-1500Ft) The bright yellow exterior of this town restaurant hides a rather plain-Jane interior. The midday menu is excellent value, though (600Ft for soup and main dish).

Galéria Restaurant & Café (☎ 350 512; Fő utca 15; mains 1190-1500Ft;) Broccoli soup, steaks (2900Ft) and lamb dishes are some of the more modern Hungarian offerings, but there's plenty of traditional *pörkölt* (stew) on the menu.

Kikötő Étterem (Bán Zsigmond út 63; mains 1400-1800Ft; May-Sep) Grilled fish and meat dishes are the speciality at this small, open-air eatery next to Albatros Kikötő.

Coop (Örvényi út 41) You can pick up self-catering supplies at this supermarket.

WORTH THE TRIP: AROUND LAKE TISZA

Don't feel stuck in Tiszafüred when exploring Lake Tisza. It has almost 80km of shoreline, and small towns and resorts are connected both by bike path and by country roads. The marinas and waterfront hotel-restaurant at **Tiszaörvény** are really an adjunct of Tiszafüred, just 2km north. Wide open water near **Abádszalok** (www.szalok.hu, in Hungarian), at the south end of the lake, makes this is an ideal place for jet-skiing and wake boarding. Around on the west side, in Poroszló, bird-watchers shouldn't miss the 1500m of boardwalk, **Tisza-tavi Water Trail** (Tisza-tavi Vízi Sétány; www.vizisetany.hu; admission free; 10am-8pm daily Jul-Aug, 10am-8pm Sat & Sun Sep-Jun). All the shoreline settlements have camping, canoe rental and food options available.

Getting There & Away

Among other destinations, direct buses connect Tiszafüred with Budapest (2300Ft, four hours, 185km, four daily), Szolnok (1200Ft, two hours, 70km, four daily) and Eger (900Ft, 1¼ hours, 55km, 10 daily).

Tiszafüred is on a spur train line that passes through the Hortobágy region on the way to Debrecen (1200Ft, 1½ hours, 73km, nine daily); from Füzesabony (450Ft, 40 minutes, 33km, 10 daily) you can connect to other points on the Budapest–Nyíregyháza line.

EASTERN PLAIN

The Hortobágy region of the eastern plain is where the myth of the lonely *pásztor* (shepherd) in billowy trousers, the wayside *csárdák* (inns) and Gypsy violinists was born – to be kept alive in literature and fine art. The horse and herding show at the national park recreates this pastoral tradition.

DEBRECEN

☎ 52 / pop 215,000

Flanked by the golden Great Church and historic Aranybika hotel, Debrecen's central square is quite pretty; a surprise given the industrial outskirts and apartment block mess you see when arriving by bus or train. During summer frequent street festivals fill the pedestrian core with revellers, but old-town bars and nightclubs create a lively scene for night crawlers on weekends year-round. The array of museums and thermal baths in the city will keep you busy for a day or two, but then you'll want to day trip out to the *puszta* to explore natural wonders, see a cowboy show, soak in the country's largest spa and shop for pottery.

History

The area around Debrecen has been settled since the earliest times. When the Magyars arrived late in the 9th century, they found a colony of Slovaks here who called the region Dobre Zliem for its 'good soil'. Debrecen's wealth, based on salt, the fur trade and cattle raising, grew steadily through the Middle Ages and increased during the Turkish occupation; the city kept all sides happy by paying tribute to the Ottomans, the Habsburgs and the Transylvanian princes at the same time.

By the mid-16th century much of the population had converted to Protestantism and churches were being erected with gusto, earning the city the nickname 'Calvinist Rome'. Debrecen played a pivotal role in the 1848–49 War of Independence, and it experienced a major building boom in the late 19th and early 20th centuries. The Great Church is still the largest house of worship in the country.

Orientation

Debrecen is an easy city to negotiate. A ring road, built on the city's original earthen walls, encloses the Inner Town (Belváros). This is bisected by Piac utca, which runs northward from the train station (Petőfi tér) to Kálvin tér, site of the Great Church and Debrecen's city centre. With the exception of Nagyerdei Park, the recreational 'Big Forest Park' some 3km north, almost all of Debrecen's attractions are within easy walking distance of Kálvin tér.

The bus station (Külső-Vásártér) is on the 'outer marketplace' at the western end of Széchenyi utca.

Information

City website (www.debrecen.hu) Lots of helpful info.
Data Net Cafe (☎ 536 724; Kossuth utca 8; per hr 900Ft; 🕑 9am-midnight) Internet and cheap international calls.
Ibusz (☎ 415 555; Révész tér 2; 🕑 8am-5pm Mon-Fri, 9am-1pm Sat) Travel agency; rents private apartments.
Kenézy Gyula Hospital (☎ 511 777; Bartók Béla út 2-26) Emergency services.
Main post office (Hatvan utca 5-9)
Maróthi György College Library (☎ 502 780; Blaháné utca 15; 🕑 9am-4pm Mon-Thu, to 2pm Fri)
OTP bank (Piac utca 16) Has a 24-hour ATM.
Tourinform (☎ 412 250; www.gotodebrecen.hu) Summer booth (Kálvin tér; 🕑 10am-6pm daily Jun-Sep); Town Hall office (Piac utca 20; 🕑 9am-8pm Mon-Fri, to 5pm Sun Jun-Aug, 9am-5pm Mon-Fri Sep-May) The unbelievably helpful town hall office has more information than you can carry about the whole region. It sells the Debrecen Tourism Card (1900Ft), which gets you 10% to 20% off admission prices for museums and spas in the area.

Sights

Many of the town's big sights are at the northern end of Piac utca, including the yellow neoclassical **Great Church** (☎ 412 694; Kálvin tér; adult/child 300/200Ft; 🕑 9am-4pm Mon-Fri, to 1pm Sat, noon-4pm Sun Apr-Oct, 10am-1pm Mon-Sat, 11.30am-1pm Sun Nov-Mar). Built in 1821, it has become so synonymous with Debrecen that mirages of its twin clock towers were reportedly seen on the Great Plain

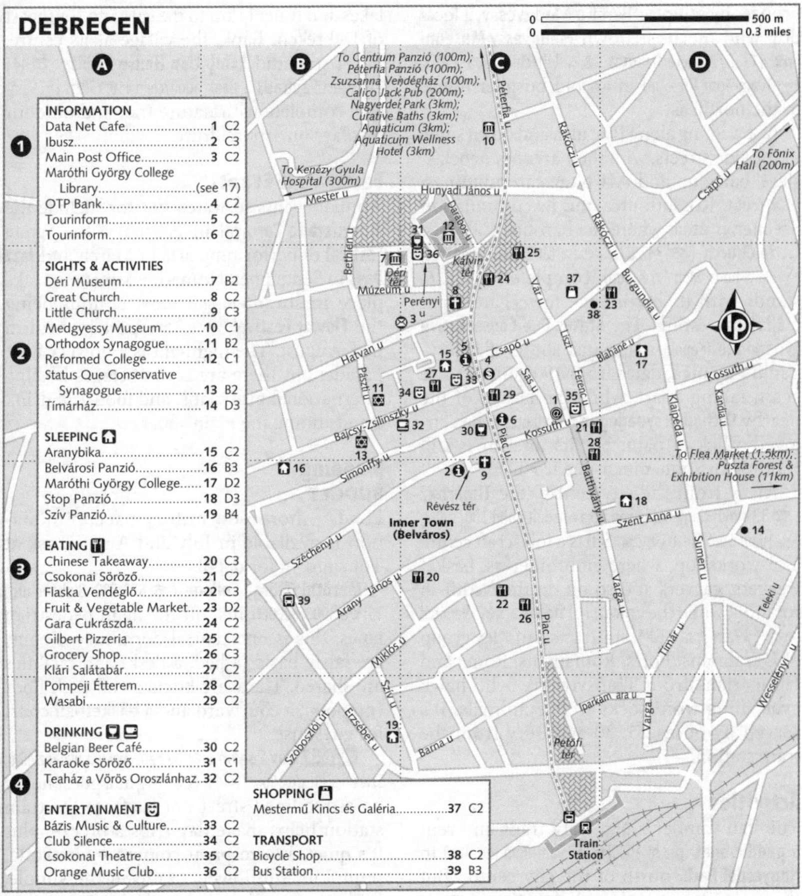

early last century. Accommodating some 3000 people, the Great Church is Hungary's largest Protestant church, and it was here that Lajos Kossuth read the Declaration of Independence from Austria on 14 April 1849. The nave is rather plain and austere aside from the magnificent organ in the loft behind the pulpit. Climb the 210 steps to the top of the west clock tower for grand views over the city.

North of the church stands the **Reformed College** (Református Kollégium; ☎ 414 744; Kálvin tér 16; adult/child 500/200Ft, guided English tours 3000Ft; ⏰ 10am-4pm Tue-Sat, to 1pm Sun), built in 1816, the site of a prestigious secondary school and theological college since the Middle Ages. Downstairs there are exhibits on religious art and sacred objects (including a 17th-century chalice made from a coconut) and on the school's history, where 'early to bed, early to rise' was the motto. Upstairs is the relatively bland 650,000-volume library and the bright, white oratory, where the breakaway National Assembly met in 1849 and Hungary's postwar provisional government was declared in 1944.

Folklore exhibits at the **Déri Museum** (☎ 322 207; Déri tér 1; adult/child 1000/500Ft; ⏰ 10am-4pm Tue-Sun Nov-Mar, to 6pm Apr-Oct), a short walk west of the Reformed College, offer excellent insights into life on the plain and the bourgeois citizens of Debrecen up to the 19th century. Mihály Munkácsy's mythical interpretations of the Hortobágy and his *Christ's Passion* trilogy take pride of place in a separate art gallery. The museum's entrance is flanked by four superb bronzes by sculptor Ferenc Medgyessy, a local boy who merits his own **Medgyessy Museum** (☎ 413 572; Péterfia utca 28; adult/child 500/250Ft; ⌚ 10am-4pm Tue-Sun) in an old burgher house to the northeast.

Just walking along Piac utca and down some of the side streets, with their array of neoclassical, baroque and Art Nouveau buildings, is a treat. Kossuth utca and its continuation Széchenyi utca, where the baroque Calvinist **Little Church** (☎ 342 872; Révész tér 2; admission free; ⌚ 9am-noon Mon-Fri & Sun), completed in 1726, stands with its bastionlike tower, are especially interesting. The **Status Que Conservative Synagogue** (Kápolnási utca), just south of Bajcsy-Zsilinszky utca, dates from 1909 and is once again falling apart, while the facade of the nearby **Orthodox synagogue** (Pászti utca 6) has enjoyed a lick of paint but its interior is still waiting for some much-needed TLC.

Away from the city centre, the **Tímárház** (☎ 321 260; Nagy Gál István utca 6; adult/child 300/150Ft; ⌚ 10am-5pm Tue-Fri, to 2pm Sat) is a folk-craft centre and workshop, where embroiderers, basket weavers, carvers and so on do their stuff in rotation, while the colourful **flea market** (Vágóhíd utca; ⌚ 7am-3pm Wed-Sun) attracts a motley group of Ukrainians, Poles, Romanians, Roma and Hungarians from Transylvania, who hawk everything from socks to live animals. It's served by buses 15, 30 and 30/y from the train station.

Activities

You can wander along leafy trails and rent a **paddle boat** (per hr 1000Ft; ⌚ 9am-8pm Jun-Aug) in **Nagyerdei Park**, north of the city centre. But the main attraction here is **Aquaticum** (☎ 514 100; www.aquaticum.hu; adult/child 2100/1600Ft; ⌚ 10am-10pm), a complex of 'Mediterranean Enjoyment Baths' with all manner of slides, waterfalls and grottos – both indoors and out. A glass dome and tropical plants make it seem a bit like a terrarium. Choose from a full menu of massages and bodywork (chocolate wrap?) from 3300Ft for 20 minutes. Go to the 2nd storey in the old building to the left to get to the **Curative Baths** (Gyógyfürdő; ☎ 346 883; adult/child 1150/930Ft; ⌚ 7am-8pm), older pools filled with nonfiltered, purely mineral (read: muddy-coloured) waters, unlike the Aquaticum's pristine blue Mediterranean variety.

If you want to see more of the great outdoors, head for the **Puszta Forest** (Erdőspuszta), a protected area of pine and acacia forests, lakes and trails 11km to the east and southeast of Debrecen. Bánk, the village at its centre, has a splendid **Exhibition House** (Tájház; ☎ 441 118; Fancsika utca 93/a, Bánk; adult/child 450/150Ft; ⌚ 9am-6pm) complete with nature trail and outdoor displays on arborculture.

Festivals & Events

Annual events to watch out for include the **Masquerade Carnival** in February, the **Spring Festival** of performing arts in March and **Jazz Days** in September. Numerous street fairs take place in summer, the most famous being the **Flower Festival** (www.flowerfestival.hu) held in mid-August. The highlight is a flowery float parade, but there are several stages hosting international musicians, and food and drink stands lining the main squares.

Sleeping

BUDGET

Loads more dormitory accommodation is available in July and August; ask at Tourinform for details.

Maróthi György College (☎ 502 780; Blaháné utca 15; s/d 3000/6000Ft) Just off the main pedestrian lanes, this is one central dormitory. Rooms are fairly basic (a bed, a desk) and facilities are shared. There are kitchens on each floor (no pots), a courtyard and a basketball court for guest use.

our pick **Szív Panzió** (☎ 322 200; www.szivpanzio.hu; Szív utca 11; s/d 6000/7800Ft) Staying at a guest house on a tree-lined street not far from the train station helps make day trips a breeze, plus it's quiet. Warm paint colours – terracotta, pumpkin, sunflower – enliven the simple, fresh rooms with low-slung beds (and stocked minibars). Guest quarters with 'French' beds (standard doubles, not two singles pushed together) go for 9800Ft. Free wi-fi and big breakfast buffet (1200Ft).

Stop Panzió (☎ 420 302; www.stop.at.tf; Batthányi utca 18; s/d/tr 6500/7900/9900Ft) Older rooms fill up because they're the right price for a good location, in a courtyard off a cafe-filled pedestrian street. The dark, old furnishings in the lobby make the place feel a bit forbidding, but the innkeeper is perfectly sweet.

MIDRANGE

Belvárosi Panzió (☎ 322 644; www.belvarosipanzio.tar.hu; Bajcsy-Zsilinszky utca 60; s/d 7000/10,000Ft; ⊠ 💻) Bright, clean and modern, this city guest house is less homey and more hotel-y than most. Some 2nd-floor rooms have a balcony, but they just look out at the building across the street. The reception has a full bar.

Péterfia Panzió (☎ 418 246; www.hotels.hu/peterfia; Péterfia utca 37/b; s/d 8000/10,000Ft; ⊠) Natural-wood furniture fills the comfy rooms, with wi-fi, and the staff make you welcome by inviting you to relax in the back garden. They'll even help you arrange sightseeing tours and airport transfers.

Centrum Panzió (☎ 442 843; www.panziocentrum.hu; Péterfia utca 37/a; s/d 8500/10,500Ft; ⊠) A bit like your grandmother's apartment, if she collected Victorian bric-a-brac. Flowery odds and ends line the reception walls and public areas; rooms are only slightly less garish, but they all have minifridge and microwave. Free wi-fi at reception, and bike rental available.

Zsuzsanna Vendégház (☎ 410 588; szallas.zsuzsanna@t-online.hu; Péterfia utca 34; s/d 9000/16,000Ft; ⊠) Of the three accommodation options in the same block, this is probably our last choice. There is a pleasant garden and free wi-fi; just ignore the odd, childish patterns on the upholstered beds.

TOP END

Aranybika (☎ 508 600; www.civishotels.hu; Piac utca 11-15; s €60-85, d €85-105;) This landmark Art Nouveau hotel has been *the* place to stay in Debrecen since construction in 1915. Superior rooms have a bit more space than standard, as well as antique reproduction furnishings.

Aquaticum Wellness Hotel (☎ 514 111; www.aquaticum.hu; Nagyerdei Park 1; s/d €80/95;) Kids' programs, babysitting, bike rental, spa services, swimming pools and loads of other amenities make Aquaticum attractive to both adults and children. And you don't have to leave the premises to get from your four-star room to the thermal park.

Eating

BUDGET

Klári Salátabár (☎ 412 203; Bajcsy-Zsilinszky utca 3; per 100g 100-300Ft; 9am-7pm Mon-Fri) Broccoli egg rolls, fried mushrooms, peas and white rice – the dishes at this self-service shopfront may not all be super healthy, but they are mostly vegetarian.

Gara Cukrászda (Kálvin tér 6; sweets 150-500Ft; 9am-6pm) Gara has some of the best cakes and ice cream (made with real fruit and loads of it) outside Budapest and has lines of eager ice-cream lovers to prove it.

Chinese takeaway (☎ 588 479; Arany János utca 28; small/large meal 600/900Ft) A genuine Chinese takeaway (no English spoken). Point to rice or noodles and have your to-go dish topped with a sampling of stir-fried mains.

Gilbert Pizzeria (☎ 537 373; Kálvin tér 5; pizzas & pasta 850-1050Ft) Some of the best pizza in town awaits, hidden, in an interior courtyard off the main square. A substantial number of the 50 choices are vegetarian.

There's a **grocery shop** (Piac utca 75; 24hr) within walking distance of the train station, and the small covered **fruit and vegetable market** (Csapó utca; 5am-3pm Mon-Sat, 5-11am Sun) is right in the city centre.

MIDRANGE

Pompeji Étterem (☎ 416 988; Batthyány utca 4; mains 1300-1800Ft) Despite the Italian name and murals, the menu is a delicious mixed bag. Sautéed chicken might be topped with mozzarella and tomato sauce, or with tzatziki and olives. Wood-fired pizzas (from 500Ft) run the gamut, too.

Flaska Vendéglő (☎ 414 582; Miklós utca 4; mains 1400-1800Ft) You can't miss the giant terracotta-red flask jutting out from the wall, and you shouldn't skip the food either. Poultry and pork top the Hungarian menu; try the *Hortobágyi palacsinta* (meat-filled pancakes with paprika sauce) or the Debreceni stuffed cabbage for traditional tastes.

Calico Jack Pub (☎ 455 999; Bem tér 15; mains 1500-2000Ft; 8am-2am Mon-Fri, 10am-2am Sat, 10am-midnight Sun) Well, shiver me timbers: the whole interior is done up like an 1882 sailing vessel (look for Jack climbing the mast). A large outside terrace and extensive beer selection make this as good a place to drink as one to eat huge meaty meals.

Csokonai Söröző (☎ 410 802; Kossuth utca 21; mains 1600-2000Ft) Medieval decor, sharp service and excellent Hungarian specialities all help to create one of Debrecen's most-recommended eating experiences. This cellar pub-restaurant also serves the odd international dish, like turkey enchiladas with beans.

TOP END

Wasabi (☎ 535 346; Piac utca 18; lunch/dinner 3490/4490Ft) It seems a bit odd for there to be a sushi conveyor belt circling a Zen interior in a Debrecen restaurant, but there it is. Choose all you can eat as more than 50 wok-cooked dishes, wraps and rolls glide by.

Drinking

Streetside cafe tables sprout with the flowers in spring; any of those on the pedestrian squares, and several along Simonffy utca, would be a good place to sip your fill.

Calico Jack Pub (☎ 455 999; Bem tér 15; ⏰ 8am-2am Mon-Fri, 10am-2am Sat, 10am-midnight Sun) A classic setting for *sör* (beer) drinking.

Belgian Beer Café (☎ 536 373; Piac utca 29; ⏰ 10am-midnight Mon-Thu, to 2am Fri & Sat) Why locals drink Belgian beer when neighbouring Slovakia and Czech Republic make such great beverages is anyone's guess. But there's no denying the popularity of this streetside cafe with its beer-hall atmosphere.

Karaoke Söröző (Perényi utca 1; ⏰ noon-midnight Sun-Thu, to 2am Fri & Sat) Trying your hand at Hungarian karaoke could get pretty hilarious, but English songs are in the repertoire, too.

Teaház a Vörös Oroszlánhaz (☎ 534 348; Bajcsy-Zsilinszky utca 14; ⏰ 1-11pm Mon-Sat, 3-11pm Sun) Hushed conversations and the smell of incense rise from this esoteric tea house with dozens of cold and hot choices.

Entertainment

Pick up a copy of the biweekly entertainment freebie *Debreceni Est* (www.est.hu) for music listings.

NIGHTCLUBS

Bajcsy-Zsilinszky utca is home to several clubs, as are the streets around Déri tér.

Club Silence (☎ 995 7701; Bajcsy-Zsilinszky utca 3-5) DJs spin house and techno tunes here most weekends, but some Saturdays see theme parties.

Bázis Music & Culture (☎ 536 414; Piac utca 11-15) Was a *Girls gone Wild* video filmed here? Coulda been – it's that kind of place.

Orange Music Club (☎ 536 414; Perényi utca 1) House parties, Depeche Mode nights, electro-funk; you never know what kind of music you'll get here.

Vigado Dance Club (☎ 346 111; Nagyerdei Park 6) Hard-rockin' club out by the Nagyerdei Park and thermal baths.

THEATRE

Csokonai Theatre (☎ 455 075; www.csokonaiszinhaz.hu; Kossuth utca 10) Three-tier gilt balconies, ornate ceiling frescoes and elaborate chandeliers: the Csokonai is everything a 19th-century theatre should be. Musicals and operas are staged here.

Debrecen Philharmonic (☎ 500 200; www.dfz.hu) The city's renowned orchestra plays at various venues around town.

Főnix Hall (Főnix csarnok; ☎ 518 400; www.fonixinfo.hu; Kassai utca 28) 'Phoenix' Hall is Debrecen's main venue for large events, whether they be concerts or sporting.

Shopping

You can't leave the city without buying – or at least trying – some of the famous Debrecen sausage available at butchers and grocery shops everywhere; the market is also a good place to procure some.

Mestermű Kincs és Galéria (Csapó utca 24) While on your way to the market, stop in at this lovely antique-cum-curio shop nearby.

Getting There & Away

In general, cities to the north and northwest are best served by train. For points south, use the bus or a transfer combination. The airport serves only chartered flights for summer holiday travel; check with Ibusz. For more on getting to Hungary from abroad, see Transport (p382).

BUS

Buses are quickest if you're going direct to the following destinations.

Destination	Price	Duration	Km	Frequency
Békéscsaba	1690Ft	3hr	135	10 daily
Eger	2040Ft	2½hr	130	6 daily
Nádudvar	675Ft	1hr	40	7 daily
Szarvas	2290Ft	3¼hr	155	2 daily
Szeged	3220Ft	5hr	230	3 daily

TRAIN

Debrecen is served by up to 20 direct trains daily.

Destination	Price	Duration	Km
Budapest Nyugati	3750Ft	3¼hr	220
Hajdúszoboszló	300Ft	15min	20
Hortobágy	675Ft	45min	40
Nyíregyháza	750Ft	45min	49
Tokaj	1350Ft	1½hr	85

Once-daily train departures leave from Debrecen to Satu Marie (2½ hours, 1032km) in Romania at 3.30pm. You have to transfer in Záhony to get to Csap (Čop) in Ukraine (where the train lines are a different size). The night train from Budapest to Moscow stops here at 9pm.

Getting Around

Tram 1 – the only line in town – is ideal both for transport and sightseeing. From the train station, it runs north along Piac utca to Kálvin tér and then carries on to Nagyerdei Park, where it loops around for the same trip southward. Most other city transport can be caught at the southern end of Petőfi tér. Trolleybuses 2 and 3 link the train and bus stations.

Ten kilometres of new bike lanes are under development in Debrecen. For bike rental, visit the **Bicycle Shop** (Kérekpárbolt; ☎ 456 220; Csapó utca 19; per day from 1200Ft; 🕑 9am-6pm Mon-Fri, to 1pm Sat).

HORTOBÁGY

☎ 52 / pop 1750

This village, some 40km west of Debrecen, is the centre of the Hortobágy region, once celebrated for its sturdy cowboys, inns and Gypsy bands. You can see the staged recreation of all this, complete with traditionally costumed *csikósok* (cowboys) at a *puszta* horse show. But you'll want to explore more of the 810-sq-km Hortobágy National Park and wildlife preserve – home to hundreds of birds, as well as plant species that are usually found only by the sea. Its importance as a cultural landscape has not just been noted in Hungary; in 1999 Unesco promoted the park to World Heritage status.

It's true that the Hortobágy has been milked by the Hungarian tourism industry, and the tacky gewgaws on sale (many made in China) are over the top. Still, dark clouds appearing out of nowhere to cover a blazing sun and the possibility of spotting a mirage may have you dreaming of a different Hortobágy – the mythical one that only ever existed in paintings, poems and active imaginations.

Orientation & Information

Buses stop on the main road (Hwy 33) near the village centre; the train station is to the northeast at the end of Kossuth utca. To get to the horse show at Máta Stud Farm, cross the train tracks from the station and find the path through the brush (to the right). This well-worn track through the fields (and eventually past Hortobágyi Club Hotel) cuts the walk to 1.5km, down from 3km if you follow the road.

Bird Park (off Hwy 33; adult/child 600/300Ft; 🕑 9am-6pm Nov-Apr) Free use of three internet terminals is included in entry to the conservation park.

National Park Information Centre (☎ 529 935; www.hnp.hu; Kossuth utca; 🕑 8am-4pm Mon-Fri Nov-Apr, 8am-5pm Mon-Fri, 10am-5pm Sat & Sun May-Oct)

OTP bank (Petőfi tér) In the shopping complex, with an ATM.

Post office (Kossuth utca 2)

Tourinform (☎ 589 321; hortobagy@tourinform.hu; Petőfi tér; 🕑 8am-5pm Mon-Fri, 9am-4pm Sat) Located in a tiny hut and offers some help.

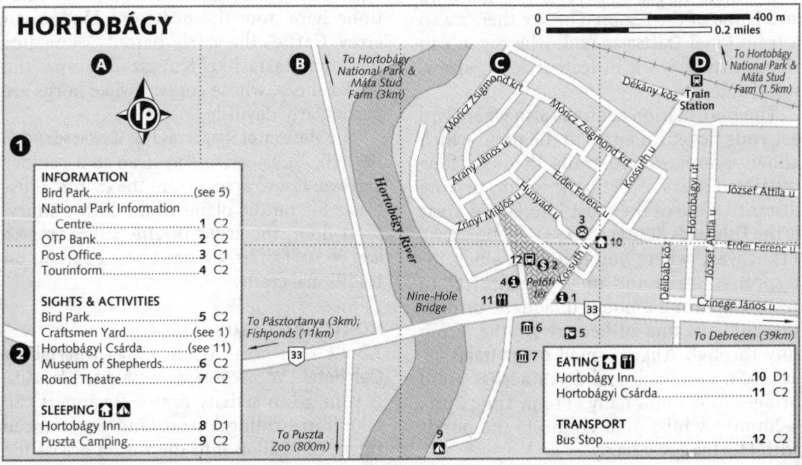

Sights & Activities

HORSE SHOW

As staged as it may be, the *puszta* show at **Máta Stud Farm** (☎ 589 369; Máta; adult/child 2400/1300Ft; 10am, noon, 2pm & 4pm Apr-Nov), 3km north of the village, *is* Hungarian. During the 1½-hour program you (and about 50 others) ride in a horse-drawn wagon train across the prairie, making stops to get out and peer into the pens of Racka sheep, see the great Grey Cattle grazing, witness a semiwild herd of horses herded past and watch Hungarian *csikósok* perform tricks. A *csikós* riding full gallop five-in-hand – standing balanced on the back of the two rear horses, with three more reined in front – is something to see. Organised as part of the national park, the stud farm also raises livestock for organic meat.

HORTOBÁGY NATIONAL PARK

With its varied terrain and water sources, the patchwork **Hortobágy National Park** (adult/child 900/500Ft) has some of the best bird-watching in Europe. Indeed, some 344 species (of the continent's estimated 400) have been spotted here in the past 20 years, including many types of grebes, herons, shrikes, egrets, spoonbills, storks, kites, warblers and eagles. The great bustard, one of the world's largest birds, standing 1m high and weighing in at 20kg, has its own reserve with limited access to two-legged mammals.

Stop first at the **National Park Information Centre** (☎ 529 935; www.hnp.hu; Kossuth utca; 8am-4pm Mon-Fri Nov-Apr, 8am-5pm Mon-Fri, 10am-5pm Sat & Sun May-Oct) to get an overview of the flora and fauna of the region. On-site there's also a traditional **Craftsmen Yard**, where you can watch artists work in leather, clay, straw, wood and iron.

The information centre is also where you get your ticket for entry to the park, which allows admission to trails through four restricted areas of the park within driving distance. One of the most interesting areas is the **Fishponds** (Halastó; off Hwy 33; dawn-dusk), 11km west, where you can walk along interpretive trails and up a watchtower to see the amazing amount of aquatic birdlife that inhabits this 20-hectare swathe. From July through August small **gauge trains** (return 600Ft) run back and forth across pond bridges four times daily (11am, 1pm, 3pm, 4.20pm). A bike path connects the ponds with Hortobágy village.

The information centre also offers 1½-hour **guided walks** (adult/child 1000/600Ft; 2pm Mon-Fri Apr-Nov) in the village area. Ask about occasional local weekend bird-watching tours, too. October is a great month to visit; between 60,000 and 100,000 common cranes stop over on the Hortobágy plain during their annual migration. For more on week-long bird-watching tours, see p68.

VILLAGE SIGHTS

The **Nine-Hole Bridge** (Kilenc-lyukú híd), built in 1833 and spanning the marshy Hortobágy River, is the country's longest stone bridge (and certainly the most sketched, painted and photographed). Just before it stands the still-operating **Hortobágyi Csárda**, one of the original eating houses (1781) used by salt traders on their way from the Tisza River to Debrecen. The inns provided itinerant Roma fiddlers with employment, though they did not originally live in this part of Hungary. Gypsy music and *csárdak* have been synonymous ever since.

Get up close with our feathered friends as they convalesce at the **Bird Park** (Madarpark; off Hwy 33; adult/child 600/300Ft; 9am-6pm Apr-Nov). Walk through the 'hospital' section of this sanctuary, among ambling storks in the park and into an aviary with hawks. Kids can learn about conservation from simple displays before they head off to the playground.

The **Puszta Zoo** (off Hwy 33; adult/child 500/300Ft; 8am-6pm Apr-Nov), with its weird and wonderful animals, is a fun place for kids of all ages. You'll find God's acid experimentations here, too: the heavy-set Hungarian Grey Cattle, the curly-haired Mangalica pig, the Rasta-like Kuvasz dog and the Racka sheep, whose corkscrewlike horns are particularly devilish.

The **Museum of Shepherds** (☎ 589 000; adult/child 500/300Ft; 9am-5pm Apr-Nov), in an 18th-century carriage house across from the *csárda*, illustrates life on the plains in the 19th century. Next door, the **Round Theatre** (Körszín; admission free; 9am-6pm Apr-Nov) has a small exhibit on traditional crafts.

HORTOBÁGY CLUB

About 2km north of the village, **Hortobágy Club Hotel** (☎ 369 020; www.hortobagyhotel.hu; Máta) is your go-to activity centre. Beginners can take horse-riding lessons and experienced riders can gallop into the sunset across the *puszta* (per hour from 3000Ft); two-hour carriage rides (per person 2000Ft) are available, too. Rent a bike here for 500/2000Ft per hour/day. The club offers occasional birdwatching tours, boating excursions and even hot-air ballooning.

Festivals & Events

The area is busiest in July, when Máta hosts the **International Equestrian Day**; on 19 to 20 August during the **Hortobágy Bridge Fair**; and on Pentecost, when the **National Herdsmen Competition & Shepherd's Meeting** is held.

Sleeping

Hortobágy is easy day-trip distance from Debrecen. There's a notice board on the west side of Petőfí tér listing private rooms.

Puszta Camping (☎ 369 300; baranyais@freemail.hu; off Hwy 33; camp sites per person/tent 800/650Ft, bungalows per person 2000Ft; May-Sep;) Occupying a quiet spot south of busy Hwy 33 and close to the river, Puszta offers basic facilities and a tiny thermal pool.

Pásztortanya (☎ 369 127; off Hwy 33; s/d 3000/6000Ft) A traditional Hortobágy-style farmhouse providing four rooms with shared facilities and an on-site restaurant. It's a solitary building 3km west of town, next to the Macskatelek airfield.

Hortobágy Inn (Fogado; ☎ 369 137; Kossuth utca 1; s/d 3500/6000Ft) The most central place to stay has seen better days, but there's a restaurant onsite and basic rooms come with balcony.

Hortobágy Club Hotel (☎ 369 020; www.hortobagyhotel.hu; Máta; s/d/apt incl breakfast €66/83/168;) As a member of Hortus Naturae Hotels in Hungary, Hortobágy Club's low-lying buildings were constructed in traditional style to blend with the environment, not that you can't see the whitewashed walls with terracotta roofs in the distance. Use of thermal pools, saunas and tennis courts is included, though horse riding and bike and canoe rental cost extra. Apartments, with kitchens, sleep four.

Eating

There's a little grocery shop just north of the post office.

Hortobágy Inn (Fogado; ☎ 369 137; Kossuth utca 1; mains 800-1500Ft; 8am-7pm) Lots of innards are on the menu at this cheaper *csárda*, across Petőfi tér from the original Hortobágyi Csárda. The bar stays open until 11pm.

Magyaros (☎ 369 020; Máta; mains 1600-2400Ft; 7am-10pm) A summer evening spent gazing at the sunset on the grassy plains from the terrace at the Hortobágy Club Hotel restaurant is one well spent. Start with the cold peach soup and next move on to a local river fish, like perch, from the menu.

Hortobágyi Csárda (☎ 589 399; Petőfi tér 2; mains 1800-3000Ft; 8am-10pm) Hungary's most celebrated roadside inn, c 1871. Sit back and admire the Hortobágy kitsch taking up every square centimetre of wall space. There's likely to be a wait as every traveller in town wants to stop here. Gypsy violinists often play as you tuck into your *bogrács gulyas* (goulash served in a small kettle) or game dishes. You can even try the meat of the famous Grey Cattle and Majolika pig, whose relatives you saw grazing on the plain. Don't miss the famous *Hortobágyi palacsinta* as an appetiser.

Getting There & Away

Seven buses stop daily at Hortobágy on runs between Debrecen (675Ft, 37 minutes, 40km) and Eger (1150Ft, two hours, 95km). Check the bus schedule carefully, as horse-show times don't correspond neatly with arrivals. One bus connects daily with Hajdúszoboszló (1050Ft, 70 minutes, 58km).

Hortobágy is on the main train line linking Debrecen (675Ft, 50 minutes, 40km), Tiszafüred (346Ft, 35 minutes, 30km) and Füzesabony (1050Ft, 1¼ hours, 60km), served by 11 trains daily, with the last train departing for Debrecen at about 10.30pm. You can connect to Eger from Füzesabony.

HAJDÚSZOBOSZLÓ

☎ 52 / pop 24,000

Thousands of visitors, many Hungarian, flock to Hajdúszoboszló, the country's largest thermal bathing centre and water park. The small town is well spread out, so at the train station or on Hősök tere you'd never suspect the hubbub to the north. Hotel after guest house after apartment rental line the streets surrounding the 40-hectare holiday spa complex.

Orientation

Almost everything you'll want or need can be found on the broad street, Szilfákalja út (Rte 4), running through town. The park-like thermal baths and water amusement centre, lumped together as the Holiday Area (Üdülőterület), occupy the northeastern

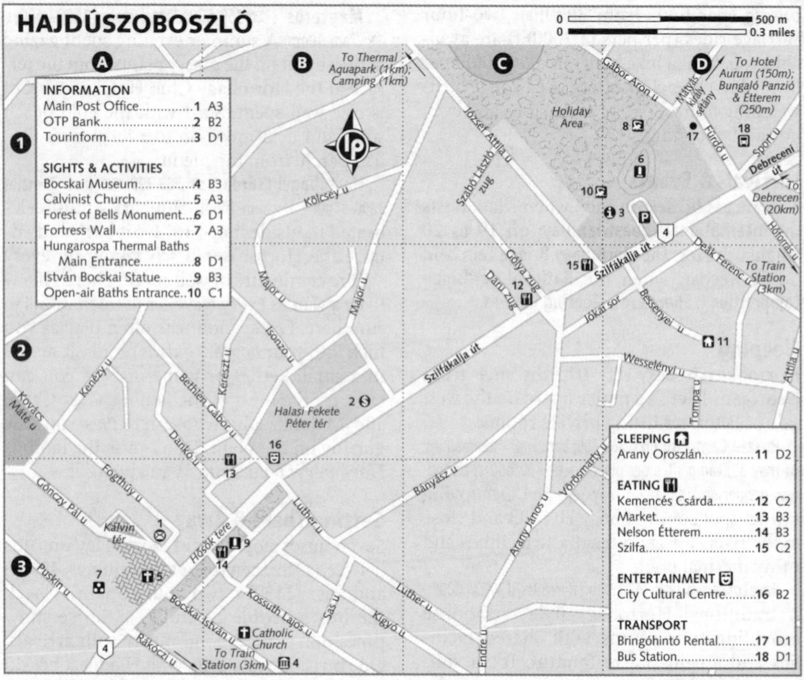

portion of Hajdúszoboszló. Hősök tere – the town centre – lies 1km southwest.

The bus station (Fürdő utca) is just north of Debreceni út. The train station (Déli sor) is a long 3km walk south via Rákóczi utca; take bus 1 or 1/a to the bus station for the closest stop to the spa and hotels.

Information

Main post office (Kálvin tér 1)
OTP bank (Szilfákalja út 10) With an ATM; next to the ABC supermarket.
Tourinform (☎ 558 929; www.hajduszoboszlo.hu; Szent István Park 1-3; 🕑 8am-6pm Mon-Fri, to 2pm Sat Jun-Sep, 9am-5pm Mon-Fri Oct-May) At the main thermal baths entrance.

Sights & Activities

Hungarospa Thermal Baths (☎ 558 558; www.hungarospa.hu; Szent István Park 1-3; adult/child 1200/900Ft; 🕑 indoor baths 7am-7pm, outside pools 8am-8pm Jul & Aug, to 7pm Jun, to 6pm May & Sep) is a complex comprising more than a dozen pools – a shallow sunbathing pool, a wave pool, themed kids' pools – set in a gigantic park, with food and souvenir stands, full restaurants and pondside rowboat rental (per hour 1000Ft). Forty different spa services are also available. Apparently the nine slides and beaches at the existing **Aquapark** (adult/child day pass 2700/1300Ft; 🕑 10am-6pm Jun-Aug), towards the back of the baths, wasn't enough. A five-billion-forint 'Aqua Palace' spa addition is scheduled to open soon after this book's publication. All of the thermal and enjoyment pools here will be undercover, making this a year-round attraction. Look for separate, skyrocket-high, rates to enter the new 'adventure' area. A camping ground and hotel are to follow.

Outside the baths' open-air entrance, the striking **Forest of Bells Monument** honouring the dead of wars throughout Hungarian history is incongruously flanked by thong (flip-flop) and swimwear stands.

In town, behind the **Calvinist church** (Kálvin tér 9; admission free), built in 1717, is a 20m stretch of wall and a small tower – all that remains of a 15th-century Gothic **fortress** destroyed by the Turks in 1660. Across Hősök tere a **statue of István Bocskai** stands – a pint-sized prince out of all proportion to his snorting stallion. Find out more about his great deeds at the **Bocskai Museum** (☎ 362 165; Bocskai István utca 12; adult/child 400/200Ft; 9am-1pm & 2-4pm Tue-Sun), a temple in memory of Prince István and his *hajdúk* (Heyduck) helpers (see the boxed text, below).

Sleeping

The choice of lodging in this tourist town is enormous (Mátyás király sétány is particularly loaded with options). Tourinform has an accommodation list online, and a glossy private-room brochure at its office. Less than a three-night stay in midsummer, if allowed, will incur a surcharge.

Thermal Camping (☎ 558 552; thermalcamping@hungarospa-rt.hu; Böszörményi út 35/a; camp sites per person/tent 1020/1020Ft) Owned by Hungarospa Thermal Baths, this camping ground is at the northern end of the holiday complex; staying here gets you reduced admission to the baths. It's a flat, basic site with some cover and a minimart, adjacent to farmers' fields (until they're ploughed under for hotels).

Bungaló Panzió (☎ 935 6497; www.hajduszoboszlo-panzio.hu; Mátyás király sétány 16; s/d 7000/12,000Ft, bungalows per 4 people 12,000Ft) Remember childhood days when your family went to a summer camp for holidays? This bungalow complex has that old-fashioned, family feel, with barbecues and ball courts. Don't worry about the kids messing up the worn indoor-outdoor carpeting. Each room has a kitchenette, while two-storey bungalows have three bedrooms but only a refrigerator. Reasonable restaurant on-site.

Arany Oroszlán (☎ 273 094; www.aranyoroszlanpanzio.hu; Bessenyei utca 14; s/d incl breakfast 9000/11,000Ft) Simple guestrooms with little more than a low-lying bed and chair are the hallmark of this contemporary, innlike guest house. The quiet off-the-main-street location is a big plus.

Hotel Aurum (☎ 271 431; www.hotelaurum.hu; Mátyás király sétány 4; s/d 21,000/32,500Ft;) Set back from the road, you approach the stately Hotel Aurum (opened mid-2008) through elegant terraces along a lamp-post-lit lane. The neoclassical exterior hides clean-lined, almost Zen rooms, each with kitchen and wi-fi.

WHAT THE HEY?

The names of Hungarian towns often reflect the heritage of original settlers, like the Jász people (of Iranian decent) in Jászberény. The Hajdúság region is no different, settled in the 15th century predominantly by the *hajdúk* (English: Heyducks or Haiduks), a community of drovers and brigands turned mercenary soldiers. When the Heyducks helped István Bocskai (1557–1606), prince of Transylvania, rout the Habsburg forces at Álmosd, southeast of Debrecen, in 1604, they were raised to the rank of nobility and some 10,000 were granted land – as much to keep the ferocious, randy brigands in check as to reward them. Thus the more than 13 town names starting with Hajdú in Hajdú-Bihar county.

Eating

Invariably your lodging will have an on-site restaurant, so you won't have to wander far for food. There are also plenty of sausage, *lángos* (deep-fried dough) and ice-cream stalls along Szilfákalja út and in the park.

Market (Bethlen Gábor utca) The partially covered market deals mainly in fresh produce, flowers and local gossip.

Szilfa (József Attila utca 2; mains 800-1500Ft) Survey the counter filled with sausages and sandwiches, then pick and buy. Primarily a takeaway, this simple eatery also has a covered terrace for escaping the summer heat.

Bungaló Étterem (☎ 935 6497; www.hajduszoboszlo-panzio.hu; Mátyás király sétány 16; mains 1000-1400Ft) Reasonable prices and a vast Hungarian menu make this family-friendly establishment especially popular. Lunchtime set menus (a soup and a main) go for 900Ft.

Nelson Étterem (☎ 270 226; cnr Hősök tere & Kossuth Lajos utca; mains 1600-2200Ft) Like a captain's luxurious cabin on a 19th-century ship, the interior of this pub-restaurant is all dark wood and brass. Upscale offerings include chicken fillet with goose liver and apricot purée, but there are simpler, vegetarian dishes, too.

Kemencés Csárda (☎ 362 221; Szilfákalja út 40/a; mains 1600-2500Ft) With its pseudo-rustic trappings and folk-dress-clad waitresses, Kemencés is cashing in on *puszta* tourism big time, but it is near the baths.

Entertainment

Hajdúszoboszló is a family town, so don't expect hip bars and pumping clubs. It's not frowned upon to drink without having a meal at any of the outdoor tables at the town's restaurants, and there are beer gardens in the park.

City Cultural Centre (☎ 557 693; Szilfákalja út 2) Ask here about organ and choral concerts in the Calvinist church.

Getting There & Away

From Hajdúszoboszló at least five buses daily depart for Nádudvar (300Ft, 30 minutes, 18km) and Miskolc (2040Ft, three hours, 120km), and up to two dozen head to Debrecen (375Ft, 30 minutes, 20km).

Trains headed from Debrecen (375Ft, 15 minutes, 20km) to Szolnok (1770Ft, 1½ hours, 100km) and Budapest (3010Ft, 2½ hours, 200km) stop at Hajdúszoboszló a couple of times an hour throughout the day.

Getting Around

Rent a two-/four-person *bringó* (pedal-powered surrey) from **Bringóhintó** (cnr Fürdő utca & Mátás király sétány; 🕑 10am-6pm Jun-Aug) for 1900/3800Ft.

NÁDUDVAR

☎ 52 / pop 9620

Though you can buy the famous black pottery elsewhere, the village of **Nádudvar** (www.nadudvar.hu), 18km west of Hajdúszoboszló, is likely to be where it originated. The characteristic black colour comes from minerals in the area's clay soil and designs are made by etching into the clay with pebbles (see opposite). The Fazekas ('Potter') family has carried on the pottery tradition for centuries and they have several businesses on the main street, Fő út. See the youngest generation's work at the studio of **István Fazekas** (☎ 480 562; www.fazekaslstván.hu; Fő út 64; 🕑 8am-6pm Mon-Fri). **Ferenc Fazekas** (☎ 480 569; www.nadudvarifazekas.hu; Fő út 152; 🕑 8am-6pm Mon-Fri) is often on hand to give a demonstration, and his wares are for sale in his workshop. The little **Fazekas Ház Museum** (Fő út 159; admission 300Ft; 🕑 8am-6pm Mon-Fri) contains 18th-century pottery made by the family and an old foot-operated potter's wheel.

Nádudvar is close enough to Debrecen to be an easy day trip, so there's no reason to stay overnight. If you get hungry, there are several eateries along Fő út to choose from. At least five buses daily, with more on weekdays, run to Hájduszoboszló (300Ft, 30 minutes, 18km) and Debrecen (675Ft, one hour, 40km).

SOUTHERN PLAIN

The Southern Plain (Dél-Alföld), spanning the lower regions of the Danube and Tisza Rivers, holds the lion's share of the Great Plain's more intriguing towns and cities. Kecskemét and Szeged are centres for fine arts and culture, with attractive architecture, absorbing museums and an above-average (for the plain) bar and restaurant scene. But the *puszta* is not far away; Bugac, in Kiskunság National Park, is one of Hungary's better hubs depicting life on the plain.

KECSKEMÉT

☎ 76 / pop 103,300

Halfway between the Danube and the Tisza Rivers in the heart of the Southern Plain is Kecskemét, a city ringed with vineyards and orchards that don't seem to stop at the limits of this 'garden city'. Colourful architecture, fine small museums and the region's excellent *barackpálinka* (apricot brandy) beckon. And Kiskunság National Park, the *puszta* of the Southern Plain, is right at the back door. Day-trip opportunities include hiking in the sandy, juniper-covered hills, a horse show at Bugac or a visit to one of the region's many horse farms.

History

Kecskemét's agricultural wealth was used wisely – it was able to redeem all its debts in cash in 1832 – and today it can boast some of the most spectacular small city architecture in the country. It was also – and still is – an important cultural centre, home to an artists' colony and the world-famous Institute of Music Education.

Orientation

Kecskemét is a city of multiple squares that run into one another without definition and can be a little confusing at first. The intercity bus and main train stations are opposite one another near József Katona Park. A 10-minute walk southwest along Nagykőrösi utca will bring you to the first of the squares, Szabadság tér. The city's other train station, Kecskemét KK (Halasi út), from where narrow-gauge trains head for Bugac, is on the southern continuation of Batthyány utca.

ISTVÁN FAZEKAS

Born into a craftsman family, István Fazekas has been a professional potter since the age of 17 and has his own studio in Nádudvar (opposite).

How long has your family been involved in the ceramics trade? At Nádudvar the Fazekas family has been making black pottery based on permissions written in the 18th century. At present four of my family are still in the business. My father and his two brothers, and from my generation only me, are working in the trade.

What makes Nádudvari pottery so special? Our clay has an extremely high content of red ferric oxides, which during the firing process yield high-quality black iron oxides. The firing takes place in wood-burning furnaces where the resulting smoke further contributes to the colouring process. In fact, this is one of the oldest firing techniques in the trade. It works today as it did some thousands of years before.

What do you see as the future of traditional folk crafts in Hungary? Youngsters, in increasing numbers, are inquiring about folk crafts. In Nádudvar there is an art school, established in 1992 by my father and a few of his friends. In addition to pottery they teach weaving, woodcarving, basketwork etc. This way perhaps our beautiful crafts will not become forgotten skills of a bygone era.

Besides Nádudvar, where do you recommend readers go to shop for handmade pottery? Hungary harbours quite a rich pottery tradition. Still today in many towns they make a wide range and complex style of folk ceramic; it is quite significant in the pottery-making of Tiszafüred (p239), Mezőtúr and Hódmezővásárhely (p269).

Information

Datanet Internet Café (Kossuth tér 6-7; per hr 300Ft; 9am-10pm) Internet access; through the courtyard.

Ibusz (486 955; Malom Centre, Korona utca 2) For daily apartment rental.

Main post office (Kálvin tér 10-12)

OTP bank (Malom Centre, Korona utca 2) Foreign exchange and ATM.

Tourinform (481 065; kecskemet@tourinform.hu; Kossuth tér 1; 8am-7pm Mon-Fri, 10am-8pm Sat & Sun Jul-Aug, 8am-6pm Mon-Fri Sep-Jun)

Sights

AROUND KOSSUTH TÉR

The late-baroque, Catholic **Great Church** (Kossuth tér 2; 9am-noon & 3-6pm Tue-Sun May-Sep, 9am-noon Tue-Sun Oct-Apr), built in 1806, dominates Kossuth tér, the southeasternmost of the main squares. Large tablets on the front honour (from left to right) a mounted regiment of Hussars that served in WWI; citizens who died in the 1848–49 War of Independence; and the Kecskemét victims of WWII. From June to August its **tower** (adult/child 300/150Ft; 9am-noon & 3-6pm Tue-Sun May-Sep, 9am-noon Tue-Sun Oct-Apr) can be climbed for views of the city's sun-bleached rooftops.

On the eastern side of Kossuth tér is the **Franciscan Church of St Nicholas** (Kossuth tér 3), dating in part from the late 13th century; the **Zoltán Kodály Institute of Music Education** (Kodály Zoltán Zenepedagógiai Intézet; 481 518; Kéttemplom köz 1; adult/child 200/100Ft; 10am-6pm) occupies the baroque monastery behind it to the east. Inside, one of the corridors is devoted to the institute's composer-namesake.

The sandy-pink **Town Hall** (Kossuth tér 1; admission free; by appointment), containing the Tourinform office, is a lovely late-19th-century building designed by Ödön Lechner. With a mixture of Art Nouveau/Secessionist and folkloric elements, he produced a uniquely Hungarian style. The exterior tilework is from the renowned Zsolnay porcelain factory (still producing china today). The carillon chimes out strains of works by Ferenc Erkel, Kodály, Mozart, Handel and Beethoven several times during the day, and its floral ceilings and frescoes of Hungarian heroes were painted by Bertalan Székely, who tended to romanticise the past. Other beautiful examples of this style are the restored **Otthon Cinema** (Széchenyi tér 4), on the corner of pedestrian Görögtemplom utca, and the Ornamental Palace (p254).

SZABADSÁG TÉR

Walking northeast into Szabadság tér you'll pass the 17th-century **Calvinist church** and the **Calvinist New College** (Református újkollégium)

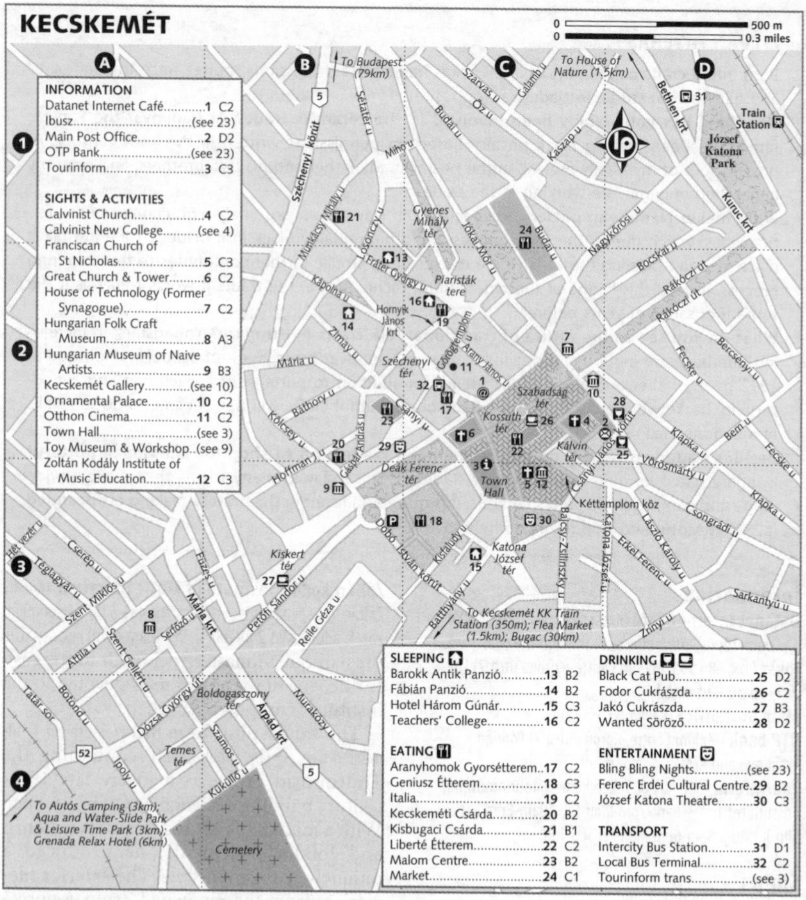

from 1912, a later version of the Hungarian Romantic style that looks like a Transylvanian castle and is now a music school. Two other buildings in the square are among the city's finest. The masterful Art Nouveau **Ornamental Palace** (Cifrapalota; Rákóczi út 1), which dates from 1902, is covered in multicoloured majolica tiles and outlined with interesting shapes. It now contains the **Kecskemét Gallery** (Kecskeméti Képtár; ☎ 480 776; Rákóczi út 1; adult/child 300/150Ft; 🕑 10am-5pm Tue-Sat, 1.30-5pm Sun). Don't go in so much for the art; climb the steps to the aptly named Decorative Hall (Díszterem) to see the amazing stucco peacock, bizarre Secessionist windows and more tiles. The **House of Technology** (Technika Háza; ☎ 487 611; Rákóczi út 2; adult/child 200/100Ft; 🕑 8am-4pm Mon-Fri), a Moorish structure dating from 1871, was once a synagogue and is now used for temporary exhibitions.

MUSEUMS

Arguably the city's most interesting museum and one of the few of its kind in Europe, the **Hungarian Museum of Naive Artists** (Magyar Naiv Művészek Múzeuma; ☎ 324 767; Gáspár András utca 11; adult/child 200/100Ft; 🕑 10am-5pm Tue-Sun mid-Mar–Oct) is in the Stork House (1730), surrounded by a white wall, just off Petőfi Sándor utca. There are lots of folksy themes here, but the warmth and craft of Rozália Albert Juhászné's work, the druglike visions of Dezső Mokry-

Mészáros and the paintings of András Süli (Hungary's answer to Henri Rousseau) should hold your attention.

Next door, the **Toy Museum & Workshop** (Szórakaténusz Játékmúzeum; ☎ 481 469; Gáspár András utca 11; adult/child 300/150Ft; ⏲ 10am-5pm Tue-Sun) has a small collection of 19th- and early-20th-century dolls, wooden trains, board games and so on, dumped haphazardly in glass cases. Much is made of Ernő Rubik, the Hungarian inventor of that infuriating Rubik's Cube from the 1970s. But the museum spends most of its time and money on organising events and classes for kids.

Some 10 rooms of an old farm complex are crammed with embroidery, woodcarving, furniture, agricultural tools and textiles at the **Hungarian Folk Craft Museum** (Magyar Népi Iparművészet Múzeuma; ☎ 327 203; Serfőző utca 19/a; adult/child 300/150Ft; ⏲ 10am-5pm Tue-Sat Feb-Nov), the granddaddy of all Kecskemét museums. Styles from across the entire region are represented and a few local handicrafts are for sale at the reception.

But don't stop there: Kecskemét is a town full of tiny museum gems. Wandering the old-town streets you'll find exhibits dedicated to photography, the ceramic arts and the history of musical instruments.

Activities

Kecskemét's main summer attraction is its **Aqua and Water-Slide Park** (☎ 481 724; Csabay Géza körút 2; adult/child 1200/900Ft; ⏲ 9am-7pm mid-May–Aug). It's loaded with fun things for the kids (five slides, huge pools, ball courts, grassy park), but it's also a thermal spa with several 'medicinal' pool and spa services. The food stand area abuts a lake, accessed for free in **Leisure Time Park** (Szabadidőpark), just north of the swimming complex.

Festivals & Events

Kecskemét is a festive town indeed, with spring (March), summer (June through August) and winter (mid-December) cultural festivals that bring classical concerts to town. Mid- to late August is especially celebratory: a weekend **International Air Show** kicks things off, followed by the **Hirős Week Festival**, with folk and popular concerts, run concurrently with the **Wine Festival**, at which vintners from all across Hungary set up tasting booths on the squares. Book accommodation ahead.

Sleeping

BUDGET

Tourinform has an extensive list of summer college accommodation.

Teachers' College (☎ 486 977; loveikollegium@tfk.kefo.hu; Piaristák tere 4; s/d 2500/5000Ft; ⏲ mid-Jun–Aug) The most central of Kecskemét's summer college accommodation, with your basic dormitory with twin beds and shared bathrooms.

Autós Camping (☎ 329 398; fax 501 199; Csabay Géza körút 5; camp sites per person/tent 800/700Ft, bungalows 5000-8000Ft; ⏲ May-Sep) Neat rows of tents and bungalows (with kitchen and bath, but no hot water) line this camping ground near the Aqua Park, 3km from the city centre. Don't expect much shade.

MIDRANGE

Barokk Antik Panzió (☎ 260 3215; www.barokkantik-panzio.hu; Fráter György utca 17; s/d incl breakfast 7500/10,500Ft; ☒) A sombre painting or two does lend a bit of an old-world feel, but we wouldn't say the rooms have actual antiques. Thankfully, they do have minibars and very modern bathrooms.

our pick **Fábián Panzió** (☎ 477 677; www.panziofabian.hu; Kápolna utca 14; s incl breakfast 8800-11,800Ft, d incl breakfast 11,000-11,800Ft; ☒ ❄) The world-travelling family that owns this pretty-in-pink guest house sure knows how to treat you. Homemade cookies and jam are a highlight of every breakfast, but they're also part of the treat that awaits returning visitors. Each morning friendly staff help their guests plan the day's excursion in a variety of languages. Teapots are available for in-room use, wi-fi is free and bikes are for rent. Rooms lack a little elbow room, but the gorgeous flower garden courtyard and amazing service make up for it. Ask about 'backpacker special' prices (excluding breakfast, with an extra bed put in a small single at a two-for-one price).

Hotel Három Gúnár (☎ 483 611; Batthyány utca 1-7; s/d incl breakfast 10,500/13,800Ft; ❄) Four multihued town houses – flowerboxes and all – have been transformed to contain 49 smallish rooms (the best are Nos 306 to 308). Simple veneer furnishings in the rooms are less cheery than the exterior facade. There's a restaurant on-site.

TOP END

Grenada Relax Hotel (☎ 503 103; www.grenadawellness.hu; Harmońia 12; s/d 14,500/17,500Ft; ☒ ❄ 💻 🏊) Wellness (sauna and indoor pools) and sport (tennis, soccer, minigolf, bowling) are the reasons to stay at this resort so far from the city centre. However, the location near the M5 motorway makes a good base for those with a car who want to tour the region and return to cool and contemporary comfort. Free wi-fi.

Eating

BUDGET

Market (Jókai Mór utca; 6am-3pm Tue-Sun) Pick up fruit and vegetables at the city's market.

Aranyhomok Gyorsétterem (☎ 503 730; aranyhomok@axelero.hu; Kossuth tér 3; mains 300-600Ft; 24hr) Locals love the quick and tasty self-service cafeteria on the ground floor of the city's ugliest hotel. Staff keep food fresh, despite being open around the clock.

Malom Centre (Korona utca 2; mains 400-800Ft; eateries 10am-10pm) The city is well set up with cheap eats since the opening of this shopping mall. Chinese, Hungarian and Italian self-service restaurants are on the 3rd floor.

MIDRANGE

Italia (☎ 484 627; Hornyik János körút 4; mains 1200-1400Ft) Italia is a little short on atmosphere, but it does a roaring trade with students from the nearby teachers' college. A full menu includes personal pizzas (from 800Ft), pasta dishes and all the fried pork varieties you can imagine.

ourpick **Liberté Étterem** (☎ 509 175; Szabadság tér 2; meals 1200-2000Ft) Artistic presentations come standard, whether you order the traditional stuffed cabbage or the mixed sautéed chicken with eggplant – yes, eggplant. This is modern Hungarian done right. Streetside tables on the pedestrian square have the best seats in town for people-watching.

Kecskemét has two restaurants that trade on folksy charm: **Kisbugaci Csárda** (☎ 322 722; Munkácsy Mihály utca 10; mains 1000-1500Ft), by far the simpler option; and the more homey **Kecskeméti Csárda** (☎ 488 686; Kölcsey utca 7; mains 1500-2000Ft), going over the top with rustic fishing gear on the walls and Gypsy music on weekends.

TOP END

Geniusz Étterem (☎ 497 668; Kisfaludy utca 5; mains 1900-3200Ft) The business-suit set can often be seen conducting meetings over a meal here. The menu changes seasonally, but options might include stuffed trout or Thai chicken. Light dishes (1300Ft to 1500Ft) are largely vegetarian.

Drinking

Western-themed pub **Wanted Söröző** (Csányi János körút 4; 10am-midnight Mon-Sat, from 4pm Sun) sits handily across from the more alternative **Black Cat Pub** (Csányi János körút 6; 11am-midnight Sun-Thu, to 2am Fri & Sat), making for quite the convivial corner.

On a summer Saturday evening it can seem like everyone in town is enjoying a coffee and ice cream from **Fodor Cukrászda** (Szabadság tér 2; 9am-9pm); those in the know go a little further afield to **Jakó Cukrászda** (Petőfi Sándor utca 7; 7am-8pm).

Entertainment

Kecskemét is a city of music and theatre; cultural festivals are on nearly year-round. Check out the free weekly *Kecskeméti Est* (www.est.hu) for entertainment listings.

Ferenc Erdei Cultural Centre (☎ 503 880; Deák Ferenc tér 1) The cultural centre sponsors some events and is a good source of information.

József Katona Theatre (☎ 483 283; www.szinhaz.hu; Katona József tér 5; ticket office 10am-1pm & 3-6pm Tue-Fri) The 19th-century theatre stages dramatic works, as well as operettas and concerts by the Kecskemét Symphony Orchestra.

Bling Bling Nights (www.blingblingnights.hu; Malom Centre, Korona tér 2) Hip-hop, house, R&B; the nightclub atop Malom Centre is definitely eclectic. DJs host most nights, but there are occasional live concerts.

Getting There & Away

BUS

Kecskemét is well served by buses, with frequent departures for even the most far-flung destinations.

Destination	Price	Duration	Km	Frequency
Baja	1770Ft	2½hr	110	5 daily
Budapest	1350Ft	1½hr	85	hourly
Debrecen	3220Ft	5½hr	235	1 daily
Eger	2290Ft	4hr	145	2 daily
Gyula	2290Ft	3¼hr	140	2 daily
Pécs	2040Ft	2½hr	130	2 daily
Szeged	1350Ft	1¾hr	85	hourly
Szolnok	1200Ft	1¾hr	75	7 daily

TRAIN

Kecskemét is on the train line linking Nyugati train station in Budapest (1770Ft, 1½ hours, 105km) with Szeged (1350Ft, one hour, 85km) at least hourly. To get to other towns north and east, you must change at Cegléd (525Ft,

20 minutes, 33km). A narrow-gauge train leaves Kecskemét KK train station, south of the city centre, at three inconvenient times (7.10am, 1.30pm and 8.05pm) daily for Bugac (750Ft, one hour, 50km) in Kiskunság National Park.

Getting Around

Buses 1, 5 and 15 link the intercity bus and train stations with the local bus terminal behind Aranyhomok Gyorsétterem, and buses 2 and 2/a connect Kecskemét KK train station with the city centre. For the Aqua and Water-Slide Park and Autós Camping, bus 22 is the best.

Rent bicycles for 2400Ft per day at **Tourinform** (☎ 481 065; kecskemet@tourinform.hu; Kossuth tér 1; 8am-7pm Mon-Fri, 10am-8pm Sat & Sun Jul-Aug, 8am-6pm Mon-Fri Sep-Jun).

KISKUNSÁG NATIONAL PARK

☎ 76

Kiskunság National Park (www.knp.hu) consists of nine 'islands' of land totalling more than 760 sq km. Much of the park's alkaline ponds, dunes and grassy 'deserts' are off-limits to casual visitors. Ask about birding and other tours at the park's main office in Kecskemét, **House of Nature** (Map p254; ☎ 482 611; www.knp.hu; Liszt Ferenc utca 19; 9am-4pm Tue-Fri, 10am-2pm Sat). The park website, http://kolon-to.org, is another good source of information.

The easiest place to get up close with this environmentally fragile area and see the famous horse herds go through their paces is at **Bugac**, on a sandy steppe 30km southwest of Kecskemét. Board a **horse-driven carriage** (adult/child incl museum & horse show 2900/1700Ft; 11.15am & 12.15pm May-Oct), walk or drive the 1.5km along the sandy track to the **Herder Museum** (admission free; 10am-5pm May-Oct), a circular structure designed to look like a horse-driven dry mill. It's filled with stuffed fauna and sheepherder's implements – carved wooden pipes, embroidered fur coats and a tobacco pouch made from a gnarled old ram's scrotum.

Walk across to the stables and arena to see the *puszta* **horse show** (admission show only 1400Ft; 12.15pm & 1.15pm May-Oct, extra show 3.15pm Jun-Aug), the park's highlight. In addition to making noble Nonius steeds perform tricks that most dogs would be disinclined to do, the *csikósok* crack their whips, race one another bareback and ride 'five-in-hand'. This is a breathtaking performance in which one *csikós* gallops five horses around the field at full tilt, while standing on the backs of the last two.

The **Juniper Trail** (2km return), behind the stables, is an interpretive track that leads you to the edge of the juniper forest and sandy hills (a restricted area). You can take an off-shoot trail to a nearby tower for a better look before heading back.

The food is surprisingly good at the entirely kitschy **Bugaci Karikás Csárda** (☎ 575 112; Nagybugac 135; mains 1600-2100Ft; 8am-8pm May-Oct), next to the park entrance. The *gulyás* (beef goulash soup) is hearty and the accompanying folk-music ensemble will get your foot tapping on the large and shady terrace. Expect a crowd after the show. If an old guy offers to take you by carriage to a better *csárda,* ignore him; it's not good.

Getting to the show ain't easy. A car is your best bet. The bus (600Ft, 50 minutes, 35km) comes in second; there's an 11am departure to Bugac that will get you to the second show. Tell your driver that you're going to Bugaci Karikás Csárda (the restaurant); at the time of publication the stops were scheduled to change and the village is 1.5km from the park entry.

Scattered around the national park's disparate sections are a whole bunch of horse farms where you can ride, sleep and eat. One of the family-friendliest is **Somodi Tanya** (☎ 377 095; www.somoditanya.hu; Fülöpháza; camp sites per person 1400Ft, r per person 3700Ft), 21km west of Kecskemét. Stay in a rustic, 100-year-old farmhouse, horse ride through the sandy national park and agricultural fields (2500Ft per hour), or just laze about in the extremely relaxing yard. Breakfast and full board are available, and there's a restaurant on-site.

KALOCSA

☎ 78 / pop 18,500

Kalocsa is a quintessential small Hungarian town – rich in history, but as quiet as a church mouse. Along with Esztergom, Kalocsa was one of the two bishopric seats founded by King Stephen in 1009 from the country's 10 dioceses. The brilliantly flowered folk art originating here – embroidery, painting and pottery – is recognised all over the country. Today the only time to see the bright tulips and daisies blooming on a girl's embroidered dress is on holidays and at festivals; otherwise, museum viewing will have to do.

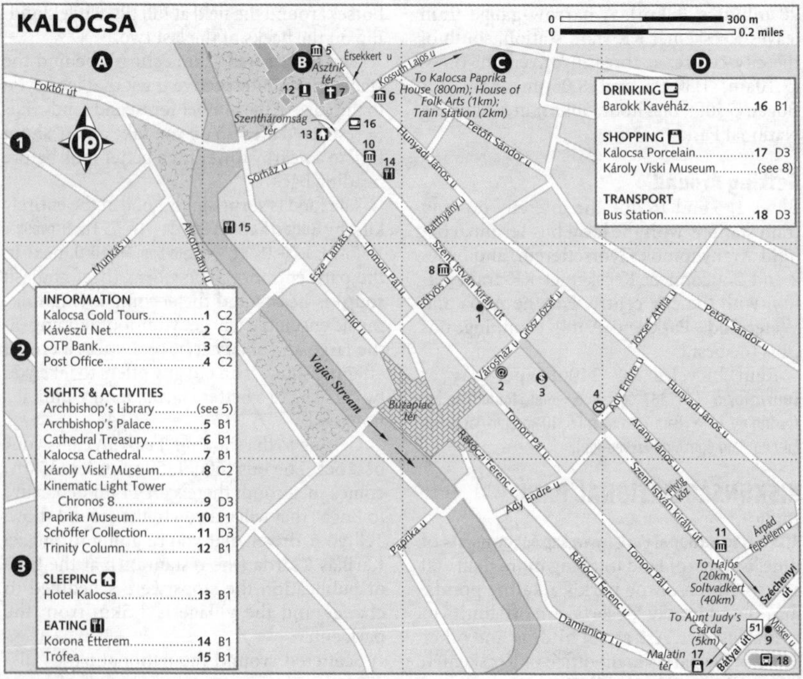

Orientation

The streets of Kalocsa fan out from Szentháromság tér. The bus station lies at the southern end of the main avenue, tree-lined Szent István király út. The train station (Mártírok tere) is a 20-minute walk northeast along Kossuth Lajos utca.

Information

There is no Tourinform office in town; the Hotel Kalocsa can arrange local tours and bicycle rental (per day 2000Ft).

City website (www.kalocsa.hu)

Kalocsa Gold Tours (☎ 465 347; www.kalocsagoldtours; Szent István király út 35; 🕓 8am-5pm Mon-Fri) Offers wine and folk-art tours in the area.

Kávészü Net (Városház utca 1; per hr 300Ft; 🕓 10am-10pm) Internet access.

OTP bank (Szent István király út 43-45)

Post office (Szent István király út 44)

Sights

KALOCSA CATHEDRAL

Almost everything of interest in Kalocsa is on or near Szent István király út, beginning at Szentháromság tér, where the **Trinity Column** (1786) is corroding into sand. **Kalocsa Cathedral** (1754), the fourth church to stand on the site, was completed by András Mayerhoffer and is a baroque masterpiece, with a dazzling pink-and-gold interior full of stucco, reliefs and tracery. Some believe that the sepulchre in the crypt is that of the first archbishop of Kalocsa, Asztrik, who brought King Stephen the gift of a crown from Pope Sylvester II, thereby legitimising the Christian convert's control over Hungary. A plaque on the south side outside memorialises this event. Franz Liszt was the first to play the cathedral's magnificent 3560-pipe organ.

The **Cathedral Treasury** (Főszékesegyházi kincstár; ☎ 462 641; Hunyadi János utca 2; adult/child 600/300Ft; 🕓 9am-5pm Tue-Sun May-Oct), just east of the cathedral across Kossuth Lajos utca, is a trove of gold and bejewelled objects and vestments. The large bust of St Stephen was cast for the Millenary Exhibition in 1896 and contains 48kg of silver and 2kg of gold.

ARCHBISHOP'S PALACE

The Great Hall and the chapel of the 1766 **Archbishop's Palace** (Érseki palota; Szentháromság tér 1) contain magnificent frescoes by Franz Anton Maulbertsch, but you won't get to see these unless a concert is being held. More than 100,000 volumes, including 13th-century codices and a Bible belonging to Martin Luther that is annotated in the reformer's hand, make the **Archbishop's Library** (Érseki könyvtár; adult/child 600/300Ft; ⌚ 9am-5pm Tue-Sun May-Oct) one of the most impressive in Hungary. Look for illuminated manuscripts, and the verses cut into palm fronds from Sri Lanka.

MUSEUMS

Virtually nothing was left undecorated by the famous 'painting women' of Kalocsa. To see examples of their work, check out the colourful interiors at the **Károly Viski Museum** (☎ 462 351; Szent István király út 25; adult/child 300/150Ft; ⌚ 9am-5pm Wed-Sun May-Sep). Look, too, for the floral embroidery and hand-painted pottery. The museum is rich in folklore and art, including that of the Swabian (Sváb), Slovak (Tót) and Serbian (Rác) peoples of the area.

The other main place to look at lavish examples of wall and furniture painting is at the **House of Folk Arts** (Népmüvészeti tájház; ☎ 461 560; Tompa Mihály utca 5-7; adult/child 600/300Ft; ⌚ 10am-5pm Tue-Sun May-Oct); the three-room museum was once a peasant's home. Choose from a huge selection of Kalocsa embroidery in the gift shop, as prices are cheaper here than on the main square.

An exhibition of the futuristic work of the Paris-based modern artist Nicholas Schöffer, who was from Kalocsa, can be seen at the **Schöffer Collection** (☎ 462 253; Szent István király út 76; adult/child 300/150Ft; ⌚ 10am-5pm Tue-Sun), though the collection would be more impressive if it was cleaned more often. You can also see some of Schöffer's work near the bus station; his **kinematic light tower Chronos 8** (1982) is a Meccano-set creation of steel beams and spinning reflecting mirrors that two decades ago was supposed to portend the art of the new century.

Festivals & Events

The embroidered folk costumes worn at the **International Danube Folklore Festival**, held mid-July, were once donned as the townswomen's Sunday best. **Kalocsa Paprika Days**, held over two weeks in mid-September, celebrate the harvest of the town's 'red gold' with kettle after kettle of paprika-laced foods, handicraft sales and entertainment (see the boxed text, below).

Sleeping

Consider visiting Kalocsa as a day trip, as the lodgings are limited.

Hotel Kalocsa (☎ 561 200; www.hotelkalocsa.hu; Szentháromság tér 4; s/d incl breakfast 15,500/20,000Ft) Carved mouldings on the furniture and tapestry drapes feel entirely appropriate in this 1780 building that used to house church offices. Your stay includes entry to the on-site thermal pool, Jacuzzi and sauna. There's a fine restaurant and cafe, too.

Eating & Drinking

Trófea (☎ 467 604; Sörház utca; mains 1000-1400Ft) What heaping portions of Hungarian specialities. A deck with outdoor seating overlooks the Vajas Stream; insect repellent is mandatory.

Aunt Judy's Csárda (Juca Néni Csárdája; ☎ 461 469; mains 1000-1500Ft) With walls decorated with traditional Kalocsa folk paintings, this *csárda* is a popular stop on tours of the area, though it's a good 5km from the town centre.

Karona Étterem (☎ 467 844; Szent István király út 6; mains 1200-1600Ft) Descend the brick stairs to the

GOING FOR THE RED GOLD

Along with Szeged, Kalocsa is the largest producer of paprika, the *piros arany* ('red gold') so important to Hungarian cuisine. It's used to season the roux of *halaszlé* (fish soup), *gulyás* (beef goulash soup), *pörkölt* (stew) and *paprikas* (dishes in a creamy paprika sauce). You can learn all about its development (first mentioned in documents way back in the 16th century), production and beneficial qualities (it's higher in vitamin C than citrus fruits) at not one, but two museums in Kalocsa: the smaller, central **Paprika Museum** (☎ 461 819; Szent István király út 6; adult/child 600/300Ft; ⌚ 10am-5pm May-Oct) and **Kalocsa Paprika House** (☎ 462 998; Kossuth Lajos utca 15; adult/child 600/300Ft; ⌚ 10am-4pm May-Oct). Both are overpriced and touristy, if informative. Maybe the true way to learn is to come to the **Kalocsa Paprika Days**, in mid-September, so you can sample both the *édes* (sweet) and *erös* (strong) versions of the spice in a range of dishes.

cellar for excellent fish soup or a pork chop stuffed with onions, garlic and paprika.

Barokk Kávéház (Szent István király út 2; ⏰ 8am-10pm) Residents linger over drinks at the cafe opposite the cathedral.

Shopping

Kalocsa Porcelain (☎ 462 017; www.porcelanfesto.hu; Malatin tér 5; admission 300Ft; ⏰ 8am-5pm Mon-Fri, 10am-2pm Sat) Tour the factory of Kalocsa Porcelain to see the making of the modern version of Kalocsa painted plates before you buy at the associated gift shop. Be warned: some find the graphic flowers rather garish.

You can buy embroidered aprons, handkerchiefs and tablecloths at both the **House of Folk Arts** (Népmüvészeti tájház; ☎ 461 560; Tompa Mihály utca 5-7; adult/child 600/300Ft; ⏰ 10am-5pm Tue-Sun May-Oct) and **Károly Viski Museum** (☎ 462 351; Szent István király út 25; adult/child 300/150Ft; ⏰ 9am-5pm Wed-Sun May-Sep). Ask at the latter for a list of private artists in the area. There's also folk-art shopping to be had at a small gift shop across from the cathedral and at festivals.

Getting There & Away

A car is handy on the far southern plain. From Kalocsa buses connect to Budapest (2040Ft, 2½ hours, 120km, 10 daily), Kecskemét (1770Ft, 2½ hours, 115km, two daily), Szeged (1770Ft, three hours, 115km, four daily) and Székesfehérvár (2780Ft, 2¾ hours, 120km, two daily), but the Kecskemét–Kiskőrös KK narrow-gauge train no longer connects with Kalocsa.

HAJÓS

☎ 78

Little white house after little white house, orange barrel-tile roof after orange barrel-tile roof. Hajós, 21km southeast of Kalocsa, isn't really a village at all but a collection of more than 1200 sharply pointed *pincék* (cellars) lined up in a seemingly endless maze of winding streets and alleys. Centuries ago a healthy Swabian population settled the region and began fermenting and storing wine; the conditions were seemingly perfect for such activities and the result is the storage cellars you see today. Light, plump whites, like Leányka, are the mainstay but some full-bodied reds are produced, too. Owners open their doors for sales and tastings at their whim. A handful may be open at any time, but the odds are best during harvest season in September.

Kovács Borház (☎ 404 947; www.kovacsborhaz.hu; Jókai utca 23/a; cellar tour 500Ft; ⏰ 10am-6pm) is a family-owned, but much larger, year-round operation, with wine tastings and sales, cellar tours and a restaurant.

A few of the larger cellars rent out apartments. Look for signs, or you can sleep in basic rooms and eat homestyle meals (mains 800Ft to 1200Ft) at **Judit Panzió** (☎ 404 832; www.juditpanzio.hu; Borbíró sor 1; s/d 3000/6000Ft).

Hajós can be reached by four buses daily from Kalocsa (450Ft, 40 minutes, 25km), Baja (525Ft, 40 minutes, 31km) and Kecskemét (1350Ft, 1¾ hours, 80km). More buses run on weekends. The athletic might try biking from Kalocsa or Baja. **Kalocsa Gold Tours** (Map p258; ☎ 465 347; www.kalocsagoldtours; Szent István király út 35, Kalocsa; ⏰ 8am-5pm Mon-Fri) offers Hajós wine tours.

BAJA

☎ 79 / pop 37,200

On the banks of the Danube, Baja is something of a local holiday centre, with a beach, bars and flood-bank forests. June and July is the high season; August can get uncomfortably hot. If you visit, you have to try the Baja version of *halaszlé* (fish soup), concocted with carp, pike-perch, catfish and the ubiquitous paprika.

WE ALL STOP FOR ICE CREAM

Who doesn't like a good ice-cream break? Tell a Kecskemét resident you're headed to Hajós and they're likely to suggest you stop at Solvadkert, about halfway, or 40km, between the two destinations. Judging from the number of cars coming and going on weekends at **Korona Cukrászda** (☎ 78-480 150; Kossuth Lajos utca 5, Solvadkert; cakes 150-450Ft; ⏰ 10am-8pm), they all sure do. Most come to the huge ice-cream parlour cafe, first opened in 1795, for their pick of creamy frozen flavours – from forest-picked blueberry to Bailey's Irish Cream – but there's also cake after cake lined up in the case. Sit at one of the marbletop tables and order a gigantic *pohár* (literally 'cup'), a sundae filled with different ice-cream flavours and syrups – yum!

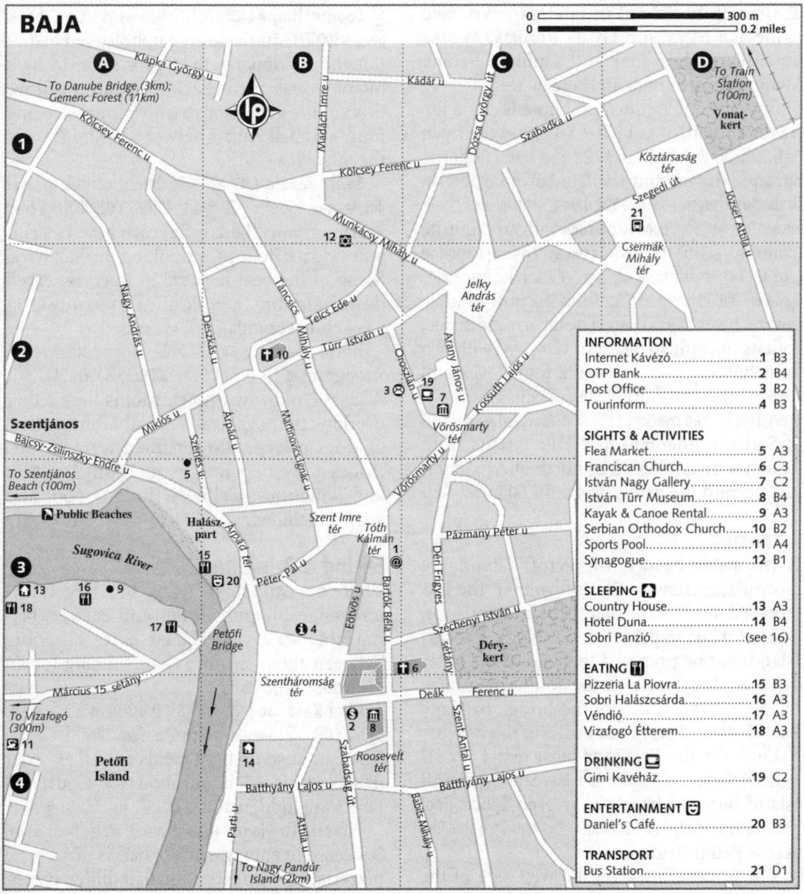

Orientation

The main square, Szentháromság tér, lies on the Kamarás-Duna (or Sugovica as it is known locally), a branch of the Danube River that cuts Petőfi and Nagy Pandúr Islands off from the main town. The bus station (Csermák Mihály tér) and train station (Vonat-kert) are north-east of the city centre off Kossuth Lajos utca.

Information

Internet Kávézó (Tóth Kálmán tér 7; per hr 500Ft; noon-9pm Mon-Fri, 9am-1pm Sat)

OTP bank (cnr Szentháromság tér & Deák Ferenc utca)

Post office (Oroszlán utca 5)

Tourinform (☎ 420 792; baja@tourinform.hu; Szentháromság tér 11; 8am-5pm Mon-Fri, 10am-7pm Sat & Sun Jun & Jul, 8am-5pm Mon-Fri Aug-May)

Sights

Hanging out at the river or at a cafe is really the thing to do here, but on a rainy day there's the **István Türr Museum** (☎ 324 173; Deák Ferenc utca 1; adult/child 350/250Ft; 10am-4pm Wed-Sat mid-Mar–mid-Dec). One exhibit covers life on the Danube, another deals with the folk groups of the area: Magyars, Germans, South Slavs (Bunyevác, Sokac) and – surprisingly for Hungary – Roma. Check out the rarely seen Roma woodcarving, South Slav black lace and the goldwork for which Baja was once famous. Enter from Roosevelt tér.

First a mansion, then an artists' colony, today the **István Nagy Gallery** (☎ 325 649; Arany János utca 1; adult/child 350/250Ft; 10am-4pm Wed-Sat mid-Mar–mid-Dec) contains artwork by members of the Alföld School of landscape art, like namesake Nagy and Gyula Rudnay. Works by cubist Béla Kádár and sculptor Ferenc Medgyessy are snuck in there as well.

Buildings of architectural note include the **Franciscan church** (Bartók Béla utca) behind the town hall, which was built in 1728 and has a fantastic baroque organ, and the late-baroque **Serbian Orthodox church** (☎ 423 199; Táncsics Mihály utca 21; admission free; ⏰ 9am-noon Wed & Thu), with an exquisite iconostasis. But the neoclassical, 1845 **synagogue** (☎ 322 741; Munkácsy Mihály utca 7-9; admission free; ⏰ 1-6pm Mon-Thu, 10am-6pm Fri, 8am-noon Sat), now a public library, beats them both. The tabernacle inside, with its Corinthian pilasters, is topped with two lions holding a crown while four doves pull back a blue-and-burgundy curtain.

A lively **flea market** (⏰ 7am-4pm Wed & Sat), full of Serbs, Romanians and Hungarians from Transylvania, takes place north of Árpád tér, just beyond the bridge to Petőfi Island.

Activities

If the **public beaches** on Petőfi Island are crowded, eschew them in favour of the less crowded ones on the mainland in Szentjános, east of Halász-part, or on Nagy Pandúr Island, but be prepared to swim to the latter or face a long walk to the southern suburb of Homokváros, across the bridge to Nagy Pandúr Island and then north to the beach.

Look for the **kayak and canoe rental** (☎ 537 2668; Petőfi-sziget; ⏰ 10am-6pm May-Sep) on Petőfi Island beach. There's a covered **Sports Pool** (☎ 326 773; adult/child 500/300Ft; ⏰ 7am-7pm Thu-Tue) across Petőfi Bridge, too.

The **Gemenc Forest**, on the west side of the Danube, is a unique reserve famed for its incredible beauty and narrow-gauge train trips. A good way to see it is to take a **boat and rail trip** (☎ 425 356; per person 4000Ft; ⏰ 9.45am Wed, Sat & Sun Jul & Aug, 9.45am Sat May-Oct), booked through Tourinform. For more on the forest, see p284.

Festivals & Events

The big event of the year is the **Baja Folk Festival**, when more than 2000 stew pots (a Guinness World Record) bubble with the famous fish soup on the second Saturday in July.

Sleeping

A whole line of guest houses sits between Március 15 sétány and the Sugovica River on Petőfi Island, including one above Vizafogó Étterem (right).

Country House (☎ 326 585; Március 15 sétány 20; r per person 3000Ft) Multicoloured upholstered beds – not the headboard, the bed – seem to be a bit of a '90s throwback, but families love this simple guest house with rooms sleeping four, and ball courts between the house and the Sugovica.

Sobri Panzió (☎ 420 654; http://sobrihalaszcsarda.hu; Március 15 sétány 20; s/d/tr 4000/6000/9000Ft) Four spartan rooms (beds only) each have exterior access to a balcony overlooking the Sugovica. Some of the best *halaszlé* in town is served downstairs, but there is loud Gypsy music on weekend evenings.

Hotel Duna (☎ 323 224; www.hotelduna.hu; Szentháromság tér 6; s/d from 8000/10,800Ft; 💻 🅿) A classic old-town hotel, rooms here either overlook the Sugovica or Szentháromság tér – as does a large, flower-filled terrace cafe. Prices vary depending on room location and amenities; wellness (indoor pool and spa) is included.

Eating & Drinking

There's a stretch of lively but largely interchangeable pubs, cafes and eateries facing the water at Halász-part. Hopping between them is more than suitable for an evening's enjoyment.

Gimi Kávéház (☎ 428 485; Oroszlan utca 2/a; mains 300-1000Ft; ⏰ 8am-8pm Mon-Thu, 9am-10pm Sat & Sun) You can nosh on light meals as well as order drinks at this neighbourhood cafe. Courtyard tables are hidden at the back.

Pizzeria La Piovra (Halász-part 2; pizzas from 800Ft) Squeezed in among a line of bars is this simple pizzeria, with unexceptional, if filling, pizzas. The view makes up for any shortcomings the pizzas may have.

Véndió (☎ 326 585; Martinovics utca 8/b; mains 1200-2200Ft) Véndió's reputation for quality international dishes, and the restaurant's excellent location down by the water, keep diners coming back for more. If only the waiters moved faster.

Locals will argue with you about which Petőfi Island restaurant has the best *halaszlé*, but most agree it's between **Vizafogó Étterem** (☎ 326 585; Petőfi-sziget 27; mains 1100-1400Ft) and **Sobri Halászcsárda** (☎ 420 654; http://sobrihalaszcsarda.hu; Március 15 sétány 20; mains 1100-1500Ft).

Entertainment

Ask staff at Tourinform about concerts around town.

Daniel's Cafe (☎ 06 20 595 5955; Halász-part 4; 🕑 10am-midnight Sun-Thu, to 2am Fri & Sat) Low, linen-and-wicker chairs provide an almost Mediterranean lounge feel. On weekends the cafe turns into a club with nightly DJs.

Getting There & Away

Though technically on the Great Plain, Southern Transdanubia is on just the other side of the Danube, making connections in that direction easy. Buses go to Kalocsa (750Ft, one hour, 45km, hourly), Szeged (1770Ft, 2½ hours, 105km, hourly) and Kecskemét (1770Ft, 2½ hours, 110km, five daily) on the plain. To the west, Mohács (900Ft, 1¼ hours, 50km) and Szekszárd (675Ft, one hour, 40km) are super close.

Baja is on a train line to Kiskunhalas (1200Ft, 1¼ hours, eight daily), from where you can transfer to Budapest (2290Ft, 2½ hours, 190km).

SZEGED

☎ 62 / pop 177,000

It's hard to put your finger on what's so appealing about Szeged. Maybe it's the shady, gardenlike main square with all the park benches, maybe it's the abundant streetside cafe seating in a pedestrian area that seems to stretch on forever, or maybe it's the interesting architecture of the old-town palaces. Then again, it could be the year-round cultural performances and lively university-town vibe. Szeged – a corruption of the Hungarian word *sziget* (island) – sits astride the Tisza River, with a thermal bath complex and park opposite the old town. Famed local edibles include Pick salami and the paprika that marries so well with spicy *halaszlé*. From here you can day trip to see the national historic park in Ópusztaszer or the ceramics in Hódmezővásárhely.

History

Remnants of the Körös culture suggest that these goddess-worshipping people lived in the Szeged area 4000 or 5000 years ago, and one of the earliest Magyar settlements in Hungary was at Ópusztaszer to the north. By the 13th century the city was an important trading centre, helped by the royal monopoly it held on the salt shipped in via the Maros River from Transylvania. Under the Turks, Szeged was given some protection as the sultan's estates lay in the area, and it continued to prosper in the 18th and 19th centuries as a royal free town.

The watery fingers of the Tisza almost wiped Szeged off the map in 1879 (see the boxed text, p265), but the town bounced back with a vengeance and an eye for uniform architecture. Since WWII Szeged has been an important university centre – students marched here in 1956 before their classmates in Budapest did.

Orientation

The Tisza River, joined by the Maros, flows west and then turns abruptly south through the centre of Szeged as a rather undignified muddy channel. The city's numerous pedestrian squares – Dóm, Dugonics, Roosevelt, Klauzál and Széchenyi – are pinned against the eastern bank of the river by inner and outer ring roads. The main train station (Indóház tér) is south of the city centre; tram 1 connects the train station with the central area. The bus station (Mars tér), to the west of the city centre, is within easy walking distance via pedestrian-only Mikszáth Kálmán utca.

You'll find an excellent source of maps at the **Map shop** (☎ 424 667; Attila utca 9), not only for Hungary but for the world, too.

Information

City website (www.szegedportal.hu)

Cyber Arena (Híd utca 1; per hr 400Ft; 🕑 24hr) Internet centre with Skype set-ups and cheap international phonecards.

Libri Bookstore (☎ 541 126; Jókai utca) Small foreign-language section that's big on Hungarian writers, historians and famous figures.

Main hospital (☎ 484 184; Kossuth Lajos Sugárút 42)

Main post office (Széchenyi tér 1)

Tourinform (☎ 488 699; http://tip.szegedvaros.hu) main office (Dugonics tér 2; 🕑 9am-5pm Mon-Fri, to 1pm Sat); booth (Széchenyi tér; 🕑 9am-9pm May-Sep) The main office, tucked away in a quiet courtyard, also sells concert tickets.

Sights

SZÉCHENYI TÉR

Ornamental trees and flowering bushes alternate with monuments and a fountain on Széchenyi tér, a square so large it's a park. The **Pál Vásarhelyi monument** immortalises the man who designed the regulation of the Tisza River. Ironically, marble plaques in the base indicate the high-water levels of the 1970 and 2006 floods. For more on architecture around the square, see the Walking Tour (p266).

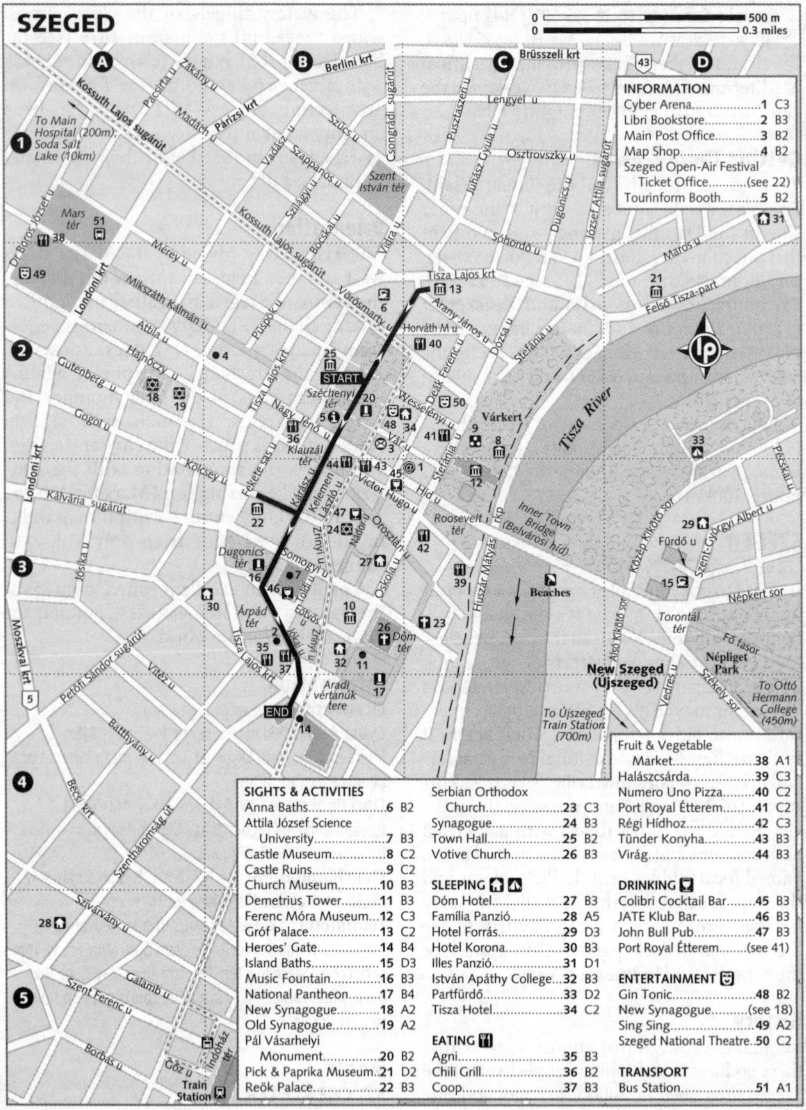

DÓM TÉR

Dóm tér, a few paces northeast of Heroes' Gate, contains Szeged's most important monuments and is the centre of events during the annual summer festival. The **National Pantheon** – statues and reliefs of 80 notables running along an arcade around three sides of the square – is a crash course in Hungarian art, literature, culture and history. Even the Scotsman Adam Clark, who supervised the building of Budapest's Chain Bridge, wins accolades, but you'll look forever for any acknowledgement of a woman.

The Romanesque **Demetrius Tower** (Dömötör-torony; admission free; by appointment), the city's oldest structure, is all that remains of a

GREAT PLAIN

church erected here in the 12th century. Adjacent stands the twin-towered **Votive Church** (☎ 429 379; adult/child 400/200Ft; ⏰ 9am-5pm Mon-Sat, 1-5pm Sun), a disproportionate brown brick monstrosity that was pledged after the 1879 flood but not completed until 1930. The interior borders on gaudy but it's still an impressive achievement; the huge nave and gigantic organ (11,500 pipes in all) dominate the entire scene. The nearby **Serbian Orthodox church** (☎ 325 278; adult/child 200/150Ft; ⏰ 8am-4pm), at the northeastern end of Dóm tér, was built in 1778 and is far more rewarding. Take a peek inside at the fantastic iconostasis: a central gold 'tree', with 60 icons hanging from its 'branches'. Ring the bell; theoretically someone will come. Back on Dóm tér, duck into the **Church Museum** (Egyházmegegyi Múzeum; Dóm tér 5; adult/child 75/40Ft; ⏰ 10am-6pm Tue-Sun) and pick through the small collection of monstrances, crosses and goblets from across the plains.

FERENC MÓRA MUSEUM

The one-time Palace of Education (1896) now houses the **Ferenc Móra Museum** (☎ 549 040; www.mfm.u-szeged.hu; Roosevelt tér 1-3; adult/child 600/300Ft; ⏰ 10am-5pm Tue-Sun). The museum contains a colourful collection of folk art from Csongrád County, bearing intelligent descriptions in several languages, and an exhibit of the 7th-century Avar people's goldwork. But the best exhibit showcases an even more obscure group, the Sarmatians, who originated in present-day Iran. Construction of the M5 motorway unearthed a 1st-century village of theirs, along with pottery, jewellery and graves.

After the 1879 flood claimed many of the walls in Szeged's riverfront **castle ruins** (c 1240), the city demolished the rest. Behind the museum you can freely see ongoing foundation excavations; for a closer look at the ancient subterranean walls, walk down into the **Castle Museum** (Varmuzéum; ☎ 549 040; Stefánia sétány 2; adult/child 300/150Ft; ⏰ 10am-5pm Tue-Sun), a small gallery with changing exhibits.

SYNAGOGUES

For many people, Szeged's most compelling sight is the Hungarian Art Nouveau **New Synagogue** (Újzsinagóga; ☎ 423 849; www.zsinagoga.szeged.hu; Gutenberg utca 13; adult/child 300/150Ft; ⏰ 10am-noon & 1-5pm Sun-Fri Apr-Sep, 10am-2pm Sun-Fri Oct-Mar), which was designed by Lipót Baumhorn in 1903. It is the most beautiful Jewish house of worship in Hungary and still very much in use. If the grace and enormous size of the exterior don't impress you, the blue-and-gold interior will. The cupola, decorated with stars and flowers (representing Infinity and Faith), appears to float skyward, and the tabernacle of carved acacia wood and metal fittings is a masterpiece. There are a few other buildings of interest in this area, the former Jewish quarter, including the neoclassical **Old Synagogue** (Ózsinagóga; Hajnóczy utca 12), built in 1843, and just south of Széchenyi tér, the remains of another old **synagogue** (Nádor utca 3), now a private house.

OTHER SIGHTS

If you'd like to know more about the making of Szeged's famed salami – from hoof to packaging – the **Pick & Paprika Museum**

THE FLOODING TISZA

Snaking its way some 600km across the Great Plain is the Tisza, Hungary's longest river. Once described by Daniel Defoe as 'three parts water and two parts fish', this wonderful natural resource has a habit of flooding on an all-too-regular basis, despite the government's best efforts to keep it from breaching its banks.

The worst flood to wash through Szeged occurred in March 1879. The river burst its banks, leaving only 300 houses, out of an estimated 6300, standing. At least 600 people died and 60,000 were left homeless. Flood protection was subsequently built, and things went swimmingly (at least flood damage was kept to a minimum) for almost a hundred years until May 1970, when the river reached its highest recorded level under flood management and gave the city another soaking. Upgrade work on flood-control barriers has been underway over the past few decades, but it seems like every few springs there's at least a minor flood. As recently as 2006, restaurants, camping grounds and swimming pools along the river were closed due to flood damage. Of course, the best solution would be to move to higher ground, but that's not much of an option on the Great Plain…

(☎ 20-980 8000; Felső Tisza-part 10; adult/child 350/250Ft; ⌚ 3-6pm Mon, 9am-5pm Tue-Fri, 9am-noon Sat) will oblige, and if that doesn't satisfy your taste buds, there's plenty on paprika, too. Pick salami can be purchased from the meat shop next to the museum.

Activities

Though recently renovated, the chalk-white, dome-topped **Anna Baths** (☎ 487 711; Tisza Lajos körút 24; adult/child 1400/1100Ft; ⌚ 6am-8pm Mon-Fri, 8am-9pm Sat & Sun) were built in 1896 to imitate the tilework and soaring ceilings of a Turkish bath. Rich architectural detail surrounds all the modern aromatherapy saunas and bubbly pools you'd expect. From July through August, the baths open for occasional special weekend evening hours.

Across the Tisza River in New Szeged (Újszeged), there is a small **public beach** on the bank south of the bridge. At the time of publication the open-air pools at the **Island Baths** (☎ 431 133; www.ligetfurdo-szeged.hu; Fürdő utca 1; ⌚ 6am-9pm Jun-Aug) were operating, but the rest of the spa was undergoing a six-million-forint renovation. **Népliget Park**, also on the island, is a great place for biking, but then, where isn't in Szeged? The whole town is outfitted with bike lanes, special traffic lights and stands. **Bike rental** (per day 2500Ft) is available from Tourinform.

About 10km west of town in the suburb of Sziksósfürdő is the thermal **Soda Salt Lake** (adult/child 800/600Ft; ⌚ 10am-6pm Mon-Fri, 8am-6pm Sat & Sun May-Sep). Alongside a conventional beach, swimming pool and rowing boats, it also has a nudist beach and camping ground.

Walking Tour

Begin your walking tour of Szeged in Széchenyi tér. The neobaroque **town hall**, with its graceful tower and colourful tiled roof, dominates the square, while statues of Lajos Tisza, István Széchenyi and the *kubikosok* (navvies) who helped regulate the Tisza River take pride of place under the chestnut trees. Take a quick detour north of the square to the **Gróf Palace** (Arany János utca), a fantastical office building completed in 1913 in Secessionist style.

Pedestrian Kárász utca leads south through Klauzál tér. Turn west on Kölcsey utca and walk for about 100m to the **Reök Palace** (Reök-palota; Tisza Lajos körút 56), a mind-blowing green-and-lilac Art Nouveau structure built in 1907 that looks like an aquarium decoration. Sadly, it's been left to the elements and is coming off second best.

Further south, Kárász utca meets Dugonics tér, site of the **Attila József Science University** (abbreviated JATE in Hungarian), named after its most famous alumnus. József (1905–37), a much-loved poet, was actually expelled from here in 1924 for writing the verse 'I have no father and I have no mother / I have no God and I have no country' during the ultra-conservative rule of Admiral Miklós Horthy. A **music fountain** in the square plays at irregular intervals throughout the day.

From the southeast corner of Dugonics tér, walk along Jókai utca into Aradi vértanúk tere. **Heroes' Gate** to the south was erected in 1936 in honour of Horthy's White Guards, who were responsible for 'cleansing' the nation of 'reds' after the ill-fated Republic of Councils in 1919. The fascistic murals have disappeared (replaced with some 'nice' but amateurish ones), but the brutish sculptures are still a sight to behold.

Festivals & Events

The **Szeged Open-Air Festival** (☎ 541 205; www.szegediszabadteri.hu; festival office, Reök-palota, Tisza Lajos körút 56; ⌚ ticket office 8am-5pm Mon-Fri) unfolds on Dóm tér from mid-July to late August, with the two towers of the Votive Church as a backdrop. The outdoor theatre here seats some 6000 people. Main events include an opera, an operetta, a play, folk dancing, classical music, ballet and a rock opera. But Szeged isn't all highbrow; others might prefer the annual **Beer Festival** at the beginning of June or the one-week **Wine Festival** at the end of May.

Sleeping

Lodging prices in Szeged are higher than the provincial average. Budget digs are sadly lacking most of the year. Tourinform has a full list of summer college accommodation online at http://tip.szegedvaros.hu.

BUDGET

Partfürdő (☎ 430 843; fax 426 659; Közép kikötő sor; camp sites per person/tent 990/350Ft, r 4600-6900Ft, apt 8000-12,000Ft) The large grassy camping ground with volleyball courts and a beach on the Tisza River looks a bit like a public park. Bungalows, containing both rooms and apartments (with kitchens), give it away.

Ottó Hermann College (☎ 544 309; iroda@linux.ohsh.u-szeged.hu; Temesvári körút 52; s/d 3000/5000Ft) On a quiet residential street, Ottó Hermann is the best of the college bunch over in New Szeged.

István Apáthy College (☎ 545 896; Eötvös utca 4; dm/s/d 3500/5500/6500Ft) This supremely central option offers bare-bones dormitory accommodation. More than 200 rooms are available in July and August, but only a handful throughout the rest of the year. Communal kitchens and laundry on each floor; wi-fi available.

MIDRANGE

Família Panzió (☎ 411 122; www.familiapanzio.hu; Szentháromság út 71; s/d/tr 8000/10,000/15,000Ft;) Families and international travellers often book up this family-run guest house with contemporary, if nondescript, furnishings in a great old-town building. The reception may be dim, but rooms have high ceilings and loads of light from tall windows. Wi-fi is free, but air-conditioning costs an extra 1500Ft.

Illes Panzió (☎ 315 641; www.illespanzio-vadaszetterem.hu; Maros utca 37; r 9900-12,900Ft;) Pretty in pink: a cheery former-mansion facade sits in stark contrast to its rooms' dark-wood veneers and woven rugs. The courtyard pool is quite pleasant, though. Walk 10 minutes to the city centre, or rent a bike (per day 2000Ft). There's an on-site restaurant, and free wi-fi.

Tisza Hotel (☎ 478 278; www.tiszahotel.hu; Wesselényi utca 1; s/d without bathroom 9900/14,900Ft, with bathroom 14,900/17,100Ft) Szeged's old-world hotel drips with crystal chandeliers and gilt mirrors, but its rooms don't match up to the public elegance. The least expensive have a shower, but the toilet is shared down the hall.

TOP END

Hotel Korona (☎ 555 787; www.hotelkoronaszeged.hu; Petőfi Sándor sugárút 4; s/d incl breakfast 13,800/18,000Ft;) Climb up the open atrium stair and you can hardly see the original 1883 building outlines hidden in this modern hotel, with lemon-yellow walls and blonde wood continuing the up-to-date trend. A full, hot breakfast is served, and you're just around the corner from entertainment on Dugonics tér.

Other places to lay your head:

Hotel Forrás (☎ 430 130; www.hotelforras.szeged.hu; Szent-Györgyi Albert utca 16-24; s/d 14,500/18,800Ft;) Spa hotel in New Szeged. Bike rental available.

Dóm Hotel (☎ 423 750; www.domhotel.hu; Bajza utca 6; s/d incl breakfast 23,100/26,600Ft;) Small and smart, in the central city core.

Eating

BUDGET

Fruit and vegetable market (5am-noon Sun-Fri, to 3pm Sat) This market is on Mars tér, site of the notorious Star Prison for political prisoners in the early 1950s.

Coop (Naplóház, Dugonics tér; mains 300-610Ft; 6am-9pm Mon-Fri, to 5pm Sat, 8am-5pm Sun) A small self-service counter with Hungarian specialities fronts this big supermarket.

Tünder Konyha (☎ 994 6546; Kelemen László utca 11; mains 300-800Ft) Lines of students snake out the door from noon to night. It's because the self-service grub is cheap, but the Hungarian dishes are pretty good, too.

Chili Grill (☎ 317 344; Nagy Jenő utca 4; mains 600-1000Ft; 11am-10pm Mon-Fri, to 6pm Sat) There are a few tables at this modern takeaway, but why not eat your turkey, bean and chilli wrap on the park benches under the trees of nearby Széchenyi tér?

MIDRANGE

Agni (☎ 477 739; Tisza Lajos körút 76; mains 1000-1300Ft) Daily lunch menus drop the prices at this little vegetarian restaurant to 750Ft for soup and a main dish, such as paprika-mushroom stew with millet.

Numero Uno Pizza (☎ 424 745; Széchenyi tér 5; mains 1000-1600Ft) We can't guarantee that this simple pizzeria is number one in the city but it's certainly up there with the best. The inner courtyard garden is also fine for a quiet drink.

our pick **Port Royal Étterem** (☎ 547 988; Stefánia utca 4; mains 1300-2200Ft) Tropical plants and live parrots are enough reason to make the pleasant terrace your destination on a steamy summer evening. Add people-watching to that as the nattily dressed come and go from the National Theatre next door, and the fact that in any season the modern kitchen turns out tasty traditional dishes, international faves and vegie options, and you have a winner. Cocktails are served till 2am on Friday and Saturday.

Régi Hídhoz (☎ 420 910; Oskola utca 4; mains 1400-2500Ft) Ask in English for a local restaurant recommendation and inevitably you will be sent to this folksy fish house. That's OK: the *halaszlé* is none too shabby and the price can't be beat. It serves meat dishes, too.

TOP END

Halászcsárda (☎ 555 980; Roosevelt tér 14; mains 2000-3500Ft) A Szeged institution that knows how to prepare the best fish in town – whole roasted pike with garlic, pan-fried frogs' legs and fillet of carp soup included. Although white tablecloths cover the tables and waiters are dressed to the nines, the outdoor terrace is pretty casual.

Drinking

There's a vast array of bars and cafes in this student town, especially around and between the squares Dugonics, Dom and Klauzál.

Port Royal Étterem (☎ 547 988; Stefánia utca 4; 11am-midnight Mon-Thu, to 2am Fri & Sat, to 11pm Sun) The Port Royal restaurant terrace is an excellent place for a frou-frou cocktail.

JATE Klub bar (Toldi utca 2; noon-midnight) A reasonably laid-back spot, attracting students with its cheap drinks and terrace.

Colibri Cocktail Bar (☎ 424 444; Deák Ferenc utca 28; 8pm-2am Wed & Thu, to 4am Fri & Sat) High energy, pretty people and an outside terrace, too; rivers of alcohol flow from under the neon lights. There's an outside terrace, too.

John Bull Pub (☎ 484 217; Oroszlán utca 6; 10am-midnight Sun-Thu, to 2am Fri & Sat) John Bull does a grand 'English pub' imitation, with carpets, proper pints and bar stools, and there's a full menu, too. Its garden is a welcome respite.

Virág (☎ 541 360; Klauzál tér 1; 8am-10pm) A cafe since 1922, Virág has steadily grown until its outdoor tables have taken over half of Klauzál tér and a second outlet had to be opened opposite. Lots of locals think this is still the best place to linger over coffee, or something harder, but there are no less than seven cafes to choose from on this one square.

Entertainment

Your best sources of entertainment information in this culturally active city are Tourinform and the free biweekly entertainment guide *Szegedi Est* (www.est.hu).

Szeged National Theatre (Szegedi Nemzeti Színház; ☎ 479 279; www.szinhaz.szeged.hu, in Hungarian; Deák Ferenc utca 12-14) Built in 1886, the theatre has always been the centre of cultural life in Szeged. Operas, ballet and classical concerts are staged.

New Synagogue (Újzsinagóga; ☎ 423 849; www.zsinagoga.szeged.hu; Gutenberg utca 13) There are free organ concerts here from late March to mid-September; it's a good chance to take in the splendour of the building without having to pay.

Sing Sing (☎ 420 314; C pavilion, Mars tér; 11pm-5am Wed, Fri & Sat) Huge warehouse rave parties here often have overtly sexy themes and dancers.

Gin Tonic (☎ 422 673; Széchenyi tér 1; 10pm-4am Wed-Fri) This central dance club pulses to a funk, house and techno beat.

Getting There & Away

BUS

The following destinations are best served by bus.

Destination	Price	Duration	Km	Frequency
Csongrád	1050Ft	1½hr	60	8 daily
Debrecen	3230Ft	5hr	230	2 daily
Gyula	2290Ft	3½hr	145	6 daily
Mohács	2290Ft	3¼hr	155	6 daily
Ópusztaszer	525Ft	45min	30	12 daily
Pécs	2780Ft	4¼hr	195	7 daily

Buses also head for Arad (1500Ft, 2½ hours), across the Romanian border, daily at 6.30am Monday to Saturday. Buses run to Novi Sad (1800Ft, 3½ hours) in Serbia at 4pm daily, and to Subotica (800Ft, 1½ hours) up to four times daily.

TRAIN

Szeged is on several rail lines, including a main one to Budapest's Nyugati train station. You have to change at Békéscsaba for Gyula. Southbound trains leave Szeged for Subotica (900Ft, 1¾ hours) in Serbia twice daily at 6.50am and 12.30pm.

Destination	Price	Duration	Km	Frequency
Békéscsaba	1500Ft	2hr	95	half-hourly
Budapest	2780Ft	2¾hr	190	hourly
Hódmező-vásárhely	525Ft	35min	30	half-hourly
Kecskemét	1770Ft	1¼hr	85	hourly

Getting Around

Tram 1 from the train station will take you north to Széchenyi tér before turning west on Kossuth Lajos sugárút. From the bus station catch bus 7/f for Sziksósfürdő and bus 2 for student accommodation in New Szeged. Rent bikes at **Tourinform** (☎ 488 699; Dugonics tér 2; 9am-5pm Mon-Fri, to 1pm Sat) for 2500Ft per day.

ÓPUSZTASZER

☎ 62 / pop 2300

About 28km north of Szeged, the **Ópusztaszer National Historical Memorial Park** (Ópusztaszeri Nemzeti Történeti Emlékpark; ☎ 275 133; www.opusztaszer.hu; per person park only 800Ft, adult/child park, galleries & panorama 2000/1700Ft; 9am-6pm Apr-Oct, 9am-4pm Tue-Sun Nov-Mar) commemorates what many consider to be the single most important event in Hungarian history: the *honfoglalás* (conquest) of the Carpathian Basin by the Magyars (see p24).

Contrary to what many people think (Hungarians included), the park does not mark the spot where Árpád, mounted on his white charger, first entered 'Hungary'. That was actually the Munkács Valley, Hungarian territory until after WWI and now in Ukraine. But according to the 12th-century chronicler known as Anonymous, it was at this place called Szer that Árpád and the six clan chieftains, who had sworn a blood oath of fidelity to him, held their first assembly, and so it was decided that a **Millennium Monument** would be erected here in 1896. (Scholars have actually determined the date of the conquest to be between 893 and 896.)

The huge park sits on top of a slight rise in the Great Plain, about 1km from the Szeged road. Pride of place goes to the monumental **panorama painting** entitled *The Arrival of the Hungarians*. Completed by Árpád Feszty for the Millenary Exhibition in Budapest in 1896, this enormous artwork, which measures 15m by 120m, was badly damaged during WWII and was restored by a Polish team in time for the 1100th anniversary of the conquest in 1996. Two **galleries** above the painting are devoted to the art and history of the area. Of particular interest here are the photos of rough-and-ready tribal Magyars dressed in their traditional 19th-century garb.

In the park grounds, besides the neoclassical monument to Árpád, there are ruins of an 11th-century **Romanesque church** and **monastery** (being excavated) and an excellent **open-air museum** (skanzen; 9am-6pm Apr-Oct, 9am-4pm Tue-Sun Nov-Mar), with a farmhouse, windmills, an old post office, a schoolhouse and cottages moved from villages around southeast Hungary. In one, the home of a rather prosperous and smug onion grower from Makó, a sampler admonishes potential gossips: 'Neighbour lady, away you go / If it's gossip that you want to know' (or words to that effect).

There are also **horse shows** (11.30am & 2.30pm Apr-Oct) celebrating the life of the nomadic Magyars of yesteryear, bows to be shot (150Ft) and horses to be ridden (300Ft per time led around the track) at the **Nomad Park**.

Pitch a tent at the park's **camping ground** (camp sites 1000Ft, 2-person cabins without bathroom 3600Ft), or visit Ópusztaszer on a day trip from Szeged. The park has several food stands. At least 12 buses travel daily between Szeged (525Ft, 45min, 30km) and Ópusztaszer, the last returning for Szeged at 8.30pm.

HÓDMEZŐVÁSÁRHELY

☎ 62 / pop 51,600

A quiet little town known for the more than 400 potters who worked here in the early 20th century, today Hódmezővásárhely (Beaver Meadow Marketplace, often shortened to Vásárhely) is home to only three ceramic artisans. You won't see much more pottery outside the town's museums than you would elsewhere, but the artistic influence is felt in the galleries, in the ceramic and bronze street signs, and at the **Autumn Weeks art festival** in October. Otherwise, there's the fascinating communist Remembrance Point to visit.

Orientation & Information

The bus station (Bocskai utca) is just off Andrássy utca, about a 10-minute walk east from Kossuth tér, the city centre. The main train station is east of the city centre, off Hódtó utca.

Main post office (Kossuth tér 8)

OTP bank (Andrássy utca 1) ATM and currency exchange.

Tourinform (☎ 249 350; www.hodmezovasarhely.hu; Szőnyi utca 1; 7am-6pm Mon-Fri, 10am-6pm Sun May-Sep, 8am-4pm Mon-Fri Oct-Apr) Has a list of local folk craft artists.

Sights

The raison d'être of the **János Tornyai Museum** (☎ 344 424; Szántó Kovács János utca 16-18; adult/child 400/200Ft; 10am-4pm Tue & Wed, to 5pm Thu-Sun) is to show off the town's folk art, like the 'hairy' embroidery done with yarnlike thread. But the collection of regional jugs, pitchers and plates is the finest, representing all three main types of pottery once made here (named after city districts): Csúcs (white

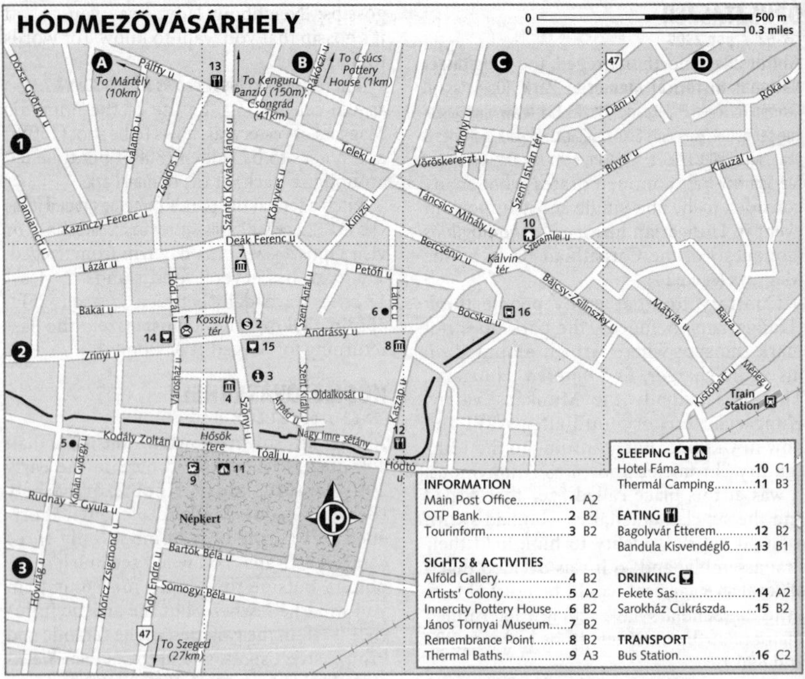

and cobalt blue), Tabán (brown) and Újváros (mustard yellow and green).

One of the few active potters in town, Ambrus Sándor opens his studio to the public as **Innercity Pottery House** (Belvárosi Fazekasház; ☎ 233 666; Lánc utca 3; admission per group 500Ft; ⏲ 10am-6pm Mon-Fri, to 2pm Sat). His museum-worthy front room showcases all three indigenous Vásárhelyi styles. It takes little coaxing for him to give a pot-throwing demonstration or to show you the newer items he has for sale. (Ring the bell.) More pottery is on display at the **Csúcs Pottery House** (Csúcsi Fazekasház; ☎ 242 224; Rákóczi utca 101; admission free; ⏲ 1-5pm Tue-Sun May-Sep), once the home of master potter Sándor Vékony.

Outsiders are not allowed into the **artists' colony** (művésztelep; Kohán György utca 2), founded in the early part of last century, but you can view selected members' work at the **Alföld Gallery** (☎ 242 247; Kossuth tér 8; adult/child 400/200Ft; ⏲ 10am-4pm Tue & Wed, to 5pm Thu-Sun). Naturally the Alföld School of alfresco painting dominates; see the Great Plain in every season through the eyes of János Tornyai, István Nagy and József Koszta. Enter from Szőnyi utca.

A combination library, cafe and museum, the **Remembrance Point** (Emlékpont; ☎ 530 940; www.emlekpont.hu; Andrássy utca 34; adult/child 800/400Ft; ⏲ 10am-6pm Tue-Sun) recalls the communist era in pictures, residents' remembrances and statuary (some great photo ops here).

Activities

Numerous horse farms in the area offer riding and accommodation. Tourinform has a comprehensive list at its office and online (www.hodmezovasarhely.hu).

The **Thermal Baths** (☎ 244 238; Népkert, Ady Endre utca 1; adult/child 990/860Ft; ⏲ 8am-8pm, outdoor pools May-Sep) have eight indoor and outdoor pools, but Mártély, about 10km to the northwest on a backwater of the Tisza, is the city's real boating, fishing and swimming centre.

Sleeping

Hódmezővásárhely has a number of private rooms (listed with Tourinform), but the town can also be easily visited as a day trip from Szeged.

Thermál Camping (☎ 245 033; Ady Endre utca 1; camp sites per person/tent 990/1090Ft, bungalows 7900Ft; ⏲ May-

Sep) This small, grassy camping ground has the advantage of being adjacent to the thermal baths. Rustic log bungalows share bathrooms and have sleeping space for eight.

Hotel Fáma (☎ 222 231; www.hotels.hu/fama; Szeremlei utca 7; s/d 8200/9200Ft;) Not much clutter in these spacious-but-simple rooms – usually just cherrywood beds and night tables – but the clean, white walls hold a certain serene appeal. Only those on ground level have air-conditioning. A courtyard garden is shared by all. There's free wi-fi and an on-site restaurant.

Kenguru Panzió (☎ 534 841; www.kengurugm.hu; Szántó Kovács János utca 78; r 10,000-15,000Ft;) Natural wood furniture and floors provide rustic flair to big, bright rooms surrounding an inner courtyard. In addition to a folksy restaurant on-site, guests have use of a pool and sauna. It's north of the city centre.

Eating & Drinking

Sarokház Cukrászda (Kossuth tér 7; cakes 120-200Ft; 9am-9pm Sun-Thu, to 10pm Fri & Sat) The 'Corner House' is a quiet cafe filled with locals gossiping about the day's events and enjoying their sweets.

Fekete Sas (☎ 249 326; Kossuth tér 5; mains 1000-1400Ft) The grand old Fekete Sas Hotel dominates the main square, but most of it is now just convention space. Enjoy a light meal or drinks at the namesake cafe to get a taste of the former glory. Mushroom and cheese crêpes are especially good. Breakfast is also served (250Ft to 550Ft).

Bandula Kisvendéglő (☎ 244 234; Pálffy utca 2; mains 1200-1800Ft) Cosy, rustic surrounds and quick service help make Bandula the best eating option in town. Huge Hungarian portions don't hurt either.

Bagolyvár Étterem (☎ 245 726; Kazap utca 31; mains 1400-2000Ft) The closest thing Hódmezővásárhely has to fine dining, the 'Owl Restaurant' serves traditional Magyar cuisine.

Getting There & Away

Buses to the resort area of Mártély (250Ft, 20 minutes, 12km) and Csongrád (675Ft, one hour, 40km) are frequent; there is a minimum of three daily departures to Kecskemét (1500Ft, two hours, 95km).

A train line through Hódmezővásárhely connects Szeged (525Ft, 35 minutes, 30km) with Békéscsaba (1050Ft, 1¼ hours, 65km) hourly.

CSONGRÁD

☎ 63 / pop 18,500

Csongrád's sleepy charm lies in its Old Castle (Öregvár) district – a quiet fishing village of thatched cottages and narrow streets on the bank of the Tisza River – which hasn't changed much since the 17th century. However, back in the 13th century Csongrád was a place of importance, gaining the title of royal capital of Csongrád County. The invading Mongols put paid to that, all but destroying the town; it wasn't until the 1920s that it once again became known as a town.

Orientation

Csongrád lies on the right bank of the Tisza River, close to where it is joined by the Körös River, some 58km north of Szeged. The Old Castle district is east of the newer, but still old, town centre. Look for the train station southwest at the end of Vasút utca, while the bus station is near the main square, Hunyadi tér.

Information

Main post office (Dózsa György tér 1)

OTP bank (Szentháromság tér 8) Has an ATM.

Tourinform (☎ 570 325; csongrad@tourinform.hu; Szentháromság tér 8; 9am-5pm mid-Jun–mid-Sep, 8am-4pm Mon-Fri mid-Sep–mid-Jun) In the cultural centre; internet access costs 200Ft per hour.

Sights & Activities

The cobblestone streets of the protected **Old Castle** (Öregvár) district begin at a little roundabout three blocks east of the church. Most of the district is made up of private homes or holiday houses, but the **Village Museum** (Tájház; Gyökér utca 1; admission free; 1-5pm Tue-Sun May-Oct) gives a good idea of how the simple fisher folk of Csongrád lived until not so long ago. It's housed in two old cottages connected by a long thatched roof and contains period furniture, household items, and lots of fish nets and traps.

Just west of the Old Castle district, **St Rókus Church** (Gróf Andrássy Gyula utca) was built in 1722 on the site of a Turkish mosque. The baroque **Church of Our Lady** (Kossuth tér), built in 1769, and the beautiful Secessionist **János Batsányi College** (Kossuth tér) are in the town centre. The town's **László Tari Museum** (☎ 481 103; Iskola utca 2; adult/child 300/150Ft; 1-5pm Tue-Fri, 8am-noon Sat, 8am-noon & 1-5pm Sun) examines

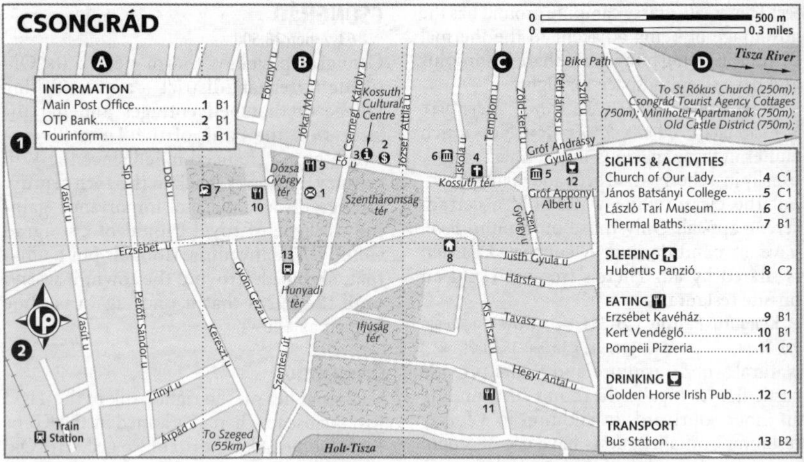

the history of Csongrád, starting with tribes that settled the region as far back as the Bronze Age.

A 7km **bike path** lines the raised bank of the Tisza River. Ask about bike, canoe and kayak rental at Tourinform. The **Thermal Baths** (Dob utca 3-5; adult/child 550/430Ft; 8am-8pm, outdoor pools 8am-8pm May-Sep), fed by a spring with water that reaches 46°C, are in a large park.

Sleeping

Hubertus Panzió (☎ 484 997; hubertuspanzio@hubertuspanzio.t-online.hu; Justh Gyula utca 5; s/d 5500/7200Ft;) It's surprising to find free wi-fi throughout a new-construction guest house in such a small town. It has air-conditioning and minibars, too – *ooooh*.

Minihotel Apartmanok (☎ 06 20 922 9319; http://minihotel.extra.hu; Gróf Andrássy Gyula utca 29; s/d 7000/8000Ft;) Pine furniture and chequered tablecloths on the kitchen tables make these two-bedded apartments quite homey. It's close to the Tisza and Old Castle district.

our pick **Csongrád Tourist Agency** (Csongrád Idegenforgalmi; ☎ 483 631; www.csongrad.net/ih; Fő utca 3; houses 6000-16,000Ft;) The most atmospheric places to stay in town are the fishing cottages in the Old Castle district rented out by the town's tourist agency. The 200-year-old houses are squat dwellings with thick whitewashed walls, clay ovens, polished wood floors and oodles of character. Each comes with a fully equipped kitchen and a bedroom or two. Only a few are heated and open in winter.

Eating & Drinking

Erzsébet Kávéház (☎ 483 106; Fő utca 3; cakes 120-200Ft; 8am-10pm) Serving inviting cakes and coffee, plus adult beverages, in smart surroundings. On summer weekends musical accompaniment plays on the terrace.

Pompeii Pizzeria (☎ 470 160; Kis Tisza utca 6; mains 800-1400Ft) Choose from among 40 pizza varieties, or opt for a South Slav grilled meat speciality. You have to look under the weeping willows to find this renovated house.

Kert Vendéglő (☎ 483 199; Dózsa György tér 6; mains 1200-2000Ft) What a pleasant garden inn, set back in a small park. An excellent array of Hungarian dishes whets most appetites.

Golden Horse Irish Pub (Gróf Andrássy Gyula utca 17/a; 10am-midnight) About the only proper place in town for a drink is east of the town centre on the way to the Old Castle district. Irish stew and fried fish (mains 900Ft to 1800Ft) are on tap along with the Guinness.

Getting There & Away

From Csongrád hourly buses run to Kecskemét (900Ft, one hour, 55km) and to Szeged (900Ft, 1½ hours, 60km) via Ópusztaszer (525Ft, 40 minutes, 34km). Direct buses also travel to Hódmezővásárhely (675Ft, one hour, 40km, nine daily) and Budapest (2290Ft, 2½ hours, 140km, eight daily).

Csongrád is on a secondary train line linking to the west with Kiskunfélegyháza (375Ft, 35 minutes, 25km), a stop on the Budapest–Szeged express train line.

SZARVAS

☎ 66 / pop 18,500

Szarvas is a pretty green town 45km northwest of Békéscsaba on a backwater of the Körös River (Holt-Körös). Its biggest drawcard is the arboretum, easily the best in Hungary. The best thing to ever happen to Szarvas was the arrival of Sámuel Tessedik, a Lutheran minister and pioneering scientist who established one of Europe's first agricultural institutes here in 1770.

Orientation

Szabadság út, the main street, bisects the town and leads westward to the Körös River and arboretum. On either side of Szabadság út are dozens of small squares organised in chessboardlike fashion by Tessedik, full of flower gardens and even small orchards. The train station is in the eastern part of town at the end of Vasút utca, while the bus station is in the town centre on the corner of Szabadság út and Bocskai István utca.

Information

K&H bank (Szabadság út 30)
Main post office (Szabadság út 9)
Panoráma Café (☎ 312 760; Kossuth tér 3/2; per hr 300Ft) In the pizzeria; has internet access.
Tourinform (☎ 311 140; www.tourinformszarvas.hu; Kossuth tér 3; 9am-6pm Mon-Fri, to 1pm Sat Jun-Aug, 9am-5pm Mon-Fri Sep-Apr) In the cultural centre.

Sights & Activities

The **Szarvas Arboretum** (☎ 312 344; http://szarvas.arbor.hu; adult/child 500/300Ft; 8am-6pm), with some 30,000 individual plants not native to the Great Plain, is Hungary's finest. On 82 hectares it contains around 1600 species of rare trees, bushes and grasses, including mammoth pines, ginkgo trees, swamp cedars, Spanish pines and pampas grass. It's about 2km northwest of the town centre across the Körös River.

The **Sámuel Tessedik Museum** (☎ 216 608; Vajda Péter utca 1; adult/child 300/150Ft; 10am-5pm Tue-Sun) has some interesting Neolithic exhibits from the goddess-worshipping Körös culture taken from burial mounds on the Great Plain, and while the section devoted to Tessedik is intriguing, it's only in Hungarian. Four blocks north, a small plaque marks the private **birthplace of Endre Bajcsy-Zsilinszky** (Vajda Péter utca 22), the resistance leader murdered by Hungarian fascists in 1944 (and namesake for countless Hungarian streets).

Just north of Tourinform in the town's dusty back alleys is one of Hungary's only working horse-driven **dry mills** (szárazmalom; ☎ 216 609; Ady Endre utca 1; adult/child 500/350Ft; 1-5pm Tue-Sun Apr-Oct), built in the early 19th century, and a **Slovakian Village House** (Szlovák tájház; ☎ 312 492; Hoffmann utca 1; adult/child 300/200Ft; 1-5pm Tue-Sun Apr-Oct) filled with hand-woven textiles and articles from everyday life.

Körös Valley Visitors' Centre (☎ 313 855; www.kmnp.hu; Anna-liget 1; adult/child 330/240Ft; 9am-5pm Tue-Sun Apr-Oct), part of Körös-Maros National Park, is 1.5km east of the town centre. Exhibits highlight the area's flora and fauna, and there's an interpretive nature trail.

Sleeping

Lux Panzió (☎ 313 417; www.aqua-lux.hu; Szabadság út 35; s/d 9500/12,000Ft;) Lux is only a stone's throw from the bus station and has large rooms with dated furniture, as well as a restaurant, fitness centre, sauna and solarium.

Halászcsárda Panzió (☎ 311 164; I ker 6; r 9500Ft;) This more rustic option has small attic rooms and is located on the edge of Elizabeth Park, creating a secluded, retreat feel.

Liget (☎ 311 954; www.ligetpanzio.hu; r incl breakfast 24,000Ft;) A sporting resort with an upscale look, with soft contemporary rooms very stylish in their earth tones. Families can enjoy all of the activities: thermal pools and saunas are included, but you can also rent canoes and arrange horse riding and guided hikes. Free wi-fi.

Eating & Drinking

Kiszely Cukrászda (cnr Szabadság út & Béke utca; ice cream 100Ft; 9am-9pm) Kiszely is a cute pastry cafe, small in size but big on ice-cream and baked-good selections.

Corner Pub (☎ 216 155; Zalke Máté utca 8; mains 1000-1600Ft) The name says it all. River stone and wood give the neighbourhood pub a rustic feel, and there's a full Hungarian menu.

Halászcsárda (☎ 311 164; I ker 6; mains 1200-2000Ft) Fish is a natural choice in this stream-filled part of the plain. Relax on the terrace overlooking the river or in the rustic inn. Swimmy soup, or fillet, it's up to you.

For a quick, cheap pizza, try **Panoráma Café** (☎ 312 760; Kossuth tér 3/2; pizzas 500-1000Ft), next to Tourinform, which has the advantage of outdoor seating, or **Belváros** (☎ 312 525; Kossuth Lajos utca 23; pizzas 500-1000Ft), an appealing, publike option on a quiet back street.

Getting There & Away

Szarvas can be reached by bus from Békéscsaba (605Ft, one hour, 45km, at least hourly), Kecskemét (968Ft, 1¾ hours, 80km, six daily), Szeged (907Ft, two hours, 75km, six daily) and Debrecen (1930Ft, three to four hours, 155km, two daily).

Szarvas is on the train line of little use that links Mezőhegyes and Orosháza.

BÉKÉSCSABA

☎ 66 / pop 66,500

Anthropologists and sausage lovers take note: Békéscsaba has a few disparate claims to fame. First, it was largely settled by Slovaks, and Slavic dishes still outnumber Magyar ones on a menu or two. Second, *csabai,* a fatty, red sausage not dissimilar to Portuguese chorizo, is both made in homes and manufactured here. Thus the best time to come is during the annual **Csabai Klobász festival** in mid-October. Other than a bit of architecture and a couple of museums, the town is rather sleepy.

History

Békéscsaba was razed and its population scattered under Turkish rule. Early in the 18th century the Habsburgs invited Slovaks to resettle the area, and it soon became a Lutheran stronghold. In 1890 Békéscsaba was the centre of the Vihar Sarok (Stormy Corner) of the Great Plain, where violent riots broke out among day labourers and harvesters. But perhaps the most significant factor in determining how the town looks today is that the railway passed through here and not neighbouring Gyula in the 19th century, and Békéscsaba eventually became the county seat.

Orientation

Békéscsaba's train and bus stations stand side by side at the southwestern end of Andrássy út, the main drag. A long stretch of this street, from Petőfi utca and Jókai utca to Szent István tér, is a pedestrian walkway. To the east of the canal lies the Parkerdő, the city's cool and leafy playground.

Information

Main post office (Irány utca)

Mihály Munkácsy Museum (☎ 323 377; Széchenyi utca 9; internet per hr 300Ft; 🕒 10am-6pm Tue-Sun Apr-Sep, 10am-4pm Tue-Sun Oct-Mar) The coffee shop in this museum has three internet computers.

OTP bank (Szent István tér 3)

Tourinform (☎ 441 261; www.turizmus.bekescsaba.hu; Szent István tér 9; 🕒 9am-6pm Mon-Fri, 10am-7pm Sat & Sun Jul & Aug, 9am-5pm Mon-Fri Sep-Jun) Truckloads of information on town and county.

Sights & Activities

The splendid **town hall** (Szent István tér 7), not open to the public, has a facade (1873) designed by the overworked Budapest architect Miklós Ybl. Walk east on József Attila utca to the canal and Árpád sor, which is lined with busts of Hungarian literary, artistic and musical greats and late-19th-century mansions.

A folklife exhibit at the **Mihály Munkácsy Museum** (☎ 323 377; Széchenyi utca 9; adult/child 800/400Ft; 🕒 10am-6pm Tue-Sun Apr-Sep, 10am-4pm Tue-Sun Oct-Mar) traces regional ethnic groups. Essentially, though, the museum exists because of the painter Munkácsy (1844–1900) and his depictions of the Great Plain; as a chronicler of that place and time (real or imagined) he is unsurpassed. Stunning temporary exhibits on historic topics like the Tatar invasion of the 1200s feature state-of-the-art (EU-funded) displays and research.

The Lutheran **Great Church**, completed in 1824, and the 18th-century **Small Church**, facing each other across Kossuth tér, attest to the city's deeply rooted Protestantism. The baroque **Greek Orthodox church** (Bartók Béla utca 51-53), dating from 1838, could easily be mistaken for yet another Lutheran church from the outside.

It's a hike to the **Slovakian Village House** (Szlovák tájház; ☎ 327 038; Garay utca 21; adult/child 300/150Ft; 🕒 10am-noon & 2-5pm Wed-Sun May-Sep), a farmhouse built in 1865 and full of folk furniture and ornamentation. A scattered few other typical peasant houses still call the neighbourhood home.

The **Árpád Thermal Baths** (☎ 549 800; Árpád sor 2; adult/child 1200/750Ft; 🕒 6am-8pm) have both indoor and huge outdoor pools; the latter are open May through September.

Sleeping

Andrássy Gyula College (☎ 325 620; e-deak@freeweb.hu; Andrássy út 56; dm/s/d without bathroom 2000/2500/3000Ft; 🕒 Jul & Aug) What to say about summer college accommodation? It's cheap, it's basic (bed, desk), and this one is close to the bus and train stations.

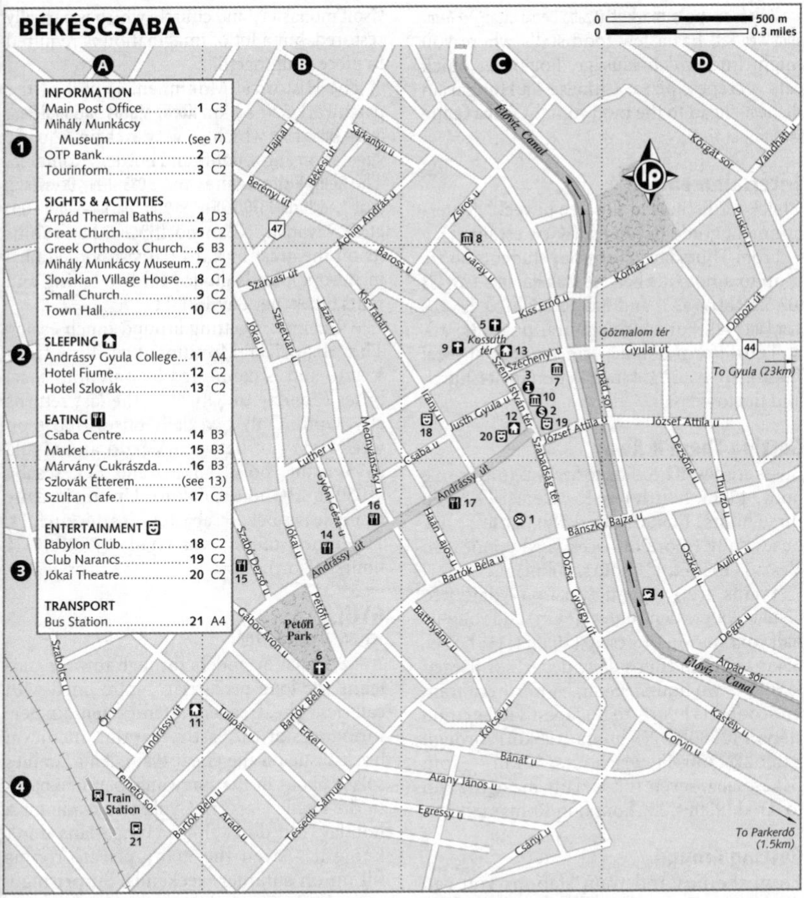

Hotel Szlovák (☎ 441 750; www.slovak.hu; Kossuth tér 10; s/d 6500/8700Ft) Enter around the back of the Slovak Cultural House and restaurant to get to this 2nd-storey hotel. The mishmash of contemporary and traditional furniture isn't stylish, but it is comfortable. Free wi-fi at reception.

Hotel Fiume (☎ 443 243; Szent István tér 2; s/d 10,100/13,600Ft) Fiume bears the old name of the Adriatic port of Rijeka (now in Croatia) and the hotel harks back to the time (1868) when the original structure was built. White upholstered Louis XV chairs sitting beneath neoclassical wallpaper and candlelike sconces set the scene in guestrooms. There's free wi-fi, and rooms come with minibar.

Eating & Drinking

Márvány Cukrászda (Andrássy út 21; cakes 100-250Ft; 🕑 8am-9pm) Those with a sweet tooth can satisfy their urges at this popular cafe, with outside seating on a pretty square.

Szultan Cafe (☎ 444 454; Andrássy út 10; mains 800-1200Ft) A mixed bag of Mediterranean choices includes salads, gyros and pizza. Terrace tables are perfect for a drink, too.

Szlovák Étterem (☎ 441 750; www.slovak.hu; Kossuth tér 10; mains 1200-1800Ft) *Strapačky* (gnocchi-like dumplings with cabbage or sheep's cheese and bacon) and other Slovak items top the menu, but you'll also find a *csabai* sausage plate on offer at this restaurant-pub. Yes, the Slovak beer is good.

Békéscsaba's **market** (Szabó Dezső utca; ⏰ 6am-4pm Wed-Sat) has a few food stalls where you might find *csabai* sausage. For other quick eats – crêpes, pizza, Chinese or Hungarian dishes – head to the food court at **Csaba Centre** (Andrássy út 37-43).

Entertainment

Check for listings in the free biweekly entertainment guide *Békési Est* (www.est.hu).

From Thursday to Saturday students booze it up to a raucous beat at **Club Narancs** (☎ 453 032; Szent István tér 3) and **Babylon Club** (☎ 326 421; Irányi utca 12). For more cultural pursuits, ask at Tourinform about performances at **Jókai Theatre** (☎ 441 527; Andrássy út 1), the Great Church and the town hall.

Getting There & Away

Buses are best if heading to Szarvas (675Ft, one hour, 45km, hourly) or Kecskemét (2290Ft, three hours, 145km, five daily). At least five buses daily (more on weekdays) connect to Vésztő (1050Ft, 1¼ hours, 60km).

Trains are frequent (up to 17 daily) to Gyula (300Ft, 15 minutes, 15km) and roughly half continue on to Vésztő (1050Ft, 1½ hours, 65km). Eleven trains daily depart for Szeged (1500Ft, two hours, 95km). A northern train line connects hourly to Budapest's Keleti train station (2780Ft, 2½ hours, 195km) through Szolnok (1500Ft, 1½ hours, 95km). From Békéscsaba, seven trains daily make the run to Arad (900Ft, 1½ hours) in Romania.

Getting Around

From the bus and train stations you can reach Szent István tér on foot via Andrássy út in about 20 minutes, or wait for bus 5 to Szabadság tér.

VÉSZTŐ

☎ 66 / pop 7900

The **Vésztő-Mágor National Historical Monument** (☎ 477 148; adult/child 370/260Ft; ⏰ 9am-6pm May-Sep, 10am-4pm Apr & Oct), 4km northwest of Vésztő, contains two burial mounds of a type found throughout Hungary (for another example, see p136) and as far east as Korea. Such mounds are not all that rare on the Great Plain, but these are particularly rich in archaeological finds. The first is a veritable layer cake of cult and everyday objects, shrines and graves dating from the 4th century BC onward. The second contains the 10th-century Csolt monastery and church, which is partially restored, but a lot of imagination is required to piece it all together.

The Historical Monument is part of the patchwork 520-sq-km **Körös-Maros National Park** (www.kmnp.hu), which is very rich in aquatic vegetation and wildlife and borders Romania. The **Réhly Visitor Centre** (☎ 483 083; Réhly, Dévaványa; exhibits adult/child 370/260Ft; ⏰ 9am-5pm Tue-Sun Apr-Oct) at Dévaványa, 38km northwest, has exhibits on the great bustard (largest bodied bird in Europe), leads guided bird-watching and rents bikes (per day 1200Ft).

A car makes getting around much easier. The Historical Monument is 4km from Vésztő and is connected by only four local buses Monday to Saturday; the last returns at 7.39pm. Only two daily buses (more on weekdays) run between Vésztő and Gyula (675Ft, one hour, 43km) and Békéscsaba (1050Ft, 1¼ hours, 60km). Up to six daily trains leave Békéscsaba for Vésztő (1050Ft, 1½ hours, 65km) via Gyula (750Ft, 1¼ hours, 48km).

GYULA

☎ 66 / pop 32,700

A lazy canal meanders through town, paralleling the long pedestrian centre lined with eateries. Theatregoers attend open-air performances at the last remaining medieval brick castle on the Great Plain. And families splash about in the sprawling, parklike baths in the Castle Garden. Gyula was made for a holiday, but don't think Hungarians don't know it – even the many private rooms fill up on summer weekends. Surprisingly enough, there are also numerous museums to keep you busy on a rainy day. This pretty little activity-filled town is about as far as you can go in southeastern Hungary; 4km further and you're in Romania.

History

Gyula refused to allow the Arad-bound railway to cross through the town in 1858; as a result the town was stuck at the end of a spur and developed at a slower pace – both a blessing and a curse. In 1950 the county seat was moved from here (after 500 years, Gyulans like to point out) to its sister city, Békéscsaba. A strong rivalry persists between the two: from who should be allocated more county money, to whose football team and sausage is better.

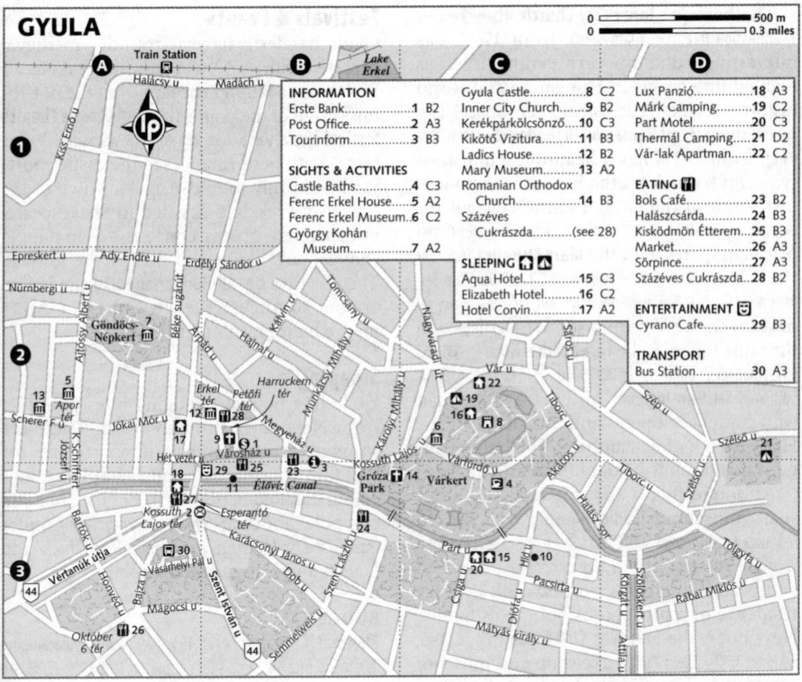

Orientation

The commercial centre of town is on Városház utca to the west. To the east, the castle and baths occupy the large Castle Garden (Várkert) area. Gyula's bus station (Vásárhelyi Pál utca) is south of Kossuth Lajos tér. Walk north through the park to the square and over the canal bridge to reach the town centre. The train station is at the northern end of Béke sugárút.

Information

Erste bank (Városház utca) Has ATM.

Post office (Eszperantó tér)

Tourinform (☎ 561 681; www.turizmus.bekesmegye.hu; Kossuth Lajos utca 7; 🕑 9am-8pm Mon-Fri, 9am-1pm & 4-8pm Sat Jun-Aug, 9am-5pm Mon-Fri Sep-May) Very helpful office located in a gallery.

Sights

Gothic **Gyula Castle** (☎ 464 117; Várfürdő utca 1; adult/child 1200/500Ft; 🕑 9am-7pm mid-Jun–Aug, 9am-5pm Tue-Sun Sep–mid-Jun), overlooking a picturesque moat near the Castle Baths, was originally built in the mid-15th century but has been expanded and renovated many times over the centuries, most recently in May 2004. Some of its 24 rooms are outfitted as living quarters would have been; others contain museum exhibits showcasing the castle's history, in particular the medieval days when the Ottoman Turks were in town and the weapons used to finally fend them off. Like any self-respecting castle, there's a thick wall to wander along, a tower to climb and a dungeon to explore, but the latter is only open during breaks in Castle Theatre performances.

Close by is the **Ferenc Erkel Museum** (☎ 361 236; Kossuth Lajos utca 17; adult/child 500/250Ft; 🕑 1-5pm Tue, 9am-5pm Wed-Sat, 9am-1pm Sun). It has a **Dürer Room** devoted to archaeological finds – pottery, jewellery and weapons – from the region.

The **György Kohán Museum** (☎ 361 795; Béke sugárút 35; adult/child 500/250Ft; 🕑 1-5pm Tue, 9am-5pm Wed-Sat, 9am-1pm Sun), in quiet Göndöcs-Népkert, is Gyula's most important art museum, with more than 3000 paintings and graphics bequeathed to the city by the artist upon his death in 1966. The large canvases of horses and women in dark blues and greens, and the relentless summer sun of the Great Plain, are quite striking.

The baroque **Inner City Church** (Harruckern tér 1; admission free; 10am-6pm), from 1777, has interesting contemporary ceiling frescoes highlighting events in Hungarian and world history – including an astronaut in space! The rarely open Zopf **Romanian Orthodox church** (Gróza Park), from 1812, has a beautiful iconostasis (you can try and get the key from the house just south of the church entrance), but for contemporary icons at their kitschy best, no place compares with the **Mary Museum** (Apor tér 11; adult/child 500/250Ft; 9am-noon & 12.30-3pm Tue-Sat, 9am-noon Sun Mar-Nov, 9am-noon Tue-Sun Dec-Feb). You've never seen the Virgin in so many guises. On the same square is the **Ferenc Erkel House** (463 552; Apor tér 7; adult/child 500/250Ft; 1-5pm Tue, 9am-5pm Wed-Sat, 9am-1pm Sun), birthplace of the man who composed operas and the music for the Hungarian national anthem. The house contains memorabilia about his life and music.

An interesting – and, for Hungary, unusual – museum is **Ladics House** (463 940; Jókai Mór utca 4; adult/child 500/250Ft; 1-5pm Tue, 9am-5pm Wed-Sat, 9am-1pm Sun), the perfectly preserved and beautifully furnished mid-19th-century residence of a prosperous bourgeois family. Next door, the **Százéves Cukrászda** (362 045; Erkel tér 1; 10am-8pm) cake shop and museum is a visual and culinary delight. Established around 1840 (no doubt Mrs Ladics bought her petits-fours here), the Regency-blue interior is filled with Biedermeier furniture and mirrors in gilt frames. It is one of the most beautiful *cukrászdá* (cake shops or patisseries) in Hungary.

Activities

Beneath the fortified brick walls, the 30-hectare Castle Garden is a grand, flower-filled setting for the **Castle Baths** (Várfürdő; 561 350; www.varfurdo.hu; Várkert utca 2; adult/child 1450/1150Ft; 8am-6pm, outdoor pools 8am-8pm May-Oct). Of course, sunbathers cover nearly every grassy spot in summer. Outside kids splash about their own recreational pool that bubbles and squirts every which way, but parents may be induced to play in the ginormous wave pool or slip down the giant slides. Some of the five 'medicinal' pools (unfiltered, untreated) have small geysers to help massage tired muscles.

Rent kayaks, canoes and row boats on the canal at **Kikötő Vizitura** (331 2331; Varosház utca 11; 10am-7pm May-Oct), from 1000Ft per hour. Bikes go for 2000Ft per day at **Kerékpárkölcsönző** (278 6657; Híd utca 2; 8am-6pm).

Festivals & Events

Gyula has festivals year-round – medieval games in July, a New Year's street dance, a Renaissance fair in February – but the not-to-miss event of the year is the **Gyula Castle Theatre festival** (Gyulai Várszínház; 463 148; www.gyulaivarszinhaz.hu), with performances in the castle courtyard from July to mid-August. Much of the first two weeks are devoted to Shakespeare, but operettas, operas, concerts – even puppet shows – are performed during the festival. There's also a big **All-Hungarian Folkdance Festival** around 20 August. See www.turizmus.bekesmegye.hu for a complete events listing.

Sleeping

Excluding holidays, lodging rates plummet from November through April. There are so many private rooms and apartments for rent that Tourinform publishes a glossy, full-colour catalogue. It's not in English, but you can poke about at **Gyula** (www.gyula.hu) under *'szálláshélyek'*, then *'maganszálláshélyek'* and *'apartmanok'* to see them online.

BUDGET

Thermál Camping (463 704; www.gyulacamping.hu; Szélső utca 16; camp sites per person/tent 1100/770Ft, s/d 5600/7600Ft) Approximately 700m from the town centre, these 400 sites have shade and barbecue areas, as well as a shared kitchen building. Motel rooms are super simple (and a bit dowdy).

Márk Camping (463 380; Vár utca 5; camp sites 2600Ft) Of Gyula's camping grounds, this is the friendliest, most central and charming (think flower gardens), but it's very small (50 sites).

Vár-lak Apartman (06 70 369 1509; www.gyulai-szallasok.hu; Vár utca 13; per person 4000Ft) Brickwork and pine beams fit in perfectly with the castle just down the street. Three new and shiny loft apartments (with full kitchens) each sleep four comfortably (two down and two up).

MIDRANGE

Lux Panzió (06 20 974 4655; www.luxpanzio.hu; Kossuth Lajos tér 2; d/tr 8000/9000Ft) So close to the restaurants and cafes in town; in fact, it's on the floor above the Sörpince. Upholstery choices are, um, bold, but overall the contemporary style suits the large rooms with kitchenettes.

Part Motel (466 303; Part utca 7; s/d 7000/10,000Ft) Just behind the back entrance to the Castle Baths, pleasant rooms here have cheery duvets and Ikea chairs. There's a great shared garden with picnic tables and a fire pit in the yard.

Aqua Hotel (☎ 463 146; aqua-hotel@axelero.hu; Part utca 7/c; s/d 7000/12,000Ft;) The exterior is not much to look at, but recently renovated rooms are up to international chainlike standards (minibar, nondescript but nice veneer furniture). You'd think you couldn't beat being right across from the Castle Baths, but you can get massages and rent bicycles here, too.

Hotel Corvin (☎ 362 044; www.corvin-hotel.hu; Jókai utca 9-11; s/d 11,500/13,900Ft;) Oenophiles take note: the Hotel Corvin has an excellent wine-bar restaurant attached. Rooms are quite swank, with unusual window designs, an array of vibrant, modern hues and solid wooden floors.

TOP END

our pick **Elizabeth Hotel** (☎ 560 240; www.elizabeth-hotel.hu; Vár utca 1; s €66, d €99-131;) What would it be like to live as a member of a noble family in a neoclassical mansion beneath the castle? See for yourself when you stay in the 1904 Almásy manor house that in 2008 became the four-star Elizabeth Hotel. Brocade bedcloths and draperies recall rich tapestries and marble covers every bit of the bathroom. Look out your full-length window onto the castle and dream. Packages that include on-site spa services or horse riding can be quite a deal. Free wi-fi.

Eating & Drinking

In warm weather, any of the streetside cafes along the pedestrian byways is a pleasant place for a leisurely drink.

Market (Október 6 tér) Gyula's produce market is southwest of the bus station.

Százéves Cukrászda (☎ 362 045; Erkel tér 1; cakes 120-280Ft; 8am-9pm) Gyula's '100-year' pastry cafe (opened in 1840) occupies a squat 16th-century Rondella tower near the castle, with a delightful terrace in summer.

Bols Café (☎ 978 7407; Kossuth Lajos utca 1; mains 800-1200Ft) Pizzas, salads and gyros are on the menu at this reasonable cafe-restaurant. Many come just to drink.

Halászcsárda (☎ 466 303; Part utca 3; mains 1100-1400Ft) When fish is what you crave: soups and such are served in a leafy, canalside garden or rustic inn.

Sörpince (☎ 362 382; Kossuth Lajos tér 2; mains 1300-1800Ft) The name means 'beer cellar' and to be sure there's plenty of *sör* (lager) to go around. But locals also swear by the traditional Hungarian dishes and there's a terrace in addition to the cellar seating.

Kisködmön Étterem (☎ 463 934; Városház utca 15; mains 1600-2400Ft) Hidden away down an uninviting alley is a wonderful restaurant. The decor looks as though it belongs in the early 1800s and poetic recipe descriptions replace the typical menu listing. 'Braid the marinated strips of meat and your husband will be struck dumb with delight.'

Entertainment

Elaborate costumes and an ancient backdrop are enough reason to see a performance during the Gyula Castle Theatre festival (see opposite).

Cyrano Cafe (Kossuth Lajos utca 3; 10am-midnight Sun-Thu, to 2am Fri & Sat) A magnet for Gyula's 20- to 30-somethings, who make the most of a night out on the town.

Getting There & Away

Buses are the preferred mode of transport for Debrecen (2040Ft, three hours, 130km, three daily) and Kecskemét (1820Ft, 3¼ hours, 145km, two daily). One daily bus goes to Szarvas (2290Ft, 1½ hours, 65km) and two to Vésztő (675Ft, one hour, 43km), with more on weekdays.

Some 17 trains daily run west on line 128, the spur between Gyula and Békéscsaba (300Ft, 15 minutes, 15km), where you can transfer on to Budapest (2780Ft, 2½ hours, 195km, hourly) or Szeged (1500Ft, two hours, 95km, 11 daily). Travelling north on this poky line will get you to Vésztő (750Ft, 1¼ hours, 48km, six daily).

Southern Transdanubia

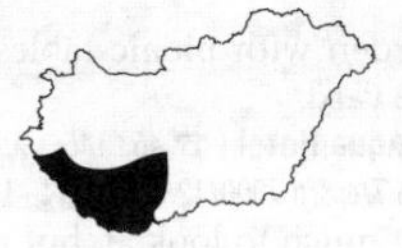

Southern Transdanubia (Dél-Dunántúl) is a region of calm, a place to savour life at a slower pace. It's only marginally touched by tourism, and touring through the countryside is like stepping back in time. The whitewashed farmhouses you'll pass, with thatched roofs and long colonnaded porticoes decorated with floral patterns and plasterwork, haven't changed in centuries.

This region has never been as important industrially as Western Transdanubia. It is thickly settled with small villages, and agriculture remains the mainstay for most people – from the fruit orchards of the Zselic region south of Kaposvár and the almonds of Pécs to the wines of Szekszárd and Villány-Siklós. The pleasant, almost Mediterranean climate helps: spring arrives early, summer is long, winter mild.

Southern Transdanubia has a lot to offer travellers. Top of the pops is Pécs. Art museums and theatres abound in a place that has been named a European Capital of Culture in 2010, and history is very much alive here. More Roman and early Christian tombs than you can shake a shovel at have been uncovered near the city's basilica, and a number of Turkish monuments have survived.

Many other towns here are worth visiting as well. Imposing castles dominate Siklós and Szigetvár, you can take advantage of curative thermal waters at Harkány, and visiting Szekszárd and Villány without tasting the local vintages would be criminal.

HIGHLIGHTS

- Viewing the wonders on exhibit at the Zsolnay Porcelain Museum and the Csontváry Museum in **Pécs** (p298 and p298)
- Sampling big, bold reds in the cellars of **Villány** and **Villánykövesd** (p293)
- Riding the **narrow-gauge train** (p285) through the Gemenc Forest in the Sárköz region
- Taking the waters at the thermal baths in **Harkány** (p292), especially in winter
- Exploring one of Hungary's best *skanzens* (open-air museums of folk architecture) in the delightfully rural village of **Szenna** (p308), southwest of Kaposvár

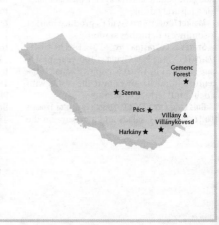

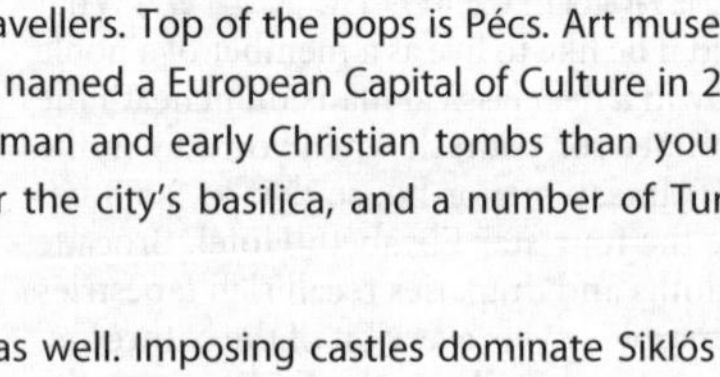

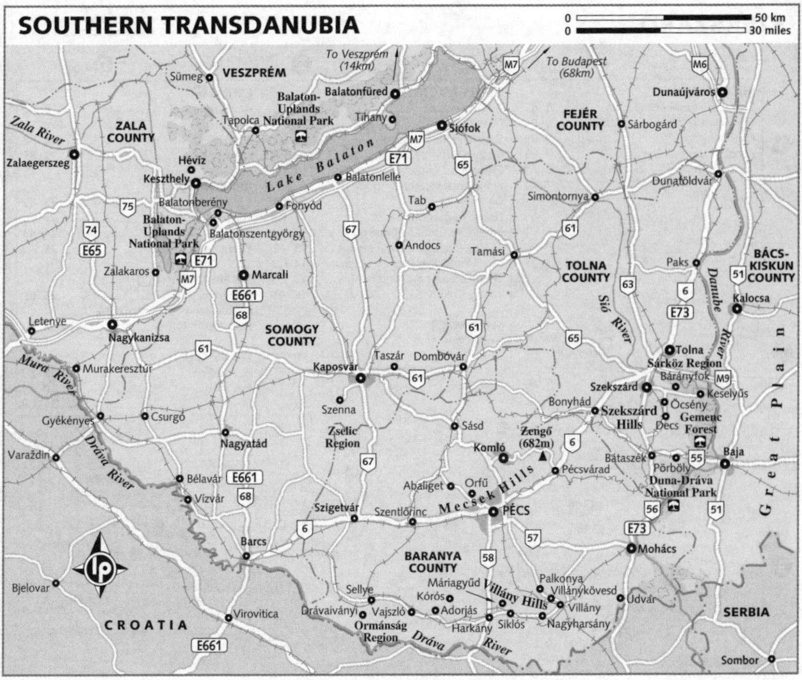

History

Southern Transdanubia was settled by the Celts and then the Romans, who built towns at Alisca (Szekszárd) and Sophianae (Pécs) and introduced grape-growing. The north–south trade route passed through here, and many of the settlements prospered during the Middle Ages.

The region was a focal point of the Turkish occupation; indeed the battle that led to the Ottoman domination of Hungary was fought at Mohács in 1526 and Pécs was an important political and cultural centre under the Turks.

Late in the 17th century the abandoned towns of Southern Transdanubia were resettled by Swabian Germans and Southern Slavs, and after WWII ethnic Hungarians came from Slovakia and Bukovina in Romania as did Saxon Germans. They left a mark that can still be seen and felt today in local architecture, food and certain traditions.

SZEKSZÁRD

☎ 74 / pop 34,700

The wine-producing city of Szekszárd lies south of the Sió River, which links Lake Balaton with the Danube, among seven of the Szekszárd Hills. It is the centre of the Sárköz folk region, but more than anything else Szekszárd is the gateway to Southern Transdanubia. In fact, you can actually see the region start in the town's main square (Garay tér), where the Great Plain, having crossed the Danube, rises slowly, transforming into the Szekszárd Hills.

Mild winters and warm, dry summers combined with favourable soil help Szekszárd produce some of the best red wines in Hungary. The premier grape here is the Kadarka, a late-ripening and vulnerable varietal that is produced in limited quantities.

History

Szekszárd was a Celtic and later a Roman settlement called Alisca. The sixth Hungarian king, Béla I, conferred royal status on the town and founded a Benedictine abbey here in 1061. The Turkish occupation left Szekszárd deserted, but the area was repopulated late in the 17th century by immigrant Swabians from Germany, and the economy was revitalised in the next century by wheat cultivation and viticulture.

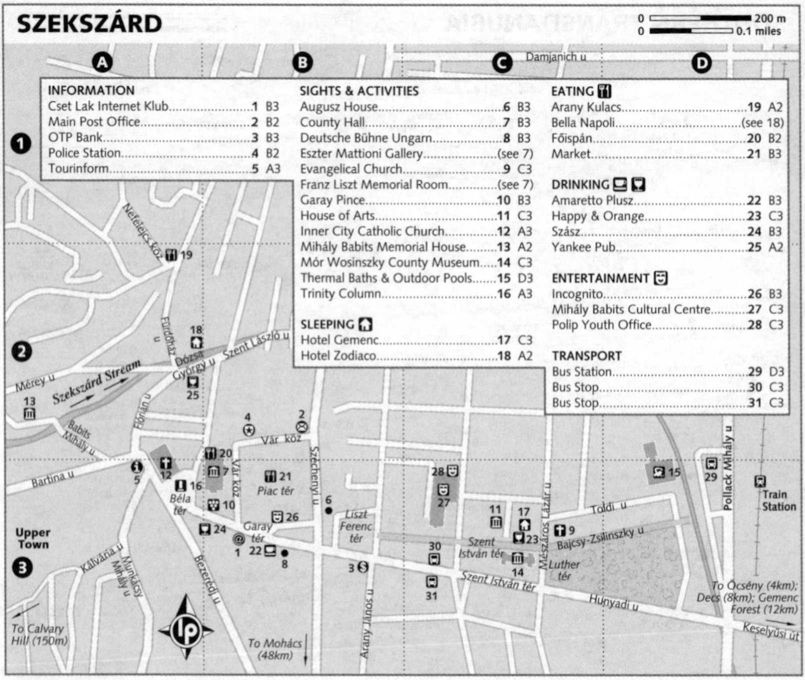

Orientation

The bus and train stations face one another across Pollack Mihály utca. Follow pedestrian Bajcsy-Zsilinszky utca west through the park to the town centre. Garay tér ascends to Béla tér.

Information

City website (www.szekszard.hu) Useful info in English.

Cset Lak Internet Klub (☎ 06 30 946 7309; Garay tér 12; 1st 15min free, then per 30min 100Ft; ⌚ 2-6pm Mon-Sat)

Main post office (Széchenyi utca 11-13)

OTP bank (Szent István tér 5-7) With ATM.

Tourinform (☎ 315 198; szekszard@tourinform.hu; Béla tér 7; ⌚ 9am-5pm daily Jun-Aug, 9am-5pm Mon-Sat, 10am-4pm Sun Sep–mid-Oct, 9am-5pm Mon-Fri, 9am-2pm Sat mid-Oct–May) Information on the town and Tolna County.

Sights

CALVARY HILL

You can get a good view over Szekszárd and its surrounds by following Munkácsy Mihály utca and then Kálvária utca from the Tourinform office southwest up to Calvary Hill (Kálvária-hegy; 205m). The hill's name recalls the crucifixion scene and chapel erected here in the 18th century by grief-stricken parents who lost their child (still remembered in a famous poem by Mihály Babits, a native of Szekszárd). The Danube and the Great Plain are visible to the east, the Sárköz region beyond the hills to the south and the Szekszárd Hills to the west. On a clear day you can see Hungary's sole nuclear power station at Paks, 30km to the north.

Today the hill is dominated by a **modern sculpture**, done by István Kiss for the city's 925th anniversary. It looked fine when unveiled in 1986 – a stylised bunch of grapes representing Szekszárd's wine, sheaves for its wheat and a large bell for Béla's 11th-century abbey. But on closer inspection, the inscriptions on the grape leaves revealed not just the names of Hungarian heroes and literary greats but those of local communist officials.

NOTABLE BUILDINGS

The neoclassical **county hall** (vármegyeháza; ☎ 419 667; Béla tér 1; adult/student & child 400/200Ft; ⌚ 9am-5pm Tue-Sun Apr-Sep, 9am-3pm Tue-Sun Oct-Mar), designed by Mihály Pollack in 1828, sits on the site of

Béla's abbey and an earlier Christian chapel; you can see the excavated foundations in the central courtyard. Upstairs is the **Franz Liszt Memorial Room** and across the hallway the **Eszter Mattioni Gallery**, whose works in striking mosaics invoke peasant themes with a twist. The square's yellow baroque **Inner City Catholic Church** (Belvárosi templom; 1805) is the largest single-nave church in Hungary. Franz Liszt stayed and performed at the eye-catching neo-Gothic **Augusz House** (Széchenyi utca 36-40) several times in the late 19th century when it was the Black Elephant Inn; today it houses a music school. Diagonally opposite is the fine **Deutsche Bühne Ungarn** (Német Színház Magyarország; ☎ 316 533; Garay tér 4), a delightful Romantic-style German theatre from 1913 that still stages performances *auf Deutsch*.

MUSEUMS

All museums in Szekszárd are free on Saturdays.

Szekszárd produced two of Hungary's most celebrated poets: Mihály Babits (1883–1941) and the lesser-known János Garay (1812–53). Although the former's avant-garde, deeply philosophical verse may be obscure (even in Hungarian) the **Mihály Babits Memorial House** (Babits Mihály Emlékház; ☎ 312 154; Babits Mihály utca 13; adult/student & child 500/300Ft; 🕒 9am-5pm Tue-Sun Apr-Sep, 10am-4pm Tue-Sat Oct-Mar), where he was born, is a good place to see how a middle-class family lived in 19th-century provincial Hungary.

The **Mór Wosinszky County Museum** (☎ 316 222; Szent István tér 26; adult/student & child 500/300Ft; 🕒 10am-6pm Tue-Sun Apr-Sep, 10am-4pm Tue-Sun Oct-Mar), purpose-built in 1895, contains objects left behind by some of the various peoples who passed through the Danube Basin ahead of the Magyars. Don't miss the fine Celtic and Avar jewellery and the large folk collection of Serbian, Swabian and Sárköz artefacts. Three period rooms – that of a well-to-do Sárköz farming family and their coveted spotted-poplar furniture, another from the estate of the aristocratic Apponyi family of Lengyel and a poor gooseherd's hut – illustrate very clearly the different economic brackets that existed side by side in the region a century ago. Also interesting are the exhibits related to the silk factory that was started in Szekszárd in the 19th century with Italian help and employed so many of the region's young women.

The Moorish flourishes of the **House of Arts** (Művészetek Háza; ☎ 511 247; Szent István tér 28; 🕒 10am-6pm Tue-Sun), behind the museum, reveals its former life as a synagogue. It is now used as a gallery and concert hall. Four of its original iron pillars have been placed outside and enclosed in an arch, suggesting the tablets of the Ten Commandments.

Activities

On a warm summer's day head for the covered **thermal baths and outdoor pools** (☎ 412 035; Toldi utca 6; adult/child 600/450Ft; 🕒 baths 11am-9pm Mon, from 6am Tue-Sun year-round, pools 9am-6pm mid-May–Aug) behind the bus station.

There are several places where you can sample local wines; central **Garay Pince** (☎ 412 828; Garay tér 19; 🕒 9am-5pm Mon-Fri, 9am-2pm Sat) has some of Szekszárd's best wines for tasting (from 300Ft per 0.1L) and buying. Tourinform has a full list of wine cellars in town.

Festivals & Events

Among the big events staged annually in Szekszárd are the **Feast of Szekszárd Stew and Wine** in late June, the **International Danube Folklore Festival** jointly sponsored with Kalocsa in mid-July, and the **Szekszárd Wine Days** in late September. See 'Events, Festivals' on the town's website (www.szekszard.hu) for details.

Sleeping

Tourinform has a list of a few **private rooms** (per person 2000-4000Ft), which are usually in the high-rise blocks near the Mihály Babits Cultural Centre.

Hotel Gemenc (☎ 311 722; hotelgemenc@vivamail.hu; Mészáros Lázár utca 1; s 6250-9950Ft, d 9500-14,400Ft, tr 11,750-16.850; ☒) Although the quintessential unrepentant socialist-era hostelry, this exceedingly ugly 92-room hotel is centrally located and has all the usual amenities – restaurant, coffee shop, weekend nightclub etc. Cheaper rooms haven't been renovated in 20 years; the more expensive ones come with fridge.

Hotel Zodiaco (☎ 511 150; info@hotelzodiaco.hu; Szent László utca 19; s/d/tr 11,500/15,500/19,000Ft; ✇ 💻) No prizes for guessing that this hotel sports an astrological theme. Facing little competition, it's by far the best place in town, with 28 large, 2nd-floor rooms 'parading' themselves around the inner courtyard of a bizarre modern block.

Eating

Market (Piac tér) The big open-air market is just off Vár köz east of county hall.

Bella Napoli (☎ 511 237; Szent László utca 19; dishes 500-1790Ft; ⌚ noon-11pm Mon-Sat) In the courtyard of the Hotel Zodiaco, Bella Napoli is a small but welcoming eatery with extra large pizzas (650Ft to 1790Ft) and decent pasta dishes (1090Ft to 1600Ft).

Arany Kulacs (☎ 413 369; Nefelejcs köz 3; entrées 690-1450Ft, mains 1050-2950Ft; ⌚ noon-midnight) For fine dining and even finer wine, head for the 'Golden Flask', probably the best restaurant in Szekszárd. Once there, choose the outside terrace with partial views of the town, or the cellarlike surroundings inside.

Főispán (☎ 312 139, 06 30 746 2824; Béla tér 1; entrées 710-2190Ft, mains 1280-2350Ft; ⌚ 11am-11pm Mon-Thu, 11.30am-midnight Fri & Sat, 11.30am-9pm Sun) Housed in a renovated wine cellar below county hall, Főispán is an atmospheric option, with a small but interesting collection of assorted wine-making implements.

Drinking

Amaretto Plusz (☎ 06 30 969 5228; Garay tér 6; ⌚ 9am-6pm or 7pm) This cafe is small in size but big on ice cream (from 130Ft) and doesn't do a bad job with cakes either.

Happy & Orange (☎ 06 70 703 1935; Mészáros Lázár utca 1; ⌚ 8am-11pm Sun-Thu, to 2am Fri & Sat) The name defeats us too (maybe they're prodemocracy Ukrainians), but this cafe with live music on weekends and internet access (per half-hour 100Ft) pushes all the right buttons.

Szász (☎ 312 463; Garay tér 18; ⌚ 10am-midnight Mon-Sat, to 4am Sun) For a drink on the town, try the central 'Saxon' pub, which attracts a relaxed crowd of all ages with its cocktails, and food, too.

Yankee Pub (☎ 887 196; Szent László utca 16; noon-midnight Mon-Thu, to 2am Fri & Sat) This funny little place with the 'log cabin' theme is opposite the Hotel Zodiaco and more boisterous than the genteel Szász.

Entertainment

For up-to-date entertainment listings, get a hold of freebie biweekly *Szekszárdi Est*.

Mihály Babits Cultural Centre (☎ 529 610; Szent István tér 10) This modern centre has information about concerts and other cultural events taking place in the county hall courtyard, the House of Arts and various other venues.

Polip Youth Office (Polip Ifjúági Iroda; ☎ 510 472; Szent István tér 10; ⌚ noon-6pm Mon-Sat) For alternative culture, including parties, see these guys in the office to the rear of the Mihály Babits Cultural Centre.

Incognito (☎ 511 010; Garay tér; ⌚ 11pm-5am Tue, Fri & Sat) This is the most central place for a night out clubbing in Szekszárd.

Getting There & Away

BUS

There are up to a dozen daily departures to Budapest (2290Ft, three hours, 154km) and Pécs (1350Ft, 1½ hours, 88km). At least five daily buses leave for Baja (750Ft, one hour, 41km) and Mohács (750Ft, one hour, 49km). From Szekszárd you can also reach Harkány (1350Ft, 2¼ hours, 88km) on at least three buses daily via Pécs, and Siófok (1500Ft, 2¼ hours, 97km) on up to eight buses daily. Some of these buses can be boarded on Szent István tér south of the Mihály Babits Cultural Centre.

Local buses bound for Keselyűs (between two and five daily) will drop you off near the Gemenc Excursion Centre in Bárányfok. Up to 10 buses daily head for Öcsény (200Ft, 12 minutes, 8km) in the Sárköz region, while departures to Decs (200Ft, 20 minutes, 12km, three to eight daily) are less frequent.

TRAIN

Only two direct trains leave Budapest's Déli train station daily for Szekszárd (2290Ft, three hours, 149km). Otherwise, take the Pécs-bound train from Budapest's Déli, Kelenföldi or Keleti train stations and change at Sárbogárd. To travel east (to Baja), west (to Kaposvár) or south (to Pécs) you must change trains at Bátaszék, 20km to the south. Öcsény (120Ft, seven minutes, 4km) and Decs (200Ft, 15 minutes, 8km) are on the train line to Bátaszék.

Getting Around

Bus 1 goes from the bus station through the centre of town to Béla tér, but it's just as easy to walk. Order a local taxi on ☎ 555 555.

AROUND SZEKSZÁRD

Gemenc Forest

The Gemenc, an 18,000-hectare flood forest of poplars, willows, oxbow lakes and dikes 12km east of Szekszárd, is part of Duna-Drava National Park. Until engineers removed some

60 curves in the Danube in the mid-19th century, the Gemenc would flood to such a degree that the women of the Sárköz region would come to the market in Szekszárd by boat.

Today the backwaters, lakes and ponds beyond the earthen dams, which were built by wealthy landowners to protect their farms, offer sanctuary to black storks, white-tailed eagles, herons, kingfishers and woodpeckers, as well as game animals like red deer and boar. Hunting is restricted to certain areas; for information contact the Budapest-based **Hungarian National Hunting Protection Association** (OMVV; ☎ 1-355 6180, 06 30 239 4659; www.vadaszativedegylet.hu; II Medve utca 34-40).

SIGHTS & ACTIVITIES

The main entrance is at the **Gemenc Excursion Centre** (Gemenci Kiránduló Központ; ☎ 74-312 552; 9am-5pm year-round) in Bárányfok, about halfway down Keselyűsi út between Szekszárd and the forest. It offers activities such as coach rides (adult/child from 1300/800Ft) and can supply you with a map of walking and cycling trails through the forest. (Keselyűsi út was once the longest stretch of covered highway in the Austro-Hungarian Empire, and in the late 19th century mulberry trees were planted along it to feed the worms at the silk factory in Szekszárd; see p283.)

Near the centre is an ornate 'gingerbread' wooden hall, built without nails for Archduke Franz Ferdinand to house his hunting trophies. Today it contains an exhibition called **Life in the Floodplain** (Élet az Ártéren; ☎ 06 30 270 2635; adult/child 500/300Ft; 9am-5pm Tue-Sun mid-Mar–mid-Oct). The hall was featured at the 1896 Millenary Exhibition in Budapest and is now in its fourth location – most recently reassembled from Szent István tér in Szekszárd.

Narrow-Gauge Train

A narrow-gauge train, which once carried wood out of the Gemenc Forest, is a fun – but difficult – way to go. The train runs from Bárányfok to Pörböly (one way adult/child 700/550Ft, two hours), some 30km to the south, via Keselyüs once daily at 3.55pm from May to October. Two other trains – at 10.40am and 1.50pm – go only as far as the Gemenc Dunapart (adult/child 570/450Ft) 11km south, where you'll need to change trains for Pörböly.

From Pörböly, a train leaves at 8.30am to Bárányfok. Two other trains leave at 9.30am and 1.30pm, but they go only as far as the Gemenc Dunapart, where you can make connections to Bárányfok

The abridged trip in itself is worthwhile, weaving and looping around the Danube's remaining bends, but it's a good idea to double-check the times with Tourinform in Szekszárd, or with the **Pörböly train station** (☎ 74-491 483; www.gemencrt.hu; Bajai út 100) before you set out.

SLEEPING & EATING

At **Trófea Üdölőház** (☎ 74-410 151; d/tr 9000/12,000Ft; ⊠), located within the excursion centre, it's possible to stay in wooden bungalows, set in the forest, with all the mod-cons. The **Trófea** (☎ 74-712 552; mains 1250-2000Ft) is a *csárda* (Hungarian-style restaurant) in the same complex, with a huge open terrace. See opposite for information on buses from Szekszárd.

Sárköz Region

The folkloric region of Sárköz, the centre of folk weaving in Hungary, consists of five towns southeast of Szekszárd between Rte 56 and the Danube, including **Öcsény** (population 2490) and **Decs** (population 4135), with its high-walled cottages, late Gothic Calvinist church and folk houses.

The Sárköz became a very rich area after flooding was brought under control in the mid-19th century. In a bid to protect their wealth and land, most families had only one child. And, judging from the displays at the **Regional & Artisan House** (Tájház és Kézművesház; ☎ 74-495 414, 06 30 360 2127; Kossuth utca 34-36; adult/child 200/100Ft; 9am-noon & 1-5pm Tue-Sat Apr-Oct, 10am-noon & 2-4pm Tue-Sat Nov-Mar), located in a peasant house in Decs, these families spent a lot of their money on lavish interior decoration and some of the most ornate (and Balkan-looking) embroidered folk clothing in Hungary. Don't miss the ingenious porcelain 'stove with eyes' (concave circles) to radiate more heat. The house was built in 1836 from earth and woven twigs, so that when the floods came only the mud had to be replaced.

Elsewhere in the Sárköz, be on the lookout for local pottery decorated with birds, the distinctive black-and-red striped woven fabric so common that it was once used as mosquito netting in this bug-infested region, and the unique *írókázás fazékok* (inscribed pots), usually made as wedding gifts.

MOHÁCS

☎ 69 / pop 18,700

The defeat of the ragtag Hungarian army by the Turks at Mohács on 29 August 1526 (p28) was a watershed in the nation's history. With it came partition and foreign domination that would last almost five centuries. It is not hyperbole to say that the effects of the battle at Mohács can still be felt in Hungary even now.

Today Mohács is a sleepy little port on the Danube that wakes up only during the annual **Busójárás festival**, a pre-Lenten free-for-all late in February or March. The town is also a convenient gateway to Croatia, with the border crossing at Udvar just 12km to the south.

Orientation

The centre of Mohács is on the west bank of the Danube; residential New Mohács, or Újmohács, is on the opposite side of the river. Szabadság utca, the main street, runs west from the Danube, with large war memorials on either end.

The bus station is on Rákóczi utca, just south of leafy Bensheim tér. The port's train station is situated about 1.5km north of the city centre, near the Strandfürdő on Bajcsy-Zsilinszky utca.

Information

K&H bank (Szentháromság tér 2) With ATM.
OTP bank (Jókai Mór utca 1) With ATM.
Post office (Széchenyi tér 2) In the southern wing of the Town Hall.
Tourinform (☎ 505 515; mohacs@tourinform.hu; Széchenyi tér 1; 🕑 7.30am-5pm Mon-Fri, 8am-5pm Sat & Sun mid-Jun–mid-Sep, 8am-4pm Mon-Fri, 8am-4.30 Mon-Fri mid-Sep–mid-Jun) Housed in the Moorish Town Hall.
Town website (www.mohacs.hu, in Hungarian) Has some information in English.

Sights

MOHÁCS HISTORICAL MEMORIAL SITE

This **memorial site** (Mohácsi Történelmi Emlékhely; ☎ 382 130, 06 20 918 2779; adult/child 550/350Ft; 🕑 9am-6pm late Mar-early Nov) at Sátorhely (literally 'encampment'), about 6km southwest of Mohács and a kilometre off route 56, was opened in 1976 to mark the 450th anniversary of the Mohács battle. It's a fitting memorial to the dead over a common grave that was only discovered in the

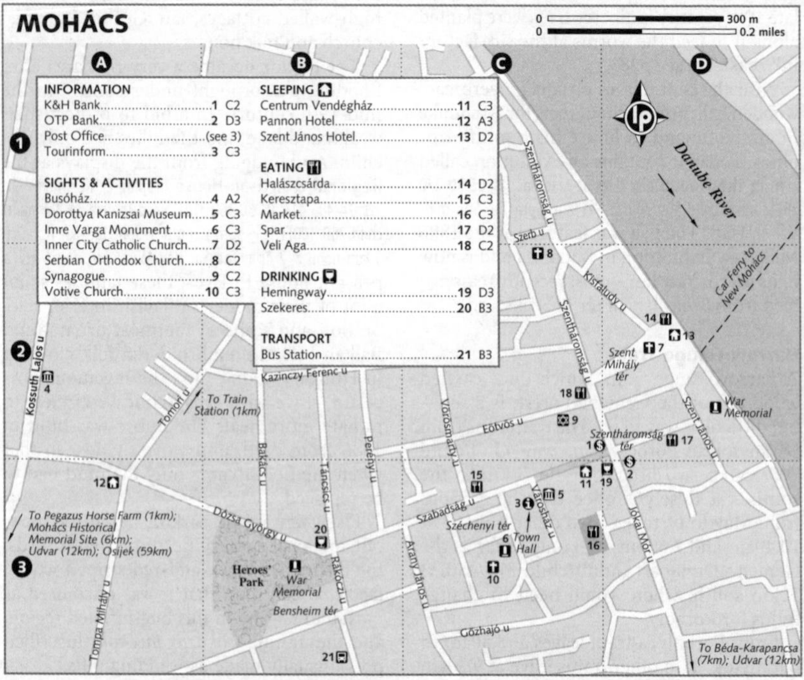

early 1970s. Scores of carved wooden markers in the shape of bows, arrows, lances and crosses lean this way and that and represent the defeated Hungarians. Those topped with turbans, crescents and scimitars and standing bolt upright are the Turks. The subterranean entrance leads to a circular courtyard with 10 panels with (somewhat one-sided) explanations in English. 'Here began the ruination of a once strong Hungary' proclaims one.

MUSEUMS

The **Dorottya Kanizsai Museum** (☎ 311 536; Városház utca 1; adult/child 300/150Ft; ⏰ 10am-3pm Tue-Sat Apr-Oct) has a large collection of costumes worn by the Sokác, Slovenes, Serbs, Croats, Bosnians and Swabians who repopulated this devastated area in the 17th century. The distinctive grey-black pottery of Mohács also figures. More interesting is the surprisingly well-balanced exhibit devoted to the 1526 battle, with both sides getting the chance to tell their side of the story.

Busóház (☎ 302 677, 06 20 331 3671; Kossuth Lajos utca 54; adult/child 300/200Ft; ⏰ 9am-5pm Mon-Fri, to noon Sat) This new museum is the place to come if you're not in Mohács just before Lent. It tells the story of the Busójárás festival, from its origins as a South Slav spring rite to a fancy-dress mummery directed at the erstwhile enemy, the Turks. The horrifying devil's and ram's-head masks are on frightening display.

OTHER SIGHTS

The city's other sights amount to a handful of houses of worship. The Byzantine-style **Votive Church** (Fogadalmi templom; Széchenyi tér 13; ⏰ 9am-noon & 1-4pm), which looks not unlike a mosque, was begun in 1926 to mark the 400th anniversary of the battle and finished 14 years later. It has some contemporary frescoes of the event and inspired modern stained-glass windows in its large dome. Outside is a striking **monument** (2000) by sculptor Imre Varga of the key players in the battle, including a rather mature-looking King Louis and his commander-in-chief, Pál Tomori.

The pulpit in the baroque **Inner City Catholic Church** (1776), on Szent Mihály tér behind the Szent János Hotel, is noteworthy. From here it's a short walk north to the **Serbian Orthodox church** (Szentháromság utca 33), which was built in 1732 and served a very large congregation of Serbs up until WWII. The church's icons and ceiling frescoes date from the 18th century.

In the courtyard of the old **synagogue** (Eötvös utca 1), a large monument with stars of David, menorahs, tablets and inscriptions in Hungarian and Hebrew honours the town's Jewish victims of fascism.

Activities

The **Béda-Karapancsa**, a 100-sq-km woodland some 7km southeast of Mohács, is where locals head to fish, hike and bike. Like the Gemenc Forest, it's part of the Duna-Dráva National Park. Purchase a good map of the area, such as *Béda-Karapancsai tájegység* (Béda-Karapancsa Region; 650Ft), from Tourinform or the ticket office at the Mohács battle site.

The Pannon Hotel (below) rents **bicycles** for 500Ft a day.

You can rent horses at the **Pegazus Horse Farm** (☎ 301 244; Eszéki út 2), just south of the city centre on the road to the battle site.

Sleeping

Centrum Vendégház (☎ 510 383, 06 30 969 4451; www.centrumvendeghaz.shp.hu; Szabadság utca 9; s/d/tr 7500/8500/11,000Ft; 💻) Located in a gated courtyard, this excellent-value *pension* (guest house) has a half-dozen bright and airy (if somewhat small) rooms in the heart – the name says it all – of town.

Pannon Hotel (☎ 510 278; www.pannonhotel.hu; Dózsa György utca 17; s/d/tr 9000/12,000/17,000Ft; ⊠ ❄ 💻) About a 1km west of Szentháromság tér, the Pannon is a cool oasis, with a dozen lovely rooms and a small garden in a former music school.

Szent János Hotel (☎ 511 010; www.hotel-szentjanos.hu; Szent Mihály tér 6-7; s 14,750-16,000Ft, d 17,250-19,750Ft; ⊠ ❄ 💻) Next to the ferry pier, the 'St James' has 49 elegant, spacious and ultra-modern rooms in an attractive new building of brick, marble and glass. The views up and down the Danube from the stunning rooftop restaurant and bar are to die for. Wheelchair accessible.

Eating

Keresztapa (☎ 303 259; Szabadság utca 22; pizzas 650-1500Ft; ⏰ 10am-10pm Sun-Tue, to 11pm Wed & Thu, to midnight Fri & Sat) The upbeat and friendly 'Godfather' near the start of Mohács' pedestrian street serves the best pizza in town.

Veli Aga (☎ 311 417; Szentháromság utca 7; entrées 390-640Ft, mains 1100-1350Ft; ⏰ 11am-10pm Mon-Thu, to 11pm Fri & Sat) These guys have got their audience well sussed, serving relatively authentic Turkish dishes like *ezo gelin çorbası* (red-lentil 'bridal' soup) and lamb pilaf to victorious visitors.

Halászcsárda (☎ 322 542; Szent Mihály tér 5; mains 1350-1850Ft) This old favourite has a beautiful terrace overlooking the Danube and a dozen different fish dishes on the menu. The resident band churns out rather insipid folk music, however.

There's a **Spar** (Szabadság utca 3 & 5; 🕑 6.30am-8pm Mon-Fri, to 5pm Sat) supermarket just west of Szentháromság tér. Fresh produce, food stalls and tacky knick-knacks are all available at the town's open-air **market** (Jókai Mór utca) to the southwest.

Drinking

Szekeres (☎ 06 30 226 1484; Dózsa György utca 2; 🕑 9am-6pm) No self-respecting Hungarian town could do without a cafe serving quality ice cream (from 130Ft) and cakes, and Szekeres does the job for Mohács.

Hemingway (☎ 322 541; Jókai Mór utca 2; 🕑 8am-11pm Mon-Thu, to midnight Fri & Sat, 10am-10pm Sun) As central as you'll find, with a huge terrace facing Szentháromság tér, Hemingway is the best place in town to enjoy a *korsó* (pint) or two during the evening.

Getting There & Away

BUS

Bus services from Mohács aren't as frequent as other towns, but to Pécs (750Ft, 1¼ hours, 48km) and Baja (600Ft, 1¼ hours, 39km) they leave almost hourly. Other destinations include Budapest (2780Ft, four hours, 196km, three daily), Villány (675Ft, one hour, 42km, three to six daily), Siklós (900Ft, 1½ hours, 55km, three to seven daily), Harkány (1050Ft, 1½ hours, 66km, five to eight daily) and Szekszárd (750Ft, one hour, 49km, five to seven daily).

TRAIN

Mohács is linked by rail with Villány (375Ft, 25 minutes, 24km) and Pécs (900Ft, 1¼ hours, 60km), with up to seven trains daily. To get anywhere else, the bus is the best (and often the only) option.

Getting Around

Local buses (150Ft) for any of the following towns will let you off at the Mohács Historical Memorial Site: Nagynyárád, Majs, Lippó, Bezedek and Magyarbóly.

A year-round car ferry (160/150/580Ft per person/bicycle/car) links Szent Mihály tér with New Mohács – and the start of the Great Plain – across the Danube.

SIKLÓS

☎ 72 / pop 10,200

Until recently, the medieval fortress at Siklós, Hungary's southernmost town, was the longest continuously inhabited castle in the country. But Siklós hardly needs superlatives to delight. Protected from the north, east and west by the Villány Hills, it has been making wine (mostly white) since the Romans settled here. Siklós is also close to Villány, famed for its big red wines, and a hop, skip and a jump to the spa centre at Harkány.

Orientation

The town centre runs from the bus station on Szent István tér along Felszabadulás utca to Kossuth tér; Siklós Castle stands watch over the town from the hill to the west.

Information

City Library (Városi Könyvtár; ☎ 579 125; Kossuth tér 15; per hr 100Ft; 🕑 1-5pm Mon, Tue & Thu, 8am-noon & 1-5.30pm Fri, 2-5pm Sat) Internet access.
K&H bank (Felszabadulás utca 48)
OTP bank (Felszabadulás utca 60-62)
Post office (Flórián tér 1) With folkloric motifs on the facade.
Tourinform (☎ 579 090; siklos@tourinform.hu; Felszabadulás utca 3; 🕑 9am-5pm Mon-Fri, 10am-7pm Sat & Sun Jun-Aug, 9am-5pm Mon-Fri Sep-May) Information on wine-makers in the area, including the free *Villány Siklós Wine Route* map-brochure.

Sights

SIKLÓS CASTLE

Though the original foundations of the **castle** (☎ 579 501; Vár körút; adult/student/child 760/480/400Ft; 🕑 9am-6pm Tue-Sun Apr-Oct, 9am-4pm Tue-Sun Nov-Mar) date back to 1249, what you see when you look up from the town is an 18th-century baroque palace, girdled by 15th-century walls and bastions. Reach it either from Kossuth tér via Batthyány Kázmér utca, or up Váralja utca from the bus station on Szent István tér.

The entrance is at the red-brick **barbican**, topped with loopholes and a circular lookout. It leads to the **Castle Museum** (Vármúzeum) in the south wing. To the right as you enter the

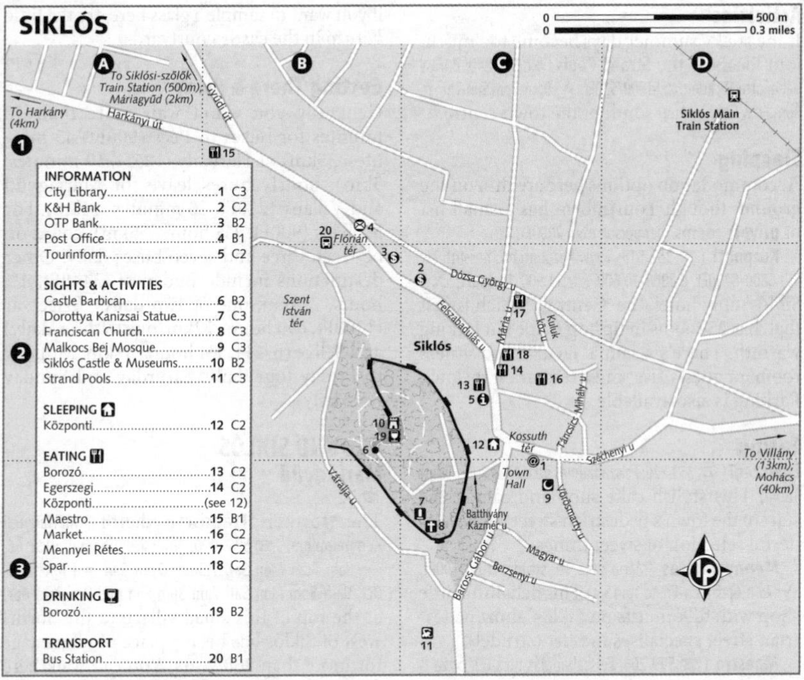

main door is an unusual exhibit devoted to the manufacture and changing styles of gloves, fans and umbrellas since the Middle Ages. The exhibit's emphasis is very much on the Hamerli and Hunor factories at Pécs, which produced some of Europe's finest kid gloves in the 19th century. The woman's mourning outfit from the 1870s, complete with black feather fan, is stylishly sombre. The cellar contains Gothic and Renaissance stone fragments from the castle. Most of the 1st floor is given over to the history of the castle; don't miss the wonderful **Sigismund Hall** (Zsigmond terem), with its Renaissance fireplace and enclosed balcony with star vaulting and fresco fragments. There's a gallery of modern art on the 2nd floor.

To the right of the museum entrance, two doors lead to the dark and spooky **cells** – a real dungeon if ever there was one. The walls here are several metres thick, and up to five grilles on the window slits discouraged would-be escapers. Woodcuts on the walls of the upper dungeon explain how the various torture devices on display were used – there's a great emphasis on impaling – but even scarier is the bold Russian graffiti dating back to the 1970s, when all was right with the Soviet world. After this the Gothic **Chapel of St John of Capistrano** (Kapisztrán Szent János kápolna) is a vision of heaven itself, with its brilliant arched windows behind the altar, web vaulting on the ceiling and 15th-century frescoed niches.

On the northern side of the courtyard is a small **Wine Museum** (Bormúzeum), basically a wine shop with farming tools and mock-ups, and a **hunting exhibit** featuring lots of heads and antlers on walls. Stairs lead to the **castle terrace**, with fine views of the Villány Hills and the towers to the north and east.

OTHER SIGHTS

The 15th-century Gothic **Franciscan church** on Vajda János tér is south of the castle; it was rebuilt after the Turks were driven out. Nearby is the small **statue of Dorottya Kanizsai**, the heroic noblewoman who presided over the burial of the dead at the battle at Mohács.

Beyond the town hall is the restored 16th-century **Malkocs Bej Mosque** (Malkocs bej dzsámija; ☎ 579 279; Vörösmarty utca 14; adult/child 300/200Ft; 🕑 10am-6pm Tue-Sun May-Sep) housing Turkish-era artefacts and temporary exhibits.

Activities

If the sticky summer days become too much, join locals at the **Strand Pools** (☎ 579 840; Baross Gábor utca 18; adult/child 800/500Ft; 9am-7pm Sun-Thu, to 8pm Fri & Sat Jun-Aug) south of the town centre.

Sleeping

Accommodation options here are thin on the ground, though Tourinform has a small list of **private rooms** (per person from 2000Ft).

Központi (☎ 352 513; www.kozponti.hu; Kossuth tér 5; s 6800-8200Ft, d 8800-10,600Ft, tr 11,900-14,400Ft;) Siklós' only hotel, the 'Central', which is just that, has 25 rooms in tip-top shape but lacking warmth. There's a sauna, Jacuzzi and fitness room for guests' use, and a restaurant (below). Parking is also available.

Eating

Egerszegi (☎ 351 226; Felszabadulás utca 22-24; 9am-10pm) This stylish cake shop and cafe at the start of the town's pedestrian street has a wonderful selection of sweet things.

Mennyei Rétes (Mária utca 10; strudel from 190Ft; 7am-6pm Mon-Fri, to 1pm Sat) This delightful little shop with folk motifs on Siklós' short pedestrian street specialises in *rétes* (strudel).

Maestro (☎ 579 206; Felszabadulás utca 69; pizza & pasta 720-1590Ft) If you're looking for something close to the bus station, try this basic eatery, serving mainly Italian fast food.

Központi (☎ 352 513; www.kozponti.hu; Kossuth tér 5; entrées 300-750Ft, mains 1250-1950Ft; 8am-10pm) One of just a few places to eat in the town centre, this hotel restaurant has an exclusively Hungarian menu and a lovely shaded terrace open in the warmer months. Set lunch weekdays is just 700Ft.

Borozó (☎ 06 20 566 9131; Felszabadulás utca 7; entrées 750-990Ft, mains 1500-1700Ft; 2-8.30pm Mon, 10am-8.30pm Tue-Sat, 2.30-11pm Sun) This one-time divey boozer is now a lovely retro-style wine bar called just that (*borozó* means wine bar) and serving hearty Hungarian dishes paired with wine.

There's a **Spar** (Mária utca 2; 6.30am-8pm Mon-Fri, to 5pm Sat) supermarket next to the Mennyei Rétes strudel shop. The town's large **market**, with everything from knock-off jeans and trainers to *čevapčiči* (spicy meatballs), is just east of the Egerszegi cafe off Kiluk köz.

Drinking

You should really save the wine tasting for Villány and the cellars at Villánykövesd, but if you want to sample a glass here, try the little *borozó* in the castle courtyard.

Getting There & Away

Generally you won't wait more than 30 minutes for buses to Pécs (900Ft, 45 minutes, 35km) or Harkány (125Ft, 10 minutes, 5km); hourly buses leave for Máriagyűd and Villány (250Ft, 20 minutes, 14km). For Mohács (900Ft, 1½ hours, 55km), count on between three and seven buses daily. Other destinations include Budapest (3440Ft, 4½ hours, 244km, one or two daily), Szigetvár (1200Ft, two hours, 72km, one to three daily) and Sellye (675Ft, 1¼ hours, 41km, Monday to Friday four daily, Saturday and Sunday one daily).

AROUND SIKLÓS

Máriagyűd

☎ 72

The former **Franciscan church** (Máriagyűdi Kegytemplom; ☎ 579 000; Vujicsics Tihamér utca 66; 8am-7pm Mon-Sat, 7.30am-7pm Sun mid-Apr–mid-Oct, 9am-5pm Mon-Sat, 7am-3pm Sun mid-Oct–mid-Apr) at the top of this small village to the northwest of Siklós has been a place of pilgrimage for more than 860 years. You can walk here from Siklós (3km) along Gyűdi út and Pécs út before turning north on Arany János utca when the church's two towers come into view and up Járó Péter utca. Direct buses from Siklós as well as Harkány-bound ones also serve the village.

Máriagyűd was on the old trade route between Pécs and Eszék (now Osijek in Croatia) and a church has stood here since the mid-12th century. Today's is a large 18th-century affair with modern frescoes on the ceiling, baroque painted altars, some beautifully carved pews and the main object of devotion, Mary and the Christ Child in gold and silver over the main altar. The most interesting time to visit is on Sunday or on a *búcsú* (a patron's festival – the Virgin Mary has lots of them) when merchants set up their stalls beside the church.

Máriagyűdi Bajor Pince (☎ 351 143, 06 30 983 2016; Tenkes utca 14; 10am-4pm Mon-Sat), in an old cellar in the square just below the church, is a good place to sample some of Siklós' white wines. If it's closed, **Máriagyűdi Bácsi Pince** (☎ 579 295, 06 70 947 7078; Járó Péter utca 35), a simple *borozó* with outside tables just to the south, should suffice.

HARKÁNY

☎ 72 / pop 3440

It's a wonder that no statue stands in honour of János Pogány at this spa town 6km west of Siklós. He was the well-digger from Máriagyűd who cured himself of swollen joints in 1823 by soaking in a hot spring he had discovered here. Wealthy landowners recognised the potential almost immediately and the following year bathing huts were erected near the 62°C spring, which has the richest sulfuric content in Hungary. Today, aside from Pécs, no town in Baranya County brings in as much money as Harkány.

Of course, all that means crowds – now topping a million visitors per year – stalls selling *lángos* (deep-fried dough topped with cheese and sour cream) in spades and an all-pervasive pong of rotten eggs. But you might like it. People come to Harkány to socialise, it's not as brash as Hajdúszoboszló on the Great Plain, and the town is on the western edge of the Villány-Siklós region, so there's plenty of wine within reach.

Orientation

Harkány is essentially the Gyógyfürdő, a 13.5-hectare green square filled with pools, fountains, grassy 'beaches' and walkways. The four streets defining the thermal complex and bordered by hotels and holiday homes of every description are Bartók Béla utca to the north, Ady Endre utca to the south, Kossuth Lajos utca, with several restaurants, to the west and

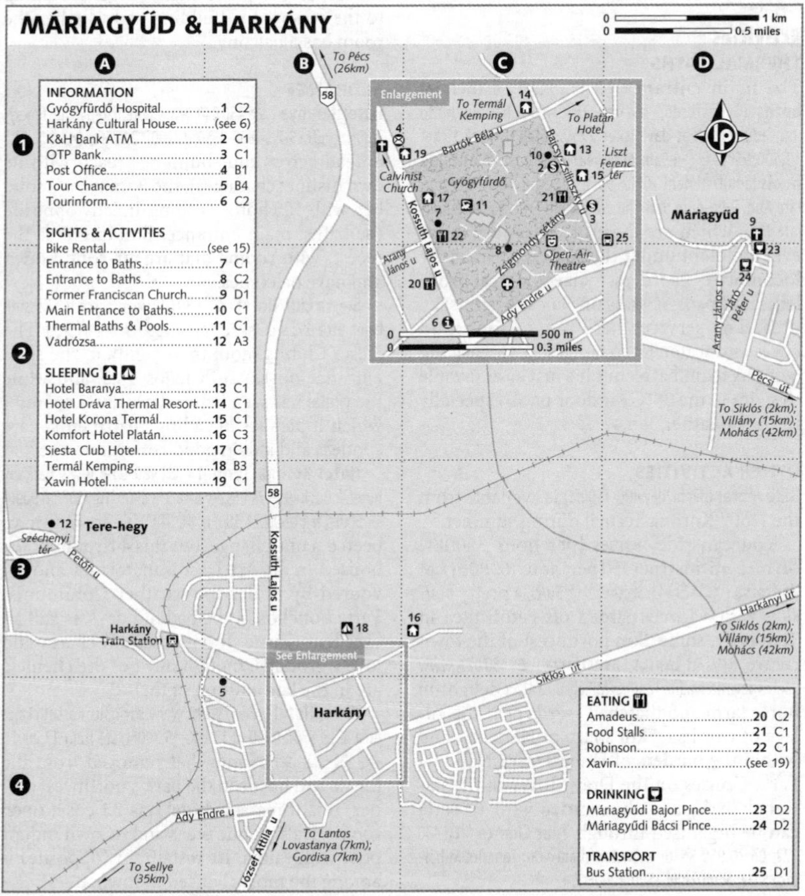

Bajcsy-Zsilinszky utca, with most of the hotels and the bus station, to the east.

Information

Harkány Cultural House (Harkányi Művelődési Ház; ☎ 480 459, 06 20 485 0185; Kossuth Lajos utca 2; 🕑 9.45am-5.45pm Mon-Thu, 10am-2pm Fri) Internet access (per hr 200Ft).
K&H bank ATM (Bajcsy-Zsilinszky utca) ATM at the spa's main entrance.
OTP bank (Bajcsy-Zsilinszky utca) Just north of the bus station.
Post office (Kossuth Lajos utca 57)
Tourinform (☎ 479 624; harkany@tourinform.hu; Kossuth Lajos utca 2/a; 🕑 9am-5pm mid-Jun–mid-Sep, 9am-4pm mid-Sep–mid-Jun) Next to Harkány Cultural House.
Town website (www.harkany.hu) Information partly in English.

Activities

THERMAL BATHS

The main entrance to Harkány's **thermal baths** (Gyógyfürdő; ☎ 480 251; www.harkanyfurdo.hu; adult/student day ticket 2250/1590Ft, week ticket 13,500/9540Ft; 🕑 9am-6pm year-round) and **outside pools** (adult/student 1090/790Ft; 🕑 9am-10pm late Jun-late Aug, 9am-6pm Sun-Thu, 9am-8pm Fri & Sat late Aug-late Jun), which are meant to cure just about every ailment under the sun (but especially locomotive disorders, gynaecological problems and psoriasis), is on Bajcsy-Zsilinszky utca. The services here range from mud cures and water-jet massages to an enticing 'winous foam bath', but it's just as enjoyable to swim in the 38°C outdoor pool, especially in cool weather.

OTHER ACTIVITIES

Bike rental (per hr/day 400/1500Ft) is available from the Hotel Korona Termál during summer.

You can ride horses (per hour 3500Ft) or hire an instructor (per hour 6000Ft) at **Vadrózsa** (☎ 479 141; Széchenyi tér 30/c), a pretty *pension* with a lovely garden off Petőfi utca in Tere-hegy, some 2km northwest of the town centre, and at **Lantos Lovastanya** (☎ 480 077; www.lantos-lovastanya.hu; Táncsics Mihály utca 4), a delightful horse farm and thatched *csárda* near the village of Gordisa, 7km south of Harkány, and within the borders of Duna-Drava National Park. Cruises on the Dráva River in the national park near the border with Croatia can be organised through **Tour Chance** (☎ 480 272, 06 30 959 3530; www.tourchance.hu; Táncsics Mihály utca 54/a; adult/child 1500/1200Ft).

Sleeping

BUDGET

Tourinform has a comprehensive list of **private rooms** (per person from 3000Ft) and apartments and will make bookings.

Termál Kemping (☎ 480 117; www.mecsektours.hu; Bajcsy-Zsilinszky utca 6; camp sites per person/tent 850/850Ft, bungalows per 2/3/4 people 6000/7000/9000Ft, pension d 3700Ft, hotel d 5300Ft; 🕑 mid-Apr–mid-Oct) This lush, green camping ground is an easy walk to the pools and a jack-of-all-trades, with tent sites, bungalows, *pension*-style rooms with kitchens, and standard hotel rooms.

Komfort Hotel Platán (☎ 580 800; www.hotelplatan.hu; Bartók Béla utca 15; s 3750-7500Ft, d 5850-12,175Ft; ⊠ 💻) A quiet, very welcoming 60-room hotel in two former trade-union holiday houses to the east of town, the Platán charges according to the season, the building and whether the room has a balcony.

MIDRANGE

Hotel Baranya (☎ 480 840; www.hotelbaranya.hu; Bajcsy-Zsilinszky utca 5-7; s 4800-8550, d 7200-12,825Ft; ⊠ ❄ 💻) Spread across four buildings (each with its own distinct character), the Baranya is a solid bet, with 105 homey rooms directly opposite the baths' main entrance. Building D is the nicest, with rooms that are air-conditioned and have balconies.

Siesta Club Hotel (☎ 480 611; www.hsch.hu; Kossuth Lajos utca 17; s 6600-7800Ft, d 7950-9900Ft; ⊠) The Siesta Club is more than handy to the spa's entrance on Kossuth Lajos utca, and while the place has seen better days, its 82 rooms – which it persists in calling apartments – are spotless and still in good condition.

Hotel Korona Termál (☎ 480 049; www.harkanyhotelek.hu; Bajcsy-Zsilinszky utca 3; s 6200-10,500Ft, d 9000-15,500Ft, tr 11,500-21,500Ft; ⊠ 💻) There may have been a name change, but this 44-room hotel, housed in an Art Deco sanatorium and favoured by under-the-weather Communist Party honchos in the bad old days, is still an excellent choice. It has a certain charm and lovely grounds, though most of the clientele are in the late autumn of their days.

Xavin Hotel (☎ 479 399; www.xavin.hu; Kossuth Lajos utca 43; s 8700-9700, d 13,900-15,300Ft, ste from 17,200Ft; ⊠ ❄ 💻 🏊) Somewhat removed from the hustle and bustle in the park's northwest corner, this three-star hotel has 33 cosy, open rooms, leafy public areas and its own indoor pool with sauna. Its restaurant (opposite) is among the most civilised in town.

TOP END

Hotel Dráva Thermal Resort (☎ 279 007; www.dravahotel.hu; Bartók Béla utca 1; s €56-80, d €74-98, ste from €120;) The long-awaited revamp of a tired old hotel with the same name is over and Harkány now has its flashiest property. The 89 ultramodern rooms are in two buildings in a pretty park just short of the camping ground, and there's an up-to-the-moment wellness centre and swimming pool. Ask for a superior room with terrace. Wheelchair accessible.

Eating & Drinking

You're not going to starve or die of thirst in this town of sausage stands and wine kiosks; if you want something on the hoof, check out the food stalls along Bajcsy-Zsilinszky utca.

Amadeus (Kossuth Lajos utca 12; ice cream from 120Ft; 9am-10pm) For something sweet on a hot day, head to Amadeus, a cafe with ice cream, cake and a terrace just north of Tourinform.

Xavin (☎ 479 399; www.xavin.hu; Kossuth Lajos utca 43; entrées 840-1920Ft, mains 1560-2890Ft; noon-11pm) The well-established and beautifully decorated restaurant of the Xavin Hotel (opposite) has silver service and an extensive Hungarian wine list.

Robinson (☎ 580 090; Kossuth Lajos utca 7; entrées 1190-2190Ft, mains 1390-3290Ft; 11am-9pm Sun-Thu, to 10pm Fri & Sat) For a decent sit-down meal, try this place with its desert-island vibe and mixed menu of Hungarian and quasi-Caribbean dishes.

Getting There & Away

While buses depart once or twice hourly for Siklós (150Ft, 10 minutes, 6km) and Pécs (900Ft, 1½ hours, 52km), other destinations are not so well served. There's a couple of buses daily to Máriagyüd (125Ft, 10 minutes, 5km), Szekszárd (1500Ft, 2¼ hours, 97km) and Mohács (750Ft, 1½ hours, 48km), and just one bus to Baja (1770Ft, 2¾ hours, 116km, daily) and Sellye (600Ft, one hour, 36km, weekdays).

In summer buses to Stuttgart (24,500Ft, 17½ hours, 1118km) via Munich (19,500Ft, 14 hours, 886km) leave Harkány on Thursday at 1.30pm and Sunday at 2.30pm. They arrive in the German city at 6.30am on Friday and 7.30am on Monday, respectively.

VILLÁNY

☎ 72 / pop 2730

Some 13km northeast of Siklós and dominated by cone-shaped Mt Szársomlyó (422m) to the west, Villány is a village of vineyards, vines and grapes. It was the site in 1687 of what has become known as the 'second battle of Mohács', a ferocious confrontation in which the Turks got their comeuppance and were driven southward by the Hungarians and slaughtered in the Dráva marshes. Serbs and Swabians moved in after the occupation and viticulture resumed. Today Villány is one of Hungary's principal producers of wine. And from the looks of the buildings in the village centre, it's surviving very nicely on plonk, thank you very much.

Orientation

Most everything in Villány lies on or just off Baross Gábor utca, the village's main street that runs north to southwest. The bus stops in the village centre near the town hall. The train station is about 1.5km to the north on Ady Endre fasor en route to Villánykövesd.

Information

OTP bank (Baross Gábor utca 28) With ATM; diagonally opposite Oportó restaurant.

Post office (Vörösmarty utca 2) In a big modern building next to Oportó restaurant.

Villány-Siklós Wine Route Association (☎ 492 181; www.borut.hu; Deák Ferenc utca 22; 8am-4pm Mon-Fri) Some 250m north of the town hall and bus stop; produces the handy *Villány Siklós Wine Route* booklet covering places to buy and sample local wines in the region, and organises tours.

Sights & Activities

The **Wine Museum** (Bormúzeum; ☎ 492 130; Bem József utca 8; admission free; 9am-5pm Tue-Sun), housed in a 200-year-old tithe cellar, has a collection of 19th-century wine-producing equipment, such as barrels and hand corkers. Downstairs in the cellars, Villány's celebrated wines age in enormous casks, and vintage bottles dating from 1895 to 1971 are kept in safes. There's a small shop at the entrance selling Villány and Siklós wines.

Many of the family **wine cellars** that line Baross Gábor utca south of the museum, including Pólya at No 58, Szende at No 87, Fritsch at No 97 and Blum at No 103, offer wine tastings. Gál is just behind the museum at Bem utca 9 and Bock around the corner from Blum at Batthyány utca 15. The hours are normally 10am to 6pm; expect to pay between 200Ft and 950Ft per *deci* (0.1L).

Arguably the best places for tastings in the area are the cellars cut into the loess soil at **Villánykövesd**, about 3.5km northwest of Villány along the road to Pécs. Cellars line the main street (Petőfi út) and the narrow lane (Pincesor) above it; most of those open to the public are along the latter. On Petőfi út, try Pinnyó at No 35 or the deep Polgár cellar at No 51. On Pincesor, Blum is at No 4-5, while Schwarzwalter is at No 16. In between, at No 13-15, is the cellar of master vintner Imre Tiffán. The cellars keep odd hours, so it's a hit-or-miss proposition.

Sleeping

Gyöngyszeme (☎ 492 710; www.gyongyszem.info; Baross Gábor utca 41-43; s/d 7000/10,000Ft;) Just round the corner from the Wine Museum, this six-room *pension* is excellent value, especially when you consider its location. It organises wine tastings, has a decent terrace restaurant just opposite and rents bicycles for 1500Ft a day.

Gere (☎ 492 195; www.gere.hu; Diófás tér 4; s/d 11,000/12,600Ft;) You shouldn't miss the chance to stay at this 13-room *pension* in the very centre of Villány. Rooms are big and cosy, and there's a peaceful garden to laze around in. Its fine restaurant serves some of the best wine in these parts.

Cabernet (☎ 493 200; www.hotelcabernet.hu; Petőfi utca 29; s/d/tr 12,000/15,000/19,500Ft) This appropriately named hostelry in Villánykövesd is worth considering if you really want to plonk (sorry) yourself in the heart of the wine area. It has 25 rooms, a restaurant and does wine tasting.

Eating

Oportó (☎ 492 582; Baross Gábor utca 33; entrées 700-1050Ft, mains 800-2300Ft; 10am-10pm) Villány's most central restaurant, Oportó is huge, has an inviting, vine-covered terrace and a great selection of local wines to accompany its selective Hungarian menu.

Fülemüle Csárda (☎ 492 939; Ady Endre fasor; mains 950-2600Ft; 11am-11pm) The 'Nightingale Inn', housed in a lovely old farm house a couple of hundred metres past the train station, is a good place to stop for a bite on your way to/from Villánykövesd.

Júlia (☎ 702 610; Baross Gábor utca 73/b; mains 1450-2160Ft; noon-10pm Thu-Sun) This intimate little restaurant serves excellent veal *pörkölt* (stew; 1750Ft) and has wine tastings.

Getting There & Around

There are one or two buses daily to Pécs (900Ft, 1½ hours, 52km), and seven to Siklós (250Ft, 20 minutes, 14km) and Harkány (300Ft, 30 minutes, 18km). Villánykövesd (125Ft, 10 minutes, 3.5km) can be reached between four and eight times daily on weekdays but only twice daily on Saturday. Trains run east to Mohács (375Ft, 25 minutes, 24km, up to seven daily) and north to Pécs (600Ft, 45 minutes, 36km, up to nine daily).

To order a taxi in Villány, ring ☎ 06 30 335 5495.

ORMÁNSÁG REGION

About 30km west of Harkány, this plain was prone to flooding by the nearby Dráva River for centuries. That – and the area's isolation ('somewhere behind the back of God,' as the Hungarians call it) – is reflected in its unusual architecture, folk ways and distinct dialect. Couples in the Ormánság usually had only one child since, under the land-tenure system here, peasants were not allowed to enlarge their holdings. That's not the only reason why the area's *talpás házak* are so small: these 'soled' or 'footed' houses were built on rollers so that they could be dragged to dry land in the event of flooding. The region is one of the most picturesque in southwest Hungary and as a repository of folklore and traditional ways, it's well worth a detour.

The shepherds of Ormánság have always been known for the items they carve from horn or wood, including crooks, pocket mirror frames and shaving kits. The oaken trousseau chests, decorated with geometrical shapes and made to hold the distinctive Ormánság bridal brocaded skirts and 'butterfly' headdresses, are unique and superior to the *tulipán ládák* (tulip chests) found in prosperous peasant houses elsewhere in Hungary.

Sellye

☎ 73 / pop 3170

In Sellye, the 'capital' of the Ormánság region, a representative 'footed house' constructed of mortar, lime and a wooden frame sits behind the **Géza Kiss Ormánság Museum** (☎ 480 201; Köztársaság tér 6; adult/child 200/150Ft; 10am-4pm Tue-Sun Apr-Oct, 10am-2pm Nov-Mar). The house has the typical three rooms but includes some big differences not normally associated with traditional dwellings: the parlour was actually lived in; the front room was a 'smoke kitchen' – without a chimney; and, to keep mosquitoes at bay, what few windows the house had were kept very small. The museum's rich collection contains Ormánság costumes and artefacts.

An **arboretum** with rare plants and 40 species of trees surrounds the Draskovich family mansion built in 1750 and now a school. It's about 100m east of the museum.

Mátyás király utca, the main drag, is southwest of the bus station, and the train station is to the southeast on Vasút utca.

Other Ormánság Villages

In **Drávaiványi**, there's a **Calvinist church** (Rákóczi Ferenc utca 1), with a colourful panelled ceiling and choir loft dating from the late 18th century. It's about 3.5km southwest of Sellye and can be reached by bus; the key is available from the house at Kossuth Lajos utca 4. **Vajszló**, 11km southeast of Sellye with several 'footed houses', is on the same train line as Sellye. Buses travel eastward from Vajszló 11km to **Kórós**, whose folk-decorated **Calvinist church** (Kossuth Lajos utca 40) is among the most beautiful in the region. The key is kept at Kossuth Lajos 31 just west of the church. Kórós is about 4km north of route No 6 via Adorjás.

Getting There & Away

Harkány is the easiest starting point for any excursion into the Ormánság by bus, with Sellye (600Ft, one hour, 36km, once daily weekdays) the first port of call. The area is also accessible from Szigetvár (675Ft, one hour, 42km) on several buses daily. Be aware that if you catch the train from Szigetvár (600Ft, 1½ hours, 39km), you must change at Szentlörinc.

PÉCS

☎ 72 / pop 156,000

Blessed with a mild climate, an illustrious past and a number of fine museums and monuments, Pécs is one of the most pleasant and interesting cities to visit in Hungary. For those reasons and more – a handful of universities, the nearby Mecsek Hills, a lively nightlife – many travellers put it second only to Budapest on their Hungary 'must-see' list.

Lying equidistant from the Danube to the east and the Dráva to the south on a plain sheltered from the northern winds by the Mecsek Hills, Pécs enjoys a microclimate that lengthens the summer and is ideal for viticulture and fruit production, especially almonds. An especially fine time to visit is during a warm *indián nyár* (Indian summer), when the light seems to take on a special quality.

History

The Romans may have settled here for the region's fertile soil and abundant water, but it's more likely that they were sold by the protection offered by the Mecsek Hills. They called their settlement Sophianae, and it quickly grew into the commercial and administrative centre of Lower Pannonia (see p23). The Romans brought Christianity with them, and reminders of that can be seen in the early clover-shaped chapels unearthed here.

Pécs' importance grew in the Middle Ages, when it was known as Quinque Ecclesiae after the five churches dotting the town; it is still called just that – Fünfkirchen – in German. King Stephen founded a bishopric here in 1009, the town was a major stop along the trade route to Byzantium and Hungary's first university opened here in 1367. The 15th-century bishop Janus Pannonius, who wrote some of Europe's most celebrated Renaissance poetry in Latin, made Pécs his home.

The city walls – a large portion of which still stand – were in such poor condition in the 16th century that the Turks took the city with virtually no resistance in 1543. The occupiers moved the local populace out and turned Pécs into their own administrative and cultural centre. When the Turks were expelled almost 150 years later, Pécs was virtually abandoned, but still standing were monumental souvenirs that now count as the most important Turkish structures in the country.

The resumption of wine production by German and Bohemian immigrants and the discovery of coal in the 18th century spurred Pécs' development. The manufacture of luxury goods (gloves, Zsolnay porcelain, Angster organs, Pannonvin sparkling wine) would come later.

Orientation

The oval-shaped inner town, about 1km wide and 700m from north to south, is almost entirely for pedestrians only. At its heart is Széchenyi tér, where a dozen streets

PÉCS

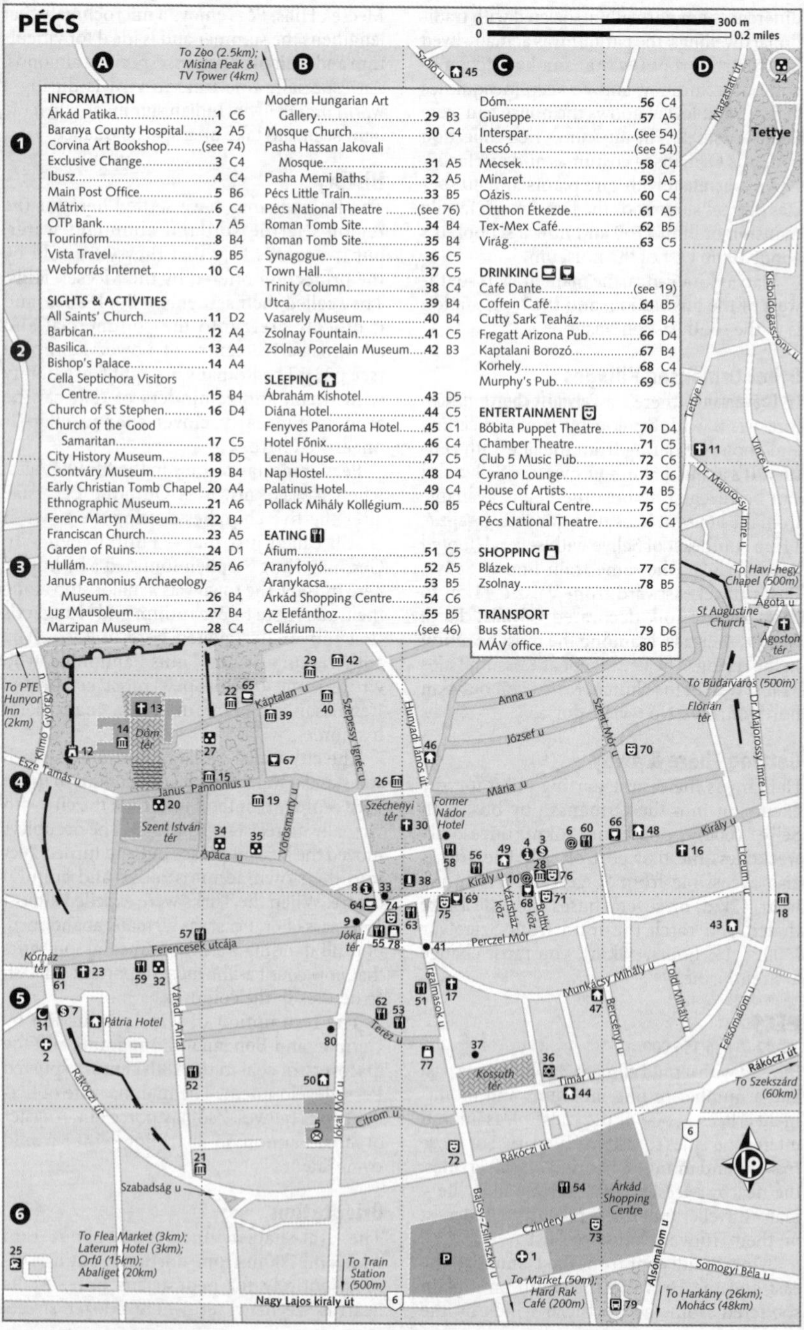

INFORMATION
Árkád Patika.....1 C6
Baranya County Hospital.....2 A5
Corvina Art Bookshop.....(see 74)
Exclusive Change.....3 C4
Ibusz.....4 C4
Main Post Office.....5 B6
Mátrix.....6 C4
OTP Bank.....7 A5
Tourinform.....8 B4
Vista Travel.....9 B5
Webforrás Internet.....10 C4

SIGHTS & ACTIVITIES
All Saints' Church.....11 D2
Barbican.....12 A4
Basilica.....13 A4
Bishop's Palace.....14 A4
Cella Septichora Visitors Centre.....15 B4
Church of St Stephen.....16 D4
Church of the Good Samaritan.....17 C5
City History Museum.....18 D5
Csontváry Museum.....19 B4
Early Christian Tomb Chapel.....20 A4
Ethnographic Museum.....21 A6
Ferenc Martyn Museum.....22 B4
Franciscan Church.....23 A5
Garden of Ruins.....24 D1
Hullám.....25 A6
Janus Pannonius Archaeology Museum.....26 B4
Jug Mausoleum.....27 B4
Marzipan Museum.....28 C4
Modern Hungarian Art Gallery.....29 B3
Mosque Church.....30 C4
Pasha Hassan Jakovali Mosque.....31 A5
Pasha Memi Baths.....32 A5
Pécs Little Train.....33 B5
Pécs National Theatre.....(see 76)
Roman Tomb Site.....34 B4
Roman Tomb Site.....35 B4
Synagogue.....36 C5
Town Hall.....37 C5
Trinity Column.....38 C4
Utca.....39 B4
Vasarely Museum.....40 B4
Zsolnay Fountain.....41 C5
Zsolnay Porcelain Museum.....42 B3

SLEEPING
Ábrahám Kishotel.....43 D5
Diána Hotel.....44 C5
Fenyves Panoráma Hotel.....45 C1
Hotel Főnix.....46 C4
Lenau House.....47 C5
Nap Hostel.....48 D4
Palatinus Hotel.....49 C4
Pollack Mihály Kollégium.....50 B5

EATING
Áfium.....51 C5
Aranyfolyó.....52 A5
Aranykacsa.....53 B5
Árkád Shopping Centre.....54 C6
Az Elefánthoz.....55 B5
Cellárium.....(see 46)
Dóm.....56 C4
Giuseppe.....57 A5
Interspar.....(see 54)
Lecsó.....(see 54)
Mecsek.....58 C4
Minaret.....59 A5
Oázis.....60 C4
Ottthon Étkezde.....61 A5
Tex-Mex Café.....62 B5
Virág.....63 C5

DRINKING
Café Dante.....(see 19)
Coffein Café.....64 B5
Cutty Sark Teaház.....65 B4
Fregatt Arizona Pub.....66 D4
Kaptalani Borozó.....67 B4
Korhely.....68 C4
Murphy's Pub.....69 C5

ENTERTAINMENT
Bóbita Puppet Theatre.....70 D4
Chamber Theatre.....71 C5
Club 5 Music Pub.....72 C6
Cyrano Lounge.....73 C6
House of Artists.....74 B5
Pécs Cultural Centre.....75 C5
Pécs National Theatre.....76 C4

SHOPPING
Blázek.....77 C5
Zsolnay.....78 B5

TRANSPORT
Bus Station.....79 D6
MÁV office.....80 B5

converge. One of these is Király utca, a traffic-free promenade of restored shops, cafes, pubs and restaurants to the east. To the northwest lies Pécs' other important square, Dóm tér. Here you'll find the cathedral, several early Christian chapels and Káptalan utca, a 'street of museums'.

Pécs' train station is in Indóház tér; from here, follow Jókai Mór utca north to the inner town. The bus station is close to the big market on Zólyom utca. Walk north along Bajcsy-Zsilinszky utca and Irgalmasok utca to the city centre.

Information

BOOKSHOPS

Corvina Art Bookshop (☎ 310 427; Széchenyi tér 7-8) Excellent selection of English-language books and guides.

INTERNET ACCESS

Mátrix (☎ 214 487, 06 70 360 2895; Király utca 15; per hr 350Ft; 🕑 9am-11pm Mon-Fri, 10am-10pm Sat, 2-10pm Sun) Super-modern facility in courtyard with 25 computers.

Tourinform (☎ 213 315; Széchenyi tér 9; 🕑 8am-6pm Mon-Fri, 10am-8pm Sat & Sun Jun-Aug, 8am-5.30pm Mon-Fri, 10am-2pm Sat May, Sep & Oct, 8am-4pm Mon-Fri Nov-Apr) Free internet access on a handful of machines.

Webforrás Internet (☎ 332 215, 06 70 520 6443; Boltív köz 2; per hr 360Ft; 🕑 10am-10pm Mon-Fri, 11am-8pm Sat & Sun) Enter at Király utca 10.

MEDICAL SERVICES

Árkád Patika (☎ 516 077; Bajcsy-Zsilinszky utca 11; 🕑 8am-8pm Mon-Sat, 10am-6pm Sun) Pharmacy in the huge Árkád shopping mall.

Baranya County Hospital (☎ 533 133; Rákóczi út 2)

MONEY

Exclusive Change (Király utca 11; 🕑 9am-7pm Mon-Fri, 10am-4pm Sat, 10am-2pm Sun) Centrally located bureau de change.

OTP bank (Rákóczi út 3) Has ATMs.

POST

Main post office (Jókai Mór utca 10) In a beautiful Art Nouveau building (1904) south of Széchenyi tér.

TOURIST INFORMATION

Tourinform (☎ 213 315; baranya-m@tourinform.hu; Széchenyi tér 9; 🕑 8am-6pm Mon-Fri, 10am-8pm Sat & Sun Jun-Aug, 8am-5.30pm Mon-Fri, 10am-2pm Sat May, Sep & Oct, 8am-4pm Mon-Fri Nov-Apr) Knowledgeable staff, copious information on Pécs and Baranya County, free internet and left-luggage service (per hour 100Ft).

TRAVEL AGENCIES

Ibusz (☎ 211 011; www.ibusz.hu; Király utca 11; 🕑 8am-5pm, to noon Sat) Changes money.

Vista Travel (☎ 518 770; www.vista.hu; Ferencesek utcája 2; 🕑 9am-5.30pm Mon-Fri) Branch of the popular Budapest agency.

Sights

SZÉCHENYI TÉR

Dominating this lovely square of largely baroque buildings is the former Pasha Gazi Kassim Mosque. Today it's the Inner Town Parish Church (Belvárosi plébánia templom), more commonly known as the **Mosque Church** (Dzámi Templom; ☎ 321 976; 🕑 10am-4pm Mon-Sat, 11.30am-4pm Sun mid-Apr–mid-Oct, 10am-noon Mon-Sat, 11.30am-2pm Sun mid-Oct–mid-Apr). It is the largest building still standing in Hungary from the time of the Turkish occupation and the very symbol of the city.

The square mosque with its green copper dome was built by the Turks with the stones of the ruined Gothic Church of St Bertalan in the mid-16th century. The Catholics moved back in the early 18th century, and the northern semicircular part was added in the 20th century. The Islamic elements on the south side are easy to spot: windows with distinctive Turkish ogee arches; a *mihrab* (prayer niche) carved into the southeast wall; faded verses from the Koran to the southwest; and lovely geometric frescoes on the corners. The mosque's minaret was pulled down in 1753 and replaced with a bell tower; bells are rung at noon and 7pm.

The **Janus Pannonius Archaeology Museum** (Janus Pannonius Régészeti Múzeum; ☎ 312 719; Széchenyi tér 12; adult/child 350/180Ft; 🕑 10am-3pm Tue-Sat Apr-Oct, 10am-2pm Tue-Sat Nov-Mar), housed in a 17th-century home of a janissary commander north of the church, traces the history of Baranya County up to the time of Árpád. It also contains much Roman stonework from Pannonia, including a bust of Marcus Aurelius.

The **Trinity Column** at the southern end of Széchenyi tér dates from 1908. The porcelain **Zsolnay Fountain**, with its lustrous glaze and four bull's head in front of the rather gloomy **Church of the Good Samaritan** (🕑 6am-6pm Mon-Fri, 8am-8pm Sat & Sun), was donated to the city by the Zsolnay factory in 1892.

KOSSUTH TÉR

This square southeast of Széchenyi tér has two important buildings: the Eclectic **town hall** (1891) to the north and **synagogue** (☎ 315 881;

adult/child 500/300Ft; 10am-noon & 12.45-5pm Sun-Fri May-Oct) to the east. The synagogue was built in the Romantic style in 1869, and a seven-page fact sheet, available in 11 languages, explains the history of the building and the city's Jewish population. Some 2700 of the city's Jews were deported to Nazi death camps in May 1944; only 150 Jews now live here. The pews hewn from Slavonian oak and Angster organ are particularly fine.

AROUND DÓM TÉR

The foundations of the four-towered **basilica** (székesegyház; ☎ 513 030; Dóm tér; adult/child 800/500Ft; 9am-5pm Mon-Sat, 1-5pm Sun Apr-Oct, 10am-4pm Mon-Sat, 1-4pm Sun Nov-Mar) dedicated to St Peter date from the 11th century and the side chapels are from the 1300s. But most of what you see today of the neo-Romanesque structure is the result of renovations carried out in 1881.

The most interesting parts of the basilica's very ornate interior are the elevated central altar and four chapels under the towers and the crypt, the oldest part of the structure. The **Chapel of Mary** on the northwest side and the **Chapel of the Sacred Heart** to the northeast contain works by 19th-century painters Bertalan Székely and Károly Lotz. The **Mór Chapel** to the southeast has more works by Székely as well as magnificent pews. The **Corpus Christi Chapel** on the southwest side (enter from the outside) boasts a 16th-century red marble tabernacle, one of the best examples of Renaissance stonework in the country.

To the southwest, the 18th-century **Bishop's Palace** (Püspöki palota; ☎ 513 030; adult/child 1500/700Ft; tours 2pm, 3pm & 4pm Thu late Jun–mid-Sep) keeps very limited hours, but have a look at the curious **statue of Franz Liszt** (Imre Varga; 1983) peering over from a balcony. Further west and to the north of the square is a long stretch of the old **city wall** that enclosed an area far too large to defend properly. The circular **barbican** (Esze Tamás utca 2), the only stone bastion to survive in Pécs, dates from the late 15th century. It is fronted by a lovely **garden** (7am-8pm May-Sep, 9am-5pm Oct-Apr).

On the southern side of Dom tér is the new **Cella Septichora Visitors Centre** (☎ 224 755; www.pecsorokseg.hu; Janus Pannonius utca; adult/child/family 1500/800/3000Ft; 10am-6pm Tue-Sun Apr-Oct, 10am-4pm Tue-Sun Nov-Mar), which links and explains a series of half a dozen early Christian burial sites that have been on Unesco's World Heritage List since 2000. The highlight is the so-called **Jug Mausoleum** (Korsós sírkamra), a 4th-century Roman tomb whose name comes from a painting of a large drinking vessel with vines found here.

Across Janus Pannonius utca from the centre, the **early Christian tomb chapel** (Ókeresztény sírkápolna; ☎ 224 755; Szent István tér 12; adult/child/family 400/200/800Ft; 10am-6pm Tue-Sun Apr-Oct, 10am-4pm Tue-Sun Nov-Mar) dates from about AD 350 and has frescoes of Adam and Eve and Daniel in the lion's den. Two **Roman tomb sites** (Apáca utca 8 & 14; adult/child/family 400/200/800Ft; by appointment) containing 110 graves from the same era are a little further south.

The small but perfectly formed **Csontváry Museum** (☎ 310 544; Janus Pannonius utca 11; adult/child 700/350Ft; 10am-6pm Tue-Sun Apr-Oct, 10am-4pm Tue-Sun Nov-Mar) exhibits the major works of master 19th-century painter Tivadar Kosztka Csontváry (see the boxed text opposite).

KÁPTALAN UTCA

Káptalan utca, running east from Dóm tér to Hunyadi János út, contains an embarrassment of excellent museums.

The **Modern Hungarian Art Gallery** (Modern Magyar Képtár; ☎ 514 040; Káptalan utca 4; adult/child 460/230Ft; noon-6pm Tue-Sun Apr-Oct, 10am-4pm Tue-Sun Nov-Mar) exhibits the art of Hungary from 1850 till today; pay special attention to the works of Simon Hollósy, József Rippl-Rónai and Ödön Márffy. More abstract and constructionist artists include András Mengyár, Tamás Hencze, Béla Uitz and Gábor Dienes.

The entry fee to the museum includes admission to the **Ferenc Martyn Museum** (Káptalan utca 6; 10am-4pm Tue-Sun), to the west, which displays works by the eponymous painter and sculptor who died in Pécs in 1986. You also get to view Erzsébet Schaár's ground-breaking **Utca** (Street; Káptalan utca 5; noon-6pm Tue-Sun Apr-Oct, 10am-4pm Tue-Sun Nov-Mar) across the street, a complete artistic environment in which the sculptor set her whole life in stone.

At the eastern end of the street, the **Vasarely Museum** (☎ 514 040; Káptalan utca 3; adult/child 700/350Ft; 10am-6pm Tue-Sun Apr-Oct, 10am-5pm Tue-Sun Nov-Mar) exhibits the work of the father of Op Art, Victor Vasarely. Although some of the works are now dated, most are evocative, tactile and just plain fun.

The **Zsolnay Porcelain Museum** (☎ 514 040; Káptalan utca 2; adult/child 700/350Ft; 10am-6pm Tue-Sun Apr-Oct, 10am-5pm Tue-Sun Nov-Mar) traces the history of the porcelain factory established in Pécs

TIVADAR KOSZTKA CSONTVÁRY

Many critics consider Tivadar Kosztka Csontváry (1853–1919), a unique symbolist artist whose tragic life is sometimes compared with that of his contemporary Vincent van Gogh, to be Hungary's greatest painter. Born in Kisszeben, now Sabinov in northeastern Slovakia, Csontváry trained and worked as a pharmacist until, at the age of 27, he heard voices telling him that he would go on to become the 'world's greatest *plein air* painter, greater than Rafael'. He allowed himself 20 years to prepare for this seemingly unachievable task by studying painting and travelling (and dispensing drugs on the side to pay the bills). Though he did some charcoal portraits and painted landscapes in the last decade of the 19th century, Csontváry produced his major works in just half a dozen years starting in 1903. His efforts met with praise at his first exhibition in 1907 in Paris, but critics panned his work at a showing in Budapest the following year. This lack of understanding and recognition by his peers pushed what was already an unstable, obsessive personality into insanity, and he died penniless and alone in Budapest. Many of Csontváry's massive (up to 30 sq metres) canvases are masterpieces. Though he belonged to no specific school of art per se, elements of postimpressionism and expressionism can be seen in such works as *East Station at Night* (1902), *Storm on the Great Hortobágy* (1903) and his most famous work, *Solitary Cedar* (1907). But arguably his best and most profound work is *Baalbeck* (1906), an artistic search for a larger identity through religious and historical themes. And while contemplating it at the museum devoted to his work in Pécs, spare a thought for one Gedeon Gerlóczy, the young architect who recognised Csontváry's genius and bought much of his œuvre at auction from his family, who were trying to flog it for the high-quality canvases the artist had used.

in 1853. At the forefront of European art and design for more than half a century, many of its majolica tiles were used to decorate buildings throughout the country and contributed to establishing a new pan-Hungarian style of architecture. Zsolnay's darkest period came when the postwar communist government turned it into a plant for making ceramic electrical insulators. It's producing art (well, knick-knacks, really) again, but contemporary Zsolnay can't hold a candle to the *chinoiserie* pieces from the late 19th century and the later Art Nouveau and Art Deco designs done in the lustrous eosin glaze. The museum was once the home of the Zsolnay family and contains many original furnishings and personal effects.

OTHER SIGHTS

Southwest of the inner town and opposite the landmark Pátria hotel is the **Pasha Hassan Jakovali Mosque** (Jakováli Hasszán Pasa dzsámija; ☎ 313 853; Rákóczi út 2; adult/child 500/250Ft; ⌚ 9.30am-5.30pm Wed-Sun late Mar-Oct). The late-16th-century mosque – complete with minaret – is the most intact of any Turkish structure in Hungary and contains a small museum of Ottoman objets d'art. The **Ethnographic Museum** (Néprajzi Múzeum; ☎ 315 629; Rákóczi út 15; adult/child 350/180Ft; ⌚ 10am-2pm Tue-Sat Apr-Oct, 10am-3pm Tue-Sat Nov-Mar) to the southeast showcases ethnic Hungarian, German and South Slav folk art of the region.

One of Pécs' most enjoyable pedestrian streets, Ferencesek utcája, runs east from Kórház tér to Széchenyi tér. On it are three beautiful old churches, including the baroque **Franciscan Church** (Ferences templom) dating from 1760 as well as the ruins of the 16th-century **Pasha Memi Baths** (Memi pasa fürdője; Ferencesek utcája 33-35).

On Király utca, another traffic-free street running east from Széchenyi tér, there's the **Marzipan Museum** (Marcipán Múzeum; ☎ 225 453; Király utca 8; adult/child 350/200Ft; ⌚ 10am-7pm), where you can make your own delectable delight or buy one from the museum shop. Just beyond is the neo-rococo **Pécs National Theatre** (☎ 226 266; Színház tér 1). Southeast of the landmark **Church of St Stephen** (Szent István templom; Király utca 44/a) is the excellent **City History Museum** (Várostörténeti Múzeum; ☎ 310 165; Felsőmalom utca 9; adult/child 350/180Ft; ⌚ 10am-3pm Tue-Sat May-Oct, 10am-2pm Tue-Sat Nov-Apr).

The suburb of Budaiváros to the northeast of the town centre is where most Hungarians settled after the Turks banned them from living within the city walls. The centre of this community was the Gothic **All Saints' Church** (Mindenszentek temploma; ☎ 512 400; Tettye utca 14), the only Christian church allowed in Pécs during the occupation and shared by three sects – who fought bitterly for every square centimetre. Apparently it was the Muslim Turks who had to keep the peace among the Christians.

ANDREA SZÁSZ

As a trained opera singer and former Magyar Rádió foreign correspondent, Andrea Szász, communications and marketing director at Pécs2010 (www.pecs2010.hu), is uniquely qualified to prepare the city and the world for Pécs' stint as European Capital of Culture in 2010.

So sing for your supper already. Why Pécs? Apart from Budapest, no other Hungarian city has as many people engaged in artistic activities as this one. But to tell you the truth, another half-dozen cities, including Budapest, Eger and Szeged, tendered for the title and were in the running. The national government nominated Pécs because our bid was the best.

What's the big idea? Well, Pécs has the strong, very solid base of culture necessary for a European Capital of Culture. I mean, we've already got the software. Now we are concentrating on the hardware.

Beg pardon? We've got five major projects on the go, including a new conference centre and conference hall and a regional library and knowledge centre. 'Museum St' (Káptalan utca) is being fully renovated, as are some 70 public squares.

***Jó munkát* (Do a good job), as you say here. Is the fear of missed deadlines keeping you awake at night?** The main focus of all this is to put Pécs on the cultural map of Europe. We have to think of the future and the opportunities the project will bring to the city. It's not just about 2010. But sometimes I do think, 'This place looks like another war zone with all the changes.' Maybe I should have stayed in Gaza or Iraq with the radio.

What's the hardest part of the job then? Winning the hearts and minds of local people. There was a lot of euphoria when we went for the bid in 2005; now people are disappointed with the pace of events. They want things now and not tomorrow and they lack a lot of civic pride. I'll consider my work a success when local people find their own way to the project and see how it can effect change in the fibre of their city.

Can a local girl do that? I'm from Kolozsvár (now Cluj-Napoca in Romania). We came to Budapest when I was 14 after a three-year wait. I feel *pécsi* because I'm working and fighting for Pécs. But local people don't see it that way. Acceptance is not complete even after all these years.

So what keeps you glued to the spot? It's the air, the ambience, the atmosphere – call it what you want – of Pécs. And I can find everything I need here, especially on the cultural front. It's small, it's human and, yes, it does have a Mediterranean feel to it. Sometimes I walk through the streets and think, 'The sea is just around the corner.'

To get a taste of the Mecsek Hills, walk northeast from the centre of Pécs to Tettye and the **Garden of Ruins** (Romkert), what's left of a bishop's summer residence built early in the 16th century and later used by Turkish dervishes as a lodge or monastery. To the northwest, up Fenyves sor and past the **zoo** (állatkert; ☎ 312 788; Dömörkapu 1; adult/student/child/family 890/690/590/2500Ft; ⏲ 9am-5pm mid-Mar–Apr & Oct, 9am-6pm May-Sep), a winding road leads to **Misina Peak** (535m) and a **TV tower** (☎ 336 900; adult/student/child 650/550/450Ft; ⏲ 9am-8pm), an impressive 194m-tall structure with a viewing platform.

Activities

The closest swimming complex to the city centre is **Hullám** (☎ 512 935; Szendrey Júlia utca 7; adult/child 800/450Ft; ⏲ indoor pool 6am-10pm, outdoor pool 9am-7pm in summer), which appears to be in a perennial state of renovation.

An easy way to see the city's highlights is from the **Pécs Little Train** (Pécsi Kisvonat; ☎ 06 70 454 5610; www.pecsikisvonat.hu; adult/child 950/500Ft; ⏲ 10am-5pm), which departs from the southeast corner of Széchenyi tér.

Festivals & Events

Among the big annual events in this party town are the **Pécs Spring Festival** (www.pecsitavaszifesztival.hu), a month-long 'everything-but-the-kitchen-sink' event starting in late March; **International Culture Week** (www.icwip.hu) in late July, which focuses on theatrical performances; **Pécs Days Heritage Festival** (www.oroksegfesztival.hu) in late September, a 10-day festival of dance and music with a couple of wine-related events; and the **European Wine Song Festival** (www.winesongfestival.hu) also in late September, and Europe's only festival exclusively for male choruses.

Sleeping

BUDGET

Ibusz (p297) can arrange **private rooms** (per person from 3500Ft); Tourinform has a list but will only book hotels. Many of Pécs' *pensions* are in the surrounding hills and difficult to get to without your own transport.

Nap Hostel (☎ 950 684, 06 30 277 0733; www.naphostel.com; Király utca 23-25; dm 2400-3850Ft, d 9600-10,500Ft; ⊠ 🖳) A new and very welcome addition to Pécs's budget accommodation scene, this place has three dorm rooms with between six and eight beds and a double with washbasin on the 1st floor of a former bank (1885). There's a large kitchen, one of the six-bed dorm rooms has a corner balcony and there's something of a garden at the rear. Enter the hostel from Szent Mór utca.

PTE Hunyor Inn (☎ 512 640; http://english.pte.hu/tartalom/213; Jurisics Miklós utca 16; s/d/tr 6200/8000/13,000Ft; 🖳) This 50-room guest house run by the Pécs University of Science is in the Mecsek foothills and a bit out of the way, but it has excellent views of the city, a laid-back air and reasonable prices. There's a pleasant restaurant attached, so it's not far to wander for a meal.

Laterum Hotel (☎ 252 113; www.laterum.hu; Hajnóczy József utca 37-39; s/d/tr/q 6500/10,000/13,500/18,000Ft; 🖳) The institutional air of this large, 64-room hotel 3km west of town is offset by exceptionally large and clean rooms, reasonable prices and an on-site restaurant.

In July and August more than a dozen of the city's colleges open up their doors to travellers; Tourinform has the complete list. The most central is **Pollack Mihály Kollégium** (☎ 315 846; Jókai utca 8; dm 2100Ft), with rooms of between two and five beds.

MIDRANGE & TOP END

Hotel Főnix (☎ 311 682; www.fonixhotel.hu; Hunyadi János út 2; s/d 7790/12,590Ft; ❄ 🖳) Főnix appears to be a hotel too large for the land it's built on and some of the 16 rooms and suites are not even big enough to swing a, well, phoenix in. Try to bag a room with a balcony; the Mosque Church is just within reach.

Lenau House (☎ 332 515; lenau@t-online.hu; Munkácsy Mihály utca 8; s/d/tr 8700/12,000/14,000Ft; ⊠ 🖳) The cultural centre of the German minority in Baranya (Branau in German) County offers accommodation on its top floor. The welcome here is hardly the warmest, but the five rooms are large and spotless with private bathroom, and the location can't be faulted.

Ábrahám Kishotel (☎ 510 422; www.abrahamhotel.hu; Munkácsy Mihály utca 8; s/d/tr 9100/12,000/14,000Ft; ❄ 🖳) This excellent little guest house, with five sparkling and very blue rooms, a well-tended, peaceful garden and a friendly welcome, has a distinct laid-back Mediterranean feel. Note that it is a religious establishment, so if you're looking for a party, head elsewhere.

Diána Hotel (☎ 328 594; www.hoteldiana.hu; Timár utca 4/a; s 9500-10,500Ft, d 13,000-14,500Ft, tr/q 18,300/20,000Ft; ⊠ ❄ 🖳) This very central *pension* offers 20 spotless room, comfortable kick-off-your-shoes decor and a warm welcome. It's a great choice overlooking the synagogue.

Fenyves Panoráma Hotel (☎ 315 996; www.hotelfenyves.hu; Szőlő utca 64; s/d from 9900/13,300Ft; ❄ 🖳) Fenyves is an old-fashioned resort hotel in the foothills to the north, with a huge terrace looking down onto the city below and, as its name would suggest, great views. Its two dozen rooms are big but rather bland.

Palatinus Hotel (☎ 889 400; www.danubiushotels.com; Király utca 5; s €60-100, d €80-120; ⊠ ❄ 🖳) The public areas of Pécs' old-world hotel on the site of the Hamerli family (of glove-making fame) mansion are exceptional, featuring plenty of marble, red carpet and Moorish flourishes. The 94 rooms, however, leave something to be desired.

Eating

RESTAURANTS

Minaret (☎ 311 338; Ferencesek utcája 35; entrées 800-1500Ft, mains 1200-2100Ft; 🕑 noon-4pm Sun & Mon, to 9pm Tue-Thu, to 11pm Fri & Sat) Boasting one of the loveliest gardens in the city, this eatery in the shadow of the Pasha Memi Baths serves predictable but tasty Hungarian favourites. Share one of the generous platters (2300Ft to 3300Ft), which include some vegetarian options.

Aranyfolyó (☎ 212 269; Váradi Antal utca 9; entrées 320-1400Ft, mains 1300-2100Ft; 🕑 11.30am-10pm Mon-Fri, from noon Sat & Sun) The two Chinese dragons guarding the door of this restaurant are a dead give-away to the cuisine on offer at the 'Golden River'. Rice and noodle dishes are a snip at 450Ft to 750Ft.

Dóm (☎ 210 088; Király utca 3; entrées 850-1950Ft, mains 1390-1990Ft, steaks 2690-3590Ft) This restaurant with wonderful *fin-de-siècle* paintings and stained-glass windows is just behind the Palatinus. It has a full range of mains, but its speciality is steak – from pepper to Chateaubriand.

our pick **Áfium** (☎ 511 434; Irgalmasok utca 2; entrées 530-1400Ft, mains 1400-1900Ft; 🕑 11am-1am) With

Croatia and Serbia so close, it's a wonder that more restaurants don't offer cuisine from south of the border. No matter – this restaurant will fill the needs (and stomachs) of most diners searching for such tastes. Don't miss the 'hatted' (actually a swollen bread crust) bean soup with trotters. Set lunch, which changes daily, is 520Ft during the week.

Az Elefánthoz (☎ 216 055; Jókai tér 6; mains 1600-2100Ft) With its enormous terrace and quality Italian cuisine, 'At the Elephant' is a sure bet for first-rate food in the city centre. It has a wood-burning stove for making pizzas (500Ft to 1800Ft) and its pasta dishes (1200Ft to 1900Ft) are exceptional.

Cellárium (☎ 314 453; Hunyadi János út 2; entrées 450-1250Ft, mains 1700-2200Ft) Below Hotel Főnix, this subterranean eatery offers excellent value for money in the city centre.

Tex-Mex Café (☎ 215 427; Teréz utca 10; mains 1750-2500Ft) For a welcome change of pace from Hungarian cuisine, duck (as it were) into this colourful cellar restaurant, serving everything from burritos and enchiladas (1900Ft to 2200Ft) to chicken mole (1900Ft).

Aranykacsa (☎ 518 860; Teréz utca 4; entrées 990-1890Ft, mains 1620-3240Ft; 🕒 11.30am-10pm Tue-Thu, to midnight Fri & Sat, to 3pm Sun) This stunning wine restaurant takes pride in its silver service and venue; the Zsolnay Room is not to be missed. The menu offers at least eight duck dishes – its name means 'Golden Duck' – including such memorables as duck liver with green apple and duck ragout with honey and vegetables.

QUICK EATS

Giuseppe (Ferencesek utcája 28; ice cream per scoop 140Ft; 🕒 11am-7pm Mon-Fri, from 3pm Sat & Sun) This place has been serving its very own Italian-style *lapátos fagyalt* (scooped ice cream) since 1992.

Otthon Étkezde (☎ 212 323; Rákóczi utca 1; set menu 550Ft; 🕒 11am-3pm Mon-Fri) Ultracheap lunch spot at the start of pedestrian Ferencesek utcája, with rib-sticking Hungarian favourites.

Oázis (Király utca 17; kebabs & dishes 450-1370Ft; 🕒 10am-11pm Mon-Thu, to 4am Fri & Sat) A cheap little kebab house serving a mix of Turkish and Middle Eastern dishes, this is a great central spot for a meal on the run.

The huge **Árkád Shopping Centre** (Bajcsy-Zsilinszky utca 11; 🕒 7am-9pm Mon-Thu & Sat, to 10pm Fri, 8am-7pm Sun), south of Rákóczi út, has a food court on the ground floor of its south side. Try the only local fast-food joint here called **Lecsó** (set meals 700-1200Ft), which serves the eponymous sauce of peppers, tomatoes and onions on just about everything.

There's an ongoing debate in Pécs over which *cukrászda* (cake shop) serves the better cakes: **Mecsek** (☎ 315 444; Széchenyi tér 16; 🕒 9am-9pm), next to the former Nádor hotel, or the **Virág** (☎ 313 793; Irgalmasok utca; 🕒 8am-10pm). Try them both and come to your own conclusions.

MARKETS & SELF-CATERING

Pécs' fruit and vegetable **market** (Zólyom utca) is next to the bus station. There is a large **Interspar** (🕒 7am-9pm Mon-Thu & Sat, to 10pm Fri, 8am-7pm Sun) supermarket in the basement of the Árkád shopping centre.

Drinking

CAFES & TEA HOUSES

Coffein Café (☎ 06 20 522 1440; Széchenyi tér 9; 🕒 8am-midnight Mon-Thu, to 2am Fri & Sat, 10am-10pm Sun) For the best views across Széchenyi tér to the Mosque Church and Király utca, find a perch at this cool cafe done up in the warmest of colours.

Café Dante (☎ 210 361; Janus Pannonius 11; 🕒 10am-1am Sun-Thu, to 3am Fri & Sat) Occupying the ground floor of the Csontváry Museum, this gem of a cafe, with its fusty living-room vibe, huge garden and occasional live music, is a good place to meet local students.

Cutty Sark Teaház (☎ 513 082; Káptalan utca 6; 🕒 2-9pm Mon-Fri, 10am-8pm Sat & Sun) Another museum (this time the Ferenc Martyn) venue, this little 'slice of England' is the place to head for a quality cuppa. It serves 52 varieties of tea.

PUBS & BARS

Korhely (☎ 535 916; Boltív köz 2) This outrageously popular *csapszék* (tavern) with the on-your-face name of 'Drunkard' has peanuts on the table, shells on the floor, a half-dozen beers on tap and a retro sorta-socialist/kinda–Latin American decor. It works.

Káptalani Borozó (Janus Pannonius utca 8-10; 🕒 10am-2am Mon-Sat, to midnight Sun) This funny little 'wine bar' opposite the Csontváry Museum has outdoor seating on a tiny terrace next to another early Christian site and serves white Cirfandli, a speciality of the Mecsek Hills, in spades. There's a story behind all those padlocks on the outside gate.

Pubs and bars line Király utca, so you should have no problem finding one that suits.

Our current favourites are **Murphy's Pub** (☎ 325 439; Király utca 2) at the western end and **Fregatt Arizona Pub** (☎ 511 068; Király utca 21) to the east.

Entertainment

MUSIC & THEATRE

Pécs is always a city of culture – not just in 2010 and because Europe said so (see the boxed text, p300). The list of theatres and concert venues is enormous for a city of its size, and most times of the year you can find something going on. For information visit the **Pécs Cultural Centre** (☎ 336 622; www.pecsikult.hu; Szécheny ter 1; ☎ 8am-4pm Mon, 9am-5pm Tue-Fri) or pick up a copy of the biweekly freebie *Pécsi Est*.

Pécs National Theatre (Pécsi Nemzeti Színház; ☎ 512 660; www.pnsz.hu; Színház tér 1; tickets 1000-1950Ft) Pécs is also renowned for its opera company and the Sophianae Ballet, both of which perform at this theatre. Advance tickets can be purchased from the theatre's **box office** (☎ 211 965; 10am-5pm Mon-Fri, 1hr before performances Sat & Sun). The **Chamber Theatre** (Kamaraszínház; ☎ 512 660; Perczel Mór utca) next door stages smaller, more experimental productions.

House of Artists (Művészetek Háza; ☎ 522 834; www.pmh.hu; Széchenyi tér 7-8; office 8am-5.30pm Mon-Fri) This jack-of-all-trades centre, going strong since the early 1980s, advertises its many cultural programs outside, including classical music concerts.

Bóbita Puppet Theatre (Bóbit Bábszínház; ☎ 210 301; www.bobita.hu; Mária utca 18) Somewhere John Malkovich would be proud to perform, the Bóbita is not just for kids.

NIGHTCLUBS

Pécs is a big university town; it goes without saying that the nightlife is good, but don't expect everything to be heaving in summer, which is the low season in these parts. Among the city's most popular discos and music clubs:

Club 5 Music Pub (☎ 212 621, 06 20 535 5090; Irgalmasok utca 24; 7pm-2am Tue-Thu, to 4am Fri & Sat) This basement bar transforms itself into a small (and very central) club on weekends.

Cyrano Lounge (☎ 06 30 650 7021; Czindery utca 6; 8pm-5am Fri & Sat) A big club, popular with a big-haired, big-nailed crowd, next to the Árkád Shopping Centre.

Hard Rak Café (☎ 502 557; Ipar utca 7; 7pm-6am Mon-Sat) In a crap part of town just south of the bus station, this warehouse (*rak* – get it?) is the place to go for rock and heavy beats.

Shopping

Flea market (Vásártér; Megyeri út; 8am-3pm Sun) About 3km southwest of the inner town, this market attracts people from the countryside, especially on the first Sunday of each month.

Pécs has been known for its leatherwork since Turkish times, and you can pick up a few bargains in several shops around the city, including **Blázek** (☎ 332 460; Teréz utca 1), which deals mainly in handbags and wallets. **Zsolnay** (☎ 310 220; Jókai tér 2) has a porcelain outlet south of Széchenyi tér.

Getting There & Away

BUS

Departures are frequent (at least once hourly) to Siklós (900Ft, 45 minutes, 55km), Mohács (750Ft, 1¼ hours, 48km), Harkány (900Ft, 1½ hours, 52km), Kaposvár (1500Ft, 1½ hours, 91km), Szigetvár (525Ft, 50 minutes, 35km) and Szekszárd (1350Ft, 1½ hours, 88km). There are four buses daily to Abaliget (525Ft, one hour, 32km) and six to 10 to Orfű (300Ft, 40 minutes, 18km) in the Mecsek Hills throughout the year, but even more in summer.

For more bus departures from Pécs, see the table, above.

International destinations served by bus include Frankfurt (26,500Ft, 18 hours, 1206km) via Nuremberg (20,000Ft, 14½ hours, 918km), which departs at 1.30pm on Sunday, arriving at Nuremberg at 4.15am and at Frankfurt just after 8am on Monday.

Destination	Price	Duration	Km	Frequency
Budapest	3010Ft	4½hr	215	5 daily
Győr	3440Ft	4½hr	256	2 daily
Kecskemét	3010Ft	4¼hr	200	2 daily
Sellye	900Ft	1½hr	57	3 daily
Siófok	2040Ft	3hr	133	3-6 daily
Szeged	3010Ft	4½hr	207	8 daily
Székesfehérvár	2540Ft	3hr	168	3-5 daily
Veszprém	2780Ft	4¼hr	183	2-3 daily
Villány	900Ft	1½hr	52	1-2 daily

TRAIN

Up to nine direct trains daily connect Pécs with Budapest (3230Ft to 4550Ft, three to four hours, 228km). You can reach Nagykanizsa (2290Ft to 2780Ft, three hours) and other points northwest via a rather circuitous but scenic 148km journey along the Dráva River. From Nagykanizsa, a half-dozen direct trains daily continue on to Szombathely (1770Ft to 1990Ft, 1½ to 2½ hours, 102km). One early morning express at 5.25am follows this route from Pécs all the way to Szombathely (3440Ft, 4½ hours). Three daily trains at 4.55am, 12.40pm (express) and 4.42pm run from Pécs to Osijek (Hungarian: Eszék). The 12.40pm express carries on to Sarajevo, arriving at 9.46pm.

The **MÁV office** (☎ 06 40 494 949; Jókai Mór utca 4; 🕑 8.30am-5pm Mon-Fri) has more information on train arrivals and departures.

Getting Around

To get to the PTE Hunyor Inn, take bus 32 from the train station or from opposite the Mosque Church. Buses 34 and 35 run direct to the Fenyves Panoráma Hotel from the train station, with bus 35 continuing onto the TV tower. For the Laterum Hotel, take bus 4 from the train station or the market near the bus station to the end of the line at Uránváros. Buses 3 and 50 from the train station are good for the flea market.

You can order a local taxi by calling ☎ 333 333 or 777 777.

MECSEK HILLS

A string of hills and valleys dotted with villages and the odd lake to the north of Pécs, the Mecsek form both the city's green lung and playground. There's good hiking here, too, but first pick up a copy of Cartographia's 1:40,000 map *A Mecsek* (No 15; 990Ft).

For transport information, see Getting There & Away (p303).

Orfű

☎ 72 / pop 760

The most accessible of the Mecsek Hills resorts and the one with the most recreational facilities, Orfű is a series of settlements on four artificial lakes, including the largest Lake Pécs (Pécsi-tó), where you can swim, row, canoe and fish; seek information from **Tourinform** (☎ 598 115; orfu@tourinform.hu; Széchenyi tér 1). There's a riding school at the **Tekeresi Lovaspanzió** (Tekeres Horse Pension; ☎ 498 032, 06 30 227 1401; www.tekeresilovaspanzio.hu; Petőfi utca 3; riding per hr 2000Ft, instructor per 10 people 6000Ft) on the lake's northern shore. From Széchenyi tér on the lake's southeastern shore you can walk south along tiny Lake Orfű to the **Mill Museum** (Malommúzeum; ☎ 06 20 466 5506; individual/family 480/1400Ft; 🕑 10am-5pm Tue-Sun May-Sep), which encompasses pump houses still in use and a horse-driven dry mill.

SLEEPING & EATING

Panoráma Camping (☎ 378 501; www.panoramacamping.hu; Dollár utca 1; camp sites per adult 650-750Ft, child 350-450Ft, 2-/4-person tent 900/1300Ft, 2-person bungalows 5300-6800Ft; 🕑 May–mid-Sep) Above the large public beach in the lake's southwestern corner, this 11-hectare camping ground has seen better days, but is large, leafy and secluded. Wheelchair accessible.

Tekeresi Lovaspanzió (Tekeres Horse Pension; ☎ 498 032, 06 30 227 1401; www.tekeresilovaspanzio.hu; Petőfi utca 3; dm 2100-2500Ft, d 6300Ft, 5-person apt 12,000Ft) At the horse-riding centre (see left), this is a kid-friendly and welcoming place with a dozen rooms. Dormitory accommodation in rooms with six to 10 beds is available mid-April to mid-October. The B&B, with well-kept rooms and apartments that feel more like home than anything else, is open year-round.

Also worth noting:

Átrium Panzió (☎ 498 288; www.hotels.hu/atrium panzio; Széchenyi tér 17; d 9800-12,000Ft; 🕑 Mar-Nov; ⊠) Has a kid's playground and front garden; the 10 rooms are spotless and there is a good restaurant.

Molnár Panzió (☎ 498 363; www.molnarpanzio.hu; Széchenyi tér 18/a; half-board per person 4900Ft) An attractive *pension* next door to the Atrium Panzió and five minutes' walk to the lake, with a dozen homey rooms.

Muskátli (☎ 498 283; www.orfumuskatli.hu; Széchenyi tér 13; mains 1300-2000Ft) Flower-bedecked restaurant near the lake has a museumlike courtyard loaded with traditional cookware and stoves.

Abaliget

☎ 72 / pop 650

Abaliget, about 3km north of Orfű and accessible by bus or on foot via a trail up and over the hill behind Panoráma Camping, is quieter and more relaxed but not as attractive; seek information from **Abaliget** (www.abaliget.hu). The main attraction here is **Abaliget Cave** (Abaligeti-barlang; ☎ 498 766, 06 30 377 3387; adult/student & child 800/600Ft; 🕑 9am-6pm mid-Mar–mid-Oct, 10am-3pm mid-Oct–mid-Mar), which, at 1.3km, is the longest cave open to the public in Southern Transdanubia. However, only 460m of the caves can be visited on a 50-minute tour. Dress warmly; the temperature is 10°C to 12°C and the humidity a very damp 97%. Next door, the new **Bat Museum** (Denevérmúzeum; ☎ 498 684, 06 30 377 3426; adult/student & child 300/200Ft; 🕑 9am-6pm mid-Mar–mid-Oct, 10am-3pm mid-Oct–mid-Mar) looks at the order Chiroptera in-depth both home and abroad.

Combined tickets with the cave are available for 950/700Ft.

There are some private rooms and *pensions* along Kossuth Lajos utca, the main drag, or try **Barlang Camping Abaliget** (☎ 498 730; camp sites per adult/child/tent 1000/500/950Ft, bungalows 3600-8100Ft) on the town's tiny lake. The camping ground is OK, but the bungalows will only do at a pinch.

The last bus for Pécs leaves at 8.15pm daily from outside the cave and museum.

KAPOSVÁR

☎ 82 / pop 66, 560

Situated in the Zselic foothills along the valley of the Kapos River, Kaposvár is, at its core, an attractive city. But don't come to 'Kapos Castle' looking for a fortress like the one at Siklós or Szigetvár; the Turks and then the Habsburgs dispatched that long ago. Instead, visit Kaposvár for its art – the city is associated with three great painters: the postimpressionists József Rippl-Rónai and János Vaszary, as well as Aurél Bernáth and Ferenc Martyn – and the Gergely Csiky Theatre, among the best in provincial Hungary.

Orientation

The train and bus stations are more or less opposite one another along busy Budai Nagy Antal utca, south of the city centre. From here, walk up Teleki utca to Kossuth tér and Fő utca, a lovely pedestrian street where most of the action is.

Information

City website (www.kaposvar.hu) Useful multilingual site on the city.

Intercafé Internet (☎ 313 223; Dózsa György utca 18; per hr 300Ft; ⌚ 7.30am-8pm Mon-Fri) Keeps bankers' hours.

Main post office (Bajcsy-Zsilinszky utca 15) Just west of Széchenyi tér.

OTP bank (Széchenyi tér 2) Has several ATMs.

Tourinform (☎ 512 921; www.tourinformkaposvar.hu; Fő utca 8; ⌚ 9am-7pm daily mid-Jun–mid-Sep, 9am-5pm Mon-Fri, 9am-2pm Sat mid-Sep–mid-Jun) Free internet access.

Sights

In among the pretty, pastel-coloured buildings lining Fő utca is the former county hall (1820) at No 10, which now houses the

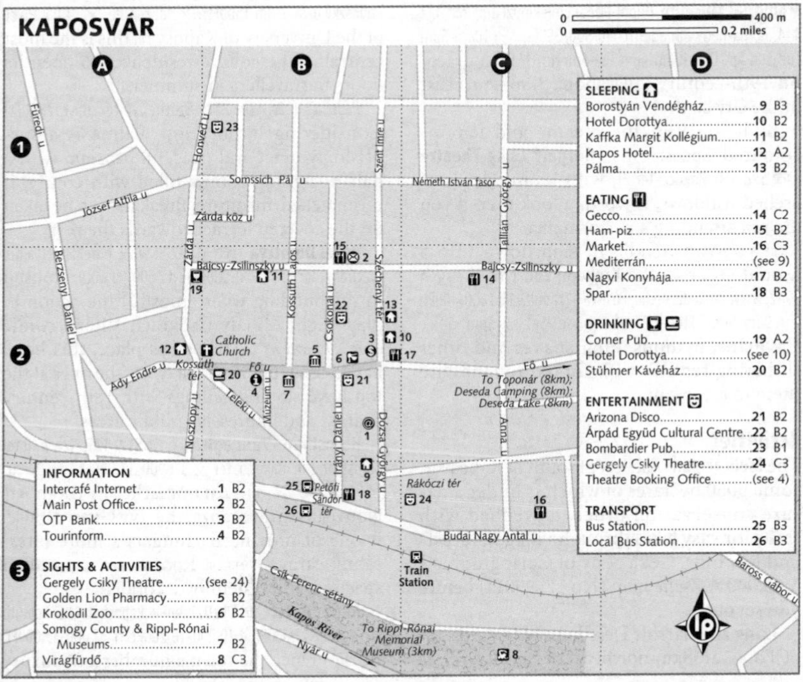

Somogy County Museum and the **Rippl-Rónai Museum** (☎ 314 114; www.smmi.hu; adult/child 400/200Ft; ⏲ 10am-4pm Tue-Sun Apr-Oct, 10am-3pm Tue-Sun Nov-Mar). In the first, you'll find a large ethnographical collection and a gallery of contemporary art on the ground floor. There is a grand collection of paintings on the 1st floor, which include works by Vaszary, Bernáth and Béla Kádár.

The folk collection is noteworthy for its wood and horn carvings (at which the swineherds of Somogy County excelled); examples of famous *kékfestő* (indigo-dyed cotton fabrics); an exhibition on the county's infamous outlaws (including the paprika-tempered 'Horseshoe Steve'); and costumes of the Croatian minority, who dressed and decorated their houses in white fabric during mourning periods as the Chinese do. The top floor is full of paintings by Ödön Rippl-Rónai, the brother of Kaposvár's most celebrated – and arguably Hungary's best – painter, József Rippl-Rónai (1861–1927).

József Rippl-Rónai was born at Fő utca 19, above the lovely **Golden Lion Pharmacy** (Aranyoroszlán Patika; ⏲ 7.30am-6pm Mon-Fri), built in 1774. Most of his work is exhibited in the **Rippl-Rónai Memorial Museum** (Rippl-Rónai Emlékmúzeum; ☎ 422 144; Róma-hegy 88; adult/child 500/250Ft; ⏲ 10am-6pm Tue-Sun Apr-Oct, 10am-4pm Tue-Sun Nov-Mar), a graceful 19th-century villa about 3km southeast of the city centre.

Built in 1911, the cream- and lemon-coloured Secessionist **Gergely Csiky Theatre** (☎ 528 450; Rákóczi tér 2), with its hundreds of arched windows, is worth a look even if you are not attending a performance.

If you can handle it, step down into a humid cellar to the **Krokodil Zoo** (☎ 06 30 264 3942; www.krokodilzoo.hu; Fő utca 31; adult/child 600/400Ft; ⏲ 9am-5pm Mon-Fri, 9am-noon Sat, 2-5pm Sun). Caymans, pythons, king snakes and other slithering reptiles with forked tongues are there to greet you.

Activities

The **Zselic region** (Zselicség) south of Kaposvár, some 9050 hectares of which is under a nature conservation order, is webbed with trails for easy **hikes** through villages, forests and low hills. Get a copy of Cartographia's 1:60,000 *A Zselic* map (No 17; 990Ft) before you set out.

Long and narrow Deseda Lake (Deseda-tó) at Toponár, 8km northeast of the city, offers **cycling**, **swimming**, other **water sports** and **tennis**, as well as some rare species of waterfowl.

In town, the new **Virágfürdő** (Flower Baths; ☎ 321 044; www.viragfurdo.com; Csík Ferenc sétány) water park has flash **outdoor pools** (adult/child 2100/1450Ft; ⏲ 9am-8pm daily mid-May–Aug) and traditional **thermal baths** (adult/child Tue-Fri 440/250Ft, Sat & Sun 680/310Ft; ⏲ 9am-7pm Tue-Sun year-round).

Festivals & Events

Kaposvár's big event is the **City of Painters Festival** (Festők Városa Hangulatfesztivál) at the beginning of June, which plays and preys on the town's nickname with dozens of graphic art exhibitions. The **Kaposvár Spring Festival** (Kaposvári Tavaszi Fesztivál) of performing arts takes place in late March and early April. **Kapos Autumn Days** (Kaposi Őszi Napok) in October celebrates the Zselic grape vintage. Tourinform's website (see p305) has more information.

Sleeping

Tourinform has information on **private rooms** (per person 2500-3000Ft), but it won't help you with making bookings.

Kaffka Margit Kollégium (☎ 502 599; Bajcsy-Zsilinszky utca 6; dm 1500Ft; ⏲ Jul & Aug; ⊠ 💻) Part of the University of Kaposvár, this is the most central of the college residences to open its doors to travellers in summer.

Pálma (☎ 420 227; Széchenyi tér 6; r 7800Ft) Considering its location, Pálma is a surprisingly quiet and peaceful *pension*, with a half-dozen big rooms filled with comfy, if mismatched, furniture. Breakfast can be taken on the covered terrace towards the rear.

Hotel Dorottya (☎ 418 055; www.hoteldorottya.hu; Széchenyi tér 8; s 5600-9800Ft, d 6600-13,600) Housed in the building where most of the action in playwright Mihály Csokonai Vitéz's comic epic *Dorottya* (1804) takes place, this hotel has 25 cosy rooms with a twist (the ones at the top have sloping ceilings with 18th-century beams) and impressive public areas.

Borostyán Vendégház (☎ 512 475; www.hotelborostyan.hu; Rákóczi tér 3; s 6900-11,900Ft, d 10,900-14,900Ft; ⊠ ❄ 💻) An upmarket 15-room Art Nouveau extravaganza, the 'Ivy Guest House' is one of provincial Hungary's more interesting caravanserais. Rooms are more than spacious and tastefully decorated.

Kapos Hotel (☎ 316 022; www.kaposhotel.hu; Kossuth tér; s 7500-12,000Ft, d 10,200-16,200Ft, tr 17,000-19,000Ft; ⊠ 💻) Once the town's number-one luxury establishment, the Kapos today is a fairly mundane 79-room block with little character. It is, however, very central and the staff are more than happy to see you.

Eating

Ham-piz (☎ 312 029; Bajcsy-Zsilinszky utca 13; burgers & pizzas 290-890Ft) Next to the main post office, this place attracts groups of gabbling students and those looking for a cheap bite to eat, with quick service and filling fast food with a Hungarian spin on it.

Nagyi Konyhája (☎ 315 433; Fő utca 35; set lunch from 530Ft; 7am-8pm Mon-Fri, 10am-4pm Sat) 'Granny's Kitchen' is like a black hole for city workers; it seems impossible for most to wander past without being sucked in by its cheap, quick and good set lunches.

Mediterrán (☎ 420 320; Rákóczi tér 3; mains 1000-1640Ft; 11am-11pm Mon-Sat) Below the Borostyán Vendégház, this colourful restaurant-cafe has a quiet courtyard and serves some decent 'Mediterranean' dishes, though it's really a tarted-up pizzeria. Pasta dishes are 600Ft to 1140Ft.

Gecco (☎ 312 993; Bajcsy-Zsilinszky utca 54; entrées 630-1760Ft, mains 1030-2020Ft) A self-proclaimed 'South American restaurant' (pedants us, we know Mexico is in *North* America), this place serves mostly toned-down dishes from 'south of the border' (nachos, fajitas etc), with the occasional attempt at a journey further south still, with things like ceviche (lemon-marinated fish salad) from Peru.

The fruit and vegetable **market** (5am-noon or 3pm Tue-Sun) is just east of Rákóczi tér. There's a large **Spar** (cnr Budai Nagy Antal utca & Irány Dániel utca; 6.30am-8pm Mon-Fri, to 5pm Sat, 8am-1pm Sun) supermarket a few steps east of the bus station.

Drinking

Stühmer Kávéház (☎ 06 30 281 8333; Fő utca 4; 7am-10pm) Fő utca's anchor tenant, this lovely cafe dating back to 1868 is a riot of *fin-de-siècle* greens and golds, Viennese-style Sachertorte and bitter espresso.

Corner Pub (☎ 526 326; Bajcsy-Zsilinszky utca 2; 10am-11pm Mon-Thu, to midnight Fri, 11am-11pm Sat & Sun) The Corner moonlights as an upmarket restaurant, but we come to this conveniently located venue with the large terrace to get wasted.

Hotel Dorottya (☎ 418 055; www.hoteldorottya.hu; Széchenyi tér 8; 8am-9pm) The drinks bar at this cosy hotel (opposite) does not exactly keep generous hours, but it's a positive delight and a step back at least two centuries.

Entertainment

Árpád Együd Cultural Centre (☎ 512 228; Csokonai utca 1) Has information on cultural events in Kaposvár, especially on festivals and events, as does the free biweekly magazine *Kapos Est* available at hotels, restaurants and bars everywhere.

Gergely Csiky Theatre (☎ 528 450; Rákóczi tér 2; tickets 300-4400Ft) At the forefront of Hungarian artistic innovation in the 1970s, this is a masterpiece of Art Nouveau/Secessionist architecture but needs a lick of paint and some TLC to keep it going. The **theatre booking office** (☎ 511 207; Fő utca 8; 9am-5pm Mon-Fri, to 2pm Sat) is at Tourinform.

Kaposvár has two central clubs that still pull in the punters (though they both close for much of the summer): the basement **Arizona Disco** (☎ 315 732; Fő utca 14), in the heart of town, and the **Bombardier Pub** (☎ 423 721; www.bombadierpub.hu; Honvéd utca 8), northwest of the city centre.

Getting There & Away

BUS

At least a dozen buses daily go to Pécs (1050Ft, 1½ hours, 65km). Other destinations include Hévíz (1500Ft, two hours, 94km, two daily), Nagykanizsa (1200Ft, 1¾ hours, 77km, two to six daily), Szekszárd (1770Ft, 2½ hours, 101km, one or two daily), Szigetvár (675Ft, 1¼ hours, 41km, two to four daily), Szombathely (2780Ft, 3½ hours, 188km, three daily) and Zalaegerszeg (2040Ft, 2½ hours, 127km, four daily).

TRAIN

You can reach Kaposvár by train from both the eastern (Siófok) and western (Fonyód) ends of Lake Balaton's southern shore. Another line links Kaposvár with Budapest (2780Ft to 3300Ft, 3½ hours, 195km) via Dombóvár to the northeast and, to the west, with Gyékényes (1050Ft, 1¾ hours, 70km) on the border with Croatia.

Getting Around

For the Deseda Lake at Toponár catch bus 8 or 18 from the local bus station opposite the intercity one. Bus 15 is good for the Rippl-Rónai Memorial Museum in Róma-hegy.

Local taxis are available by calling ☎ 555 555.

AROUND KAPOSVÁR

Szenna

☎82 / pop 760

This village 9km southwest of Kaposvár contains the smallest but one of the best *skanzen* in the country, the **Open-Air Ethnographical Collection** (Szabadtéri Néprajzi Gyűtemény; ☎484 223; Rákóczi utca 2; adult/student & child 500/250Ft; 🕓10am-6pm Tue-Sun Apr-Oct, to 4pm Tue-Sun Nov-Mar). What makes it unique is that its centrepiece, the large 18th-century Calvinist church (1815), with its 'crowned' pulpit, coffered and painted ceiling, loft and pews, still functions as a house of worship for villagers.

Half a dozen *porták* (farmhouses with outbuildings) from central Somogy County and the Zselic region surround the 'folk baroque' church – as they would in a real village – and the caretaker will point out the most interesting details: the 'smoke' kitchens with stable doors; the woven-wall construction of the stables and barns; lumps of sugar suspended from the ceiling to soothe irritable children (bread soaked in the Hungarian fruit brandy *pálinka* was given to those particularly pesky); a coop atop the pigsty to keep the chickens warm in winter; and ingenious wooden locks 'so secure that even God couldn't get in'.

Buses to/from Kaposvár (200Ft, 20 minutes, 9km, up to a dozen daily) depart from/arrive at the main bus stop opposite the *skanzen*.

SZIGETVÁR

☎73 / pop 11,200

Szigetvár, a quiet town 40km south of Kaposvár, contains the remains of one of Hungary's most celebrated castles as well as a handful of important Turkish-era monuments to gawp at. And when it's time to cool off, the town's popular thermal spa has reopened after a long hiatus and is now a flashy water park.

Szigetvár began life as a Celtic settlement before the Romans moved in and renamed it Limosa. The strategic importance of the town was recognised early on, and in 1420 a fortress was built on a small island – Szigetvár means 'island castle' – in the marshy areas of the Almás Stream. But Szigetvár would be indistinguishable today from other Southern Transdanubian towns had the events of September 1566 not taken place (see the boxed text, p310).

Orientation

The bus and train stations are close to one another, a short distance south of the town centre at the end of Rákóczi utca. To reach the town centre follow this road north into lovely Zrínyi tér. Vár utca on the northern side of the square leads to the castle.

Information

Main post office (József Attila utca 27-31)

OTP bank (Vár utca 4) Has an ATM.

Szigetvár Youth Information Office (Szigetvári Ifjúsági Információs Iroda; ☎414 715; József Attila utca 9; per hr adult/student 100/50Ft; 🕓9am-5pm Mon-Fri, to 2pm Sat) Internet access in the Vigadó building.

Sights

ZRÍNYI CASTLE

Out hero Miklós Zrínyi probably wouldn't recognise his four-cornered **castle** (☎311 442; Vár utca; adult/child 600/400Ft; 🕓9am-5pm Tue-Sun May-Sep, 9am-3pm Tue-Sun Apr & Oct) that he so valiantly fought to save more than 400 years ago. The Turks strengthened the bastions and added buildings; the Hungarians rebuilt much of the castle again in the 18th century. Today there are only a few elements of historical interest left: walls from up to 6m thick and linked by four bastions; the square **Baroque Tower** crowning the southern wall; the 16th-century **Sultan Suleiman Mosque** (Szulejmán pasa dzsámija), with its truncated minaret; and, attached to it, a summer mansion built by Count Andrássy in 1930 now housing the **Castle Museum** (Vár Múzeum).

Naturally, the museum's exhibits focus on the siege and its key players: Zrínyi's praises are sung throughout and there's a detailed account of how Suleiman built a bridge over the Dráva River in 16 days to attack Szigetvár. The mock-ups of the battle, especially the Turkish encampment (complete with carpets), are quite effective. The mosque, completed in the year of the siege, contains an art gallery of little interest, but the arches, prayer niches and Arabic inscriptions on the walls are worth a look. At the entrance to the castle is a statue of the impish-looking **Sebestyén Tinódi**, the beloved 16th-century poet and wandering minstrel who was born in Szigetvár.

OTHER SIGHTS

The ogee windows (called 'donkey's back arches' in Hungarian) and hexagonal roof of the baroque **parish church** (plébaniatemplom; Zrínyi

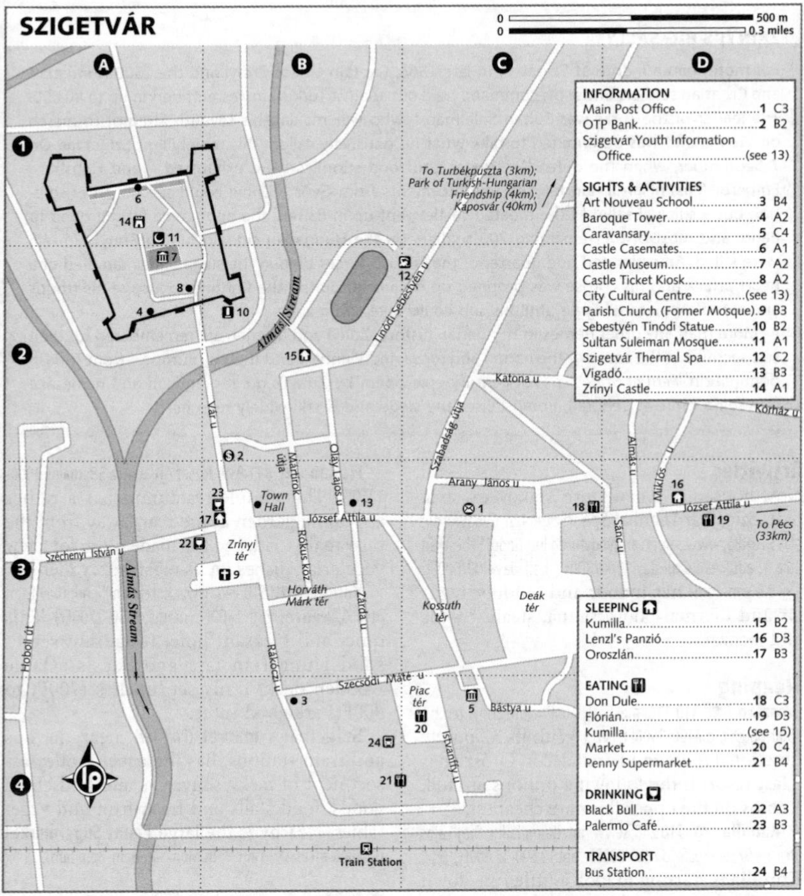

tér 9) are the only exterior signs that this was once the Pasha Ali Mosque, built in 1589. The altarpiece of the Crucifixion and the ceiling frescoes depicting the deaths of Zrínyi and Suleiman were painted by István Dorffmeister in 1788.

Not far from the bus station, the 16th-century **Caravansary** (Karavánszeráj; ☎ 06 30 561 2237; Bástya utca 3; adult/child 100/60Ft; ⏲ 10am-4pm Tue-Sun May–mid-Oct), also known as the Turkish House (Török-ház), contains an exhibit of reproduced Turkish miniatures.

Two other buildings in town worth a look include the splendid **Art Nouveau school** (Rákóczi utca 18), northwest of the bus station, which dates back to 1901, and the flamboyant **Vigadó** (József Attila utca 9) containing the City Cultural Centre (Városi Művelődési Ház). The building was designed by maverick architect Imre Makovecz in his unusual 'organic' style.

Some 4km north of Szigetvár on Rte 67, a Turkish-era battlefield is now the **Park of Turkish-Hungarian Friendship** (Török-Magyar barátság parkja; ⏲ dawn-dusk), with interesting tomblike memorials in the shape of domes and turbans, enormous bronzes of both Suleiman and Zrínyi and a hexagonal *şadirvan* (ablutions fountain) decorated with Iznik tiles.

The Catholic church at Turbékpuszta, about 3km northeast of Szigetvár, was originally built as a **tomb for Sultan Suleiman**. But according to local tradition, only the sultan's heart lies within; his son and successor, Selim II, had the body exhumed and returned to Turkey.

ZRÍNYI'S BIG SALLY

For more than a month at Szigetvár in late 1566, Captain Miklós Zrínyi and the 2500 Hungarian and Croatian soldiers under his command held out against Turkish forces numbering up to 80,000. The leader of the Turks was Sultan Suleiman I, who was making his seventh attempt to march on Vienna and was determined to take what he derisively called 'this molehill' of Szigetvár. On 7 September, when the defenders' water and food supplies were exhausted – and Habsburg Emperor Maximilian II had refused reinforcements from Győr – Zrínyi could see no other solution but a suicidal sally. As the moated castle went up in flames, the opponents fought hand to hand, and most of the remaining 200 soldiers on the Hungarian side, including Zrínyi himself, were killed. An estimated one-quarter of the Turkish forces died in the siege; Suleiman died of a heart attack and his corpse was propped up on a chair during the fighting to inspire his troops and avoid a power struggle until his son could take command.

More than any other heroes in Hungarian history, Zrínyi and his men are remembered for their self-sacrifice in the cause of the nation and for saving Vienna – and thereby Europe – from Turkish domination. *Peril at Sziget*, a 17th-century epic poem by Zrínyi's great-grandson and namesake (himself a brilliant general), immortalises the siege and is still widely read here.

Activities

Now housed in a new Imre Makovecz–style hall, **Szigetvár Thermal Spa** (Szigetvári Gyógyfürdő; ☎ 510 485; www.szigetvarigyogyfurdo.hu; Tinódi Sebestyén utca 1; adult/child all day 1300/800Ft, half-day 900/600Ft; 8.30am-7pm) has indoor and outdoor regular and thermal pools, sauna, steam rooms and Jacuzzi.

Sleeping

Oroszlán (☎ 310 116; mexbor@t-online.hu; Zrínyi tér 2; s 5800-6800Ft, d 7100-8500Ft;) With its 32 purely functional rooms and drab decor, Oroszlán is a last resort if the following options are full. Rooms on the upper floor are cheapest.

Kumilla (☎ 510 248; www.hotelkumilla.hu; Olay Lajos utca 6; s 5750-7800Ft, d 7800-8800Ft, apt 10,600-12,600Ft;) Kumilla is starting to look a little run-down but with its peaceful location backing onto a small stream, views of the castle and newly opened thermal spa, and 30 fan-cooled rooms and apartments, it's an excellent option.

Lenzl's Panzió (☎ 413 045; www.panzio-szigetvar.hu; József Attila utca 63; s 6000-6900Ft, d 7800-10,800Ft, tr 11,700-14,700Ft) This very friendly chaletlike *pension* has 17 small but attractive rooms (some with balcony), free parking and a restaurant. Again, climb the steps for the cheapest rooms.

Eating

Don Dule (☎ 311 450; József Attila utca 41; entrées 750-990Ft, mains 990-1390Ft; 1-10pm Sun-Thu, to 11pm Fri & Sat) This place serves not-often-seen *lepények* (pies stuffed with meat or cheese; 570Ft to 710Ft) as well as more ambitious mains, but it's still the best spot in town for pizza (500Ft to 1120Ft).

Flórián (☎ 311 939; József Attila utca 58; mains 1000-1850Ft) This simple restaurant has a rather appealing garden at the rear, away from the busy main road, and has made room for a few vegetarian dishes on its meat-heavy menu.

Kumilla (☎ 510 248; www.hotelkumilla.hu; Olay Lajos utca 6; entrées 750-1400Ft, mains 1050-2200Ft) This quiet and pleasant hotel restaurant serves solid Hungarian fare and boasts a large wooden deck. Daily set lunches (700Ft to 800Ft) are good value.

Szigetvár's **market** (Piac tér), near the bus and train stations, has the usual motley assortment of tacky souvenirs and household goods, food stalls and fresh fruit and vegetables. Nearby is the large **Penny Supermarket** (Rákóczi utca; 7am-9pm Mon-Sat, 8am-8pm Sun).

Drinking

Palermo Café (☎ 06 30 997 8428; Zrínyi tér 2; 9am-10pm Sun-Thu, 8am-2am Fri & Sat) Szigetvár is not known for its nightlife, but this is one very central place for a quiet drink during the evening. There are great views of the mosque church from the terrace.

Black Bull (☎ 312 218; Széchenyi István utca 2; 7am-10pm Mon-Sat, from 9am Sun) The Bull serves average pizza (990Ft to 1140Ft), but it's also a popular place for a beer.

Getting There & Away

BUS

Up to 10 buses depart daily for Pécs (600Ft, 50 minutes, 35km), and two to six run to Kaposvár (675Ft, 1¼ hours, 40km). There are also buses to Hévíz (2290Ft, 3½ hours,

156km, one daily), Nagykanizsa (1770Ft, 2½ hours, 107km, four to five daily), Sellye (525Ft, one hour, 31km, one to three daily) and Siklós (1200Ft, two hours, 72km, one to three daily).

TRAIN

Szigetvár is on the train line linking Pécs (525Ft, 45 minutes, 34km) and Nagykanizsa (1770Ft, 2¼ hours, 114km). The 84km-long stretch from Barcs to Nagykanizsa follows the course of the Dráva River and is very scenic, especially around Vízvár and Bélavár. If you're trying to leave Hungary from here, get off at Murakeresztúr (two stops before Nagykanizsa), through which trains pass en route to Zagreb and Ljubljana.

NAGYKANIZSA

☎93 / pop 51,300

Lying on a canal linking the Zala River to the north with the Mura River on the Croatian border, Nagykanizsa is not especially noted for its sights (nothing remains of its castle, which was blown to smithereens by the Habsburgs in the 18th century); the town is almost totally focused on light industry (eg light bulbs and furniture manufacture). But if you think of it as a convenient stepping stone, you'll be – quite literally – on the right track. From Nagykanizsa you can easily reach Western Transdanubia, both the northern and southern shores of Lake Balaton, Italy, Slovenia, Croatia and the beaches of the Adriatic.

History

Nagykanizsa hosted a succession of settlers, including Celts, Romans, Avars and Slavs, before the arrival of the Magyars. Early in the 14th century Charles Robert, the first Anjou king of Hungary, ceded the area to the Kanizsay family, who built a castle in the marshes of the canal west of today's city centre. The castle was fortified after the fall of Szigetvár but, despite the heroics of one Captain György Thury, it too was taken by the Turks and remained an important district seat for 90 years under their rule. Development didn't really come for a couple more centuries until the construction of the Budapest–Adriatic railway line through the city and the discovery of oil in the Zala fields to the west.

Orientation

To reach the city centre from the train station, walk north along Ady Endre utca for about 1.5km until you reach Fo utca, the main drag. The bus station is in the city centre on the west side of Erzsébet tér.

Information

Main post office (Ady Endre utca 10)
OTP bank (15 Deák Ferenc tér)
Tourinform (☎313 285; http://tourinform.nagykanizsa.hu; Csengery út 1-3; 🕑8.30am-5pm Mon-Fri, 9am-1pm Sat) Free internet access.

Sights & Activities

The **György Thury Museum** (☎314 596; Fő utca 5; adult/child 500/25Ft; 1-5pm Tue & Wed, 10am-5pm Thu-Sun) has a surprisingly interesting interactive exhibit called 'People, Roads & Connections' tracing the history of Nagykanizsa and southern Zala County. Absolutely nothing connected with wood, the woods and forestry is overlooked, with exhibits on everything from antique saws and charcoal-burning equipment to household utensils made of bark and exquisite hunting knives. The contemporary illustrations of Kanizsa Castle are fascinating, especially the idealised Turkish one from 1664 showing 14 minarets within the castle walls.

The neoclassical **synagogue** (Fő utca 6) built in a courtyard in 1810 is in poor condition, having most recently served as a storeroom for the Thury museum. Outside the western entrance a cenotaph remembers the 2700 Jews who were rounded up here in late April 1944 and deported to death camps in Germany. The condition of the **Jewish cemetery** (Ady Endre utca) opposite the train station is just as bad.

The interesting baroque building opposite the Centrál hotel is the so-called **Iron Man House** (Vasemberház; Erzsébet tér 1) dating from the mid-18th century. It is named after the suit of armour on the facade that once advertised an ironmonger's.

The Franciscan **Lower Town Church** (Alsóvárosi templom; Nagyváthy utca), just south of Fo utca, was begun in 1702 but not completed for another 100 years. It has ornate stuccowork, a rococo pulpit and a holy water font carved from the burial stone of the Turkish general Pasha Mustafa.

Even if you're not going to see a film, have a look at the **Apolló Cinema** (cnr Sugár út & Rozgonyi utca), formerly the Municipal Theatre, located within a small park. It's a unique example of

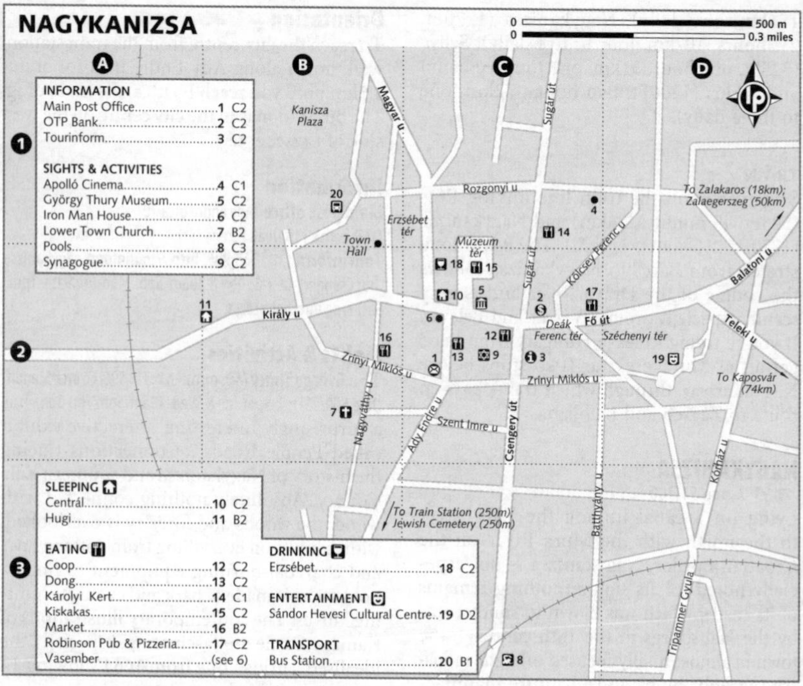

Art Nouveau and Hungarian folk architecture designed by István Medgyaszay in 1926. He also did the exquisite Petőfi Theatre (p225) in Veszprém.

There are **pools** (Csengery út 49; adult/child outdoor pools 500/270Ft, indoor pool 500/270Ft; outdoor pools 6am-7pm Jun-Aug, indoor pool 11am-8pm Mon, 6am-8pm Tue-Fri, 6am-7pm Fri, 9am-6pm Sat & Sun year-round), about 700m south of Tourinform. If you prefer your water thermal, head for the spa at **Zalakaros**, 18km to the northeast near the Little Balaton (Kis-Balaton). The Zalakaros spring, which gushes out of the ground at an incredible 92°C, was discovered by workers drilling for oil in the early 1960s, and now a half-dozen hotels surround it.

Sleeping

Hugi (/fax 336 100, 06 30 265 7120; Király utca 7; s/d/tr 5000/8500/13,800Ft;) Within easy walking distance west of the city centre is this solid guest house, with secure parking, large rooms and surprisingly little road noise considering its location on a main street.

Centrál (314 000; www.hotelcentral.hu; Erzsébet tér 23; s/d/tr 13,000/16,000/18,000Ft;) The Central, in a beautiful building erected in 1912, takes careful aim at the business market, making it somewhat overpriced for what is on offer. The three dozen rooms, however, are modern and quite comfortable. Wheelchair accessible.

Eating & Drinking

Robinson Pub & Pizzeria (310 519; Deák Ferenc tér 10; pizzas 450-1100Ft; 11am-midnight) A rather dark but fashionable place popular with Nagykanizsa's young bloods.

Károlyi Kert (310 487; Sugár út 5; pizzas 750-1300Ft) With its large terrace facing a peaceful park and the lovely Apolló Cinema, this place serves big pizzas in a relaxed atmosphere.

Dong (310 350; Ady Endre utca 5; entrées 200-720Ft, mains 900-1800Ft; 10am-10pm Mon-Sat) If you can't go on without that fix of rice and/or noodles, this Chinese eatery opposite the main post office will oblige.

Vasember (314 555; Erzsébet tér 1; entrées 350-990Ft, mains 770-2190Ft; 11am-10pm Mon-Thu, to 11pm Fri & Sat, to 8pm Sun) The 'Iron Man' cellar restaurant, in the central building of that name, offers consistently good Hungarian cuisine and steaks. Set lunch is 670Ft.

Kiskakas (☎ 321 600; Múzeum tér 6; entrées 880-1200Ft, mains 1050-2200Ft; 11am-11pm Mon-Sat, to 4pm Sun) Tucked away in a quiet courtyard/parking lot is the 'Little Rooster', an upmarket spot with a Hungarian menu and covered outdoor seating area.

Erzsébet (☎ 06 30 361 4831; Erzsébet tér 21; 7am-10pm Mon-Fri, 8am-10pm Sat, 8am-8pm Sun) This refined cafe-bar has street-side seating suitable for coffee and *rétes* (strudel), the house speciality, during the day in the warmer months and drinks at night.

The fruit and vegetable **market** (Nagyváthy utca) is just south of Király utca. There's a large **Coop** (cnr Fő utca & Csengery út; 6.15am-6pm Mon-Fri, to noon Sat, 7-10am Sun) supermarket just up from Tourinform.

Entertainment

Sándor Hevesi Cultural Centre (☎ 311 468; Széchenyi tér 5-9) The modern cultural centre just east of Tourinform distributes brochures and leaflets and can tell you what's on in Nagykanizsa. Information on the town is also listed in the free biweekly *Zalai Est*.

Getting There & Around

There's a bus running every 30 to 60 minutes to the Zalakaros spa (300Ft, 30 minutes, 18km). There are also hourly buses to Zalaegerszeg (900Ft, 1½ hours, 51km). Other services from Nagykanizsa include Keszthely (900Ft, 1½ hours, 52km, six daily), Kaposvár (1200Ft, two hours, 77km, four daily), Pécs (2290Ft, three hours, 142km, five daily) and Szombathely (1770Ft, 2½ hours, 114km, six daily).

From Nagykanizsa, a half-dozen daily trains go north to Szombathely (1770Ft, 2¼ hours, 102km) and three head south to Zagreb. Trains run direct to Budapest's Déli (via Kelenföld) and Keleti train stations (3230Ft, 4½ hours, 221km) and the southern shore resorts, but if you're headed for the western or northern sides (eg Keszthely or Balatonfüred), you must change at Balatonszentgyörgy.

Nagykanizsa is an easy city to get around on foot, but you may prefer to wait and ride. From the train station, bus 18 goes to the bus station and city centre.

Northern Uplands

Forested hiking trails, superb wine regions, traditional folk culture and castle ruins high in the hills beckon you to the Uplands. OK, so the highest peak here – Kékes in the Mátra Hills – is just more than a whopping 1000m. In a country as flat as a *palacsinta* (pancake), these foothills of the Carpathians soar above most of Hungary. Explore Bükk National Park on foot, with its minimal human habitation (but readily available accommodation). Or go caving in the largest stalactite system in Europe, the 25km-long Baradla-Domica caves in Aggtelek. After a few exertion-filled days, why not sip the eminently drinkable Bull's Blood red wine in the beautifully baroque town of Eger, or the sweet ambrosia-like white Aszú near the Tisza River in Tokaj.

But the five ranges of the Uplands – Cserhát, Mátra, Bükk, Aggtelek and Zemplén – are not only about nature and her products. This is a land where the folkways of the Palóc and Mátyo people hold strong in traditional villages like Hollókő and Mezőkövesd. As reminders of far too many battles won and lost, ageing castles and evocative ruins punctuate the landscape above numerous towns. History buffs will want to read up on the anti-Habsburg national uprising of the 18th century; many related events took place in this region. Outdoor recreation, culture, history – must be time to head for the hills.

HIGHLIGHTS

- Savouring **Eger** (p330), the unequalled jewel of the Uplands – a spa town of legendary wine, baroque architecture and easygoing temperament
- Taking a narrow-gauge forest railway trip up the mountain to the lakeside resort town of **Lillafüred** (p343)
- Attending a medieval festival at **Boldogkő Castle** (p347) ruins, perched high on a craggy cliff
- Hiking through the lush green forests of the Bükk Hills after visiting the famous white stallions in **Szilvásvárad** (p338)
- Staying overnight and listening to the silence in **Hollókő** (p319), a tiny village where folk art and tradition live on

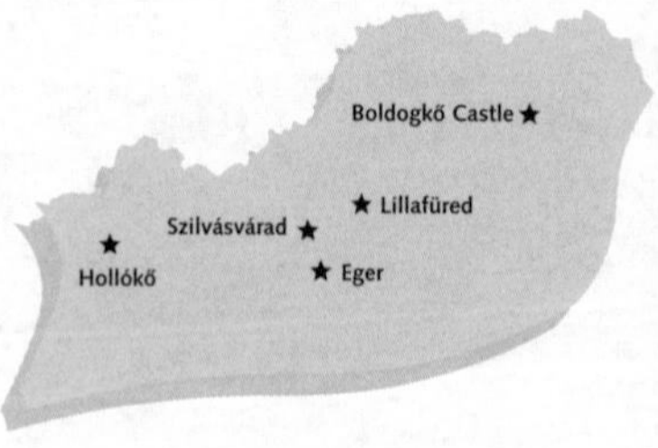

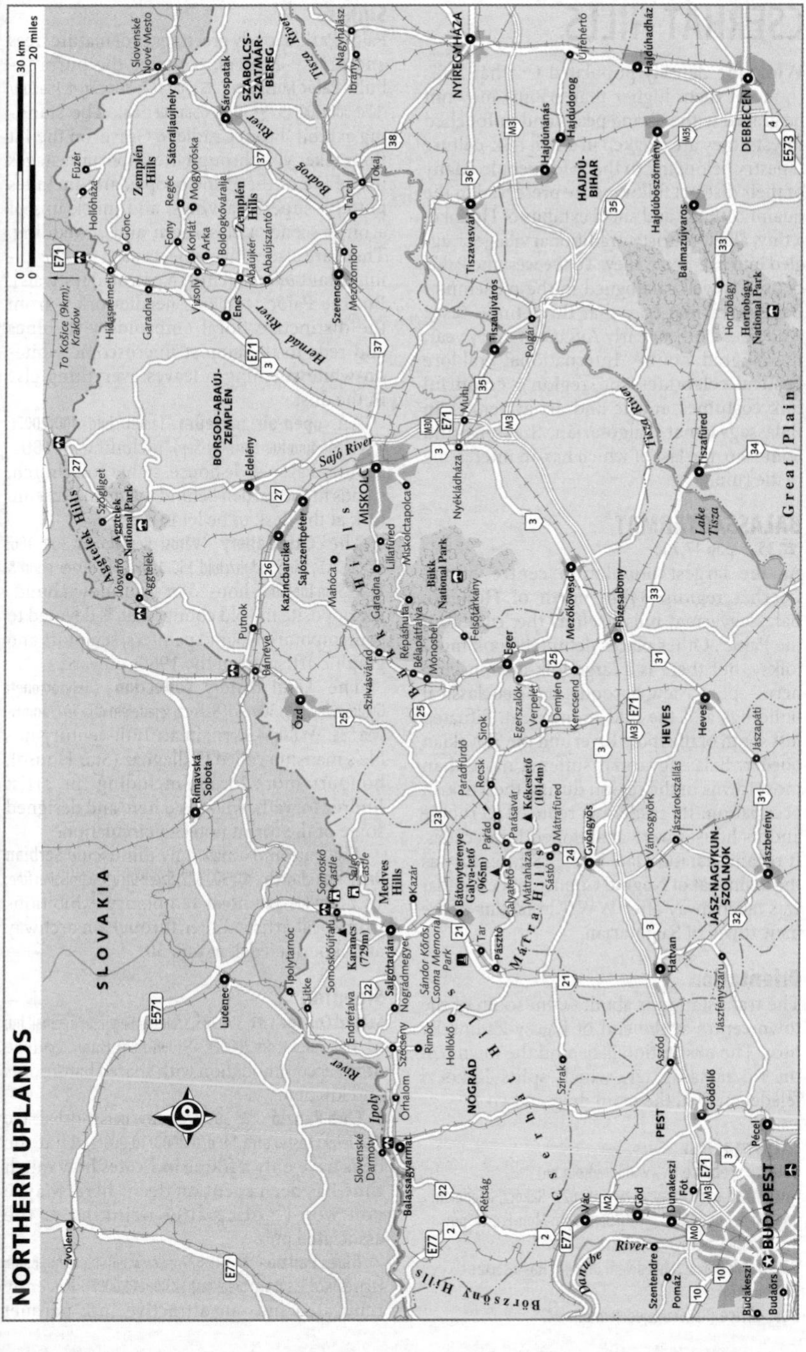
NORTHERN UPLANDS
0 30 km
0 20 miles
SLOVAKIA
Zvolen
Lučenec
Rimavská Sobota
Slovenské Nové Mesto
Slovenské Darmoty
To Košice (9km); Kraków
E77
E571
E71
Ipoly River
Balassagyarmat
Örhalom
Szécsény
Endrefalva
Litke
Ipolytarnóc
Rimóc
Hollókő
Nógrádmegyer
Salgótarján
Somoskőújfalu
Somoskő Castle
Salgó Castle
Karancs (729m)
Medves Hills
Kazár
Sándor Kőrösi Csoma Memorial Park
NÓGRÁD
Cserhát Hills
Rétság
Szirák
Pásztó
Tar
Bátonyterenye
Galya-tető (965m)
Galyatető
Mátraháza
Mátra Hills
Sástó
Mátrafüred
Parád
Parádfürdő
Parasávár
Recsk
Kékestető (1014m)
Gyöngyös
Sirok
Egerszalók
Verpelét
Demjén
Kerecsend
Eger
Ózd
Bánréve
Putnok
Szilvásvárad
Mónosbél
Bélapátfalva
Répáshuta
Bükk Hills
Bükk National Park
Felsőtárkány
Garadna
Mahóca
Lillafüred
Miskolctapolca
MISKOLC
Sajószentpéter
Kazincbarcika
Edelény
Aggtelek
Jósvafő
Aggtelek Hills
Aggtelek National Park
Szögliget
BORSOD-ABAÚJ-ZEMPLÉN
Sajó River
Nyékládháza
Muhi
Mezőkövesd
Füzesabony
HEVES
Heves
Jászapáti
Jászárokszállás
Vámosgyörk
JÁSZ-NAGYKUN-SZOLNOK
Jászberény
Jászfényszaru
Hatvan
Aszód
Gödöllő
PEST
Pécel
BUDAPEST
Budakeszi
Budaörs
Pomáz
Szentendre
Danube River
Vác
Göd
Dunakeszi
Fót
Börzsöny Hills
Hidasnémeti
Garadna
Hernád River
Encs
Vizsoly
Abaújkér
Abaújszántó
Boldogkőváralja
Arka
Korlát
Fony
Regéc
Mogyoróska
Gönc
Hollóháza
Füzér
Zemplén Hills
Sátoraljaújhely
Sárospatak
Bodrog River
SZABOLCS-SZATMÁR-BEREG
Szerencs
Mezőzombor
Tarcal
Tokaj
Tisza River
Ibrány
Nagyhalász
NYÍREGYHÁZA
Tiszavasvári
Tiszaújváros
Polgár
Hajdúnánás
Hajdúdorog
Újfehértó
Hajdúhadház
HAJDÚ-BIHAR
Hajdúböszörmény
Balmazújváros
Hortobágy
Hortobágy National Park
DEBRECEN
E573
Tiszafüred
Lake Tisza
Great Plain
M0
M2
M3
M30
M35

CSERHÁT HILLS

While the densely populated Cserhát Hills (none of them higher than 650m) may not be graced with soaring peaks and untouched forests, they are cloaked in a rich folk-culture tapestry belonging to the Palóc people. Many of their distinct folkways are preserved in the quaint cottages and small exhibits of Hollókő, a tiny, albeit touristy, traditional village snuggled into a remote valley. To the west the Palóc culture is well catalogued in the museum at Balassagyarmat (say that three times fast). And in late July or early August of every year, the Nógrád County International Folklore Festival celebrates the region's colourful folk costumes, music and art at venues in Balassagyarmat, Salgótarján, Szécsény and Somoskő, the last of which has an interesting castle ruin.

BALASSAGYARMAT

☎ 35 / pop 17,700

As the largest population centre of the Cserhát region, 34km north of Hollókő, Balassagyarmat bills itself as the 'capital of the Palóc'. Other places definitely look more folksy, but there is a large folk-art museum here – plus a few baroque and neoclassical buildings and the odd monument. Situated just south of the Ipoly River and the Slovakian border, Balassagyarmat suffered more than most towns in the region during the Turkish occupation. Its castle was reduced to rubble and its houses were abandoned for decades. It regained stature late in the 18th century as the main seat of Nógrád County, but even that was taken away after WWII in favour of the 'new town' of Salgótarján.

Orientation

The train station is about 600m south of the town centre at the end of Bajcsy-Zsilinszky utca. The bus station is behind the town hall on Köztársaság tér, which splits Rákóczi fejedelem útja, the main drag, in two.

Information

County website (www.nogradtour.hu)

Imre Madách Library (☎ 300 622; Rákóczi fejedelem útja 50; per hr 100Ft; ⏰ 7.30am-7pm Mon-Fri, 1-5pm Sat) Internet access.

OTP bank (Rákóczi fejedelem útja 44) Has a secure 24-hour ATM.

Post office (Rákóczi fejedelem útja 24)

Sights

Palóc Park, a lovely green space of mature trees and grassy corners, contains the purpose-built **Palóc Museum** (☎ 300 168; Palóc liget 1; adult/child 600/300Ft; ⏰ 10am-6pm Tue-Sun). The standing exhibit 'From Cradle to Grave' on the 1st floor takes you through the important stages in the life of the Palóc people, and includes pottery, superb carvings, and mock-ups of a birth scene, a classroom and a wedding. There are also votive objects used for the all-important *búcsúk* (church patronal festivals). But the Palóc women's needlework – from the distinctive floral embroidery in blues and reds to the almost microscopic white-on-white stitching – leaves everything else in the dust.

An **open-air museum** (adult/child 400/200Ft; ⏰ 10am-4pm Tue-Sun May-Sep), including an 18th-century Palóc-style house, stable and church, stands in the garden behind the main museum (ask at the desk to be let in).

The **City Gallery** (Városi Képtár; ☎ 300 186; Köztársaság tér 5; adult/child 150/100Ft; ⏰ 10am-noon & 12.30-5pm Tue-Sun), housed in a run-down building opposite the old county hall, is devoted to contemporary Nógrád painters, sculptors and graphic artists from the 1960s onward.

The **Local History Collection** (Helytörténeti Gyűjtemény; ☎ 300 663; Rákóczi fejedelem útja 107; admission free; ⏰ 8am-4.30pm), in an 18th-century noble's mansion called Csillagház (Star House), honours more locals, including the artist Endre Horváth, who lived here and designed some of the forint notes in circulation.

The cute and amazingly minuscule **Serbian Orthodox church** (☎ 300 622; Szerb utca 5; admission free; ⏰ 2-6pm Tue-Sun) hosts temporary exhibitions from local artists. Enter through an archway at Rákóczi fejedelem útja 30.

Sleeping

Szalézi College (☎ 301 765; szalezikollegium@freemail.hu; Ady Endre utca 1; dm 2000Ft; ⏰ Jun-Aug) Basic college dorm accommodation with shared bathrooms and kitchen.

Club Panzió (☎ 301 824; www.gosser-club-panzio.hu; Teleki László utca 14; d/tr 8000/10,000Ft) That the beds have only a frame indicates how much time has been spent on decor here. Maybe you won't notice after drinking at the associated pub.

Blues Panzió (☎ 545 6776; www.euroblues.hu; Baltik Frigyes utca 3; s/d incl breakfast 12,000/14,000Ft) Recently renovated into an attractive inn; parquet

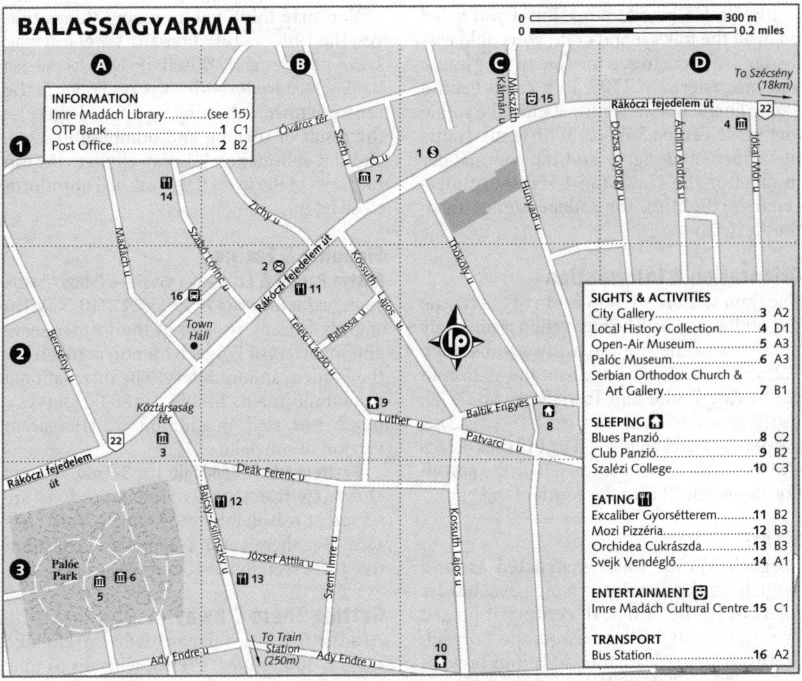

floors and hand-carved beds stand neat and tidy against fresh white walls. The restaurant is quite nice, too.

Eating

Orchidea Cukrászda (☎ 311 450; Bajcsy-Zsilinszky utca 12; ice cream 120Ft; ⌚ 9am-9pm) Enjoy excellent ice cream and cakes opposite Palóc Park.

Excaliber Gyorsétterem (☎ 313 6612; Rákóczi fejedelem útja 22; mains 350-550Ft; ⌚ 11am-2.30pm Mon-Fri) Every painted inch of this vaulted cellar depicts a surreal medieval fantasy world. And, oh yeah, it has self-serve stews and *főzelék* (creamed vegetables), too.

Mozi Pizzéria (☎ 315 405; Bajcsy-Zsilinszky utca 8; pizzas 600-1400Ft; ⌚ closed Sun) The wonderful smell of wood-fired pizzas here is a good indication of the taste to come. After your pie, you can catch a movie at the attached *mozi* (movie theatre).

Svejk Vendéglő (☎ 300 999; Szabó Lőrinc utca 16; mains 1000-1400Ft) Given such a Czech restaurant name, it's surprising that there are so few Slavic specialities on the mostly Hungarian menu. But you can guzzle genuine Pilsner and Budvar in the large covered beer garden.

Entertainment

Check out the free biweekly *Nógrádi Est* (www.est.hu) magazine, which covers Balassagyarmat, or stop at the **Imre Madách Cultural Centre** (☎ 300 622; Rákóczi fejedelem útja 50; ⌚ 8am-8pm Mon-Fri, 1-8pm Sat & Sun) to find out what's on.

Getting There & Away

Some 12 daily buses link Budapest (1200Ft, two hours, 78km) with Balassagyarmat. At least eight daily buses go to Szécsény (375Ft, 25 minutes, 21km), where you can change for Hollókő. Five connect with Salgótarján (900Ft, 1¼ hours, 52km).

Balassagyarmat can be reached twice a day by very slow train from Budapest's Keleti station (1280Ft, 2½ hours, 80km). Coming from elsewhere, you have to change at Aszód (300Ft, 25 minutes, 16km), on the Budapest–Nyíregyháza line.

SZÉCSÉNY

☎ **32 / pop 6600**

Bordering on comatose, Szécsény is justifiably given a miss by travellers headed for its tiny, but much better-known, neighbour to the southeast, Hollókő (16km). But if you're fed up of all the folk art and craft, you could easily day-trip here to see the fine manor house and monastery. In 1705, in a camp behind where Forgách Manor now stands, the ruling diet made Ferenc Rákóczi II of Transylvania the prince of Hungary and the commander in chief of the *kuruc* (anti-Habsburg mercenaries) fighting for independence from the Austrians.

Orientation & Information

The train station is 1.5km north of the centre, just off Rákóczi út. The bus station is on Király utca, east of the firewatch tower on Fő tér. Follow Rákóczi út north from the station to get to Ade Endre and **Tourinform** (☎ 370 777; szecseny@tourinform.hu; Ady Endre utca 4; ⏰ 8am-4.30pm Mon-Sat, closed Sat also Oct-May). The **OTP bank** (Rákóczi út 86) is northwest of the town hall; the **post office** (Dugonics utca 1) is to the south of the bank.

Sights

Forgách Manor was constructed around 1760, from the remains of a medieval border fortress. In the mid-19th century it passed into the hands of the aristocratic Forgách family, who made further additions to what is now **Ferenc Kubinyi Museum** (☎ 370 143; Ady Endre utca 7; adult/child 600/150Ft; ⏰ 10am-4pm Tue-Sun). On the ground floor a few rooms are done up much the way the females of the Forgách family would have liked to see them. Other exhibit subjects include Bronze Age relics, the history of area fortresses and Szécsény's role in the Rákóczi revolution. Displays trace castle history in the northeast **bastion** *(bástya)*, from where part of the original 16th-century wall is seen to the west and south.

Parts of the Gothic **Franciscan church and monastery** (☎ 370 076; Haynald Lajos utca 7-9; adult/child 300/150Ft; ⏰ by tour 9am-4pm Tue-Sat) date from the 14th century. In the church sanctuary (the oldest section) a guide will point out the 500-year-old carvings of saints, flowers and fruits on the vaulted ceiling. You can also see where Muslims carved out a *mihrab* (prayer niche) in the south wall during occupation. In the 17th-century baroque monastery you might see the monks' cells, library, dining hall and Gothic oratory, or the Rákóczi Room, where the newly appointed prince and military commander met with his war cabinet in 1705.

You may think you're seeing things but, yes, the 19th-century **firewatch tower** (tűztorony; Rákóczi út 86; adult/child 200/100Ft; ⏰ 10am-4pm Tue-Sun May-Sep, 10am-4pm Mon-Fri Oct-Apr), on Fő tér in the centre of town, is leaning (by three degrees) – the result of shelling and bombing in 1944, and clay subsidence. You can climb to the top for views of the town if you ask at Tourinform to be let in.

Sleeping & Eating

Bástya Panzió & Étterem (☎ 372 427; http://bastyapanzio.hu; Ady Endre utca 14; s/d 5500/8500Ft) Stay (in slightly frumpy rooms) at the former servants' quarters of Forgách Manor, across from the Franciscan monastery. The international restaurant (mains 1400Ft to 1800Ft) serves a number of salads in addition to a Hungarian version of souvlaki.

Gesztenyéskert Vendéglő (☎ 372 600; Rákóczi út 87; mains 850-1000Ft) Sturdy Hungarian faves are served at reasonable prices on a covered terrace. But there's not a namesake 'chestnut' tree to be seen in the concrete 'garden'.

Getting There & Away

At least five buses depart daily for Hollókő (300Ft, 30 minutes, 17km), with up to nine on Saturday. Direct buses also connect to Balassagyarmat (300Ft, 25 minutes, 18km, hourly), Salgótarján (525Ft, one hour, 34km, hourly) and Budapest (1770Ft, two hours, 103km, three daily).

Szécsény is on a minor train line linking it with Balassagyarmat (300Ft, 30 minutes, 19km) and Ipolytarnóc (675Ft, 1½ hours, 41km) nine times daily.

IPOLYTARNÓC

☎ 32 / pop 570

Squeezed between the Ipoly River and the Slovakian border, equidistant from Szécsény and Salgótarján (25km), is tiny Ipolytarnóc. It'd be inconsequential if it weren't for the unusual **Ipolytarnóc Nature Preserve** (☎ 454 113; adult/child 800/450Ft; ⏰ 9am-4pm Apr-Oct), gratuitously nicknamed 'ancient Pompeii' by all and sundry. You won't find any houses or people frozen in time, but you can see prehistoric footprints dating back 20 million years. It seems that around this time a volcano decided to blow its top, and the subsequent lava flows and ash fall sealed for all posterity animal tracks, subtropical trees and leaves, and even shark teeth. While many other such fossilised remains are located across the continent, Ipolytarnóc is particularly celebrated for its diversity of flora and fauna; there are an impressive 5000 leaf prints and 2000 animal footprints (including those of an ancient rhinoceros). It is widely believed that the area was once the site of a river flowing into a tropical sea.

To see the fossils, you have to take a tour, which departs 700m from the visitor centre every hour on the half-hour. A few imbedded imprints lie along the 1½-hour walk through the forest, but the most impressive tracks are under cover in a EU-funded building towards the end. Ancient bears and cats that left their mark are brought back in a high-tech movie on a giant screen above.

Back at the multi-million-forint visitor centre, opened in 2008, you can watch a feature-length 3-D film about prehistoric times for 900Ft. Numerous trails in the preserve are free for your walking.

At the entry to the preserve, **Christina Park Hotel** (☎ 454 066; www.cphotel.hu; Kossuth Lajos utca 56; r incl breakfast 18,900-24,000Ft; ⊠ ⁘), also shiny and new, is the only place to eat (mains 1200Ft to 1600Ft) or sleep. Burgundy accent walls, with understated leaf-print art, stand behind scrolled iron-and-wood beds. Natural tile mosaics cover bathroom walls – pretty stylish sleeps for the boonies.

Buses connect with Salgótarján (450Ft, 50 minutes, 26km) at least three times daily (more on weekdays). Ipolytarnóc is best reached from Szécsény (375Ft, 39 minutes, 22km) by the nine daily trains from there and Balassagyarmat (650Ft, 1¼ hours, 41km). The preserve is about 2km east of the village, on Kossuth Lajos utca.

HOLLÓKŐ

☎ 32 / pop 380

Hollókő (Raven Rock) is a love-or-hate kind of place. Some think the two-street village nestled in a valley 16km southeast of Szécsény deserves kudos for holding on to its traditional architecture and old customs. The village has burned to the ground many times since the 13th century (most recently in 1909), but the residents have always rebuilt their houses exactly to plan with wattle and daub – interwoven twigs plastered with clay and water. Others see the homogeneous houses as a staged tourist trap run by Budapest entrepreneurs (admittedly there are some crap souvenirs). Unesco agreed with the former view in 1987 when it put Hollókő on its World Heritage List of cultural sites – the first village in the world to receive such an honour.

What sets Hollókő apart is its restored 13th-century castle and the architecture of the so-called Old Village (Ófalu), where some 60 houses and outbuildings have been listed as historic monuments. Stay in the village after the day trippers have gone home and watch the sun set behind the old church steeple for full effect. Today you won't see women wearing the traditional Palóc dress – wide, red-and-blue, pleated and embroidered skirts, and ornate headpieces – except on important feast days, such as Easter, or during a festival.

Orientation

The bus stops on Kossuth Lajos utca at Dósza György utca; from there the old village is downhill. Follow József Attila utca up to the castle (or climb the stairs up from the lower village). You come through the New Village on the way here; if you have a car, it's easier to stay there since the Old Village streets are narrow, uneven cobblestone filled with sightseers.

Information

ATM (cnr József Attila & Sport utca)
Post office (Kossuth Lajos utca 72; 🕑 8am-4pm Mon-Fri)
Tourinform (☎ 579 011; holloko@tourinform.hu; Kossuth Lajos utca 68; 🕑 8am-6pm Mon-Fri, 10am-6pm Sat & Sun May-Sep, to 4pm Sep-May) At the time of writing a new info centre was under construction at Kossuth Lajos utca 44.
Town website (www.holloko.hu, in Hungarian)

Sights

The Old Village's folk architecture is the main attraction. Stroll down one cobblestone street and up the other, past whitewashed houses with carved wooden porches and red-tiled roofs. Few people live in the Old Village any more, and there's something of a fishbowl effect for those who do. (We know one resident who had a tourist just walk in on him in his underwear!) Many of the old buildings today contain crafts shops (see Shopping, p321).

VILLAGE CHURCH

A little wooden **church** (Kossuth Lajos utca), the focus of the village's spiritual and social life, is on the corner where Petőfi utca, the Old Village's 'other' street, branches off from Kossuth Lajos utca. Built as a granary in the 16th century

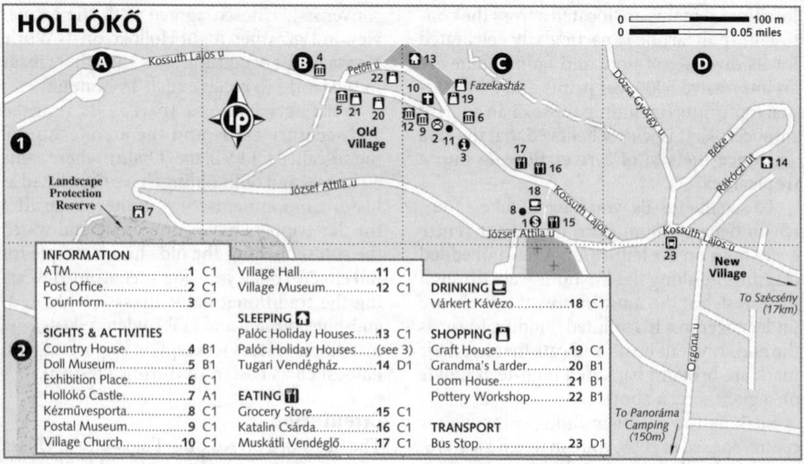

and sanctified in 1889, it is a fairly austere affair both inside and out. Like many churches throughout the country, a locked gate bars entry to the main nave but you can see in.

MUSEUMS

The five minuscule museums may not be worth their paltry admission fees except that they occupy traditional houses on Kossuth Lajos utca. The **Postal Museum** (Postamúzeum; ☎ 379 288; Kossuth Lajos utca 80; adult/child 250/150Ft; 🕑 10am-6pm Apr-Oct) is a branch of the one in Budapest. If you skip one, make this it. Next door, the **Village Museum** (Falumúzeum; ☎ 379 258; Kossuth Lajos utca 82; adult/child 250/150Ft; 🕑 10am-6pm Apr-Oct) is the usual three-room peasant house, with local folk pottery, painted furniture, embroidered pillows and, in the back yard, an interesting carved wine press dating from 1872. A nature exhibition at the **Country House** (Tájház; ☎ 06 30 529 6439; Kossuth Lajos utca 99-100; adult/child 250/150Ft; 🕑 10am-5pm daily Apr-Oct, Sat & Sun Nov-Mar) deals with the flora, fauna and human inhabitants of the Eastern Cserhát Landscape Protection Reserve, part of which surrounds the village.

The **Exhibition Place** (Kiállítóhely; ☎ 370 547; Kossuth Lajos utca 79; adult/child 250/150Ft; 🕑 10am-5pm Apr-Oct) spotlights the work of a local master woodcarver, Ference Kellemen. The **Doll Museum** (Babamúzeum; ☎ 379 088; Kossuth Lajos utca 96; adult/child 250/150Ft; 🕑 10am-5pm Apr-Oct) exhibits more than 200 porcelain dolls in traditional costumes from all across Hungary. Some are for sale.

HOLLÓKŐ CASTLE

At 365m on Szár-hegy (Stalk Hill), **Hollókő Castle** (Hollókői Vár; ☎ 06 30 968 1739; adult/child 600/300Ft; 🕑 10am-5.30pm Apr-Oct) commands a striking view of the surrounding hills. The fortress was built at the end of the 13th century and strengthened 200 years later. Captured by the Turks, it was not liberated until 1683 by the Polish king Jan Sobieski (r 1674–96). It was partially destroyed after the war of independence early in the 18th century but the shell is fairly intact. Climb up to the top of the pentagonal keep to look out across fields and forested hills without a trace of human occupation.

Activities

Learn to make straw roses, dipped candles or handmade cloth dolls the old-fashioned way at **Kézművesporta** (☎ 379 273; www.hollokotourism.hu; Kossuth Lajos utca 53; per craft 250-800Ft; 🕑 10am-4pm Wed-Fri, to 5pm Sat & Sun).

There are some gentle **walks** into the hills and valleys of the 140-hectare landscape protection reserve to the west and south of the castle. *A Cserhát*, the 1:60,000 map (No 8) from Cartographia, will help you plan your route.

Festivals & Events

Hollókő marks its calendar red for the annual **Easter Festival** in late March or April, the **Nógrád Folklore Festival** and **Palóc Homespun Festival** held at the open-air theatre in July, and the **Castle Days**, a touristy medieval tournament at the castle in late June, August and September.

Sleeping

There are quite a number of private rooms in the New Village.

Panoráma Camping (☎ 378 077; Orgona utca 31; camp sites per person/tent 800/800Ft, bungalows 6000Ft) Four-bed bungalows (shared facilities) and sites gather round the campfire area set up for outdoor feasts. There are good views from this camping ground above the village.

our pick **Tugari Vendégház** (☎ 379 176; www.holloko-tugarivendeghaz.hu; Rákóczí út 13; r 6000-8400Ft) Though technically on the edge of the New Village, this 70-year-old cottage is charmingly traditional. Red duvets and curtains add folksy contrast to pine beds and whitewashed walls. You can tell the cheerful owners Adam and Tünde worked in the London hospitality industry before coming home to start this guest house – they provide electric kettles in every room and will deliver a king's breakfast basket discreetly to your door for 1000Ft. Note that private baths may be down the hall; guests share a full kitchen.

Palóc Holiday Houses (Palóc üdülőházak; ☎ 579 010; holoközal@mail.datanet.hu; d 12,000Ft) Throughout the village, traditional houses that could easily double as folk museums are available for rent by the room. Some of the whitewashed cottages with dark beams have glorious antiques – hand-carved beds, hanging lanterns – and others are plainer. All have full kitchens and ceramic stoves for heating. Though the text is in Hungarian, you can see some of the pictures at www.holloko.hu – click under *'szállashelyek'* (accommodation) and *'Palóc üdülőházak'*.

Eating & Drinking

Remember, this is a day-tripping village so plan ahead; places close early. There's a small grocery store up on József Attila utca, opposite the footpath to Kossuth Lajos utca.

Katalin Csárda (☎ 06 30 499 0558; Kossuth Lajos utca 67-69; mains 1100-1800Ft; 🕑 11am-6pm Sun-Fri, to 8pm Sat) Come here for classic Hungarian fare served in a quaint village house. The family members who run the rustic Katalin are extra accommodating and will change dishes to suit your needs.

Muskátli Vendéglő (☎ 379 262; Kossuth Lajos utca 61; mains 1520-2000Ft; 🕑 11am-6pm Wed-Sun) The homemade dishes at Muskátli are the best in the village. Unfortunately the traditional cottage restaurant is often closed for group functions.

Várkert Kávézo (Kossuth Lajos utca 44; 🕑 10am-6pm) You can buy bottles of wine and snacks to go at this modern cafe in the future info centre building.

Shopping

While some of the folk crafts in village shops are genuine, there is no guarantee they are locally made or handcrafted – beware 'Made in China' stickers. Shops generally open from 10am to 5pm unless there is a busload of tourists expected.

Loom House (Szövőház; ☎ 379 273; Kossuth Lajos utca 94) Textiles here are all locally woven and embroidered in Palóc tradition. It's interesting to watch the women demonstrate how their enormous loom works (adult/child 250/150Ft), and to give it a go yourself.

Craft House (Míveshág; ☎ 380 016; Petőfi utca 4) This artisans' workshop is an excellent place to admire and buy Palóc folk dress and costumes.

Pottery Workshop (Fazekas műhely; ☎ 06 70 456 7116; Petőfi utca 7) Ceramic pots and plaques made and fired on-site.

Grandma's Larder (Nagymama Kamrája; Kossuth Lajos utca 86) Jams, jellies, wines and spices fill the shelves in this pantrylike shop.

THE GOOD PALÓC PEOPLE

The Palóc people are a distinct Hungarian group living in the fertile hills and valleys of the Cserhát Hills (Cserhátalja). Ethnologists are still debating whether they were a separate people who later mixed with the Magyars, or a Hungarian ethnic group that, through isolation and Slovakian influence, developed its own unique ways. What's certain is that the Palóc continue to speak a distinct dialect of Hungarian (unusual in a country where language differences are virtually nonexistent). Hollókő, with its uniformly traditional cottages, is undoubtedly Palóc central. Villages like **Rimóc** (www.rimoc.hu, in Hungarian) and **Kazar** may have more mixed architecture, but they preserve their traditions with small ethnographic exhibits and elaborate celebrations on church feast days and at festivals. There's a **Tourinform office** (☎ 32-341 360; www.kazar.hu, in Hungarian; Diófa út 13; 🕑 8am-4pm Mon-Fri) in Kazar. For more information on Palóc lands, check out www.palocut.hu.

Getting There & Away

One bus a day (3.15pm) heads directly from Budapest (1350Ft, 2¼ hours, 88km) to Hollókő. Otherwise, you have to change in Szécsény (241Ft, 30 minutes, 17km, at least five daily).

SALGÓTARJÁN

☎32 / pop 39,700

After an idyllic day in the rural villages of the Cserhát, arriving in the industrial city of Salgótarján, 25km east of Szécsény, is quite the contrast. This is a town where the communist's ideal of architecture lives on, and a place to see its square corners and strong lines first hand. Ravaged by fire in 1821 and by serious flooding 70 years later, Salgótarján can boast almost no buildings that predate last century. This is a possible base (ie it's the closest town) for exploring Salgó and Somoskő Castles, and the prehistoric Ipolytarnóc Nature Preserve (p318) isn't too far.

The surrounding Medves Hills have been mined for coal since the 19th century, and it's on this that Salgótarján's success is based. As in Miskolc, the communists found the coal miners and steelworkers here sympathetic to their cause, and were supported after WWII (though this didn't stop the dreaded ÁVH secret police from shooting over 100 citizens here during the 1956 Uprising). For its support, Salgótarján was made the county seat in 1950 and rebuilt throughout the 1960s.

A NOBLE NIGHT'S REST

So you always thought you were meant to be royalty (or is that just us?). Try the noble life for a night at the **Hotel Kasthély Szírak** (☎32-485 300; www.kastelyszirak.hu; Petőfi utca 26, Szírak; palace ste 41,000Ft). To get the full effect stay in one of the four suites in the gleaming white palace proper: enter through the antechamber, past the Louis XV chairs, to reach your monumental hand-carved tester canopy bed. Szírak, 33km south of Hollókő, is isolated. Your evening's entertainment will be a spa visit or a stroll around the hillside forested grounds. Just imagine all those poor peasants below.

Orientation

Because it has virtually swallowed the village of Somoskőújfalu some 10km to the north, Salgótarján feels like a large city. The train and bus stations are a short distance apart to the southwest of the city centre.

Information

OTP bank (Rákóczi út 12)

Post office (Fő tér 1) Located closer to the end of Klapka György tér, despite its official address.

Tourinform (☎512 315; salgotarjan@tourinform.hu; Fő tér 5; 8am-5pm Mon-Sat Jun-Aug, from 9am Sep-May) In the Attila József Cultural Centre. Helpful staff provides information on the surrounding area.

Sights & Activities

The **Mining Museum** (☎420 258; Zemlinszky Rezső utca 1; adult/child 600/300Ft; 9am-3pm Tue-Sun Apr-Sep, 10am-2pm Tue-Sun Oct-Mar), the city's only real sight, and not a great one at that, is a short walk southwest of the train and bus stations. Rooms are filled with geological maps and samples, old uniforms and a statue of St Barbara (the patron of miners) standing proudly next to communist banners calling for the nationalisation of the mines. Across the street you can wander through a 280m-long mine, 'worked' by performers (in unrealistically clean overalls).

Aside from the museum, Salgótarján's attractions amount to a plethora of communist architecture. The **Town Hall**, which closely resembles a Spam can, is a particular marvel. Salgótarján is also one of the few cities in Hungary that still has **socialist monuments** prominently displayed, in Fő tér. The monument to the west of the square depicts a supporter of Béla Kun's 1919 Republic of Councils running with a rifle in hand; the other, to the east, in front of the cultural centre, shows a couple of socialist youths looking rather guilty as they set doves free.

There's a small open-air **thermal bath** (☎430 991; Tóstrand, Kemping út; adult/child 900/700Ft; 8am-6pm May-Sep), 5km north of the centre off Rte 21.

Festivals & Events

Jazzy strains resound off Salgótarján's concrete facades during the **International Dixieland Festival** held in May.

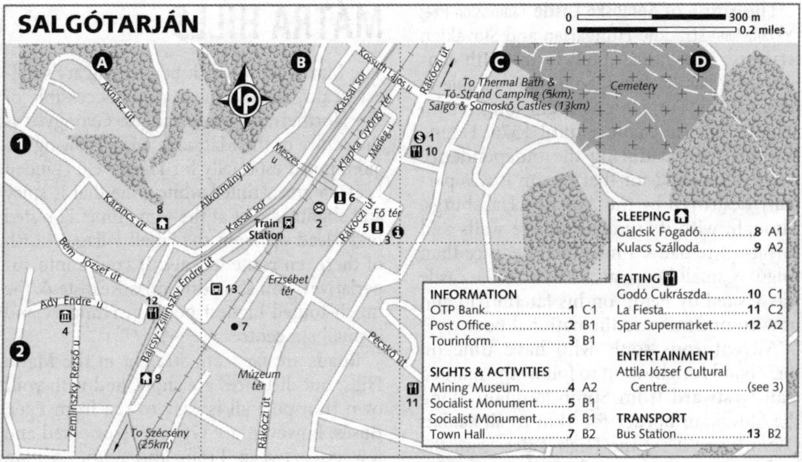

Sleeping & Eating

Galcsik Fogadó (☎ 422 660; www.galcsikhotel.hu; Alkotmány út 2; s/d incl breakfast 7900/10,900Ft;) Patterned bedspreads brighten rooms – as if the canary-yellow walls weren't enough. The breakfast room is a pleasant atrium; the Hungarian restaurant (mains 1100Ft to 1800Ft) has a terrace.

Godó Cukrászda (☎ 416 068; Rákóczi út 12; cakes 100-300Ft; 10am-9pm Mon-Sat, 9am-9pm Sun) Queue for cake and ice cream then plonk yourself down on the patio to enjoy a summer treat.

La Fiesta (☎ 512 622; Pécskő út 15; mains 900-1600Ft) Two eateries in one. The rustic, publike dining room menu has the expected paprika-based stews and chicken kiev. The more formal restaurant (dinner only) serves chateaubriand and pastas additionally.

More places to lay your head:

Tó-Strand Camping (☎ 430 168; Tóstrand, Kemping sor; camp sites per person/tent 800/750Ft, bungalows per person 1500Ft, motel r 4500Ft) Shaded tent sites, wood bungalows and a year-round motel near the thermal bath. Take bus 46 or 63 from Rákóczi út.

Kulacs Szálloda (☎ 511 739; pentasystem@freemail.hu; Bartók Béla út 14; s/d 9500/12,500Ft) The newest and nicest rooms in town, but it backs up to Rte 21.

Both the Galcsik and Kulacs lodging places have decent eateries. There's a large **Spar supermarket** (cnr Bajcsy-Zsilinszky Endre út & Bem József út).

Entertainment

Ask about concerts and such at Tourinform, or check directly with the **Attila József Cultural Centre** (☎ 310 503; Fő tér 5; 8am-7.45pm Mon-Fri, 10am-6pm Sat & Sun), Salgótarján's premier cultural venue.

Getting There & Away

Buses leave Salgótarján for Balassagyarmat (900Ft, one hour, 51km, five daily) and Szécsény (423Ft, one hour, 34km, hourly). Three to twelve buses a day head to Ipolytarnóc (450Ft, 45 minutes, 26km).

A train line links Salgótarján with Somoskőújfalu (200Ft, 10 minutes, 6km, 10 daily) and with Hatvan (900Ft, 1½ hours, 59km, 11 daily), on the main Budapest–Miskolc trunk line.

AROUND SALGÓTARJÁN

Salgó & Somoskő Castles

The freely accessible ruins of **Salgó Castle** lie 8km northeast of Salgótarján city centre. It was in the 13th century that the fortress was first constructed atop a basalt cone some 625m up in the Medves Hills. After Buda Castle fell to the Turks in 1541, Salgó served as an important border fortress until it, too, was taken. Gutted by fire, it fell into ruin after the Turks abandoned it in the late 16th century. The castle is best remembered for the visit made by Sándor Petőfi in 1845, which inspired him to write *Salgó,* one of his best-loved poems. Today you can make out the inner courtyard, tower and bastion from the ruins, and views of Somoskő and into Slovakia are excellent from this peaceful spot.

The ruins of **Somoskő Castle** (admission free; 7am-7pm) straddle Hungarian and Slovakian territory, 4km north. Built in the 14th century from basalt blocks, Somoskő was able to hold off the Turkish onslaught longer than Salgó Castle, not falling until 1576. Ferenc Rákóczi used it during the independence war in 1706, and for that reason it was partially destroyed by the Austrian Habsburgs. Though, with its semi-complete walls and turrets, it remains a more solid edifice than Salgó. A small house at the base of the castle was visited by Petőfi on his fateful trip and now commemorates the national poet.

Adventurous souls who have time on their hands might want to follow the marked trail westward from Somoskőújfalu along the Slovakian border for 4km to **Mt Karancs** (729m); you'll see the High Tátra from the lookout tower on top of what's known locally as the 'Palóc Olympus'. Cartographia's 1:60,000 *Karancs, Medves* map (No 11) covers these hills.

To get to Salgó Castle, catch bus 11/b (at least 12 daily) anywhere along Rákóczi út in Salgótarján and stay on until the terminus in Salgóbánya (35 minutes), the city's old mining district. Follow the path leading off Vár út to the west (about 20 minutes). Bus 11/a (at least eight daily) heads for the village of Somoskő (30 minutes); the castle is up Városoldal utca. Few buses run between the villages.

Buddhist Stupa

Travelling along Rte 21 towards Pásztó, some 22km south of Salgótarján, you might think you've driven through a black hole and arrived in Southeast Asia. There, on a hillside to the north of the village of **Tar**, is a full-sized Buddhist stupa (the largest of its kind in Europe) with a revolving prayer wheel containing sacred texts, its little chimes tinkling and coloured pennants fluttering in the gentle breeze. The Dalai Lama consecrated **Sándor Kőrösi Csoma Memorial Park** in 1992, in memory of the early-19th-century Hungarian Franciscan monk who became a Hungarian Bodhisattva (Buddhist saint). There's a gift shop selling Indian crafts and a **snack bar** (9am-7pm Tue-Sun Apr-Sep, 10am-4pm Tue-Sun Oct-Mar). Buses to Tar, a couple of kilometres to the south, and to Pásztó stop along the highway just below the stupa.

MÁTRA HILLS

The Mátra Hills, which boast Hungary's tallest peaks, are the most easily accessible of the Northern Uplands ranges. Gyöngyös is the centre of the Mátraalja wine-growing region, noted especially for Hárslevelű (Linden Leaf), a green-tinted white wine that is spicy and slightly sweet at the same time. Forested hikes lead off from the small villages north of there, en route to Eger. If you're into superlatives, you shouldn't miss Kékestető, the much-touted highest point in Hungary and a small ski centre.

Roads are far from straight in the Mátra Hills, but distances are short, and with your own transport all is easy to see from Eger. Buses, however, are Gyöngyös-oriented and few go between 11am and 2pm, so plan carefully. For general information on the Mátra Hills, see www.matrahegy.hu.

GYÖNGYÖS

☎ 37 / pop 33,600

A colourful, small city at the base of the Mátras, Gyöngyös (from the Hungarian word meaning 'pearl') is the gateway to the hills. With its museum, ancient churches and rich medieval library, it's easy to let the delights of the hills wait a short while. Or you may simply want to hang out on the pastel-shaded square and sample a glass or two of the region's fine wines.

Orientation

The bus station is on Koháry út, a 10-minute walk southeast of Fő tér, the main square. The main train station is on Vasút utca, near the eastern end of Kossuth Lajos utca. The narrow-gauge train departs from near the Mátra Museum at the start of Dobó István utca.

Information

Ibusz (☎ 311 861; www.ibusz.hu; Kossuth Lajos utca 6; 8am-5pm Mon-Fri) Books private rooms and apartments.

OTP bank (Fő tér 1)

Post office (Páter Kiss Szaléz utca 9-11) Accessed from Mátyás király utca.

Tourinform (☎ 311 155; gyongyos@tourinform.hu; Fő tér 10; 9am-6pm Mon-Fri, 10am-7pm Sat & Sun May-Sep, 9am-5pm Mon-Fri Oct-Apr) Opposite the Town Hall.

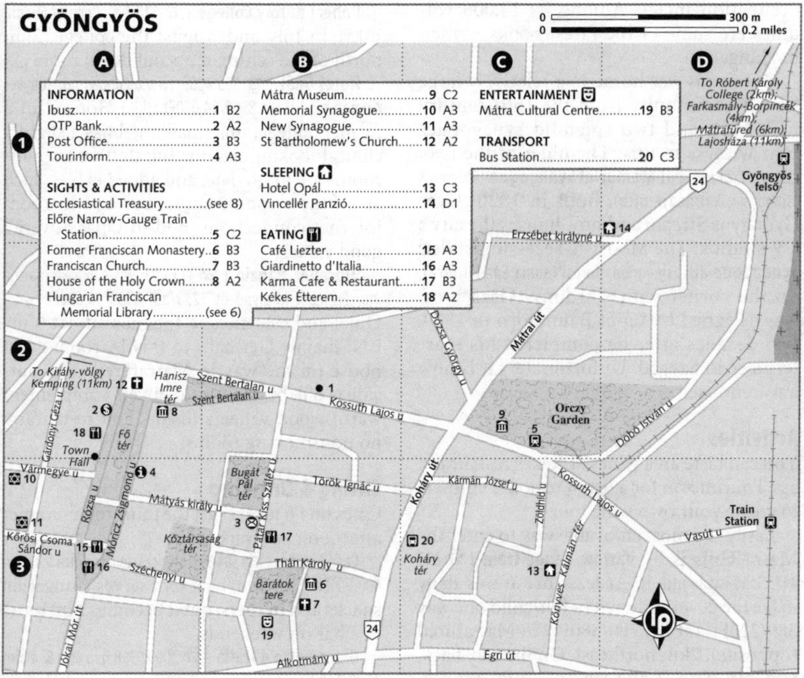

Sights

It's hard to believe the fine old Orczy manor house that now holds the **Mátra Museum** (☎ 311 447; www.matramuzeum.hu; Kossuth Lajos utca 40; adult/child 1000/500Ft; 9am-5pm Tue-Sun Apr-Oct, 10am-4pm Tue-Sun Nov-Mar) began as a family hunting lodge in the 1760s. In addition to the requisite natural history exhibits (including a mini mammoth fossil), there's the history of Gyöngyös in the 18th and 19th centuries, area ethnography and a room dedicated to the 1800 local Jewish Holocaust victims. Recently refurbished, the displays are all very well done, with English summaries. City lore has it that the wrought-iron railings enclosing the elaborate flower gardens were made from gun barrels taken during the *kuruc* uprising.

St Bartholomew's Church (Szent Bertalan út 1) is on the west side of Hanisz Imre tér. It was built in the 14th century and is the largest Gothic church in Hungary. You'd hardly know it though, with the baroque restoration (including an unusual upper-storey gallery inside) that was carried out 400 years later. Look for the twin Gothic-arch windows on each side, which are original. To the southeast the so-called **House of the Holy Crown** (Szent Korona-ház), which served as a safe house for St Stephen's Crown three times from 1806 to 1809 during the Napoleonic Wars, contains the city's **Ecclesiastical Treasury** (Egyházi Kincstár; ☎ 311 143; adult/child 400/200Ft; 10am-noon & 2-5pm Tue-Sun), a rich collection of liturgical objects and church plate.

The **Franciscan church** (Barátok tere 1) was built around the same time as St Bartholomew's but it, too, has undergone some major changes, with the light frescoes and baroque tower added in the 18th century. The one-nave basic Gothic form was retained. The church's most celebrated occupant – well, second-most famous to the faithful – is János Vak (Blind) Bottyán, a heroic but sight-challenged commander who served under Ferenc Rákóczi II during the war of independence. The former **Franciscan monastery** (built 1730), which is attached to the church, contains the **Hungarian Franciscan Memorial Library** (Magyar Ferencesek Műemlék Könyvtára; ☎ 311 361; Barátok tere 2; admission free; 2-6pm Tue-Fri), the only historical archive in Hungary to have survived the Turkish occupation intact. Among its 14,000 volumes are some of the rarest books written in Hungarian.

Gyöngyös was home to a relatively large Jewish community from the 15th century to WWII, and two splendid synagogues bear witness to this. The older of the two, the neoclassical **Memorial Synagogue** (Műemlék zsinagóga; Vármegye utca), built in 1820, faces Gyöngyös Stream and now houses the city's TV studios. The Moorish-Secessionist **New Synagogue** (Új zsinagóga; Kőrösi Csoma Sándor utca), on the corner with Gárdonyi Géza utca, was designed by Lipót Baumhorn in 1930, two decades after he completed his masterpiece in Szeged. Unfortunately it is now a warehouse.

Activities

You can taste area wines at Kékes restaurant; ask Tourinform for a list of regional vintners to create your own wine tour.

Easily the most enjoyable way to enter the Mátra Hills is by **narrow-gauge train** (☎ 312 447; Dobó István utca 1). At least five trains daily make the 20-minute run (adult/child one way 380/220Ft, return 700/380Ft) to Mátrafüred (opposite), 7km northeast. On the way back, you can get off at Farkasmály-Borpincék, where there's a row of wine cellars, and then jump onto any bus coming down Rte 24 to return the 4km to Gyöngyös.

A second train chugs along the 11km (40 minutes) to Lajosháza twice a day from May through September. The slow ride gives you a good feel for what's on offer further into the hills, but the terminus offers no real destination beyond being a trekking trailhead. For example, the **yellow square trail** leads 4.4km east along the Nagy-völgy (Big Valley) past a series of water catchments and down into Mátraháza (p328). Check out www.matrahegy.hu for more suggestions.

Sleeping

For such a pretty town, there's a surprising dearth of accommodation here, but Mátrafüred (opposite) is only 8km north.

Király-völgy Kemping (☎ 364 185; www.kiralyvolgykemping.hu; Táncsics Mihály út 40; camp sites per person/tent 700/800Ft; ⏲ May-Sep) A leafy camping ground on the southern edge of the hills, Király-völgy has two dozen sites and its very own babbling brook. Take the bus 11km west to Gyöngyöspata.

Róbert Károly College (☎ 518 100; Bene út 69; dm 2000Ft) In July and August the college, 2km north of the centre, rents out dorm rooms.

Hotel Opál (☎ 505 400; www.opalhotel.hu; Könyves Kálmán tér 12; s/d 8500/14,000Ft; 💻) Housed in a former college, this small hotel has a slightly clinical-looking exterior. But staff are friendly, rooms are up to date, and added extras, such as a fitness room, sauna, bar and in-room internet connections, add to Opál's overall good value.

Vincellér Panzió (☎ 311 691; www.vincellerpanzio.hu; Erzsébet királyné út 22; r/apt 8900/14,500Ft; 🅿) Quiet and closeness to the hills attract tourists (mainly German) to this 14-room guest house on the way to Mátrafüred. The outside is old, but colourful duvets complement warm wood veneers inside. Full restaurant; no nonsmoking rooms.

Eating & Drinking

Cafes on Fő tér are just the thing for a summer afternoon beverage.

Café Liezter (☎ 304 591; Móricz Zsigmond utca 5; snacks 600-900Ft) This convivial spot serves Hungarian snacks and burgers, but it becomes a bit more of a bar on weekends.

Giardinetto d'Italia (☎ 300 709; Rózsa utca 8; mains 1100-1600Ft) How can you beat a real-deal Italian restaurant, in Hungary, that has Blues Brothers statues kicking back at the entrance? The garden at Giardinetto is good for both drinks and food.

Karma Cafe & Restaurant (☎ 301 701; Páter Kiss Szaléz utca 22; mains 1300-1800Ft) At 11pm on Saturday night Indian-inspired cuisine gives way to a DJ beat (the bar stays open until 4am). The dharma decorations stick around full time.

Kékes Étterem (☎ 311 915; Fő tér 7; mains 2100-2800Ft) Try a glass of local Hárslevelű with your pork cutlet in a wild forest mushroom sauce. With a full list of regional specialities, Kékes is simply tops in town.

Entertainment

For entertainment listings, pick up a copy of the free biweekly *Gyöngyösi Est* (www.est.hu) magazine.

Mátra Cultural Centre (Mátra Művelődési Központ; ☎ 312 281; Barátok tere 3; ⏲ 8am-9pm Mon-Sat) Described as a 'Finnish functionalist-style building', with huge colourful stained-glass windows, this is where Gyöngyös entertains itself.

Getting There & Away

BUS

You won't wait for more than an hour for buses to/from Budapest (1200Ft, 1½ hours, 79km) or Eger (900Ft, one hour, 52km). Three midafternoon buses (between 1pm and 4pm) traverse the hills (via Parád) from Gyöngyös to Eger (1050Ft, 1¾ hours, 61km). In the Mátra Hills, destinations include the following:

Destination	Price	Duration	Km	Frequency
Kékestető	375Ft	45min	18	11 daily
Mátrafüred	200Ft	10min	6	half-hourly
Mátraháza	300Ft	15min	15	half-hourly
Parád	525Ft	1¼hr	30	9 daily
Recsk	600Ft	1¼hr	35	9 daily
Sirok	675Ft	1¾hr	42	5 daily

TRAIN

Gyöngyös is on a dead-end spur, 13km from the Vámosgyörk stop (250Ft, 14 minutes), where you can switch to the Budapest–Miskolc trunk line. Hourly trains connect Vámosgyörk with Budapest (1350Ft, 1½ hours, 87km). You'd have to change a second time, in Füszabony, to get to Eger by train.

GYÖNGYÖS TO EGER

Rte 24 wends its way through the Mátra Hills north of Gyöngyös to Parásavér and then cuts eastward onto Eger (60km); if you're travelling under your own steam, it's one of the prettiest drives in the country. The section to Mátraháza is popular with bikers, who constantly attack the road and its hairpin corners with wanton abandon on weekends. Excellent if you're into bikes, but potentially annoying if you're not.

Take the narrow-gauge train that terminates in Mátrafüred for the idyllic approach. From Gyöngyös, buses to (and between) Mátrafüred, Mátraháza and Kékestető (Hungary's highest point) are frequent. The further east you go, the more sporadic runs become. If you make time to stop at each village, it can be all but impossible to follow this whole route in one day by bus. Buses that run between the villages usually terminate in Gÿongyös. For information on getting there and away, see above.

Mátrafüred

☎ 37 / pop 980

Hungarians come to the village of Mátrafüred (www.matrafured.hu), 8km north of Gyöngyös, to breathe the forest air and walk in nature at 340m. The many easy trails in the area are the draw. Buy a Mátra hiking map at any of the trinket stands on Béke utca.

You can change money at the ATM near the **post office** (Béke utca 5; 8am-noon & 12.30-3.30pm Mon-Fri).

The **Palóc Doll Museum** (☎ 320 137; Pálosvörösmarti út 2; adult/child 300/250Ft; 9am-5pm), south of the narrow-gauge train stop, is well worth a visit. Rita Juhász Lovás is not only an artist with her sculpted cloth dolls, she's an ethnographer too – replicating each of the region's 17 Palóc village costumes for different stages of life. A few traditional folk rooms are also replicated, and crafts are for sale.

Off Akadémia utca, the red trail leads less than 1km north up to the small ruins of **Bene Castle** (Benevár). From the west side of the village, off Hegyalja utca, you can follow the **yellow triangle trail** past Közmáry watchtower and Dobogó Hill, up to the next watchtower and bus stop at Sástó (2.5km, 300m elevation change). Or take the bus up to Sástó and walk down to Mátrafüred.

SLEEPING & EATING

Back streets west of Rte 24 have the bulk of signs advertising private rooms (per person from 2500Ft), while holiday hotels surround the park. Food stands selling full meals and sweets congregate at the intersection of the main route and Béke utca.

Diana Panzió (☎ 06 30 565 8320; kalandvar@t-online.hu; Turista utca 1; s/d/tr 7000/10,000/14,000Ft; ☒) Your host knows all the hiking routes and is happy to point them out on the wall-mounted map, or to rent you a mountain bike (2000Ft per day). Basic rooms all have small refrigerators; the three apartments (12,000Ft to 20,000Ft) have equipped kitchens. After your day's exertion, relaxing in the sauna or garden, or playing billiards here might be just the thing.

Gyöngyvirág (☎ 520 001; www.gyongyvirag.hu; Béke utca 8; s/d/apt 7500/8500/12,000Ft;) A heated pool, minigolf and a playground make this otherwise institutional-looking hotel kid central. Parents on a budget will love the self-catering apartment, and the Hungarian eatery (mains 1000Ft to 1600Ft) is quite reasonable.

Anna Hotel (☎ 320 317; www.anna-hotel.hu; Üdülő sor 55; s/d 15,000/19,000Ft; ☒) The citrusy wall colours might distract you enough that you don't notice there's little room to stretch beyond the modern modular beds. A full wellness centre (fitness, sauna, whirlpool), stocked minibars and free wi-fi attest to this being one of the newest places to stay in the village. There's a fancy restaurant, too.

Fekete Rigó (Blackbird; ☎ 320 052; Avar utca 2; mains 800-1200Ft) An easy-going choice for dining, with a lovely beer garden nestled in among trees. The fruit and ham-stuffed pork (yes, meat-stuffed meat) is actually pretty good.

Sástó

☎ 37

About 3km north of Mátrafüred, Sástó (Sedge Lake) is little more than the reedy lake and an ever-extending recreation and camping complex. Rowing boats and a 54m-high lookout tower are just the beginning. At the **Oxygen Adrenalin Park** (☎ 316 480; www.adrenalin-park.hu; Sástó-kobány; 9am-7pm Mon-Fri, to 9pm Sat & Sun Jun-Aug, 10am-4pm Mon-Fri, to 5pm Sat & Sun Sep-May) you can ride a chain-assist, roller-coasterlike bobsled, climb a rope coarse, ride a four-wheeler, do a mini bungy jump, go to a petting zoo, swoop down a zip line or scale a rock wall. Activities cost between 350Ft and 1000Ft apiece.

With all that adrenaline, you can well imagine that **Mátra Camping** (☎ 374 025; www.matrakemping.hu; Sástó-kobány; camp sites per person/tent 1050/800Ft, motel r 5500Ft, bungalows with/without bathroom 9600/5500Ft; Apr-Oct) is far from quiet. Tents are pitched willy-nilly in a field; snack stands clutter up the clearing's edge. 'Comfortable' wood bungalows come with bathrooms and TVs, while the 'uncomfortable' (as they put it) variety have shared facilities; both sleep three. Motel rooms have two twin beds, but only one person has room to move at a time.

The plain-Jane guest quarters at the **Panorama Panzió** (☎ 600 074; www.adrenalin-park.hu/panzio; Sástó-kobány; s/d 7500/10,000Ft) are much nicer – trimly made beds and crisply painted walls. Music plays on the terrace on summer evenings, when the restaurant is open daily (mains 1000Ft to 1800Ft). October through April, it opens only on weekends.

In addition to the food stands in the park, there's a small grocery at the camping ground.

Mátraháza

☎ 37 / pop 540

Holiday-makers have been coming to Mátraháza since the first hotel was built in the 1920s. On a slight incline 715m above sea level, the village is about 5km north of Sástó. It has a smidge of an alpine feel, and is smaller and more secluded than Mátrafüred (with correspondingly fewer services). Both short walks in the immediate area and more adventurous hiking further afield start here. The **post office** (8am-3.30pm Mon-Fri) is near the turn-off to Kékestető, and there's an ATM at the bus station along the main road through the village.

Follow the **yellow trail** (triangle then square) 4.4km west through the hills to Lajosháza and the terminus of a narrow-gauge train (p326), or the **red trail** south through Kalló Valley (Kalló-völgy) past the Bene Castle ruins to Mátrafüred (4.5km). The real test is the 3.4km **red and blue cross trail** that leads first through a gentle valley before climbing steeply the last kilometre to Kékestető.

SLEEPING & EATING

Vörösmarty Fogado (☎ 374 042; vorosmarty-fogado@t-online.hu; s/d 4000/6000Ft, cabins 4000Ft) Share a kitchen and garden with other guests at this lived-in boarding house in the woods. The A-frame cabins out back are tinier than tiny, but have four beds (and nothing else). It's set back from Rte 24, 2km from Mátraháza.

Pagoda Pihenő Panzió (☎ 374 023; www.pagodapanzio.hu; s/d 6000/10,000Ft) You can't miss the odd pagodalike building in the centre of Mátraháza village. It's one of three old buildings that house so-so rooms (what garish furniture choices) among the trees; ask for one with a balcony. There's a rustic terrace restaurant and picnic tables in the park surrounds.

Hotel Ozon (☎ 374 004; www.hotelozon.hu) At the time of writing Ozon was a hotel under reconstruction, about halfway between Sástó and Mátraháza. Look for new apartments to have full kitchens.

Kisvendéglő Tölgy (☎ 322 7711; mains 1590-1700Ft; 11am-8pm Thu-Sun) The large covered deck is just the place to enjoy a carb-loaded meal of dumplings and cheese before heading up the nearby trail to Kékestető. Service is super friendly.

Kékestető

☎ 37 / pop 80

Every Hungarian knows that Kékestető, 4km west of Mátraháza, is the highest point in the country; that it's only 1014m doesn't seem to deter enthusiasm. Hikers (or skiers) line up one after another to have their picture taken next to the red, white and green painted rock that marks the spot. You do have quite a view on clear days, which only gets better if you take the elevator up the nine-storey **TV tower** (☎ 367 086; adult/child 400/270Ft; 9am-6pm May-Sep, 9am-5pm Oct-Apr).

If they're not staying at the nearby Sanatorium, most visitors take a look around, maybe stop at one of the few eateries, and then hike back down. Following the **blue and red cross trail** through the forest, crossing over the road, gets you to Mátraháza in 3.4km (you can also take a shortcut, 2km, down the ski hill). The even more scenic 7km **green trail** leads past waterfalls and valleys to Mátrafüred.

Things liven up when snow falls (roughly late December until March) and the **Ski Centre** (day lift ticket adult/child 4500/3500Ft; 9am-4pm) opens up. Two tow-lifts serve eight runs, including one advanced, and skis are for rent (from 3000Ft per day). **Ski mobile rides** (per hr 7500Ft; 11am-2pm) are offered nearby.

The uncomplicated log cabin lodge rooms at **Kékesi Vendégház** (☎ 567 007; info@matracentrum.hu; s/d 5000/9000Ft; 10am-8pm Wed-Sun), opposite the ski lift from Mátraháza, are your best bet for sleeping. They rent mountain bikes (2000Ft per day) there, plus there's a wonderful hearty-Hungarian restaurant (mains 1300Ft to 2400Ft) and deck downstairs. **Tető Étterem** (mains 600-1000Ft; 10am-6pm) offers self-service cafeteria options at the top of the other run.

Buses stop at the Sanatorium; follow the road, or the trail on the other side of the turn-around, up to be king of the hill.

Parásavér

☎ 36 / pop 510

Parásavér, 12km north of Mátraháza, is where the country's most odoriferous – and effective? – *gyógyvíz* (medicinal drinking water) is bottled. Stop for a glass at the public fountain, if you can stand the stench of this sulphuric brew.

Nearly three hectares of parkland surround the 58-room **Kastélyhotel Sasvár** (☎ 444 444; www.sasvar.hu; Kossuth Lajos utca 1; r incl breakfast 35,000-43,000Ft;). Miklós Ybl, the same man responsible for the Hungarian State Opera House in Budapest, constructed the Renaissance-style hunting manor and its out buildings in 1882. Rooms range from the romantic (swagged canopies and dusty rose silk) to the utilitarian. A stay includes spa admission, plus tennis, bowling and billiards. A grand meal is to be had at the silver service restaurant (mains 2600Ft to 4200Ft), but a more reasonable full-board buffet is available.

Parád & Parádfürdő

☎ 36 / pop 2200

Five kilometres further west, Parád and Parádfürdő run into one another and effectively make up one long village. The **Coach Museum** (Kocsimúzeum; ☎ 364 387; Kossuth Lajos utca 217; adult/child 450/250Ft; 9am-5pm Tue-Sun), housed in the red marble Cifra Istálló (Ornamental Stables) of Count Károlyi, is an excellent small museum. Silk brocade richly decorates the 19th-century diplomatic and state coaches; the bridles contain as much as 5kg of silver. (For the record, the word 'coach' comes from Kocs, a small village in Transdanubia, where these lighter horse-drawn vehicles were first used in place of the more cumbersome wagons.) The stables can arrange **horse riding** (per hr from 3000Ft) as well.

The lovely **Erzsébet Királyné Park Hotel** (Queen Elizabeth Park Hotel; ☎ 444 044; www.erzsebetparkhotel.hu; Kossuth Lajos utca 372; s/d 16,500/20,500Ft;) is more hotel than palace, but it was also designed by the very busy Miklós Ybl in 1893. Tasteful furnishings reflect today's pared-down interpretations of imperial classics. Bathe in the thermal waters of the Elizabeth's own medicinal pools or do laps in the Olympic-sized swimming pool outdoors before retiring to the cafe or the formal restaurant for a bite to eat.

Recsk

☎ 36 / pop 2900

From Parádfürdő the road continues for 2km to Recsk, a place that lives on in infamy as the site of Hungary's most brutal forced-labour camp, set up by Mátyás Rákóczi in 1950 and closed down by the reformer Imre Nagy in 1953. In honour of those who slaved and died here, the **Recsk Forced-Labour Death Camp** (Recski Kényszermunka Haláltábor; ☎ in Budapest 1-312 6105; adult/child 300/200Ft; 9am-5pm May-Sep, 9am-3pm Sat & Sun Oct-Apr) has been partially reconstructed near the quarry, about 5km south of the village. It's now a peaceful spot, which makes it all that more poignant.

Sirok

☎ 36 / pop 2070

Effectively the last town in the Mátra Hills, Sirok lies 8km to the east of Recsk. The freely accessible small ruins of an early-14th-century **castle** perched on a mountaintop due north of the village provide superb views of the Mátra and Bükk Hills and the mountains of Slovakia. Some of the rooms at **Vár Panzió** (☎ 361 061; www.varpanzio.hu; Dobó István utca 30; d/q 7400/14,000Ft) have distant views of the ruins. Otherwise they are super simple, with thin pine beds and not much else. The family-owners serve a bevy of roast meats at their little restaurant (mains 1200Ft to 1600Ft).

BÜKK HILLS

Perhaps the prettiest and most verdant of the hills that line the Northern Uplands, much of Bükk is a 43,000-sq-km national park. The range takes its name from the beech trees growing here. Karst formations, upland plateaus, thick pine forests and abundant wildlife attract hikers and bikers to hillside villages like Szilvásvárad (also known for the Lipizzaner horses) and Lillafüred. Southern slopes support wine production, including the famous Bull's Blood red. Sample it in the baroque treasure of a town, Eger, one of the country's true treasures. To the east, the valleys around industrial Miskolc have been scarred by ore mining. But you needn't linger when you can go to the nearby cave-spa town, Miskolctapolca.

Cartographia (www.cartographia.com) puts out a 1:40,000 Bükk map and an atlas; **Topograf** (www.topgraf.hu) produces both hiking (green) and cycling (brown) tourist maps. For information on the national park, contact the **Bükk National Park Directorate** (☎ 36-411 581; www.bnpi.hu).

NORTHERN UPLANDS' TOP FIVE FORTRESSES

- Boldogkő (p347) – classic castle ruins rising from solid rock
- Eger (opposite) – a monumental history museum
- Sárospatak (p352) – romantic palace in superb condition
- Hollókő (p319) – intact fortress with far-reaching views
- Füzér (p356) – lonely ruin high above villages and pastures

EGER

☎ 36 / pop 58,300

Lavished with wonderfully preserved baroque architecture, Eger is a jewel box of a town with loads to see and do. Explore the bloody history of Turkish conquest and defeat at the hilltop castle, climb a Turkish minaret, hear an organ performance at the ornate Basilica… But best of all may be traipsing from cellar to cellar in the Valley of Beautiful Women, tasting the celebrated Eger Bull's Blood (Egri Bikavér) red wine from the cask and bottle. Flanked by the Northern Uplands' most inviting ranges, hiking and horse riding excursions are never far away: plan to spend an extra day or two.

History

It was here that the Hungarians fended off the Turks for the first time during the 170 years of occupation in the siege of Eger in 1552. The Turks came back in 1596 and this time captured the city, turning it into a provincial capital, and erecting several mosques and other buildings, until they were driven out at the end of the 17th century. All that remains of this architectural legacy is a lonely little minaret pointing its long finger towards the heavens in indignation.

Eger played a central role in Ferenc Rákóczi II's attempt to overthrow the Habsburgs early in the 18th century, and it was then that a large part of the castle was razed by the Austrians. Having enjoyed the status of an episcopate since the time of King Stephen in the 11th century, Eger flourished in the 18th and 19th centuries, when the city acquired most of its wonderful baroque architecture.

Orientation

Dobó István tér, the centre of Eger, is just a couple of minutes on foot to the east of the renovated bus station on Pyrker János tér. To reach the city centre from the main train station on Vasút utca, walk north on Deák Ferenc utca and then head along pedestrian Széchenyi István utca, Eger's main drag. The Egervár train station, which serves Szilvásvárad and other points north, is on Vécseyvölgy utca, and about a five-minute walk north of Eger Castle.

AS STRONG AS A BULL

The story of the Turkish attempt to take Eger Castle is the stuff of legend. Under the command of István Dobó, a mixed bag of 2000 soldiers held out against more than 100,000 Turks for a month in 1552. As every Hungarian kid in short trousers can tell you, the women of Eger played a crucial role in the battle, pouring boiling oil and pitch on the invaders from the ramparts. (A painting by Bertalan Székely called *The Women of Eger* in the castle's art gallery pays tribute to these brave ladies.)

If we're to believe the tale, it seems that Dobó sustained his weary troops with a ruby-red vintage of the town's wine. When they fought on with increased vigour – and stained beards – rumours began to circulate among the Turks that the defenders were gaining strength by drinking the blood of bulls. The invaders departed, for the time being, and the name Bikavér (Bull's Blood) was born.

Information

City website (www.eger.hu, in Hungarian)
Egri Est Café (☎ 411 105; Széchenyi utca 16; per hr 300Ft; ⌚ 11am-midnight Sun-Thu, to 2am Fri & Sat) A cafe-bar with internet access in the rear.
Ibusz (☎ 311 451; www.ibusz.hu; Széchenyi István utca 9) Rents private flats.
Magvető Könyvesbolt (☎ 517 757; Bajcsy-Zsilinszky utca 4; ⌚ 9am-5pm Mon-Fri, to 1pm Sat) Small bookstore with a selection of English titles, and maps.
Markhót Ferenc Megyei Hospital (Kórház; ☎ 411 444; Markhót Ferenc utca 1/3; ⌚ 24hr)
OTP bank (Széchenyi István utca 2)
Post office (Széchenyi István utca 20-22)
Tourinform (☎ 517 715; eger@tourinform.hu; Bajcsy-Zsilinszky utca 9; ⌚ 9am-5pm Mon-Fri, to 1pm Sat & Sun mid-Jun–mid-Sep, closed Sun mid-Sep–mid-Jun) Covers both town and surrounds.

Sights

EGER CASTLE

The best view of the city can be had by climbing up the cobblestone lane from Dózsa György tér to **Eger Castle** (Egri Vár; ☎ 312 744; www.egrivar.hu; Vár 1; combined ticket adult/child 1200/600Ft; ⌚ exhibits 9am-5pm Tue-Sun Apr-Oct, 10am-4pm Tue-Sun Nov-Mar), erected in the 13th century after the Mongol invasion. Much of the castle is of modern reconstruction, but you can still see the foundations of 12th-century **St John's Cathedral**. Models and drawings in the **István Dobó Museum**, housed in the former Bishop's Palace (1470), show how it once looked. Learn the history of the castle there. On the ground floor, a statue of Dobó takes pride of place in the **Heroes' Hall**. The 19th-century building on the northwestern side of the courtyard houses the **Eger Art Gallery**, with several works by Mihály Munkácsy. In 2005 reconstruction was completed on the medieval **Dobó Bastion** (1549), which collapsed in 1976. Currently it contains a weapons display. Other exhibits, including the **Waxworks** (adult/child 400/300Ft) and **Minting Exhibit** (adult/child 400/300Ft) cost extra.

You can also just wander the **castle grounds** (adult/child 400/200Ft; ⌚ 8am-8pm Apr-Aug, 8am-7pm Sep, 8am-5pm Oct-Mar), which are open Monday, when most exhibits are closed.

ESZTERHÁZY TÉR

A highlight of the town's amazing architecture is the **Basilica** (Bazilika; Eszterházy tér; admission free; ⌚ 9am-4pm Mon-Fri), a neoclassical monolith completed in 1836 and designed by József Hild, the same architect who later worked on the cathedral at Esztergom. A good time to see the place is when the ornate altars and a soaring dome create interesting acoustics for the half-hour **organ concert** (admission 500Ft; ⌚ 11.30am Mon-Sat, 12.45pm Sun May-Oct).

To the right of the main church steps, behind the István Dobó statue, is the entry to the **Town under the Town** (☎ 06 20 961 4019; Eszterházy tér; tour adult/child 800/400Ft; ⌚ 10am-9pm Apr-Sep, 10am-5pm Oct-Mar). A history-oriented tour leads through the caverns that once were the archbishop's cellars. Several of the guides speak English; ask ahead.

Directly opposite the Basilica is the sprawling Zopf-style **Lyceum** (Líceum; ☎ 520 400; Eszterházy tér 1; ⌚ 9.30am-3.30pm Tue-Sun Apr-Sep, 9.30am-1pm Sat & Sun Oct-Mar), dating from 1765. Because the pages are linen not paper, you're allowed to touch a 17th-century book in the 20,000-volume **library** (adult/student 700/350Ft), which contains hundreds of priceless manuscripts and codices. The trompe l'oeil ceiling fresco (1778) depicts the Counter-Reformation's Council of Trent (1545–63) and a lightning

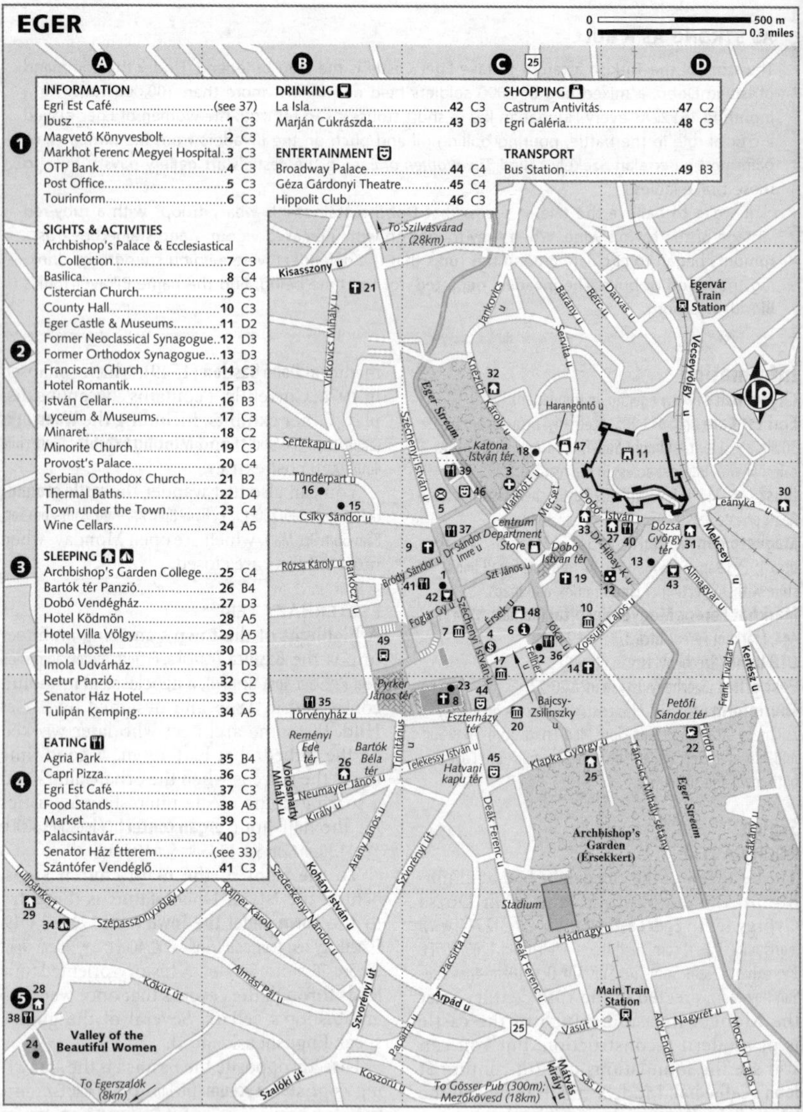

bolt setting heretical manuscripts ablaze. The **Astronomy Museum** (adult/student 800/650Ft), on the 6th floor of the east wing, contains 18th-century astronomical equipment and an observatory. Climb three more floors up to the observation deck to try out the camera obscura, the 'eye of Eger', designed in 1776 to spy on the town and to entertain townspeople. Unless you have a specific interest, entry to both is overpriced.

Northeast of the cathedral in the **Archbishop's Palace** (Érseki Palota; Széchenyi István utca 5) is the **Ecclesiastical Collection** (Egyházi Gyűjtemény; ☎ 421 332; adult/child 400/300Ft; 9am-5pm Tue-Sat Apr-Oct, 8am-4pm Mon-Fri Nov-Mar), with priceless vestments, church plates and liturgical objects.

OTHER SIGHTS

The theatrical baroque altar sculpture of St Francis Borgia in gilt and white stucco at the **Cistercian church** (Széchenyi István utca 15), built in 1743, is well worth a look. As is the enormous iconostasis of gold leaf and braid at the **Serbian Orthodox Church** (☎ 320 129; Vitkovics Mihály utca 30; admission 400Ft; ⏰ 10am-4pm Thu-Sun); enter from Széchenyi utca 59.

Only nonclaustrophobes will brave the 97 narrow spiral steps to the top of the super-skinny **Minaret** (☎ 410 233; Knézich Károly utca; admission 200Ft; ⏰ 10am-6pm Apr-Oct). This, the last Turkish remnant in town, is topped incongruously with a cross. Mecset utca south of the minaret leads to central Dobó István tér, site of the town's market in medieval times. On the southern side of the square stands the **Minorite church** (☎ 312 744; Dobó István tér 6; admission free; ⏰ 9am-5pm Tue-Sun), built in 1771 and one of the most glorious baroque buildings in Hungary. The altarpiece of the Virgin Mary and St Anthony of Padua is by Johann Kracker, the Bohemian painter who also did the fire-and-brimstone ceiling fresco in the Lyceum library. Statues of István Dobó and his comrades-in-arms routing the Turks in 1552 fill the square in front of the church.

Kossuth Lajos utca is a fine, tree-lined street with dozens of architectural gems. The first of interest is the former **Orthodox synagogue** (Kossuth Lajos utca 17), built in 1893 and now a furniture store backing onto a shopping mall. Another, former **neoclassical synagogue** (Dr Hibay Károly utca 7) dating from 1845 is around the corner. You'll pass several outstanding baroque and Eclectic buildings, including the **county hall** (megyeháza; Kossuth Lajos utca 9), with a wrought-iron grid above the main door of Faith, Hope and Charity by Henrik Fazola, a Rhinelander who settled in Eger in the mid-18th century. Walk down the passageway, and you'll see two more of his magnificent works: baroque wrought-iron gates decorated on both sides that have superseded the minaret as the symbol of Eger. The gate on the right shows the seal of Heves County and has a comical figure on its handle. The more graceful gate on the left is decorated with grapes. The **Franciscan church** (Kossuth Lajos utca 14) was completed in 1755 on the site of a mosque. The wrought-iron balcony and window grids of the rococo **Provost's Palace** (Kispréposti palota; Kossuth Lajos utca 4) were also done by Fazola.

Activities

WINE TASTING

You can taste Eger's famous wines at many places around town, including at restaurants at the base of the castle and in the **István Cellar** (☎ 313 670; Tündérpart 5; ⏰ 1-10pm Tue-Sun Apr-Oct, 2-9pm Tue-Sun Nov-Mar) and wine shop. But why bother drinking in town when you can do the same in the wine cellars of the evocatively named Valley of the Beautiful Women (Szépasszony-völgy)?

Wines are stored, not made in the valley, and more than two dozen *pincek* (cellars) have been carved into the horseshoe-shaped rock. For an average of 100Ft you can take a 1-decilitre taste of a range of reds, like Bull's Blood, and whites, such as Olaszrizling and Hárslevelű. Bring an empty plastic bottle (water bottle, gallon jug, new petrol container…don't laugh, we've seen it) to have filled with the house cask wine for about 350Ft per litre. A handful of the cellars are local, family-owned operations with a son or a daughter pouring; others are run by large consortiums and staffed with uniform-wearing college students (note the one with a castlelike facade). The outdoor cellar tables fill up on a late summer afternoon, locals cook *gulyás* (beef goulash soup) in the park and you hear notes from a gypsy violin floating up from the restaurants at the valley's entrance (or maybe a drunk guy serenading his girlfriend…). It's a not-to-be-missed experience.

The valley is a little over 1km southwest across Rte 25, off Király utca. A taxi back to the centre runs about 1000Ft.

OTHER ACTIVITIES

After strolling in the **Archbishop's Garden** (Érsekkert; enter from Petőfi Sándor tér 2), once the private reserve of papal princes, you can further unwind in the nearby **Thermal Baths** (☎ 413 356; Fürdő utca 1-3; adult/child 1250/1050Ft; ⏰ 6am-8pm Apr-Oct, 9am-7pm Nov-Mar). Admission gains you access to a variety of open-air pools, but in summer months (June through August) you have to pay 700Ft extra to get into the 'adventure' complex with the newest whirligigs – bubbling massage pools, a castle-themed kids' pool etc. In late 2009 the 1617 Turkish indoor bath building should reopen after total reconstruction, plus a multi-million-forint addition. Another big new spa complex is 8km outside of town at Egerszalók (p336).

Rent bicycles from the **Hotel Romantik** (☎ 413 903; Jókai utca 6; per day 3000Ft; 8am-8pm).

Tours

Tourinform organises **historic walking tours** (per person 250Ft; 10am Sat Jun-Oct) of the baroque city centre and **evening wine tours** (adult/child 5000/3500Ft; 6.30pm Thu Jun-Aug) with tastings, in both English and German. Sign up in advance.

Festivals & Events

Annual events include the **Spring Festival** in late March/April, the **Border Fortress Merrymaking Festival and Games** at the castle at the end of July, **Baroque Weeks** in late July/August, the **Agria International Folkdance Meeting** in August and the **Feast of Eger** in mid-September.

Sleeping

Tourinform publishes a glossy booklet of accommodation available, not only in the city (including private rooms), but also in the surrounding area.

BUDGET

Tulipán Kemping (☎ 410 580; Szépasszonyvölgy utca 71; camp sites per person 1450Ft, 4-bed bungalows 6000Ft) Many of the caravan and tent sites here are in an open, shadeless field. But you're surrounded by vineyards, stumbling distance from valley wine cellars. The bungalow is just a cabin (no bath or kitchen).

our pick **Retur Panzió** (☎ 416 650; www.returvendeghaz.hu; Knézich Károly utca 18; s/d 4000/6000Ft) You couldn't find sweeter hosts than the daughter and mother who own this *panzió* (guest house) under the eaves. Walking up three flights of stairs, you enter a cheery shared kitchen/eating area central to four rooms. Out back is a huge flower garden with tables and fire pit at your disposal. You can't beat the central location, near the Minaret, for the price.

Imola Hostel (☎ 520 430; www.imolanet.hu/hostel; Leányka utca 2; s 3000-5000Ft, d 6000-8000Ft) Former student housing has been modernised and updated. Large desks and comfy beds fill the smart twin rooms. Each floor shares a kitchen and an internet computer.

A number of colleges offer dormitory accommodation from June to August; **Archbishop's Garden College** (Érsekkerti Kollégium; ☎ 520 432; Klapka György utca 12; dm 3000Ft) is the most central option, and is in an old-town building full of character.

MIDRANGE

Atrium Apartmanház (☎ 418 427; www.atriumapartment.eu; Neumayer János út 8; s/d/tr 6500/10,000/12,500Ft) Your home in the city. Each loft apartment has at least one bedroom, a kitchenette (coffee-maker, fridge, microwave), cool tile floors and free wi-fi.

Bartók tér Panzió (☎ 515 556; www.bartokpanzio.com; Bartók Béla tér 8; s/d/tr incl breakfast 7000/9000/12,900Ft) The owners run Bartók tér and St Kristoff Panzió, down the street (Arany Janos 1), as one. Guests share breakfast at this, the main guest house. Both have big, but unmemorable rooms; Bartók's are a little quieter.

Dobó Vendégház (☎ 421 407; www.dobovendeghaz.hu; Dobó utca 10; s/d incl breakfast 8000/11,700Ft) Tucked into the old-town pedestrian streets, Dobó Vendégház is a sightseeing special. White linens on pine beds look especially snappy given the pop of colour from mango-and-orange pillows. Check out the impressive Zsolnay porcelain collection in the breakfast room.

Hotel Villa Völgy (☎ 321 664; www.hotelvillavolgy.hu; Tulipánkert utca 5; s/d 12,900/17,500Ft) Awaken to a view of the vineyards in this well-bred, modern-design villa in the wine valley. Neoclassical columns surround the glass-enclosed pool. There's free wi-fi.

TOP END

Senator Ház Hotel (☎ 320 466; www.senatorhaz.hu; Dobó István tér 11; s/d 15,000/19,000Ft) Warm and cosy rooms with traditional white furnishings fill the upper floors of this delightful 18th-century inn on Eger's main square. The ground floor is shared between a quality restaurant and a reception that could easily moonlight as a history museum. Free wi-fi.

Yet more options:

Imola Udvarház (☎ 516 180; www.imolanet.hu/udvar-bemut.htm; Dósza György tér 4; s/d incl breakfast 19,000/22,000Ft) Sleek and stylish apartments, great castle views.

Hotel Ködmön (☎ 515 803; www.szepasszonyvolgy.eu; Szépasszonyvölgy utca 1; r incl breakfast 24,500-35,000Ft) Four-star, spa-service hotel opened in the valley in 2008.

Eating

BUDGET

Lining the entry path to the Valley of the Beautiful Women are eight interchangeable food-stand-like eateries, with waiters that come to your covered picnic table and who menus to point at (mains 600Ft to 1100Ft).

Market (Katona István tér; 6am-6pm Mon-Fri, to 1pm Sat, to 10am Sun) Eger's large covered market has more fruit and vegies than you could possibly carry away.

Agria Park (Törvényház utca 4; mains 300-800Ft; 10am-10pm) Chinese, Hungarian and Greek self-service restaurants are among your choices on the upper floor of the Agria Park shopping centre.

Capri Pizza (☎ 410 877; Bajcsy-Zsilinszky utca 4; pizzas 550-1100Ft) Beans feature on a surprising number of the pizzas at this hole-in-the-wall. White pizzas (sans sauce) and vegetarian available, too.

MIDRANGE

There are several *csárdák* (rustic, Hungarian-style inns) among the wine cellars and food stands in the Valley of the Beautiful Women. At the end of the day they can be much of a muchness; you'll most certainly be serenaded by a gypsy violinist.

Egri Est Café (☎ 411 105; Széchenyi István utca 16; mains 1200-1600Ft; 11am-midnight Sun-Thu, to 2am Fri & Sat) University students fill up this cafe at weekends, to drink as much as to eat the basic Hungarian and Italian dishes.

our pick **Palacsintavár** (☎ 413 986; Dobó István utca 9; mains 1400-1600Ft) Pop art and postcards line the walls and groovy music fills this eclectic eatery. Entrée-sized *palacsintak* (crêpelike 'pancakes') here are served with an abundance of fresh vegetables, and range in flavour from Asian to Italian.

Szántófer Vendéglő (☎ 517 298; Bródy Sándor utca 3; breakfasts 600-800Ft, mains 1400-1800Ft; 8am-10pm) The best choice in town for hearty, home-style Hungarian. Farming equipment and cooking utensils hang like prize kills on the walls; a covered courtyard out back is perfect for escaping the heat.

Senator Ház Étterem (☎ 320 466; www.senatorhaz.hu; Dobó István tér 11; entrées 350-500Ft, mains 1400-2500Ft) The antique-filled dining rooms are charming, but the outdoor seats are the hot seat of Eger's main square. The soups and salads and desserts are especially exquisite; try the cream of garlic soup.

TOP END

Fehérszarvas Vadásztanya (☎ 411 129; Klapka György utca 8; mains 1800-3500Ft) With its game specialities and cellar setting, autumn and winter are really the best seasons to enjoy the city's white-tablecloth choice. Cold fruit soups and goose liver pâte are particular specialities here.

Drinking

The open-air tables at the wine cellars of the Valley of the Beautiful Women are clearly the best place to drink in town; they serve by the carafe in addition to by the decilitre.

Marján Cukrászda (☎ 312 784; Kossuth Lajos utca 28; 9am-10pm May-Sep, 9am-8pm Oct-Apr) Linger over coffee and sweets on the big terrace south of Dózsa György tér.

Gösser Pub (☎ 349 2133; Mátyás Király utca 56; 10am-midnight Thu-Sun, to 2am Fri & Sat) Sick of wine? Stop in for a Magyar pint at this local beer bar. There's live music Saturday nights.

La Isla (☎ 405 0817; cnr Széchenyi István utca & Foglár utca; 10am-midnight Sun-Thu, to 2am Fri & Sat) As much a Latin cocktail bar as a cafe, this is a fine place to kick back after a hard day's sightseeing.

Entertainment

Eger has a year full of cultural programs listed in the free monthly magazine, *Belváros*, available at Tourinform. For music concerts *(zene)*, pick up the free *Egri Est* (www.est.hu) listings magazine.

Géza Gárdonyi Theatre (☎ 310 026; Hatvani kapu tér 4; box office 2-7pm Mon-Fri) Dance, opera and drama are staged at the town's theatre.

Broadway Palace (Pyrker János tér 3; 10pm-6am Wed, Fri & Sat) This bizarre cavelike DJ dance club beneath the cathedral steps parties hard on weekends.

Hippolit Club (☎ 411 031; Katona István tér 2; 10pm-5am Fri & Sat) Eger's classic club, where the dance floor heaves until the wee hours, is downstairs from the Elefanto restaurant.

Shopping

Egri Galéria (☎ 517 518; Érsek utca 8) A lovely little gallery, Egri sells locally made jewellery, fine art, pottery and other collectibles.

Castrum Antikvitás (☎ 311 613; Harangöntő utca 2; 9am-5pm Mon-Fri) Search for that undiscovered treasure in the piles of antiques hidden away in this store's several rooms.

Getting There & Away

BUS

Bus services are good, and there are direct buses to the following destinations.

Destination	Price	Duration	Km	Frequency
Debrecen	2290Ft	2½hr	131	7 daily
Gyöngyös	900Ft	1hr	52	hourly
Kecskemét	2060Ft	4½hr	166	3 daily
Miskolc	1050Ft	1½hr	68	8 daily
Szeged	3220Ft	5¾ hr	237	2 daily
Szilvásvárad	450Ft	45min	29	hourly

The only bus that goes through the Bükk Hills via Felsőtárkány to Miskolc leaves on Sunday at 8.30am.

TRAIN

Up to seven direct trains a day connect to/from Budapest's Keleti train station (2290Ft, 2½ hours, 142km). Otherwise, Eger is on a minor train line linking Putnok and Füzesabony, so you have to change at the latter for Miskolc (1200Ft, 1½ hours, 74km) or Debrecen (1770Ft, three hours, 120km).

Getting Around

From the main train station, bus 11, 12 or 14 will drop you off at the city centre or at the bus station.

AROUND EGER

Egerszalók

☎ 36 / pop 1990

Every house in rural **Egerszalók** (www.egerszalok.hu), 8km from Eger, seems to be painted a more vibrant hue than the next – rich plum, sage green, golden yellow… A line of *pincek*, ripe for tastings, and little hostelries line the route to this colourful village. But the real attraction (and probable reason for the spruce-up) is the **Salt Hill Thermal Spa** (☎ 688 500; www.egerszalokfurdo.hu; Forrás út 4; adult/child 2400/1200Ft; 10am-6pm Mon-Thu, to 8pm Fri-Sun), 1km or so to the south. Since 1961, when oil prospectors struck thermal water instead black gold, 69°C water has been streaming down the hill, creating a cascade of white minerals hardening into the 'salt hill'. Mid-2008 saw completion of the upscale new 17-bath spa complex. Outdoors the organic-shaped pools have different temperatures and mineral contents, complemented by jets and waterfalls in view of the hill. (Note that they've diverted waters to create three new mineral formations – in the meantime it looks kind of bare.) Inside, several tiered pools are set in a faux crystalline mountain complete with waterslide. Cavelike chambers and a waterfall in the main passage contain waters from 40°C (ouch) to 7°C (double ouch!). And kids can play in their own giggles-and-squirts fun pool while parents indulge in seaweed baths or marine massages.

At the time of writing the original open-air **thermal baths** (☎ 515 300; adult/child 700/500Ft; 3-9pm Wed-Sun), off to one side, had not been completely absorbed in the complex and could be entered separately.

A huge Salt Hill Spa hotel and restaurant is scheduled to open sometime in 2009 (there's a snack bar in-spa), but you have plenty of other options. The **D & A Apartmanházak** (☎ 786 776; www.dandaonline.hu; Forrás út 1; r 11,000-13,000Ft), across from the baths, has full kitchens, food delivery service, bike rentals and Budapest airport transfers. In town, the pale apricot **Thermál Panzió & Étterem** (☎ 474 532; jager70@freemail.hu; Széchenyi út 4; mains 1100-1500Ft, s/d incl breakfast 6000/9000Ft;) serves solid Hungarian fare and makes up simple rooms above. The meet-me-at-the-Kasbah guestrooms, Arabian Nights–inspired spa and Northeast African restaurant make the upscale **Shiraz Hotel** (☎ 574 500; www.shiraz.hu; Széchenyi út 31; mains 2000-3000Ft, s/d incl breakfast 27,700/32,700Ft) a destination in itself. Other eat-and-drinkeries, including wine cellars, can be found on Ady Endre utca between Salt Hill and town.

Bus schedules direct from Eger to the spa (the 'Egerszalók, gyögyfürdő' stop when searching www.menetrendek.hu) were still being sorted out at the time of writing. Buses connect the village with Eger (200Ft, 13 minutes, 8km) at least 10 times daily.

Mezőkövesd

☎ 49 / pop 18,000

Some 18km southeast of Eger, Mezőkövesd is not much of a town, but it is the centre of the Matyó, a Magyar people famous for their fine embroidery, wood painting and folk dress. Here you have the opportunity to see some of the most distinctive folk art in Hungary.

From the Mezőkövesd bus station on Rákóczi utca, walk south for 50m and then east along Mátyás király út for 600m to Szent László tér, where you'll find **Tourinform** (☎ 500 285; www.mezokovesd.hu; Szent László tér 23; 9am-5pm

NORTHERN UPLANDS

Mon-Fri, 10am-2pm Sat mid-Jun–Aug, 10am-4pm Mon-Fri Sep–mid-Jun). From the train station, head north on Dósza György út and west on Mátyás király. There's an **OTP bank** (Mátyás király út 149) at the bus station end of town and the **post office** (Alkomány utca 1) is behind Tourinform.

SIGHTS & ACTIVITIES

At the stop-worthy **Matyó Museum** (☎ 311 824; Szent László tér 8; adult/child 600/300Ft; 9am-5pm Tue-Sun Apr-Oct, 9am-3pm Tue-Sat Nov-Mar), displays illustrate the regional differences and historical development of local needlework: from white-on-white stitching and intricate patterns of blue-and-red roses, to the metallic fringe that was banned in the early 1920s because the high cost was ruining some families.

A short distance southwest of Szent László tér, follow Eötvös utca south through Hősök tere to the small streets of the **Hadas District** (www.mezokovesd.tajhaz.hu), a back-in-time world of whitewashed cottages and thatched roofs. Interesting lanes to stroll along include Patkó köz and Kökény köz, but the centre of activity is Kis Jankó Bori utca, named after Hungary's own 'Grandma Moses', who lived and stitched here (1867–1954). The family's 200-year-old cottage is now the **Bori Kis Jankó Memorial House** (Kis Jankó Bori Emlékház; ☎ 411 873; Kis Jankó Bori utca 22; adult/child 200/100Ft; 10am-6pm daily Jul–mid-Aug, 10am-4pm Apr-Jun & mid-Aug–Oct, 10am-2pm Sat & Sun Nov-Feb). 'Aunt Bori', as she was known locally, is credited with creating 100 rose embroidery patterns. She and her apprentices broke with tradition by eschewing symmetry and improvising on traditional designs, stitching intensely bright flowers flowing across dark backgrounds (as opposed to the simpler, graphic floral designs on white in Kalocsa – see p257). Aunt Bori's embroidered jackets, linens and costumes decorate the simple two-room peasant house.

You can see occasional embroidery demonstrations and dance performances at the **House of Folk Art & Dance** (☎ 411 686; Kis Jankó Bori utca 5-7). Check out traditional Matyó wood-painting techniques at **Szabolcs Kovacs Furniture Folk Artist** (☎ 500 288; Kis Jankó Bori utca 6-8). Several other artists – making intricately decorated honey cakes, painted enamel etc – have their studios on this street, or on Mogyoró köz, where you may be able to buy the crafts direct (the museum also sells some). Studios are generally open the same hours as Aunt Bori's house, though they are subject to the owner's whim.

The best time to visit is during a festival, when you can see some townsfolk in full traditional regalia. Matyó folk costumes are some of the most easily recognisable in Hungary; married women wear something akin to pompoms on their head and layer after layer of petticoat is piled up under dark-coloured embroidered skirts. Think that's fancy? You should see a wedding. Come at Easter time or check online (www.mezokovesd.hu) for program schedules.

About 3km west of centre, the thoroughly modern **Zsóry Thermal Baths** (☎ 412 844; www.zsory-furdo.hu; Napfürdő utca 2; adult/child 1200/900Ft; 8.30am-6pm, outdoor pools to 8pm Jun-Aug only) attract a lot of local attention.

NORTHERN UPLANDS

SLEEPING & EATING

With Eger so close, you may not want to overnight in Mezőkövesd, but there are plenty of private rooms and holiday rentals. There's also camping, accommodation and restaurants around Napfürdő utca, near the spa.

Tulipános Vendégház (☎ 411 686; www.tulipan.ini.hu; Mogyoró köz 1; r 6000Ft) Sleep in the heart of the Hadas District. This self-catering cottage home has three fairly modern double rooms, booked separately, that share a kitchen and garden.

Rozmaringos Vendégház (☎ 06 30 935 0827; www.hidakapus.hu; Kis Jankó Bori út 42; r 6000Ft) An older home in the historic district, rooms here have antiques and a dark-wood character. There are shared bathrooms and kitchen.

Pizza Néró (☎ 415 676; Eötvös utca 9; mains 800-1100Ft; 10am-11pm Sun-Thu, to 2pm Fri & Sat) Simple pizzas and pastas served close to the Hadas District.

Hungária (☎ 416 800; Alkotmány út 2; mains 900-1500Ft, steaks 3000Ft) Hungária's interior may be a bit stiff, but the chicken cordon bleu and other fried meat dishes are solid. There's a huge dessert menu, too. It's near Tourinform.

GETTING THERE & AROUND

Buses run to/from Eger (375Ft, 30 minutes, 20km) and trains to Miskolc (675Ft, 40 minutes, 44km) at least every hour. From near the Matyó Museum and the bus station, local bus 5 runs along Mátyás király út to the thermal baths.

NORTHERN UPLANDS

SZILVÁSVÁRAD

☎ 36 / pop 1750

Home to graceful white stallions, carriage races, a narrow-gauge train and forest trails, Szilvásvárad makes an excellent day's excursion from Eger, 28km to the south. But hikers and horse lovers especially may want to extend their stay in this peaceful, green village in the hills.

Orientation

Szilvásvárad has one main street, Egri út, that runs east and north through the village. Szalajka Valley is south of the small centre and the Lipizzaner Stud Farm is north. If you take the train, get off at the Szilvásvárad-Szalajkavölgy stop, and walk northeast for about 10 minutes to the centre. The main train station is 3km north.

Information

ABC (Egri út 8) Grocery store and ATM.

Information stand (www.szilvasvarad.hu; Szalajka-völgy; 10am-6pm Jun-Oct) The rest of the year, check with Tourinform in Eger.

Post office (Egri út 12)

Sights & Activities

The open-air **narrow-gauge train** (☎ 564 004; Szalajka-völgy 6; 1 way adult/child 300/150Ft; Apr-Oct) chugs up 5km (15 minutes) into the Szalajka Valley seven times daily from May to September (10 times daily on the weekend). Departures in April and October leave when enough people gather.

The little forest train ride ends at Szalajka-Fátyolvízesés. From there, you can walk for 15 minutes to **Istállóskő Cave**, where Stone Age pottery shards were discovered in 1912, or climb 958m **Mt Istállóskő**, the highest peak in the Bükk Hills. To return to Szilvásvárad, either board the train for the return trip or walk back 1¼ hours down along shady trails, past the veil waterfall, trout-filled streams and fish ponds. Towards the end of the path, there's an inconsequential **Forestry Museum** (☎ 355 112; adult/child 400/200Ft; 8.30am-4.30pm Tue-Sun) and a turn-off where you can veer for a 2.1km hike to the **Millennium Tower** (adult/child 300/200Ft; noon-7pm May-Oct), which you can climb for great valley views.

At the mouth of the Szalajka Valley, south of the narrow-gauge train station, you come upon a line of paid amusements, like a trampoline jump and (non-Lipicai) **pony rides** (per round 400Ft; 11am-5pm May-Oct). The **mountain bike rental shop** (☎ 06 30 335 2695; per hr/day 200/2000Ft; 9am-6pm) sells gear and maps as well as renting mountain bikes.

Continue north of the train station back towards town and you'll see a number of souvenir and food stands near the open and closed **racecourses** (www.menesgazdasag.hu), where festivals, Lipizzaner parades and coach races take place.

Learn more about these intelligent horses north in town by visiting the tiny **Horse Museum** (☎ 355 135; Park utca 8; adult/child 400/200Ft; 9am-noon & 1-4pm Thu-Sun). Exhibits focus on bloodlines, but the real sight is the breeding

THE MAGNIFICENT WHITE STALLIONS

The celebrated white Lipizzaner horses, or Lipicai in Hungarian, are well known for their graceful, ballet-like dressage movements at the Spanish Riding School in Vienna. In Szilvásvárad they are bred as carriage horses; as a result they are bigger and stronger than those raised for riding and show at Lipica in Slovenia, and those destined for the Spanish Riding School from Graz, Austria.

When you walk around the Szilvásvárad stables at the stud farm or the Horse Museum, you'll notice charts on each horse's stall with complicated figures, dates and names. It's all to do with the horse's lineage. Some six families with 16 ancestors (including Spanish, Arabian and Berber breeds) can be traced back to the Habsburg reign in the early 18th century; their pedigrees read like those of medieval nobility. Only about 3000 were registered in the world at the time of writing.

A fully mature Lipizzaner measures about 15 hands (that's about 152cm), weighs between 500kg and 600kg and lives an average of 25 to 30 years. Lipizzaners are not born white, but grey, or even brown. The celebrated 'imperial white' coat does not come about until they are between five and 10 years old, when their hair loses its pigment. Think of it as part of the maturing process. We could all be so lucky as to get more attractive as we age.

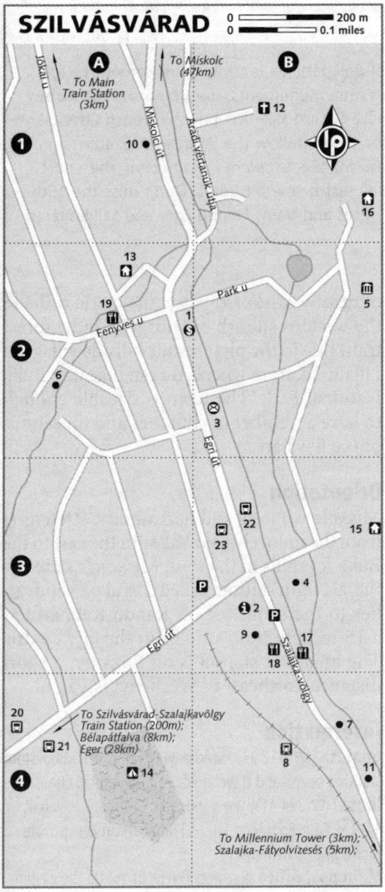

INFORMATION
ABC & ATM 1 A2
Information Stand 2 B3
Post Office 3 B2

SIGHTS & ACTIVITIES
Covered Racecourse 4 B3
Horse Museum 5 B2
Lipizzaner Stud Farm 6 A2
Mountain Bike Rentals 7 B4
Narrow-Gauge Train Station 8 B4
Open Racecourse 9 B3
Orbán House 10 A1
Pony Rides 11 B4
Round Church 12 B1

SLEEPING
Eden Panzió 13 A2
Hegyi Camping 14 A4
Szalajka Liget Hotel 15 B3
Szilvásvaradi Kasthely Hotel 16 B1

EATING
Csobogó Étterem 17 B3
Lovas Étterem 18 B3
Táltos Vigadó 19 A2

TRANSPORT
Bus Stop 20 A4
Bus Stop 21 A4
Bus Stop 22 B3
Bus Stop 23 B3

mares who live here in an 18th-century stable. The stallions at the **Lipizzaner Stud Farm** (Lipicai Állami Ménesgazdaság; ☎ 564 400; www.menesgazdasag.hu; Fenyves utca; adult/child 300/200Ft; ⌚ 10am-noon & 2-4pm Thu-Sun) can also be visited. Arrange ahead for horse rides up the into protected areas of the Bükk Plateau (3000Ft per hour) or for coach rides (from 5000Ft per hour). Riding packages include overnighting in a cottage in the hills.

The Protestant **Round Church** (Aradi vértanúk útja 33; admission free; ⌚ 2-6pm Tue-Sun), with its Doric columns and dramatic dome raised in 1841, looks to some like a provincial attempt to duplicate the basilica at Eger. Displays in a 17th-century **Orbán House** (☎ 355 133; Miskolci utca 58-60; adult/child 400/200Ft; ⌚ 9am-5pm Tue-Sun mid-Apr–Oct) are devoted to the flora, fauna and geology of Bükk National Park.

Sleeping

More guest houses and private rooms for rent can be found along the main street, Egri út.

Hegyi Camping (☎ 355 207; www.hegyicamping.com; Egri út 36/a; camp sites 1800Ft, 2-/3-/4-bed bungalows 5500/6500/7400Ft; ⌚ May-Oct) A small, shady camping ground close to walks. White-and-wood bungalows are a bit dated.

Eden Panzió (☎ 564 007; www.edenpanzio.hu; s 7500-9500Ft, d 10,000-12,000Ft) Each of the brightly hued rooms (cornflower blue, Dijon yellow) has light wood furnishings and minibars. Friendly guest-house owners will arrange bicycle rental and horse riding. There's a Jacuzzi and sauna on-site.

Szalajka Liget Hotel (☎ 564 300; www.szalajkaliget.hu; Park utca 25; r/house 20,000/38,000Ft;) Rooms are surprisingly bland and neutral at this full-blown resort with huge outdoor pool and playground, indoor whirlpools and sauna, spa services, bike rental and beer garden. Holiday houses (with kitchen) sleep four and there's free wi-fi.

Szilvásváradi Kasthely Hotel (☎ 564 065; Park utca 6) At the time of writing, this hotel was under extensive reconstruction. Look for the old manor house to reopen as a top-notch lodging.

DETOUR: BÉLAPÁTFALVA

On the way to Szilvásvárad, you pass the village of Bélapátfalva (and its giant cement factory). Nearby is one of Hungary's most preserved Romanesque monuments: the **Bélháromkút Abbey Church** (☎ 354 784; adult/child 300/150Ft; ⌚ 10am-4pm Tue-Sun mid-Mar–Oct), built by French Cistercian monks in 1232. Walk east from the village centre for 1.5km (follow the 'Apátság Múzeum' signs) along Apátság utca; another sign gives the address for the *templom kulcsa* (key). The church, built in the shape of a cross, is set in a peaceful dell just below Mt Bélkő. Don't miss the 19th-century painted Calvary scene nearby. Most of the buses and trains linking Eger and Szilvásvárad stop at Bélapátfalva.

Eating

Numerous food stands and eateries line the entrance to Szalajka Valley, near the narrow-gauge rail station; most of them serve *fustolt pistrang* (smoked trout), the area speciality.

Táltos Vigadó (☎ 355 108; Fenyves út 2; mains 890-1100Ft) Hearty Hungarian faves top the menu at this rustic, neighbourhood inn. Sit outside if you can't ignore all the trophy animals staring at you.

Csobogó Étterem (☎ 06 20 952 2632; Szalajka-völgy; mains 1500-1800Ft) Next to a stream-powered waterwheel under the valley trees is a truly lovely place to dine. In summer you can watch your grilled dishes being fired nearby on the open outdoor pit.

Lovas Étterem (☎ 355 555; Szalajka-völgy; mains 1650-2500Ft; ⌚ 10am-8pm) The dining room walls here serve as an informal gallery of coach racing and Lipicai glory. As the main restaurant in town, Lovas host loads of events – from dances to sleigh rides with hot drinks in winter.

Getting There & Away

Buses connect with Eger (450Ft, 45 minutes, 30km) at least hourly, travelling via Bélapátfalva (200Ft, 10 minutes, 7km). Two buses a day go direct to Budapest (2290Ft, three hours, 152km).

There's been talk of discontinuing service on the small spur rail line from Eger (525Ft, one hour, 34km). At the time of writing, there were still six trains a day, but none go between 10am and 2pm.

MISKOLC

☎ 46 / pop 184,100

Miskolc, Hungary's third-largest city, is a sprawling metropolis ringed by refineries and cardboard-quality housing blocks. Not so attractive in its own right, the location at the foot of the Bükk Hills makes this the jumping-off point for trips to the thermal cave baths of nearby Miskolctapolca, the castle ruins in the western suburb of Diósgyőr and a forest train ride to the picturesque hillside village of Lillafüred, from where you can hike into Bükk National Park. The town is sizeable enough to have a number of churches and museums, plus a few bars.

Orientation

Miskolc is a long and narrow city, stretching from the unlovely Sajó Valley in the east to the Bükk foothills in the west. Miskolc's state-of-the-art train station, called Tiszai pályaudvar, lies to the southeast on Kandó Kálmán tér, a 15-minute tram ride from the city centre. The huge bus station is on Búza tér, a short distance northeast of Széchenyi István út.

Information

Géniusz (☎ 412 932; Széchenyi István út 107) Bookstore stocking novels and travel guides on Hungary in English.
Ibusz (☎ 324 411; www.ibusz.hu; Széchenyi István út 14; ⌚ 8am-5pm Mon-Fri, to 11am Sat) Brokers private rooms and apartments.
Main post office (Kazinczy Ferenc út 16) On the eastern side of Hősök tere.
OTP bank (Széchenyi István út 15) Opposite the Dark Gate.
Planet Café (Bajcsy-Zsilinszky utca 2-4; per hr 400Ft; ⌚ 10am-10pm) Internet access and wi-fi in the Szinva-park mall.
Tourinform (☎ 350 425; www.miskolc.hu; Városház tér 13; ⌚ 9am-7pm Mon-Fri, 10am-8pm Sat & Sun Jun-Sep, 9am-5pm Mon-Fri, 9am-1pm Sat Oct-May) Bundles of information on the city and its surrounds.

Sights

The main drag, Széchenyi István út, is lined with some fairly interesting old buildings, especially those around the so-called **Dark Gate** (Sötétkapu), an 18th-century vaulted passageway.

The tourist board likes to vaunt Miskolc as the 'city of churches', but they aren't far wrong. The **Hungarian Orthodox Church** (Deák Ferenc tér 7), a splendid late-baroque structure, has a Greek Orthodox iconostasis (1793) that is 16m high with 88 icons. A guide will escort you to the impressive **Ecclesiastical Museum** (☎ 415 441; adult/child 300/150Ft; ⏰ 10am-6pm Tue-Sun Apr-Sep, 10am-4pm Tue-Sat Oct-Mar) near the main gate. Look out for the Black Madonna of Kazan, presented to the church by Catherine the Great, and the jewel-encrusted Mt Athos Cross, brought to Miskolc by Greek settlers in the 18th century. To the southeast stands the large **Orthodox Synagogue** (Kazinczy Ferenc utca 7), designed in 1861 by Ludwig Förster, architect of the Great Synagogue in Budapest. It is the only synagogue still in use in the county.

The Calvinist **Plank Church** (Petőfi tér) is a 1938 replica of a 17th-century Transylvanian-style wooden church. It has been completely rebuilt and renovated after being badly damaged by fire in 1997. In a cemetery below the Avas Hill is the large Gothic **Avas Calvinist church** (Avas-hegy), with a painted wooden interior (1410). The bell tower dates from the mid-16th century. The key is in the parish office at Papszer utca 14.

The **Ottó Herman Museum** (☎ 346 875; Papszer utca 1; adult/child 600/300Ft; ⏰ 10am-4pm Tue-Sun), south of the city centre, has large collections of Neolithic finds (many from the Bükk region), plus ethnographical and mineral collections (yawn).

For more nearby sights, see Around Miskolc (p343).

Activities

Your open-air carriage hugs the cliff (with a precipitous drop on the other side) as the train climbs the hill. The journey, one of the most enjoyable forest train trips in Hungary, connects Miskolc with the resort town of Lillafüred (p343). This little **narrow-gauge train** (Map p344; ☎ 530 593; www.laev.hu; adult/child return 1000/800Ft) leaves from Dorttya út in western Miskolc on weekdays at 10.20am and 12.40pm; on weekends there are additional 12.40pm and 2pm departures. More trips are scheduled in July and August.

After the 30-minute ride to Lillafüred, the train carries on 6km (one hour) further to Garadna, another Bükk National Park hiking destination.

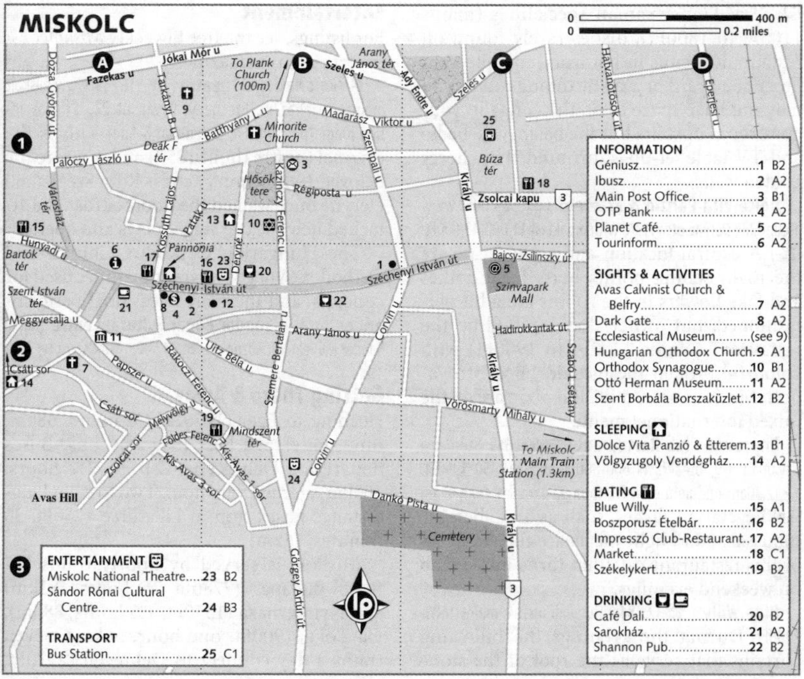

South of the centre, you can stroll up leafy **Avas Hill** along the narrow lanes past some of the more than 800 wine cellars cut into the limestone. (The best approach is via Mélyvölgy utca, off Papszer utca, or Földes Ferenc utca, off Mindszent tér.) You can also taste a few of the choice local wines at **Szent Borbála Borszaküzlet** (☎ 411 188; Széchenyi István út 14; 🕑 9am-5pm Mon-Fri, to 1pm Sat) in a courtyard off the main street.

Festivals & Events

The city has a calendar full of cultural events, including **Miskolc City Festival** mid-May.

Sleeping & Eating

For more pleasant surrounds while you sleep, check into lodging in nearby Miskolctapolca and Lillafüred.

Völgyzugoly Vendégház (☎ 353 676; www.volgyzugolyvendeghaz.hu; Toronyalja utca 61; s/d 6000/8000Ft) Bold hues and avant-garde artwork pep up the five rooms at this small boarding house. The owner is a JRR Tolkien fan. There's free wi-fi in-room.

Székelykert (☎ 411 222; www.szallasinfo.hu/szekelykert; Földes Ferenc utca 4; s/d/tr 9000/12,000/14,000Ft; 💻) Try Transylvanian specialities (mains 1100Ft to 1800Ft), dishes rarely found on restaurant menus in Hungary, in a pleasant inner courtyard or a rustic dining room. You may not have space to do the conga in your guestroom upstairs but the basic twin-beds-and-TV-table set-up is surrounded by cheery golden walls.

Dolce Vita Panzió & Étterem (☎ 505 045; www.freund.hu; Déryné utca 7; s/d with breakfast 11,000/13,000Ft; ❄) A central location and a good cafe are the main selling points here. Lace doilies and fake flowers in the rooms are a bit old-fashioned, but owners have spiffed up the restaurant (mains 1450Ft to 1900Ft) with colourful broken-tile mosaics. Beef stroganoff, Mexican bean chilli and pizza are on the mixed international menu.

Impresszó Club-Restaurant (☎ 509 669; Széchenyi István út 3-9; breakfasts 600-800Ft, mains 1450-1990Ft; 🕑 7.30am-midnight Mon-Fri, from 9.30am Sat, from 11am Sun) Vegetarian dishes, such as an aubergine moussaka, and light meals are the strengths of this restaurant-cafe that turns into a club on weekend evenings.

Blue Willy (☎ 323 844; Hunyadi utca 4; mains 1600-2200Ft) During the evenings the billowing curtains that serve as the roof of the stone courtyard create a relaxed Mediterranean feel. Inside is almost airy with high ceilings and large oceanic photos. Expect updated Magyar classics on offer.

Miskolc's large **market** (Zsolcai kapu; 🕑 8am-3pm) is east of Búza tér, or you can head to **Boszporusz Ételbár** (Széchenyi István út 21-23; mains 500-800Ft; 🕑 11am-8pm Mon-Sat) for Hungarian cheap eats.

Drinking

Have your pick of drink cafes along Déryné utca. Impresszó restaurant also has a killer cocktail list.

Sarokház (☎ 320 588; Széchenyi István út 2; 🕑 8am-10pm Mon-Fri, 10am-midnight Sat, 10am-10pm Sun) The 'Corner' coffee house has an old-world theme and some pretty tasty pastries to go along with the assortment of java and juice.

Cafe Dali (Déryné utca 10; 🕑 10am-11pm Mon-Thu, 10am-midnight Sat, 11am-10pm Sun) With big couches, a funky decor and chilled tunes, Dali is perfect for lolling around sipping cocktails.

Shannon Pub (☎ 413 904; Széchenyi István út 2; 🕑 10am-11pm Mon-Thu, 10am-midnight Sat, 11am-10pm Sun) Beer it up at this town's imitation Irish pub.

Entertainment

For listings, see the free biweekly *Miskolci Est* (www.est.hu) magazine.

Miskolc National Theatre (☎ 516 735; www.miskolcinemzetiszinhaz.hu; Széchenyi István út 23; 🕑 box office 10am-7pm Mon-Fri, 3-7pm Sat & Sun) This is the original theatre (built 1857) and is where the beloved 19th-century actress Róza Széppataki Déryné once walked the floorboards. The attached new theatre stages plays and operas.

The Hungarian Orthodox Church and Orthodox Synagogue are sometimes used for concerts, and there are occasional performances at the **Sándor Rónai Cultural Centre** (Rónai Sándor Művelődési Központ; ☎ 342 408; Mindszent tér 3).

Getting There & Away

Heading to Eger (1770Ft, 1½ hours, 68km, nine daily), it's best to go by bus. Buses depart for Debrecen (1210Ft, 2¼ hours, 100km) at least every hour. Two to eight long-distance buses stop in Lillafüred (250Ft, 30 minutes, 16km).

Miskolc is served by hourly trains between Budapest (2780Ft, 2½ hours, 182km) and Nyíregyháza (1350Ft, 1½ hours, 88km), via Tokaj (900Ft, one hour, 56km). Seven trains a day connect to Debrecen (2170Ft,

1½ hours, 137km). About 12 trains leave Miskolc each day for Sárospatak (1200Ft, 1¼ hours, 74km) and Sátoraljaújhely (1350Ft, 1½ hours, 84km).

Two trains a day depart Miskolc for Košice in Slovakia (1¼ hours).

Getting Around

Tram 1 begins at the train station and travels the centre of the city (Városház tér is near Tourinform) before reaching the narrow-gauge train at stop 18 (LÁEV) and turning around at the terminus Diósgyőr. You can transfer from there to bus 5 to Lillafüred. Tram 2 also tracks from the train station through the centre, but it ends up in the industrial quarter of Diósgyőr-Kóház.

AROUND MISKOLC

Diósgyőr

☎46 / pop 6500

The reason to visit this suburb of Miskolc, 7km to the west, is the four-towered **Diósgyőr Castle** (☎533 355; www.diosgyorivar.hu; Vár utca 24; adult/child 900/450Ft; 9am-6pm May-Oct, 9am-5pm Nov-Apr). Begun in the 13th century, the castle was heavily damaged early in the 18th century and was only restored – very insensitively in some parts – in the 1950s. Tour the castle's history display, ruined rooms and ramparts. The wax museum and medieval weapon stash exhibits cost 200Ft extra. The castle hosts numerous summer events, including plays staged in the castle courtyard, the **International Folk Festival** in mid-July, and **Medieval Castle Days** in mid-August.

You can soak in the sight of the impressive fortress at the open-air **Castle Baths** (☎530 292; Vár utca 26; adult/child 900/500Ft; 9am-6pm Jun-Aug).

Talizmán Étterem (☎378 627; Vár utca 14; mains 1200-1800Ft), on a pedestrian street lined with chestnut trees, serves folksy faves. The restaurant at **Várkert Panzió** (☎532 248; www.diosgyorivarkert.hu; Tapolcarét 2; s/d 12,000/15,000Ft), beyond the baths, has slightly better food (mains 1200Ft to 2000Ft), but is only open Thursday through Sunday. Real wood furnishings fill the upstairs room at the attractive stonefront Várkert. Quick snacks are available in the castle courtyard, where costumed docents also sell crafty gifts.

Diósgyőr is part of Miskolc public transport: Tram 1 terminates here and local bus 5 connects with Lillafüred, 15 minutes further west, at least hourly. From the bus and tram stops, the castle is east on Nagy Lajos Király útja and south on Vár utca.

Lillafüred

☎46 / pop 480

The mountain feel of Lillafüred, a tiny resort at the junction of two valleys formed by the Garadna and Szinva Streams, is in stark contrast to the urban sprawl of Miskolc only 12km to the east. Take the narrow-gauge train up to feel the change unfold. Other than a couple of caves and a palatial hotel and gardens, there are no sights. It's just a nice spot to enjoy some fresh air, and a good springboard for walks and hikes. The village is in the eastern expanses of Bükk National Park.

The Hotel Palota has a Tourinform brochure stand; otherwise the Miskolc branch can provide information.

ACTIVITIES

The **narrow-gauge train** (☎530 593; www.laev.hu; adult/child return to Miskolc 1000/800Ft, to Garadna 2000/1600Ft) chugs down to Miskolc's Dorttya út (11.55am, 2.25pm departures) or continues an hour further west into the park at Garadna (10.55am, 1.15pm departures). More trips are scheduled on weekends, and daily June through August.

Below the Palota hotel, stone steps and terraces lead down to the 20m **waterfall** *(vízesés)* and to **Anna Cave** (☎334 130; www.bnpi.hu; adult/child 750/500Ft; 10am-3pm mid-Apr–mid-Oct), sometimes called Petőfi Cave. On a 25-minute tour of the labyrinth of tunnels, you'll come across fossilised leaves, branches and even entire trees. Tours depart on the hour (technically only if 25 people have gathered, but fewer may be OK in July and August).

István Cave (☎334 130; adult/child 750/500Ft, minimum 10 people; 9am-3pm mid-Apr–mid-Oct) is about 500m up the mountain road leading to Eger, past the souvenir and food stands. Hour-long tours (on the hour) take in stalagmites, stalactites, sinkholes and large chambers.

Jade-coloured **Foundry Lake** (Hámori-tó) was named after the proto-blast furnace set up here by a German named Frigyes Fazola in the early 19th century to exploit the area's iron ore. **Row boats** (10am-6pm May-Sep) cost 300Ft per person per half-hour, while paddle boats cost 700Ft. The Palota hotel rents out bicycles for 2000Ft per day, but only to guests when they're busy.

A lovely walk leads along the red/green trail from the east side of the car park, south of István Cave, to **Fehérkő Overlook** (3km, 1¼ hours). When the green triangle veers off, follow it up a steep incline and narrow trail for panoramic views of Szinva Valley. Longer hikes can be undertaken from the terminus of the narrow-gauge train at Garadna, but accommodation is sparse in those parts and hikers had better be prepared to camp rough if they miss the train. Be sure to have a copy of a Bükk map from Cartographia or Topograf and carry extra water.

The Hotel Palota organises guided hikes.

SLEEPING & EATING

Sidle up to any of the several food stalls serving *lángos* (deep-fried dough with toppings) and sausage near the narrow-gauge train station, or climb uphill towards István Cave for even more food-stand options with covered seating and fuller menus.

Lillafüred Camping (☎ 333 146; http://kovatt.lillacamp.hu/camping.htm; Erzsébet sétány 39; camp sites per person/tent 1000/800Ft; ⏲ May-Sep) This small, shady camping ground is tent and caravan only. There's a shared fridge and wash station in addition to bathrooms.

Lillafüred Panzió (☎ 379 299; www.lillapanzio.eoldal.hu, in Hungarian; Erzsébet sétány 7; s/d 6000/8000Ft) Well hidden among lush trees above the central village is a straightforward *pension*, with

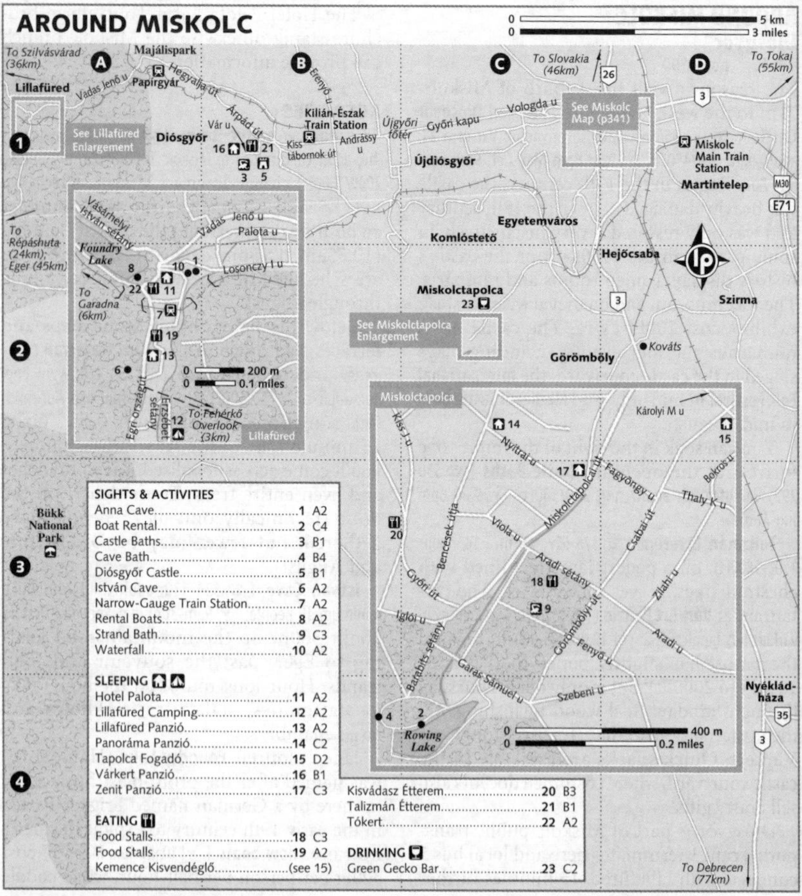

WORTH THE TRIP: RÉPÁSHUTA

Nearly central in Bükk National Park, **Répáshuta** (www.repashuta.hu) makes an excellent base for exploring area caves and, further afield, the Bükk Plateau. The long and windy hillside village has a handful of *panzió* or private rooms, a game restaurant, a folk craft exhibition and a grocery store. Just 24km from Lillafüred, buses connect to Miskolc (675Ft, 1¼ hours, 41km) two to eight times a day. The hilly drive from Eger through Répáshuta to Miskolc is extremely enjoyable, but the bus only makes the journey once weekly, on Sunday morning.

clean and simple rooms, friendly staff and a basic restaurant.

Hotel Palota (☎ 331 411; www.hunguesthotels.hu; Erzsébet sétány 1; s/d from 22,000/27,000Ft; 💻 🅿) Dominating Lillafüred with its regal air, fancy turrets and formal gardens, the 'Palace' hotel is a piece of old-world luxury. Look out from traditional rooms onto views of the lake or forest. Stained-glass windows and an enormous fireplace decorate the upscale Mátyás restaurant (mains 2700Ft to 4200Ft), where waiters look like they're dressed to serve a medieval banquet. There's also a wine cellar and grill-terrace restaurant on-site. Services include guided hikes, bike rental, saunas, billiards, a fitness centre and more.

Tókert (☎ 533 560; Erzsébet sétány 3; breakfasts 600-800Ft, mains 1700-2300Ft; 🕒 7am-11pm) In the shadow (in every sense) of the Palota hotel, this multilevel terrace restaurant has great views of the lake. Both game and fish dishes are pretty good; try the basil fried tomatoes.

GETTING THERE & AWAY

From Miskolc you can reach Lillafüred by narrow-gauge train (p341), or from the end station of tram 1 at Diósgyőr, transfer to bus 5. Two to eight long-distance buses stop in Lillafüred en route between Miskolc (250Ft, 30 minutes, 16km) and Répáshuta (375Ft, 40 minutes, 24km).

Miskolctapolca

☎ 46 / pop 4700

This leafy spa town, now a suburb 7km southwest of Miskolc, has long been attracting visitors; the curative waters here have been known since the Middle Ages. Today's **Cave Bath** (Barlangfürdő; ☎ 561 361; www.barlangfurdo.hu; Pazár István sétány 1; adult/child 2100/1400Ft; 🕒 9am-7pm mid-Jul–Aug, 9am-6pm Sep–mid-Jul) is unique in the country. Go with the flow from the atrium pool through a series of cave pools that, because of the skylights, at times feel like you're in a not-too-hot volcano. Outdoor pools have a few jetted bubbles and a climbing apparatus for the kids. Choose from a full complement of medical, spa and fitness services. Special events – like night bathing or musical theme nights – are held often.

Next to the cave baths, the little Rowing Lake has **boat rental** (per hr 600Ft; 🕒 10am-6pm May-Sep).

Can't get enough swimming? Dip into the pretty **Strand Bath** (Strandfürdő; ☎ 368 127; Miskolctapolcai út 1; 🕒 9am-6pm May-Sep), open-air pools surrounded by the city's large park.

NORTHERN UPLANDS

SLEEPING

Miskolctapolca is a holiday town. The landscaped parks and shady lanes provide an agreeable break from city life, thus the accommodation options pretty much everywhere. Tourinform in Miskolc (p340) can help.

Panoráma Panzió (☎ 431 970; www.panoramapanzio.olh.hu; Nyitrai utca 5; s 4500-6500Ft, d 6500-9500Ft) Being willing to walk up a small hill gets you a big price break. The modern, multilayer exterior – in red and smoky grey – gives way to more mix-and-match interiors. Guests share a kitchen and garden.

Tapolca Fogadó (☎ 562 215; www.tapolcafogado.hu; Csabai utca 36; s/d 8000/11,000Ft) Steep peaks and a towering turret give the Tapolca a romantic, rustic-castle feel. Many rooms have interesting triangular windows beneath slanted, wood-panelled eaves. Natural beds and floors complete the all-wood look.

Zenit Panzió (☎ 561 560; www.zenitpanzio.hu; Miskolctapolcai út 25; d/tr 13,500/16,700Ft) It's not just the big yellow house that makes this *panzió* homey; there's the warm staff that will help you rent a car, too. Ask for a room with a balcony, or enjoy the communal terrace. There's free wi-fi.

EATING & DRINKING

Choose among numerous food stalls and snack bars on Aradi sétány.

Kisvádasz Étterem (☎ 422 329; Győri utca 15; mains 1300-2000Ft) Formal-looking waiters serve a little stiffly from a menu packed with Hungarian specialities.

Kemence Kisvendéglő (☎ 562 215; Tapolca Fogadó, Csabai utca 36; mains 1600-2400Ft) Everything from pork in a paprika-sour-cream sauce with gnocchi-like dumplings to the honey-and-apple grilled chicken tastes good at this rustic guest-house eatery.

Green Gecko Bar (☎ 06 20 926 9292; Miskolctapolcai út 99; 🕑 8pm-2am Mon-Sat) Hip young things make the trek from Miskolc for this upscale bar (yes, it's painted green). More than 50 shots and mixed drinks are on the menu.

GETTING THERE & AWAY

Miskolctapolca is part of Miskolc public transport: bus 2 runs between here (stop says 'Tapolca Strandfürdő') and Búzá tér, near the Miskolc bus station.

AGGTELEK HILLS

It can be a little unnerving leaving Miskolc behind and heading northwest along Rte 26 towards the Slovak border. One giant chemical factory after another lines the road, and it's hard to resist turning around and looking for greener pastures. But don't be put off by all the twisted steel and rusting pipes; just to the north are the Aggtelek Hills, an area with hardly a hint of urban intrusion. Here, rolling forested hills and meadows hide the occasional rural village, and life still follows the seasons.

This region is also home to the **Aggtelek National Park** (http://anp.nemzetipark.gov.hu), a hilly karst region encompassing some 200 sq km, and Europe's largest stalactite caves.

AGGTELEK

☎ 48 / pop 580

The tiny village of Aggtelek is the main gateway to the Baradla-Domica caves, a network of some 25km of passageways (6km of them in Slovakia) that has been a dual-nation Unesco World Heritage Site since 1995. A trip underground to see the array of red-and-black stalactite drip stones, stalagmite pyramids and enormous chambers is the highlight. Six kilometres east, the village of Jósvafő also has accommodation and a cave entrance.

Orientation

There are three entrances to the Baradla Cave system: at Aggtelek village; at Jósvafő, 6km to the east; and at Vörös-tó (Red Lake), just before Jósvafő. Guided tours of the Baradla Cave system depart from these points.

Information

Aggtelek National Park Directorate (Aggteleki Nemzeti Park Igazgatósága; ☎ 506 000; http://anp.nemzetipark.gov.hu; Tengerszem oldal 1) The national park office is in neighbouring Jósvafő.

Post office (☎ 343 156; Kossuth utca 37) Has an ATM, too.

Tourinform (☎ 503 000; aggtelek@tourinform.hu; Baradla oldal 3; 🕑 8am-6pm Apr-Sep, 8am-4pm Oct-Mar) Supplies info and sells maps.

Activities

Baradla Cave (Baradla-baling; Baradla oldal 1; 🕑 9am-6pm Apr-Sep, 10am-3pm Oct-Mar), northwest of Tourinform, has tours that depart year-round. Most allow you to listen to a short organ recital or some other form of music in the Concert or Giants' Halls and, if the water is high enough, take a boat ride on the underground river Styx. The temperature at this level is usually about 10°C with humidity over 95%, so be sure to bring a warm top. One-hour tours (adult/child 2100/1300Ft) start at the Aggtelek entrance at 10am, 11.30am, 1pm and 3pm, with additional tours at 9am, noon and 5pm from April to September. More advanced tours have to be booked ahead: the four-hour Keresztély Raisztour (4000/2400Ft; 3.6km) includes an unpaved section without illumination (torches provided); the Long tour (6000/3600Ft; 7km) takes in the entire main cave section from Aggtelek, including the Red Lake, and ends in Jósvafő.

A two-hour tour (2500Ft) of the Red Lake section alone leaves from the Vörös-tó entrance, halfway between Aggtelek and Jósvafő, at 10am, noon and 2pm year-round. You can also buy reduced-price tickets that combine Aggtelek and Jósvafő cave tours or guided park walks over two consecutive days.

You can join up with some excellent **hiking trails** above the Tourinform office in Aggtelek, affording superb views of the rolling hills and valleys. A relatively easy three-hour (7km) walk along the **Baradla Trail**, tagged yellow, will take you from Aggtelek to Jósvafő. There are other treks lasting five to six hours, and these routes can be used for cycling and horse riding. A 20km **bicycle route** links Aggtelek and Szögliget to the northeast, but unfortunately you'll have to bring your own bike.

The park directorate organises a number of programs, including the three-hour Aggtelek **guided walk** (Baradla oldal 1; adult/child 1000/600Ft; 1pm Apr-Sep), as well as various ecotours, booked ahead at the Aggtelek and Jósvafő cave entrances.

The **Hucul Stud Farm** (Hucul Menes; Táncsics utca 1; 8am-5pm Apr-Oct), part of the national park, in Jósvafő has horses for hire (3000Ft per hour) and offers hour-long carriage rides for 6000Ft.

Festivals & Events

Main events in Aggtelek and its vicinity are the **International Opera Festival** in Baradla Cave in June and the **Gömör-Torna Festival of folk and world music** in July.

Sleeping & Eating

There are a number of small boarding houses in both Aggtelek and Jósvafő. All sleeping possibilities listed here have restaurants (Tengerszem is the best). There are food stalls (pizza, gyros, *lángos*) in the car park near the Aggtelek cave and a coffee shop near the Vörös-tó entrance.

Baradla Hostel & Camping (☎ 503 005; szallas@anp.hu; Baradla oldal 2; dm adult/student 2000/1800Ft, camp sites per person/tent 900/1000Ft) Simple four-bedded dorm rooms located near the Baradla Cave entrance. The building is not exactly new, and the camping ground is just a big, shadeless field, but it'll do.

Tengerszem Szállo (☎ 506 005; tengerszem_szallo@t-online.hu; Tengerszem oldal 2, Jósvafő; s/d 7500/13,000Ft) A gable end facing front and bright red window shutters create a downright alpine-esque appeal. Heavy pine beds and nightstands fit right into the lodge look. Cuddle up in a large leather chair by the stone fireplace when winter comes. It's near the Jósvafő cave entrance.

Cseppkő Szállo (☎ 343 075; http://hotelcseppko.freeweb.hu; Gyömrői út 2; s/d incl breakfast 8900/14,000Ft;) On a scenic hill above the Aggtelek cave entrance, this ugly concrete hotel has surprisingly decent rooms. The restaurant, bar, bowling alley, tennis court, indoor swimming pool, and terrace with splendid views make the place.

Getting There & Away

Direct buses connect to Miskolc (1050Ft, 1½ hours, 62km) and Budapest (3230Ft, five hours, 240km) once daily; more buses run to Miskolc in July and August. All buses to Aggtelek stop at Jósvafő first.

Aggtelek can also sort-of be reached by train from Miskolc (750Ft, 1¼ hours, 49km, nine daily); you want the one heading for Tornanádaska. A local bus meets each of the trains at the Jósvafő-Aggtelek train station, some 14km east of Jósvafő, and takes you to either town.

Getting Around

Five local buses a day link Aggtelek (stopping outside the Cseppkő hotel) and Jósvafő (stopping at the cave entrance) via Vörös-tó.

ZEMPLÉN HILLS

The microclimate on the southern and eastern slopes of the Zemplén Hills is just right for creating world-renowned Tokaj wine. The 'wine of kings' most know is a golden sweet dessert nectar, but the area also produces some wonderful, apple-scented dry whites. That Tokaj is also a pretty little town makes this the hills' star. But the northern Zemplén, on the border with Slovakia, is full of hiking opportunities and romantic castle ruins like Füzér and Boldogkő. And the Eurovelo 11 cycling route skirts the hills, entering from Slovakia near Göncs, and continuing east to Sátoraljaújhely before beginning to follow the Tisza River's path south at Tokaj.

For more on the region, check out www.zemplen.hu. Make sure to invest in one of Cartographia's *Zempléni-hegység* (1:40,000) maps.

BOLDOGKŐVÁRALJA

☎ 46 / pop 1190

The picturesque Hernád Valley, which basically runs from Szerencs to Hidasnémeti, near the Slovakian border, is dotted with quaint wine-producing towns, perfect for sampling the region's fine vintages. Boldogkőváralja, 39km north of Tokaj, would be just another of these charming places if it weren't for its impressive castle ruins, seamlessly grafted to a rocky outcrop above the valley. Heading north on the train, sit on the right-hand side to see the dramatic fortress as it comes into view.

KARÓLY BUZÁS

The founding president of the Trail and Hiking Information Association (TUTI; Turista és Természetjáró Információs Egesült), Károly Buzás organises and leads several biking events annually. He helped mark the Eurovelo 11 route in Hungary in 2008.

What is best and worst about cycling in Hungary? Compared to the past, cycling is galloping today. We are part of the ECF (European Cycling Federation); the Eurovelo has come to Hungary. The worst in all this is that great opportunities are not explored. In many places they call a portion of a road separated by a yellow line a 'bike route'.

Do you have a favourite bike route? I have not been on all of our bike roads, but my favoured destination is the Zemplén Hills. I love it not only for the scenery but also for the kindness and hospitality of the people living there. I also appreciate Bereg County. In many places there are no biking facilities but some low-traffic, country roads, which are quite enjoyable. I also love Szigetköz [Western Transdanubia]. OK, I love whichever bike road I am on…

What's been your most memorable accomplishment since organising TUTI? The Eurovelo's Norway to Greece Route was a tremendous experience for which I was the Hungarian coordinator. We hosted 40 foreign bikers on 17 stopovers. Indeed, it was a super community effort throughout and I had a delightful experience.

Atop a basalt mountain, **Boldogkő Castle** (adult/child 500/300Ft; ⏲ 10am-6pm Apr-Oct), literally 'Happy Rock' Castle, is exactly what most people imagine a castle to be: impossibly perched on solid rock, strong walls and turrets commanding 360-degree views of the southern Zemplén Hills, the Hernád Valley and nearby vineyards. Originally built in the 13th century, the castle was strengthened 200 years later, but gradually fell into ruin in the 17th century. A few rooms have been reconstructed to contain small exhibits on area minerals and medieval armaments, but walking through the uneven courtyard up onto the ramparts and looking out over the surrounding countryside in the late afternoon is much more satisfying. It's easy to see how the swashbuckling lyric poet Bálint Balassi (1554–94) produced some of his finest work here.

Boldogkőváralja doesn't hold much reason to linger, but **Bodóvár Panzió** (☎ 306 065; www.bodovar.hu; Kossuth Lajos utca 61; s/d 9000/11,000Ft; 🏊), at the bottom of the road to the castle, has a heated pool and hot tub great for soaking after a hike. Some of the just-OK rooms (with fake chenille upholstered beds) have views of the castle. At the restaurant (mains 1100Ft to 1800Ft), tasty Hungarian dishes like pork steak with green beans, bacon and sour cream can be paired with a local Tokaj wine. There's free wi-fi.

Boldogkőváralja is not the easiest place to get to without a vehicle. By train, you have to switch (no wait) at Abaújszántó (200Ft, 10 minutes, 7km, six daily) to get to Szerencs (375Ft, 30 minutes, 21km, 10 daily), where you can connect to Tokaj, Miskolc, Debrecen and Budapest. Buses require just as many, but less convenient transfers.

TOKAJ

☎ 47 / pop 5100

The sweet and sultry wines produced here have been known since the 15th century. Today Tokaj is a picturesque little town of old buildings, wine cellars and nesting storks. Sitting riverfront provides the advantage of recreation opportunities, and the disadvantage of occasional flooding. The 66-sq-km Tokaj-Hegyalja wine-producing region, a microclimate along the southern and eastern edges of the Zemplén Hills, was declared a World Heritage Site in 2002. For more information on the qualities of Tokaj wines, see p53.

Orientation

Tokaj's centre lies west of where the Bodrog and Tisza Rivers meet. The train station is 1.2km south of the town; walk north for 15 minutes along Baross Gábor utca and Bajcsy-Zsilinszky utca to Rákóczi Ferenc út, the main thoroughfare. Buses arrive and depart from along Serház utca east of Kossuth tér.

Information

Integral Internet & Lan Club (☎ 352 157; Bajcsy-Zsilinszky utca 34; per hr 500Ft; ⏲ 10am-9pm Mon-Fri) Internet cafe inside Millennium Hotel.

OTP bank (Rákóczi Ferenc út 35)
Post office (Rákóczi Ferenc út 24)
Tourinform (☎ 552 070; www.tokaj.hu; Serház utca 1; 9am-6pm Mon-Fri, 10am-7pm Sat & Sun Jun-Aug, 9am-5pm Mon-Fri Sep-May)

Sights

The **Tokaj Museum** (☎ 522 070; Bethlen Gábor utca 13; adult/child 400/200Ft; 10am-4pm Tue-Sun), in the 18th-century Greek Trading House, leaves nothing unsaid about the history of Tokaj and the production of its wines. There's also a superb collection of Christian liturgical art, including icons, medieval crucifixes and triptychs, and Judaica from the former Great Synagogue, and temporary exhibits by local artists.

The 19th-century Eclectic **Great Synagogue** (Serház utca 55), which was used as a German barracks during WWII, is once again gleaming after a total reconstruction. It is now used as a conference and cultural centre.

The bells of several small churches on Kossuth tér make for an especially sonorous Sunday morning.

Activities

WINE TASTING

The correct order for sampling a flight of Tokaj wines is dry to sweet: Furmint, dry Szamorodni, sweet Szamorodni and then the Aszú wines. The latter, dessertlike wines have a rating of four to six *puttony* (a measure of how much of the sweet essence of noble rot grapes has been used). A basic flight of six Tokaj wines costs around 2600Ft; an all-Aszú tasting can run as much as 6000Ft. Private *pincek* and restaurants for tastings are scattered throughout town. The granddaddy of them all is the 600-year-old **Rákóczi Cellar** (Rákóczi Pince; ☎ 352 408; Kossuth tér 15; 11am-7pm), where bottles of wine mature in long corridors (one measures 28m by 10m). **Erzsébet Cellar** (☎ 06 20 802 0137; www.erzsebetpince.hu; Bem utca 16; 10am-6pm) is a smaller, family-run affair that usually needs to be booked ahead online. **Hímesudvar** (☎ 352 416; www.himesudvar.hu; Bem utca 2; 10am-4pm) is a 16th-century wine cellar with shop northwest of the town centre.

Smaller cellars line Hegyalja utca, off Bajcsy-Zsilinszky utca at the base of the vine-covered hill above the train station. A small, wheeled **wine train** (per ride 500Ft; May-Oct) departs from Tourinform, at varying hours, and rolls around town allowing time to stop at cellars.

OTHER ACTIVITIES

There's a grassy riverfront beach for swimming at **Tutajos Beach Camping** (☎ 06 30 239 6300; admission 300Ft; 9am-7pm Jun-Aug), across the Tisza River Bridge from town.

Rent canoes, kayaks and bicycles from **Vízisport-telep** (☎ 352 645; Horgász utca 3; per day 1000Ft; 8am-8pm); inquire inside the restaurant.

From May through October hour-long **sightseeing boat tours** (☎ 352 465; Kikötő; adult/child 960/720Ft; 11am & 3pm) ply the Tisza and Bodrog waters.

Festivals & Events

The **Tokaj Wine Festival**, held in late May, attracts oenophiles from far and wide, as do the **Vintage Days** during harvest season, on the first weekend of October. In mid-July the **Hegyalja Festival** rocks Tokaj out with bands from across Europe.

DETOUR: REGÉC

Most of the Zemplén towns and villages to see and stay in ring the base of the small mountains. Heading into the hills takes a little more work but it's often worth the effort. Even if villages have few services, they usually have at least a home or two that rent rooms and have a small grocery. You could create any number of adventures with a Cartographia Zemplén Hills map in hand. For example, the blue trail leads from Boldogkőváralja, on the castle's northern side, to **Regéc** (www.regec.hu, in Hungarian), about 17km (5¼ hours) away, skirting mountains in a moderate hike. A short but steep side trail (red L), 1km before the village, climbs up to the 14th-century **Regéc castle ruins** (Regéci vár; 689m). This trail is part of the 1128km-long **National Blue Tour** (Országos Kéktúra; www.kektura.eu) hiking route. From here you could follow the road west 10km to Fony (where there's a train station) or continue east 26km (seven hours) on the blue trail to Sátoraljaújhely (p354). Of course, you can also cheat and drive to Regéc via Fony; the windy mountain road continues over to the east side of the hills.

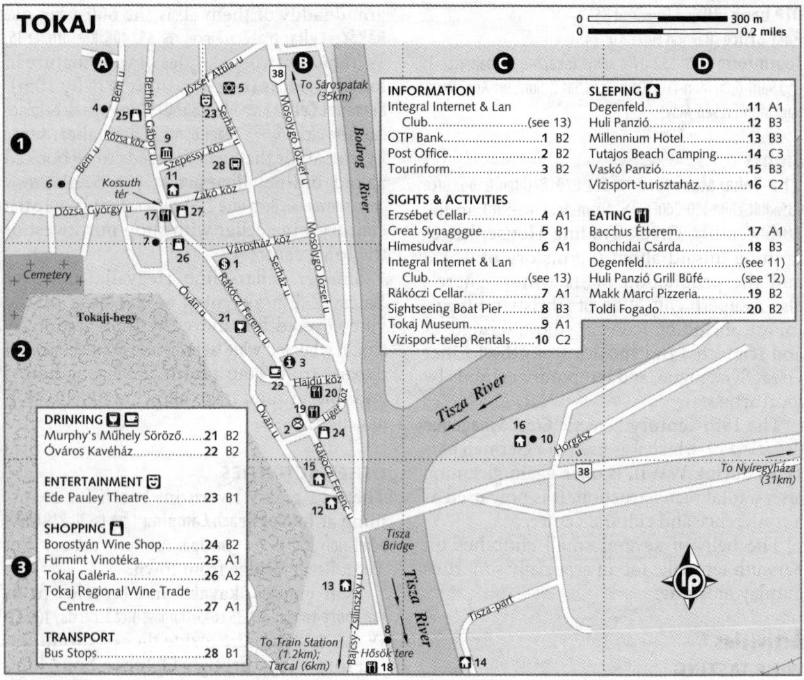

Sleeping

Private rooms on offer along Hegyalja utca are convenient to the train station and are surrounded by vineyards. Be prepared for bugs if you're camping.

Tutajos Beach Camping (☎ 06 20 969 1088; Honfoglalas 24; camp sites/bungalows per person 300/2200Ft; ⏲ Apr-Oct) Shady tent sites and basic bungalows are adjacent to a beach with boat rental. Showers cost 100Ft for four minutes.

Vízisport-turisztaház (☎ 352 645; Horgász utca 3; camp sites/dm 1000/2000Ft) Three- to four-bed rooms share a bathroom at this bare-bones hostel (beds only, no kitchen or common room). Rent bikes, canoes and kayaks here at the confluence of the Tisza and Bodrog Rivers; it organises canoe trips, too. There's a restaurant on-site.

Huli Panzió (☎ 352 791; www.hulipanzio.hu; Rákóczi út 16; s/d 4000/8000Ft; ❄) A sunny yellow covers both the walls and the flowered duvet covers in 12 down-to-earth rooms. What do you need besides a sturdy wood bed and table? Oh, there are minifridges and the possibility of air-con (1500Ft). Enjoy breakfast (800Ft) at the ground-floor restaurant.

Vaskó Panzió (☎ 352 107; http://vaskopanzio.fw.hu; Rákóczi út 12; r 8000Ft) The supremely central Vaskó has eight cute rooms, with window sills bedecked with flower pots. It's above a private wine cellar and the proprietor can organise tastings.

Degenfeld (☎ 552 173; www.degenfeldpalota.hu; Kossuth tér 1; s/d 7300/10,000Ft; ❄) Rooms aren't as elegant as you'd expect given the buttoned-up restaurant and wine cellar downstairs. But the simple polished wood floors and leather chairs seem to suit the four former palace rooms well enough. There are free cable internet connections.

Millennium Hotel (☎ 352 247; www.tokajmillennium.hu; Bajcsy-Zsilinszky utca 34; s/d 13,000/15,900Ft; ❄ 💻) Equidistant from the train station and town centre, the only drawback to the Millennium Hotel's location is the busy road out front. Burled wood wardrobes with black trim give the rooms an almost Art Deco charm and there's a pleasant beer garden, too.

Eating

Makk Marci Pizzeria (☎ 352 336; Liget köz 1; pizzas 780-990Ft) This cheap and friendly pizzeria is good for a basic meal.

Huli Panzió Grill Büfé (☎ 352 791; Rákóczi út 16; breakfasts 600-800Ft, mains 1100-1600Ft; 🕑 8am-10pm) When everything in Tokaj seems touristy and over the top, stop in to this simple counter-service restaurant for a hot breakfast or grilled meat.

Bonchidai Csárda (☎ 352 632; Bajcsy-Zsilinszky utca 21; mains 1500-2100Ft) Eight types of *halászlé* (fish soup) are just the beginning of the offerings made from the water's bounty. Sit on the large terrace overlooking the marina on the Tisza River or inside the rustic inn.

our pick **Degenfeld** (☎ 553 050; Kossuth tér 1; mains 1650-2500Ft) Experts' wine pairings accompany each exquisite item, such as the pork loin medallions with wild mushroom stew, on your choice of two set menus. Ordering a la carte, you might start with the wine cream soup with raisins; this, one of provincial Hungary's finest restaurants, is in Tokaj after all.

And then there's the following:

Bacchus Étterem (☎ 352 054; Kossuth tér 17; mains 1100-1800Ft; 🕑 8am-10pm) Hungarian staples and pizza on the main square.

Toldi Fogado (☎ 353 403; Hajdú köz 2; mains 1490-1790Ft) Quasi-fine dining, good duck dishes.

Drinking

Just look around for the nearest *borozó* (wine bar) to sate your thirst.

Óváros Kávéház (☎ 552 124; Rákóczi út 38; 🕑 9am-10pm) Enjoy a full selection of hot beverages to warm you on chilly mornings. The coffee house has a pleasant, cherrywood interior, but not much outdoor seating.

Murphy's Műhely Söröző (☎ 06 20 945 8562; Rákóczi út 42; 🕑 2-10pm) Should your palate tire of all that wine, turn your taste buds hopsward at this Irish 'workshop' pub.

Entertainment

Ede Pauley Theatre (☎ 352 003; www.szinhaz.tokaj.hu; Serház utca 55) From folk dance to full drama, something's always on at Tokaj's shiny new theatre.

Shopping

Wine, wine and more wine – from a 10L plastic jug of new Furmint to a bottle of six-*puttony* Aszú – is available in shops and cellars throughout Tokaj. **Furmint Vinotéka** (☎ 353 340; Bethlen Gábor utca 14; 🕑 9am-6pm) is perhaps the most helpful, with some information in English. You can also head to the shop at the Rákóczi cellar, the **Borostyán wine shop** (☎ 352 313; Rákóczi út 11; 🕑 10am-9pm Mon-Fri, to 10pm Sat & Sun) or the **Tokaj Regional Wine Trade Centre** (☎ 552 173; Kossuth tér 1; 🕑 10am-8pm).

For handmade folk crafts, look into **Tokaj Galéria** (☎ 352 039; Rákóczi út 45; 🕑 9.30am-6pm Tue-Sat).

Getting There & Away

Bus travel in the Zemplén Hills requires frequent changes and careful timing; few buses run daily. Tokaj is well connected by rail, however. Up to 16 trains a day head west through Miskolc (544Ft, one hour, 56km) to Budapest Keleti (3750Ft, 2½ hours, 238km), and east through Nyíregyháza (525Ft, 35 minutes, 32km) to Debrecen (1480Ft, two hours, 81km). If you want to travel north to Sárospatak (430Ft, one to two hours, 44km) and Sátoraljaújhely (544Ft, two hours, 54km), catch the Miskolc-bound train and change at Mezőzombor.

Getting Around

Cycling is an excellent way to get around Tokaj, and the Hegyalja region in general – especially if you're wine tasting. Most lodgings can arrange rental in this bike-friendly town, or rent from **Vízisport-telep** (☎ 352 645; Horgász utca 3; per day 1000Ft; 🕑 8am-8pm).

A LONG & WINEY ROAD

Including Tokaj, there are 28 villages in the Tokaj-Hegyalja region that have wine cellars to sample. Pick up a wine map at Tourinform in Tokaj, or check out **Tokaj Wine Routes** (www.tokaji-borut.hu) to help plan a do-it-yourself itinerary. Picture-pretty **Tarcal** (www.tarcal.hu), 6km west, is a good place to start. Especially since you can stay in the restored **Gróf Degenfeld Castle Hotel** (☎ 580 400; www.hotelgrofdegenfeld.hu; Terézia kert 9; s/d from €107/120;), with vineyards and parklands as a backdrop. The owners rank among the top vintners in the region so there's plenty of excellent wine at hand, but you can also rent a bicycle there and toodle off to visit another of the dozen or so local cellars and restaurants. What are you waiting for? Tarcal is easily accessed by train from Tokaj (200Ft, five minutes, 6km, hourly).

SÁROSPATAK

☎ 47 / pop 14,000

An attractive small town on the Bodrog River, Sárospatak means 'Muddy Stream' (ok, so it's not a *big* river). Here beneath the Zemplén Hills, 35km northeast of Tokaj, you'll find the finest example of a Renaissance fort extant in Hungary. The town is also known for its centuries-old college, and its long history.

History

The daughter of King Andrew of Hungary, Szent Erzsébet (St Elizabeth), anointed for her charitable works as the young wife of a nobleman in Germany, was born here in 1207. Sárospatak became a free, royal wine-producing town in the early 15th century. The list of alumni of the town's illustrious Calvinist College reads like a who's who of Hungarian literary and political history, and includes the patriot Lajos Kossuth, the poet Mihály Csokonai Vitéz and the novelist Géza Gárdonyi.

Orientation

The bus and train stations sit cheek-by-jowl at the end of Táncsics Mihály utca, northwest of the city centre. Walk southeast through shady Iskola-kert to join up with Rákóczi út, the main drag.

Information

Main post office (Rákóczi út 45)
OTP bank (Eötvös utca 3)
Tourinform (☎ 315 316; www.sarospatak.hu; Szent Erzsébet utca 3; 9am-7pm Mon-Fri, 10am-8pm Sat May-Oct, 9am-5pm Mon-Fri Nov-Apr) Loads of area info and free internet access.

Sights

The **Rákóczi Castle** (☎ 311 083; Szent Erzsébet utca 19-21; grounds free, combined admission adult/child 1000/700Ft; 10am-6pm Tue-Sun) should be your first stop. The oldest part of the castle, the five-storey **Red Tower** (Vörös-torony), dates from the late 15th century – inside you'll find rooms from this period in almost immaculate condition. Note that this can only be visited by guided tour.

The **Renaissance palace wing** *(palotaszárny)*, connected to the Red Tower by a 17th-century loggia known as the **Lorántffy Gallery**, was built in the 16th century and later enlarged by its most famous owners, the Rákóczi family of Transylvania. Today, along with some 19th-century additions, it contains the **Rákóczi Museum**, devoted to the uprising and the castle's later occupants. Bedrooms and dining halls overflow with period furniture, tapestries, porcelain and glass. Of special interest is the small five-windowed bay room on the 1st floor near the **Knights' Hall**, with its stucco rose in the middle of a vaulted ceiling. It was here that nobles put their names *sub rosa* (literally 'under the rose' in Latin) to the *kuruc* uprising against the Habsburg emperor in 1670. The expression, which means 'in secret', is thought to have originated here.

The **Castle Church** (☎ 311 183; Szent Erzsébet utca 7; adult/child 200/100Ft; 9am-5pm Tue-Sun) is one of Hungary's largest Gothic hall churches (those within castle walls), and has flip-flopped from serving Catholics to Protestants and now back since the 14th century. The enormous baroque altar was moved here from the Carmelite church in Buda Castle late in the 18th century; the 200-year-old organ from Kassa (now Košice in Slovakia) is still used for concerts throughout the year. The statue by Imre Varga outside the church depicts **St Elizabeth**, riding side-saddle, and her husband Ludwig IV on foot.

The history of the celebrated **Calvinist College** (Református Kollégium; ☎ 311 057; Rákóczi út 1; adult/child 400/200Ft; 9am-5pm Mon-Sat, to 1pm Sun) is told in words and displays at the **Comenius Memorial Museum** in the last of the college's original buildings, an 18th-century physics classroom. The collection is named after János Amos Comenius, a Moravian humanist who organised the education system here late in the 17th century and wrote the world's first illustrated textbook for children, *Orbis Pictus* (World in Pictures). The main reason for visiting the college is to see its 75,000-volume **Great Library Hall** (Nagy Könyvtárterem) in the main building, a long oval-shaped room with a gallery and a trompe l'oeil ceiling simulating the inside of a cupola.

Sárospatak counts a number of buildings designed by the 'organic' architect Imre Makovecz, including the anthropomorphic **Cultural House** (Művelődés Háza; ☎ 311 811; Eötvös utca 6), the **Hild Udvar shopping mall** on Béla Király tere and the cathedral-like **Árpád Vezér College** at Arany János utca 3–7.

Activities

Tasting a flight of eight wines costs 2000Ft at **Rákóczi Wine Cellar** (Rákóczi Pince; ☎ 312 310, 311

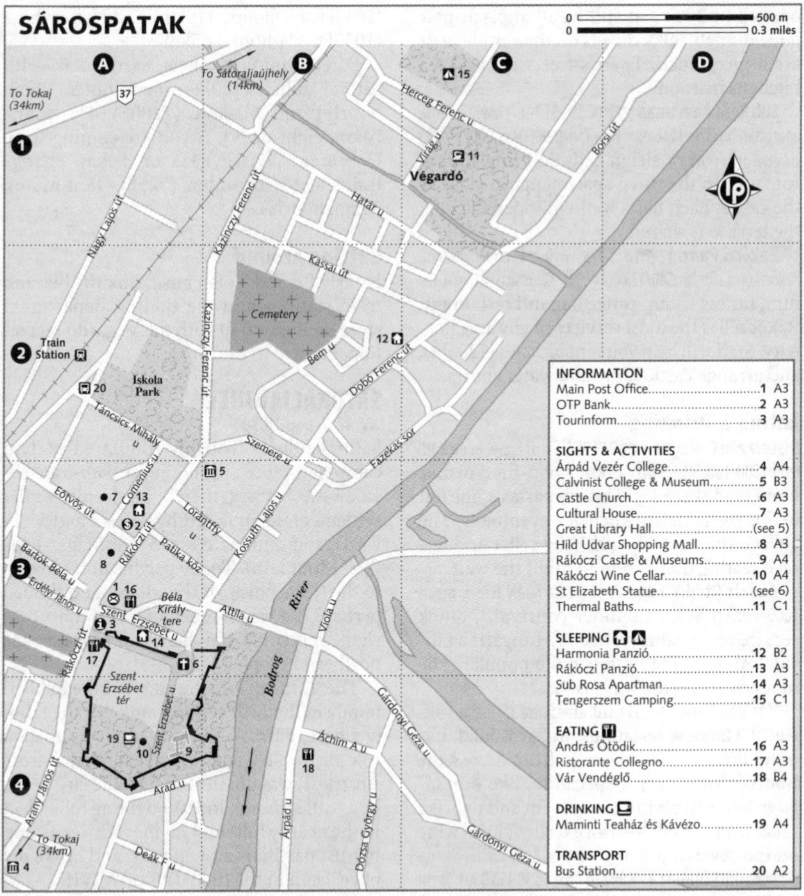

902; Szent Erzsébet utca 26; 10am-5pm daily May-Sep, 10am-5pm Mon-Fri Oct-Apr). You can visit the cellar without tasting for 250Ft.

The hugely popular **thermal baths** (311 639; adult/child 900/650Ft; 8am-6pm) are in the Végardó recreational complex about 2km northeast of the city centre. At the time of writing, new indoor and outdoor pools were under construction.

Festivals & Events

In mid-May **St Elizabeth Days** is a popular weekend festival celebrating the saint in the castle quarter. Sárospatak hosts some of the events of the **Zemplén Arts Days** in mid-August along with other Zemplén towns, including Sátoraljaújhely and Füzér.

Sleeping

You can certainly see everything in Sárospatak as a day trip from Tokaj, but it's a bit hard to do without a vehicle so you may want to stay over.

Tengerszem Camping (312 744; Herceg Ferenc utca 2; www.tengerszem-camping.hu; camp sites 1000Ft, bungalows 6000-10,000Ft;) Basic bungalows sleep two to five with shared facilities near the thermal baths. Superior apartments (13,500Ft) really are: the new whitewashed buildings with kitchenettes and cable TV ring the swimming pool. There's a restaurant and grocery on-site.

Harmonia Panzió (889 111; www.harmoniapanzio.hu; Dobó Ferenc utca 39; s/d 5000/10,000Ft;) You can tell this purpose-built guest house was opened in 2008 – it still has that clean new *panzió* smell. Silky duvets on the simple beds are a nice touch. There's free wi-fi and tea kitchens in-room.

Sub Rosa Apartman (☎ 06 30 955 1487; www.subrosaapartman.hu; Szent Erzsébet utca 7; d/tr 9000/13,000Ft; ☒) Scrolled iron or sleigh beds do bring a bit of romance to the three apartments so close to the castle. Each has a well-equipped kitchen; the terrace is shared.

Rákóczi Panzió (☎ 511 423; www.rakoczipanzio.com; Rákóczi utca 30; s/d 6500/12,000Ft;) Sauna, solarium, fitness room, coffee bar and restaurant: Rákóczi has the most services of any area hostelry. Staff will help you rent bicycles (1200Ft), and arrange castle tours and water sports.

Eating & Drinking

Ristorante Collegno (☎ 314 494; Szent Erzsébet utca 10; mains 800-1600Ft) Really good wood-fired pizzas, homemade bread and hearty pastas come out of this rustic Italian kitchen – eventually. The college students who pack the cellar and terrace seating don't seem to mind the wait.

András Ötödik (☎ 312 415; Béla Király tere 3; mains 1000-1700Ft) With its inner courtyard, quick service and healthy range of Hungarian cuisine, Andrew the Fifth is quite popular. The modern art on the walls is local.

Vár Vendéglő (☎ 311 370; Árpád utca 35; mains 1800-2600Ft) The best restaurant in Sárospatak has quite the view of the castle from across the Bodrog River. Try a speciality, like *harcsapaprikás* (catfish in a sour cream and paprika sauce), and enjoy with an excellent local wine on the covered patio.

Maminti Teaház és Kávézo (☎ 06 30 453 3501; Szent Erzsébet utca 26/a; 10am-10pm Thu-Sun, 1-10pm Mon & Wed) More than 100 varieties of teas and coffees are on offer in the castle garden.

Entertainment

Be sure to ask Tourinform about organ concerts at the Castle Church. Sárospatak is included in the free biweekly *Miskolci Est* (www.est.hu) listings magazine.

Getting There & Away

Much of the Zemplén region is not easily accessible by bus without multiple transfers. Only two buses a day travel between Sárospatak and Tokaj (600Ft, one hour, 38km); six a day (more on weekdays) head to Sátoraljaújhely (250Ft, 25 minutes, 12km). Two daily buses also travel to Debrecen (2040Ft, 2¾ hours, 119km) and Nyíregyháza (1050Ft, 1½ hours, 65km).

Direct trains connect Sárospatak with Sátoraljaújhely (200Ft, nine minutes, 10km, hourly) and Miskolc (1200Ft, 1¼ hours, 74km, eight daily). If you are coming from Debrecen, Nyíregyháza or Tokaj, change trains at Mezőzombor (525Ft, 45 minutes, 31km, hourly).

Getting Around

Hourly Borsod Volan buses link the bus and train stations and the Bodrog department store on Rákóczi út with the Végardó recreational centre to the north.

SÁTORALJAÚJHELY

☎ 47 / pop 18,300

Sátoraljaújhely (roughly translated as 'tent camp new place', pronounced *shah*-toor-all-ya-ew-we-hay – so there!) is a sleepy frontier settlement surrounded by forests and vineyards, and dominated by 514m Magas-hegy (Tall Mountain). Today's sights don't live up to the town's historical heritage, and though perhaps not worth much of a visit in its own right, you could stay here and trek into the northern Zemplén Hills.

The town fell into the hands of the Rákóczi family in the 17th century and, like the family's base, Sárospatak, played an important role in the struggle for independence from Austria. It was not the last time the city would be a battleground. In 1919 fighting took place in the nearby hills and ravines between communist partisans and Slovaks, and broke out once again in the final days of WWII.

Orientation

The bus and train stations sit side by side 1km south of the city centre. From there, follow Fasor utca north past the old Jewish cemetery to Kossuth Lajos utca. This will lead you to Hősök tere and then Széchenyi tér. Slovakia is not far beyond (5km).

Information

Main post office (Kazinczy Ferenc utca 10)
OTP bank (Széchenyi tér 13)
Tourinform (☎ 321 458; www.satoraljaujhely.hu; Kossuth tér 5; 10am-7pm Jun-Aug, 8am-4.30pm Mon-Thu, to 2pm Fri Sep-May) Can help with Zemplén-wide info.
Zemplén Computer (Dózsa György utca 2; per hr 300Ft; 8.30am-12.30pm & 1.30-5pm Mon-Fri) Offers internet access.

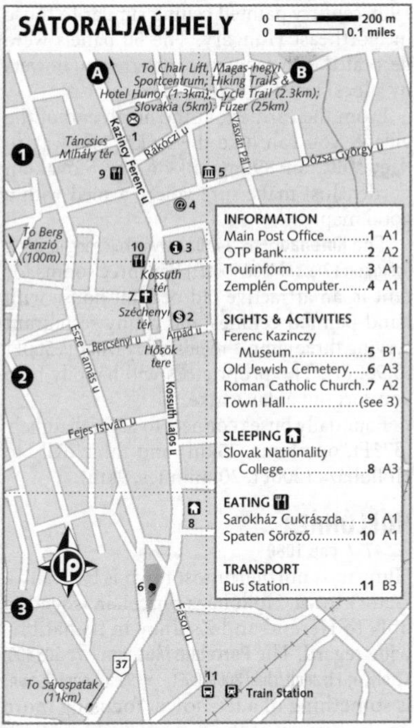

Sights & Activities

The central **Roman Catholic Church** (Széchenyi tér 10), rebuilt in the late-baroque style in 1792, is not very interesting in itself, though it was here that the teachings of Martin Luther were first read aloud in public in Hungary. The **Town Hall** (Kossuth tér 5) is where in 1830 the anti-Habsburg Hungarian president-to-be, Lajos Kossuth, gave his first public speech.

The **Ferenc Kazinczy Museum** (☎ 322 351; Dózsa György utca 11; adult/child 600/300Ft; 🕑 8am-4pm Mon-Sat) covers the history of the city to the 19th century, with emphasis on the Hungarian-nationalist Rákóczi family, and the namesake 19th-century language reformer and patriot Kazinczy, who did much of his research locally.

Pilgrims pay their respects on 16 July each year at the **old Jewish cemetery**, where the *zaddik* (miracle-working rabbi) Moses Teitelbaum (1759–1841) is buried.

The **chair lift** (libegő; ☎ 322 346; Torzás út; return adult/child 1100/550Ft; 🕑 10am-5pm daily May-Aug, 10am-4pm Tue-Wed & Fri-Sun Sep-Apr) to the top of Magas-hegy is the longest in Hungary (1332m). A 25-minute ride up doesn't get you much of a view. For that you have to hike up a bit further then climb five flights to the top of the **observation tower** *(kilátó)*. From the hilltop, you can follow the **red triangle trail** west and then the **green trail** south, past the cavalry, to get back to the centre of town (2.5km). Or go further into the forested hills, if you've bought a Cartographia *Zempléni-hegység* hiking map.

If you get off the chair lift mid-hill at the **Magas-hegyi Sportcentrum**, you can take the green trail north down a gentler slope to get you back to the chair-lift car park (1.5km). From late 2009 the sport centre should have a year-round bob sled up and running.

A kilometre north of the chairlift, at the Locsa Field picnic area, a 13.5km one-way, signposted **cycle trail** begins. It follows the base of the hills, so there's little elevation change. Rent bicycles (2000Ft per day) at the **Hotel Hunor** (☎ 521 521; Torzsás út 25; 🕑 8am-8pm).

Sleeping & Eating

A plethora of private rooms are available in the area (from 2500Ft per person). Restaurant pickin's are slim in the city centre.

Slovak Nationality College (☎ 322 568; zoja kollegium@freemail.hu; Kossuth Lajos utca 31; dm 2500Ft; 🕑 mid-Jun–mid-Aug) Forty-six four-bed dorm rooms are for rent in summer.

Berg Panzió (☎ 321 518; www.bergpanzio.hu; Felsó Zsolyomka 27; s/d 3000/6000Ft) The location at the edge of the hills is perfect for those who want to hike up (or return down from) Magas-hegy. Plain vanilla rooms are almost dormlike; there's a pizza-pub on-site.

Hotel Hunor (☎ 521 521; www.hotelhunor.hu; Torzsás út 25; s/d 9800/13,500Ft;) The stone-and-wood rugged exterior fits right in with the locale at the base of Magas-hegy. Rooms are awfully boring in comparison, but who wants to stay inside when you can swim, play tennis, hike, bike or get a massage at or near this hotel. Fine Tokaj wines are offered with the Hungarian dishes at the restaurant (mains 1600Ft to 2200Ft).

Sarokház Cukrászda (☎ 322 742; Táncsics Mihály tér 2; cakes 100-200Ft; 🕑 7.30am-6pm Mon-Fri, to 4pm Sat & Sun) Soothe your sweet tooth at this pastry cafe.

Spaten Söröző (☎ 321 527; Kossuth tér 10; mains 1000-1600Ft) A basic beer pub, Spaten also serves stick-to-your-ribs Hungarian mains.

Getting There & Away

Four daily buses roll along to Füzér (375Ft, one hour, 25km) and five daily to Hollóháza (450Ft, one hour, 29km) to the north.

Direct trains connect Sátoraljaújhely with Sárospatak (200Ft, nine minutes, 10km, hourly) and Miskolc (1350Ft, 1½ hours, 84km). If you're approaching from the south or east (Debrecen, say, or Nyíregyháza or Tokaj), you must change at Mezőzombor (675Ft, 50 minutes, 41km, hourly).

AROUND SÁTORALJAÚJHELY

Füzér

☎ 47 / pop 540

An easy excursion, about 25km northwest of Sátoraljaújhely on the edge of the Zemplén Hills, can be made to Füzér, an idyllic little village where life is still ruled by the seasons. Aside from the chance to experience rural Hungary, the highlight here is what remains of the hilltop **Füzér Castle** (admission free; 9am-6pm), dating from the 13th century. Its position, high above the village and sticking out like a sore – but proud – thumb among lush green pastures, is arguably the most dramatic in all Hungary. To reach the ruins from the village bus stop, follow the steep, marked trail 370m up. The castle's claim to fame is that it was chosen as a 'safe house' by Péter Perényi for the Hungarian coronation regalia from Visegrád for a year or so after the disastrous defeat at Mohács in 1526. Like most castles in the area, it was heavily damaged by the Austrians after the unsuccessful *kuruc* revolt in the late 17th century, but parts of the chapel, a tower and the outer walls remain.

Down in the village centre, the medieval **Calvinist church** (Árpád utca; by appointment) has a 19th-century painted ceiling similar to those in Northeast Hungary. The 50 panels were decorated with geometric patterns and flowers by a local artist in 1832.

From the car park at the north end of the village, you can hike the 3.5km one way to **Nagy Milic**, an 893m hill on the Slovakian border. Just make sure you're armed with a good map.

The **Koronaőr** (☎ 340 020; www.koronaor.hu; Dózsa György utca 2/a; s/d 4000/6000Ft) has three rooms for rent in an attractive old peasant house with hand-painted ceilings and a tiny restaurant serving three simple meals a day (mains 500Ft to 900Ft). The proprietors will happily help you sort out a day's hike.

Four daily buses connect to Sátoraljaújhely (375Ft, one hour, 25km) and three daily to Hollóháza (200Ft, 20 minutes, 9km).

HOLLÓHÁZA

☎ 47 / pop 1080

Hungary's northernmost town is basically a factory town. Hollóháza porcelain is second only to Herend and Zsolnay in its nationwide regard. The **Porcelain Museum** (☎ 505 400; Károlyi út 11; adult/child 800/400Ft; 9am-5pm Tue-Sun) is something of a let-down, focusing more on the history of the factory building than the craft. But there is a **shop** (9am-5pm Mon-Sat). Otherwise, there's not a whole lot here besides the workers' houses and goats grazing on the hills.

Buses run to Füzér (200Ft, 20 minutes, 9km, three daily) and Sátoraljaújhely (450Ft, one hour, 29km). If you're driving you can continue around to Abaújvár, the west side of the Zemplén lowlands and back to Tokaj (75km).

Northeast

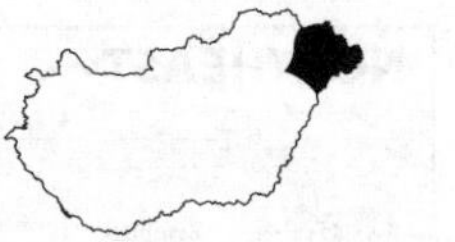

If you want to experience Hungarian village life – steeped in folk culture, replete with dirt roads, horse-drawn carts and little old churches – the Northeast is the place. Traditions are long-kept in the Bereg Region, where some women still eke out a living embroidering pillowcases in age-old patterns, and men work the land. Rural folk art, churches and a cemetery resembling a 'shipyard' of grave markers are the attractions here. Hospitality is at its height in the furthest corners of the Northeast; you'll never be welcomed into even the poorest home without a shot of *pálinka* (fruit-based firewater that Hungarians call 'brandy') and a chocolate.

Not far off, the larger towns of Nyírség have history to offer and more ecclesiastical treasures – Nyírbátor prides itself on not one but two noteworthy, originally Gothic churches, and the iconic art in Máriapócs is downright miraculous. Since distances are short (and regional transport so inadequate) a great way to explore is to hire a car and trip out from the capital, Nyíregyháza. The spa town with a pleasant pedestrian centre has most of the creature comforts, and a few activities of its own. In the leafy Sóstófürdő park you can soak in four different thermal-bath complexes and step into the region's village past at an excellent open-air museum. Here in the Northeast, remembrances of rural life are never far from mind.

HIGHLIGHTS

- Staying the night in a peaceful rural village like **Csaroda** (p366) or **Túristvándi** (p366)
- Gazing at the patterns on the painted wooden ceiling in the 'peasant's cathedral' in **Tákos** (p365)
- Walking between the bizarre boat-shaped grave markers in Szatmárcseke's **cemetery** (p366)
- Being awed by the gilt iconostasis and ornate painting at the **Greek Catholic Cathedral** (p362) in Máriapócs
- Immersing yourself in the thoroughly modern Aquarius Adventure Baths before having dinner on a lakeside terrace in **Nyíregyháza** (p358)

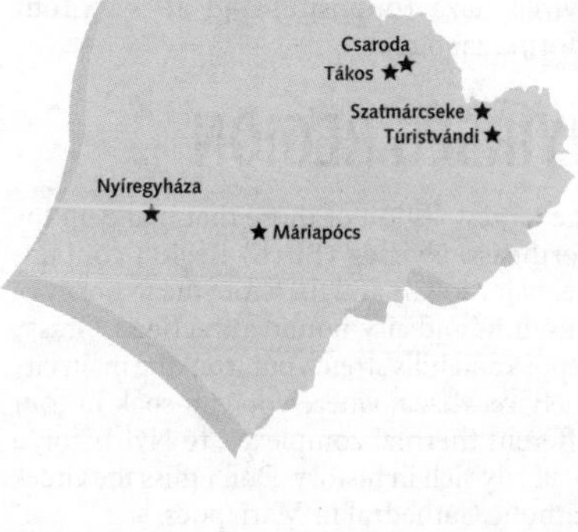

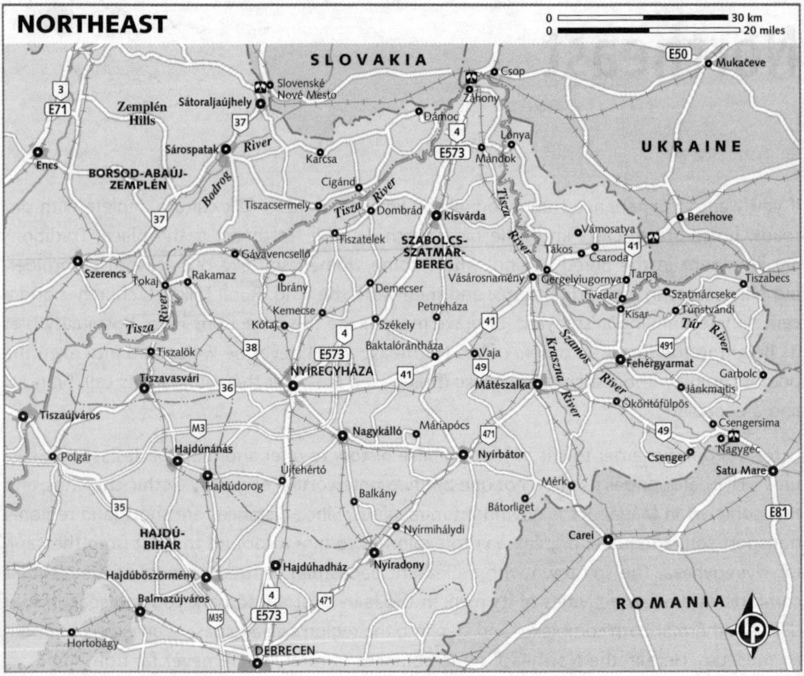

Getting There & Around

The best way to see the small region is under your own steam, be it by car, motorbike or bicycle. The Hungarian world to the west is connected by rail to Nyíregyháza, and from there by really slow train to towns like Nyírbátor and Vásárosnamény. Though villages are fairly close together, bus services in Bereg are hardly worth mentioning.

Note that areawide information is available at the county Tourinform office in Nyíregyháza (opposite) and at www.tourinform.szabolcs.net.

NYÍRSÉG REGION

The largest region of those that make up the Northeast, Nyírség (Birch) Region contains the major towns and therefore the majority of museums and city-bound attractions. Grassy steppes and hills stretch out from the main city of Nyíregyháza, where you can soak in four different thermal complexes, to Nyírbátor, a small city rich in history. Don't miss the Greek Catholic Cathedral in Máriapócs.

NYÍREGYHÁZA

☎ 42 / pop 116,800

You have to look at Nyíregyháza from the inside out: stand in the old town centre and notice the checkerboard of well-tended squares and gardens; survey the forests, pavilions and reedy shore at the park in Sóstófürdő (Salt Lake Thermal Baths). The problem is, what rings these pleasant views is the ugly high-rises and industrial architecture of a commercial and administrative centre. Still, give Nyíregyháza a chance; the town's spas and low-key lifestyle make up for the ugliness. And this is the most citified springboard for visiting other towns and villages in the Northeast region.

History

For centuries Nyíregyháza was the private domain of Transylvanian princes. Under Soviet rule the town prospered due to the establishment of a food-processing industry in the area. After a downturn, Nyíregyháza has recently remade itself as something of a holiday destination, spiffing up its thermal bathing complexes north of town.

Orientation

Nyíregyháza's centre is made up of a handful of interconnecting squares, including Országzászló tér, Kálvin tér, Kossuth tér and Hősök tere, and is surrounded by both an inner and an outer ring road. Streets running north lead to Sóstófürdő, the city's sprawling 600-hectare recreational area, 5km north.

The main train station, on Állomás tér, is about 1.5km southwest of the centre at the end of Arany János utca. The bus station is on Petőfi tér, just north of the train station, at the western end of Széchenyi utca.

Information

Hospital (Kórház; ☎ 465 666; Szent István utca 68)
Ibusz (☎ 311 817; www.ibusz.hu; Országzászló tér 4) Brokers private rooms and flats.
Main post office (Bethlen Gábor utca 4)
Net Café Bar (☎ 508 670; Európa Hotel, Hunyadi utca 2; 🕑 8am-midnight Mon-Sat, 2-10pm Sun) More than 20 internet terminals, and full liquor selection.
OTP bank (Dózsa György utca 2) Has an ATM.
Tourinform (☎ 504 647; www.tourinform.szabolcs.net; Országzászló tér 6; 🕑 9am-5pm Mon-Fri, 10am-5pm Sat & Sun May-Sep, 9am-5pm Mon-Fri Oct-Apr) The county Tourinform office provides info on the town and the entire Northeast region.
Tourinform Water Tower (☎ 411 193; www.sostogyogyfurdo.freeweb.hu; Víztorony, Sóstófürdő; 🕑 8.30am-4.30pm May-Sep) A seasonal info stand near the spas.

Sights & Activities

DOWNTOWN

It is worth taking the time to check out the architecture in the centre: the eclectic **County Hall** (Hősök tere) dating from 1892; the blue-and-white **Art Nouveau building** (Országzászló tér), which houses a bank and offices; and the restored **Korona Hotel** (Dózsa György utca 1-3). At the time of writing, the bizarre **Mihály Váci Cultural Centre** (☎ 411 822; Szabadság tér 9; 🕑 9am-5pm Mon-Fri), built in 1981 (a wobbly looking, bridgelike structure inspired by 'the principles of Japanese metabolism', so we're told), was under reconstruction.

Hősök tere is also home to **Lovers' Lock Gate**, an unusual amorous display. The idea is for partners to declare their love by engraving their names on a padlock, then latch it to the gate standing mid-square. Both partners keep a copy of the key, just in case things turn sour.

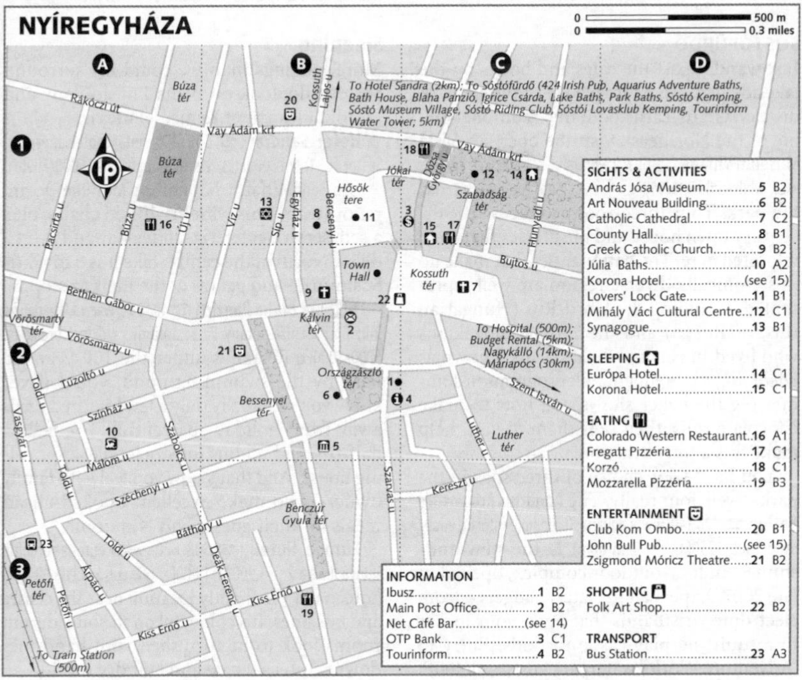

There are many houses of worship in the inner city. Dominating Kossuth tér, the 1904 neo-Romanesque **Catholic cathedral** (☎ 409 691; Kossuth tér 4; admission free; 6.30am-6pm Mon-Fri) has arabesque pastel-coloured tiles inside. The **Greek Catholic church** (☎ 415 901; Bethlen Gábor utca 5; admission free; 8am-4pm), built in 1895, contains a rich liturgical collection of vestments and plates. The **synagogue** (☎ 417 939; Mártírok tere 6; admission free; 8am-2pm Mon-Thu) still functions as a house of worship and has a small collection of Jewish artefacts.

The huge **András Jósa Museum** (☎ 315 722; Benczúr Gyula tér 21; adult/child 500/300Ft; 9am-4pm Tue-Sat, to 2pm Sun) is the basic, fairly boring, town history museum. Exhibitions span from the Iron Age to the 19th century.

Spending time at the nothing-fancy, in-town **Júlia Baths** (Júlia Fürdő; ☎ 315 800; http://juliafurdo.sostort.hu; Malom utca 19; adult/child 1200/1000Ft; 10am-8pm Mon-Fri, 9am-8pm Sat & Sun) is like visiting a museum in a way. You get to see how spa culture in Hungary used to be – the older local neighbourhood women gossiping in the shaded pool, and the retired guys inside religiously dunking first in piping-hot then icy-cold pools to reinvigorate themselves.

NORTHEAST

SÓSTÓFÜRDŐ

Just wander past the cafes and hotels on the lakeside paths in Nyíregyháza's inviting park district. Or, to learn about the traditional folk life of the Northeast, visit the open-air **Sóstó Museum Village** (Sóstói Múzeumfalu; ☎ 500 552; Tölgyes utca; adult/child 300/150Ft; 9am-6pm Tue-Sun) across the park. Tour three-room cottages, a 19th-century town house and businesses that were relocated here. The nationalities that make up this ethnically diverse region are well represented, including the Uhro-Rus (Hungarian Rus, or Rusyn) and the Tirpák, Slovakians who lived in isolated 'bush farms' known as *bokor tanyák*. Frequent folk programs in summer (eg the baker shows you how to make chocolate rolls, then sells them to you) help make this a top attraction.

You have your choice of three spas in the park – well, four really. The **Aquarius Adventure Baths** (☎ 726 140; www.aquariusfurdo.hu; Sóstói út; adult/child 1400/1250Ft; 9am-8pm) is the new-and-shiniest indoor-outdoor complex, opened in late 2007. Expect all the latest gadgets – from electronic wristbands that open your locker to a squirting play castle for kids. Entry to 'Adventure World' waterpark costs 800/400Ft extra, and add another 1000Ft (for both adults and children) for 'Sauna World'.

Park Baths (Parkfürdő; ☎ 475 736; http://parkfurdo.sostort.hu; Bernát utca 1-3; adult/child 800/600Ft; 8am-7pm, open-air baths May-Sep only) is the original spa. Two indoor 'medicinal' pools (aka unfiltered) and the large athletic swimming pool remain open year-round.

A portion of the southern half of the Salt Lake itself has been cordoned off for swimming at the **Lake Baths** (Tófürdő; ☎ 479 701; http://tofurdo.sostort.hu; Blaha Lujza sétány; adult/child 800/600Ft; 8am-8pm Jun-Aug); there's also a grassy strand perfect for sun worshipping and football kicking.

Last but not least, there's the **Bath House** (Fürdőház; ☎ 411 191; www.furdohaz.hu, in Hungarian; Víztorony; adult/child 800/600Ft; 2-9pm Mon-Fri, 10am-9pm Sat & Sun). The large thermal swimming pool and associated cold pool and whirlpool are mainly frequented by guests of the attached Fürdőház Panzió, but you can horn in.

The **Sóstó Riding Club** (☎ 475 202; www.sostoilovasklub.hu; Tölgyes utca; per hr 2500-3000Ft), next to the Sóstó Museum Village, hires horses to be ridden with a guide in the ring or out in the fields (for experienced riders only).

Sleeping

More lodgings than we could list surround Sóstófürdő; look on Blaha Lujza sétány and Sóstói út (north of Kemecsei utca).

Hotel Sandra (☎ 505 400; info@hotelsandra.hu; Sóstói út 31; dm 3000Ft, s/d without bathroom 6000/7000Ft; Jun-Aug) What a happening college dorm: renovated rooms with bright red chairs, plus a self-service cafeteria, coffee bar and even a disco. North of the centre, take bus 8 towards Sóstófürdő and get off at the Etelköz stop.

our pick **Blaha Panzió** (☎ 403 342; www.blahapanzio.hu; Blaha Lujza sétány 7, Sóstófürdő; s/d incl breakfast 6000/8000Ft) Relaxing under the 100-year-old oaks by the swimming pond, you'd never know you're actually only a few hundred yards away from holiday-spa central. The yellow half-timber building looks a lot like a sprawling house. And that's how you feel with family owners who make excellent booked-ahead meals for their guests only – at home.

Európa Hotel (☎ 508 670; www.europahotel.hu; Hunyadi utca 2; s/d 9000/11,000Ft;) This so-so hotel has a very handy location near the centre and bus lines. It's colourful on the outside, but rooms look to be furnished with hand-me-downs. Internet cafe and laundry on site.

Korona Hotel (☎ 409 300; www.korona.cs.hu; Dózsa György utca 1-3; s/d 12,800/13,900Ft; ⊠ ▣) Like a big blue wedding cake with frilly white icing, the Korona Hotel has decorated Nyíregyháza's main square since 1895. At these prices, the ho-hum rooms could use an update, but you do have easy access to John Bull Pub, Soho Pizzeria and all of downtown at your doorstep.

A large green space allows for plenty of room to play on the ball courts at **Sóstó Kemping** (☎ 500 692; www.hotelsosto.hu; Sóstói út 76, Sóstófürdő; camp sites per person/tent 900/700Ft, 4-person bungalows 6400Ft; ▣), while horse riding is the activity of choice at **Sóstói Lovasklub Kemping** (☎ 475 202; www.sostoilovasklub.hu, Sóstófürdő; Tölgyes utca; camp sites per person 1250Ft, bungalows per person 1800Ft). Both camping grounds are in forested areas; the former has more services – restaurant, sauna and wi-fi hot spots.

Eating & Drinking

Several food stalls line the pedestrian paths near where Sóstói út meets Blaha Lujza sétány in Sóstófürdő. The old town pedestrian squares may have more ice-cream shops per square metre than anywhere in Hungary.

Korzó (Jókai tér 7; ⏲ 9am-9pm) This new-in-2008 shopping centre has both a large supermarket and self-service eateries (meals 300Ft to 800Ft), including one dedicated to fabulous *főzelék* (creamed vegetables; see p52).

Colorado Western Restaurant (☎ 444 200; Búza tér 15; mains 1190-1500Ft) True to the name, Colorado cooks up beef-and-bean chilli and steaks (2500Ft to 4000Ft). But it also serves an inventive Hungarian menu, with suggested wine pairings, in rustic surrounds.

our pick **Igrice Csárda** (☎ 444 200; Blaha Lujza sétány 41, Sóstófürdő; mains 1200-1900Ft) As the sun sets and you look out over the reeds to the lake beyond, glass of dry white Olaszrizling in hand, you might be tempted to think you've found the best terrace in town – and you have. Just avoid the place when cold weather forces you inside, unless you like synthesised Hungarian music played directly in your ear. Try the turkey breast with locally made plum jam or the grilled plate for two, which actually serves three.

424 Irish Pub (☎ 726 222; Blaha Lujza sétány 1, Sóstófürdő; ⏲ 11am-midnight Sun-Thu, to 2am Fri & Sat) The only thing Irish about this place is the Guinness sign hanging out front, but that takes nothing away from this cute pavilion pub with views of the lake.

For a decent slice of pie, both the central **Fregatt Pizzéria** (☎ 420 100; Szabadság tér 4; pizza 500-800Ft) and **Mozzarella Pizzéria** (☎ 424 008; Kiss Ernő utca 10; pizza & pasta 550-1000Ft) will do. Stick with the pizza at the latter; it's much better than the pasta.

Entertainment

Pick up a calendar of events at Tourinform; something always seems to be on.

Zsigmond Móricz Theatre (☎ 400 375; www.moriczszinhaz.hu; Bessenyei tér 13) Though most performances here are dramatic (and in Hungarian), you will find the occasional dance or operetta.

For music, try the following:

Club Kom Ombo (Rákóczi út 8; ⏲ 8pm-5am Tue, Fri & Sat) A trendy dance club that mixes it up with DJs and live bands.

John Bull Pub (Dózsa György utca 1-3; ⏲ 11am-midnight Sun-Thu, to 2am Fri & Sat) Live music Friday and Saturday.

Shopping

If you're going further east, you can buy hand-embroidered treasures direct from the ladies who make them. Stopping here? Check out the **Folk Art Shop** (Népművészeti Bolt; ☎ 261 6753; Kossuth tér 8) in the Metropol shopping centre.

Getting There & Away

BUS

Heading west to Eger (2040Ft, 2½ hours, 132km, two daily), buses are most convenient. Regionally, only two buses go to Nagykálló (250Ft, 30 minutes, 16km) daily, and there are 10 on the weekend; to Máriapócs (525Ft, 45 minutes, 30km) there are at least hourly departures on working days, but only two on Saturday and Sunday. At least three buses connect daily with Nyírbátor (600Ft, one hour, 40km).

CAR

Hire a car at **Budget Rental** (☎ 06 30 255 4793; www.budget.hu; Váci Mihály utca 41; ⏲ 8.30am-5pm Mon-Fri).

TRAIN

The Tisza Express train to Kyiv (22 hours) stops here every day at 10pm. To get to the Ukrainian border town of Csop (Čop), 14km from Uzhgorod, you have to change in Záhony (1050Ft, 80 minutes, 66km, hourly). Direct destinations include the following:

Destination	Price	Duration	Km	Frequency
Budapest (Keleti station)	4160Ft	3hr	270	7 daily
Budapest (Nyugati station)	3650Ft	4hr	270	hourly
Debrecen	750Ft	45min	49	hourly
Kisvárda	675Ft	43min	43	hourly
Máriapócs	450Ft	1hr	30	8 daily
Nyírbátor	600Ft	1½hr	38	8 daily
Tokaj	525Ft	35min	32	half-hourly
Vásárosnamény	900Ft	1¾hr	59	8 daily

Getting Around

Take bus 7 or 8 from the train or bus station to reach the centre of the old town (Egyház or Kossuth Lajos utca stops); bus 8 carries on to the last stop at Sóstófürdő.

AROUND NYÍREGYHÁZA

Nagykálló

☎ 42 / pop 10,600

This little town 14km southeast of Nyíregyháza has some interesting buildings on its pretty central square, Szabadság tér: a baroque **Calvinist church** (daytime) on the south side, with a free-standing Gothic bell tower; and the brilliant-yellow former **County Hall** (Szabadság tér 13), which was constructed in the Zopf style (1780) and later turned into a notorious mental asylum that is still in operation.

Most visitors to Nagykálló are Orthodox Jewish pilgrims who come to pay their respects at the **tomb of Isaac Taub** (☎ 06 30 248 6379; Nagybalkányi út; by appointment), especially on the anniversary of his death on 7 Adar in the Hebrew calendar (February/March). Known as the 'Wonder Rabbi of Kálló' (a *zaddik* in Yiddish), Isaac Taub was an 18th-century philosopher who advocated a humanistic approach to prayer and study. Note that unless you call ahead, the cemetery gates, less than 1km due south of Szabadság tér, will be locked.

In late July, Nagykálló hosts the popular **Téka Tábor**, a week-long folk festival 'camp' (meals available) held in a bizarre, winged, barnlike structure in Harangodi, some 2km north of the centre. Contact the **Rákóczi Cultural Centre** (☎ 263 141; Báthory utca 1; 9am-5pm Mon-Fri) for more information.

Óbester Étterem (☎ 264 946; Korányi Ferenc utca 1; mains 1100-1600Ft), serving Hungarian staples, is really your only option for a meal; its outside tables on the main square are popular on summer evenings. **Üvegtigris Kávézó** (Kossuth Lajos utca 2; 7am-9pm) is mostly for coffee and adult beverages, but it sells ice cream.

Eight daily trains link with Nyíregyháza (250Ft, 20 minutes, 14km), via Máriapócs (300Ft, 35 minutes, 16km) and Nyírbátor (375Ft, 50 minutes, 24km).

Máriapócs

☎ 42 / pop 2,200

The village of Máriapócs contains one of the country's most beautiful churches – and not a whole lot else. The **Greek Catholic Cathedral** (☎ 385 142; Kossuth tér 25; admission free; 8am-5pm) here has been an important pilgrimage site from at least 1696, when the **Black Madonna icon** first shed tears (she wept again in 1715 and in 1905). That the painting floating angelically above the altar on the north side of the building is not the original, but a 19th-century copy, does little to take away from the breathtaking church. (The real icon is in St Stephen's Cathedral in Vienna.) Every inch of this ornate house of worship is covered in gilt detail or decorative paint; the gold iconostasis soars some

WHEN WERE THERE GREEKS IN HUNGARY?

Well, never. The Greek Catholic religion, also called Uniate or Byzantine Catholic, has nothing to do with Athens or Thessaloniki. Historically, the Hungarian counties in and surrounding the Carpathian Mountains (now primarily in the Ukraine) were home to the Slavic-speaking Carpatho-Rusyn people. What set them apart primarily was their religion. In 1646, at the Union of Uzhgorod, a group of Orthodox churches in Kárpátalja (Sub- or Transcarpathia) accepted the authority of Rome, creating a unique Eastern Rite Catholic church. The traditions of Orthodoxy remain – plain chant liturgies, onion-dome architecture, icon screens and married priests – but the leader of the church is the pope, and the theology Catholic. The label 'Greek' was a misnomer that grew out of the original association with Constantinople. Today, Máriapócs remains the most venerated of Greek Catholic pilgrimage sites – just as it was when this author's great-grandfather served as a Greek Catholic priest in the region.

NORTHEAST

15m up to the vaulted ceiling. The current building, which was constructed on the site of a small wooden church, dates from the mid-18th century. Feast days and festivals are cause for pilgrimage and celebration here from March through November, but the biggest annual event is the **Feast of the Nativity** in honour of the Virgin Mary's birth on September 8.

True to any village home, all of the heavily furnished guest quarters at the **Pócsi Mária Vendégház** (☎ 06 20 590 4461; www.mariapocsivendeghaz.hu; Petri utca 6; s/d 3000/6000Ft) have an icon of Mary hanging on the wall. The shared garden is quite lovely and you're just down the road from the church (next to the post office). There's a small grocery store and a pastry cafe on Kossuth Lajos utca.

From Nyíregyháza (525Ft, 45 minutes, 30km) buses run to the village at least hourly on weekdays, but only twice on Saturday and Sunday. One bus connects the village proper with Nyírbátor (250Ft, 30 minutes, 10km). There are eight daily trains from Nyíregyháza (450Ft, one hour, 30km) that call at Nagykálló (300Ft, 35 minutes, 16km) en route to Máriapócs, carrying on to Nyírbátor (200Ft, 15 minutes, 8km) and vice versa. Problem is, the Máriapócs train station is 4km south of the town centre. Local buses run between the centre and the station, but they are not very reliable.

NYÍRBÁTOR

☎ 42 / pop 13,200

Nyírbátor is a fairly sleepy, not overly attractive town, but anyone with a passion for medieval or Transylvanian history should put it on the itinerary. Several of the town's Gothic buildings were originally constructed in the latter part of the 15th century by István Báthory, the ruthless Transylvanian prince whose family is synonymous with this town and its sights.

Orientation & Information

The train and bus stations are on Ady Endre utca, which is in the northern part of town, less than 1km from the centre (Szabadság tér) via Kossuth Lajos utca. Check out www.nyirbator.hu for information about the town.

Main post office (Szabadság tér)

OTP bank (Zrínyi utca 1) Located across from Szabadság tér; has an ATM.

BLOODY FAMILIES

Did you know István Báthory palled around in battle with Vlad the Impaler (aka Dracula) and was disposed as Prince of Transylvania in 1493 for extreme cruelty? You may have heard of his grand, grandniece, Erzsébet Báthory, who was accused of killing peasant girls and bathing in their blood for beauty (see the boxed text, p188).

Sights

Walking into the **Calvinist church** (☎ 281 749; 🕑 9am-5pm Mon-Sat, 8-10am & 1-5pm Sun), on a small hill just off Báthory István utca, is like drawing a breath of crispy mountain air. Its refreshingly plain interior and long lancet windows, which flood the nave with light, allow the church's masterpiece – the ribbed vault – to gain your undivided attention. István Báthory's remains lie in a marble tomb at the back of the church; the family's coat of arms embellished with wyverns (dragonlike creatures) is on top of the tomb. The 17th-century wooden **bell tower**, standing apart from the church (as was once required of Calvinists in this overwhelmingly Catholic country), has a Gothic roof with four little turrets.

Across the main road stands the starkly white, 15th-century **Báthory Várkastély** (☎ 510 216; Nyírbátor vár utca 1; adult/child 400/200Ft; 🕑 10am-6pm Tue-Sun), a small fortified palace with a striking 2nd-storey loggia. Recently refurbished, the building is mostly used as an event centre, but a couple of rooms are outfitted in Renaissance style. It's located north off Szentvér utca.

The **Minorite church** (Károlyi Mihály utca 19; 🕑 9-11am & 4-5pm Mon-Sat) was originally late-Gothic, but, like so many Hungarian churches, it was ravaged by the Turks in 1587 and rebuilt in the baroque style 130 years later. Five spectacular altars carved in Presov (now eastern Slovakia) in the mid-18th century fill the nave and chancel. The most interesting is the first on the left, the Krucsay Altar of the Passion (1737), with its diverse portrayals of fear, longing, devotion and faith.

Engaging exhibits showcase the trades of the town's heyday – barrel-making, leatherworking, hat-making and potteryworking – at the **István Báthory Museum** (☎ 510 218; Károlyi Mihály utca 21; adult/child 300/150Ft; 🕑 9am-5pm Tue-Sat Jun-Aug, 9am-5pm Mon-Fri Sep-May) in the 18th-century monastery next to the church.

In early July, actors, musicians and puppets perform during the **Week of the Winged Dragon International Street Theatre Festival**. Mid-August, the **Nyírbátor Music Festival** hosts concerts in the town's churches.

Sleeping

Napsugár Panzió (☎ 283 878; Zrínyi utca 15; s/d 6000/8000Ft) Altogether average, this modern guest house has eight fairly up-to-date rooms, a not-too-bad fitness centre and an adequate bar out front.

Bástya Wellness Hotel (☎ 281 657; www.bastyawellnesshotel.xls.hu; Hunyadi utca 10; s/d 6960/9540Ft;) Stone walls on the exterior and in the grottolike underground pool seem to hint at a medieval theme. But the rooms are something else entirely – we're just not sure what. Let's call it tacky eclectic.

Hotel Hódi (☎ 283 556; evahodi@hotmail.com; Báthory István utca 11; s/d 11,900/12,900Ft;) In some of the individually decorated rooms, 19th-century settees stand next to antique ceramic stoves. And marble tiles line the conservatory pool beneath a leaded-mirror dome and tilework. Hódi is nothing if not over-the-Olde-Worlde-top.

Eating & Drinking

Both Hotel Hódi and Bástya Wellness Hotel have half-decent restaurants.

Csekő Kávéház & Pizzéria (☎ 381 289; Bajcsy-Zsilinszky utca 62; cakes 150-200Ft, mains 620-1250Ft) Once inside the door, go right and ogle the cream-filled cakes in the cafe case or go left and sit down in a light-filled eatery. Unexpected options include main-dish salads like the 'Mexican' with chicken and beans, and the savoury crêpes stuffed with fillings like seafood in a sour cream sauce.

Kakukk (☎ 281 050; Szabadság tér 21; mains 1100-1600Ft) A lunchtime set menu (around 550Ft for soup and main) packs 'em in at midday, but basic Hungarian specialities are served all day.

Portside Pub (Radnóti út 5; noon-midnight Sun-Thu, to 2am Fri & Sat) Ahoy matey, come aboard this fun young bar that impersonates a pirate ship.

THE ROMA

The Roma, or Gypsy people (*'cigány'*, which has a derogatory connotation in Hungarian), have been a conspicuous minority in Hungary for at least 500 years. One of the highest concentrations of the marginalised group resides in the Northeast, where the population was hard hit by area factory shutdowns. Though minority rights legislation has been on the books for more than 15 years, results are mixed: groups like Microsoft have come in to set up Roma-oriented knowledge centres, and the language is now officially taught in schools, but as recently as 2006 the UN Committee on the Elimination of Discrimination Against Women condemned a hospital in Fehergyarmat for sterilising a Roma woman without her informed consent.

Getting There & Away

Three buses a day connect to Nyíregyháza (600Ft, one hour, 40km) via Nagykálló (484Ft, 30 minutes, 37km). One daily bus goes into Máriapócs (250Ft, 30 minutes, 10km) proper; the others stop at the train station (*vasútállomás*).

Eight daily trains from Nyíregyháza (600Ft, 1½ hours, 38km) call at Nagykálló (375Ft, 50 minutes, 24km) and Máriapócs (200Ft, 45 minutes, 8km) first. Trains also arrive direct from Debrecen (900Ft, 1¼ hours, 58km, 10 daily).

BEREG REGION

Folksy blue and red flowers from the 1600s bloom in fresco on a Csaroda church wall, a kerchief-clad grandmother sits by the fence in Tákos selling her needlework, and row after row of boat-shaped wooden grave markers stand sentinel in Szatmárcseke. The pleasures of far, far northeastern Hungary are simple and rural ones. Regular flooding of the Tisza and Szamos Rivers cut Bereg off from the rest of Hungary, and isolation discouraged development and preserved folkways.

Bring your sense of adventure; the simple life is not always easy. Each small village has only one sight, and the guy who keeps the church key may not be home. English is spoken rarely, and rural lodgings, if they exist, are far from five-star. An intrepid, and potentially rewarding experience is to be had if you track down someone to rent you a room, and you can always base yourself in the region's only sizeable town, Vásárosnamény. Keep an eye out for the two- to three-colour (usually black and red and/or blue) graphic cross-stitch and plum products for which the area is famous. Remember that having your own transport is key, as a negligible number of buses connect the villages, and they go on weekdays only.

VÁSÁROSNAMÉNY

☎ 45 / pop 9330

Once upon a time Vásárosnamény was an important trading post on the Salt Road, which ran from the forests of Transylvania, via the Tisza River and across the Great Plain to Debrecen. Today it's a nondescript little town, but it does offer the closest city services for Bereg villages – including a new thermal bath and a small Tisza riverfront holiday centre.

The **OTP Bank** (Szabadság tér 28-31) and ATM are right near the **Tourinform** (☎ 570 206; vasarosnameny@tourinform.hu; Szabadság tér 33; ⏰ 8am-4pm Mon-Fri, 9am-1pm Sat), where the friendly staff will help you plan your rural excursions. Pick up an *Iranyi Bereg* (Golden Bereg) guide, in English and German, here. Fifteen minutes of internet usage is free.

The **Bereg Museum** (☎ 576 146; Szabadság tér 26; adult/child 300/150Ft; ⏰ 10am-6pm Tue-Sun), inside a former palace, contains a really excellent collection of Bereg cross-stitch, pottery, iron stoves and painted Easter eggs. A whole room is dedicated to how local textiles are woven. You can buy examples of cross-stitch and plum jam in the Tourinform office or at the **Folkart Shop** (Népművészeti Bolt; ☎ 06 30 555 6673; Szabadság tér 2).

The five indoor and outdoor pools at **Szilva Thermal Baths** (☎ 470 180; www.szilvafurdo.hu; Beregszászi út 1/b; adult/child 900/700Ft; ⏰ 10am-8pm) opened in 2007 near the town centre. The slides and rides at **Atlantika Waterpark** (☎ 570 112; www.atlantika.hu; Gulácsi út; adult/child 2500/2000Ft; ⏰ 9am-6.30pm Jun-Aug) are 2km east across the Rte 41 bridge in Gergelyiugornya, near the Tisza-part (Tisza bank) **beach**, where there are concession stands and **boat rental** (☎ 06 30 958 1150; off Tiszavirág sétány; per day 1200-12,000Ft; ⏰ 8am-8pm Jun-Aug).

Tourinform can help arrange bike rental.

Sleeping & Eating

A number of small lodgings have rooms for rent on Gulácsi út and Tiszavirág sétány in the Gergelyiugornya area. From June through August food stands and bars open on the waterfront there.

Diófa Camping (☎ 712 298; Gulácsi út 71; camp sites per person/tent 900/800Ft, r 6000Ft; 🅿) Not only does this small camping ground have an indoor pool and game room with billiards, it's right across the street from the water park. Pitch your tent in the field, or bunk in an above-average motel room. Full restaurant on site.

Szeles Apartman & Söröző (☎ 396 423; www.szelestei.hu; Kölcsey út 5; r 6000-8000Ft) Bare-bones apartments border on the sterile, but at least they're awfully clean. Don't expect anything beyond white walls, a kitchen and unadorned beds. Downstairs the comfy *söröző* (pub) has loads more character; there's a branch of the bar in an open-air pavilion at the Tisza-part beach.

Winkler Ház Panzió-Étterem (☎ 470 945; www.winkler.hu; Rákóczi utca 5; breakfasts 500-800Ft, mains 1200-1700Ft; ⊠) You can tell this restaurant is tops in town by the number of people who pack in for weekday lunches. Check out the poignant black-and-white photographs of area characters done by Rádi Bálint. Hand-woven neutral textiles are the highlight of pleasantly plain guestrooms (singles/doubles with breakfast 8000/10,000Ft) that have pine panelling and plaid tablecloths; each has a minibar.

Getting There & Away

Eight daily trains connect with Nyíregyháza (900Ft, 1¾ hours, 59km). The up to six weekday-only buses that link Vásárosnamény with Tákos (200Ft, 15 minutes, 8km) continue on to Csaroda (250Ft, 20 minutes, 13km); three keep going to Tarpa (375Ft, 40 minutes, 20km). To get to Szatmárcseke and Túristvándi, you have to change in Fehergyarmat, but runs are few and far between.

TÁKOS

☎ 45 / pop 410

A village must for anyone interested in folk art, Tákos is 8km northeast of Vásárosnamény on Rte 41. The 18th-century wattle-and-daub **Calvinist church** (☎ 701 718; Bajcsy-Zsilinszky utca 25; admission 200Ft; ⏰ 7am-7pm) has a spectacularly painted coffered ceiling of blue and red flowers, a beaten earth floor and an ornately carved 'folk baroque' pulpit sitting on a large millstone. Outside the church, which villagers call the 'barefoot Notre Dame of Hungary', stands a perfectly preserved **bell tower** (1767). The keeper of the keys, who is almost as old as the church, lives in a house just north of the church at Bajcsy-Zsilinszky utca 29.

The **provincial house** (tájház; 7am-7pm), opposite the church, sells snacks and works by local craftspeople. You'll often find grandmothers on chairs out front cross-stitching away, their work displayed on the fence behind them.

CSARODA

45 / pop 660

A lovely **Romanesque church** (484 905; Kossuth utca 2; admission 100Ft; 10am-6pm Mon-Fri Mar-Oct) from the 13th century stands in this village, which is slightly larger than Tákos and some 3km east. The church is thought to have been founded by King Stephen in the 11th century, following his plan to have at least one church for every 10 villages in his domain. The building is a wonderful hybrid with both Western- and Eastern-style frescoes (some from the 14th century), as well as some fairly crude folk murals dated 9 July 1647. On the walk from the car park or bus stop, you'll pass two wooden **bell towers** of a much more recent vintage.

Julia Udvar (645 484; József Attila utca 54; 9.30am-8pm Apr-Oct) is one of the best places in all of Bereg to buy needlework – for both selection and reasonable prices. The small snack bar sells pillowcases, table runners, tablecloths, book marks and ornaments by a cooperative of four local women who've continued the tradition to the next generation.

You can find repose in these peaceful rural surrounds at **Székely Vendégház** (484 830; József Attila utca 48; s/d 3000/6000Ft). The long, yard-oriented traditional peasant house-turned-lodging – with thick whitewashed walls, dark wood and red geraniums – has more than a little rustic appeal. The owners can usually help you arrange a meal.

TARPA

45 / pop 2280

A bit more of a town, with actual stores and streetlights, Tarpa lies 16km east and south of Csaroda. It's known for its plum products, but one of Hungary's last examples of a working, horse-driven, 19th-century **dry mill** (szárazmalom; 488 331; Árpád utca 36; adult/child 200/100Ft; by appointment) is also here. Nearby is a decorated **Calvinist church** (Kossuth utca 13; admission free; 8am-noon Mon-Fri).

Shop for homemade *szilva lekvár* (plum jam) and *pálinka* at **Bereg Kincsei** (488 488; Kölcsey utca 10; 10am-4pm). It also sells cross-stitch and other folk crafts. For other plummy sights in the area, including fruit farms and restaurants, ask for a Szilva Route map at Tourinform in Vásárosnamény (p365). You can also check out www.szilvaut.hu (in Hungarian).

The rustic rooms all have refrigerators at **Riviera Vendégfogadó** (42-313 032 for reservations; riviera@chello.hu; Árpád utca 24; s/d incl breakfast 7500/10,000Ft), which is a traditional peasant-house lodging. Order dinner ahead for 1500Ft, or eat hearty Hungarian food at **Kuruc Vendéglő** (488 121; Kossuth út 25).

On a bend in the river, **Tivadar**, 5km south of Tarpa, is a quiet little beachfront settlement with alternative lodging, a camp site and an eatery or two.

SZATMÁRCSEKE

44 / pop 1600

To get to this village, site of a **cemetery** (temető; Táncsics utca) with intriguing prow-shaped **grave markers**, cross the river at Tivadar, turn east and carry on another 7km northeast. The 600 carved wooden markers that resemble up-ended boats are unique in Hungary; the notches and grooves represent a complicated language detailing marital status, social position and so on. No one knows how the tradition (which is carried on today) started, but scholars generally agree it's not of Finno-Ugric (ancestral Hungarian) origin. One of the few stone markers in the cemetery is that of native son Ferenc Kölcsey (1790–1838), who wrote the words to 'Himnusz', the Hungarian national anthem.

TÚRISTVÁNDI

44 / pop 770

About 4km due south of Szatmárcseke is the village of Túristvándi and its pride and joy, a wonderfully restored 18th-century working **water mill** (vízimalom; 434 110; Zrínyi út 4; adult/child 200/100Ft; 8am-4pm Apr-Sep). On 20 August, locals celebrate a **Pasta Festival**, serving dishes made from mill-ground flour.

Across the bridge on the same pleasant stream, you can sleep and eat at **Vízimalom** (721 082; www.turvizimalom.hu; Malom utca 3; camp sites per person & tent 1000Ft, s/d 4000/8000Ft; camping Mar-Oct, lodge year-round). The 100 camp sites are along the shady water's edge. In addition to an unexpectedly international restaurant (Indian, Chinese and Hungarian mains 900Ft to 1400Ft), there's a snack bar and a rustic 30-room lodge. You'll have plenty to do, with a swimming hole out back, a kid's playground and canoe hire for 1000Ft per hour. In the early autumn you can help the proprietors make plum jam.

DETOUR: ERDŐHÁT'S FORGOTTEN VILLAGE

Nagygéc is a small ruined village that stands as a memorial in the far reaches of Erdőhát (a region with a name meaning 'Behind the Woods' of Transylvania). On 13 May 1970 the village suffered severe flooding and residents were evacuated. Even though the village had successfully dealt with floods since the Middle Ages (Nagygéc was first mentioned in a charter dating from 1280), the communist government mandated that villagers disperse and Nagygéc be left to the elements. Today, not much remains. The former centrepiece, a Protestant church with 13th-century Romanesque and 15th-century Gothic features, lies in ruin, ready to topple. At its entrance a sign reads: 'National memorial place. A memento for the deliberate destruction of villages, and a symbol of the will to preserve and restore'.

RÉTKÖZ REGION

Squeezed up against Ukraine, between the Lónya stream and the Tisza River, the Rétköz is a small, ethnically distinct region. Once a reedy swampland (providing great materials for basket-making and thatched roofs), the waters have been drained for agriculture. The area is known for strong clan ties and a wealth of folk tradition and craft, such as the Rétköz homespun cloth, but neither is easy for the traveller to find today.

KISVÁRDA

☎ 45 / pop 18,400

The centre of the Rétköz is Kisvárda, 45km northeast of Nyíregyháza. You can get a peek at area culture at the museum, and the small brick fortress, with a thermal bath next door, is mildly interesting. This is also a possible stop if you're continuing on to Ukraine.

Orientation & Information

Flórián tér, the town centre, is 2km northeast along Bockskai utca from the bus and train stations.

Main post office (Somogyi Rezső utca 4)

OTP bank (cnr Mártírok útja & Szent László utca) Has an ATM.

Sights & Activities

The yellow, Zopf-style **town library** (Flórián tér; internet access free; 9.30am-12.30pm & 1-6pm Mon-Fri, 8am-noon Sat) takes pride of place on the main square. To the east, the **Rétköz Museum** (☎ 405 154; Csillag utca 5; adult/child 300/150Ft; 8.30am-noon & 1-4.30pm Tue-Fri, 10am-2pm Sat) is in the Secessionist former synagogue (1900) with blue-and-yellow stained glass and wrought-iron gates in the shape of menorahs. Recreated village rooms and workshops (a smithy, loom etc) occupy the ground floor and a few crafts are for sale. **Agni Sipi's Shop** (Sipi Agni Boltja; Szent László utca 19) sells some regional weaving and small shepherd dolls.

The small brick **Kisvárda Castle** (☎ 405 239; Várkert; performances only) is about 10 minutes' walk from the centre of town, at the end of the street northwest of Flórián tér. Though part of one wall dates from the 15th century, most of the castle has been heavily restored. It's used for plays and concerts; ask at the **House of Arts** (☎ 500 451; Flórián tér 20; 8am-5pm Mon-Fri) for schedules.

Next to the castle ruins, the **Castle Baths** (Várfürdő; www.varfurdo.eu; Városmajor utca 43; adult/child 1000/800Ft; 9am-7pm May-Sep) have an assortment of outdoor thermal pools, with castle-themed bridges and such, plus sauna and sunbathing areas.

Sleeping & Eating

Várfürdő Camping (☎ 420 063; www.varfurdo.eu; Városmajor utca 43; camp sites per person/tent 1500/500Ft, bungalows 2600Ft; May-Sep) Basic field camping and wood cabins, located at the Castle Baths.

Bástya Panzió (☎ 421 100; www.bastya-panzio.hu; Krucsay Márton utca 2; r 4500-5500Ft) Tiny rooms for just as minuscule a price. The simple lodging above a main-street shopping arcade couldn't be more central.

Szent László utca has a number of small, quick eateries and a grocery store; **Várda Étterem** (☎ 405 119; Szent László utca 11-13; mains 900-1250Ft) is more of a sit-down option with solid Hungarian fare.

Getting There & Away

Three to seven daily buses head to Vásárosnamény (450Ft, one hour, 29km). Otherwise, Kisvárda is on the train line connecting Nyíregyháza (675Ft, 43 minutes, 43km) with Záhony (375Ft, 30 minutes, 23km) up to 18 times daily. Transfer at the latter to get into Ukraine. Local buses to Flórián tér await arriving trains.

Directory

CONTENTS

ACCOMMODATION

Except during the peak summer season (ie July and most of August) in Budapest, most of Lake Balaton, the Danube Bend and the Mátra Hills, you should have no problem finding accommodation to fit your budget in Hungary. Camp sites are plentiful, university and college dormitories open their doors to guests during summer and other holiday periods (some do so the entire year), the number of hostels and decent hotels is on the increase, and family-run *pensions* are everywhere. Although they are decreasing in number, private rooms are another option in many towns, particularly near tourist centres.

In this book, budget accommodation – camp sites, hostels, *pensions* and cheap hotels – is anything under 7500Ft a night in the provinces and under 13,500Ft in Budapest; midrange (usually *pensions* and hotels) is between 7500Ft and 15,500Ft in the counties and 13,500Ft to 30,000Ft in the capital; and top end is anything over 15,500Ft outside Budapest and over 30,000Ft in Budapest. Prices in this book are full price in high season (except for Budapest, where price ranges cover all seasons) and include bathroom. Exceptions are noted in specific listings.

The price quoted should be the price you pay, but it's not as cut and dried as that. Tourist offices and travel agencies usually charge a small fee for booking a private room or other accommodation, and there's usually a surcharge on the first night if you stay for less than three nights. Tourist tax (see the boxed text, opposite) is often not quoted in the advertised price. Some top-end hotels in Budapest do not include the 15% Value Added Tax (VAT) in their rack rates; make sure you read the fine print. As a general rule, hotels and *pensions* include breakfast in their rates, but it's best to check before signing in. It can almost always be added for anything between 800Ft and 2000Ft, however.

Parking is rarely a problem in Hungary's provinces, but in Budapest it's another matter altogether. For this reason we have only included the parking symbol (P) in the Budapest chapter.

With the Hungarian economy in trouble at the time of writing, it is unclear whether accommodation prices will rise or fall in the coming years. It is, however, certain that room rates will remain more expensive over the summer months compared to the winter period (aside from Christmas and New Year).

BOOK YOUR STAY ONLINE

For more accommodation reviews and recommendations by Lonely Planet authors, check out the online booking service at www.lonelyplanet.com/hotels. You'll find the true, insider lowdown on the best places to stay. Reviews are thorough and independent. Best of all, you can book online.

TOURIST TAX

Most cities and towns levy a local tourist tax on accommodation of between 300Ft and 400Ft per night for persons aged between 18 and 70 (those outside this range are usually exempt). Some hotels and *pensions* advertise their prices exclusive of the tax, so don't be surprised when it comes time to pay that a little extra has been added on. Where possible, we've included the tax in Sleeping prices quoted in this book.

Camping

The handy *Hungary Camping Map* published by the Hungarian National Tourist Office (HNTO; p380) lists some 425 camp sites of various sizes across the country, and these are the cheapest places to stay. Small, private camp sites accommodating as few as a dozen tents are usually preferable to the large and very noisy 'official' sites. Prices for two adults plus tent start from as low as 1800Ft off the beaten track in Western Transdanubia and rise to five times that amount on Lake Balaton in the height of summer.

Most camp sites open from April or May to September or October, and sometimes rent bungalows *(üdölőházak* or *faházak)* from 1500Ft to 15,000Ft, depending on their facilities. In midsummer the bungalows may all be booked, so it pays to check with the local Tourinform office before making the trip. A Camping Card International will sometimes get you a discount of up to 10%. Camping 'wild' is prohibited in Hungary.

For more information, contact the **Hungarian Camping & Caravanning Club** (MCCC; Map p84; ☎ 1-267 5255; mccc@mccc.hu; VIII Maria utca 34, 2nd fl) in Budapest. A useful website is www.camping.hu.

Farmhouses

'Village tourism', which means staying at a farmhouse, can be even cheaper than a private room in a town or city, but most of the places are truly remote and you'll usually need your own transport. For information contact Tourinform, the **National Federation of Rural & Agrotourism** (FATOSZ; Map p84; ☎ 1-352 9804; www.falusiturizmus.eu, in Hungarian; VII Király utca 93) or the **Centre of Rural Tourism** (Map pp80-1; ☎ 1-321 2426; www.falutur.hu; VII Dohány utca 86) in Budapest.

Hostels

The youth hostel *(ifjúsági szállók)* scene in Budapest has exploded in the last couple of years, leaving backpackers with a massive array of options. However, in the rest of Hungary quality hostels are a rare breed. Generally, the only official year-round hostels are in Budapest. The **Hungarian Youth Hostel Association** (MISZSZ; www.miszsz.hu) lists a number of places across the country associated with Hostelling International (HI), but unfortunately the HI card (or equivalent) doesn't get you far, as not all HI-associated hostels provide discounts to HI card-holders. Useful websites with online booking include www.youthhostels.hu and www.hihostels.hu.

Dormitory beds in a hostel cost between 3000Ft and 6000Ft per person and doubles 6000Ft to 15,500Ft in Budapest; the prices drop considerably in the countryside. A HI card is not required, although holders will sometimes get 10% off the price or not be required to pay the tourist tax. There's no age limit at hostels, which usually remain open all day. Hostels almost always have cooking and laundry facilities, as well as free or very cheap internet access.

Hotels

Hotels, called *szállók* or *szállodák*, run the gamut from luxurious five-star palaces to the run-down old socialist-era hovels that still survive in some towns.

A cheap hotel will often be more expensive than a private room, but it may be the answer if you're only staying one night or if you arrive too late to get a private room through an agency. Two-star hotels usually have rooms with a private bathroom; it's always down the hall in a one-star place. Three- and four-star hotels – many of which are new or newly renovated old villas – can be excellent value compared with those in other European countries.

For the big splurge, or if you're romantically inclined, check out Hungary's network of castle hotels *(kastély szállók)* or mansion hotels *(kúria szállók)*.

Pensions

Privately run *pensions* (*panziók*), which have formed the biggest growth area in the Hungarian hospitality trade over the past decade, are really just little hotels of up to a dozen or so rooms, charging from an average

PRACTICALITIES

- Budapest counts three English-language weekly newspapers: the long-established tabloid *Budapest Sun* (www.budapestsun.com; 399Ft), appearing on Thursday, with a useful classified section and *Style* arts and entertainment supplement; the *Budapest Business Journal* (www.bbjonline.hu; 1250Ft), an almost archival publication of financial news and business, appearing on Monday; and the *Budapest Times* (www.budapesttimes.hu; 580Ft), with good reviews and opinion pieces.
- Magyar Radio (www.radio.hu) runs three main stations: MR1-Kossuth (107.8FM), which has jazz, news and talk-back; MR2-Petőfi (94.8FM), with a wide range of popular music; and MR3-Bartók (105.3FM), offering classical music. Budapest Rádió, the external arm of Hungarian Radio, broadcasts on 88.1FM.
- Plug your hairdryer or travel kettle into a standard European adaptor with two round pins before connecting to the electricity supply (220V, 50Hz AC).
- Hungary uses the metric system for weights and measures (see the conversion table on the inside front cover).

10,000Ft for a double with shower. They are usually modern and clean, and often have an attached restaurant. As they are often located outside the centre, *pensions* are usually best for those travelling under their own steam, and visitors from Austria and Germany seem to favour them. A useful website (in Hungarian only) is www.panzio.lap.hu.

Private Rooms

Hungary's 'paying-guest service' *(fizetővendég szolgálat)* offers a great deal and is still relatively cheap, but with the advent of *pensions* it's not as widespread as it once was. There has, however, been an increase in apartment rental options in the provinces – these make a great deal if you're looking to save on eating out all the time. Expect to pay anywhere between 3000Ft and 6000Ft (6000Ft and 8500Ft in Budapest) per person depending on the class and location of the room; apartments normally start at around 6000Ft. Private rooms at Lake Balaton are always more expensive, even in the shoulder seasons. Single rooms are often hard to come by, and you'll usually have to pay a 30% supplement on the first night if you stay less than three or four nights.

Tourinform offices, city information centres and an ever-decreasing number of travel agencies such as Ibusz normally have a list of private rooms and apartments for a particular town or region. There are often several places in one town offering rooms, so ask around if the price seems higher than usual or the location inconvenient. In resort areas look for houses with signs reading '*szoba kiadó*' or '*Zimmer frei*', advertising private rooms in Hungarian or German.

If you decide to take a private room, you'll share a house or flat with a Hungarian widow, couple or family. The toilet facilities are usually communal, but otherwise you can close your door and enjoy as much privacy as you please. All first- and some second- and third-class rooms have shared kitchen facilities. In Budapest you may have to take a room far from the city centre. Some Tourinform offices and agencies also have entire flats or holiday homes for rent without the owner in residence. These can be a good deal if there are four or more of you travelling together.

University Accommodation

From 1 July to 20 August (or later) and sometimes during the Easter holidays, Hungary's cheapest rooms are available at vacant student dormitories, known as *kollégium* or *diákszálló,* where beds in double, triple and quadruple rooms start as low as 1200Ft per person. There's no need to show a student or hostel card, and it usually won't get you a discount anyway. Facilities are usually – but not always – basic and shared.

ACTIVITIES

Hungary offers an extensive range of activities, from cycling and canoeing to birdwatching and 'taking the waters' at one of the nation's many thermal spas. For details, see the Activities chapter (p66).

BUSINESS HOURS

With rare exceptions, opening hours, or *nyitvatartás,* of any concern are posted on the front door of businesses; *nyitva* means 'open' and *zárva* 'closed'. In this guidebook, reviews only include business hours if they differ from the standard hours listed below.

Grocery stores and supermarkets open from about 6am or 7am to 6pm or 7pm Monday to Friday and 7am to 3pm Saturday; an ever-increasing number also open 7am to noon Sunday. Department stores generally open from 10am to 6pm Monday to Friday, with late-night shopping (until 8pm) on Thursday, and on Saturday they usually close at 1pm. Many private retail shops close early on Friday and throughout most of August. Almost all towns and cities have at least one 'nonstop' – a convenience store that is open around the clock (or very early/late), and sells basic food items, drinks and tobacco. Most of the hyper-supermarkets outside the big cities, such as Tesco, open on Sunday.

Restaurant opening hours vary tremendously across the country but are essentially from 10am or 11am to 11pm or midnight daily. Bars are equally variable but are usually open from 11am to midnight Sunday to Thursday and until 1am or 2am on Friday and Saturday. Nightclubs usually open from 4pm to 2am Sunday to Thursday and until 4am on Friday and Saturday; some only open on weekends.

Banking hours are varied, depending on the institution and location, but banks usually operate from 7.45am to 5pm or 6pm Monday, 7.45am to 4pm or 5pm Tuesday to Thursday and from 7.45am to 4pm on Friday. The main post office in any town or city opens from 8am to 6pm weekdays, and until noon on Saturday. Branch offices close much earlier – usually at 4pm – and are almost never open on weekends.

CHILDREN

Travelling with children in Hungary poses few major problems: the little 'uns receive discounts on public transport and entry to museums and attractions; shops like DM, the nationwide German-owned health and cosmetic store, stock basic supplies for children; and the general public attitude to kids is one of acceptance. Outside upmarket hotels, babysitters are almost impossible to organise, however. All car-rental firms in Hungary have children's safety seats for hire for about €20 per rental; make sure you book them in advance. The same goes for highchairs and cots (cribs).

Museums catering specifically to children are few and far between in Hungary, but there are plenty of other entertainment options. Many thermal parks across the country have slides, wave pools and designated kiddie pools, and shallow Lake Balaton is perfect for a family holiday. Some towns, such as Pécs, have puppet theatres, and everyone loves a steam-train trip (p393. For ideas on how to keep the pack happy in Budapest, see p107.

For general information, Lonely Planet's *Travel with Children* is a good source.

CLIMATE CHARTS

In general, winters in Hungary are cold, cloudy and damp or windy, and summers are warm – sometimes very hot (see p16 for more information). July and August are the hottest months (average temperature 26°C) and January the coldest (-4°C). The number of hours of sunshine averages between 1900 and 2500 a year – among the highest in Europe. The average annual precipitation is about 600mm.

The climate charts in this chapter (p372) show you what to expect and when to expect it. For information on specific weather conditions nationwide, contact the **national weather forecast service** (☎ 1-346 4600; www.met.hu, in Hungarian).

COURSES

Language

The granddaddy of all Hungarian language schools is the **Debrecen Summer University** (Debreceni Nyári Egyetem; ☎ 52-532 594; www.nyariegyetem.hu; Egyetem tér 1) in Debrecen. It organises intensive two- and four-week courses in July and August; 80-hour, two-week intensive courses in January; and a superintensive two-week course in May/June. The two-/four-week (60-/120-hour) summer courses cost €520/950; board and lodging in a triple room costs €290/580 (singles and doubles are available at extra cost). There's also now a Budapest branch (p107).

For details on reliable schools in Budapest teaching Hungarian to foreigners, see p107.

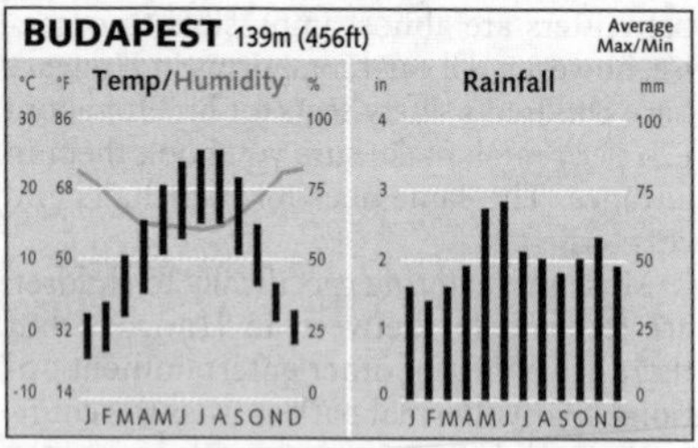

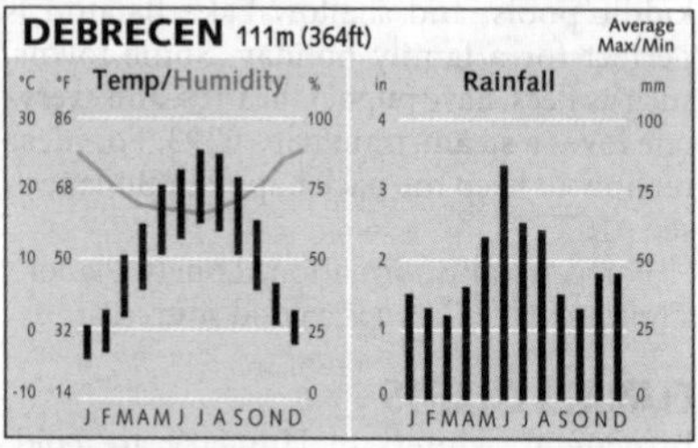

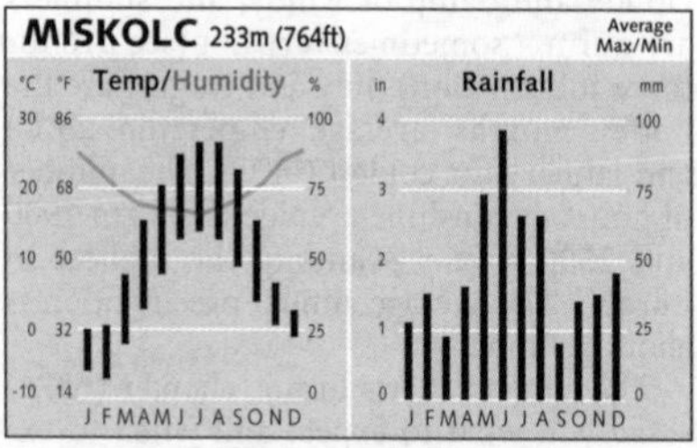

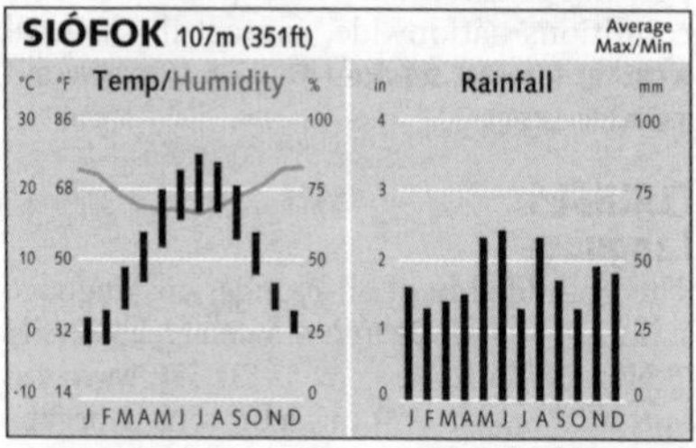

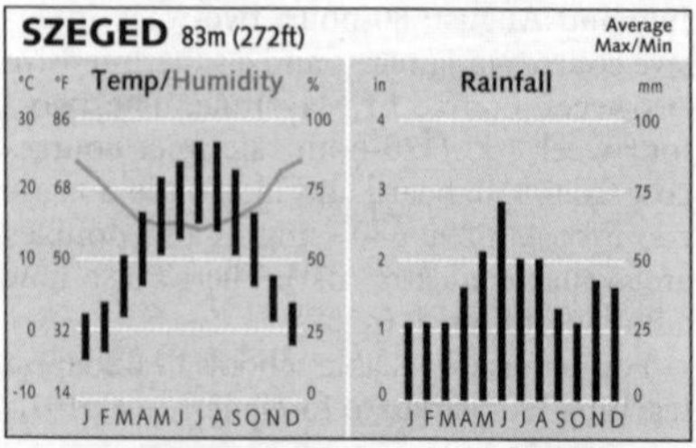

CUSTOMS REGULATIONS

Duty-free shopping within the EU was abolished in 1999 and Hungary, as an EU member, now adheres to the rules. You cannot, for example, buy tax-free goods in, say, Poland or France and take them to Hungary. However, you can still enter an EU country with duty-free items from countries outside the EU.

The usual allowances apply to duty-free goods purchased at airports or on ferries originating outside the EU: 500 cigarettes, 100 cigars or 500g of loose tobacco; 1L of still wine and 1L of spirits; 100mL of perfume; 250cc of eau de toilette. You must declare the import/export of any amount of cash, cheques, securities etc exceeding the sum of 1,000,000Ft.

When leaving the country, you are not supposed to take out valuable antiques without a 'museum certificate', which should be available from the place of purchase.

DANGERS & ANNOYANCES

As a traveller, you are most vulnerable to pickpockets, dishonest waiters, car thieves and scams.

Pickpocketing is most common at popular tourist sights, inside foreign fast-food chains, near major hotels and in flea markets. The usual method on the street is for someone to distract you by running into you and then apologising profusely – as an accomplice takes off with the goods.

Most Hungarian car thieves are not after fancy Western models because of the difficulty in getting rid of them. But Volkswagens, Audis and the like are very popular, and are easy to dismantle and ship abroad. Don't leave anything of value, including luggage, inside the car.

For important telephone numbers to know in an emergency anywhere in Hungary, see the boxed text on p379.

Scams

Beware of the capital's so-called *konzumlányok*, attractive 'consume girls' in collusion with rip-off bars and clubs who will see you relieved of a serious chunk of money (see p76).

It is not unknown for waiters to try to rip you off once they see/hear that you are a foreigner. They may try to bring you an unordered dish, make a 'mistake' when tallying the bill, or add service to the bill and then expect an additional tip. If you think there's a discrepancy, ask for the menu and check the bill carefully. If you've been taken for more than 15% or 20% of the bill, call for the manager. Otherwise, just don't leave a tip (see p377).

Some readers have mentioned border patrol guards on trains requesting additional ID in the form of credit cards, then using the name and numbers for fraud. Be aware that you are only required to present your passport as proof of identification. Other travellers have recorded problems on the Budapest metro.

DISCOUNT CARDS

Hostel Cards

The Hungarian Youth Hostel Association (p369) and branches of the Express travel agency chain issue HYHA cards valid for a year to Hungarian citizens and residents for 2300Ft, which includes a 300Ft NeoPhone phonecard. The card provides a 10% discount on some youth hostels connected with the association.

Hungary Card

Those planning on travelling extensively in the country might consider buying a **Hungary Card** (☎ 1-266 3741, 267 0896; www.hungarycard.hu; 6540Ft, valid for 13 months), which gives free admission to many museums nationwide; a 50% discount on a half-dozen return train fares and some bus and boat travel, as well as other museums and attractions; up to 20% off selected accommodation; and 50% off the price of the Budapest Card (p73) and Balaton Card (p197). The **Hungary Card Light** (2400Ft, valid for 13 months) is a thinner version of the Hungary Card. Cards are available at Tourinform offices nationwide.

Regional Cards

A number of regions in Hungary offer regional-specific discount cards. These include, among others, the Budapest Card (p73), Balaton Card (p197) and Badacsony Card (p209).

Student, Youth & Teacher Cards

The **International Student Identity Card** (ISIC; www.isic.org; 1800Ft), a plastic ID-style card with your photograph, provides bona fide students many discounts on certain forms of transport, and cheap admission to museums and other sights. If you're aged under 26 (30 in some countries) but not a student, you can apply for ISIC's International Youth Travel Card (IYTC; 1300Ft) or the Euro<26 card (2200Ft) issued by the **European Youth Card Association** (EYCA; www.euro26.org), both of which offer the same discounts as the student card. Teachers can apply for the International Teacher Identity Card (ITIC; 1300Ft).

EMBASSIES & CONSULATES

Hungarian Embassies & Consulates

Hungarian embassies (and consulates as indicated) around the world include the following. For further information (and a longer list), see www.mfa.gov.hu.

Australia Canberra (☎ 02-6282 2555; cbr.missions@kum.hu; 17 Beale Cres, Deakin, ACT 2600); Sydney (☎ 02-9328 7859; hunconsyd@kum.hu; Ste 405, Edgecliff Centre, 203-233 New South Head Rd, Edgecliff, NSW 2027)

Austria (☎ 01-537 80 300; vie.missions@kum.hu; 1 Bankgasse 4-6, A-1010 Vienna)

Canada Ottawa (☎ 613-230 2717; mission.ott@kum.hu; 299 Waverley St, Ottawa, ON K2P 0V9); Toronto (☎ 416-923 8981; consulate.tor@kum.hu; Ste 501, 425 Bloor St East, Toronto, ON M4W 3R4)

Croatia (☎ 01-489 0906; mission.zgb@kum.hu; Pantovčak 255-257, 10000 Zagreb)

France (☎ 01 45 00 94 97; mission.par@kum.hu; 5 bis, square de l'Avenue Foch, 75116 Paris)

Germany Berlin (☎ 030-203 100; infober@kum.hu; Unter den Linden 76, D-10117 Berlin); Munich (☎ 089-911 032; muc.missions@kum.hu; Vollmannstrasse 2, 81927 Munich)

Ireland (☎ 01-661 2902; mission.dub@kum.hu; 2 Fitzwilliam Place, Dublin 2)

Netherlands (☎ 070-350 04 04; mission.hga@kum.hu; Hogeweg 14, 2585 JD The Hague)

Romania (☎ 021-312 0073; mission.buc@kum.hu; Strada Dr Prof Dimitrie Gerota 63-65, Bucharest 70202)

Serbia (☎ 011-244 0472; blg.missions@kum.hu; ul Krunska 72, Belgrade 11000)

Slovakia (☎ 012-59 20 52 00; mission.pzs@kum.hu; ul Sedlárska 3, 81425 Bratislava)

Slovenia (☎ 01-512 1882; huemblju@siol.net; Konrada Babnika ulica 5, 1210 Ljubljana-Sentvid)

South Africa (☎ 012-342 3288; missionprt@kum.hu; 959 Arcadia St, Hatfield, 0083 Pretoria)

UK London embassy (☎ 020-7201 3440; office.lon@kum.hu; 35 Eaton Pl, London SW1X 8BY); London consulate (☎ 020-7235 5218; konz.lon@kum.hu; 35/b Eaton Pl, London SW1X 8BY)

Ukraine (☎ 044-230 8000; mission.kev@kum.hu; ul Rejtarskaja 33, Kyiv 01034)

USA Washington (☎ 202-362 6730; www.huembwas.org; 3910 Shoemaker St NW, Washington, DC 20008); New York (☎ 212-752 0669; nyf.missions@kum.hu; 223 East 52nd St, New York, NY 10022); Los Angeles (☎ 310-473 9344; mission.los@kum.hu; Ste 410, 11766 Wilshire Blvd, Los Angeles, CA 90025); Chicago (☎ 312-670 4079; consulate.chi@kum.hu; Ste 750, 500 North Michigan Ave, Chicago, IL 60611)

Embassies & Consulates in Hungary

Selected countries with representation in Budapest (where the area code is ☎ 1) are listed here. The opening hours indicate when consular or chancellery services are available, but be sure to confirm these times before you set out as they change frequently.

Australia (Map pp80-1; ☎ 457 9777; www.australia.hu; XII Királyhágó tér 8-9, 4th fl; 9-11am Mon-Fri)
Austria (Map pp80-1; ☎ 479 7010; www.austrian-embassy.hu; VI Benczúr utca 16; 9-11am Mon-Fri)
Canada (Map pp80-1; ☎ 392 3360; www.dfait-maeci.gc.ca; II Ganz utca 12-14; 8.30-11am & 2-3.30pm Mon-Thu)
Croatia (Map pp80-1; ☎ 354 1315; hrvhu@mail.euroweb.hu; VI Munkácsy Mihály utca 15; 10am-6pm Mon, Tue, Thu & Fri)
France (Map pp80-1; ☎ 374 1100; www.ambafrance-hu.org; VI Lendvay utca 27; 9am-12.30pm Mon-Fri)
Germany (Map p83; ☎ 488 3500; www.budapest.diplo.de; I Úri utca 64-66; 9am-noon Mon-Fri)
Ireland (Map p84; ☎ 301 4960; www.irishembassy.hu; Bank Center, Granite Tower, 5th fl, V Szabadság tér 7; 9.30am-12.30pm & 2.30-4.30pm Mon-Fri)
Netherlands (Map pp80-1; ☎ 336 6300; www.netherlandsembassy.hu; II Füge utca 5-7; 10am-noon Mon-Fri)
Romania (Map pp80-1; ☎ 384 7689; roembbud@mail.datanet.hu; XIV Thököly út 72, enter from Izsó utca; 8.30am-12.30pm Mon-Fri)
Serbia (Map pp80-1; ☎ 322 9838; ambjubp@mail.datanet.hu; VI Dózsa György út 92/b; 10am-1pm Mon-Fri)
Slovakia (Map pp80-1; ☎ 460 9010; slovakem@axelero.hu; XIV Stefánia út 22-24; 8.30am-noon Mon-Fri)
Slovenia (Map p77; ☎ 438 5600; II Cseppkö utca 68; 9am-noon Mon-Fri)
South Africa (Map p77; ☎ 392 0999; II Gárdonyi Géza út 17; 9am-12.30pm Mon-Fri)
UK (Map p86; ☎ 266 2888; www.britishembassy.hu; V Harmincad utca 6; 9.30am-12.30pm & 2.30-4.30pm Mon-Fri)
Ukraine (Map p77; ☎ 422 4120; uakovetseg@t-online.hu; XII Istenhegyi út 84/b; 9am-noon Mon-Wed, by appointment only Fri)
USA (Map p84; ☎ 475 4400; www.usembassy.hu; V Szabadság tér 12; 1-4.30pm Mon-Thu, 9am-noon & 1-4pm Fri)

FESTIVALS & EVENTS

Hungary's most outstanding annual events include the following. For more detailed coverage, pick up a copy of the HNTO's annual *Events Calendar* brochure, available from Tourinform offices.

February/March

Busójárás (www.mohacs.hu) Pre-Lenten carnival involving anthropomorphic costumes, held in Mohács on the weekend before Ash Wednesday.

March

Budapest Spring Festival (www.festivalcity.hu) Hungary's largest cultural festival, with some 200 events staged at 60 venues throughout the capital.

March/April

Hollókő Easter Festival (www.holloko.hu) Traditional costumes and folk traditions welcome in spring at this World Heritage–listed village.

May

Balaton Festival (keszthely@tourinform.hu) Pop and classical music and street theatre usher in the summer season at Keszthely.

June

Hungarian Dance Festival (www.hungariandancefestival.hu) The nation's most prestigious festival of dance, held biannually in Győr.

June/July

Sopron Festival Weeks (www.prokultura.hu) Theatre, quiet music, folk dancing and a handicraft fair, held in Sopron.

July

International Danube Folklore Festival Authentic folk music and dance, with performers from around Hungary and Europe, held in Kalocsa and Szekszárd.
Szeged Open-Air Festival (www.szegediszabadteri.hu) The most celebrated open-air festival in Hungary, with opera, ballet, classical music and folk dancing, held in Szeged.
Week of the Winged Dragon International Street Theatre Festival (www.szarnyas-sarkany.hu) Some 50 music and puppet performances are held in and around historical buildings in Nyírbátor in the Northeast.

August

Debrecen Flower Carnival (www.debrecen.hu) Week-long spectacular in Debrecen kicked off by a parade of flower floats on St Stephen's Day (20 August).
Formula One Hungarian Grand Prix (www.hungaroring.hu) Hungary's prime sporting event, held in Magyoród, 24km northeast of Budapest.
Haydn Festival A week of classical music performance at the Esterházy Palace in Fertőd.
Hortobágy Bridge Fair This 100-year-old fair in Hortobágy has dance, street theatre, folklore performances and the occasional horse and pony.

Jászberény Summer (www.jaszbereny.hu) Some 10 days of folk music and dancing, including the celebrated Csángo Festival, held in Jászberény.
Sziget Music Festival (www.sziget.hu) Now one of the biggest and most popular music festivals in Europe, held on Budapest's Hajógyár Island.
Zemplén Art Days (www.zemplenfestival.hu) Classical music festival launched by the Ferenc Liszt Chamber Orchestra and held in venues around Zemplén, especially Sárospatak.

September

Debrecen Jazz Days (www.debrecen.hu) Held in Debrecen, this is the oldest jazz festival in the country and attracts performers from all over the world.
Budapest International Wine Festival (www.winefestival.hu) Hungary's foremost wine-makers introduce their wines to festival-goers in mid-September in the Castle District.

October

Budapest International Marathon (www.budapestmarathon.com) Eastern Europe's most celebrated foot race goes along the Danube and across its bridges in early October.

November

Miskolc Autumn Cultural Days (www.miskolc.hu) Jazz, pop and rock music, literary and theatrical performances, and exhibitions of photography and industrial art take place throughout Miskolc for a week.

FOOD

Hungary has a varied, world-class cuisine and a wine-making tradition that goes back to the time of the Romans. For details, see the Food & Drink chapter (p51).

GAY & LESBIAN TRAVELLERS

There's not much gay life beyond Budapest (p124) unless you take it along with you, but the Budapest-biased freebie pamphlet **Na Végre!** (At Last!; www.navegre.hu) lists a handful of venues in the *vidék* (countryside). Pick it up at gay venues in Budapest or contact the organisation directly. Other useful websites, though primarily focused on Budapest, include www.budapestgayvisitor.hu and http://budapestgayguide.net.

The **Háttér Gay & Lesbian Association** (☎ 1-329 3380, 06 80 505 605; www.hatter.hu, in Hungarian; 🕑 6-11pm) has an advice and help line operating daily. **Budapest gayguide.net** (☎ 06 30 932 3334; http://budapestgayguide.net; 🕑 4-8pm Mon-Fri) can offer advice and/or provide information via email or telephone, while the **Labrisz Lesbian Association** (☎ 1-252 3566; www.labrisz.hu) has info on Hungary's cultural lesbian scene.

HOLIDAYS

Public Holidays

Hungary celebrates 10 *ünnep* (public holidays) each year.

New Year's Day 1 January
1848 Revolution/National Day 15 March
Easter Monday March/April
International Labour Day 1 May
Whit Monday May/June
St Stephen's/Constitution Day 20 August
1956 Remembrance Day/Republic Day 23 October
All Saints' Day 1 November
Christmas holidays 25 & 26 December

School Holidays

Hungarian school holidays fall during autumn (first week of November), over the Christmas and New Year period (12 days from around 22 December to 2 January), over Easter (one week in March/April) and, of course, in summer (11 weeks from 15 June to 31 August).

INSURANCE

A travel insurance policy to cover theft, loss and medical problems is a good idea. There is a wide variety of policies available, so check the small print.

You may prefer a policy that pays doctors or hospitals directly rather than requiring you to pay on the spot and claim later. If you have to claim later, make sure you keep all documentation. Some policies ask you to call back (reverse charges) to a centre in your home country where an immediate assessment of your problem can be made.

For information on vehicle insurance, see p389, and for health insurance, p394.

INTERNET ACCESS

Most people make constant use of internet cafes and free web-based email such as **Yahoo** (www.yahoo.com) or **Hotmail** (www.hotmail.com) when travelling.

The internet is now well established in Hungary, with blue 'eMagyarország Pont' signs throughout the country announcing that you can log on somewhere in the vicinity – be it via a free access terminal, at a commercial internet cafe or at a wi-fi hotspot. Many libraries in Hungary have free (or almost free) terminals, and most towns have at least one commercial internet cafe; Budapest has an overabundance of such places. Cafes open and close at a rapid rate, so check with local tourist offices if those mentioned in the book no longer exist. Expect to pay anything between 300Ft and 600Ft per hour.

Most hostels have at least one terminal available to guests, either free or for a nominal sum; the same cannot be said for hotels, but you may be able to use the reception's computer if you ask nicely. For those travelling with a laptop, many hotels offer wireless internet access, either free or for a small fee. The internet icon in this guidebook (💻) indicates a computer terminal is available for guest use.

Be aware that your modem may not work once you leave your home country. The safest option is to buy a reputable 'global' modem before you leave home, or buy a local PC-card modem if you're spending an extended time in any one country. For more information on travelling with a portable computer, see www.teleadapt.com.

If you are travelling with your own notebook or hand-held computer, remember that the power-supply voltage in Hungary may vary from that at home, risking damage to your equipment. The best investment is a universal AC adaptor for your appliance, which will enable you to plug it in anywhere. You'll also need a plug adaptor for European outlets; it's often easiest to buy these before you leave home.

For the best websites to check out before arriving in Hungary, see p18.

LEGAL MATTERS

Those violating Hungarian laws, even unknowingly, may be expelled, arrested and/or imprisoned. Penalties for possession, use or trafficking in illegal drugs in Hungary are severe, and convicted offenders can expect long jail sentences and heavy fines.

Another law that is taken very seriously here is the 100% ban on alcohol when driving. Do not think you will get away with even a few glasses of wine at lunch; police conduct routine roadside checks with breathalysers and if you are found to have even 0.001% of alcohol in your blood, you could be fined up to 150,000Ft on the spot. If the level is over 0.08%, you will be arrested and your licence almost certainly taken away. In the event of an accident, the drinking party is automatically regarded as guilty.

The legal age for voting, driving an automobile and drinking alcohol is 18. In 2004 the age of consent for gays and lesbians was lowered to 14 to come into line with that of heterosexual couples.

MAPS

Hungary's largest map-making company, **Cartographia** (www.cartographia.hu), publishes a useful 1:450,000-scale sheet map (640Ft) of the country, and its 1:250,000 *Magyarország autó-atlasza* (Road Atlas of Hungary; 2890Ft) is indispensable if you plan to do a lot of travelling in the countryside by car. The latter comes with 24 handy city maps. Bookshops in Hungary generally stock a wide variety of maps, or you can go directly to the **Cartographia** (Map p84; ☎ 1-312 6001; VI Bajcsy-Zsilinszky út 37; 🕐 10am-6pm Mon-Fri; Ⓜ M3 Arany János utca) outlet in Budapest.

Cartographia also produces national, regional and hiking maps (average scales 1:40,000 and 1:60,000), as well as city plans (1:11,000 to 1:20,000; around 660Ft each). Smaller companies such as Topográf, Magyar Térképház and Nyír-Karta also publish excellent city and specialised maps.

Since 1989 many streets, parks and squares have been renamed.

MONEY

The Hungarian currency is the forint (Ft) and today there are coins of 5Ft, 10Ft, 20Ft, 50Ft and 100Ft; in March 2008 the 1Ft and 2Ft coins were dropped from circulation. Notes come in seven denominations: 200Ft, 500Ft, 1000Ft, 2000Ft, 5000Ft, 10,000Ft and 20,000Ft.

The green 200Ft note features the 14th-century king Charles Robert and his castle at Diósgyőr near Miskolc. The hero of the independence wars, Ferenc Rákóczi II, and Sárospatak Castle are on the burgundy-coloured 500Ft note.

The 1000Ft note is blue and bears a portrait of King Matthias Corvinus, with Hercules Well at Visegrád Castle on the verso. The 17th-century prince of Transylvania Gábor Bethlen is on his own on one side of the 2000Ft bill and meeting with his advisers on the other.

The 'greatest Hungarian', Count István Széchenyi, and his family home at Nagycenk

> **A HEALTHY MIX OF MONIES**
>
> Although Hungary is now part of the EU, it will retain its own currency until at least 2013 (depending on the country's economic performance). Prices in shops and restaurants are uniformly quoted in forint, but many hotels and guest houses and even MÁV, the national rail company, give their rates in euros. In such cases, we have followed suit and you can usually pay in either euros or forint.

are on the purple 5000Ft note. The 10,000Ft note bears a likeness of King Stephen, with a scene in Esztergom appearing on the other side. The 20,000Ft note has Ferenc Deák, the architect of the Compromise of 1867, on the recto and the erstwhile House of Commons in Pest (now the Italian Institute of Culture on VIII Bródy Sándor utca) on the verso.

ATMs

ATMs accepting most credit and cash cards are everywhere in Hungary, even in small villages, and all of the banks listed in the Information sections in this guide have them. The best ones to use are the Euronet ATMs as they dispense sums in units of 5000Ft. Many of the ATMs at branches of Országos Takarékpenztár (OTP), the national savings bank, give out 20,000Ft notes, which can be difficult to break.

Cash

Nothing beats cash for convenience – or risk. It's always prudent to carry a little foreign cash, though, preferably euros or US dollars, in case you can't find an ATM nearby or there's no bank or travel agency open to cash your travellers cheques. You can always change cash at a hotel.

Credit Cards

Credit cards, especially Visa, MasterCard and American Express, are widely accepted in Hungary, and you'll be able to use them at many restaurants, shops, hotels, car-rental firms, travel agencies and petrol stations. They are not usually accepted at museums, supermarkets, or train and bus stations.

Many banks, including K&H and PostaBank (represented at post offices nationwide), give cash advances on major credit cards.

International Transfers

Having money wired to Hungary through an agent of **Western Union Money Transfer** (☎ 1-235 8484; www.intercash.hu) is fast and fairly straightforward, and the procedure generally takes less than 30 minutes. You should know the sender's full name, the exact amount and the reference number when you're picking up the cash. The sender pays the service fee (US$37 for US$500 sent, US$47 for US$1000).

Moneychangers

It is easy to change money at banks, post offices, tourist offices, travel agencies and private exchange offices. Look for the words *valuta* (foreign currency) and *váltó* (exchange) to guide you to the correct place or window.

There's no black market in Hungary to speak of but exchange rates can vary substantially, so it pays to keep your eyes open. And while the forint is a totally convertible currency, you should avoid changing too much as it will be difficult exchanging it beyond the borders of Hungary and its immediate neighbours.

Taxes & Refunds

ÁFA, a value-added tax of between around 5% and 17%, covers the purchase of all new goods in Hungary. It's usually included in the price but not always, so it pays to check. Visitors are not exempt, but non-EU residents can claim refunds for total purchases of at least 44,001Ft on one receipt, as long as they take the goods out of the country (and the EU) within 90 days. The ÁFA receipts (available from where you made the purchases) should be stamped by customs at the border, and the claim has to be made within 183 days of exporting the goods. You can then collect your refund – minus commission – from the **Global Refund** (www.globalrefund.com) desk in the departure halls of Terminals 2A and 2B at Ferihegy International Airport in Budapest, and at branches of the Ibusz chain of travel agencies in Budapest, Debrecen, Nyíregyháza, Békéscsaba, Szeged, Pécs and nine border crossings. You can also have it sent by bank cheque or deposited into your credit-card account.

Tipping

Hungary is a very tip-conscious society, and virtually everyone routinely tips waiters, hairdressers and taxi drivers. Doctors and dentists accept 'gratitude money', and even petrol-station attendants who pump your petrol and thermal-spa attendants who walk you to your changing cabin expect something. If you were less than impressed with the service at the restaurant, the joyride in the taxi or the way your hair was cut, leave next to nothing or nothing at all. He or she will get the message – loud and clear.

The way you tip in restaurants is unusual. You never leave the money on the table, but tell the waiter how much you're paying in total. If the bill is, say, 2700Ft, you're paying with a 5000Ft note and you think the waiter deserves a gratuity of around 10%, first ask if service is included (some restaurants in Budapest and other big cities add it to the bill automatically, which makes tipping unnecessary). If it isn't, say you're paying 3000Ft or that you want 2000Ft back.

Travellers Cheques

You can change travellers cheques – American Express, Visa, MasterCard and Thomas Cook are the most recognisable brands – at most banks and post offices. Banks and bureaux de change generally don't take a commission, but exchange rates can vary; private agencies are always the most expensive. OTP has branches everywhere and offers among the best rates; Ibusz is also a good bet. Travel agents usually take a commission of 1% to 2%. Shops never accept travellers cheques as payment in Hungary.

POST

The **Hungarian Postal Service** (Magyar Posta; www.posta.hu), whose logo is a jaunty, stylised version of St Stephen's Crown, has improved greatly in recent years, but the post offices themselves are usually fairly crowded and service can be slow. To beat the crowds, ask at kiosks, newsagents or stationery shops if they sell *bélyeg* (stamps).

Postal Rates

Postcards and letters up to 30g sent within Hungary cost 70Ft (100Ft for priority mail), while for the rest of Europe letters up to 20g cost 200Ft (230Ft priority) and postcards 150Ft (170Ft priority). Outside Europe, expect to pay 220Ft (250Ft priority) for letters up to 20g and 170Ft (190Ft priority) for postcards.

To send a parcel, look for the sign 'Csomagfeladás' or 'Csomagfelvétel'. Packages sent within Hungary cost around 830Ft for up to 20kg. Packages going abroad must not weigh more than 2kg or you'll face a Kafkaesque parade of forms to fill in and queues; try to send small ones. You can send up to 2kg in one box for 4000Ft surface mail to Europe and 4900Ft to the rest of the world. Airmail rates are higher and cost 5850Ft and 6790Ft, respectively.

Sending & Receiving Mail

To get in and out of the post office with a minimum of fuss, look for the window marked with the symbol of an envelope. Make sure the destination of your letter is written clearly, and simply hand it over to the clerk, who will apply the stamps for you, postmark it and send it on its way.

Hungarian addresses start with the name of the recipient, followed on the next line by the postal code and city or town, and then the street name and number. The postal code consists of four digits. The first one indicates the city, town or region (eg '1' is Budapest, '6' is Szeged), the second and third are the district, and the last is the neighbourhood.

Mail addressed to poste restante in any town or city will go to the *főposta* (main post office), which is generally listed under Information in the relevant section in this book. When collecting poste restante mail, look for the sign *'postán maradó küldemények'* and be sure to have identification on you. Since the family name always comes first in Hungarian usage (see the boxed text, p41), have the sender underline your last name, as letters are very often misfiled under foreigners' first names.

SHOPPING

Hungarian shops are well stocked with generally high-quality products. Books and folk-music CDs are affordable, and there is an excellent selection, especially of much-loved classical music. Traditional products include folk-art embroidery and ceramics, pottery, painted wooden toys and boxes, dolls, basketry and porcelain (especially that from Herend and Zsolnay). Feather or goose-down pillows and duvets (comforters), ranked second only to the Siberian variety, are of exceptionally high quality and good value.

Some of Hungary's 'boutique' wines (see p53) make good, relatively inexpensive gifts; a bottle of dessert Tokaj always goes down well. *Pálinka* (fruit-flavoured brandies) and Unicum are stronger options.

Foodstuffs that are expensive or difficult to buy elsewhere – potted goose liver, saffron, dried forest mushrooms, jam (especially the apricot variety), prepared meats like Pick salami, and the many types of paprika – make wonderful gifts (that is, if you are allowed to bring them into your home country). Be aware that in supermarkets and outdoor markets, fresh food is sold by weight or by *darab* (piece). When ordering by weight, you specify by kilograms or *deka* (decagrams – 50dg is equal to 0.5kg or a little more than 1lb).

TELEPHONE

You can make domestic and international calls from public telephones, which are usually in good working order; they take either coins or phonecards. Telephone boxes with a black-and-white arrow and red target on the door and the word 'Visszahívható' display a telephone number, so you can be phoned back.

Local & International Calls

All localities in Hungary have a two-digit telephone area code, except for Budapest, which has just a '1'. Local codes appear under the heading name of each city and town in this book.

To make a local call, pick up the receiver and listen for the neutral and continuous dial tone, then dial the phone number (seven digits in Budapest, usually six elsewhere). For an intercity landline call within Hungary and whenever ringing a mobile telephone, dial ☎ 06 and wait for the second, more melodious, tone. Then dial the area code and phone number. Cheaper or toll-free blue and green numbers start with ☎ 06 40 and 06 80, respectively.

The procedure for making an international call is the same as for a local call, except that you dial ☎ 00, then the country code, the area code and the number. The country code for Hungary is ☎ 36.

EMERGENCY NUMBERS

Ambulance (☎ 104)
Central emergency number (☎ 112; English spoken)
Fire (☎ 105)
Police (☎ 107)
24-hour car assistance (☎ 188)

USEFUL TELEPHONE NUMBERS

Domestic operator/inquiries (☎ 198; English spoken)
Information Plus (☎ 197; English spoken, any inquiry)
International operator/inquiries (☎ 199; English spoken)
Time/speaking clock (☎ 180; in Hungarian)

Mobile Phones

Hungary uses GSM 900 and 1800, which is compatible with the rest of Europe and Australia, but not with the North American GSM 1900 or the totally different system in Japan (though some North Americans have GSM 1900/900 phones that do work here). In Hungary you must always dial ☎ 06 when ringing mobile telephones, which have specific area codes depending on the telecom company: **Pannon GSM** (☎ 06 20; www.pgsm.hu), **T-Mobile** (☎ 06 30; www.t-mobile.hu) or **Vodafone** (☎ 06 70; www.vodafone.hu).

If you have a GSM phone, check with your service provider about using it in Hungary, and beware of calls being routed internationally. If you're going to spend more than just a few days here and expect to use your phone quite a bit, consider buying a rechargeable SIM card. Pannon offers prepaid SIMs for 2600/3900Ft with 1300/2500Ft worth of credit; T-Mobile's cost 4000Ft with 2500Ft worth of credit; and Vodafone's are 1680Ft with 500Ft worth of credit. Recharge cards, available from mobile phone stores and supermarkets, come in denominations of 900Ft, 1800Ft and 3600Ft. Local calls using a local SIM card cost between 25Ft and 40Ft.

Phonecards

Phonecards, which are available from post offices, newsagents, hotels and petrol stations, come in message units of 30/120 and cost 500/2000Ft, but these are by far the most expensive way to go. As everywhere else these days, there is a plethora of phonecards on offer. Among the most widely available are T-Com's Barangoló, which comes in denominations of 1000Ft and 5000Ft; **NeoPhone** (www.neophone.hu), with cards also valued at 1000Ft and 5000Ft; and Pannon, offering cards for 1000Ft, 3000Ft and 5000Ft. It can cost as little as 8Ft per minute to the USA, Australia and New Zealand using such cards.

TIME

Hungary lies in the Central European time zone and is one hour ahead of GMT. Clocks are advanced one hour at 2am on the last Sunday in March and set back at the same time on the last Sunday in October.

Without taking daylight-saving times into account, when it's noon in Budapest it's 3am in San Francisco, 6am in New York, 11am in London, noon in Paris, 1pm in Bucharest, 2pm in Moscow, 8pm in Tokyo, 9pm in Sydney and 11pm in Auckland.

An important note on the complicated way Hungarians tell time: like a few other European languages, Magyar tells the time by making reference to the next hour – not the previous one as we do in English. Thus 7.30 is *fél nyolc óra* ('half eight'; sometimes written as f8). Also, the 24-hour system is often used in giving the times of movies, concerts and so on. So a film at 7.30pm could appear on a listing as 'f8', 'f20', '½8' or '½20'. A quarter to the hour has a ¾ symbol in front (thus '¾8' means 7.45), while a quarter past is ¼ of the next hour (eg '¼9' means 8.15).

TOURIST INFORMATION

The **Hungarian National Tourist Office** (HNTO; www.hungarytourism.hu or www.hungary.com) has a chain of more than 140 tourist information bureaus called **Tourinform** (☎ within Hungary 06 80 630 800, from abroad +36 30 30 30 600; www.tourinform.hu) across the country. They are usually the best places to ask general questions and pick up brochures – and can sometimes provide more comprehensive assistance. The main **Tourinform office** (Map p86; ☎ 1-438 8080; hungary@tourinform.hu; V Sütő utca 2; ⏰ 8am-8pm) is in Budapest.

If your query is about private accommodation, flights or international train travel, or you need to change money, you could turn to a commercial travel agency, such as Ibusz, arguably the best for private accommodation, or Express, which issues student, youth, teacher and hostel cards, and sells discounted Billet International de Jeunesse (BIJ) train and cheap air tickets. See the Information sections under the various cities and towns in this book for details.

The HNTO has offices in a number of countries worldwide, including the following.

Austria (☎ 01-585 20 1215; www.ungarn-tourismus.at; Opernring 5, 2nd fl, A-1010 Vienna)

Czech Republic (☎ 283 870 742; www.madarsko.cz; Schnirchova 29, 17000 Prague 7)

France (☎ 01 53 70 67 17; www.hongrietourisme.com; 140 Ave Victor Hugo, 75116 Paris)

Germany (☎ 030-243 1460; www.ungarn-tourismus.de; Wilhelmstrasse 61, D-10117 Berlin)

Netherlands (☎ 070-320 9092; www.hongaarsverkeersbureau.nl; Laan van Nieuw Oost Indie 271, 2593 BS The Hague)

UK (☎ 020-7823 0413; www.gotohungary.co.uk; 46 Eaton Place, London SW1X 8AL)

USA (☎ 212-695 1221; www.gotohungary.com; Ste 7107, 350 Fifth Ave, New York, NY 10118)

TRAVELLERS WITH DISABILITIES

Hungary has made great strides in recent years in making public areas and facilities more accessible to the disabled. Wheelchair ramps, toilets fitted for the disabled and inward opening doors, though not as common as they are in Western Europe, do exist, and audible traffic signals for the blind are becoming commonplace in the cities.

For more information, contact the **Hungarian Federation of Disabled Persons' Associations** (MEOSZ; Map pp78-9; ☎ 1-388 5529, 388 2387; www.meoszinfo.hu; III San Marco utca 76) in Budapest.

VISAS

Citizens of virtually all European countries, as well as Australia, Canada, Israel, Japan, New Zealand and the USA, do not require visas to visit Hungary for stays of up to 90 days. Nationals of South Africa (among others) still require visas. Check current visa requirements at a consulate, at any HNTO or Malév Hungarian Airlines office, or on the website of the **Hungarian Foreign Ministry** (www.mfa.gov.hu), as requirements often change without notice.

Visas are issued at Hungarian consulates or missions, Ferihegy International Airport and the International Ferry Pier in Budapest. They are rarely issued on international buses and never on trains. Be sure to retain the separate entry and exit forms, which are issued with the visa that is stamped in your passport.

Short-stay visas (€60), which are the best for tourists as they allow stays of up to 90 days, are issued at Hungarian consulates or missions in the applicant's country of residence. Be sure to get a short-stay rather than a transit visa; the latter – also available for €60 – is only good for a stay of five days.

Short-stay visas are only extended in emergencies (eg medical ones; 5000Ft) and this must be done at the *rendőrkapitányság* (central police station) of any city or town 15 days before the original one expires.

You are supposed to register with the local police if staying in one place for more than 30 days; staff at your hotel, hostel, camp site or private room booked through an agency will do this for you. In other situations – if you're staying with friends or relatives, for example – you or the head of the household will have to take care of this within 72 hours of moving in. Address registration forms for foreigners *(lakcímbejelentő lap külföldiek részére)* are usually available at post offices.

WOMEN TRAVELLERS

Women should not encounter any particular problems while travelling in Hungary. If you do need assistance and/or information, ring the **Women's Line** (Nővonal; ☎ 06 80 505 101; 6-10pm Thu-Tue) or **Women for Women Against Violence** (NANE; ☎ 1-267 4900; www.nane.hu).

Transport

CONTENTS

GETTING THERE & AWAY

ENTERING HUNGARY

Border formalities with Hungary's four EU neighbours – Austria, Romania, Slovenia and Slovakia – are virtually nonexistent. However, as a member state that forms part of the EU's external frontier, Hungary must implement the strict Schengen border rules, so expect a somewhat closer inspection of your documents when travelling to/from Croatia, Ukraine and Serbia.

Flights, tours and rail tickets can be booked online at www.lonelyplanet.com/travel_services.

Passport

Everyone needs a valid passport or, for citizens of the EU (but *not* Denmark, Ireland, Latvia, Sweden or the UK), a national identification card to enter Hungary. For information on visas, see p380.

AIR

Airports & Airlines

Hungary has two international airports, but the vast majority of international flights land at **Ferihegy International Airport** (BUD; ☎ 1-296 7000; www.bud.hu) on the outskirts of Budapest. **Balaton Airport** (SOB; ☎ 83-354 256; www.flybalaton.hu) receives Ryanair flights from Dusseldorf, Frankfurt and London Stansted, and is located 15km southwest of Keszthely near Lake Balaton.

Malév Hungarian Airlines (MA; ☎ in Hungary 06 40 21 21 21, from abroad 1-235 3888; www.malev.hu), the national carrier, connects Ferihegy's Terminal 2A with the Middle East and all of the main cities in Continental Europe and the British Isles. It also flies to New York, Toronto and Beijing. Most other international airlines use Terminal 2B, which is next door to 2A and within easy walking distance. The super-discount European carriers use Terminal 1, about 5km to the west.

AIRLINES FLYING TO & FROM HUNGARY

Aside from Malév, the major airlines entering Hungary's airspace include the following.

Aeroflot (SU; ☎ 1-318 5955; www.aeroflot.com; hub Moscow)
Air Berlin (AB; ☎ 06 80 017 110; www.airberlin.com; hub Köln)
Air France (AF; ☎ 1-483 8800; www.airfrance.com; hub Paris)
Alitalia (AZ; ☎ 1-483 2170; www.alitalia.it; hub Rome)
Austrian Airlines (OS; ☎ 1-296 0660; www.aua.com; hub Vienna)
British Airways (BA; ☎ 1-777 4747; www.ba.com; hub London)
CSA Czech Airlines (OK; ☎ 1-318 3045; www.csa.cz; hub Prague)
EasyJet (U2; www.easyjet.com; hub London)
EgyptAir (MS; www.egyptair.com; hub Cairo)
El Al (LY; ☎ 1-266 2970; www.elal.co.il; hub Tel Aviv)
Finnair (AY; ☎ 1-296 5486; www.finnair.com; hub Helsinki)

THINGS CHANGE...

The information in this chapter is particularly vulnerable to change. Check directly with the airline or a travel agent to make sure you understand how a fare (and ticket you may buy) works and be aware of the security requirements for international travel. Shop carefully. The details given in this chapter should be regarded as pointers and are not a substitute for your own careful, up-to-date research.

CLIMATE CHANGE & TRAVEL

Climate change is a serious threat to the ecosystems that humans rely upon, and air travel is the fastest-growing contributor to the problem. Lonely Planet regards travel, overall, as a global benefit, but believes we all have a responsibility to limit our personal impact on global warming.

Flying & Climate Change

Pretty much every form of motor travel generates CO_2 (the main cause of human-induced climate change) but planes are far and away the worst offenders, not just because of the sheer distances they allow us to travel, but because they release greenhouse gases high into the atmosphere. The statistics are frightening: two people taking a return flight between Europe and the US will contribute as much to climate change as an average household's gas and electricity consumption over a whole year.

Carbon Offset Schemes

Climatecare.org and other websites use 'carbon calculators' that allow jetsetters to offset the greenhouse gases they are responsible for with contributions to energy-saving projects and other climate-friendly initiatives in the developing world – including projects in India, Honduras, Kazakhstan and Uganda.

Lonely Planet, together with Rough Guides and other concerned partners in the travel industry, supports the carbon offset scheme run by climatecare.org. Lonely Planet offsets all of its staff and author travel.

For more information check out our website: lonelyplanet.com.

German Wings (4U; ☎ 1-526 7005; www.germanwings.com; hub Köln)
LOT Polish Airlines (LO; ☎ 1-266 4771; www.lot.com; hub Warsaw)
Lufthansa (LH; ☎ 1-411 9900; www.lufthansa.com; hub Frankfurt)
Ryanair (FR; www.ryanair.com; hub London)
SAS (SK; www.flysas.com; hub Copenhagen)
Tarom Romanian Airlines (RO; www.tarom.ro; hub Bucharest)
Turkish Airlines (TK; ☎ 1-266 4291; www.thy.com; hub Istanbul)
Wizz Air (W6; ☎ 06 90 181 181; www.wizzair.com; hub Katowice)

Tickets

Competition in European skies has resulted in cheap fares offered by both no-frills airlines and full-service carriers. Discounted web fares are often the best deals for short-haul hops, but as a general rule travel agents still offer the best options for long-haul flights.

Reliable, online bookers are listed here.

Australia & New Zealand

From this far away consider purchasing a round-the-world ticket or multistop ticket offered by the likes of Qantas and British Airways; travel agents will be able to inform you of the most up-to-date prices.

There are no direct flights from either Australia or New Zealand to Hungary; most fly via London or Frankfurt, with a small minority stopping in at other European capitals.

For the location of Australian branches of STA Travel, call ☎ 1300 733 035 or visit www.statravel.com.au. **Flight Centre** (☎ 133 133; www.flightcentre.com.au) also has offices throughout Australia. For online bookings, try www.travel.com.au. In New Zealand, both **Flight Centre** (☎ 0800 243 544; www.flightcentre.co.nz) and **STA Travel** (☎ 0508 782 872; www.statravel.co.nz) have branches throughout the country.

Continental Europe

Malév flies nonstop to Budapest from a plethora of European cities, including almost all of the capitals on the continent. Many national airlines duplicate Malév's coverage, as do the likes of what Hungarians call the *fapados* (wooden-bench) airlines – the super discount carriers such as Air Berlin, EasyJet, Ryanair and Wizz Air.

Recommended agencies for France include **Anyway** (☎ 0892 893 892; www.anyway.fr); **Lastminute** (☎ 0892 705 000; www.lastminute.fr); **Nouvelles Frontiéres** (☎ 0825 000 747; www.nouvelles-frontieres.fr); **OTU Voyages** (www.otu.fr), which specialises in student and youth travellers; and **Voyageurs du Monde** (☎ 01 40 15 11 15;

www.vdm.com). Recommended German agencies include **Expedia** (www.expedia.de); **Just Travel** (☎ 089 747 3330; www.justtravel.de); **Lastminute** (☎ 01805 284 366; www.lastminute.de); and **STA Travel** (☎ 01805 456 422; www.statravel.de) for travellers under the age of 26. In the Netherlands, try **Airfair** (☎ 020 620 5121; www.airfair.nl).

Middle East

Malév flies to/from Tel Aviv, Damascus and Beirut two or three times per week.

UK & Ireland

Discount air travel is big business in London. Advertisements for many travel agencies appear in the travel pages of the weekend broadsheet newspapers, in *Time Out,* in the *Evening Standard* and in the free online magazine *TNT* (www.tntmagazine.com).

No-frills airline Ryanair connects Budapest with Bristol, East Midlands, Liverpool, Glasgow and Dublin, and Balaton with London Stansted, while EasyJet links the Hungarian capital with London Luton and London Gatwick. Wizz Air has also gotten in on the game, flying between London Luton and Budapest.

Recommended travel agencies include the following.

Flight Centre (☎ 0870 890 8099; flightcentre.co.uk)
Flightbookers (☎ 0870 814 4001; www.ebookers.com)
North-South Travel (☎ 01245-608 291; www.northsouthtravel.co.uk) North-South Travel donates part of its profit to projects in the developing world.
Quest Travel (☎ 0870 442 3542; www.questtravel.com)
STA Travel (☎ 0870 160 0599; www.statravel.co.uk) For travellers under the age of 26.
Trailfinders (www.trailfinders.co.uk)
Travel Bag (☎ 0870 890 1456; www.travelbag.co.uk)

USA & Canada

Discount travel agents in the USA are known as consolidators (although you won't see a sign on the door saying 'Consolidator'). San Francisco is the ticket consolidator capital of America, although some good deals can be found in Los Angeles, New York and other big cities. The following agencies are recommended for online bookings in the USA.

Cheap Tickets (www.cheaptickets.com)
Expedia (www.expedia.com)
Lowest Fare (www.lowestfare.com)
Orbitz (www.orbitz.com)
STA Travel (www.sta.com) For travellers under the age of 26.
Travelocity (www.travelocity.com)

In Canada, **Travel Cuts** (☎ 800 667 2887; www.travelcuts.com) is the national student travel agency, and for online bookings try www.expedia.ca and www.travelocity.ca.

LAND

Hungary is well connected with all seven of its neighbours by road, rail and even ferry, though most transport begins or ends its journey in Budapest.

As elsewhere in Europe, timetables for both domestic and international trains and buses use the 24-hour system. Also, Hungarian names are sometimes used for cities and towns in neighbouring countries on bus and train schedules (see p407).

Bus

Crossing the continent is cheapest by bus, but it is also the least comfortable. Most international buses are run by **Eurolines** (www.eurolines.com) and link with its Hungarian associate, **Volánbusz** (☎ 1-382 0888; www.volanbusz.hu).

Eurolines has passes that allow unlimited travel between 35 European cities, including Budapest. Adults pay between €199 and €329 for 15 days and between €299 and €439 for 30 days, depending on the season, and those under 26 pay €169 to €279 for 15 days and €229 to €359 for 30 days.

Car & Motorcycle

Europe is well covered by national and international motorways. Drivers of cars and riders of motorbikes will need the vehicle's registration papers, liability insurance and an international driver's permit in addition to their domestic licence. Gasoline and parts for modern cars are generally easily available in almost all European countries.

For specific information on car and motorcycle travel within Hungary, see p388.

Train

By far the most comfortable and often most environmentally friendly way to get to Hungary is by train. The country is well connected to its neighbouring countries, with international services arriving and departing at least once a day. On long hauls, sleepers are almost always available in both 1st and 2nd class, and couchettes are available in 2nd class. Not all express trains have dining or even buffet cars; make sure you bring along snacks and drinks as vendors can be few and far between. Most international journeys require seat reservations.

Magyar Államvasutak (☎ 1-371 9449; www.mav.hu), which translates as Hungarian State Railways and is universally known as MÁV, links up with the European rail network in all directions. Its trains run as far as London (via Munich and Paris), Stockholm (via Hamburg and Copenhagen), Moscow, Rome and Istanbul (via Belgrade). Almost all international trains bound for Hungary eventually arrive and then depart from Budapest's Keleti station. For more information on the city's stations, see p131.

The *Thomas Cook European Timetable* is the trainophile's bible, giving a complete listing of train schedules, supplements and reservations information. It is updated monthly and is available from Thomas Cook outlets. In the USA, call ☎ 800 367 7984.

CLASSES, COSTS & RESERVATIONS

InterCity (IC) and EuroCity (EC) trains crisscross Hungary on their way to various parts of Europe both east and west. Seat reservations for international destinations cost €3 one way where they are compulsory. Tickets are normally valid for 60 days from purchase and stopovers are permitted. On overnight trips there is usually a choice between a couchette or a more expensive sleeper. Long-distance trains have a dining car or snacks available.

Budapest is the country's main train hub and has good connections to much of Central Europe. Destinations that can be reached from the capital include Berlin (€58, 12 hours), Belgrade (€26, 7½ hours), Bratislava (€16, 2½ hours), Frankfurt (€78, 15 hours), Munich (€58, seven to nine hours), Prague (€38, seven hours), Sofia (€77, 18 hours), Venice (€55, 14 hours), Vienna (€26, three hours), Warsaw (€58, 12 hours) and Zurich (€78, 12 hours). All prices quoted are full-price, one-way, 2nd-class fares; 1st-class seats are around 50% more expensive than 2nd class. Examples of two-berth sleeper prices are €149/100/94/75 to Frankfurt/Venice/Sofia/Warsaw.

Substantial discounts to a number of European capitals are available on tickets purchased more than three days in advance. Note that a limited number of seats on any one train are discounted, so book early to take advantage of the savings.

TRAIN PASSES

Inter Rail (www.interrailnet.com) Global Passes cover much of Europe and can be purchased by nationals of European countries (or residents of at least six months). A pass offers 1st-/2nd-class travel for five days within a 10-day period (€329/249), 10 days within a 22-day period (€489/359), 22 continuous days (€629/469), or one month (€809/599). Discounts are available for those under 26.

It's almost impossible for a standard **Eurail pass** (www.eurailnet.com) to pay for itself in Hungary. If you are a non-European resident, you may consider one of its combination tickets allowing you to travel over a fixed period for a set price. These include the Hungary N' Slovenia/Croatia pass, Austria N' Hungary pass and Romania N' Hungary pass, offering five/10 days of travel on those countries' rail networks for around US$250/370 for adults and US$170/260 for youths; children aged between four and 11 travel half-price. Buy the pass before you leave home.

For information on individual Hungary passes, see p393.

Croatia, Slovenia, Serbia & Bulgaria

BUS

From late June to September a bus connects Budapest with Pula (one way 10,900Ft, 9¾ hours) every Saturday, travelling via Rijeka (9900Ft, 8¼ hours) and then carrying on to Porec (10,900Ft, 11½ hours); overnight buses on Friday also serve Dubrovnik (11,900Ft, 14 hours) and Split (11,900Ft, 13 hours).

One bus daily year-round services Subotica (Szabadka in Hungarian; 3900Ft, 4½ hours), while buses run to Sofia (12,500Ft, 13½ hours) on Tuesday, Thursday and Sunday.

TRAIN

You can get to Budapest from Zagreb (six to 7½ hours) on three trains that pass through Siófok on Lake Balaton's southern shore: the *Maestral*, the IC *Kvarner* and the EN *Venezia*. The last begins in Venice (14 hours) and passes through Ljubljana (nine hours).

Trains between Budapest and Belgrade (7¼ hours) via Subotica are the *Beograd* and the IC *Avala*. Two daily trains make the 1¾-hour journey between Subotica and Szeged. For Sofia (27½ hours), a change in Belgrade is required.

Romania

BUS

Only a handful of buses connect Budapest with Romania, including the daily service to Cluj-Napoca (6000Ft, 9½ hours).

TRAIN

From Bucharest to Budapest (13½ to 16 hours) you can choose from three direct trains: the *Dacia,* the EN *Ister* or the *Pannonia.* All go via Arad (5½ hours) and some require seat reservations.

There are two daily connections from Cluj-Napoca to Budapest (seven hours) via Oradea: on the *Ady Endre* and the *Corona.* The EC *Traianus* and IC *Kőrős* link Budapest with Timişoara (4¾ hours).

Slovakia, Czech Republic & Poland

BUS

From Népliget station there are buses to Bratislava (Pozsony in Hungarian; 3700Ft, four hours) daily, and overnight services on Tuesday and Friday to Prague (9900Ft, 7½ hours).

Kraków (3900Ft, 7¼ hours) is served every Wednesday and Saturday throughout the year.

TRAIN

In addition to the EC 170, Budapest can be reached from Prague (seven to 7½ hours) on the EC 174, the EC *Jaroslav Hašek,* the EN *Galileo Galilei,* and the *Pannónia,* which then carries on to Bucharest. All of these, plus the IC *Moravia,* pass through Bratislava (2¾ hours) on their travels.

The IC *Hernád* and EC *Bem József* connect Košice (3¼ hours) with Budapest via Miskolc; the former continues onto Siófok and Keszthely while the latter originates in Warsaw (12¼ hours) and passes through Kraków (9¼ hours). The 2km hop from Slovenské Nové Mesto to Sátoraljaújhely is only a four-minute ride on the train; two of the four trains that make the daily journey continue to Budapest.

Ukraine & Russia

BUS

On Monday and Friday there are overnight buses to Kyiv (14,900Ft, 20 hours) via Lviv (12,900Ft, 11 hours).

TRAIN

The *Tisza Express* is the only direct train linking Kyiv (26 hours) and Budapest. The Tisza, which begins its journey in Moscow (37¾ hours), also passes through Lviv (15 hours). Note that EU, US, Canadian and Japanese citizens no longer require a visa for visits of up to 90 days to Ukraine.

Western Europe

BUS

From Népliget station there are buses to many cities across Western Europe.

Vienna (5900Ft, 3½ hours) is served by up to five buses daily, and Berlin (17,900Ft, 13¾ hours) by up to two buses on Tuesday, Friday and Saturday. There's a long-distance bus that runs throughout the year up to four times a week to Amsterdam (26,900Ft, 21½ hours) via Frankfurt (24,900Ft, 14 hours) and Düsseldorf (25,900Ft, 17¼ hours) that continues on to Rotterdam (26,900Ft, 22¾ hours).

Buses to London via Brussels and Lille (30,900Ft, 24¾ hours) depart on Monday, Wednesday, Friday and Sunday. Paris (26,900Ft, 20¼ hours) is connected with Budapest on Monday, Wednesday and Friday throughout the year.

Other destinations include Athens (21,000Ft, 24 hours, up to three times weekly), Venice (13,900Ft, 10¼ hours, Wednesday) and Zürich (22,900Ft, 23 hours, one daily).

TRAIN

Seven trains daily link Vienna's Westbahnhof with Budapest (three hours) via Hegyeshalom and Győr; some also depart from the city's Südbahnhof. Two trains that pass through Vienna (and Salzburg; six hours) – the EN *Kálmán Imre* and EC 62 – come from Munich (7½ to 10 hours). Other trains departing from the Westbahnhof include the EC 26 from Cologne (9½ hours) and Frankfurt (seven hours), the EN *Wiener Walzer* from Zürich (nine hours) and the IC 345 to Belgrade (11 hours). The early-morning EC *Lehár Ferenc* departs from Vienna's Südbahnhof. None of these trains require a reservation, though it's highly recommended in summer.

Hourly trains leave Vienna's Südbahnhof every day for Sopron (one to 1½ hours) via Wiener Neustadt, which is easily accessible from Vienna. Six daily milk trains make the 2½- to three-hour trip from Graz to Szombathely.

The EC 170 and 174 travel from Berlin to Budapest (11¾ hours) via Dresden, Prague and Bratislava.

RIVER

A hydrofoil service on the Danube River between Budapest and Vienna (5½ to 6½ hours) operates daily from late April to early October; passengers can disembark at Bratislava with advance notice. Services leave from both Budapest and Vienna at 9am. Adult one-way/return fares for Vienna are €89/109 and for Bratislava €79/99. Students with ISIC cards receive a €10 discount, and children between two and 14 years of age travel for half-price. Taking a bicycle costs €20 one way.

In Budapest, ferries arrive and depart from the International Ferry Pier (Nemzetközi hajóállomás) on V Belgrád rakpart, between Elizabeth Bridge (Erzsébet híd) and Liberty Bridge (Szabadság híd) on the Pest side. In Vienna, the boat docks at the Reichsbrücke pier near Mexikoplatz.

For information and tickets, contact **Mahart PassNave** (☎ 1-484 4013; www.mahartpassnave.hu; V Belgrád rakpart) in Budapest and **Mahart PassNave Wien** (☎ 01-72 92 161/2; Handelskai 265) in Vienna.

GETTING AROUND

Hungary's domestic transport system is efficient, comprehensive and inexpensive. In general, almost everything runs to schedule and the majority of Hungary's towns and cities are easily negotiated on foot.

AIR

There are no scheduled flights within Hungary and chartering a plane can be an expensive prospect. Hungary is small enough to get everywhere by train within the span of a day.

BICYCLE

Hungary offers endless opportunities for cyclists: challenging slopes in the north, much gentler terrain in Transdanubia and flat though windy (and hot in summer) cycling on the Great Plain.

Outside the tourist hotspots and summer high season, hiring a bike can prove a problem. Your best bets are camping grounds, resort hotels and – very occasionally – bicycle repair shops. See the Activities sections under the various cities and towns in this book for guidance.

Remember when planning your itinerary that bicycles are banned from all motorways and national highways with a single digit, and bikes must be equipped with lights and reflectors. Bicycles can be taken on many trains and boats, but not on buses.

For more information, see p68.

BOAT

From April to late October the Budapest-based shipping company Mahart PassNave (left) runs excursion boats on the Danube from Budapest to Szentendre, Vác, Visegrád and Esztergom; and hydrofoils from Budapest to Visegrád, Nagymaros, Esztergom and Komárom between May and September. For details, see p140.

Mahart also schedules excursions once a month from May to September on the country's southern stretch of the Danube River. Boats sail from Budapest to places like Kalocsa (adult/child return 13,990/6990Ft), Solt (11,990/5990Ft) and Mohács (15,990/7990Ft) on the Great Plain. There are also weekend sailings between mid-May and mid-September from Budapest to Százhalombatta. The 2006 floods ended services on the Tisza River (ie Sárospatak to Tokaj and Szeged to Csongrád), but they may restart in the coming years. Additionally, the BKV (Budapest Transport Company) runs passenger ferries on Budapest's stretch of the Danube between mid-April and mid-October (see p132).

Over summer, Lake Balaton is well served by ferries; for more information, see p195.

BUS

Hungary's **Volánbusz** (www.volanbusz.hu) network is a good – and sometimes necessary – alternative to trains. In Southern Transdanubia and many parts of the Great Plain, buses are essential unless you are prepared to make several time-consuming changes on the train. For short trips around the Danube Bend or Lake Balaton areas, buses are preferable to trains. There is only one type of class on Hungarian buses.

In most cities and large towns it is usually possible to catch at least one direct bus a day

---

BUS TIMETABLE SYMBOLS

Symbol	Meaning
✕	Monday to Saturday (except public holidays)
⊗	Monday to Friday (except public holidays)
✕̄	Monday to Thursday (except public holidays)
☐	first working day of the week (usually Monday)
⊤	last working day of the week (usually Friday)
⊙	Saturday & public holidays
⊕	Saturday, Sunday & public holidays
╪	Sunday & public holidays
⊞	day before the first working day of the week (usually Sunday but Monday when Sunday is a public holiday)
▼	school days
▽	working days during school holidays (mid-June to August; first week of November; Christmas & New Year; one week in March/April)

---

to fairly far-flung areas of the country – for example, Pécs to Sopron (six hours, 287km) or Eger to Szeged (five hours, 245km).

National buses arrive and depart from Budapest's *távolságiautóbusz pályaudvar* (long-distance bus stations), not the local stations, which are called *helyiautóbusz pályaudvar*. Outside the capital the stations are often found side by side or in the same building. Arrive early to confirm the correct departure bay or *kocsiállás* (stand), and be sure to check the individual schedule posted at the stop itself; the times shown can be different from those shown on the *tábla* (main board).

Tickets are usually purchased directly from the driver, who gives change and will hand you a receipt as a ticket. There are sometimes queues for intercity buses (especially on Friday afternoon), so it's wise to arrive early. Smoking is not allowed on buses in Hungary, though a 10- or 20-minute rest stop is made about every two or three hours. Seats on Volánbusz are spaced far enough apart for you to be able to fit your pack or bag between your knees.

Posted bus timetables can be horribly confusing if you don't speak Hungarian. The things to remember when reading a timetable are that *indulás* means 'departures' and *érkezés* means 'arrivals'. Some timetable symbols are shown in the table, p388.

Numbers one to seven in a circle refer to the days of the week, beginning with Monday. Written footnotes you might see include *naponta* (daily), *hétköznap* (weekdays), *munkanap* (working days), *szabadnap* (Saturday), *munkaszünetes nap* (Sunday and holidays), *szabad és munkaszünetes nap* (Saturday, Sunday and holidays), *szabadnap kivételével naponta* (daily except Saturday), *munkaszünetes nap kivételével naponta* (daily except holidays) and *iskolai nap* (school days).

A few of the larger bus stations have left-luggage rooms, but they generally close early (around 6pm). Check your bag at the train station, which is almost always nearby; the left-luggage offices there keep much longer hours.

Costs
Bus fares are calculated by distance. At the time of writing, Volánbusz charged the following prices.

Fare	Distance
125Ft	for up to 5km
200Ft	for 10km
750Ft	for 50km
1500Ft	for 100km
2780Ft	for 200km
3830Ft	for 300km

CAR & MOTORCYCLE
Automobile Associations
In the event of a breakdown, the so-called **Yellow Angels** (Sárga Angyal; ☎ nationwide 24hr 188) of the **Hungarian Automobile Club** (Map pp80-1; Magyar Autóklub; ☎ 1-345 1800; www.autoklub.hu, in Hungarian; II Rómer Flóris utca 4/a, Budapest) do basic car repairs free of charge if you belong to an affiliated organisation such as AAA in the USA, or AA or RAC in the UK. Towing, however, is still very expensive even with these reciprocal memberships. The number to ring in an emergency is ☎ 188.

For 24-hour information on traffic and public road conditions around Hungary, contact **Útinform** (☎ 1-336 2400, 322 2238; www.kozut .hu). In the capital, ring **Fővinform** (☎ 1-317 1173; www.fovinform.hu).

Driving Licence

Foreign driving licences are valid for one year after entering Hungary. If you don't hold a European driving licence and plan to drive here, obtain an International Driving Permit (IDP) from your local automobile association before you leave – you'll need a passport photo and a valid local licence. It is usually inexpensive and valid for one year. Be aware that an IDP is not valid unless accompanied by your original driving licence.

Third-party liability insurance is compulsory in Hungary. If your car is registered in the EU, it is assumed you have it. Other motorists must show a Green Card or they will have to buy insurance at the border.

Fuel

Ólommentes benzin (unleaded petrol 95/98 octane) is available everywhere. Most stations also have *gázolaj* (diesel).

Hire

In general, you must be at least 21 years old and have had your licence for a year to rent a car. Drivers under 25 sometimes have to pay a surcharge. All of the big international firms have offices in Budapest, and there are scores of local companies throughout the country, but don't expect many bargains. For details of options in Budapest, see p130.

Insurance

All accidents should be reported to the police (☎ 107) immediately. Several insurance companies handle auto liability, and minor claims can be settled without complications. Any claim on insurance policies bought in Hungary can be made to **Allianz Hungária** (☎ 06 40 421 421, 01-237 2372; www.allianz.hu) in Budapest. It is one of the largest insurance companies in Hungary and deals with foreigners all the time.

Road Conditions

Roads in Hungary are generally good – in some cases excellent nowadays – and there are several basic types. Motorways, preceded by an 'M' (including the curiously named M0 half-ring road around Budapest), will eventually total eight. At present they link

ROAD DISTANCES (KM)

	Békéscsaba	Budapest	Debrecen	Dunaújváros	Eger	Győr	Kaposvár	Kecskemét	Miskolc	Nyíregyháza	Pécs	Sopron	Szeged	Székesfehérvár	Szolnok	Szombathely	Veszprém
Budapest	203																
Debrecen	130	226															
Dunaújváros	210	67	277														
Eger	220	128	130	194													
Győr	327	123	350	142	251												
Kaposvár	314	189	381	146	317	201											
Kecskemét	124	85	191	86	158	208	190										
Miskolc	228	179	98	246	61	303	368	199									
Nyíregyháza	179	245	49	311	145	368	434	240	93								
Pécs	283	198	367	131	326	241	67	176	377	416							
Sopron	414	217	436	229	338	87	220	295	390	455	287						
Szeged	94	171	224	158	245	294	251	86	286	273	189	381					
Székesfehérvár	258	66	292	55	194	87	126	134	245	310	153	174	206				
Szolnok	107	97	129	148	121	220	252	62	162	179	238	307	130	163			
Szombathely	404	222	448	211	350	105	178	280	402	467	245	70	352	156	319		
Veszprém	292	110	336	99	238	77	127	168	289	355	166	143	240	44	207	111	
Zalaegerszeg	392	224	450	216	352	154	124	268	403	468	190	124	342	161	321	54	119

the capital with Vienna via Győr (M1) and Croatia via the southern shore of Lake Balaton (M7). They also run along the eastern bank of the Danube Bend (M2), part of the way to Slovakia as far as Miskolc (M3), and en route to Szeged and Serbia via Kecskemét as far as Kiskunfélegyháza (M5). National highways (dual carriageways) are designated by a single digit without a prefix and fan out mostly from Budapest. Secondary/tertiary roads have two/three digits.

Road Rules

You must drive on the right-hand side of the road. Speed limits for cars and motorbikes are consistent throughout the country and strictly enforced: 50km/h in built-up areas (from the town sign as you enter to the same sign with a red line through it as you leave); 90km/h on secondary and tertiary roads; 110km/h on most highways and dual carriageways; and 130km/h on motorways. Exceeding the limit will earn you a fine of between 5000Ft and 30,000Ft, which must be paid by postal cheque or at any post office.

The use of seat belts in the front (and in the back – if fitted – outside built-up areas) is compulsory in Hungary, but this rule is often ignored. Using a mobile phone while driving is prohibited, but again this law is universally ignored. A law that is taken very seriously is the one requiring all drivers to use their headlights throughout the day outside built-up areas. Motorcyclists must illuminate headlights too, but at all times and everywhere. They also must wear helmets – a law that is strictly enforced.

There is a 100% ban on alcohol when you are driving, and this rule is taken very seriously by all (see p376). It may not be much fun while on holiday, but you'll have to follow the lead of Hungarians and take turns with a companion in abstaining at meal and other times.

In any case, when driving in Hungary you'll want to keep your wits about you; this can be quite a trying place for motorists. It's not that drivers don't know the highway code; everyone has to attend a driver's education course and pass an examination. (That 'T' on the roof or back of a vehicle indicates *tanuló vezető*, or 'learner driver', by the way – not 'taxi'.) But overtaking on blind curves, making turns from the outside lane, running stop signs and lights, and jumping lanes in roundabouts are everyday occurrences.

Though many cities and towns have a confusing system of one-way streets, pedestrian zones and bicycle lanes, parking is not a big problem in the provinces. Most centres now require that you 'pay and display' when parking your vehicle – parking disks, coupons or stickers are available at newsstands, petrol stations and, increasingly, automated ticket machines. In smaller towns and cities a warden (usually a friendly pensioner) will approach you as soon as you emerge from the car and collect 200Ft or so for each hour you plan to park. In Budapest, parking on the street costs between 120Ft and 600Ft per hour, depending on the neighbourhood.

You must obtain a motorway pass or *matrica* (vignette) to access Hungary's motorways. Passes, which cost 1170Ft for four days, 2550Ft for 10 days and 4200Ft for a month, are available at petrol stations, post offices, and some motorway entrances and border crossings.

HITCHING

Hitching is never entirely safe in any country and we don't recommend it. Travellers who decide to hitch are taking a small but potentially serious risk. Hitchhiking is legal everywhere in Hungary except on motorways. Though it isn't as popular as it once was (and can be very difficult here), the road to Lake Balaton is always jammed with hitchhikers in the holiday season. There is a ride-sharing service in the capital called Kenguru (p131) that matches drivers and passengers for a fee.

LOCAL TRANSPORT

Urban transport is well developed in Hungary, with efficient bus and, in many cities and towns, trolleybus services. It usually runs from about 5.30am to 9pm in the provinces and a little longer in the capital.

You'll probably make extensive use of public transport in Budapest, but little (if any) in provincial towns and cities: with very few exceptions, most places are quite manageable on foot, and bus services are not all that frequent except in the largest settlements. Generally, city buses meet incoming long-distance trains; hop onto anything waiting outside when you arrive and you'll get close to the city centre.

You must purchase transport tickets (usually from 150Ft) at newsstands or ticket windows beforehand and validate them once aboard. Travelling without a ticket (or 'riding black') is an offence; you'll be put off and fined on the spot. Don't try to argue; the inspector has heard it all before.

Boat

Budapest and Lake Balaton have ferry systems – see p132 and p195, respectively, for more details.

Bus

Buses are the mainstay of public transport in most – if not all – villages, towns and cities in Hungary. They are generally well frequented by the local community and are a cheap and efficient way of getting to further-flung places.

Metro

Budapest is the only city in Hungary with a metro. See p134 for more details.

Taxi

Taxis are plentiful on the streets of most Hungarian cities and, if you are charged the correct fare, very reasonably priced. Flag fall varies, but a fare between 6am and 10pm is from 200Ft (in Budapest from 300Ft), with the charge per kilometre about the same, depending on whether you booked it by telephone (cheaper) or hailed it on the street. The best places to find taxis are in ranks at bus and train stations, near markets and around main squares. But you can flag down cruising taxis anywhere at any time. At night, vacant taxis have an illuminated sign on the roof.

Tram

Hungary's larger cities – Budapest, Szeged, Miskolc and Debrecen – have the added advantage of a tram system. The capital also has a suburban railway known as the HÉV.

TOURS

A number of travel agencies, including Vista and Ibusz (p75), as well as Cityrama and Program Centrum (p108), offer excursions and special-interest guided tours (horse riding, cycling, bird-watching, Jewish culture etc) to every corner of Hungary.

By way of example, Cityrama has a three- to 4½-hour tour by boat and bus to Szentendre or by bus to Gödöllő (€38 to €44; children under 12 years free or half-price); and an 8½-hour tour of the Danube Bend by coach and boat, with stops at Visegrád and Esztergom (€56). Cityrama also offers day trips to Lake Balaton (Balatonfüred and Tihany) and Herend (€72, nine to 10 hours), as well as to Kecskemét and a traditional Hungarian farm on the Southern Plain (€72, eight hours). Program Centrum offers similar tours at almost the same prices, as well as a nine-hour tour of the Eger wine region (€87). Vista has a six-day tour of the country that takes in parts of the Northern Uplands, Great Plain, Southern Transdanubia and Lake Balaton region. The tour includes accommodation and breakfast and costs €599 per person for double-sharing.

TRAIN

MÁV (www.mav.hu) operates reliable and relatively comfortable train services on just under 8000km of track, exactly a third of which is electrified. Most Hungarian trains are hardly what you could call luxurious, but they are generally clean and punctual. All the main railway lines converge on Budapest, though many secondary lines link provincial cities and towns. There are three main stations in Budapest. In general, Keleti station serves destinations in the Northern Uplands and the Northeast; Nyugati station serves the Great Plain and Danube Bend; and Déli station serves Transdanubia and Lake Balaton. But these are not hard and fast rules; confirm the departure station when you buy your ticket. The 24-hour number for domestic train information is ☎ 06 40 49 49 49 nationwide or ☎ 1-371 94 49 in Budapest. Online, check www.elvira.hu for fares and times.

Depending on the station, departures and arrivals are announced by loudspeaker/Tannoy or on an electronic board and are always on a printed timetable – yellow for *indul* (departures) and white for *érkezik* (arrivals). On these, fast trains are marked in red and local trains in black. The number (or sometimes letter) next to the word *vágány* indicates the 'platform' from which the train departs or arrives; for symbols and abbreviations used, see the table on p388.

If you plan to do a lot of travelling by train, get yourself a copy of MÁV's official timetable (*Menetrend;* 1000Ft), which is available at most large stations. It also has explanatory notes in several languages, including English.

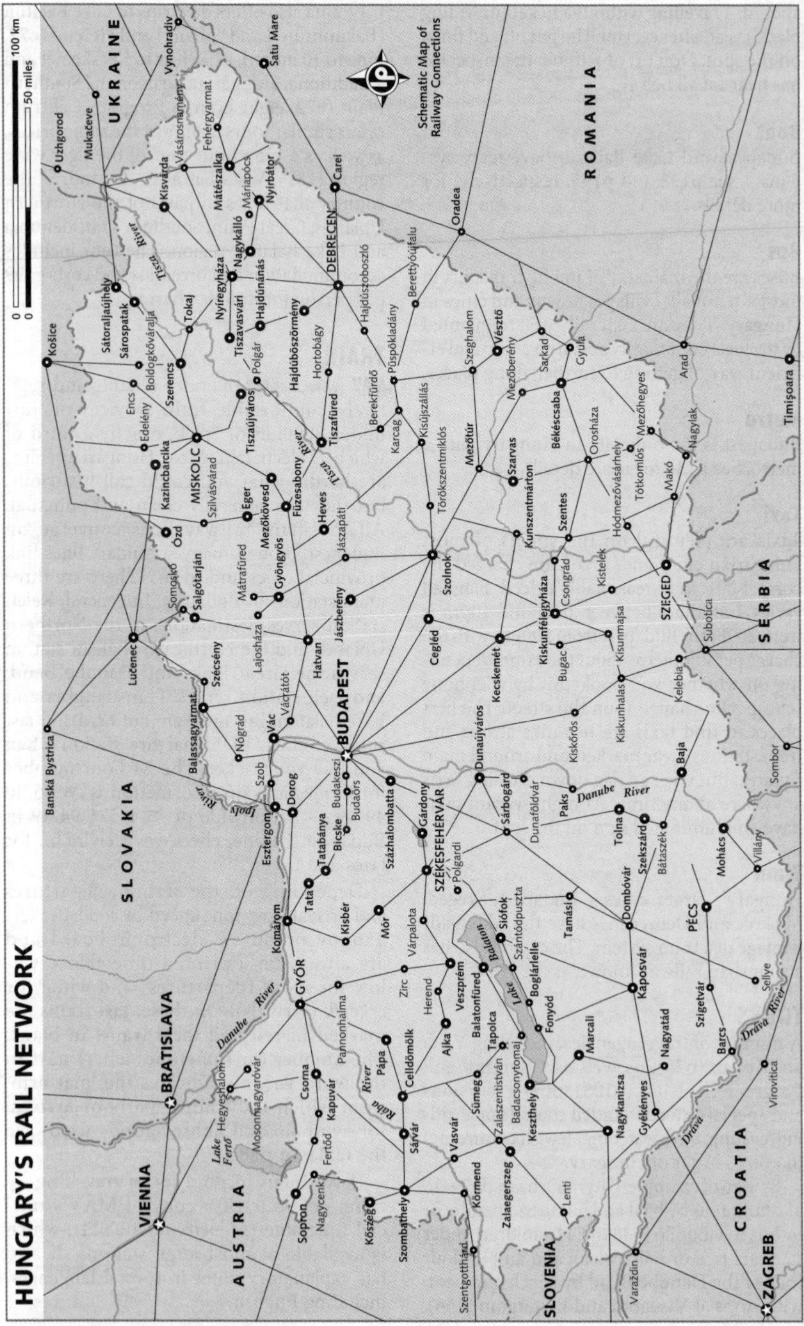
HUNGARY'S RAIL NETWORK
Schematic Map of Railway Connections
0 50 miles
0 100 km
UKRAINE
SLOVAKIA
AUSTRIA
ROMANIA
SERBIA
CROATIA
SLOVENIA
VIENNA
BRATISLAVA
BUDAPEST
ZAGREB
Danube River
Tisza River
Ipoly River
Rába River
Dráva River
Lake Balaton
Lake Fertő
Uzhgorod
Mukačeve
Vynohradiv
Satu Mare
Carei
Oradea
Arad
Timişoara
Subotica
Sombor
Košice
Banská Bystrica
Lučenec
Varaždin
Virovitica
Sátoraljaújhely
Sárospatak
Tokaj
Boldogkőváralja
Encs
Szerencs
Edelény
Kazincbarcika
MISKOLC
Szilvásvárad
Ózd
Eger
Mezőkövesd
Füzesabony
Tiszaújváros
Kisvárda
Vásárosnamény
Fehérgyarmat
Mátészalka
Máriapócs
Nyírbátor
Nagykálló
Nyíregyháza
Hajdúnánás
Tiszavasvári
Polgár
Hajdúböszörmény
DEBRECEN
Hajdúszoboszló
Berettyóújfalu
Püspökladány
Hortobágy
Tiszafüred
Berekfürdő
Karcag
Kisújszállás
Törökszentmiklós
Szolnok
Mezőtúr
Szeghalom
Vésztő
Mezőberény
Sarkad
Gyula
Békéscsaba
Szarvas
Orosháza
Mezőhegyes
Nagylak
Tótkomlós
Hódmezővásárhely
Makó
Kunszentmárton
Szentes
Csongrád
Kistelek
SZEGED
Kiskunfélegyháza
Kecskemét
Cegléd
Bugac
Kiskunmajsa
Kiskunhalas
Kelebia
Kiskőrös
Dunaújváros
Paks
Dunaföldvár
Sárbogárd
Baja
Tolna
Szekszárd
Bátaszék
Mohács
Villány
PÉCS
Sellye
Szigetvár
Barcs
Dombóvár
Tamási
Kaposvár
Nagyatád
Marcali
Nagykanizsa
Gyékényes
Heves
Jászapáti
Jászberény
Hatvan
Gyöngyös
Mátrafüred
Lajosháza
Salgótarján
Somoskő
Szécsény
Balassagyarmat
Nógrád
Vác
Vácrátót
Szob
Esztergom
Dorog
Budakeszi
Budaörs
Bicske
Tatabánya
Tata
Komárom
Kisbér
Mór
Százhalombatta
Gárdony
SZÉKESFEHÉRVÁR
Polgárdi
Várpalota
Siófok
Szántódpuszta
Balatonfüred
Boglárlelle
Fonyód
Veszprém
Zirc
Herend
Ajka
Tapolca
Badacsonytomaj
Keszthely
Zalaszentiván
Sümeg
Celldömölk
Pápa
Pannonhalma
GYŐR
Csorna
Kapuvár
Mosonmagyaróvár
Hegyeshalom
Fertőd
Sopron
Nagycenk
Kőszeg
Szombathely
Sárvár
Vasvár
Körmend
Szentgotthárd
Zalaegerszeg
Lenti

All train stations have left-luggage offices, some of which stay open 24 hours. You sometimes have to pay the fee (150/300Ft per six hours/one day) at another office or window nearby, which is usually marked *pénztár* (cashier).

Some trains have a carriage especially for bicycles; on other trains, bicycles must be placed in the first or last cars. You are able to freight a bicycle for 25% of a full 2nd-class fare.

Classes

Express ('Ex' on the timetable) trains usually require a seat reservation. The InterCity (IC) trains, the fastest and most comfortable in Hungary, and EuroCity (EC) ones levy a supplement, which generally includes a seat. *Gyorsvonat* (fast trains), indicated on the timetable by boldface type, a thicker route line and/or an 'S', often require a seat reservation. *Személyvonat* (passenger trains) are the real milk runs and stop at every city, town, village and hamlet along the way.

Most domestic links between smaller towns normally only offer 2nd-class services only.

Costs

Tickets for *egy útra* (one way) and *oda-vissza* (return) journeys in 1st and 2nd class are available at stations and certain travel agencies throughout the country. Train fares are calculated by distance. At the time of writing, MÁV charged the following prices.

Fare	Distance
125Ft	for up to 5km
200Ft	for 10km
750Ft	for 50km
1500Ft	for 100km
2780Ft	for 200km
3830Ft	for 300km

To travel 1st class costs around 25% more.

Passengers holding a ticket of insufficient value must pay the difference plus a fine of 2000Ft. If you buy your ticket on the train rather than at the station, there's a 500Ft surcharge. You can be fined 500Ft for travelling on a domestic IC train without having paid the supplement, and the same amount for not having a seat reservation when it is compulsory.

Reservations

On Hungarian domestic trains, seat reservations may be compulsory (indicated on the timetable by an 'R' in a box), mandatory only on trains departing from Budapest (an 'R' in a circle) or available without needing to book (just a plain 'R').

Express trains usually require a seat reservation costing 130Ft, while the IC ones levy a surcharge of between 200Ft and 480Ft, which includes the reservation.

Special Trains

Some 16 *keskenynyomközű vonat* (narrow-gauge trains), for the most part run by Állami Erdei Vasutak (ÁEV; State Forest Railways) on 220km of track, can be found in many wooded and hilly areas of the country. They are usually taken as a return excursion by holiday-makers, but in some cases can be useful for getting from A to B (eg Miskolc to Lillafüred and the Bükk Hills).

An independent branch of MÁV runs vintage *nosztalgiavonat* (steam trains) in summer, generally along the northern shore of Lake Balaton (eg from Keszthely to Tapolca via Badacsonytomaj) and along the Danube Bend from Budapest to Szob or Esztergom. For information, contact **MÁV Nostalgia** (☎ 1-238 0558; www.mavnosztalgia.hu) at Keleti train station.

The only other train line in Hungary is called **GySEV** (www.gysev.hu) and links Győr, Szombathely and Sopron with Ebenfurth in Austria.

Train Passes

The Hungary pass from Eurail, available to non-European residents only, costs US$104/147 for five/10 days of 1st-class travel in a 15-day period and US$79/99 for youths in 2nd class. Children five to 11 pay half-price.

The **Inter Rail Hungary Pass** (www.interrail.com) offers 1st- and 2nd-class travel for three, four, six or eight days within a month and is only available to non-Hungarian European residents. Discounts for those under 26 are also available – see the website for prices.

TRANSPORT

Health

CONTENTS

Good travel health depends on your predeparture preparations, your daily health care while travelling and the way you handle any medical problem that develops while you are on the road. Although the potential dangers might seem frightening, in reality few travellers experience anything more than an upset stomach.

BEFORE YOU GO

A little planning before departure, particularly for pre-existing illnesses or conditions, will save you trouble later. See your dentist before a long trip, carry a spare pair of contact lenses or glasses, and take your optical prescription with you. Bring any medications in their original, clearly labelled containers. A signed and dated letter from your physician describing your medical conditions and medications, including their generic names, is also a good idea. If you are carrying syringes or needles, be sure to have a physician's letter documenting their medical necessity.

INSURANCE

If you're an EU citizen, a European Health Insurance Card (EHIC), available from health centres, covers you for most medical care. It will not cover you for nonemergencies or emergency repatriation. Citizens from other countries should find out if there is a reciprocal arrangement for free medical care between their country and Hungary.

In Hungary, foreigners are entitled to first-aid and ambulance services only when they have suffered an accident and require immediate medical attention; follow-up treatment and medicine must be paid for.

If you do need health insurance while travelling (see p375), consider a policy that covers you for the worst possible scenario, such as an accident requiring an ambulance or an emergency flight home. Find out in advance if your insurance plan will make payments directly to providers or reimburse you later for overseas health expenditures. The former option is generally preferable, as it doesn't require you to pay out of pocket in a foreign country.

RECOMMENDED VACCINATIONS

Hungary doesn't require any vaccination of international travellers, but the World Health Organization (WHO) recommends travellers be covered for diphtheria, tetanus, measles, mumps, rubella and polio, regardless of their destination. Since most vaccines don't produce immunity until at least two weeks after they're given, visit a physician or clinic at least six weeks before departure.

INTERNET RESOURCES

The WHO's online publication *International Travel and Health* is revised annually and is available at www.who.int/ith. Other useful websites:

Age Concern (www.ageconcern.org.uk) Advice on travel for the elderly.
Fit for Travel (www.fitfortravel.scot.nhs.uk) General travel advice for the layperson.
Marie Stopes (www.mariestopes.org.uk) Information on women's health and contraception.
MD Travel Health (www.mdtravelhealth.com) Travel-health recommendations for every country; updated daily.

It's usually a good idea to consult your government's travel-health website before departure, if one is available.

Australia (www.smarttraveller.gov.au)
Canada (www.travelhealth.gc.ca)
UK (www.dh.gov.uk/en/home)
USA (www.cdc.gov/travel)

IN TRANSIT

DEEP VEIN THROMBOSIS

Blood clots may form in the legs (deep vein thrombosis or DVT) during plane flights, chiefly because of prolonged immobility. The longer the flight, the greater the risk. The chief symptom of DVT is swelling or pain in the foot, ankle or calf, usually – but not always – on just one side. When a blood clot travels to the lungs, it may cause chest pain and breathing difficulties. Travellers with any of these symptoms should seek medical attention immediately.

To prevent the development of DVT on long-haul flights, you should walk about the cabin, contract the leg muscles while sitting, drink plenty of fluids and avoid alcohol.

JET LAG & MOTION SICKNESS

To avoid jet lag (common when crossing more than five time zones), try to drink plenty of nonalcoholic fluids and eat light meals. Upon arrival, get exposure to natural sunlight and readjust your schedule (for meals, sleep and so on) as soon as possible.

Antihistamines such as dimenhydrinate (Dramamine) and meclizine (Antivert, Bonine) are usually the first choice for treating motion sickness. A herbal alternative is ginger.

IN HUNGARY

AVAILABILITY & COST OF HEALTH CARE

Medical care in Hungary is generally adequate and good for routine problems but not complicated conditions. Treatment at a *rendelő intézet* (public outpatient clinic) costs little, but doctors working privately will charge much more. Very roughly, a consultation in an *orvosi rendelő* (doctor's surgery) costs from 5000Ft while a home visit is from 10,000Ft.

Most large towns and all of Budapest's 23 districts have a *gyógyszertár* or *patika* (rotating 24-hour pharmacy). A sign on the door of any pharmacy will help you locate the closest one.

ENVIRONMENTAL HAZARDS

Insect Bites & Stings

Tick-borne encephalitis is spread by *kullancs* (ticks), which burrow under the skin. In recent years, it has become a common problem in parts of Central and Eastern Europe, especially eastern Austria, Germany, Hungary and the Czech Republic. Encephalitis is a serious infection of the brain, and vaccination is advised for campers and hikers, particularly in Transdanubia and the Northern Uplands between May and September.

Lyme disease is another tick-transmitted infection not unknown in Central and Eastern Europe. The illness usually begins with a spreading rash at the site of the tick bite and is accompanied by fever, headaches, extreme fatigue, aching joints and muscles, and mild neck stiffness. If untreated, these symptoms usually resolve themselves over several weeks, but over subsequent weeks or months disorders of the nervous system, heart and joints might develop.

Mosquitoes are a real scourge around Hungary's lakes and rivers in summer; the blood-thirsty beasties might not carry malaria but can still cause irritation and infection. Just make sure you're armed with a DEET-based insect repellent, or *rovarírtó,* and wear long-sleeved shirts and long trousers around sundown.

Bees and wasps cause real problems only to those with a severe allergy (anaphylaxis), in which case an 'epipen' or similar adrenaline injection should be carried.

Bed bugs lead to very itchy, lumpy bites. Spraying the mattress with crawling-insect killer after changing bedding will get rid of them.

Scabies are tiny mites that live in the skin, particularly between the fingers. They cause an intensely itchy rash. Scabies is easily treated with lotion from a pharmacy; other members of the household also need treating to avoid spreading scabies between asymptomatic carriers.

TRAVELLING WITH CHILDREN

All travellers with children should know how to treat minor ailments and when to seek medical treatment. Make sure the children are up to date with routine vaccinations, and discuss possible travel vaccines well before departure, as some vaccines are not suitable for children under the age of one.

In hot, moist climates, any wound or break in the skin is likely to let in infection. The area should be kept dry.

Remember to avoid contaminated food and water. If your child has vomiting or diarrhoea, the lost fluid and salts must be replaced. It may be helpful to take rehydration powders for reconstituting with boiled water.

Children should be encouraged to avoid and mistrust any dogs or other mammals because of the risk of rabies and other diseases. Any bite, scratch or lick from a warm-blooded, furry animal should immediately be thoroughly cleaned. If there is any possibility that the animal is infected with rabies, medical assistance should be sought immediately.

WOMEN'S HEALTH

If using oral contraceptives, remember that some antibiotics, diarrhoea and vomiting can stop the pill from working and lead to the risk of pregnancy. Time zones, gastrointestinal upsets and antibiotics do not affect injectable contraception.

Travelling during pregnancy is usually possible but always consult your doctor before planning your trip. The riskiest times for travel are during the first 12 weeks of pregnancy and after 30 weeks.

SEXUAL HEALTH

Emergency contraception is most effective if taken within 24 hours of unprotected sex. The **International Planned Parent Federation** (www.ippf.org) can advise about the availability of contraception in different countries.

The number of registered AIDS cases in Hungary and those who are HIV-positive is relatively low (just over 1100), though Hungarian epidemiologists estimate the actual number of those infected with HIV to be around 3000 or more. That number could multiply substantially as Budapest claims its less-than-distinctive title of 'sex industry capital of Eastern and Central Europe'. An AIDS line to contact in Budapest is the **Anonymous AIDS Association** (☎ 1-466 9283; www.anonimaid.hu; 5-8pm Mon, Wed & Thu, 9am-noon Tue & Fri).

HEALTH

Language

CONTENTS

Hungarian *(Magyar)* is a member of the Ugric group of the Uralic family of languages; it is related very distantly to Finnish (with five million speakers), Estonian (one million) and about a dozen other minority languages in Russia and western Siberia (with far fewer speakers). It's not an Indo-European language, meaning that English is actually closer to French, Russian or Hindi in vocabulary and structure than it is to Hungarian. As a result you'll come across very few recognisable words – with the exception of borrowings like *disko*, *szex* or *hello*, which is the slangy way young Hungarians say 'goodbye'.

There are also a fair number of misleading homophones (words with the same sound but different meanings) in Hungarian: *test* is not a quiz but 'body'; *fog* is 'tooth'; *comb* is 'thigh'; and *part* is 'shore'. *Ifjúság*, pronounced (very roughly) 'if you shag', means 'youth'; *sajt* (pronounced 'shite'), as in every visiting Briton's favourite *sajtburger*, means 'cheese'.

For more Hungarian words and phrases than there is space for here, get a copy of Lonely Planet's *Hungarian Phrasebook*.

PRONUNCIATION

Hungarian may seem daunting with its long words and strange-looking accents, but it's surprisingly easy to pronounce. Like English, Hungarian isn't always written the way it's pronounced, but if you stick to the phonetic guides that accompany each phrase or word you can't go wrong.

The Hungarian alphabet has 44 letters and is based on the Latin alphabet. It includes accented letters and consonant combinations. The stroke over a vowel in the pronunciation guides (eg ā) means you say it as a long vowel sound.

The letters **ö** and **ő**, and **ü** and **ű**, are listed as separate pairs of letters in dictionaries (following **o**, **ó** and **u**, **ú** respectively). The consonant combinations **cs**, **dz**, **dzs**, **gy**, **ly**, **ny**, **sz**, **ty** and **zs** also have separate entries.

Vowels

Letter	Pronunciation Guide	
a	o	as in 'hot'
á	aa	as in 'father'
e	e	as in 'bet'
é	ay	as the 'ai' in 'air'
i	i	as in 'hit'
í	ee	as in 'meet'
o	aw	as in 'law' but short
ó	āw	as in 'awl'
ö	eu	as the 'u' in 'curt' but short
ő	ēū	as the 'er' in 'her' (British)
u	u	as in 'pull'
ú	ū	as in 'rule'
ü	ew	like **i** but with rounded lips (like **u** in French *tu*)
ű	ēw	as in 'strewn'

Remember, always pronounce **y** as in 'yes', but without a vowel sound. We've used an apostrophe (as in **n'**, **d'**, **t'**) to show this **y** sound when it falls at the end of a syllable. You'll also see double consonants like **bb**, **dd** or **tt** – draw them out a little longer than you would in English.

Consonants

Letter	Pronunciation Guide	
c	ts	as in 'rats'
cs	ch	as in 'cheese'
dz	dz	as in 'adze'
dzs	j	as in 'joke'
gy	dy/d'	as the 'du' in 'dune' (British)
j/ly	y	as in 'yes'

ny	n'	as the 'ny' in 'canyon'
r	r	as in 'run' (but rolled)
s	sh	as in 'ship'
sz	s	as in 'sit'
ty	ty/t'	as the 'tu' in 'tube' (British)
zs	zh	as the 's' in 'pleasure'

Syllables & Word Stress

In this language guide, the syllables in the pronunciation guides are separated by a dot (eg *kawn*·tsert) so you'll have no problem isolating each unit of sound. Accents don't influence word stress, which always falls on the first syllable of the word. We've used italics to show stress, which should make things even easier.

ACCOMMODATION

Where's a ...?
Hol van egy ...? — hawl von ed' ...

camp site
kemping — *kem*·ping

guesthouse
panzió — *pon*·zi·āw

hotel
szálloda — *saal*·law·do

room in a private home
fizető vendégszoba — *fi*·ze·tēū ven·dayg·*saw*·bo

youth hostel
ifjúsági szálló — *if*·yū·shaa·gi *saal*·lāw

What's the address?
Mi a cím? — mi o tseem

May I see it?
Megnézhetem? — *meg*·nayz·he·tem

I'll take it.
Kiveszem. — *ki*·ve·sem

I'd like to book a ... room, please.
Szeretnék egy ... szobát foglalni.
se·ret·nayk ed' ... *saw*·baat *fawg*·lol·ni

single
egyágyas — *ed'*·aa·dyosh

double
francia ágyas/ duplaágyas — *fran*·tsi·o *aa*·dyosh/ *dup*·lo·aa·dyosh

twin
kétágyas — *kayt*·aa·dyosh

How much is it per ...?	*Mennyibe kerül egy ...?*	*men'*·nyi·be *ke*·rewl ed' ...
night	*éjszakára*	*ay*·so·kaa·ro
person	*főre*	*fēū*·re

CONVERSATION & ESSENTIALS

Be Polite!

As in many other Western languages, verbs in Hungarian have polite and informal forms in the singular and plural. The polite address (marked as 'pol' in this section) is used with strangers, older people, officials and service staff. The informal address (marked as 'inf' in this language guide) is reserved for friends, children and sometimes foreigners, but is used much more frequently and sooner than its equivalent in, say, French. Almost all young people use it among themselves – even with strangers. In the following phrases, the polite 'you' (*Ön* and *Önök*) is given except for situations where you might wish to establish a more personal relationship.

Note that when you want to say 'Hello', 'Hi', or 'Bye', the word will change depending on whether you are speaking to one person or more than one. Look for the markers 'sg' (singular) or 'pl' (plural) to determine which word to use.

Hello.
Szervusz. (sg) — *ser*·vus
Szervusztok. (pl) — *ser*·vus·tawk

Hi.
Szia/Sziasztok. (sg/pl) — *si*·o/*si*·os·tawk

Good ...
Jó ... kívánok. — yāw ... *kee*·vaa·nawk

morning
reggelt — *reg*·gelt

afternoon/day
napot — *no*·pawt

evening
estét — *esh*·tayt

Goodbye.
Viszontlátásra. (pol) — *vi*·sawnt·laa·taash·ro
Szia. (inf sg) — *si*·o
Sziasztok. (inf pl) — *si*·os·tawk

Good night.
Jó éjszakát. — yāw *ay*·y·so·kaat

Yes.
Igen. — *i*·gen

No.
Nem. — nem

Please.
Kérem. (pol) — *kay*·rem
Kérlek. (inf) — *kayr*·lek

Thank you (very much).
(Nagyon) Köszönöm. (*no*·dyawn) *keu*·seu·neum
You're welcome.
Szívesen. *see*·ve·shen
Excuse me. (to get attention)
Elnézést kérek. *el*·nay·zaysht *kay*·rek
Excuse me. (to get past)
Bocsánat. *baw*·chaa·not
Sorry.
Sajnálom. *shoy*·naa·lawm
How are you?
Hogy van? (pol) hawd' von
Hogy vagy? (inf) hawd' vod'
Fine. And you?
Jól. És Ön/te? (pol/inf) yāwl aysh eun/te
What's your name?
Mi a neve? (pol) mi o *ne*·ve
Mi a neved? (inf) mi o *ne*·ved
My name is ...
A nevem ... o *ne*·vem ...
I'm pleased to meet you.
Örvendek. *eur*·ven·dek
Where are you from?
Ön honnan jön? (pol) eun *hawn*·non yeun
Te honnan jössz? (inf) te *hawn*·non yeuss
I'm from ...
Én ... jövök. ayn ... *yeu*·veuk

Local Lingo

Great!
Nagyszerű! *nod'*·se·rēw
Maybe.
Talán. *to*·laan
Just a minute.
Egy pillanat. ed' *pil*·lo·not
No problem.
Nem probléma. nem *prawb*·lay·mo
Clear. (as in 'understood')
Világos. *vi*·laa·gawsh

DIRECTIONS

Where's (the market)?
Hol van (a piac)? hawl von (o *pi*·ots)
What's the address?
Mi a cím? mi o tseem
How do I get there?
Hogyan jutok oda? *haw*·dyon *yu*·tawk *aw*·do
How far is it?
Milyen messze van? *mi*·yen *mes*·se von
Can you show me (on the map)?
Meg tudja mutatni nekem (a térképen)? meg *tud*·yo *mu*·tot·ni *ne*·kem (o *tayr*·kay·pen)
It's straight ahead.
Egyenesen előttünk van. e·dye·ne·shen *e*·lēūt·tewnk von

SIGNS

Bejárat	Entrance
Kijárat	Exit
Nyitva	Open
Zárva	Closed
Foglalt	Reserved/Occupied
Felvilágosítás/Információ	Information
Belépni Tilos	No Entry
Tilos	Prohibited
Tilos a Dohányzás	No Smoking
Toalett/WC	Toilets
Férfiak	Men
Nők	Women

Turn ...
Forduljon ... *fawr*·dul·yawn ...
at the corner
a saroknál o *sho*·rawk·naal
at the traffic lights
a közlekedési lámpánál o *keuz*·le·ke·day·shi *laam*·paa·naal
left/right
balra/jobbra *bol*·ro/*yawbb*·ro

north	*észak*	*ay*·sok
south	*dél*	dayl
east	*kelet*	*ke*·let
west	*nyugat*	*nyu*·got

HEALTH

Where's the nearest ...?
Hol a legközelebbi ...? hawl o *leg*·keu·ze·leb·bi ...
dentist
fogorvos *fawg*·awr·vawsh
doctor
orvos *awr*·vawsh
hospital
kórház *kāwr*·haaz
medical centre
orvosi rendelő *awr*·vaw·shi *ren*·de·lēū
(night) pharmacist
(éjszaka nyitvatartó) gyógyszertár (*ay*·so·ko *nyit*·vo·tor·tāw) *dyāwd'*·ser·taar

I have a headache.
Fáj a fejem. *faa*·y o *fe*·yem
I have a sore throat.
Fáj a torkom. *faa*·y o *tawr*·kawm

I have (a) ...	*... van.*	... von
asthma	*Asztmám*	*ost*·maam
diarrhoea	*Hasmenésem*	*hosh*·me·nay·shem
fever	*Lázam*	*laa*·zom
nausea	*Hányingerem*	*haan'*·in·ge·rem

EMERGENCIES

Help!
Segítség! she·geet·shayg
Could you please help?
Tudna segíteni? tud·no she·gee·te·ni
Can I use your phone?
Használhatom a telefonját? hos·naal·ho·tawm o te·le·fawn·yaat
Call the police!
Hívja a rendőrséget! heev·yo o rend·ēūr·shay·get
I'm sick.
Rosszul vagyok. raws·sul vo·dyawk
Call a doctor!
Hívjon orvost! heev·yawn awr·vawsht
Where's the police station?
Hol a rendőrség? hawl o rend·ēūr·shayg
Where are the toilets?
Hol a vécé? hawl o vay·tse
I'm lost.
Eltévedtem. el·tay·ved·tem
Go away!
Menjen el! men·yen el

I'm allergic to ...
Allergiás vagyok ... ol·ler·gi·aash vo·dyawk ...
antibiotics
az antibiotikumokra oz on·ti·bi·aw·ti·ku·mawk·ro
penicillin
a penicillinre o pe·ni·tsil·lin·re

antiseptic
fertőzésgátló fer·tēū·zaysh·gaat·lāw
contraceptives
fogamzásgátló faw·gom·zaash·gaat·lāw
painkillers
fájdalomcsillapító faa·y·do·lawm·chil·lo·pee·tāw

LANGUAGE DIFFICULTIES

Do you speak (English)?
Beszél (angolul)? (pol) be·sayl (on·gaw·lul)
Beszélsz (angolul)? (inf) be·sayls (on·gaw·lul)
Does anyone speak (English)?
Beszél valaki (angolul)? be·sayl vo·lo·ki (on·gaw·lul)
I (don't) understand.
(Nem) Értem. (nem) ayr·tem
What does ... mean?
Mit jelent az, hogy ...? mit ye·lent oz hawd' ...
Could you please write it down?
Leírná, kérem. le·eer·naa kay·rem

NUMBERS

0	*nulla*	nul·lo
1	*egy*	ed'
2	*kettő/két*	ket·tēū/kayt
3	*három*	haa·rawm
4	*négy*	nayd'
5	*öt*	eut
6	*hat*	hot
7	*hét*	hayt
8	*nyolc*	nyawlts
9	*kilenc*	ki·lents
10	*tíz*	teez
11	*tizenegy*	ti·zen·ed'
12	*tizenkettő*	ti·zen·ket·tēū
13	*tizenhárom*	ti·zen·haa·rawm
14	*tizennégy*	ti·zen·nayd'
15	*tizenöt*	ti·zen·eut
16	*tizenhat*	ti·zen·hot
17	*tizenhét*	ti·zen·hayt
18	*tizennyolc*	ti·zen'·yawlts
19	*tizenkilenc*	ti·zen·ki·lents
20	*húsz*	hūs
21	*huszonegy*	hu·sawn·ed'
22	*huszonkettő*	hu·sawn·ket·tēū
30	*harminc*	hor·mints
31	*harmincegy*	hor·mints·ed'
32	*harminckettő*	hor·mints·ket·tēū
40	*negyven*	ned'·ven
41	*negyvenegy*	ned'·ven·ed'
42	*negyvenkettő*	ned'·ven·ket·tēū
50	*ötven*	eut·ven
60	*hatvan*	hot·von
70	*hetven*	het·ven
80	*nyolcvan*	nyawlts·von
90	*kilencven*	ki·lents·ven
100	*száz*	saaz
200	*kétszáz*	kayt·saaz
1000	*ezer*	e·zer

How much? *Mennyi?* men'·yi
How many? *Hány?* haan'

SHOPPING & SERVICES

Where is ...?
Hol van ...? hawl von ...
an ATM
egy bankautomata ed' bonk·o·u·taw·mo·to
a foreign exchange office
egy valutaváltó ügynökség ed' vo·lu·to·vaal·tāw ewd'·neuk·shayg
the market
a piac o pi·ots
a shopping centre
egy bevásárlóközpont ed' be·vaa·shaar·lāw·keuz·pawnt
a supermarket
egy élelmiszeráruház ed' ay·lel·mi·ser·aa·ru·haaz

LANGUAGE

'd like to ...
zeretnék ... se·ret·nayk ...

change a travellers cheque
beváltani egy utazási csekket be·vaal·to·ni ed' u·to·zaa·shi chek·ket

change money
pénzt váltani paynzt *vaal*·to·ni

Do you accept ...?
Elfogadnak ...? el·faw·god·nok ...

credit cards
hitelkártyát hi·tel·kaar·tyaat

travellers cheques
utazási csekket u·to·zaa·shi *chek*·ket

Where can I buy ...?
Hol tudok venni ...? hawl *tu*·dawk *ven*·ni ...

I'd like to buy ...
Szeretnék venni ... se·ret·nayk *ven*·ni ...

I'm just looking.
Csak nézegetek. chok *nay*·ze·ge·tek

How much is this?
Mennyibe kerül ez? men'·yi·be *ke*·rewl ez

Could you write down the price?
Le tudná írni az árát? le *tud*·naa *eer*·ni oz *aa*·raat

What time does it open/close?
Mikor nyit/zár? mi·kawr nyit/zaar

Where's the nearest public phone?
Hol a legközelebbi nyilvános telefon?
hawl o *leg*·keu·ze·leb·bi *nyil*·vaa·nawsh *te*·le·fawn

I want to buy a phonecard.
Szeretnék telefonkártyát venni.
se·ret·nayk *te*·le·fawn·kaar·tyaat *ven*·ni

Where's the local internet cafe?
Hol van a legközelebbi internet kávézó?
hawl von o *leg*·keu·ze·leb·bi *in*·ter·net *kaa*·vay·zāw

I'd like to ...
Szeretném ... se·ret·naym ...

check my email
megnézni az e-mailjeimet *meg*·nayz·ni oz *ee*·mayl·ye·i·met

get internet access
rámenni az internetre *raa*·men·ni oz *in*·ter·net·re

TIME & DATE

What time is it?
Hány óra? haan' *āw*·ra

It's (one/10) o'clock.
(Egy/Tíz) óra van. (ed'/teez) *āw*·ra von

Five past (10).
Öt perccel múlt (tíz). eut *perts*·tsel mūlt (teez)

Quarter past (10).
Negyed (tizenegy). ne·dyed (*ti*·zen·ed')

Half past (10).
Fél (tizenegy). fayl (*ti*·zen·ed')

now	*most*	mawsht
today	*ma*	mo
tonight	*ma este*	mo *esh*·te
yesterday	*tegnap*	*teg*·nop
tomorrow	*holnap*	*hawl*·nop
afternoon	*délután*	*dayl*·u·taan
evening	*este*	*esh*·te
morning	*reggel*	*reg*·gel
night	*éjszaka*	*ay*·so·ko

Monday	*hétfő*	*hayt*·fēū
Tuesday	*kedd*	kedd
Wednesday	*szerda*	*ser*·do
Thursday	*csütörtök*	*chew*·teur·teuk
Friday	*péntek*	*payn*·tek
Saturday	*szombat*	*sawm*·bot
Sunday	*vasárnap*	*vo*·shaar·nop

January	*január*	*yo*·nu·aar
February	*február*	*feb*·ru·aar
March	*március*	*maar*·tsi·ush
April	*április*	*aap*·ri·lish
May	*május*	*maa*·yush
June	*június*	*yū*·ni·ush
July	*július*	*yū*·li·ush
August	*augusztus*	*o*·u·gus·tush
September	*szeptember*	*sep*·tem·ber
October	*október*	*awk*·tāw·ber
November	*november*	*naw*·vem·ber
December	*december*	*de*·tsem·ber

TRANSPORT

Public Transport

Where's the ticket office?
Hol a jegypénztár? hawl o *yed'*·paynz·taar

What time does it leave?
Mikor indul? mi·kawr *in*·dul

What time does it get to (Eger)?
Mikor ér (Egerbe)? mi·kawr ayr (*e*·ger·be)

How long does the trip take?
Mennyi ideig tart az út? men'·yi *i*·de·ig tort oz ūt

How long will it be delayed?
Mennyit késik? men'·yit *kay*·shik

Please stop here.
Kérem, álljon meg itt. *kay*·rem *aall*·yawn meg itt

How much is it?
Mennyibe kerül? men'·yi·be *ke*·rewl

local bus station
helyi buszállamás he·yi *bus*·*aal*·law·maash
long-distance bus station
távolsági autóbusz-államás *taa*·vawl·shaa·gi *o*·u·tāw·bus·*aal*·law·maash

Which ... goes (to Budapest/the Parliament)?
Melyik ... megy (Budapestre/a Parlamenthez)?
me·yik ... med' (*bu*·do·pesht·re/o *por*·lo·ment·hez)

bus
busz bus
metro line
metró *met*·rāw
train
vonat *vaw*·not
tram
villamos *vil*·lo·mawsh
trolleybus
trolibusz *traw*·li·bus

When's the ...?
Mikor megy ...? *mi*·kawr med' ...
first
az első oz *el*·shēū
last
az utolsó oz *u*·tawl·shāw
next
a következő o *keu*·vet·ke·zēū

A ... ticket to (Eger).
Egy ... jegy (Eger)be. ed' ... yej (*e*·ger)·be
one-way
csak oda chok *aw*·do
return
oda-vissza *aw*·do·*vis*·so

Is this taxi available?
Szabad ez a taxi? *so*·bod ez o *tok*·si
Please put the meter on.
Kérem, kapcsolja be az órát. *kay*·rem *kop*·chawl·yo be oz *āw*·raat
How much is it to ...?
Mennyibe kerül ... ba? *men'*·yi·be *ke*·rewl ... bo
Please take me to (this address).
Kérem, vigyen el (erre a címre). *kay*·rem *vi*·dyen el (*er*·re o *tseem*·re)
How much is it?
Mennyit fizetek? *men'*·nyit *fi*·ze·tek

Private Transport

I'd like to hire a/an ...
Szeretnék egy ... bérelni. *se*·ret·nayk ed' ... *bay*·rel·ni
car
autót *o*·u·tāwt
motorbike
motort *maw*·tawrt

ROAD SIGNS

Autópálya Kijárat	Exit Freeway
Behajtani Tilos	No Entry
Bejárat	Entrance
Egyirányú	One Way
Elsőbbségadás Kötelező	Give Way
Megállni Tilos	No Standing
Terelőút	Detour
Útépítés	Road Work Ahead
Várakozni Tilos	No Parking

Is this the road to (Sopron)?
Ez az út vezet (Sopronba)? ez oz ūt *ve*·zet (*shawp*·rawn·bo)
Where's a petrol station?
Hol van egy benzinkút? hawl von ed' *ben*·zin·kūt
Please fill it up.
Kérem, töltse tele. *kay*·rem *teult*·she *te*·le
I'd like ... litres.
... litert kérek. ... *li*·tert *kay*·rek

petrol/gas
benzin *ben*·zin
diesel
dízel/gázolaj *dee*·zel/*gaa*·zo·lay
leaded
ólmozott *āwl*·maw·zawtt
LPG
folyékony autógáz *faw*·yay·kawn' *o*·u·tāw·gaaz
regular
normál *nawr*·maal
premium unleaded
ólommentes szuper *āw*·lawm·men·tesh *su*·per
unleaded
ólommentes *āw*·lawm·men·tesh

(How long) Can I park here?
(Meddig) Parkolhatok itt?
(*med*·dig) *por*·kawl·ho·tawk itt
I need a mechanic.
Szükségem van egy autószerelőre.
sewk·shay·gem von ed' *o*·u·tāw·se·re·lēū·re
The car/motorbike has broken down (at Sopron).
Az autó/A motor elromlott (Sopronnál).
oz *o*·u·tāw/o *maw*·tawr *el*·rawm·lawtt (*shawp*·rawn·naal)
The car/motorbike won't start.
Az autó/A motor nem indul.
oz *o*·u·tāw/o *maw*·tawr nem *in*·dul
I have a flat tyre.
Defektem van.
de·fek·tem von

TRAVEL WITH CHILDREN

Is there a ...?
Van ...?
von ...

I need a/an ...
Szükségem van egy ...
sewk·shay·gem von ed' ...

baby change room
babapelenkázó szobára
bo·bo·pe·len·kaa·zāw *saw*·baa·ro

baby seat
babaülésre
bo·bo·ew·laysh·re

(English-speaking) babysitter
(angolul beszélő) bébiszitterre
(*on*·gaw·lul *be*·say·lēū) *bay*·bi·sit·ter·re

booster seat
gyerekülésre
dye·rek·ew·laysh·re

disposable nappies/diapers
eldobható pelenkára
el·dawb·ho·tāw *pe*·len·kaa·ro

highchair
etetőszékre
e·te·tēū·sayk·re

potty
bilire
bi·li·re

stroller
ülő gyerekkocsira
ew·lēū *dye*·rek·kaw·chi·ro

Are children allowed?
Beengedik a gyerekeket?
be·en·ge·dik o *dye*·re·ke·ket

Do you mind if I breastfeed here?
Megengedi, hogy itt szoptassak?
meg·en·ge·di hawd' itt *sawp*·tosh·shok

Glossary

Can't find the word you're looking for here? Try the Language chapter (p397) or the glossary in the Food & Drink chapter (p60).

ÁEV – Állami Erdei Vasutak (State Forest Railways)
ÁFA – value-added tax (VAT)
Alföld – the Great Plain; same as *Nagyalföld* and *puszta*
aluljáró – underpass
Ausgleich – German for 'reconciliation'; the *Compromise of 1867*
autóbusz – bus
áutóbuszállomás – bus station
Avars – a people of the Caucasus who invaded Europe in the 6th century
ÁVO – Rákosi's hated secret police in the early years of communism; later renamed ÁVH

bal – left
bélyeg – stamp
benzin – petrol
BKV – Budapest Közlekedési Vállalat (Budapest Transport Company)
bokor tanyák – bush farms
bolhapiac – flea market
borozó – wine bar; any place serving wine
Bp – commonly used abbreviation for Budapest
búcsú – farewell; also a church patronal festival
büfé – snack bar

centrum – town or city centre
čevapčiči – spicy Balkan meatballs
Compromise of 1867 – agreement that created the Dual Monarchy of Austria-Hungary
Copf – a transitional architectural style between late baroque and neoclassicism (*Zopf* in German)
csárda – a Hungarian-style inn or restaurant
csatorna – canal
csikós – 'cowboy' from the *puszta*
csomagmegőrző – left-luggage office
cukrászda – cake shop or patisserie

D – map/compass abbreviation for *dél*
Dacia – Latin name for Romania and lands east of the Tisza River
db or **drb** – piece (measurement used in markets)
de – in the morning; 'am'
dél – south
du – in the afternoon/evening; 'pm'

É – map/compass abbreviation for *észak*
Eclectic – an art and architectural style popular in Hungary in the Romantic period, drawing from sources both indigenous and foreign
élelmiszer – grocery shop or convenience store
előszoba – vestibule or anteroom; one of three rooms in a traditional Hungarian cottage
em – abbreviation for *emelet*
emelet – floor or storey
erdő – forest
érkezés – arrivals
észak – north
eszpresszó – coffee shop, often also selling alcoholic drinks and snacks; strong, black coffee; same as *presszó*
étkezde – canteen that serves simple dishes
étterem – restaurant

falu – village
fasor – boulevard, avenue
felvilágosítás – information
fogas – pike-perch-like fish indigenous to Lake Balaton
főkapitányság – main police station
földszint – ground floor
folyó – river
forint – Hungary's monetary unit; see also *HUF*
főváros – main city or capital
főzelék – a traditional way of preparing vegetables, where they're fried or boiled and then mixed into a roux with milk
fsz – abbreviation for *földszint*
Ft – abbreviation for *forint*

gázolaj – diesel fuel
gémeskút – Hungarian for *shahoof*
gulyás or **gulyásleves** – a thick beef soup cooked with onions and potatoes and usually eaten as a main course
gyógyfürdő – bath or spa
gyógyszertár – pharmacy
gyógyvíz – medicinal drinking water
gyorsvonat – fast trains
gyűjtemény – collection
gyula – chief military commander of the early Magyar

hajdúk – Hungarian for *Heyducks*
hajó – boat
hajóallomás – ferry pier or landing
ház – house
hegy – hill, mountain

hegyalja – hill country
helyi autóbusz pályaudvar – local bus station
HÉV – Helyiérdekű Vasút (suburban commuter train in Budapest)
Heyducks – drovers and outlaws from the *puszta* who fought as mercenaries against the Habsburgs
híd – bridge
HNTO – Hungarian National Tourist Office
hőforrás – thermal spring
honfoglalás – conquest of the Carpathian Basin by the Magyars in the late 9th century
HUF – international currency code for the Hungarian *forint*
Huns – a Mongol tribe that swept across Europe under Attila in the 5th century AD

Ibusz – Hungarian national network of travel agencies
ifjúsági szálló – youth hostel
illeték – duty or tax
indulás – departures

jobb – right (as opposed to left)

K – abbreviation for *kelet*
kamra – workshop or shed; one of three rooms in a traditional Hungarian cottage
kastély – manor house or mansion (see *vár*)
kb – abbreviation for *körülbelül*
kékfestő – cotton fabric dyed a rich indigo blue
kelet – east
kemping – camping ground
képtár – picture gallery
kerület – city district
khas – towns of the Ottoman period under direct rule of the sultan
kijárat – exit
kincstár – treasury
kirándulás – outing
Kiskörút – 'Little Ring Road' in Budapest
kocsma – pub or saloon
kolostor – monastery or cloister
komp – ferry
könyvesbolt – bookshop
könyvtár – library
konzumlányok – 'consume girls'; attractive young women who work in collusion with bars and clubs to rip off unsuspecting male tourists
kórház – hospital
körülbelül – approximately
körút – ring road
korzó – embankment or promenade
köz – alley, mews, lane
központ – centre
krt – abbreviation for *körút*
kúria – mansion or manor
kuruc – Hungarian mercenaries, partisans or insurrectionists who resisted the expansion of Habsburg rule in Hungary after the withdrawal of the Turks (late 17th/early 18th centuries)

lángos – deep-fried dough with toppings
lekvár – fruit jam
lépcső – stairs, steps
liget – park

Magyarország autóatlasza – road atlas of Hungary
Mahart – Hungarian passenger ferry company
Malév – Hungary's national airline
MÁV – Magyar Államvasutak (Hungarian State Railways)
megye – county
menetrend – timetable
mihrab – Muslim prayer niche facing Mecca
MNB – Magyar Nemzeti Bank (National Bank of Hungary)
Moorish Romantic – an art style popular in the decoration of 19th-century Hungarian synagogues
mozi – cinema
műemlék – memorial, monument
munkavállalási engedély – work permit

Nagyalföld – the Great Plain; same as *Alföld* and *puszta*
Nagykörút – 'Big Ring Road' in Budapest
népművészeti bolt – folk-art shop
Nonius – Hungarian breed of horse
nosztalgiavonat – vintage steam train
Ny – abbreviation for *nyugat*
nyitva – open
nyugat – west

ó – abbreviation for *óra*
önkiszolgáló – self-service
óra – hour; 'o'clock'
orvosi rendelő – doctor's surgery
osztály – department
OTP – Országos Takarékpenztár (National Savings Bank)
Ottoman Empire – the Turkish empire that took over from the Byzantine Empire when it captured Constantinople (Istanbul) in 1453, and expanded into southeastern Europe

pálinka – fruit brandy
palota – palace
pályaudvar – train or railway station
Pannonia – Roman name for the lands south and west of the Danube River
panzió – *pension*, guest house
part – embankment
patika – pharmacy
patyolat – laundry

pénztár – cashier
pénzváltó – exchange office
piac – market
pince – wine cellar
plébánia – rectory, parish house
polgármester – mayor
pörkölt – stew
porta – type of farmhouse in Transdanubia
presszó – same as *eszpresszó*
pu – abbreviation for *pályaudvar*
Puli – Hungarian breed of sheepdog with shaggy coat
puszta – literally 'deserted'; other name for the Great Plain (see *Alföld* and *Nagyalföld*)
puttony – the number of 'butts' of sweet Aszú essence added to other base wines in making Tokaj wine

Racka – sheep on the Great Plain with distinctive corkscrew horns
rakpart – quay, embankment
rendőrkapitányság – police station
repülőtér – airport
Romany – the language and culture of the Roma (Gypsy) people

sebesvonat – swift trains
Secessionism – art and architectural style similar to Art Nouveau
sedile (pl **sedilia**) – medieval stone niche with seats
sétány – walkway, promenade
shahoof – distinctive sweep-pole well found only on the Great Plain (Hungarian: *gémeskút*)
skanzen – open-air museum displaying village architecture
söröző – beer bar or pub
spahi – name given to a member of the Turkish irregular cavalry. The officers of the spahis were granted fiefs by the Sultan, and were entitled to all income from the fief in return for military service to the Sultan.
stb – abbreviation of '*s a többi*' (and so on); equivalent to English 'etc'
strand – grassy 'beach' near a river or lake
sugárút – avenue
szálló or **szálloda** – hotel
székesegyház – cathedral
személyvonat – passenger trains that stop at every city, town, village and hamlet along the way
sziget – island
színház – theatre
szoba kiadó – room for rent
szűr – long embroidered felt cloak or cape traditionally worn by Hungarian shepherds

Tanácsköztársaság – the 1919 communist 'Republic of Councils' under Béla Kun
táncház – dance house; folk music and dance workshop
tanya – homestead or ranch; station
tartózkodási engedély – residence permit
távolsági autóbusz pályaudvar – long-distance bus station
templom – church
tér – town or market square
tere – genitive form of *tér,* as in Hősök tere (Square of the Heroes)
tilos – prohibited, forbidden
tiszta szoba – parlour; one of three rooms in a traditional Hungarian cottage
tó – lake
toalett – toilet
Treaty of Trianon – 1920 treaty imposed on Hungary by the victorious Allies, which reduced the country to one-third of its former size
Triple Alliance – 1882–1914 alliance between Germany, Austria-Hungary and Italy – not to be confused with the WWI Allies (members of the *Triple Entente* and their supporters)
Triple Entente – agreement among Britain, France and Russia, intended as a counterbalance to the *Triple Alliance,* lasting until the Russian Revolution of 1917
turul – eaglelike totem of the ancient Magyars and now a national symbol

u – abbreviation for *utca*
udvar – court
ünnep – public holiday
úszoda – swimming pool
út – road
utca – street
utcája – genitive form of *utca,* as in Ferencesek utcája (Street of the Franciscans)
útja – genitive form of *út,* as in Mártíroká útja (Street of the Martyrs)
üzlet – shop

vá – abbreviation for *vasútmegállo*
vágány – platform
vár – castle
város – city
városház or **városháza** – town hall
vasútállomás – train station
vasútmegállo – train station
vendéglő – a type of restaurant
vm – abbreviation for *vasútállomás*
Volánbusz – Hungarian bus company
vonat – train

WC – toilet (see *toalett*)

zárva – closed
Zimmer frei – German for 'room for rent'
Zopf – German and more commonly used word for *Copf*

Alternative Place Names

On a lot of bus and train timetables, Hungarian-language names are used for cities and towns in neighbouring countries. Many of these are in what once was Hungarian territory, and the names are used by the Hungarian-speaking minorities who live there. You should at least be familiar with the more important ones (eg Pozsony for Bratislava, Kolozsvár for Cluj-Napoca, Bécs for Vienna).

ABBREVIATIONS
(C) Croatian, (E) English, (G) German, (H) Hungarian, (R) Romanian, (S) Serbian, (Slk) Slovak, (Slo) Slovene, (U) Ukrainian

Alba Iulia (R) – Gyula Fehérvár (H), Karlsburg/Weissenburg (G)

Baia Mare (R) – Nagybánya (H)
Balaton (H) – Plattensee (G)
Banská Bystrica (Slk) – Besztercebánya (H)
Belgrade (E) – Beograd (S), Nándorfehérvár (H)
Beregovo (U) – Beregszász (H)
Braşov (R) – Brassó (H), Kronstadt (G)
Bratislava (Slk) – Pozsony (H), Pressburg (G)

Carei (R) – Nagykároly (H)
Cluj-Napoca (R) – Kolozsvár (H), Klausenburg (G)

Danube (E) – Duna (H), Donau (G)
Danube Bend (E) – Dunakanyar (H), Donauknie (G)
Debrecen (H) – Debrezin (G)

Eger (H) – Erlau (G)
Eisenstadt (G) – Kismárton (H)
Esztergom (H) – Gran (G)

Great Plain (E) – Nagyalföld, Alföld, Puszta (H)
Győr (H) – Raab (G)

Hungary (E) – Magyarország (H), Ungarn (G)

Kisalföld (H) – Little Plain (E)
Komárom (H) – Komárno (Slk)
Košice (Slk) – Kassa (H), Kaschau (G)
Kőszeg (H) – Güns (G)

Lendava (Slo) – Lendva (H)
Lučenec (Slk) – Losonc (H)

Mattersburg (G) – Nagymárton (H)
Mukačevo (U) – Munkács (H)
Murska Sobota (Slo) – Muraszombat (H)

Northern Uplands (E) – Északi Felföld (H)

Oradea (R) – Nagyvárad (H), Grosswardein (G)
Osijek (C) – Eszék (H)

Pécs (H) – Fünfkirchen (G)

Rožnava (Slk) – Rozsnyó (H)

Satu Mare (R) – Szatmárnémeti (H)
Senta (S) – Zenta (H)
Sibiu (R) – Nagyszében (H), Hermannstadt (G)
Sic (R) – Szék (H)
Sighişoara (R) – Szegesvár (H), Schässburg (G)
Sopron (H) – Ödenburg (G)
Štúrovo (Slk) – Párkány (H)
Subotica (S) – Szabadka (H)
Szeged (H) – Segedin (G)
Székesfehérvár (H) – Stuhlweissenburg (G)
Szombathely (H) – Steinamanger (G)

Tata (H) – Totis (G)
Timişoara (R) – Temesvár (H)
Tirgu Mureş (R) – Marosvásárhely (H)
Transdanubia (E) – Dunántúl (H)
Transylvania (R) – Erdély (H), Siebenbürgen (G)
Trnava (Slk) – Nagyszombat (H)

Uzhhorod (U) – Ungvár (H)

Vác (H) – Wartzen (G)
Vienna (E) – Wien (G), Bécs (H)
Villány (H) – Wieland (G)
Villánykövesd (H) – Growisch (G)

Wiener Neustadt (G) – Bécsújhely (H)

The Authors

NEAL BEDFORD **Coordinating Author, Destination Hungary, Getting Started, Itineraries, Environment, Danube Bend, Western Transdanubia, Lake Balaton Region, Directory, Transport**

With Hungary only a short train ride away from his adopted home Vienna, it was only a matter of time before Neal began exploring the country. Following the lead of so many Austrians, he started with trips to Sopron for cheap dental work – and even cheaper wine – but soon found himself expanding his horizons and heading for the likes of Lake Balaton, Budapest and the wide open *puszta* (plain). After dozens of trips, and a few travel guides on Hungary under his belt, he can safely say he's seen almost every corner of the country, but knows in his heart that Hungary will always remain foreign and fascinating.

LISA DUNFORD **Activities, Great Plain, Northern Uplands, Northeast**

Ever since Lisa learned as a child that her grandfather came from Hungary, she's been hooked. It started with writing book reports in school and collecting folk costumes from family. But it moved on to a degree in international affairs, learning the language, and a year spent studying in Budapest. She travelled to the country often while working in nearby Bratislava and spent time researching family history in the Northeast. What she found were cousins and new and dear friends, who attended her wedding in the church where her great-grandfather was ordained. She returns annually to visit, explore and write about Hungary.

STEVE FALLON **History, The Culture, Food & Drink, Budapest, Southern Transdanubia**

Steve, who has worked on every edition of *Hungary,* first visited Magyarország in the early 1980s and immediately fell in love with thermal baths, Tokaj wine and the voice of Marta Sebestyén. Not able to survive on just the occasional fix, he moved to Budapest in 1992, where he could enjoy all three in abundance and in *magyarul* (Hungarian). Now based in London, Steve returns to Hungary regularly for all these things and more, including *pálinka* (fruit brandy), Art Nouveau and the best nightlife in the region.

LONELY PLANET AUTHORS

Why is our travel information the best in the world? It's simple: our authors are passionate, dedicated travellers. They don't take freebies in exchange for positive coverage so you can be sure the advice you're given is impartial. They travel widely to all the popular spots, and off the beaten track. They don't research using just the internet or phone. They discover new places not included in any other guidebook. They personally visit thousands of hotels, restaurants, palaces, trails, galleries, temples and more. They speak with dozens of locals every day to make sure you get the kind of insider knowledge only a local could tell you. They take pride in getting all the details right, and in telling it how it is. Think you can do it? Find out how at **lonelyplanet.com**.

Behind the Scenes

THIS BOOK

This 6th edition of Lonely Planet's *Hungary* was written by Neal Bedford, Steve Fallon and Lisa Dunford. Steve wrote the first three editions and was joined by Neal for the 4th and 5th editions. This guidebook was commissioned in Lonely Planet's London office, and produced by the following:

Commissioning Editors Fiona Buchan, Lucy Monie
Coordinating Editors Carolyn Boicos, Stephanie Pearson
Coordinating Cartographer Valeska Cañas
Coordinating Layout Designer Paul Iacono
Senior Editors Helen Christinis, Katie Lynch
Managing Cartographer Alison Lyall
Managing Layout Designer Laura Jane
Assisting Editors Kate Daly, Justin Flynn, Kristin Odijk
Assisting Cartographer Owen Eszeki
Cover Designer Marika Mercer
Project Managers Chris Girdler, Craig Kilburn
Language Content Coordinator Quentin Frayne

Thanks to Lucy Birchley, Sally Darmody, Bruce Evans, Penelope Goodes, Lauren Hunt, Trent Paton, Branislava Vladisavljevic, Clifton Wilkinson

THANKS

NEAL BEDFORD

Special thanks to my co-authors Steve and Lisa for their energy, ideas and support on this book. Ditto to Fiona Buchan, a wonderful – and thankfully patient! – CE who is always a pleasure to work with.

In Hungary, the good people in Tourinform offices across the country must be thanked for lightening my workload time and time again, as do the excellent chaps at the Hullám Hostel, who took the time to show me their Kál Basin. Gratitude goes to Bea Szirti for her insights into her homeland.

For her translation skills, and all-round Hungarianness, *köszi* must go to Zsuzsa Gáspár. I extend all my love and thanks to Karin Strobl for her support and guidance when it mattered most.

LISA DUNFORD

My dearest thanks to my cousins Gabi Jensen and Iren Berecz, who make arriving in Budapest like coming home. Olika, I adored the time spent with you and William in Nyíregyháza. The whole Fábián family is welcome to show up on my Texas doorstep anytime; Zsuzsana, Zsuzsi, Etienne, Tom and Lily – thank you. And Noémi, I appreciated your help immensely. Gerard Gorman, Kati Ingrice and Ambrus Sándor, your expertise was invaluable. Fee, thanks for including me, and for your hurricane-force understanding. Thanks, too, to my friends and colleagues, Neal and Steve, two *hajok* who passed in the night. I hope we get together soon. Billy, you know none of this would be possible without you…*icau*.

BEHIND THE SCENES

THE LONELY PLANET STORY

Fresh from an epic journey across Europe, Asia and Australia in 1972, Tony and Maureen Wheeler sat at their kitchen table stapling together notes. The first Lonely Planet guidebook, *Across Asia on the Cheap,* was born.

Travellers snapped up the guides. Inspired by their success, the Wheelers began publishing books to Southeast Asia, India and beyond. Demand was prodigious, and the Wheelers expanded the business rapidly to keep up. Over the years, Lonely Planet extended its coverage to every country and into the virtual world via lonelyplanet.com and the Thorn Tree message board.

As Lonely Planet became a globally loved brand, Tony and Maureen received several offers for the company. But it wasn't until 2007 that they found a partner whom they trusted to remain true to the company's principles of travelling widely, treading lightly and giving sustainably. In October of that year, BBC Worldwide acquired a 75% share in the company, pledging to uphold Lonely Planet's commitment to independent travel, trustworthy advice and editorial independence.

Today, Lonely Planet has offices in Melbourne, London and Oakland, with over 500 staff members and 300 authors. Tony and Maureen are still actively involved with Lonely Planet. They're travelling more often than ever, and they're devoting their spare time to charitable projects. And the company is still driven by the philosophy of *Across Asia on the Cheap*: 'All you've got to do is decide to go and the hardest part is over. So go!'

SEND US YOUR FEEDBACK

We love to hear from travellers – your comments keep us on our toes and help make our books better. Our well-travelled team reads every word on what you loved or loathed about this book. Although we cannot reply individually to postal submissions, we always guarantee that your feedback goes straight to the appropriate authors, in time for the next edition. Each person who sends us information is thanked in the next edition – and the most useful submissions are rewarded with a free book.

To send us your updates – and find out about Lonely Planet events, newsletters and travel news – visit our award-winning website: **lonelyplanet.com/contact**.

Note: we may edit, reproduce and incorporate your comments in Lonely Planet products such as guidebooks, websites and digital products, so let us know if you don't want your comments reproduced or your name acknowledged. For a copy of our privacy policy visit lonelyplanet.com/privacy.

STEVE FALLON

First and foremost, I'd like to thank my excellent friend Bea Szirti for her helpful suggestions and more pedestrian assistance on the ground. Thanks also to Ildikó Nagy Moran for steering me in the right direction on more than one occasion. Péter Lengyel and Balázs Váradi showed me the correct wine roads to follow, and Brandon Krueger, Adrian Zador and Erik D'Amato once again provided useful insights into what's on in Budapest after dark.

I'd like to dedicate my part of the book to my (not always so) civil partner Michael Rothschild, with love and gratitude and long memory, as well as to the memory of Erzsébet 'Zsóka' Tiszai, my friend and one-time Hungarian teacher, whose life travels came to an end as I wrote. *Nyugodj békében kedves barátom.*

OUR READERS

Many thanks to the travellers who used the last edition and wrote to us with helpful hints, useful advice and interesting anecdotes:

René Andreasen, Jan Beagley, Victoria Bei, Daan Bijdevaate, Pierre Biver, Susan Biver, Peter Bognar, Joannes Bressellers, Philip Butterill, Jocelyn Chan, Tamara Curd, Anthony Esposito, Alison Farmer, Ralph Go, Elizabeth Gray, Aubrey Groves, Laura Heckman, Tess Hildebeast, Julian Hofrichter, Charles Holmes, Robby Hoskens, Nick Islin, Yael Katzin, Pat Maguire, Anne Matheson, M Mcgrath, Ivani Monteiro, Colin Nelson, Nicholas Olesen, Andrea Patterson, Antony Penny, B Q, Pirjo Rantanen, Riccardo Ricci, Shimon Rumelt, Dave Silverstone, Stan Smidt, John Spencer, Heiko Stribl, Jesse Sutton, Viktor Szabo, Arthur Tybandha, Katia Waegemans, Ronald Wian

ACKNOWLEDGMENTS

Many thanks to the following for the use of their content:

Globe on title page ©Mountain High Maps 1993 Digital Wisdom, Inc.

Internal photographs: by Lisa Dunford p12 (#2); Kubeš/isifa Image Service s.r.o./Alamy p8; Christopher Cormack/Imagestate Media Partners Limited - Impact Photos/Alamy p9; blickwinkel/Alamy p10. All other photographs by Lonely Planet Images, and by Bruce Yuan-Yue Bi p5; Martin Moos p6 (#1), p7 (#2); John Elk III p6 (#3); David Greedy p9 (#2), p11 (#2); Roberto Soncin Gerometta p10 (#3), p12 (#1).

Index

000 Map pages
000 Photograph pages

000 Map pages
000 Photograph pages

INDEX

INDEX

000 Map pages
000 Photograph pages

N

O

P

R

INDEX

000 Map pages
000 Photograph pages

INDEX

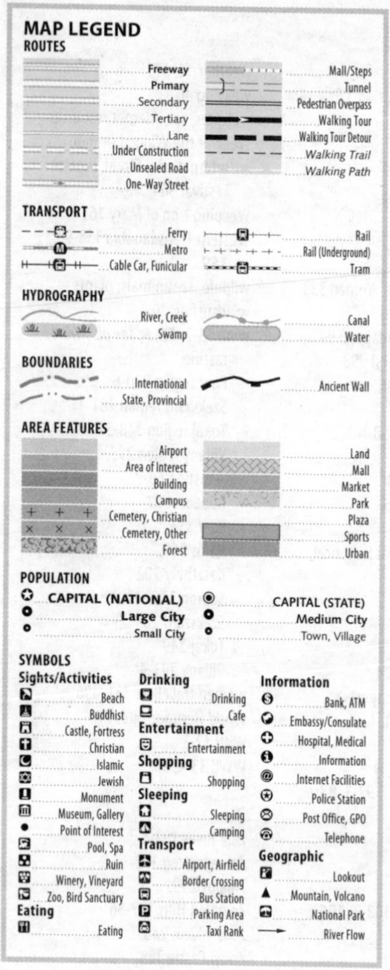

LONELY PLANET OFFICES

Australia

Head Office
Locked Bag 1, Footscray, Victoria 3011
☎ 03 8379 8000, fax 03 8379 8111
talk2us@lonelyplanet.com.au

USA

150 Linden St, Oakland, CA 94607
☎ 510 250 6400, toll free 800 275 8555
fax 510 893 8572
info@lonelyplanet.com

UK

2nd fl, 186 City Rd,
London EC1V 2NT
☎ 020 7106 2100, fax 020 7106 2101
go@lonelyplanet.co.uk

Published by Lonely Planet Publications Pty Ltd
ABN 36 005 607 983

Cover photograph: St Stephen's Basilica, Budapest, Bruce Bi/Lonely Planet Images. Many of the images in this guide are available for licensing from Lonely Planet Images: www.lonelyplanetimages.com.

Printed by Hang Tai Printing Company, Hong Kong.
Printed in China.